ACTION LEARNING AND RESEARCH

ACTION LEARNING AND ACTION RESEARCH: GENRES AND APPROACHES

EDITED BY

ORTRUN ZUBER-SKERRITT

Griffith University, Australia and North-West University, South Africa

AND

LESLEY WOOD

North-West University, South Africa

United Kingdom – North America – Japan – India – Malaysia – China

Emerald Publishing Limited
Howard House, Wagon Lane, Bingley BD16 1WA, UK

First edition 2019

Reprints and permissions service
Contact: permissions@emeraldinsight.com

British Library Cataloguing in Publication Data
A catalogue record for this book is available from the British Library

ISBN: 978-1-78769-538-2 (Print)
ISBN: 978-1-78769-537-5 (Online)
ISBN: 978-1-78769-539-9 (Epub)
ISBN: 978-1-78769-540-5 (Paperback)

Printed and bound by CPI Group (UK) Ltd, Croydon, CR0 4YY

ISOQAR certified
Management System,
awarded to Emerald
for adherence to
Environmental
standard
ISO 14001:2004.

ISOQAR
REGISTERED
Certificate Number 1985
ISO 14001

INVESTOR IN PEOPLE

Contents

Introduction

Part I: Action Learning

Part II: Action Research

Conclusion

Foreword

Mary Brydon-Miller

While on a recent visit to North-West University in South Africa hosted by one of the editors of this volume, Professor Lesley Wood, I had the opportunity to visit some local schools. We arrived at the school in Rustenburg to find that classes had been dismissed because there was no water. But while we were visiting the school, a community volunteer, John, arrived with two huge plastic tanks of water and the children who were still nearby gathered around to fill their bottles. Water shortages like this are a serious challenge for schools in this part of the country, but school leaders are working to address the problem through creative solutions like including systems for gathering rainwater in new school developments. And children are engaged in learning about the environment, working together on school gardening projects and monitoring weather stations located on the school grounds. These schools are the site of a Participatory Action Learning (AL) and Action Research (AR) project and are my partners in a global climate change education initiative. AL and AR are also at the centre of a campaign to protect local beaches on Panglao Island in the Philippines, to develop a social enterprise partnership between a motorway services site and local non-profit organizations in Southwest England, and in the creation of a new teacher mentoring program in my own hometown of Louisville, Kentucky.

All of these projects reflect the core tenets of AL/AR described in this book. And for the researchers and practitioners involved in these projects, and all those like them around the world, this volume is an important and timely contribution to finding more effective ways of engaging in community-based education, research and activism.

Key points raised by the editors and authors of this book concern what these strategies have in common as forms of AL/AR and what distinguishes them from one another. By sharing a focus on creating opportunities for community participation in order to address pressing economic, social, cultural and environmental issues, all these forms of AL/AR are founded on the understanding that human relationships and a shared commitment to serving as agents of positive change underlie everything we do in AL/AR. Adaptability and willingness to innovate and embrace the emergent nature of knowledge and understanding are additional

Action Learning and Action Research: Genres and Approaches, vii–viii
doi:10.1108/978-1-78769-537-520191021

hallmarks of all forms of AL/AR, as illustrated by the variety of approaches included in this volume. These approaches are used not only for community engagement but also in a wide variety of fields for personal, professional and organizational development, in small project teams or at large scale in a whole organization – nationwide or globally.

Contributions by many of the key figures in the world of AL/AR, as well as by rising leaders in the field, provide readers with a wealth of opportunities to explore the major themes and many variations of AL/AR. Researchers, practitioners, consultants and community partners new to AL/AR will find this book an invaluable guide to understanding and engaging in this approach to research, but even those of us who've been working in this area for many years will find new insights and inspiration.

Mary Brydon-Miller

Acknowledgments

We sincerely thank three groups of people. One is the authors of this book for their collaboration, cooperation and excellent contributions to this volume. Another is our critical friends who kindly read and commented on the first draft chapters of this book, providing us with constructive critique and suggestions for improvement: from Austria, Stephan Laske; from Colombia, Doris Santos; from Israel, Victor Friedman; from New Zealand, Jan Robertson; from Singapore, Hairon Salleh; from South Africa, Annette Wilkinson and useful suggestions from Rod Waddington, Ansurie Pillay, Bruce Damons, Ansie Kitching, Corne Kruger, Elsabe Wessels, Marinda Neetlingh, Karen Venter and Akpovire Oduaran; from the United Kingdom, Mary McAteer and Mike Pedler; and from the United States, Davydd Greenwood and Margaret Riel. The third group is our ALARA friends in Brisbane, in particular Bob Dick and Ron Passfield.

We also acknowledge the helpful comments and suggestions for improving the quality of our work from Maureen Todhunter, our friend and professional copy-editor; and the assistance we received from proof-reader, Jo Anne Pomfrett; and from graphic designer, Anna Ng. Thanks also to the production team of Emerald who have provided excellent technical and editorial support.

The writing of this book was enabled by funding from the National Research Fund in South Africa (NRF: 93316). Any statements, conclusions and findings contained therein are those of the authors; and the NRF cannot be held responsible thereto.

Reviewers' Comments

This edited collection takes on the valuable but difficult task of identifying the non-negotiable or defining characteristics of action learning (AL) and action research (AR). The task is difficult because the 'action' approach values multiple perspectives and worldviews and encourages participants to own and create their knowledge. This results in a family of approaches as AL/AR evolves to serve practitioners in their learning process. As editors, Zuber-Skerritt and Wood have invited a wide range of perspectives from AL/AR advocates/scholars who have contributed to the evolution of the now many genres. They close with embracing their goal of deepening understanding AL/AR as philosophy, methodology, theory of learning and process for community engagement. This book does an excellent job of challenging action researchers to critically think through their traditions in contrast to other approaches. The chapters provide a solid foundation for AL and AR approaches to create understandings and knowledge based on values and worldviews that uphold inclusion and will further develop the quality of social sciences and our democratic world.

Margaret Riel, PhD, Director, Center for Collaborative Action Research,
Pepperdine University, Los Angeles, CA, USA

The author list for this edited book reads like a 'who's who' in action learning (AL) and action research (AR). These authors are leaders in the field internationally, bringing years of research and theoretical and professional experience to their writing. Many of these authors influenced my own action research PhD in coaching leadership over two decades ago and I wish such a text had been available then. It offers extensive perspectives on the subject, with strong validation of research methodologies. AR has been generally misunderstood in universities and not highly regarded as a research paradigm. Supervision of action research postgraduate studies can be problematic, and for the AL/AR scholar/researcher may feel murky and difficult to negotiate. But this complexity typically matches the wicked problems, often those of justice, social relationships and environmental sustainability, that ALAR seeks to address. In this way, the paradigm is true to its early beginnings in Kurt Lewin's work – in pursuit of social justice.

This is a text for leaders of organizations, schools and community groups, who want to engage the people who are affected by problems in the creation of the solutions. It offers readers inclusivity of perspectives and will be a beneficial read for beginning action researchers and their supervisors, more experienced action researchers wanting further critical perspectives and challenge, and for leaders in the field wanting to engage in participatory AL/AR.

Jan Robertson, PhD, Adjunct Professor, Griffith University; Academic Leadership Consultant and Author of *Coaching Leadership: Building Educational Leadership Capacity Through Partnership*, New Zealand.

In bringing together an impressive range of authors and perspectives from across the globe, Zuber-Skerritt and Wood have produced a text that celebrates the rich diversity and multi-perspective nature of action learning (AL) and action research (AR), while demonstrating the coherent framework in which these approaches operate. This important book will make a real contribution to the understanding and work of practitioners from a range of disciplines and contexts. It is clearly and coherently structured, with chapters that are accessible to novice AL/AR practitioners, yet offer critical challenge to those who are more experienced.

As a typology of these approaches, it is comprehensive and cogent. Presenting a critical discussion of each approach, it offers readers an opportunity to 'see inside' the practice and theory of these approaches in a range of contexts, each with its own complexity and challenges. Topics for discussion and reflection at the end of each chapter help the reader develop deeper understanding of the topic concerned, and more importantly, address the issue of values underpinning our actions, learnings and research. In this way, the book becomes more than the sum of its parts, clearly illustrating the power and potency of (and indeed great need for) such approaches in our contemporary world.

Mary McAteer, PhD, Director of Professional Learning Programs, Edge Hill University, Lancashire, UK.

This fine publication addresses a real need among followers (and critics) of action research, by clarifying and demystifying the most common genres of and approaches to action learning and action research (AL/AR). It filters and illustrates, and explains what AL/AR is and what it is not. The book re-establishes AL/AR as practical, collaborative, emancipatory, interpretive and critical – a philosophy, methodology and approach to learning and development for addressing complex global challenges.

In structuring the publication, the editors effectively weave together the rich voices of leading scholars of AL/AR. The result is a coherent assembly of diverse ideas and experiences that produce a wealth of distinctive, informative nuances.

This work can become an important reference on the shelves of researchers, authors and other practitioners. It has the potential to motivate and empower a wide readership to study, acknowledge, adopt and adapt AL/AR – further establishing its rightful place as a research paradigm suitable for bringing true social change in our times.

Annette Wilkinson, PhD, Professor, University of the Free State, South Africa.

I have learned that whenever Ortrun Zuber-Skerritt publishes something, it is worth paying attention. Zuber-Skerritt and Lesley Wood have put together an edited collection that is unusual in being integrated around a principled overview of the fields of action research (AR) and action learning (AL). The overview distinguishes usefully between action learning and action research, and makes a case for their synergies and differences in ways that enhanced my understandings greatly. This is accomplished by the editors' having recruited the principal exponents of the genres that are the topics of each chapter and asked them to reflect synthetically on their particular areas of work. The result is both a panoramic view of AL and AR and a

deep dive into many of the varieties of practice. The writing is clear, pedagogically adept, and analytically cogent. The editors and the contributors deserve great credit for having put together such a useful and thoughtful overview of these fields.
Davydd Greenwood, PhD, Goldwin Smith Professor of Anthropology,
Cornell University, USA.

Forty years ago I applied for a Chair in Management and Business Education. In my application lecture I discussed the potential of Action Learning (AL) and Action Research (AR). Obviously, I do not remember any details of my speech. But still today I can recall that several colleagues on the appointment committee strongly questioned the value and the scientific character of AL and AR. Today, 40 years later we can find a large and differentiated body of research and practical experiences, and a broad range of contexts where AL and AR have proven their theoretical and empirical strengths. No longer are there serious doubts about the scientific relevance of these approaches.

This book is of great merit to its editors, Ortrun Zuber-Skerritt, the Australian Doyenne of AL and AR, and her colleague Lesley Wood, having collected contributions from outstanding scholars and experienced practitioners in the field of AL & AR from all over the world. This is not just a collection of articles. Presented within a well substantiated framework, the chapters reveal the evolution of this participatory, transformational paradigm, unfolding the great utility, diversity and richness of the various genres of AL and AR, and thus offering a very useful, comprehensive guide. Readers will benefit greatly from the didactic of every chapter – not only illustrating the what, why, *and* how *of each genre, but also offering topics for further discussion and reflection, and tips for further reading. This rich collection on AL and AR can be very useful for not only emerging scholars and other newcomer practitioners but also for more experienced scholars, looking for their own way of adapting this approach creatively and constructively – at this time when AL and AR have such methodological relevance for resolving small and large scale difficulties in our complex world.*
Stephan Laske, PhD, Emeritus Professor, University of Innsbruck, Austria.

This book brings together a collection of interesting works from established scholars to bring to light various genres and approaches in the fields of action learning and action research. From the conceptual discussions and practical exemplars, readers of this book who are new to action learning and action research will gain a clearer understanding of the what, how *and* why *of action learning and action research. Readers with greater familiarity and experience in the field will gain a deeper appreciation of the field's traditions as well as new curiosity – or wondering into the future – about how action learning and action research can be relevant and integrated to new genres and approaches. This book is also a timely reminder of how the participatory paradigm can be a forceful counter response to the growing neoliberalism of the twenty-first century.*
Hairon Salleh, PhD, Associate Professor, Policy and Leadership
Studies, National Institute of Education, Nanyang Technological
University, Singapore.

This book presents the self-reflective process of a group of Action Learning (AL) and Action Research (AR) practitioners and advocates. Readers are invited to become involved in this self-reflective process as the authors analyse the origins and development of most of the main genres of AL and AR through their own experiences while seeking to address global and local problems in complex contemporary times. Each chapter illustrates the diversity of ways to think and act collaboratively to address difficult situations through the various types of AL and AR. Together the chapters serve to demystify AL and AR and how they can be used or adapted to create conceptual and practical knowledge for, and while achieving, sustainable social change.

Professor Doris Santos, Universidad Nacional de Colombia, Bogotá DC,
Colombia, South America.

I welcome the appearance of this new survey of action learning and action research, compiled by leading scholars from Australia, USA, UK, Ireland, South Africa and Austria. This book promises some interesting excursions into intriguing aspects of action learning and action research practice in a difficult field of work.

Professor Mike Pedler, Emeritus Professor of Action Learning at Henley
Business School, University of Reading, UK.

About the Authors

Mary Brydon-Miller, PhD, is a Professor in the Department of Educational Leadership, Evaluation, and Organizational Development in the College of Education and Human Development at the University of Louisville, USA. She also holds the honorary title of Extraordinary Professor in the research entity of Community-based Educational Research at North-West University, South Africa. She is a participatory action researcher who conducts work in both school and community settings. Her current research focuses on research ethics in educational and community settings. She is the Editor, with David Coghlan, of the *SAGE Encyclopedia of Action Research* and has recently completed work on a book on ethical challenges in the context of participatory research with her colleague Sarah Banks from Durham University, UK. Her next major project focuses on working with middle-school students from around the world to engage as citizen scientists to better understand the impacts of global climate change.

Danny Burns, PhD, is a Professor of International Development at the Institute of Development Studies (IDS), University of Sussex, UK. He was formerly Professor of Social and Organizational Learning at the University of the West of England where he co-directed the SOLAR action research centre with Susan Weil. Danny has written extensively on action research, including two books: *Systemic Action Research: A strategy for whole system change* (2007) and *Navigating Complexity in International Development: Facilitating sustainable change at scale* (2015). He has directed more than 25 action research projects and teaches a successful short course on action research with Joanna Howard at IDS.

David Coghlan, PhD, is a Professor Emeritus and Fellow Emeritus at Trinity Business School, Trinity College Dublin, Ireland. He specializes in organization development and action research and is active in both communities internationally. He has published over 170 articles and book chapters. Recent books include *Conducting Action Research* (Sage, 2018); *Inside Organizations* (Sage, 2016); *Organizational Change and Strategy* (Routledge, 2016); *Doing Action Research in Your Own Organization* (4th ed., Sage, 2014); and *Collaborative Strategic Improvement through Network Action Learning* (Edward Elgar, 2011). He is co-editor of *The Sage Encyclopedia of Action Research* (2014) and of the four-volume sets, *Fundamentals of Organization Development* (Sage, 2010) and *Action Research in Business and Management* (Sage, 2016). He serves on the editorial advisory boards of *Journal of Applied Behavioral Science*; *Action Research*; *Action Learning: Research and Practice*; *Systemic Practice and Action Research*; and *The OD Practitioner*, among others.

Bob Dick, DLitt, is an Independent Scholar, an occasional academic, a coach and mentor and a consultant in community and organizational change. He has been a practitioner and an academic for almost a half century, and continues to work in both fields. In both he uses concepts and processes from action research, action learning, action science, narrative and community and organization development to help people (including himself), organizations and communities to improve their work, learning and life. The single most important book he read as a practitioner was *Theory in Practice*, the 1974 book in which Argyris and Schön introduced the foundational elements of action science to the world. Since then, action science has been a core influence on his work. It influences much of what he does and how he does it. Bob resides in Brisbane's leafy western suburbs with the love of his life, Camilla.

Robin R. Hurst, EdD, SPHR, is an Assistant Professor of Adult Learning and Human Resource Development in the School of Education at Virginia Commonwealth University (VCU), Richmond, USA. She came to VCU after more than 20 years of experience in human resource management, and training and organizational development, with both multinational and domestic organizations. Robin has consulted with numerous organizations in organizational development, leadership development using action learning, ethical decision-making and continuous improvement. Robin holds an MA in Human Resource Development and an EdD in Human and Organizational Learning from the George Washington University. She has presented at both national and international conferences in the areas of action learning in graduate education, organizational culture development in cross-border mergers and acquisitions, organizational identity, transformational learning in student study abroad programs and moving training evaluation to a higher level. She has published her work in international journals, and has served as an Associate Editor for *Organizational Culture: An International Journal*.

Stephen Kemmis, PhD, is a Professor Emeritus in the School of Education, Charles Sturt University, Wagga Wagga, NSW, Australia. He is co-author with Wilfred Carr, of *Becoming Critical: Education, knowledge and action research* (Falmer, 1986); with Jane Wilkinson, Christine Edwards-Groves, Ian Hardy, Peter Grootenboer and Laurette Bristol, of *Changing Practices, Changing Education* (Springer, 2014); with Robin McTaggart and Rhonda Nixon, of *The Action Research Planner: Doing Critical Participatory Action Research* (Springer, 2014); and, with Christine Edwards-Groves, of *Understanding Education: History, Politics and Practice* (Springer, 2018).

Michael Marquardt, EdD, is a Professor Emeritus of Human and Organizational Learning and International Affairs at George Washington University, USA. He was the co-founder and first President of the World Institute for Action Learning (WIAL), and now serves as Chair of the WIAL Global Advisory Committee. Mike is the author of 26 books and over 100 professional articles in the fields of leadership, learning, globalization and organizational change including *Action Learning for Developing Leaders and Organizations; Optimizing the Power of Action Learning; Leading with Questions; Building the Learning Organization* (selected as Book of the Year by the Academy of HRD); *The Global Advantage;*

Action Learning in Action; Global Leaders for the 21ˢᵗ Century; Global Human Resource Development; Technology-based Learning; and *Global Teams.* Over one million copies of his publications have been sold in nearly a dozen languages worldwide. Mike also served as the Editor of the UNESCO Encyclopedia volume on Human Resources and is an editor and/or advisor for several leading professional journals around the world. He has been a keynote speaker at international conferences in Australia, Japan, Philippines, Malaysia, South Africa, Singapore and India as well as throughout North America.

Robin McTaggart, BSc, MEd Melbourne; PhD Illinois, is an Adjunct Professor in the Griffith Institute of Educational Research. He is co-author, with Stephen Kemmis and Rhonda Nixon, of *The Action Research Planner: Doing Critical Participatory Action Research* (Springer). He has published widely in the field of action research and taught the theory and practice of action research and program evaluation in several countries, fields and cultures. Originally a Victorian high school chemistry and biology teacher, he was Professor of Education and Head of the School of Administration and Curriculum Studies at Deakin University, Geelong, Australia and also Adjunct Professor in Management at the University of South Australia. Subsequently he was Dean of Education and Pro Vice Chancellor for Quality Assurance at James Cook University and an Australian Universities Quality Agency Auditor.

Rhonda Nixon, PhD, is an Assistant Superintendent of Curriculum and Teacher Professional Learning, in a medium-sized school district in Alberta, Canada and she is an Adjunct Professor at the University of Alberta. She is a critical participatory action researcher who continues to conduct such research in her field. In her previous jurisdiction and work as a PhD student at the University of Alberta, and later, as a Professor at the University of Victoria, British Columbia, Canada, she provided school stories of critical participatory action research within the book by Kemmis, McTaggart and Nixon (2014) *The Action Research Planner: Doing Critical Participatory Action Research.* She continues to work on teacher professional learning from a critical participatory action research stance. Her goal is to ensure that teachers' and leaders' practices are about improving life chances of students locally and globally.

Ron Passfield, PhD, is an Emeritus Professor with the Australian Institute of Business, Adelaide, Australia. He was a Founding Executive Member (1991) of the Action Learning, Action Research Association (ALARA) and President for five years. He has used action learning and action research in multiple contexts for more than 40 years. Over the past decade, Ron and his colleague, Julie Cork, have conducted more than 50 longitudinal action learning programs ranging from four to six months for managers in multiple roles and locations. The program is focused on people management and is designed to help managers to create a workplace culture that is conducive to mental health. Participants covered many managerial roles within public services such as police, doctors, nurses, engineers, accountants and scientists. Ron is the author of the mindfulness blog: www.growmindfulness.com.

Peter Posch, PhD, is a retired Professor of Education and an Associate Member of the Institute of Instructional and School Development at the University of Klagenfurt, Austria. He holds a teaching degree in English and Geography, a PhD in Education and a *venia docendi* in Education. He has been involved in several research and development projects based on action research nationally and internationally, for example, the International Environment and School Initiatives Project. He still serves on the Editorial Boards of *Educational Action Research* and *International Journal for Lesson and Learning Studies*. Recent publications on action research include the co-authored book *Teachers Investigate Their Work: An Introduction to Action Research across the Professions* (3rd ed., Routledge, 2018).

Franz Rauch, PhD, is an Associate Professor (tenured) and the Head of the Institute of Instructional and School Development at the University of Klagenfurt, Austria. He holds a master's degree in Natural Sciences (teaching certification), a PhD in Education and a *venia docendi* in Education. He has been involved in research and development projects based on action research nationally (e.g., University Courses for Teachers, Program IMST and Network ECO-Schools) and internationally (e.g., EC Projects PROFILES, PARRISE and ARTIST) for many years. He is one of the editors of the *Educational Action Research* journal and serves on editorial boards of other journals (such as *The Journal of Environmental Education*). Recent publications on action research include *Networking for Education for Sustainable Development in Austria: The Austrian ECOLOG-schools program* (Educational Action Research, 2016, 1). He is co-editor of *Action Research, Innovation and Change* (Routledge, 2014) and *Promoting Change through Action Research: International Case Studies in Education, Social Work, Health Care and Community Development* (Sense, 2014). His further research and development areas are education for sustainable development/environmental education, networks in education, school development, science education and continuing education for teachers.

Richard Teare, PhD, is Co-founder and President, Global University for Lifelong Learning (GULL), a non-profit international network movement that works with other organizations to facilitate self-help in communities and the workplace. Earlier, he held professorships at four UK universities and he is currently an Adjunct Professor, Caribbean Maritime University, Jamaica. Richard has been an Emerald journal editor for more than 30 years and his academic publications include 23 authored, co-authored and edited books on aspects of community development, service management and organizational learning. Among these, he is the author of *Lifelong Action Learning: A Journey of Discovery and Celebration at Work and in the Community* (Amazon, 2018) and co-author of *Lifelong Action Learning for Community Development* (Sense, 2013) and *Designing Inclusive Pathways with Young Adults* (Sense, 2015) the first and second in a series of books about GULL's work with communities.

Amanda Trosten-Bloom, MSc, Principal, Corporation for Positive Change, USA, is a widely acclaimed Appreciative Inquiry Consultant specializing in high-engagement whole system change. Her award-winning work has included community-based action research and strategic planning. Her publications include *The Power of Appreciative Inquiry*; *Appreciative Leadership*; *Appreciative Team Building*; *The Encyclopedia of Positive Questions*; and numerous articles.

Maria Giovanna Vianello, MBA, MSc, is an Organizational Development Professional and an International Coach Federation (ICF) Executive Coach working for Novartis, based in Singapore. With two decades of experience in the design and delivery of Learning, Organizational and Leadership Development initiatives, she has a demonstrated track record driving innovative science-based solutions for complex organizational issues at Fortune 100 companies in the global market, thoroughly applying Appreciative Inquiry principles within multiple different business contexts. Awarded 2013 and 2015 "Most Influential HR Leader in Asia," Maria Giovanna progressively experienced a combination of international and local business partnering, supporting the development of organizations across Asia, South America, USA, Europe and Africa. Maria Giovanna develops, executes and customizes extremely innovative Change Management, Organizational Development, Talent Acquisition and Talent Development strategies. She considers simplicity, data analysis and cost efficiency as key success factors in every initiative she has implemented, achieving huge consensus among key stakeholders within the academic and corporate environment. In her role as ICF Executive Coach, Maria Giovanna supports leaders in improving emotional intelligence and influencing skills through her extensive experience in nonverbal communication.

Jack Whitehead, PhD, is a Visiting Professor in Education at the University of Cumbria in the UK. He is a former President of the British Educational Research Association and Distinguished Scholar in Residence at Westminster College, Utah, USA. He is a Visiting Professor at Ningxia University in China and a member of the editorial board of the *Educational Journal of Living Theories* (EJOLTS http://ejolts.net/node/80). Since 1973 his research program in Higher Education has focused on the creation of the living-educational-theories that individuals use to improve their practice and to explain their educational influences in their workplaces. His website can be accessed at http://www.actionresearch.net.

Diana Whitney, PhD, a leading figure in the fields of Appreciative Inquiry and Large Scale Change, has been at the forefront of positive change theory and practice in the USA and worldwide for three decades. She founded the international consultancy, Corporation for Positive Change, and co-founded the social constructionist think tank, the Taos Institute. Her work – designing and facilitating strategic culture transformation, merger integration and leadership development with Fortune 100 companies – has gained her a worldwide following. She is a prolific and award-winning author of dozens of chapters and articles and 20 books, including *The Power of Appreciative Inquiry*; *Appreciative Leadership*; *Appreciative Inquiry: A Positive Revolution in Change*; and *Positive Approaches to Peacebuilding*.

Lesley Wood, DEd, is a Research Professor in the Faculty of Education and Director of the research niche area, Community-based Educational Research at North-West University, South Africa. She is a National Research Foundation rated researcher whose interests lie in researching participatory ways to facilitate psycho-social wellness within various educational communities. She has received international recognition for her work in action research and HIV and AIDS, having been awarded an Honorary Doctorate in 2014 by Moravian College, Pennsylvania, USA. She has published over 80 articles, chapters and books, and has received several internationally funded grants for her projects.

Stefan Zehetmeier, PhD, is an Associate Professor at the University of Klagenfurt, Austria. He has experience with action research in diverse contexts for more than 15 years. As researcher and teacher educator, he was involved in several Austrian large-scale teacher professional development programs based on action research Moreover, he was involved in national and international research and development projects based on action research. His further research interests include mathematics and science teacher education, school development, evaluation and impact analysis of teacher professional development programs.

Ortrun Zuber-Skerritt, PhD, is an Adjunct Professor at Griffith University, Australia; Honorary Research Fellow at North-West University, South Africa; and Pro Chancellor, Global University for Lifelong Learning (GULL), USA. After her undergraduate and postgraduate education in German universities, she obtained four doctoral degrees while living in Australia: PhD in Literature and Applied Linguistics (University of Queensland, 1976), PhD in Higher Education (Deakin University, 1986), DLitt in Management Education (International Management Centres, UK, 1992) and an Honorary Doctorate in Professional Studies (GULL, USA, 2008). Ortrun has published 42 books, over 70 book chapters, over 60 refereed journal articles and more than 100 professional and conference papers, and has produced over 50 educational video programs. She has been awarded over $1.2 million in competitive R&D grants and has led action research and leadership development programs in many universities in Australia, New Zealand, Hong Kong, Singapore, Japan, Sweden, Holland, Austria, Germany, England, the United States, Canada, Fiji, South America and South Africa. In 2018 she was appointed an Officer of the Order of Australia, a prestigious national honour for "distinguished service to tertiary education in the field of action research and learning as an academic, author and mentor, and to professional bodies."

List of Acronyms

ACT	Acceptance and Commitment Therapy
AERA	American Educational Research Association
AI	Appreciative Inquiry
AI 4-D cycle	Discovery, Dream, Design and Destiny (Destiny, aka Delivery)
AIDS	Acquired Immune Deficiency Syndrome
AL	Action Learning
ALAR	Action Learning and Action Research
ALARA	Action Learning and Action Research Association
ALARPM	Action Learning, Action Research and Process Management
ALS	Action Learning Set
AR	Action Research
ARNA	Action Research Network of the Americas
BBP	Basic Business Philosophy
BRC	British Red Cross
BSc	Bachelor of Science
BTU	British Thermal Unit
CARN	Collaborative Action Research Network
CCM	Church and Community Mobilization
CEO	Chief Executive Officer
COMBER	Community-Based Educational Research
CPAR	Critical Participatory Action Research
CPM	Confident People Management Program
DBA	Doctor of Business Administration
DEd	Doctor of Education
DFID	Department for International Development (UK)
DLitt	Doctor of Letters
EAR	Educational Action Research
EC	European Community
EdD	Doctor of Education
EJOLTS	*Educational Journal of Living Theories*
ENSI	International Environment and School Initiatives Project
GCWAL	Global Centre for Work-Applied Learning
GLE	Granada Learning Experience
GM	General Manager
GULL	Global University for Lifelong Learning
HDI	Human Development Institute

HDWFD	Hunter Douglas Window Fashions Division
HIC	Hospital International Communications
HIV	Human Immunodeficiency Virus
HR	Human Resources
HRD	Human Resource Development
HRO	High Reliability Organization
ICF	International Coaching Federation
IDP	Internally Displaced People
IDS	Institute of Development Studies
IFAL	International Federation of Action Learning
IFR	*International Financial Review*
IMCA	International Management Centres Association
IMST	Innovations Make Schools Top Program
INGO	International Non-governmental Organization
IUS	*Institut für Unterrichts- und Schulentwicklung* (Institute for Instructional and School Development)
JWCS	Joy to the World Community Services
LAL	Lifelong Action Learning
LfT	Learning for Transformation
LL	Lifelong Learning
MA	Master of Arts
MAPP	Mindfulness All-Party Parliamentary Group
MARC	Mindful Awareness Research Center
MASA	Mindfulness, Action Learning, Self-Awareness, Agency Model
MBA	Master of Business Administration
MBSR	Mindfulness Based Stress Reduction
MEd	Master of Education
MHCD	Mental Health Centre of Denver
MPhil	Master of Philosophy
MSc	Master of Science
MTSF	Medium Term Strategic Framework
NEARI	Network Educational Action Research Ireland
NGO	Non-governmental Organization
NRF	National Research Foundation
OD	Organizational Development
PALAR	Participatory Action Learning and Action Research
PAR	Participatory Action Research
PASA	People Against Sexual Abuse (renamed Positive Attitudes, Solutions and Actions)
PFL	*Pädagogik und Fachdidaktik für Lehrkräfte* (Teacher Education in Subject Areas)
PhD	Doctor of Philosophy
PM	Process Management
PNG	Papua New Guinea
PRIA	Participatory Research in Asia
ProFil	*Professionalität im Lehrberuf* (Professionalism in the Teaching Profession)

PV	Personal Viability
RANIR	Refugee Action Network for IDP [Internally Displaced People] and Refugees
R&D	Research and Development
SAAGG	South Asian Academy for Good Governance
SAR	Systemic Action Research
S-ART	Self-Awareness, Self-Regulation and Self-Transcendence Model
Seven Cs	Communication, Collaboration, Commitment, Coaching, Critical and self-critical attitude, Competence, Character
SOS	Sense of Self
SPHR	Senior Professional in Human Resources
SPIRAL	Systemic Participatory Inquiry Research and Action Learning
Three Es	Emancipation, Empowerment, Emergence
Three Rs	Relationships, Reflection, Recognition
TSR	Training, Service and Revenue
TUC	Trade Union Council
UK	United Kingdom
UNESCO	United Nations Educational, Scientific and Cultural Organization
US	United States
USA	United States of America
USAID	US Agency for International Development
USIP	United States Institute of Peace
VCU	Virginia Commonwealth University [USA]
VSO	Voluntary Service Overseas
WIAL	World Institute for Action Learning
WV	World Vision
WVI	World Vision International
WVL	World Vision Lebanon
WVSL	World Vision Sri Lanka
WVM	World Vision Mongolia

List of Tables

List of Figures

Introduction

Chapter 1

Introduction to Action Learning and Action Research: Genres and Approaches

Ortrun Zuber-Skerritt and Lesley Wood

Chapter Outline

In this chapter we introduce the book's main aim: to provide a platform for the world's leading scholars of Action Learning and Action Research to explain the what, why and how of their respective action learning and action research genres. In seeking to provide a typology of action learning and action research, as editors of this book we asked the authors of each chapter to address these aspects of their particular genre: (1) what it is (and is not); (2) for what purposes and in which contexts it is best suited; and (3) what processes are most effective for conducting research. We explain why this book is necessary, based on our own experience as learners, researchers, supervisors, examiners, authors and leaders of action learning and action research. We also explain the importance of action learning and action research in their many forms for addressing increasingly complex global challenges that confront humankind in the twenty-first century. We argue that, and illustrate how, in this era, action learning and action research approaches are ideal for resolving complex problems of personal, professional, organizational and community development and sustainability and learning through the experience. We also discuss potential pitfalls and challenges of action learning and action research and how to overcome them. This is important for demystifying both and for identifying why they have been misunderstood and misused, and therefore criticized or totally rejected as a valid learning/research methodology by some academic researchers. We explain how the authors contributing to this book reflect on their rich and diverse experience, on their practical and theoretical work through which they have contributed new genres, and on their insights and conclusions over a lifetime of learning through active research and development (R&D). Finally, we outline the contents and structure of this book, before reflecting on and drawing conclusions from this chapter about why and how action learning and action research need to be clarified as a valuable contribution to learning and research, conceptually and practically.

Action Learning and Action Research: Genres and Approaches, 3–16
Copyright © 2019 by Ortrun Zuber-Skerritt and Lesley Wood
All rights of reproduction in any form reserved
doi:10.1108/978-1-78769-537-520191003

Introduction

Action Learning (AL) and Action Research (AR) are useful and increasingly popular approaches to improve personal, professional, team, organization and community development. They are based on a participatory paradigm of working together for the common good. Many approaches to AL and AR have evolved over time and the main ones are discussed by the authors in this book. AL and AR each have many definitions, so to start this book let us clarify and introduce these concepts as a basis for further discussion.

Action is almost an all-embracing term. In this book its temporal scope includes past, present and future. It refers to something done in the past that has affected or can affect our present insight, learning and knowledge and enables and compels us to plan our future action in light of this insight, learning and knowledge.

Action learning is learning from and through action or concrete experience, and through reflecting on this experience and taking action as a result of this learning. It is learning from and with each other in AL 'sets' to address a major, complex, practical problem in the workplace, organization, community or other site of collective activity. One of the early definitions of AL is Reg Revans' (1982) equation for learning: $L = P + Q$, that is, learning is programmed knowledge plus questioning insight.

> P is the concern of the traditional academy; Q is the field of action learning .... On the whole, however, programmed knowledge, P, already set out in books or known to expert authorities, is quite insufficient for keeping on top of a world like ours today, racked by change of every kind. Programmed knowledge must not only be expanded: it must be supplemented by questioning insight, the capacity to identify useful and fresh lines of inquiry. This we denote by Q, so that learning means not only supplementing P but developing Q as well. It is arguable which is more important ...; the evidence is that a surfeit of P inhibits Q, and that experts, loaded with P, are the greatest menace to adaptation to change by questioning, Q. (p. 16)

According to Revans (1982, 1991), AL is a process by which groups of people (managers, academics, teachers, students or 'learners' generally) work on real problems, issues or concerns, carrying real responsibility in real conditions and contexts. The solutions people come up with may require changes to be made in the organization, and such changes often pose challenges to senior management or to others who seek, for whatever reason, to preserve the status quo. Nevertheless, the benefits of pursuing and sustaining such change are potentially great because the people involved actually own their own shared problems, their own shared solutions, and so are highly likely to be collectively committed to achieving and sustaining improved outcomes.

Action research was arguably first conceptualized by Kurt Lewin (1951) and further developed by Kolb (1984), Carr and Kemmis (1986) and subsequently many others. In brief, AR consists of a spiral of cycles of action and research with four major phases: *planning, acting, observing* and *reflecting*. Planning includes identifying and defining the problem and analytical approach and on this basis preparing a strategic plan. Acting refers to implementing the strategic plan. Observing entails watching, perceiving and evaluating the action by appropriate research methods and processes. Reflecting refers to thinking back critically, not just about the results of the evaluation but about the whole action, research process and outcomes, that is, the previous three phases of planning, acting and observing. This in turn may lead to identifying a new problem/issue or way to address it, and hence, a new cycle of planning, acting, observing and reflecting.

Here the basic assumption is that people can learn and create knowledge (1) on the basis of their own concrete experience; (2) through observing and reflecting on that experience; (3) by forming abstract explanatory or analytical concepts, principles and generalizations; and (4) by testing the implications of these concepts in new situations, which will lead to new concrete experience and hence, the beginning of a new cycle (Kolb, 1984).

The aims of AR are (1) to improve practice and contribute to conceptual and practical knowledge by improving our understanding of a situation and its complexity; and (2) if warranted, to suggest and make positive changes to the environment, context and conditions in which that practice takes place, to achieve and sustain desirable improvement and effective development. Thus, AR is an approach to social science research that is:

- *practical*, that is, the results and insights gained from the research are not only theoretically important to the advancement of knowledge in the field, but also lead to practical immediate improvements during and after the research process;
- *participative and collaborative*, that is, the researcher is not considered to be an outside expert conducting an inquiry with 'subjects', but doing research with and for the people concerned with the practical problem/issue;
- *emancipatory*, that is, not hierarchical; all people concerned are equal 'participants' contributing to the inquiry;
- *interpretive*, that is, social inquiry is assumed to result not in the researcher's positivist statements based on right *or* wrong answers to the research question, but in solutions based on the views and interpretations of the people involved in the inquiry. Research validity is achieved by certain methods, such as triangulation and participant confirmation or member check; and
- *critical*, that is, the 'critical community' of participants not only search for practical improvements in their work or other collective activity within the given socio-political constraints, but also act as critical and self-critical change agents of those constraints where needed.

AR is therefore a philosophy, methodology, theory and process of learning and development. It can be used not only to enable practical and emancipatory outcomes, but also to generate relevant and authentic theory that has real meaning for those involved (Wood, 2013; Wood & Zuber-Skerritt, 2013;

Zuber-Skerritt, 2011). AR is making a vital contribution to knowledge creation and knowledge democracy by those using it to help address increasingly complex, global challenges confronting humankind in this twenty-first century. As such, it is gaining in popularity worldwide.

Even so, as experienced action researchers, postgraduate supervisors, examiners of theses and reviewers of articles and books, we recognize that this emerging paradigm of AR in the social sciences has been widely misunderstood and misused by some researchers, students, educators and practitioners. This stems from confusion around (1) the research and development (R&D) paradigm that underpins the practice of AR; and (2) the many AL and AR genres that have emerged over time.

Aims, Scope and Contributions of This Book

This book makes timely and valuable contributions to knowledge about the theory, practice and process of AL and AR by clarifying what constitutes AL and AR in their many forms and what does not. We believe this clarification will help in strengthening and moving AL and AR into the future, based on inclusive values and worldviews, as an appropriate and valuable approach to R&D in the human and social sciences.

Therefore, this book aims to provide an inclusive overview of the most common genres and approaches of AL and AR, explaining their differences while also highlighting what they share – their adherence to the basic epistemological, ontological and axiological principles of AL and AR. By 'genre' we mean a type, style or category of AL and AR, whereas 'approach' signifies a way of dealing with a problem, dilemma, difficult situation or a question of academic debate.

Most of the authors contributing to this book are internationally acclaimed as leaders in their fields and individually have published work that outlines the essentials of AL and AR. However, this is a seminal work whose very purpose is to collectively present a wide variety of types and foci in the large family of AR, expressly to offer a comprehensive guide to AL and AR. The authors of each chapter therefore focus on a specific variation of AL and/or AR and discuss the *what, why* and *how* of the particular approach, including potential challenges and ideas on how to overcome them, to identify and illustrate the utility and distinctive qualities of these varied yet closely related AL/AR types.

As editors of this book, we conceived its content and design on the basis of recognizing a real need for the overview this book provides, particularly through the many requests we receive for such guidance from postgraduate students, beginning researchers, established researchers who are newcomers to AR, thesis examiners and reviewers of articles. AL and AR have, after all, begun to flourish across recent years. We recognize that this overview may also motive researchers, educators and practitioners working inside or outside the AL/AR paradigm to adopt/adapt the genres discussed here, or to create their own variants that better suit their particular contexts. Importantly, this creation/adaptation can encourage further development of theory, practice and process of AL and AR because by their very nature AL and AR are an ever evolving paradigm and praxis – one of their distinctive strengths. In summary then, the unique contributions of this publication are providing an inclusive overview of the existing genres and approaches in the fields of AL and AR, and stimulating thought and ideas about possible new future directions.

This chapter proceeds with five main sections that consider (1) the AL and AR paradigms, based on distinctive philosophical and methodological assumptions; (2) the need for transforming research in this twenty-first century to most effectively address increasingly complex, 'wicked' problems locally and globally; and (3) the usefulness of identifying and clarifying the wide variety of genres and approaches of AL and AR, by world experts, to enable expansion of their use and adaptation. Since this is the book's introductory chapter, we also include (4) a brief summary of the contents and structure of this book, and in the final par (5) our reflections on why and how AL and AR need to be clarified in the way presented in this book, as a valuable contribution to learning and research, conceptually and practically.

Learning and Research Paradigms in the Social Sciences

In the social sciences there are many approaches to inquiry, with diverse understandings especially on the role of the researcher. In the AL and AR paradigm, the researcher is recognized as not an outside, unattached, objective expert, but a co-researcher with participants who are actively involved in the whole process from problem definition, through trial and error, to final solution. Solutions to complex human and social problems cannot be 'delivered' by experts; solutions need to be created by and with those who are affected by the problems, particularly if these solutions are to be sustainable. Any complex problem always has at least several possible solutions, depending on the social, economic, political, cultural and/or historical situation, context and conditions and participants' preferences as to process and desired outcome. Participatory paradigms like AL/AR take this complexity into consideration. For example, critical theory recognizes that history and power relations shape reality, and that knowledge is mediated by values and context. Constructivism proposes that reality and knowledge are socially constructed. A participatory paradigm subsumes these ideas but reaches further.

AL and AR are underpinned by a participatory paradigm that understands reality through the sharing of experiences of people in relationship with each other, and where the researcher's subjectivity is an inevitable and important part of the research process. Thus, in an AL and AR approach, the solution is created with and by the participants in the team project, including the researcher/facilitator as a co-researcher who joins the group to better understand their situation (like an anthropologist), and becomes part of the collaborative inquiry and action to help improve the situation for and with those involved. The aim and purpose of AL/AR are, through seeking to address shared concerns, identifying and exposing ineffective/inefficient, unjust or harmful practices that are detrimental to people and/or the environment, and taking action to bring about sustainable positive outcomes. In many respects, then, AL and AR are linked into traditions of activism: citizens' direct action and community organizing. All participants in AL/AR projects are practitioners and co-researchers who become actively involved practically, intellectually and emotionally in the cause for which the research is conducted. It is precisely this commitment that is a necessary part of being an engaged practitioner or member of a community of practice.

Participatory paradigms recognize that knowledge is socially constructed and created from within, and for, a particular group and context. The researcher's role is to describe, analyse and explain the situation or case, in as convincing and trustworthy a manner as possible. The aim is not to establish generalizable laws for multiple contexts, but to know, understand, improve or change a particular social situation or context and to advocate for the benefit of the people who are also the 'participants' (not 'subjects') in the inquiry and who are directly affected by the results and solutions. Variables are not predetermined and controlled, but are taken on board as they are identified from the emerging meanings. These are multiple and dynamic. Rigour is achieved through triangulation and/or use of multiple methods and perspectives, and through participant validation. Therefore, this kind of inquiry is more complex and difficult to conduct if it is to be high quality, systematic and valid to those involved. But it is eminently worthwhile as it promotes the positive transformation of its participants, including the researcher, and thus greater likelihood of sustainable positive outcome.

Validity in a participatory paradigm is more personal and interpersonal than methodological, and should be based on an "interactive dialectic logic" (Reason & Rowan, 1981, p. 244) rather than a dichotomy of 'subjective' or 'objective' truth. This dichotomy can be overcome by the concept of 'perspective', that is, taking a personal view from some distance, and *after* an interactive dialectic using multiple data sets, respondents and co-inquirers. In brief, the action learner/ researcher is interested in perspectives, rather than truth per se, and in giving a credible account of how the participants in the project view themselves and their experiences in the language they themselves use. For example, action learners/ researchers use terms like 'problem', 'issue' or 'concern', rather than 'hypothesis', and personal narrative such as 'we argue', rather than the abstracted passive voice of 'it is argued'.

Several points need to be mentioned about these dichotomies and the observation that experience often escapes the hold of cold logic. First, there are other participatory paradigms in the social sciences, for example, feminist, poststructural and postmodern paradigms. Here we include them in the new, emerging paradigm for reasons of necessary brevity and simplicity. Second, these are observations of paradigms in their most absolute forms. In practice, there is no such purity.

The AL and AR paradigms of learning and knowledge creation can be explained in terms of ontology (assumptions about the nature of being/reality), epistemology (assumptions about the nature of knowledge and knowing), axiology (assumptions about beliefs, values and worldviews) and methodology (consequent strategy for approach to inquiry), as authors discuss in the following chapters.

Bawden and Williams (2017) emphasize the importance of worldview transformations and conclude:

1. Transforming the way that we view the world around us (our worldviews) is a necessary prerequisite if we want (or need) to profoundly change the way we do things (our paradigms) in and to that world.
2. The complex, messy and systemic nature that characterizes the most pressing global issues of the day is dictating precisely such epistemic transformations, given that the currently dominant worldview globally is not only patently inadequate to the task of addressing these pressing issues, but also can clearly be identified as contributing to the emergence and persistence of these issues.
3. Systemic issues demand systemic worldviews, which form the foundations of systemic/holistic paradigms.

The AL and AR paradigms are based on a systemic/holistic worldview, that is, an alternative to the traditional, positivist scientific paradigm. It is particularly suited to human and social research and development for achieving positive, transformational change. By its very nature, the AL/AR paradigm (with its inherent principles and processes) is evolutionary, as explained in more detail in our concluding Chapter 14.

This introductory chapter is based on (1) our perspective and professional experience using AL and AR; and (2) our theoretical framework that is informed by aspects and principles from several existing theories, including grounded theory, action theory, critical educational theory, systems theory, personal construct theory, complexity theory, hope theory and experiential learning theory. In our experience, this framework has worked very effectively in many organizational and community change programs, proving to be appropriate, powerful, emancipatory and successful in terms of their aims and objectives (Wood, 2013; Zuber-Skerritt, 2011). We have published widely about these projects, as AR requires of us to create and contribute to knowledge.

AL and AR for Addressing 'Wicked' Problems in our Turbulent World through Relationships

In the twenty-first century, people across the globe experience and are increasingly aware of so-called 'wicked' problems. These problems are difficult or impossible to solve because what's needed to address them is contradictory, incomplete and changing in ways that are difficult to identify. 'Wicked' problems are not evil; they resist resolution. Why, then, are the approaches of AL and AR especially helpful in working to address the complex, wicked problems of the twenty-first century? As Bob Dick (2012) states:

> We are now in a different era. As globalization and complexity generate turbulence, a greater proportion of problems and issues become intractable – 'wicked'. The best time to plan something in

detail is when it's over, because only then do we know what really happened. In a fast-changing world there are not even any guarantees that a similar solution will fit a 'similar' future problem. More flexibility and more trial and error are needed. It is here that action learning and action research have much to offer. As well as engaging flexibly and participatively with the issues, they can help to develop more facilitative leadership and more flexible approaches to wicked problems. (p. 30)

The authors contributing to this book demonstrate how the various AL and AR approaches can be used for personal, professional, organizational and community development that is both beneficial and sustainable.

Sustainability

What do we mean by 'sustainable development'? In today's world, huge concerns –from overpopulation and unjust distribution of wealth, through global warming and intensity of natural disasters, to peak oil and nuclear catastrophe – raise deep alarm about the future of humankind on earth. This has projected the issue of 'sustainability' into common conversation. The concentration of wealth, power and influence in the hands of an ever smaller minority produces ever greater inequality across societies. It corrodes social, political and economic wellbeing and justice, rooted in understanding that human beings are interdependent and thus need to be inclusive, compassionate and caring so that all may live worthwhile lives. Working to achieve such justice with universal care for the quality of all life, requires that we work together to subvert neoliberalism, the dominant paradigm that promotes and sustains present problems of inequality and destruction of the ecological environment. It requires moving away from egocentrism to recognize that flourishing of society and nourishing of planet earth where we live are inevitably interdependent. This shift from neoliberalism towards a more just, sustainable world therefore also requires a shift in research paradigms in the social and human sciences. This shift takes learning and knowledge creation away from the dominant Western research paradigm of positivism. It shifts to an alternative, non-positivist paradigm of inquiry, such as AR and its derivatives, that recognizes the inevitable interdependence of human beings and their – our – dependence on the physical environment that sustains all life on earth.

Smith and Sharicz (2011) synthesize the literature on sustainability and adopt a similar environmental–social–economic perspective in the form of "Triple Bottom Line" (TBL) sustainability for organizations. They define this as:

The result of the activities of an organization, voluntary or governed by law, that demonstrate the ability of the organization to maintain viable business operations (including financial viability as appropriate) whilst not negatively impacting any social or ecological systems. (pp. 73–74)

Sustainability is also spiritual. Mofid (2011) distils beautifully the concept of spiritual sustainability: "Sustainability is dealing justly with future generations." He argues:

> Many sages, philosophers and theologians throughout history have reminded us that there are two forces at work in society, the material and the spiritual. If either of these two is neglected or ignored they will appear to be at odds with one another: society will inevitably become fragmented, divisions and rifts will manifest themselves with increasing force and frequency.
>
> It is clear that this is exactly what has happened today. We have a situation of disequilibrium and disharmony. Only the reawakening of the human spirit will save us from our own worst extremes. Physical wealth must go hand in hand with spiritual, moral and ethical wealth ....
>
> Above all else, the purpose of the economy is to provide [for] basic human needs as well as the means of establishing, maintaining, and nurturing *human relationships* while dealing justly with future generations (sustainability) and ethically with all life on earth (ecological balance). (http://www.commondreams.org/view/2011/11/01-8)

Relationships

Relationships – among human beings and with the physical environment in which we live – are one of the most important factors in AL and AR. Therefore, at the beginning of every AL or AR project or program (consisting of several team projects), we need to spend time on team and relationship building. Without it, there is much more likely to be disagreements, disharmony and much time wasted later, often leading to poor quality or failure of project outcomes. One powerful example of facilitating team and relationship building is Bob Dick's 'Turning Points' Exercise (http://www.aral.com.au/resources/turningpoints.pdf), which we have often conducted at the start of AR projects or programs and have always found to be immensely helpful for building positive relationships and mutual understanding among participants.

An AL set or an AR team is a living organism that communicates internally mainly through relationships – an energy field, shared understanding, and therefore a set of relationships inside which its members live with mutual respect, trust, love and care. An AL/AR team is a support to each of its members. Its members recognize differences among them – through life experience, beliefs, culture, race, gender, sexual orientation and other sources of diversity – as sources of shared learning and team strength. This is not only a religious way of thinking, or a personal belief system, but also a socioeconomic message with potential to profoundly change the world.

A community of action learners and action researchers is a network of relationships without a specific structure. It is built on community, collaboration,
cooperation and work for the common good. In many parts of the world, people
live in societies where the dominant value system rooted in neoliberalism builds
in individualism, competition and greed – resulting in oppressive economic systems, environmental devastation, unnecessary suffering, toxic environments and
mental health issues in the workplace and beyond. In our own research, we have
observed team members shift from individual consciousness at the beginning of a
project, to creating new ways of thinking, acting, being and knowing (Kearney &
Zuber-Skerritt, 2011, 2012) that we call 'collective consciousness'. This means
thinking as one cohesive unit whose members collectively acknowledge and pursue their shared interests and both have access and give access to the consciousness of the others.

Savary and Berne (2017) observed similarly: "When someone on the team
made a good suggestion, everyone on the team seemed to recognize its value, so it
became easy to implement with minimal discussion, without people taking sides,
pro and con ..." (p. 53).

This unity or union of project team members takes on a life of its own. It
forms a new entity that is necessarily more complex than any of the individuals
in the team, and their shared consciousness becomes richer than that of any individual team member. We agree with Savary and Berne's (2017) statement:

> Love is the most powerful force or energy in the universe. That
> power is multiplied in relationships. Love's potency is released most
> powerfully among people who have formed a relationship (a *union*).
> People who truly unite for a purpose beyond themselves become
> 'differentiated' as they unite and work together in a shared con-
> sciousness to achieve their larger purpose .... In a true relationship,
> no one's individuality is lost. It is increased. That is the beauty of
> connections. These unions that enjoy a collective consciousness
> become the launching pads for the next stage of evolution, as we
> learn consciously how to create them and use them. (pp. 54–55)

Main Genres of AL and AR Discussed in this Book

We now turn to the book's contents and structure, outlining the main genres of
AL and AR presented by the contributors in each chapter. Following this first
introductory chapter where, as editors, we open the book, until the final chapter
(Reflections and Conclusions) where we close the book, the chapters are arranged
in two parts. Part I sets out the main genres of AL and Part II sets out the main
genres of AR.

Part I has four chapters on AL. AL is learning by doing and reflecting on what
went well and what did not go well and why. It is learning from and with each
other in small groups or 'action learning sets' on issues/projects of mutual concern and for the common good. From experience we believe that before engaging
in an AR project or program, it is easier for beginners to start with an AL team

project for understanding, experiencing and reflecting on the values, philosophy, methodology and processes of both AL and AR. Zuber-Skerritt (2011) has defined the commonalities of and differences between AL and AR:

> The main *difference* between action learning and action research is the same as that between learning and research generally. Both include learning, searching, problem solving, inquiry and reflection on action. However, action research is more systematic, rigorous, scrutinisable, verifiable, always made public (e.g. in publications, oral or written reports) and grounded in a certain methodology and rigorous research methods of collecting, analysing and verifying data. (pp. 5–6)

Chapter 2 by Robin Hurst and Michael Marquardt provides an overview of *action learning*. Chapter 3 by Richard Teare focuses on *lifelong action learning*, which is deliberate, conscious, intentional and sustainable. He offers examples of self-directed lifelong action learners in developing countries and in other poor, marginalized contexts, all of whom have no access to formal education. In Chapter 4, Ron Passfield argues and illustrates that *action learning and mindfulness* have much in common and are particularly suited for addressing issues of *mental health in the workplace*, a new significant global issue. In Chapter 5, Ortrun Zuber-Skerritt discusses the *integration of action learning with action research (ALAR)*, in concept, praxis, history and applications. All chapters in Part I use verifiable, evidence-based data as a preparation for AR.

Part II presents the eight specific genres of AR that are used most commonly. Through the theme of *demystifying action research*, Chapter 6 by David Coghlan takes readers on an experiential journey through the main tenets and practices of AR that all kinds of AR have in common. Chapter 7 by Jack Whitehead focuses on the contribution to knowledge creation and knowledge democracy of *AR for self-study and living-educational-theories*. In Chapter 8, Franz Rauch, Stefan Zehetmeier and Peter Posch present an overview of *educational AR* conducted by individuals, AR teams and school/faculty wide. *Systemic AR* discussed by Danny Burns in Chapter 9 is another special genre with an imperative for positive change and development in a whole system. In Chapter 10, Bob Dick introduces *action science* based on the foundational work of Argyris and Schön, and also discusses the latest developments in this AR genre. In Chapter 11, Diana Whitney, Amanda Trosten-Bloom and Maria Giovanna Vianello present *Appreciative Inquiry* as life-affirming AR for co-creating positive personal and social change in organizations and communities. Chapter 12 by Stephen Kemmis, Robin McTaggart and Rhonda Nixon, explains the genre of *critical participatory AR* in the tradition of the Frankfurt and Deakin Schools of critical theory (Carr & Kemmis, 1986; Kemmis, McTaggart, & Nixon, 2014), and also considers recent developments in the participatory AR paradigm. The last chapter in Part II, Chapter 13 by Lesley Wood, is also in the participatory paradigm and introduces the fairly new genre of *participatory action learning and action research* (PALAR).

Chapter 14 concludes this book, returning to editors Ortrun Zuber-Skerritt and Lesley Wood. Here we bring together the arguments presented in this Introduction chapter with the explanations provided about the various AL and AR genres by the authors of the 12 chapters in Parts I and II. We present an inclusive overview of the main principles and processes of AL and AR in the transformative worldview, which have to underpin the approaches of all AL/AR irrespective of their genre. We also highlight the need for AR designs to be flexible and dynamic, so that they can be adapted for specific problems and contexts. We conclude the chapter and therefore the book in true AR style, with personal reflections on our learning through preparing/editing this book.

At the end of each chapter, we include a section on 'Topics for Discussion' with questions to stimulate self-critical reflection and debate in small groups; and a section on 'Further Reading' to provide guidance and suggestions on useful literature for in-depth study and further work. We illustrate the structure of the book in Fig. 1.1.

Reflections and Conclusions

Early in the twentieth century when social scientists attempted to be accepted as the equals of their colleagues in the natural sciences, they adopted the one dominant, positivist paradigm from the natural sciences. This paradigm is still dominant in social science research, but it does not stand alone. Over time, some researchers in the social sciences have recognized that people's behaviour is inspired and shaped by factors different from what does and does not influence inorganic matter. Human beings think, know, reflect, feel and emote, so therefore they behave and react differently, not just from other living creatures but also from each other. This is especially so in different environments, contexts, cultures and traditions where people are subject to different influences.

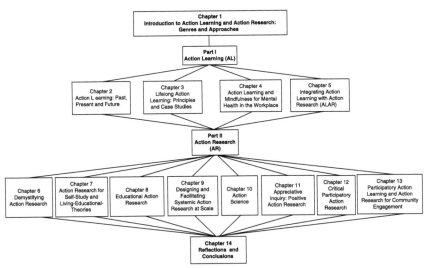

Fig. 1.1:   Structure of This Book.

Hence, in the social sciences, as researchers have further developed or transformed understandings and methodologies to take into account their growing awareness of different kinds of knowledge, humanness, beliefs, values and worldviews, so too research paradigms have evolved. With evolving understanding of 'knowledge' – what it is and how/why it is created and used – ever more researchers in the social sciences appreciate that research on human issues, concerns and problems has to use methodologies that are appropriate to address or help solve the complex and often 'wicked' problems that now appear to touch every quarter of human life. The 'research lens' of AR, which actively supports those involved in the problem to help identify and address it sustainably, ensures the adaptability and therefore the utility of this research paradigm. It is why so many different approaches to AL and AR have been created over time and are still being invented and further developed.

However, among beginning researchers and their supervisors and examiners who are new to AR, many have found these developments confusing, especially if these people have not properly used or explained certain processes, procedures and methods. Problems are even more important and more serious if these researchers actually have adhered to the AR paradigm but have been criticized by traditional 'positivist' researchers and examiners who assess all research narrowly from their perspective and paradigm and do not accept AR as an alternative and more appropriate approach to human and social inquiry, learning, development and knowledge creation.

Each of the following chapters demonstrates how and why this approach has been taken with success (or failure) in a particular genre of AL and AR. We trust that reading the chapters in this book will demystify AL and AR for our readers and will clarify their understanding of both in their various forms. We hope that this clarification will enable readers to not only use AL and AR effectively in their R&D projects, but also develop new variants best suited to their particular contexts, participants and problems. Such is the positive contribution – and the evolution – of this affirmative paradigm for our times!

Topics for Discussion

1. In your view/experience, what are the main characteristics, commonalities of and differences between AL and AR?
2. How would you describe your research paradigm?
3. Why do you think relationships are important in AL and AR?

Further Reading

Wood, L. (in press). *Participatory action learning and action research*. Abingdon, Routledge.

Wood, L. (2013). Action research for the 21st century: Exploring new educational pathways. *South African Journal of Higher Education, 28*(2), 660–672.

Wood, L., & Zuber-Skerritt, O. (2013). PALAR as a methodology for community engagement by faculties of education. *South African Journal of Education, 33*(4), 1–15.

Zuber-Skerritt, O. (2018). An educational framework for participatory action learning and action research (PALAR). *Educational Action Research, 26*(4), 513–532.

References

Bawden, R., & Williams, M. (2017). The learning conference and worldview transforma-
tions. In O. Zuber-Skerritt (Ed.), *Conferences as sites of learning and development:
Using participatory action learning and action research approaches* (pp. 74–85).
London: Routledge.

Carr, W., & Kemmis, S. (1986). *Becoming critical: Education, knowledge and action research.*
London: Falmer Press.

Dick, B. (2012). Action research and action learning for an uncertain and turbulent world.
In O. Zuber-Skerritt (Ed.), *Action research for sustainable development in a turbulent
world* (pp. 29–44). Bingley: Emerald Publishing Limited.

Kearney, J., & Zuber-Skerritt, O. (2011). *Actioning change and lifelong learning in community development.* Melbourne: Action Learning and Action Research Association.
Retrieved from http://www.alara.net.au/files/ALARA%20Monograph%20No%20
1%20JKearney%20&%20OZuberSkerritt%20201106s.pdf

Kearney, J., & Zuber-Skerritt, O. (2012). From learning organization to learning community: Sustainability through lifelong learning. *The Learning Organization, 19*(5),
400–413.

Kemmis, S., McTaggart, R., & Nixon, R. (2014). *The action research planner: Doing critical
participatory action research.* Dordrecht: Springer.

Kolb, D. (1984). *Experiential learning: Experience as the source of learning and development.* Princeton, NJ: Prentice Hall.

Lewin, K. (1951). *Field theory in social science: Selected theoretical papers.* New York, NY:
Harper & Row.

Mofid, K. (2011). Global crises are spiritual: A time for awakening. Retrieved from http://
www.commondreams.org/view/2011/11/01-8

Reason, P., & Rowan, J. (Eds.). (1981). *Human inquiry: A sourcebook of new paradigm
research.* Chichester: John Wiley & Sons.

Revans, R. (1982). *The origins and growth of action learning.* Bromley: Chartwell-Bratt.

Revans, R. (1991). Action learning: Reg Revans in Australia [Video series produced by
Ortrun Zuber-Skerritt (now on DVD)]. Brisbane: Video Vision, University of
Queensland. Retrieved from https://www.alarassociation.org/?q=about-al-and-ar/
reg-revans-and-action-learning

Savary, L., & Berne, P. (2017). *Teilhard de Chardin on love: Evolving human relationships.*
Mahwah, NJ: Paulist Press.

Smith, P. A. C., & Sharicz, C. (2011). The shift needed for sustainability. *The Learning
Organization, 18*(1), 73–86.

Wood, L. (in press). *Participatory action learning and action research.* Abingdon, Routledge.

Wood, L. (2013). Action research for the 21st century: Exploring new educational pathways. *South African Journal of Higher Education, 28*(2), 660–672.

Wood, L., & Zuber-Skerritt, O. (2013). PALAR as a methodology for community engagement by faculties of education. *South African Journal of Education, 33*(4), 1–15.

Zuber-Skerritt, O. (2011). *Action leadership: Towards a participatory paradigm.* Dordrecht,
Springer International.

Zuber-Skerritt, O. (2018). An educational framework for participatory action learning and
action research (PALAR). *Educational Action Research, 26*(4), 513–532.

Part I

Action Learning

Part I of this book consists of four chapters on Action Learning (AL), that is, learning by doing, reflecting on what went well and what did not – and why, and learning from and with each other in small groups or 'action learning sets' on issues/projects of mutual concern and for the benefit of the common good. We argue that AL is a useful introduction to Action Research (AR) for understanding, experiencing and reflecting on the values, philosophy, methodology and processes of both AL and AR.

In brief, Chapter 2 provides an overview of action learning. Chapter 3 focuses on lifelong action learning (LAL) that is deliberate and sustainable, with examples of self-directed learners in poor, marginalized contexts and in developing countries, who have no access to formal education. Chapter 4 argues and illustrates that action learning and mindfulness are particularly well suited for addressing mental health issues in the workplace, a new and significant global issue. Chapter 5 discusses the integration of action learning with action research (ALAR), in concept, praxis, history and applications.

Chapter 2

Action Learning: Past, Present and Future

Robin R. Hurst and Michael Marquardt

Chapter Outline

The story of Action Learning today begins in the coalmines of Wales in the 1940s when Reg Revans began exploring new ways of solving problems by involving the miners themselves rather than bringing in outside experts. Over the next 40 years, Revans practised and wrote about action learning, bringing it to Europe, Asia and Australia. Jack Welch brought action learning to General Electric and the United States in the 1980s. Action learning, however, was little known and practised until several action learning books were published and conferences convened in the 1990s. Through the efforts of organizations such as the International Federation of Action Learning and the World Institute for Action Learning, action learning quickly became the leadership development and problem-solving methodology of thousands of corporations and government agencies around the world. Research on action learning continues to identify ever more powerful ways for action learning to be used in virtual, national and global settings. The chapter not only explores the history of action learning, and action learning in its present state, but also provides predictions of action learning in the future. This chapter is significant because it identifies the main strengths and challenges of action learning to date, and provides a vision of its future potential value and impact worldwide.

Introduction

Action Learning today had its beginnings in the coalmines of Wales during the 1940s when Reg Revans, considered the "father of Action Learning" and its principal pioneer, had the novel idea to involve the miners themselves in examining and exploring both the problems faced in the mine and potential solutions to the dilemmas, rather than involving outside experts. This focus on involving the workers in problem solving by 'brainstorming problems' and taking action, and reflecting on the results of their actions, became the basis upon which action

Action Learning and Action Research: Genres and Approaches, 19–33
Copyright © 2019 by Robin R. Hurst and Michael Marquardt
doi:10.1108/978-1-78769-537-520191005

learning has evolved. Revans took his new philosophy to organizations in other countries such as Belgium, where he worked for several years to help improve the country's economic development (Boshyk, Barker, & Dilworth, 2010). He also used action learning to assist the University of Manchester in a project with the Hospital International Communications (HIC) project, which involved hospitals in London (Boshyk et al., 2010; Eason, 2017). The success of these projects, which used employees involved in the problems to aid in the solutions, paved the way for action learning as a discipline, and for its use as a powerful problem solving and management development tool.

Although Revans developed and applied many of the principles of action learning when he began working in the coalmines of Wales and in the hospitals of London in the 1940s, he did not actually use the term 'action learning' publicly or in his writings until 1972, when he was aged 65 (Boshyk, 2011, 2012). He was initially reluctant to define the concept of action learning, because he felt a definition might constrain the evolution and development of the action learning process. Revans (1982a) did, however, finally define action learning:

> Action learning is a means of development, intellectual, emotional, or physical, that requires its subject, through responsible involvement in some real, complex and stressful problem, to achieve intended change sufficient to improve observable behavior henceforth in the problem field. In action learning, people learn with and from each other by mutual support, advice and criticism during their attacks upon real problems, intendedly to be solved in whole or in part. (pp. 626–627)

Other descriptions of action learning have emerged as scholars and practitioners on both sides of the Atlantic embraced the concept and began studying and applying the model in the workplace. Dilworth and Willis (2003) described action learning as "a process of reflecting on one's work, and beliefs in a supportive/confrontational environment of one's peers for the purpose of gaining new insights and resolving real business and community problems in real time" (p. 11). Yorks, O'Neil and Marsick (1999) define action learning as:

> An approach to working with and developing people, that uses work on an actual project or problem as the way to learn. Participants work in small groups to take action to solve their problem and learn how to learn from action. (p. 3)

Marquardt (1999) describes action learning as:

> Both a process and powerful program that involves a small group of people solving real problems while at the same time focusing on what they are learning and how their learning can benefit each group member and the organization as a whole. (p. 4)

Marquardt, Banks, Cauwelier, and Ng (2018) state:

> Action learning is a powerful problem-solving tool that has the amazing capacity to simultaneously build successful leaders, teams, and organizations. It is a process that involves a small group working on real problems, taking action, and learning as individuals, as a team, and as an organization while doing so. (p. 4)

The theme running through each of these definitions of action learning is that real-world problems become a focal point for learning and for taking action. These definitions also focus on reflection as a means of learning (Dilworth & Willis, 2003). Reflection is a way of making meaning out of what has occurred or is occurring (Schön, 1987). Collaboration with others to understand meaning is also crucial to action learning. Dilworth and Willis (2003) contend it is the dialogue between group/set members that actually aids in providing the meaning to the problem, as well as the pathway to finding the solutions. Marquardt (2014) argues that fresh questions provide the basis for understanding the problem, as well as for potential solutions.

Action learning groups may be formed around a single problem or several problems. In the single-problem group, one topic is identified and all group members focus their energies on solving that problem. These single-problem sets are sometimes referred to as 'in-company action learning', although in some instances the problem is brought by a partner, customer, or other stakeholder organization. In multiple-problem sets, each group member brings a problem to the group for fellow members to help solve. Some organizations use the multiple-problem format (also referred to as the open-group approach, peer coaching, or learning circles) to help managers resolve leadership issues they are facing in their roles. This approach is also commonly used to bring together individuals from different environments to help one another.

Action Learning: The Past

Reg Revans, who is recognized as the founding father of action learning, often repeated the story that he first became aware of some of the key elements of action learning when his father told him about his investigations into the sinking of the 'unsinkable' Titanic. In his interviews with the engineers who built the Titanic, Revans' father discovered that the engineers never expressed their doubts before the sinking because they feared asking a 'dumb question'. Later on, Revans would advocate the importance of creating an action learning environment in which fresh, fearless questions could be asked when seeking to solve a problem. His later experiences in the Cavendish Laboratories at Cambridge University enabled Revans to understand the power of ideas from people with different perspectives, rather than expertise alone, in solving problems. His work in the coalmines of Wales supported his belief that rather than relying on outside expertise, people who had a stake in the problems were better able to solve them.

Each of these experiences enabled Revans to develop the basic principles and elements of action learning.

Revans (1983) claimed, "the organization that continues to express only the ideas of the past is not learning, and training systems intended to develop our young may do little more than to make them proficient in yesterday's technique" (p. 1). Revans presented the learning equation: $L = P + Q$ to represent action learning in its simplest form, meaning that Learning is equal to the programmed knowledge of set/group members, added to the questioning and insight of set/group members, along with others involved in the problem-solving process (Revans, 1983).

Revans (1983) developed a number of assumptions about action learning as part of this process, including:

- *Learning is cradled in the task.* Action learning, itself, is part of the task.
- *Formal instruction is not sufficient to solve all problems.* This does not imply that formal instruction should be cast aside, but only that formal learning alone may not be sufficient to solve the problems at hand. This is where the continued questioning of assumptions is important in problem solving.
- *Problems require insightful and 'fresh' questions in order to solve the problem.* Once again, Revans calls for set/team members to look beyond traditional questions, and think outside the conventional norms of problem solving.
- *Learning involves doing.* Managers and leaders must engage in problem solving and action in order to learn, whether this is a novel approach, or one that may not conform to the managers' past experiences.
- *Learning is voluntary.* A change in one's behavior is dependent on the individual. Managers and set/team members may not agree on the correct course, but they learn changes in behavior on their own volition, not at the will of others.
- *Urgent problems provide the spur for learning.* When the problem is urgent, the need for solution to the problem is also urgent. This may inspire managers/team members to look at different options.
- *Action must be taken, and feedback is important to learning.* Learning is reinterpreted from past experiences. However, the premise of action learning is that there may be a reinterpretation of past experiences in the acquisition of new knowledge. This new knowledge helps in the solution to the new problems.
- *The contribution of peers and/or sets is important in the process.* Learning with and from each other is the cornerstone of action learning. New ideas generated from multiple folks involved in the process of problem solving help to generate new ideas in problem solving. These new ideas may spark other ideas which lead to solutions to the real problem. Learning with and from each other is a pillar upon which action learning is based.

During the 1970s and 1980s, as action learning moved beyond the work of just Revans and traversed to other parts of the world, different approaches or schools of action learning appeared. Marsick and O'Neil (1999) categorized these different approaches into the (1) scientific, (2) experiential and (3) critical reflection schools of action learning. A discussion of each follows.

Scientific school of action learning

Those whose work is most closely based on Revans' work fall into this school. Probably because Revans began his professional career as a physicist, he based his thinking on the scientific method. He conceptualized action learning as a model of problem solving in three stages that he called Systems Alpha, Beta and Gamma, with System Alpha being analogous to a situation analysis. This form of action learning shares many features with Action Research, but it is intentionally biased towards learning. Questioning is central to Revans' (1982b, 1983) learning theory. Questioning insight occurs when people question their direct experience (Morris, 1991). Revans (1983) describes it as "intuition, things crossing the mind, insight" (p. 102). Programmed knowledge is "expert knowledge, knowledge in books, what we are told to do because that is how it has been done for decades" (Weinstein, 1995, p. 44). Revans embraces the notion that the key to learning is in finding the right question/s to ask. Questions that help people get started along this path include the following: "What are we trying to do? What is stopping us from doing it? What can we do about it?" (Revans, 1978, p. 17).

Experiential school of action learning

Other practitioners of action learning saw Kolb's experiential learning cycle as its theoretical base. In Kolb's (1984) experiential learning cycle, action, reflection, theory and practice are of equal importance. Proponents of this school see the starting point for learning as the action learning group members, who then reflect on experience with the support of others, followed by further action, to change – rather than simply repeat – previous patterns. Action learning enables learning in each stage of the experiential learning cycle (McGill & Beaty, 1992). Advocates of this school typically use a design that ensures the amount of attention given to learning is higher than it is in the normal accidental and informal task and learning experience (Mumford, 1991). Learning is the reason for the action learning session. Action learning programs help create the ability to learn how to learn in a number of ways. For example, time is scheduled for learning reviews at each meeting. Members review the projects, their own learning process, and relevant issues that emerge from group dynamics and the work of others. Members may keep learning logs, or negotiate personal development plans and learning agreements (Mumford, 1996).

Critical reflection school of action learning

This school holds that the kind of reflection undertaken in the Experiential School is useful, but not sufficient. Practitioners in this school believe participants also need to reflect on the assumptions and beliefs that shape practice. Taking time to reflect can be powerful, and critical reflection can be more powerful, because attention is directed to the root of the problem (O'Neil & Marsick, 1994). These practitioners explain the process and results of critical thinking in different ways. Weinstein (1995) talks about participants examining what they believe and value, and how they are changing and moving, and gaining a better understanding of their own insights. She feels that when critical reflection occurs, the process may be deeply disturbing for those who do not want to change existing structures, status or beliefs. Re-formulation of the existing problem commonly occurs when people uncover misperceptions, norms and expectations that were hidden (Marsick & Watkins, 1992; Pedler, 1996; Weinstein, 1995). Critical reflection can also extend beyond the individual participants' underlying assumptions, and can lead specifically to the examination of organizational norms.

Different Conceptions of Action Learning

As action learning began to be practised in the United States, managers in many US organizations, such as General Electric and Boeing, modified the action learning process to fit their organization and the types of problems they wanted to address (Boshyk, 2012; Dilworth & Boshyk, 2010; Willis, 2011). Boshyk (2012) contends that the *Americanized* version of action learning is no more than what some refer to as 'organizational development', combining Lewin's (1946) concepts with some of the principles of action learning. This is due to the prevalence of more action research and organizational development concepts adopted and promoted by American scholars over the years.

The International Management Centre was formed in 1984 and thousands of action learning practitioners have graduated from it, in collaboration with academic institutions in the UK, Australia, Papua New Guinea, Malaysia, Hong Kong, South Africa, Netherlands and Switzerland. The Action Learning, Action Research and Process Management Association (ALARPM) was founded in 1991 in Australia with the specific goal of promoting the study, practice, research, and teaching of action learning, action research and process management together as a professional discipline.

From the 1980s, action learning has been incorporated into masters and doctoral programs in many universities, including the University of Michigan, Business School of the Netherlands, Virginia Commonwealth University, George Washington University, Columbia University and American University. As action learning was introduced into the business curriculum, Boshyk (2012) noted it is an improvement on more traditional lecture-based programs:

> In its Americanized form, team members do learn and teams do assist organizations in addressing difficult problems – it is just that they fall short of their potential. It is as if many US companies have grasped the outward form of Action Learning, that is, teams working on problems, without, however, attending to its essence. (p. 12)

The 'Americanized version' in business curriculum does not usually involve the implementation of team recommendations and at the same time does not maximize individual development and behavioral change.

Action Learning: The Present State

Before the beginning of the twenty-first century, most action learning was conducted in English speaking countries, many of which Revans visited before his death in 2003. Over the past 20 years, however, action learning has expanded rapidly. It has now become the fastest growing management development/problem solving methodology in the world as more and more organizations in many fields around the globe have seen the benefits of the process (Marquardt et al., 2018).

Since the mid-1990s, scores of publications on the subject have appeared, and have been translated from English into many languages such as Korean, Italian, Japanese, Chinese, Thai, Portuguese, Russian, Arabic, Spanish and Farsi (Marquardt, 2011). A *Business Week* article published in October 2005 proclaimed, "Action learning is one of the top management ideas in the history of management" (Byrnes, 2005, p. 71). A 2009 study by the *Corporate Executive Board* found that 77 per cent of learning executives chose action learning as the 'top driver' of leadership development (Corporate Executive Board, 2009) in their organizations. Two organizations are leading in the effort to bring action learning throughout the world: the World Institute for Action Learning (WIAL) and The International Federation of Action Learning (IFAL). Both organizations contribute to the field of action learning, and provide guidance and research.

Action learning has been used by numerous government ministries from around the world to develop specific social or economic sectors of the country. For example, the Ministry of Education in Malaysia is currently using action learning to transform the country's higher education institutions as the "stepping stone to developing its people and bringing Malaysia to *developed country status* by the year 2020" (Marquardt & Yeo, 2012, p. 114). Selected universities throughout Malaysia created action learning teams to solve specific challenges that they were facing in their communities as well as challenges experienced with their students and faculties. Each university created action learning teams that have been given the resources, training and coaching to develop break-through strategies and actions. Action learning was then applied in university classrooms and offices to transform the academic culture and to influence the national culture (Marquardt & Yeo, 2012).

In addition to the explosive growth of action learning in corporations and government agencies, more and more universities around the world have developed programs to train action learning coaches, including Rikkyo University in Tokyo, La Rochelle Business School in France and Uganda Martyrs University in Nkozi. Government agencies have also implemented action learning programs, most notably the governments of Jamaica, Trinidad and Tobago, Brazil, China, Singapore, Malaysia, India, Saudi Arabia, Sweden, Nigeria and South Africa (Marquardt et al., 2018).

Marquardt and Yeo (2012) surveyed hundreds of action learning programs around the world and identified six categories in which action learning is being used: (1) talent and leadership development; (2) organizational learning and restructuring; (3) sales and marketing; (4) environment and sustainability; (5) product and service innovation; and (6) corporate culture and ethics.

Talent and Leadership Development

Talent management, which includes hiring, developing and retaining of skilled people, has become a key organizational requirement and challenge of the twenty-first century. Leaders of organizations realize they must have top-flight talent to succeed in the hypercompetitive and increasingly complex global economy. The Global Leadership Program at Boeing using action learning debuted in 1999 as one of several tools to enhance Boeing's ability to operate as a global company and to develop leadership competencies within the executive population. The action learning program is targeted to develop executive skills within three categories of global competencies: (1) most critical competencies (adapting, thinking globally, building relationships, inspiring trust, leading courageously, aligning the organization, influencing and negotiating); (2) very important competencies (shaping strategy, fostering open and effective communication, attracting and developing talent, driving stakeholder success, demonstrating vision, using sound judgment); and (3) important competencies (driving execution, inspiring and empowering, working cross-functionally, focusing on quality and continuous improvement, applying financial acumen). Anglo American Mining, one of the world's largest diversified mining and natural resource groups with operations in South Africa, South America and Australia, has consistently used action learning for developing foundational broad management skills, knowledge and awareness across Anglo American countries.

Organizational Learning and Restructuring

Deutsche Bank, an international bank with its headquarters in Frankfurt, Germany, employs more than 80,000 people in 72 countries, with a large presence in Europe, the Americas, Asia Pacific and in the emerging markets of Africa. Revenues in 2009 exceeded $30 billion. In 2010 Deutsche Bank received the Bank of the Year Award, the financial industry's most coveted award, from the prestigious *International Financial Review* (IFR magazine), an award it also won in 2003 and 2005. A few years ago, Deutsche Bank faced tremendous changes in its business and staff structure, with critical implications for corporate culture. Organizational change was critical, and action learning was employed to work on the following problems:

- reconfiguration along divisional product lines;
- shift from regional to global operational structure;
- shift from multinational to global leadership structure;
- acquisition of several US entities and their leadership model; and
- change in corporate language from German to English.

To solve these problems, Deutsche Bank recognized that it needed to develop its leadership and its problem-solving capabilities. Existing leadership development programs were focused on individual, not organizational, development. As a result, little knowledge was transferred to the workplace, meaning that the learning was not applied to deal with business challenges. In addition, the cost of off-the-job training and development was high and climbing. In searching for a tool that would develop leaders while simultaneously resolving these challenges, Deutsche Bank chose action learning because of its 'just-in-time' learning and self-managed learning efficiency.

Key business challenges were identified and a six-month action learning program was begun. The CEO, program director and/or program manager selected the problems confronting Deutsche Bank that were best suited for both the bank and the action learning participants. These problems need to meet four criteria: to be

- of strategic importance to the bank;
- a potential source of significant organizational change;
- strategic – not tactical – in nature, to 'stretch' participants; and
- broad in scope, offering rich learning opportunities.

Twenty participants were selected. Following a two-day introduction to action learning, the four groups met over a period of six to eight weeks on a part-time basis working on their problem. The final two days of the program included the presentation of actions taken as well as capturing the learning that could be applied throughout Deutsche Bank. The program was considered a great success, having attained innovative and cost-effective actions for each of the company's four problems.

Sales and Marketing

Toyota distributors selected 160 General Managers (GMs) from throughout Japan to participate in the Lexus action learning launch. Action learning projects were begun in September 2004 and continued until April 2005. Emphasis was placed on establishing the Lexus concept and developing the Lexus marketing strategy. The action learning project was also designed to create a new style of leadership for the leaders of Lexus, developing the leadership competencies of the GMs by moving them from directive bosses to participative, team-oriented leaders. This shift in thinking gave rise to impressive results:

- sales within the first few months exceeded expectations, and by 2009 the HS 250h became the top selling sedan in Japan;
- Lexus Japan's network of 143 new dealerships became profitable in 2007; and
- under the guidance of the GMs, strong Toyota teams were developed throughout Japan.

Environment and Sustainability

Organizations around the world are trying to 'go green' and let their customers know that they care about saving the environment and are therefore socially responsible. DuPont used action learning teams in its Sabine River Works

Project. The Sabine River Works consumes a large amount of energy, but its energy efficiency achievements have set an example for the entire DuPont Company. As a result of the strategies developed by action learning teams, CO_2 emissions dropped by 40 per cent and British Thermal Unit consumption per pound of production decreased by 50 per cent, while production increased by 20 per cent. In 2009, the company's energy savings were worth $8 million. The plant achieved these savings by improving burner efficiency and converting waste streams into fuel. Sabine's Site Manager Bobby Laughlin noted, "Our teams did outstanding work in making meaningful and sustainable changes in our energy usage by assessing our opportunities for improvement and implementing a variety of creative solutions" (DuPont, 2011, as quoted in Marquardt & Yeo, 2012, p. 98).

Product and Service Innovation

The GMs and Human Resource Director of the Morgan's Hotel Group met in Las Vegas to identify problems that (a) were critically important for the growth and development of Morgan's Hotel Group, and (b) would be appropriate and meet the criteria for the action learning process. The problems chosen affected three critical aspects of the company's business, namely, employees, guests and owners/shareholders. The action learning groups identified numerous powerful actions to solve six key challenges of the hotel, namely,

- expanding and improving the value-added responsibilities of the concierge;
- developing recognition programs and awards for frequent-stay guests;
- developing a performance matrix for shareholders;
- promoting and developing employees;
- creating employee recognition programs; and
- maintaining guest relations during hotel renovation.

The ideas generated during this session helped the hotel chain to achieve higher occupancy, as well as review and resolve problems and challenges which faced the group (Marquardt & Yeo, 2012).

Corporate Culture and Ethics

Panasonic, like many organizations, has used action learning for leadership development and problem solving. But this company has found other great value in action learning – its ability to build (1) a culture imbued with high ethical standards; (2) a commitment to continuing learning; and (3) deep respect for others – as these values are inherent within the principles and practice of action learning. Accordingly, all new employees at Panasonic are introduced to action learning and participate in action learning problem solving as part of their orientation. Panasonic was eager to make action learning a part of every employee's experience because top management discovered how well it matches with the following four components of the Basic Business Philosophy (BBP) of Panasonic's

Founder, Konosuke Matsushita. These components are (1) courtesy and humility; (2) cooperation, team spirit and collective wisdom; (3) *sunao* mind or understanding the truth without bias or self-interest; and (4) adaptability and untiring effort to improve.

Action Learning: The Future

The future for action learning appears to be even more glorious than the past and the present. Practitioners and researchers continue to learn more and more how to improve the power and speed of action learning within action learning groups, as well as innovative applications that occur following the action learning sessions.

What enables action learning to be powerful is its relative simplicity in practice, but relative complexity in the theories underlying action learning. Simply stated, action learning works so well because it has the unique ability to interweave a wide array of organizational, psychological, sociological, anthropological, educational and political theories that form a foundation and synergy unavailable in any other source. In addition to social sciences, action learning also incorporates a number of the physical sciences such as physics, mathematics, systems engineering and biology.

Probably no science will have more impact on the future of action learning than neuroscience. As we better understand the brain and how it influences our behaviour, we will better understand why action learning works and how it can be improved. Rock and Cox (2012) have classified the main social triggers that activate an individual's primary threat response through their relationship to the five domains of status, certainty, autonomy, relatedness and fairness. Each of these domains comes into play when we use action learning. For example, action learning neutralizes the status threat by encouraging the problem presenter to be an equal member of the group. Once the problem is presented, anyone can ask a question of anyone else, and the team is accountable for working on the challenge together. Even the problem presentation helps to reduce the status threat, as the problem presenter is asked to present his or her challenge very succinctly, reducing the biases and assumptions that are introduced. The action learning team is then responsible for drawing out the needed information through questioning. This reduction in status stops the fight-or-flight response and ensures people are productive and effective.

Similarly, action learning reduces the relatedness threat response. For people to do their best, most creative and effective work, they need to be in what Rock and Cox (2012) call a 'toward state', not hindered by fear or threat. Feeling positive about those you are working with is key to this. Feeling relatedness, or socially connected and included, is a core value for humans. When leaders ask good questions, as they do in action learning, it engages the listener's prefrontal cortex, the rational part of the brain that deals with decision making and working memory. A connection is formed between the questioner and the responder. Through asking a question, the questioner is implying, "I care about your opinion; I want your viewpoint; I value your insights." Therefore, questions increase the levels of relatedness and connection in the group.

While subtle, fairness is interwoven through the action learning process. Action learning coaches ask a number of questions to every member of the group, giving each person an opportunity to answer. Coaches are encouraged to stop those who elaborate on their replies, ensuring that each person has a chance to give an answer before discussing the details. Similarly, coaches hold to time in a multi-problem action learning session, giving each problem presenter equal opportunity to work on his or her challenge.

In addition to the impact of increased research and better applications of action learning, three other factors greatly influence the use of action learning: (1) greater virtual practice of action learning teams; (2) technology in the workplace; and (3) globalization and culture.

Virtuality: more and more of the learning and more and more of the work of the organization are being done by individuals and teams located in different physical locations and across different time zones. A number of benefits accrue to the organization that can unite highly qualified people without location restrictions. These include greater ability to leverage skills throughout the organization, better capability to provide customers with the 'best and brightest', more balance between work and home relationships, and the opportunity of cutting costs and time. The necessity of most effectively utilizing the knowledge and talents of people throughout the organization who have the necessary capabilities to interact with specific customers has resulted in more and more organizations creating action learning teams that can work together virtually as effectively as they could face-to-face.

Technology: organizations are continuously seeking more effective ways to capitalize on the power of technology – to increase production, decrease costs, expand knowledge, adapt successes, or incorporate company-wide resources. Technology has significant impact on the structure, management and functioning of every organization. It demands new patterns of work organization and affects individual jobs, the formation and structure of groups as well as the nature of supervision and managerial roles (Waddill & Marquardt, 2011). Action learning has the ability to develop learners' understanding and harness the power of technology to maximize both the internal and external operations of an organization. Technology, such as Skype, Zoom and other formats may replace the face-to-face meetings so important to action learning today. Virtual reality simulations may aid teams in predicting the 'what if' and 'what then' questions. Several organizations, including Goodrich, Kirin, Microsoft and Krones Bottling, have already begun using action learning groups to leverage technology for business success.

Globalization: as organizations globalize, the presence of multiple cultures in action learning groups will occur more frequently. Instead of seeing cultural differences as barriers, however, these differences can be seen and utilized as the source of synergy, which contributes to a variety of perspectives that can actually augment the power and success of action learning programs. Action learning recognizes that diversity rather than expertise is more valuable as the problems become more complex and more difficult to understand and solve.

Conclusions

Action learning began as a simple concept to involve workers in problem solving, take action and then reflect on that action. As organizations began to see results from the process, action learning was successfully adopted by numerous companies, mainly in Europe, to aid in solving difficult problems. The concept found its way to the United States in the 1980s and was embraced by many Fortune 500 companies as not only a process for problem solving, but also a way to help develop leadership skills in 'real-time' situations. Action learning has now gained an international reputation for problem solving and leader development, so we can foresee it gaining additional prominence as a problem solving and leader/manager development strategy in the future. Whether on-site, face-to-face, or virtual, the essence of action learning will remain the same: question assumptions and everything else, take action and reflect on that action, and then question again. The process and results envisioned by Revans in the 1940s are relevant to action learning today and in the future.

Topics for Discussion

1. As teams become more dispersed globally, and technology has become a cornerstone of virtual meetings, how do you think this will affect the effectiveness of action learning sets in solving problems? What actions can be taken to ensure that virtual teams are successful in action learning?
2. What is the role of the action learning coach in virtual teams? What are the challenges the coach will face in working with virtual teams? How can these challenges be mitigated to ensure members of the action learning set will perform at their highest level?
3. In today's work environment, global teams comprised of individuals from many different cultures are the norm. How can you ensure that cultural differences will be addressed and appreciated in action learning sets?

Further Reading

Albers, C. (2008). Improving pedagogy through action learning and scholarship of teaching and learning. *Teaching Sociology, 36*, 79–86.

Leonard, H. S., & Lang, F. (2010). Leadership development via action learning. *Advances in Developing Human Resources, 12*(2), 225–240.

Marquardt, M., Banks, S., Cauwelier, P., & Ng, C. (2018). *Optimizing the power of action learning: Real-time strategies for developing leaders, building teams, and transforming organizations* (3rd ed.). Boston, MA: Nicholas Brealey Publishing.

O'Neil, J., & Marsick, V. (2007). *Understanding action learning*. New York, NY: AMACON.

References

Boshyk, Y. (2011). Ad fontes – Reg Revans: Some early sources of his personal growth and values. In M. Pedler (Ed.), *Action learning in practice* (4th ed., pp. 81–91). Farnham: Gower.

Boshyk, Y. (2012). New dimensions in action learning: Reinventing leadership development. PowerPoint from presentation at MIT Sloan Management, Action Learning Conference, August 1–2. Retrieved from http://mitsloan.mit.edu/actionlearning/media/document/conference2012/YuryBoshyk.pdf

Boshyk, Y., Barker, A., & Dilworth, R. (2010). Milestones in the history and worldwide evolution of action learning. In Y. Boshyk & R. Dilworth (Eds.), *Action learning: History and evolution* (pp. 117–204). Basingstoke: Palgrave Macmillan.

Byrnes, N. (2005). Star search: How to recruit, train, and hold on to great people: What works, what doesn't. *Business Week*, October 10, p. 71.

Corporate Executive Board. (2009, March 19). What drives leadership bench strength? *Learning and Development Roundtable*. Washington, DC: Corporate Executive Board.

Dilworth, R., & Boshyk, Y. (2010). Action learning in different national organizational contexts and cultures. In Y. Boshyk & R. Dilworth (Eds.), *Action learning: History and evolution* (pp. 205–233). Basingstoke: Palgrave Macmillan.

Dilworth, R., & Willis, V. (2003). *Action learning: Images and pathways*. Malabar, FL: Krieger Publishing Company.

Eason, K. (2017). Action learning across the decades: Case studies in health and social care settings in 1966 and 2016. *Leadership in Health Services, 30*(2), 118–128.

Kolb, D. (1984). *Experiential learning: Experience as the source of learning and development*. Upper Saddle River, NJ: Pearson Education.

Lewin, K. (1946). Action research and minority problems. *Journal of Social Issues, 2*(4), 34–46.

Marquardt, M. (1999). *Action learning in action: Transforming problems and people for world-class organizational learning*. Palo Alto, CA: Davies-Black Publishers.

Marquardt, M. (2011). *Optimizing the power of action learning: Real-time strategies for developing leaders, building teams, and transforming organizations* (2nd ed). Boston, MA: Nicholas Brealey Publishing.

Marquardt, M. (2014). *Leading with questions: How leaders find the right solutions by knowing what to ask*. San Francisco, CA: Jossey-Bass.

Marquardt, M., Banks, S., Cauwelier, P., & Ng, C. (2018). *Optimizing the power of action learning: Real-time strategies for developing leaders, building teams, and transforming organizations* (3rd ed.). Boston, MA: Nicholas Brealey Publishing.

Marquardt, M., & Yeo, R. (2012). *Breakthrough problem solving with action learning: Concepts and cases*. Stanford, CA: Stanford University Press.

Marsick, V., & O'Neil, J. (1999). The many faces of action learning. *Management Learning, 30*(2), 159–176.

Marsick, V., & Watkins, K. (1992). *Informal and incidental learning in the workplace*. New York, NY: Routledge.

McGill, I., & Beaty, L. (1992). *Action learning: A practitioner's guide*. Abingdon: Routledge.

Morris, J. (1991). Minding our Ps and Qs. In M. Pedler (Ed.), *Action learning in practice*, pp. 71–80. Aldershot: Gower.

Mumford, A. (1991). Individual and organizational learning: The pursuit of change. *Industrial and Commercial Training, 23*(6), 31–37.

Mumford, A. (1996). Effective learners in action learning sets. *Employee Counseling Today, 8*(6), 3–10.

O'Neil, J., & Marsick, V. (1994). Action learning coaches. *Advances in Developing Human Resources, 16*(2), 202–221.

Pedler, M. (1996). *Action learning for managers*. London: Lemos & Crane.

Revans, R. (1978). Action learning takes a healthcare approach. *Education and Training*, *20*(10), 295–299.

Revans, R. (1982a). *The origins and growth of action learning*. London: Chartwell-Bratt.

Revans, R. (1982b). What is action learning? *Journal of Management Development*, *1*(3), 64–75.

Revans, R. (1983). *The ABC's of action learning*. London: Chartwell-Bratt.

Rock, D., & Cox, C. (2012). SCARF in 2012: Updating the social neuroscience of collaborating with others. *NeuroLeadership Journal*, *4*, 1–14.

Schön, D. (1987). *Educating the reflective practitioner: Toward a new design for teaching and learning in the professions*. San Francisco, CA: Jossey-Bass.

Waddill, D., & Marquardt, M. (2011). *The e-HR advantage: The complete handbook for technology-enabled human resources*. Boston, MA: Nicholas Brealey Publishing.

Weinstein, K. (1995). Action learning: The classic approach. As quoted in Y. Boshyk (2000) *Business driven action learning: Global best practices* (pp. 3–18). London: Palgrave Macmillan Business.

Willis, V. (2011). Digging deeper: Foundations of Revans' gold standard of action learning. In M. Pedler (Ed.), *Action learning in practice* (4th ed., pp. 71–80). Farnham: Gower.

Yorks, L., O'Neil, J., & Marsick, V. (1999). *Advances in developing human resources*, *1*(2), v–ix.

Chapter 3

Lifelong Action Learning: Principles and Case Studies

Richard Teare

Chapter Outline

Why is it that in the twenty-first century, the place where a person is born *still* determines their life chances? Since 2007, the Global University for Lifelong learning (GULL) has been refining a practical, networkable system that focuses on the needs of the many who would like to develop themselves but face barriers in accessing traditional forms of education. The chapter outlines how lifelong action learning (LAL) can be provided to the low paid, the marginalized and the millions of people who are living in poverty. The suitability and adaptability of LAL to different cultures and contexts in the community and the workplace is exemplified by a case study analysis of GULL's work over the past 10 years and by earlier experience with corporate workplace applications. The chapter concludes that locally led and self-funded LAL networks offer a cost-effective solution to the problem, and that an array of different agencies (including universities) can help to facilitate the creation of a more equitable, inclusive and global paradigm for learning.

Introduction

Despite all the advances made leading up to the twenty-first century, it is still the case that *the place where a person is born largely determines his or her life chances*. Given this reality, I argue that a practical, networkable system for lifelong action learning (LAL) is needed, because if the poorest aspire to develop themselves (without pre-qualification or the means of paying fees and related study costs) they face a significant barrier. Imagine then, a different way – one without those barriers – where the Global University for Lifelong Learning (GULL) serves as a vehicle for self-directed development and knowledge transfer (Teare, 2007). Workplace organizations work with GULL too – from leadership development to supporting frontline workers with modest incomes.

Action Learning and Action Research: Genres and Approaches, 35–52
Copyright © 2019 by Richard Teare
All rights of reproduction in any form reserved
doi:10.1108/978-1-78769-537-520191006

The purpose of this chapter is to present an integrated concept and genre for LAL that aims not only at *action* (i.e., development, positive change and improvement of practice) but also at *Action Learning* (AL) that is self-directed, reflexive, transformative, sustainable and *lifelong*. Zuber-Skerritt and Teare (2013) sought to address the question: *How might we encourage those in low income and subsistence communities to discover and fully utilize their talents along with other like-minded people?* One outcome was to propose: (1) an overarching conceptual framework of learning and development in the twenty-first century supported by two main pillars, (2) LAL and (3) action leadership development. These are grounded in (4) personal and shared development for individual and social transformation and change. All four elements contribute to the central focus on a (5) 'better world'.

This chapter builds on the discussion in that book and argues that the model of LAL as a new genre is particularly suitable for work-based learning in communities as well as organizations. The aim here is to illustrate the transformational potential of self-directed LAL. This can be likened to a journey of the human spirit – it elicits a deep form of change – such that participants become more confident and hopeful that they can change themselves and the circumstances around them. Further, a systemized approach to LAL can be inclusive so that every person has an opportunity to advance and improve their prospects. This is arguably more important to the many who live in grinding poverty than learning how to read and write, as finding solutions that make life more tolerable is more pressing for them.

In the main body of this chapter, I (1) introduce and summarize the genre of LAL as an integration and synthesis of lifelong learning (LL) and AL; (2) discuss why the system of LAL used in GULL is an appropriate and effective approach to learning and development, especially in developing countries; and (3) demonstrate how and why LAL has been used in the workplace and communities.

Lifelong Action Learning

GULL uses the term 'LAL' as it integrates LL that is mainly personal, with AL that is mostly collaborative. These two facets have in common that knowledge can be created by anybody who learns how to create knowledge through experiential learning and by solving real-life problems. The integrated LAL concept includes the time and space of LL in a person's life, their cultural context and the process of AL (Zuber-Skerritt & Teare, 2013).

GULL provides an enabling framework for LAL and, at the beginning, guidance from a facilitator helps to establish a starting point so that individuals, groups and larger communities of participants can begin to analyse and improve their real-life situations. Beyond this, GULL aims to help learners to take charge of their own lives and work, discussing with and reflecting on with others what has or has not worked; why, why not and how; what needs to be done next and how; and to what end. As a result of this approach to problem-solving through trial and error, discussion, reflection and learning, participants are able to apply their learning from one task to other tasks. This is sometimes referred to as 'double-loop learning' as it is reflected in changes made to goals, assumptions, values and/or standards for performance through mindful appreciation of the change process.

Effective self-directed change is linked to the time spent thinking about the actions needed for transformational learning to occur. This is because critical reflection is a core component of holistic change and for GULL, it is the essence of 'professional learning' – a collaborative and holistic process that helps the learner to make deeper level behavioural changes (Zuber-Skerritt, Fletcher, & Kearney, 2015). The concept of professionalism is generally considered to encompass mastery of a body of knowledge and skills and the appropriate mental framework to apply it effectively in different situations. In exploring this concept, it can be observed that professional learning applies across the spectrum of human activity, from technically qualified professionals like medics to unqualified subsistence farmers with technical mastery based on traditional knowledge. Furthermore, professional learning is a challenging, active process because to adapt, change, learn and re-learn, a practitioner must think and act differently. It also requires an open mind and a willingness to learn from work – whether it is paid or voluntary – and from others.

GULL's Approach to LAL for Personal and Community Development

To help participants to begin thinking about their personal learning needs, they start their GULL journey by writing a personal learning statement (week 1). As they consider this, they are also asked to identify who they know who they could ask to journey with them. GULL terms this support person or persons a 'learning coach' and it is an important, voluntary role. Ideally, all participants will enlist one or more individuals to coach them – perhaps someone at work and someone from their wider network of contacts. The learner is also asked to consider the potential support roles of their network of family, friends and colleagues so that they can create a personal web of support. This is especially important if the learner is seeking to make adjustments to ways of working (e.g., improving time management skills) and/or to develop new skills (e.g., developing personal coaching skills so as to encourage and help others).

Next, participants use GULL's diary format to record, reflect on and learn from activities and inputs over a five-week cycle. The objective is to enable participants to learn by reflecting on activities at work or in the community – as these activities occur. The diary format draws on four weekly summaries and one monthly summary, with learning coach and reviewer support (organized by the learner) to enable the participant to fully utilize their work or community role as a vehicle for personal and professional development. Normally, participants review progress (in week 7) and then repeat the cycle (beginning with a personal learning statement update) to consolidate use and understanding of the process of AL and working with a web of support. As participants continue at level 2 with a second diary format reflection cycle, they typically gain confidence and proficiency by using AL to help themselves and other stakeholders in the process.

After completing a second foundation cycle (level 2), participants move to progression levels 3–5 and the emphasis changes from personal (P) to technical (T). At this point, the learner aims to use work (paid or voluntary) as a vehicle for personal learning, and at the same time, to explore ways of making improvements in work-related activity.

GULL's experience is that LAL is applicable in any context – no matter how challenging – but it must be operationalized differently in each instance according to participants and their circumstances. Typically, workplace settings are characterized by an abundance of available data and computing resources but the commodity in short supply is 'time'. In contrast, communities often rely on natural resources and they don't have much computing power but they generally do have much more time to give to the cycle of learning: reflect, take action, review and improve.

In the following two sections, a characterization of GULL system applications in the workplace and then in community settings helps to illustrate both the differences across applications and the importance of customization to the context, needs and objectives of the application. The analysis drew on some 50 case studies and generated a number of categories each with unique characteristics as well as commonalities. The purpose was to document GULL's progress over a 10-year period, as reflected by the title of the book that followed: *Lifelong action learning: A journey of discovery and learning at work and in the community* (Teare, 2018). The analysis is entirely grounded in longitudinal observation, reflection and post experience re-formulation of GULL's approaches to integrating life, work and learning in response to the widest possible spectrum of need. This chapter extends the analysis by reflecting on the characteristics of different community and workplace applications of LAL.

Workplace

I have long held the view that workplace environments possess most of the elements needed to provide a rich and continuing source of opportunity for personal and professional growth. But how does LAL relate to the world that practitioners inhabit? In the late 1980s and 1990s, I worked on a number of university-led workplace learning initiatives with large corporations, and later did so via an independent organization. The outcomes are written-up in a number of books, for example: Teare, Davies, and Sandelands (1998) and Prestoungrange, Sandelands, and Teare (2000).

Business-led Development

Business leaders know that if they are able to create some thinking space for their employees, these employees are likely to come forward with ideas that will help the business, as illustrated by the applications in Table 3.1. Over the years I have facilitated many individual and group projects that have resolved what historically have been intractable problems. A memorable example is the concept of a personal 'business challenge' as an executive development take-away with proven

Table 3.1:   Example Applications: Business-led Development.

Application	Main Driver
Air Niugini, Papua New Guinea (PNG) (Airline)	*Service enhancement.* The chief executive wanted to enable Air Niugini staff to make advances in service delivery with employee participation at all organizational levels and the airline used the GULL system to develop their own Academy
Compass Group, UK (Catering)	*Business challenges.* Compass Group's executive development program featured a personal business challenge as the entry point to an AL pathway adopted by more than 60 leaders from around the world. All participants wrote-up and evaluated their work (for a company case book) and this demonstrated a significant return on investment
Granada Group, UK (Media, hotels and catering)	*Cross-functional development.* The Granada Learning Experience (GLE) provided a cross-functional, business-focused forum for senior managers. The GLE drew on a customized curriculum so that non-specialists (e.g., finance) could gain a grounding while specialists explored new thinking/techniques
Sonesta Resorts, St Maarten (Hotels)	*Customer responsiveness.* Resort managers used GULL's AL approach to develop their own integrated customer service and satisfaction tracking system. A related outcome was an array of industry awards

return on investment (the Compass Group application). Prior to introducing the 'business challenge', the executive development events didn't lead anywhere because participants felt 'swamped' by problems when they returned to work.

GULL was able to assist Sonesta Resorts (St Maarten) to transform its social media profile by linking the personal and professional development of departmental managers with the creation of a cross-departmental customer service and guest satisfaction tracking system. This work led to multiple industry awards and much higher resort occupancy levels, average room rates and profitability. The main reasons why a small group of managers was able to achieve so much in a relatively short time are listed in Table 3.2. All three benefits and related characteristics were easy to discern in this application.

Table 3.2:   Example Benefits: Business-led Development.

Benefits	Characterized by
Encourages innovative thinking and behaviour and challenges 'stasis' (state of inactivity or equilibrium)	Bold ideas that are more likely to generate breakthroughs than routine, familiar approaches
Incentivizes effort that yields a benefit for the organization and its stakeholders	Employees challenging themselves and their colleagues to explore new/different ways of working
Promotes active, collaborative learning as a core business process	Self-directed individuals and teams who think and work proactively – rather than reactively

People-focused Development

Senior leaders who themselves have risen up the ranks and/or are concerned about retaining and developing their frontline staff, tend to view 'inclusion' as a key issue for learning and development. The example applications in Table 3.3 include a long-running and fruitful collaboration with Eurest, USA. A divisional President has been the GULL champion since 2008, and though we sought to involve training and human resource specialists, we found it was quicker and easier to integrate the organization and oversight of personal and professional development with day to day operations, led by operators.

Table 3.3:   Example Applications: People-focused Development.

Application	Main Driver
Eurest, USA (Catering)	*Retention and career development.* The Division President, Eurest Dining Services USA wanted to establish a development and progression pathway for frontline employees that equips them with the skills needed for self-directed learning at work
Interbrew UK (now InBev) (Brewing)	*Personal and professional development.* Building on a pilot initiative "Competing for the future through action learning," Interbrew UK sought to facilitate personal development and responsibility, linked to key business projects
Sodexo (formerly Sodexho), USA (Catering and facilities management)	*Skills development.* The company's corporate university offered work-based AL to all staff so that they could self-audit and determine what new skills to acquire via work-based projects

Eurest focuses on the provision of development pathways for hourly paid workers who are the least well educated and qualified staff. These workers typically respond with great enthusiasm. They quickly realize that they have more potential than they are using, and that GULL's self-directed approach enables them to make improvements that help them develop and advance inside the company. Eurest is maintaining year on year growth and so GULL's development initiative is playing a key role in retaining operatives and preparing them to demonstrate readiness for promotion to a supervisory role. The outcome is 'win–win'. Eurest has a cost-effective way of filling vacancies from within the company, and as the participants are learning how to learn at work, they are more fulfilled and committed to the company. When we meet with participants annually at celebration events, they say that they are much happier at work and that they are motivated and confident about continuing their learning journey. Table 3.4 summarizes the reported benefits.

Organization-led Development

A desire to establish a corporate school or academy is more often than not an outcome of organization-led development. The examples in Table 3.5 reflect this as each application sought to focus initially on systematic development.

Table 3.4:   Example Benefits: People-focused Development.

Benefits	Characterized By
Fosters personal and professional development by creating opportunities to reflect, adjust and improve	Self-sustaining culture that enables individual and shared learning for optimal performance
Engenders a sense of fulfilment as participants develop and begin to release their fullest potential	Happier employees who are motivated to self-actualize at work and beyond
Releases the potential in people as they gain confidence from personal and professional development.	Committed employees who are energized by learning and less likely to leave the organization

A personal highlight in this category was an extended period of involvement with a group of all-inclusive resorts in five Caribbean islands. The starting point with Sandals was to explore ways of integrating learning at work in a demanding environment where staff often spend six long days at work (with split-shift duties) – making part-time, off-site study practically impossible.

At Sandals, hundreds of employees registered for GULL pathways and paid their own fees. We based the fees on the salaries of staff so as to ensure that the fees were genuinely affordable and the initiative led to many remarkable personal and project-related outcomes. The benefits highlighted in Table 3.6 include a more systematic, organization-led response to keeping up with the pace of external change and valuing self-directed development in an environment where formal opportunities for learning are limited.

Table 3.5:   Example Applications: Organization-led Development.

Application	Main Driver
Heathrow Airport Holdings (formerly BAA, UK) (Airport owners and operators)	*To become a more effective learning organization.* BAA wanted to enable its managers in diverse specialisms (e.g., airport fire services, property development, terminal management, retail and operations research) to work together on AL pathways with inputs from company specialists and mentor support
Sandals Resorts International, Caribbean (Luxury all-inclusive resorts)	*Workplace learning.* The patterns of work in all-inclusive resorts makes it difficult to study part-time and so hundreds of staff at resorts in the Turks and Caicos Islands, Jamaica, The Bahamas, Antigua and St Lucia enrolled in self-funded GULL pathways that were designed to integrate learning and work
The Salvation Army International (Church and social development)	*Organizational effectiveness.* A small team based at the International headquarters in London developed a pathway for its Project Officers – in all world locations. The main purpose was to provide a framework that would enable staff to self-audit and work collaboratively with others to enhance personal effectiveness

Table 3.6:   Example Benefits: Organization-led Development.

Benefits	Characterized By
Views organization-led learning as a core strategy in keeping pace with the rate of external change	Proactive, fast-paced but integrated initiatives that sustain incremental improvement
Fosters a dynamic, inclusive curriculum that embraces all aspects of organizational learning and development	Employees who are curious, ask questions, challenge each other and collaborate in the quest for solutions
Encourages self-directed development – even if formal opportunities for learning are limited	Employees who initiate improvements – without waiting to be asked

Community

Community development is normally characterized by initiatives for individuals and groups of people led from outside the host community. The process is typically led by an external facilitator with the aim of strengthening the community's own capacity to sustain development in the longer term. However, this rarely seems to unfold as planned because dependency on the change agent tends to occur. GULL's main purpose is to provide a practical system to facilitate the transition from dependency to self-help, and we do this in partnership with what GULL terms 'affiliate organizations' that are locally led. These organizations provide inputs on specific aspects of community development and to illustrate this, the applications in this section reflect an array of different starting points, as determined by the need and situation.

Cause-led Development

Given the multiplicity of challenges facing low income communities, I have encountered a variety of 'cause-led' development initiatives provided by faith-based organizations, single-issue agencies (such as anti-corruption) and social entrepreneurs as illustrated in Table 3.7. A fascinating and effective self-help approach is the concept of 'Personal Viability' (PV) developed and refined over more than 20 years by the Human Development Institute (HDI) in PNG.

HDI focuses on preparing subsistence community participants to become self-reliant and financially independent. This is a critical issue in a country like PNG where the formal employment sector is small and the majority of people still live a subsistence lifestyle. Table 3.8 exemplifies the benefits and associated characteristics of a pathway based on 'PV' and LAL that begins by participants learning how to use money wisely in the context of sustainable micro-enterprise.

Table 3.7:   Example Applications: Cause-led Development.

Application	Main Driver
El Alfarero Bible School, Bolivia (Applied theology)	*Christian mission.* El Alfarero was established in 2001 and in 2013 began a mission training program for graduates prior to affiliating with GULL in 2014. El Alfarero wants its students to apply their learning by setting-up or developing Christian outreach projects and GULL's outcomes-based approach is used to certify this
HDI, PNG (Community development)	*Personal viability.* HDI has trained more than 20,000 people in 'PV' since 1996 and in November 2008, affiliated with GULL. PV-GULL now facilitates a step-by-step lifelong approach to attaining self-reliance and financial independence for subsistence communities throughout the Pacific Island region
South Asian Academy for Good Governance (SAAGG), Sri Lanka	*Good governance.* In post-conflict Sri Lanka, SAAGG aims to advance the cause of good governance by providing a pathway for its anti-corruption activists and champions to facilitate and influence positive societal change

Table 3.8:   Example Benefits: Cause-led Development.

Benefits	Characterized By
Encourages competent entrepreneurship as participants make progress towards financial independence	Gradual progress from dependency to self-reliance as participants discover and use latent gifts and talents
Fosters a sense of optimism and self-confidence arising from holistic development	Participants who are able to visualize prosperity with their mind and use money wisely as a tool to attain it
Enables participants to understand and learn to accept alternative viewpoints and beliefs	Changing perspectives and a willingness to accept and work with others with different values and beliefs

Young Adult Development

In locations where education and training is not routinely provided and/or cannot be funded without family support, a young person living from day-to-day is at risk – not least because their life prospects are restricted. In these circumstances, access to skill-related training is helpful but insufficient on its own, as mentoring (and/or counselling) and personal development are needed to deal with trauma, substance abuse and other debilitating impacts of life outside a traditional family support network. I have been privileged to work with agencies with considerable expertise and dedication in helping young adults to discover for themselves their innate talent and then use it to create or find work and attain self-reliance.

Among the example applications in Table 3.9, Joy to the World Community Services (JWCS) stands out as a beacon of hope for orphaned children and

Table 3.9:   Example Applications: Young Adult Development.

Application	Main Driver
JWCS, Malaysia (Social care and enterprise)	*Social enterprise.* JWCS cares for orphans – more than half of whom are young adults. JWCS uses an approach termed 'TSR' – training, service and revenue. The aim is to equip young adults with the life and professional skills needed to secure employment and self-reliance
Nicodemus Trust, Guatemala (Marginalized youth)	*Self-reliance.* A high proportion of Guatemalan children live in poverty and the Nicodemus Trust helps vulnerable young adults aged 18–25 by providing a pathway with mentors and skills training to equip them for work opportunities
World Vision Lebanon (WVL) (Young adults)	*Peace-building.* Given the scale of regional conflict, WVL helps young people who are affected by insecurity and lack of opportunity. One response with GULL was to initiate a youth-led peace-building project utilizing dance, drama, music and puppet shows

young adults. Its founder realized that to fund his orphanage operations (which he described as the 'House of Joy'), everybody would need to work and that his role was to 'talent spot' and enable young adults to practise and develop their potential.

The JWCS approach to equipping young adults for life is based on 'training, service and revenue' (TSR) coupled with personal development to foster professional habits, attitudes and behaviours. Given the background of participants (e.g., neglect, abandonment and physical abuse) prior to moving into the House of Joy, holistic healing and development are vitally important. GULL's system complements TSR by using LAL and introducing tools for self-directed personal development along with other benefits as outlined in Table 3.10.

Non-governmental Organization-led Development

The overwhelming majority of community development is led by non-governmental organizations (NGOs) and GULL has supported national and international NGOs in Africa, Asia, Central and South America and the Pacific region. As noted earlier, the best and most effective initiatives are designed to enable communities to take control of their own future development with technical support from the NGO as needed. Table 3.11 outlines several of the applications led by the international NGO World Vision in conjunction with GULL.

An outstanding application has been 'LfT', an AL process that fully integrates GULL's pathway approach for balanced personal and technical development. Its cascade-style design encourages NGO staff to think and act differently and to use training interventions as the starting point for community-led LAL. As Table 3.12 shows, this better equips communities to draw on the expertise provided by NGOs and to take their own action.

Table 3.10:   Example Benefits: Young Adult Development.

Benefits	Characterized By
Self-directed personal development and coaching balances and blends with skills training	Work-ready young adults who know how to adapt themselves so that they create or secure paid work
Holistic development can be introduced in numerous ways so that the process engages with the need	Creativity in learning and development that harnesses the innate skills, talents and vitality of young adults
Adult mentoring can be integrated with self-directed development for attitudinal and behavioural change	Confident young adults who are learning how to learn and how to overcome adversity

Table 3.11:   Example Applications: NGO-led Development.

Application	Main Driver
Learning for Transformation (LfT) (developed by a former World Vision regional leader)	*Community-led change.* LfT is a community-based development process that integrates GULL's narrative format for personal reflection and change through AL. The LfT components are: development thinking; personal development; facilitation skills; conscientization – creating awareness – and mobilizing small groups
LfT, World Vision Mongolia (WVM)	*NGO staff development for community-led change.* WVM began with LfT-GULL in late 2014 and by mid-2016, 225 staff were participating. GULL's narrative format enabled them to monitor their own personal change and effectiveness in using new-to-them community development tools
LfT, World Vision Sri Lanka (WVL)	*NGO staff development for community-led change.* WVL began their LfT-GULL journey at the end of 2012 and by early July 2016, more than 200 staff had completed the LfT with GULL process
World Vision (WV) (International NGO)	*Empowering community volunteers.* GULL has worked with WV national offices in Burundi, El Salvador, Haiti, Kenya, Lebanon, Mexico, Mongolia, PNG, Rwanda, Sri Lanka and the US Global Center with a focus on equipping, empowering and certifying the impact of WV's community volunteers

Table 3.12:   Example Benefits: NGO-led Development.

Benefits	Characterized By
Active learning supports agency-led training for community development as it reduces dependency	More systematic self-directed learning, ownership of development and effective use of natural resources
Engenders a desire to advance, improve, apply learning and facilitate learning for others	Shared learning and organic 'cascading' as early adopter participants facilitate for new groups
Enhances connectivity within communities and awareness of what can be accomplished corporately	Participants accomplishing more than they imagined possible for themselves, their families and others

Poverty Alleviation

The UK-based NGO Tearfund has for many years, provided training and logistical support to the 'Church and Community Mobilization' (CCM) process authored and developed by a Kenyan. This indigenous African system has had a greater impact than any other development program I have encountered because it uses African Church networks to bring communities together (both Christian and Muslim groups) and equips them with the confidence and skills needed to make even more effective use of their own natural resources and individual skills and talents. To date, GULL has supported CCM in 16 African countries and there have been astonishing outcomes, briefly summarized in Table 3.13.

Table 3.13:   Example Applications: Poverty Alleviation.

Application	Main Driver
CCM (with support from Tearfund UK)	*Community self-help.* CCM has been used to facilitate community-led change in every part of the continent of Africa. CCM training is supported by Tearfund UK and since 2008, by GULL with certification based on evidence of impact. As the participants live in poor communities, this is their only development option and it inspires them
CCM, Uganda	*Community mobilization.* In January 2012, the largest procession ever seen in Soroti, Uganda assembled in the town centre and more than 1,000 CCM participants marched from there to the GULL graduation ceremony venue (1)
Msalato Theological College (a faculty of St John's University), Tanzania	*Applied theology.* CCM has been operating in Tanzania for many years and in November 2016, the third graduation event since the involvement of GULL began in 2008 took place at a Theology college. This was the first CCM with GULL graduation for experienced church pastors to be held in conjunction with an African host university
Tearfund (International NGO)	*Poverty alleviation.* CCM is an effective, self-help approach to poverty alleviation and GULL has supported Tearfund since 2008 by recognizing the efforts of thousands of CCM participants in Burundi, Burkina Faso, Chad, D R Congo, Ivory Coast, Kenya, Liberia, Niger, Nigeria, Rwanda, Sierra Leone, South Sudan, Sudan, Tanzania, Uganda and Zimbabwe

The integration of GULL with CCM is helping to address the lack of educational opportunity for thousands of people who don't have the money and/or the basic educational qualifications needed to participate in further and higher education. That said, CCM is a rigorous and lengthy practical process that begins with personal mindset change. Living with grinding poverty is infinitely challenging, and it is important that CCM participants believe they can address the controllable aspects of poverty themselves. They cannot easily influence levels of political corruption. But if there is water in the ground, they can – and do – dig their own wells, create dams, establish fish pools (an excellent protein source) and their self-organized water security means the community can grow more food than ever before, and sell their surpluses so they can buy what they cannot easily make themselves. Above all, CCM brings hope through self-directed development, and with GULL it meets a deeply felt need for more systemized learning and development with recognized professional certification (see Table 3.14).

The Role of Self-directed Networks

In the book, *Lifelong action learning for community development* (Zuber-Skerritt & Teare, 2013), the first of two books I have co-authored with the sub-title: *Learning and development for a better world*, we sought to explain and illustrate how indigenous communities can be strengthened by adopting a LAL approach that builds on traditional knowledge, culture and language. GULL's system harnesses the potential of people to bring about positive change together, characterized by greater self-reliance, financial independence and by cascading learning to others. It is a self-directed and sustainable process for learning and growth and detailed case studies show that over time, poor communities can achieve remarkable breakthroughs with benefits for participants and for the wider community.

The second book in the series, *Designing inclusive pathways with young adults* (Kearney, Wood, & Teare, 2015), built on the first book's conceptual framework for LAL by focusing on the design and implementation of pathways with and for

Table 3.14:   Example Benefits: Poverty Alleviation.

Benefits	Characterized By
Meets a deeply felt need for learning and development that is rarely met (lack of money and poor infrastructure)	Enthusiasm for learning and a resolve to continue, build momentum and find solutions to poverty
Participants are incentivized by the prospect of recognition to attain practical outcomes	Joyful determination to make best use of innate skills to secure self-reliance and financial independence
Encourages action leadership as first phase participants become skilled self-directed learners	People and communities who are committed and able to sustain self-help (based on LL)

young adults. As with the first book, the second draws on approaches used by GULL, with examples from nine countries. The aim was to illustrate how access to purposeful learning and development can be provided to marginalized young people during the period from their mid-teens to mid-twenties using applications based on micro-enterprise, peace-building, music and the creative arts.

There are many indicators that GULL's involvement has helped to sustain self-directed development and is appreciated by participants who say the prospect of recognition is all they need to keep going. Yet, reaching subsistence communities and marginalized youth is really difficult. It takes time to build trusting relationships with NGO representatives, and they in turn have to convince their colleagues that GULL can add value to their work in the field. Ten years on, I know that GULL's system, structure and process works in any setting, no matter how difficult, and in any culture and language. However, the greatest challenge remains. That is, to reach people in relatively remote places. To achieve this, stable networks are needed that are led and facilitated by people who see the need for GULL and are committed to ensuring that GULL's role can thrive inside their network.

A source of personal encouragement in the quest to establish enduring networks is the interest shown and now, active involvement, of a group of public universities in South Africa. They see and accept that GULL's practical self-help and recognition system can assist with their own community engagement efforts and sit alongside (as a parallel system) their own largely campus-based academic structure. As universities are inherently long-term, stable institutions, I hope that GULL can secure more university affiliations in the coming years. In fact, some academics are already advocating this kind of development, as exemplified by Nyland, Davies and Clarke, cited in Teare (2018):

> The case for devising a new curriculum is self-evident ... [The challenge centres on] the problem of delivering institutionally-based learning and accreditation to very poor communities who cannot afford to pay for it [and] the thorny issue of whether the knowledge taught is actually 'real' and relevant to the people and communities who need it. A new view of the university in its community is needed to improve access to what learning can offer. In a globalized world where mass migration flows are commonplace, it is clear that the old system is broken and cannot serve the needs of the majority. The next stage requires not merely a scaling-up of existing provision but a wholesale re-thinking of learning for those billions of people who can view the benefits of advanced industrial society (via their hand-held devices and computers) but who cannot achieve it. (pp. 135–136)

The starting point is usually training, community projects, technical assistance and/or other inputs (as depicted in Fig. 3.1) and they assume personal relevance when participants take ownership of the principles and apply them. In fact, participants are required to do this in order to qualify for a GULL professional award. More than this, participants must gather evidence of their personal

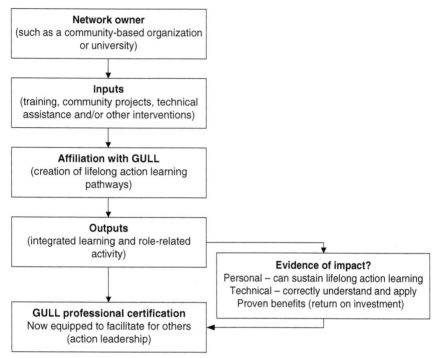

Fig. 3.1:   Creating Self-sustaining Networks for Inclusive LAL.

change and the positive influence and impact that their GULL journey has made. This is a holistic challenge that requires honesty, self-examination, courage and a commitment to action – all of which indigenous self-help systems value. In part, this is why GULL is able to play a valued role in support of systems like 'CCM', 'LfT' and 'PV'. These systems share a similar objective – encouraging self-directed change via a process that is action-oriented and equips people for life by helping them to recognize, release and use their gifts, skills and talents to their fullest potential. Every human being can do this and so GULL offers this prospect: universal access to LAL. No one is excluded because everyone can advance and improve.

Conclusion

I conclude with an illustration given by a World Bank representative at GULL's launch event in the State Function Room, Parliament House, Port Moresby, PNG on 5 October 2007 (Ateng, 2007). He said:

> We people from the third world – I'm a Kenyan – often feel like we are sinking into a swamp – we lift our hands in the air and hope that someone will come along and pull us out. GULL is different – it is like a low hanging branch – you reach up and pull yourself out.

This encapsulates the essence of GULL using LAL, and I hope that the kind of self-help the GULL program offers can be extended much more widely in the coming years. If 'pulling out' of poverty was easy, it would be happening already and so a change in program emphasis is needed, from over-reliance on training to equipping people to identify and create their own solutions. This transition requires a system, structure and process – elements that GULL has refined these past 10 years – and stable, self-funding national and regional networks are all that is needed. If you think you can help with this, please let me know!

Topics for Discussion

1. What role can LAL play in locations where access to further and higher education is limited?
2. What are the common features and the differences between community and work-based applications of LAL?
3. How could inclusive, self-directed networks for LAL be established in your locality, and which entities could play a role in facilitating this?

Further Information and Reading

Kearney, J., Wood, L., & Teare, R. (2015). *Designing inclusive pathways with young adults.* Rotterdam, The Netherlands: Sense Publishers.

Zuber-Skerritt, O., & Teare, R. (2013). *Lifelong action learning for community development: Learning and development for a better world.* Rotterdam, The Netherlands: Sense Publishers.

Also see http://www.gullonline.org/case-studies/community/church-community-mobilization/index.html and Chapter 4: Q1 Professionalizing Community Mobilization; Q2 Recognizing the Mobilizers; Q3 Addressing Poverty; and Q4 Sustaining Self-directed Development.

References

Ateng, B. (2007). Mr Benson Ateng. Retrieved from http://www.gullonline.org/media/gull-story/inauguration/benson-ateng/index.html

Kearney, J., Wood, L., & Teare, R. (2015). *Designing inclusive pathways with young adults: Learning and development for a better world.* Rotterdam, The Netherlands: Sense Publishers.

Prestoungrange, G., Sandelands, E., & Teare, R. (2000). *The virtual learning organization: Learning at the workplace campus.* London: Continuum.

Teare, R. (2007). *The GULL story Part 1: Mission.* Global University for Lifelong Learning. Retrieved from http://www.gullonline.org/about/mission/index.html

Teare, R. (2018). *Lifelong action learning: A journey of discovery and celebration at work and in the community.* Retrieved from Amazon.com. Independently published.

Teare, R., Davies, D., & Sandelands. E. (1998). *The virtual university: An action paradigm and process for workplace learning.* London: Cassell.

Zuber-Skerritt, O., Fletcher, M., & Kearney, J. (2015). *Professional learning in higher education and communities: Towards a new vision of action research*. London: Palgrave Macmillan.

Zuber-Skerritt, O., & Teare, R. (2013) *Lifelong action learning for community development: Learning and development for a better world*. Rotterdam, The Netherlands: Sense Publishers.

Chapter 4

Action Learning and Mindfulness for Mental Health in the Workplace

Ron Passfield

Chapter Outline

In this chapter I explore the relationship between Action Learning and mindfulness, and show that they are complementary and mutually reinforcing because they share the common intermediate goals of developing 'self-awareness' and building 'agency' for managers and non-managerial employees. I argue these two personal competencies are conducive to mental health in the workplace. I also demonstrate how this is realized in two recent doctoral studies that used action learning as an intervention to address organizational environments that were damaging to the mental health of management and non-managerial employees. I propose that a toxic work environment, where self-awareness and agency are thwarted, requires two forms of organizational intervention used in concert – action learning and mindfulness training – if the damage to the mental health of all concerned is to be reduced or eliminated. I propose the *MASA (Mindfulness, Action Learning, Self-awareness, Agency) Model* to illustrate the dynamic relationships amongst the various elements in the model and I suggest that the model can serve as a framework for organizational interventions designed to address toxic work environments.

Introduction

On the surface, action learning and mindfulness may appear antithetical. Action learning involves taking action to achieve an improved state in the future in an external situation. Mindfulness, on the other hand, involves being still, present in the moment and internally focused. However, on closer and more carefully considered inspection, action learning and mindfulness can be seen to be complementary and mutually reinforcing.

Action learning is learning by doing and engaging with others in reflection on actions taken to improve a situation and the outcomes realized, both intended and unintended. Members of the action and reflection group are often called

Action Learning and Action Research: Genres and Approaches, 53–68
Copyright © 2019 by Ron Passfield
All rights of reproduction in any form reserved
doi:10.1108/978-1-78769-537-520191007

an action learning 'set'. The norms of such an action learning group can be summarized as 'supportive challenge' – being prepared to challenge perspectives and assumptions but doing so in a way that builds self-esteem rather than diminishes it.

Mindfulness involves inner awareness in-the-moment that is curious and open. Jon Kabat-Zinn (2005), creator of the globally recognized Mindfulness Based Stress Reduction (MBSR) Program, describes mindfulness as "moment-to-moment, non-judgmental awareness, cultivated by paying attention in a specific way, that is, in the present moment, and as non-reactively, as non-judgmentally, and as open-hearted as possible" (p. 108).

The Mindful Awareness Research Center (MARC, n.d.) emphasizes the role of 'acceptance' in mindfulness development and defines 'mindful awareness' as "paying attention to present moment experiences with openness, curiosity, and a willingness to be with what is" (p. 1).

Mindfulness is developed through meditation and mindfulness practices that focus on some aspect of our internal reality – on our thoughts, feelings or sensations. Meditation can involve recall and investigation of a past event as well as being in touch with the present reality of our mental state and its bodily manifestation. An endless array of meditations can be employed to build mindfulness, for example, mindful breathing, walking meditation, gratitude meditation, standing or sitting meditation, compassion meditation, open awareness, self-compassion meditation or various forms of somatic meditation.

The Private Sector Working Group (2016, p. 9) operating under the auspices of the UK Mindfulness All-Party Parliamentary (MAPP) Group drew on mindfulness research to maintain that mindfulness training within organizations supports wellbeing and resilience because it:

- equips individuals with self-awareness that helps them to understand resilience and actively participate in its development;
- enables people to recognize the signs of stress and respond more effectively;
- develops discernment between activities that nurture or deplete internal resources;
- recognizes the power of thoughts and finds ways of skillfully working with them; and
- supports a culture where relationships are valued.

The Complementarity and Mutual Reinforcement of Action Learning and Mindfulness

The primary goal of action learning is future improvement in a situation, whether in business, government, education or community. Mindfulness, on the other hand, has the primary goal of awareness in the present moment. Yet despite their different time focus and end goals, action learning and mindfulness are complementary and mutually reinforcing.

Their complementarity can be explained in terms of their relationship to an individual's external and internal environment. Action learning focuses on the outside (the external environment) and, in the process, develops an individual's internal environment; mindfulness works from the inside (the internal environment) and develops an individual's conscious action in the external environment.

The mutual reinforcement involved in action learning and mindfulness is born out by the fact that although they have different primary end goals, they share two common intermediate goals: 'self-awareness' and 'agency'. Both of these intermediate goals contribute to mental health in the workplace. In the following discussion, I explore how self-awareness and agency contribute to mental health, and how, in turn, both action learning and mindfulness contribute to each of these intermediate goals. These relationships are illustrated in Fig. 4.1 which provides a framework for the subsequent discussion.

Self-awareness and Mental Health

Intuitively we know that self-awareness is essential for mental health and that deficiencies in a 'sense of self' (SOS) to some degree characterize many common mental illnesses such as depression and anxiety. Some may speak of people with emotional problems in the workplace as "having lost touch with reality" or "lacking in self-awareness" or having "lost themselves." Being lost was poignantly expressed by Avicii, Swedish DJ and singer-songwriter, who committed suicide at the age of 28 in early 2018, when he wrote the lines, "All this time I was finding myself, and I didn't know I was lost," in the song, *Wake Me Up*.

Russ Harris (2009), a proponent and practitioner of the mindfulness-based Acceptance and Commitment Therapy (ACT), argues that self-awareness – being able to view 'self-as-context' – is critical to achieving mental health and optimum effectiveness. ACT, incorporating 'acceptance' and 'commitment' as core elements of its therapeutic approach, places considerable emphasis on the 'observing self' (the part of a person that does all the noticing) and challenges the accuracy of the resultant observations.

We know too from research that delusions (false beliefs about oneself) underpin some forms of depression. Moe and Docherty (2014) explored the relationship between SOS and schizophrenia, and established that certain

Fig. 4.1:   The MASA Model.

facets of SOS were deficient. It is particularly relevant that the deficient facets involved "certain aspects of agency and relatedness to others'. They undertook their study based on the wealth of evidence that suggests SOS is the "foundation upon which individuals experience their daily lives" and that "a disrupted SOS is thought to represent a platform for the experience of psychiatric symptoms, social cognitive deficits, and other abnormalities of consciousness" (p. 161).

Developing Self-awareness through Action Learning and Mindfulness

Both action learning and mindfulness develop self-awareness as an intermediate goal to their respective end goals. They each seek to help participants free themselves from false assumptions, from entrenched negative thoughts and stories, from narrow perspectives on what people can achieve, and from the delusion of "knowing it all." When used in concert, action learning and mindfulness are complementary and mutually reinforcing.

Developing Self-awareness through Action Learning. Action learning develops self-awareness through the norm of supportive challenge by peers in an action learning set, along with the challenge of doing something of significance about something important, which forces participants to redefine their roles, their values and how they perceive themselves. In one longitudinal action learning program, the facilitators likened the learning journey to the story of *The Wonderful Wizard of Oz*.

In discussing what is definitive about action learning, Reg Revans (1982) explains that action learning, involving real commitment to action in the here-and-now, causes participants to "become aware of their own values" and entails a "voyage of self-discovery" that enables them to "fix attention upon this inner and personal self." In the process of taking action after disclosing their own motives for change to others in their action learning set, participants are "obliged to explore that inner self otherwise taken for granted and never questioned." Critical but supportive colleagues help the action learner to assess their own ideas and outcomes in an often-hostile organization environment and this, in turn, will "purge them of any lingering self-deception." Thus, action learning involves "development of the self by the mutual support of equals" who are also engaged in the "struggle to understand themselves" (pp. 630–633).

Revans (1991), in an interview in Brisbane, spoke about the need to develop 'questioning insight' to be able to deal with the complexity of reality. He maintained that we cannot rely on what we know, or on the knowledge of experts, so we need to admit what we do not know and ask fresh questions. Revans suggested that admitting what you do not know, rather than trying to convince others of how much you do know, is the beginning of learning and the road to wisdom. He argued that expert knowledge, although necessary, is insufficient and does not equip us with how to deal with new conditions that are complex, uncertain and/or ambiguous. Revans (1991) also pointed out that action learning places emphasis foremost on what you do not know and then explores how to address this ignorance. He maintained very strongly that if you assume that you know all there is to know about a subject because of your expert qualifications, you are going to get into trouble not only yourself, but others as well. Action learning, then, demands self-awareness through exploring what we do not know, rather than boasting about how much we do know.

Developing Self-awareness through Mindfulness. Vago and Silbersweig (2012) undertook a systematic review of 300 articles on mindfulness and developed the *Self-Awareness, Self-Regulation, Self-Transcendence* model as an integrated, systems-based model, incorporating neurobiology, that explains "the mechanisms by which mindfulness reduces biases related to self-processing and creates a healthy sustainable mind" (p. 1). They contend that this model reveals the progressive development of mindfulness through the correction of self-narratives that distort inner and outer reality:

> Mindfulness is described through systematic mental training that develops meta-awareness (self-awareness), an ability to effectively modulate one's behaviour (self-regulation), and a positive relationship between self and other that transcends self-focused needs and increases prosocial characteristics (self-transcendence). (p. 1)

Emeritus Professor Jon Kabat-Zinn (2017), a global leader in the mindfulness movement, explains that the brain creates narratives – stories about who you are, how you compare with others and what is wrong with you – that lead to self-distortion and emotional states such as loneliness, depression and anxiety. After more than 30 years in the field of clinical practice, he maintains in this video presentation that meditation liberates people from this incessant "narrative network mode" and changes the way the brain experiences reality. In an interview with Krista Tibbett, Kabat-Zinn (2011) stated that mindfulness meditation results in a new level of self-awareness, "you change your relationship to who you think you are as a person and in particular to the story of who you are or think you are."

In line with the contention by Revans that "admitting what we do not know" counters self-deception and opens the way for creative solutions, Kabat-Zinn (2011) maintained in the interview:

> So rather than just sort of keeping tabs on what we know, it's really helpful to be aware of how much we don't know. And when we know what we don't know, well, then that's the cutting edge of which all science unfolds.

Here Kabat-Zinn explained further that, when you "rest in awareness" through mindfulness meditation, insight or solutions come to you. In a conversation with Daniel Goleman about his MBSR Program, reported in Goleman's (2013) book, *Focus*, Kabat-Zinn pointed out that people who engaged in mindfulness meditation changed their behaviour (e.g., stopped smoking) of their own accord once they started "paying attention to their own inner states." This happened despite the changed behaviour not being the focus of their meditation efforts. Just developing self-awareness about their own feelings and stimuli enabled them to see what needed to be changed in their lives.

Goleman (2018a) stated that one of the most effective means to develop self-awareness is mindfulness meditation "which actually reshapes the brain circuitry involved in emotion recognition and regulation." He maintained that the mindfulness research incorporated in his recent co-authored book (Goleman & Davidson, 2017) provides 'strong evidence' to demonstrate the neurobiology of mindfulness and its impact on self-awareness. However, he argued more recently in a video presentation (Goleman, 2018b) that mindfulness meditation needs to be supplemented by external input to overcome an individual's 'blind spots'. He suggests that this external challenge can be achieved through '360 Degree Feedback' methods. I would argue that an action learning set is a more effective and supportive way to provide the requisite challenge because of the norms underpinning action learning and the relative freedom from political contamination.

As people engage in mindfulness meditation and action learning, they realize they are on a journey of self-discovery where the limitations of their thoughts, feelings and actions are exposed, and they are forced to confront themselves and their behaviour. This enhanced level of personal insight enables both managers and non-managerial employees to develop agency.

Agency and Mental Health

Agency in a work context means having the capacity to shape the work environment and control the way work is done. Fundamental to agency is an individual's need for a sense of control, evidenced even at an early age, for example, by a 13-month-old toddler insisting on feeding themselves with a spoon.

Neuroscientist Tali Sharot (2017) maintains through her research and that of her colleagues:

> The brain has evolved to control our bodies so that our bodies can manipulate our environments .... Our biology is set up so that we are driven to be causal agents; we are internally rewarded with a feeling of satisfaction when we are in control, and internally punished with anxiety when we are not. (p. 102)

Sharot demonstrates through research findings that we have a very high need for control. She argues, for example, that aerophobia – the fear of flying – is essentially about the loss of control; we are in the "hands of the pilot and the plane." She suggests that suicide is an extreme response to the sense of being out of control, unable to control anything in one's internal or external environment. She discusses examples of research projects in different contexts that provide evidence of the effectiveness of the fundamental principle of letting go to empower others by giving them a sense of agency.

Sharot (2017) maintains that "control is tightly related to influence" and influence expands when we provide others with a sense of agency – the capacity to control their environment, and gain power over the way things are done. She argues:

> The message, perhaps ironically, is that to influence actions, you need to give people a sense of control. Eliminate the sense of agency and you get anger, frustration, and resistance. Expand people's sense of influence over their world and you increase their motivation and compliance. (p. 87)

This leads us to a discussion of how action learning and mindfulness build agency in an organization and contribute to the development of an organizational culture conducive to mental health and wellbeing for managers and non-managerial employees.

Building Agency in the Workplace through Action Learning

In my experience with facilitating action learning programs over four decades, the need to develop a sense of agency applies not only to non-managerial employees but also to managers as well. Hence, I discuss separately how action learning builds the capacity for agency for managers and for non-managerial employees.

Building Managerial Agency through Action Learning. Agency is a defining characteristic of action learning, which involves learning with and through action and reflection on the consequences of action, both intended and unintended. Action learning is typically conducted in groups within a workplace, where employees are collaborating to improve the work environment and the way the work is being done.

Reg Revans, the acknowledged father of action learning, argued that the best way to improve a workplace and the way the work is done, is to involve the people who have the "here and now" responsibility for the work – not only managers, but also employees. Revans is famous for his work with colliery managers in the UK and managers of leading industrial companies in Belgium. He also undertook ground-breaking interventions with nurses in hospitals.

Over the past decade my colleague, Julie Cork, and I have co-facilitated more than 50 longitudinal (four to six months), action learning programs with managers at various levels and from different disciplines in the Queensland government throughout the Australian state of Queensland. The program, called Confident People Management (CPM), focuses on developing people management skills for managers and leaders, and helps them to exercise agency with respect to developing a productive and healthy organization culture.

One of the consistent findings about this action learning program, drawn from self-reports and external reviews, is that the action-learning based, manager development program is an intervention that builds the confidence of managers to take up the authority and responsibility that derive from their managerial position. Participants develop an awareness of how their words and actions, as well as their omissions, shape the team culture daily. They become conscious of their power to develop a positive and productive culture within their team, thus shaping their work environment and the way the work is done – and, in this sense, building agency for themselves.

As the CPM Program is project-based, it provides managers with the opportunity to enhance the sense of agency experienced by their non-managerial employees, by engaging them in the process of changing their work environment and the way the work is done.

Building the Agency of Non-managerial Employees through Action Learning. Reg Revans famously suggested that you do not get a Professor of Medicine to solve the problems of nurses having to look after dying children. You get the nurses themselves to explore together the issues they are confronting, identify what creative solutions they could adopt, and take action to implement these identified solutions.

Austin, Smythe and Swann (2016) reported an action learning intervention in a hospital setting that put Reg Revans' ideas into practice. The doctoral research undertaken by Dr Diana Austin found that the way to address the seemingly intractable problem of midwives experiencing trauma after the death of a baby and/or mother – before, during or after birth – was to have the midwives work in an 'action group' of colleagues affected by a 'critical incident', who then gathered information about traumatic events and reactions, from each other, from interviews with other affected parties, and from external health professionals. The affected midwives were able to share with each other their raw feelings and powerful insights in the safe, supportive environment of an action learning set. For some, it was the first time that they had spoken to anyone about the trauma they were experiencing from involvement in a critical incident leading to the death of a baby and/or mother.

The action learning group identified the unconscious rules of the health professionals and management as the major impediment to improving the midwives' work situation. Austin's (2016) research resulted in the creative solution of an illustrated "Critical Incidents eBook" that addresses and challenges the fundamental assumptions underlying these unconscious rules. The e-book is now accessible to all health professionals throughout New Zealand and the world.

Austin et al. (2016), in their presentation 'Learning for Change and Innovation World Congress' in Adelaide, explained that the action learning by the action group led to some key changes in the work environment for midwives (and other health professionals), and changed the way critical incidents and the health professionals involved were treated. This transformation to a supportive culture was detailed further in Austin, Ferkins, Swann and Smythe (2017). The changes realized were:

- destructive assumptions and unconscious rules were surfaced and challenged;
- the 'conspiracy of silence' about the personal impact of trauma after a critical incident was unearthed, challenged and removed;

- the e-book support package was created and made accessible to all;
- new supportive processes were implemented, and self-compassion was encouraged;
- a collaborative ethos was established that replaced the old ethos of 'going-it-alone' when suffering trauma after a critical incident; and
- the focus after a critical incident shifted from personal blaming to systemic inquiry for identifying how processes, procedures and communication could be improved to prevent a recurrence of the incident.

This doctoral study demonstrates very clearly how managerial and employee agency developed through action learning can contribute to improved health outcomes for both managers and their staff.

Building Agency in the Workplace through Mindfulness

It took a manager with robust self-esteem and a keen sense of agency to undertake an action learning project that challenged deeply entrenched unconscious rules, gave a sense of agency to the disempowered midwives and other health professionals and provided an environment conducive to retention and development of professional competence. This is where mindfulness has a role to play, not only in building a manager's sense of agency and willingness to 'let go' of control, but also in developing the capacity of non-managerial employees to take up the responsibility that a new level of agency entails.

Building Managerial Agency through Mindfulness. Managers need to cope with their own thoughts and emotions when offering agency (some control and power) to non-managerial employees. A natural fear of losing control can impede the delegation of authority and responsibility. There is also the ongoing concern when things do not turn out as hoped for, or mistakes are made. Managers need self-awareness and self-management skills, developed through mindfulness, if they are to remain calm and to resist the temptation to curtail the agency of non-managerial employees to prevent any reoccurrence of mistakes.

The more positive and healthy perspective is to encourage honesty when mistakes are made, to undertake a systemic analysis of what went wrong (rather than an inquisition of the individual involved) and to enable all concerned to learn from what happened. This requires considerable self-awareness on the part of the manager and a willingness to trust non-managerial employees – a trust that helps to develop a constructive, mentally healthy environment. This does not preclude the manager from ensuring that adequate training is provided to non-managerial employees to undertake the tasks assigned to them.

The manager's calmness, self-control and empathy in an apparent crisis (developed through mindfulness practices), will inspire non-managerial employees and build their trust, confidence and risk-taking as they move outside their comfort zone and take up the opportunities presented by their increased agency, that is, increased authority and responsibility over their work environment and how work is done.

Building the Capacity of Non-managerial Employees for Agency through Mindfulness. Mindfulness builds the capacity of non-managerial employees to contribute effectively in an organization by taking up the authority, responsibility and opportunity provided by increased agency. Like the manager, non-managerial employees need to develop self-awareness (understanding their own thoughts and emotions) and self-management (keeping their thoughts and emotions under control). It is natural for non-managerial employees to feel fearful as they move outside their comfort zone (typically based on dependence), exercise more independence and judgment and take on increased responsibility for outcomes.

Some non-managerial employees are reluctant to agree on outcomes and outputs in advance, even while having control over how they are achieved, because this freedom of choice and agency brings with it a new level of responsibility. Self-awareness and self-management developed through mindfulness, and the support of an empathetic manager, can help non-managerial employees to take on the responsibility associated with increased agency.

Mindfulness, too, enables non-managerial employees to develop clarity in relation to their role and responsibilities, while enabling them to develop creative solutions. It also helps them to build resilience – to 'bounce back' from difficulties and setbacks when pursuing specific goals and outcomes in the workplace. Relationships in the workplace are enhanced as non-managerial employees develop social skills through mindfulness training and become better able to contribute to the team effort and collaborative endeavours.

Hence mindfulness training better equips managers to provide the psychological and productivity benefits of giving increased agency to non-managerial employees. On the other hand, non-managerial employees trained in mindfulness are more able to take up the responsibilities and opportunities entailed in increased agency and to enjoy the satisfaction and wellbeing that results. Hence, mindfulness training has the potential to develop sustainable managerial agency, as well as the agency of non-managerial employees, in an organization.

The following case study and related reflection provide the opportunity to consider the combined effect of action learning and mindfulness in terms of developing both self-awareness and agency for managers and non-managerial employees.

Improving a Toxic Work Environment through Action Learning: A Doctoral Case Study

Waddington and Wood (2018) discuss the processes and results of Rod Waddington's doctoral study that employed action learning to improve a toxic work environment in a technical and vocational education environment. The doctoral study and related article tracks his intervention as Human Resource Development (HRD) manager in a college in South Africa with five campuses.

The college was characterized by a toxic workplace that resulted in both physical and psychological problems for managers and non-managerial employees. Waddington and Wood (2018) discussed the toxicity of the organization in terms of the 'toxic triangle' (leaders, followers and the work environment) described by Padilla, Hogan and Kaiser (2007). The action learning intervention set out to address the three elements that contributed to toxicity in the workplace – toxic leaders, toxic followers and a toxic organizational context (systems, processes and procedures that enabled toxicity to develop and grow). Toxic leaders – identified as displaying narcissistic tendencies and traits – micromanaged, abused and bullied non-managerial employees, failed to address poor behaviour (in part, because of favouritism), threw tantrums and undermined engagement, productivity and wellness of managers and non-managerial employees.

Developing an Action Learning Intervention

In his doctoral study, Waddington was able to create an action learning group (action learning set) comprising a representative group of nine managers who managed campuses or divisions and reported to the Corporate Centre where the HRD manager worked. In the article co-authored with Wood (2018), Waddington explained his approach to the action learning intervention in terms of engaging people who were directly impacted by, and were contributing to, the toxic organizational environment:

> I had to learn to adopt an inclusive, participative, democratic paradigm to guide a bottom-up approach. I thus recruited other managers as participants, co-researchers and change agents to constitute an action learning set .... The goal was to improve our common practice as managers so that we could reduce toxicity in the workplace through promoting life-enhancing values, thereby bringing about organizational development and improving wellness in the college. (p. 9)

The resultant action learning intervention developed the self-awareness of the participating managers and enabled them to build agency for themselves and their non-managerial employees.

Developing Self-awareness through the Action Learning Intervention. The creative processes of drawing and storytelling employed in this research captured the experiences and feelings of the managers who formed the action learning group. This provided a safe environment for exchanging information that was self-disclosing and uncomfortable, and left them vulnerable. In the first instance, the managers in the participating group were invited to identify events that contributed to their experience of trauma and stress.

The storytelling or narrative that followed the drawings enabled the managers to articulate what they each had been feeling for a long time but had denied, submerged and kept hidden from others. The process gave them permission to be honest in their communication with each other because it helped them to realize they were not alone in their experience of personal hurt, dissatisfaction, stress and, in some cases, trauma.

The participating managers identified different feelings – a strong sense of abandonment through lack of support, devalued because they were not listened to, dehumanized because they were verbally abused and hopelessness because there was no positivity or direction provided. Hence participants started to admit their own feelings as well as the part they themselves played in perpetuating the toxic environment. This growth in self-awareness enabled them to move from helplessness and self-blame to take up the 'agency and responsibility' offered to them through the action learning process.

Building Agency through the Action Learning Intervention. After the first round of personal disclosure, the participating managers were asked to develop a picture of a changed workplace that incorporated the values that had been denied through the toxicity of the work environment. This shared personal vision enabled the managers to tap into a sense of empowerment and hope that they could create an environment conducive to improved physical and mental health and to the development of an organization characterized by wellness and mutual respect. This process thus led to a keen sense of agency.

The focus of conversation amongst the managers moved from negative thoughts and feelings to discussion focused on hope and aspiration. A key outcome was the development of a sense of responsibility, not only for their own area of responsibility but also for the organization as a whole. This was reflected in the managers' agreement to initiate a 'values campaign' in their areas of responsibility, based on five core values – inclusiveness, participation, trust, empowerment and consultation. They developed an agreed format for posters to be used as part of this 'values advocacy'. Through the processes of drawing, sharing and reflecting, participants built trust in each other, changed their mindset, developed better coping skills and increased resilience as proactive change managers.

Reflections on Waddington's Action Learning Intervention

My reflections on the action learning intervention described by Waddington and Wood (2018) relate to how ongoing training in mindfulness, for participating managers and non-managerial employees, could have contributed to the outcomes of the intervention, including its sustainability. In discussing the potentiality of mindfulness training in the context of the intervention, I am mindful of the earlier discussion of how mindfulness develops self-awareness and builds agency.

If participants in an action learning intervention were trained in mindfulness and related meditation practices, they could bring to the intervention a greater capacity to contribute openness and honesty, make the most of the opportunities for increased agency and contribute to the sustainability of the intervention through their enhanced resilience.

One of the outcomes that Waddington's action learning intervention in an educational setting in South Africa had in common with Austin's action learning intervention in a health setting in New Zealand, is the personal disclosure by participants of what they were experiencing and feeling and what contributed to their pain and suffering. In the case of the college, the participating managers identified the core factors negatively impacting their mental health to be the style of management and resultant toxicity of the workplace; in the health setting, midwives identified the core factors to be the unconscious rules and the resultant lack of support they experienced following a critical incident that led to personal trauma. In both cases, participants had suffered in silence and not shared with others what was happening for them; they were engaged in a conspiracy of silence. The collaborative environment provided by action learning enabled them to feel safe and to be open about what they really thought and felt.

If mindfulness training had preceded these interventions (and continued throughout), participants could have been more aware of themselves and more willing to share at a deeper level. Mindfulness brings with it self-awareness and increased insight into factors impacting thoughts, feelings and reactions (Goleman, 2018a). Participants would also be better placed to support each other through the disclosure experience. If participants in these action learning programs had been exposed to mindfulness over a reasonable period and had undertaken regular practice, they would have brought a higher level of resilience to the action learning intervention. This, in turn, would contribute to the ability to sustain the outcomes of the intervention as participants would be better able to manage setbacks and difficulties.

Conclusion

In exploring the relationships amongst action learning, mindfulness and mental health in this chapter, a key conclusion emerged. It is the potential of action learning, in combination with mindfulness training, to reduce the negative impacts of a toxic work environment.

The *Mindful Nation UK* report produced by the UK MAPP Group (2015) drew on neuroscience research to explore the potential role of mindfulness in health, education, the workplace and the UK Criminal Justice System. The Report stated that mindfulness training alone will not fix dysfunctional organizations that create toxic environments for employees where they are devalued, overworked and subject to public, caustic criticism. Mindfulness training can, however, build resilience and increase the capacity of employees to contribute to the organization where reasonable stressors exist. It is not designed to build employees' capacity to endure unreasonable workloads or a toxic environment (Achor & Gielan, 2016).

The *Mindful Nation UK* report was cognizant of the very relevant views expressed by the Trade Union Congress (TUC) in its 2013 document titled, *Work and Wellbeing: A Trade Union Resource*. In this resource, the TUC expressed concern that wellbeing programs were being used as a substitute for addressing more fundamental issues such as workload, hours of work and inappropriate management style. In their discussions with the working group developing the *Mindful Nation UK* report, the TUC was particularly concerned about the need to address toxic work environments and not assume that mindfulness training for staff will change the level of toxicity by osmosis, that is, by unconscious assimilation of the values, ideas and skills of mindfulness by managers who create toxic environments. The working group recognized the validity of the TUC's concerns with its statement in the Report that, "Mindfulness will only realise its full potential when it is part of a well-designed organizational culture which takes employee wellbeing seriously" (p. 45).

Despite this assertion and the statement that "as an isolated intervention it [mindfulness] cannot fix dysfunctional organizations," the recommendations of the report relating to mindfulness training in the workplace still failed to include the need for an explicit intervention in the organizational culture (pp. 45–46). As organizations help managers and leaders to grow in mindfulness through mindfulness training, they also need to design interventions to directly address the culture of the organization in a planned, constructive way that creates values and behaviour consistent with those espoused in mindfulness programs. This strongly suggests that mindfulness training as an intervention should be developed in concert with an action learning intervention.

The *MASA (Mindfulness, Action Learning, Self-awareness, Agency) Model* presented in Fig. 4.1 illustrates the complementarity and mutual reinforcement of action learning and mindfulness, and the potential for effective intervention in toxic work environments when the two are used in concert. When action learning is used together with ongoing mindfulness training, the potential benefits of the intervention are enhanced considerably, and sustainability of the positive outcomes is increased.

Mental health in the workplace is a complex dimension of organizational life. However, interventions combining action learning and mindfulness training, with a conscious focus on the development of self-awareness and agency, can create a culture that nurtures mental health and wellness in the workplace.

Topics for Discussion

1. What impact has a lack of self-awareness had on your work team?
2. In your experience, how have staff responded to an increased sense of agency?
3. What needs to happen to sustain the benefits of an action learning intervention?

Further Reading

Doidge, N. (2015). *The brain's way of healing: Remarkable discoveries and recoveries from the frontiers of neuroplasticity*. Brunswick, Australia: Scribe Publications.

Good, D. J., Lyddy, C. J., Glomb, T. M., Bono, J. E., Brown, K. W., Duffy, M. K., … Lazar, S. W. (2015). Contemplating mindfulness at work: An integrative review. *Journal of Management*, *42*(1), 1–29. Retrieved from http://journals.sagepub.com/doi/10.1177/0149206315617003

Passfield, R. (2018). *Grow Mindfulness – A blog on mindfulness research, practices and benefits*. Retrieved from www.growmindfulness.com

Sinclair, A. (2016). *Leading mindfully: How to focus on what matters, influence for good, and enjoy leadership more*. Crows Nest: Allen & Unwin.

References

Achor, S., & Gielan, M. (2016). Resilience is about how you recharge, not about how you endure. *Harvard Business Review*, June 24. Retrieved from https://hbr.org/2016/06/resilience-is-about-how-you-recharge-not-how-you-endure

Austin, D. (2016). *Critical incidents eBook: Support tool for health professionals.* Auckland, NZ: University of Auckland. Retrieved from https://indd.adobe.com/view/f81e3740-3568-4693-8abe-9d5f701515f0

Austin, D., Ferkins, L., Swann, J., & Smythe, L. (2017). After the event: Debrief to make a difference. *O & G Magazine, 19*(2), 55–56.

Austin, D., Smythe, L., & Swann, J. (2016). Helping you, helping me: Facilitating wellbeing following critical incidents in health care. Presentation at the Learning for Change and Innovation World Congress, Adelaide, South Australia, 7–9 November.

Doidge, N. (2015). *The brain's way of healing: Remarkable discoveries and recoveries from the frontiers of neuroplasticity.* Brunswick, Australia: Scribe Publications.

Goleman, D. (2013). *Focus: The hidden driver of excellence.* London: Bloomsbury.

Goleman, D. (2018a). *How self-awareness pays off.* Retrieved from https://www.linkedin.com/pulse/how-self-awareness-pays-off-daniel-goleman/

Goleman, D. (2018b). Mindfulness and the 12 competencies of emotional intelligence. Video presentation during the online Mindfulness at Work Summit, 11–20 June 2018. Retrieved from https://atworksummit.mindfulleader.org/

Goleman, D., & Davidson, R. J. (2017). *Altered traits: Science reveals how meditation changes your mind, brain and body.* New York, NY: Penguin Publishing.

Good, D. J., Lyddy, C. J., Glomb, T. M., Bono, J. E., Brown, K. W., Duffy, M. K., … Lazar, S. W. (2015). Contemplating mindfulness at work: An integrative review. *Journal of Management, 42*(1), 1–29. Retrieved from http://journals.sagepub.com/doi/10.1177/0149206315617003

Harris, R. (2009). *ACT made simple: An easy-to-read primer on acceptance and commitment therapy.* Oakland, CA: New Harbinger Publications.

Kabat-Zinn, J. (2005). *Coming to our senses: Healing ourselves and the world through mindfulness.* New York, NY: Hyperion.

Kabat-Zinn, J. (2011, January 27). *Opening to our lives: An interview with Krista Tibbett.* Retrieved from https://onbeing.org/programs/jon-kabat-zinn-opening-lives/

Kabat-Zinn, J. (2017). *How the brain creates the narratives of your life.* Video retrieved from https://www.youtube.com/watch?v=DVtkl-l_Cdg

Mindful Awareness Research Center (MARC). (n.d.). *About MARC.* Los Angeles, CA: UCLA. Retrieved from http://marc.ucla.edu/about-marc.

Moe, A. M., & Docherty, N. M. (2014). Schizophrenia and the sense of self. *Schizophrenia Bulletin, 40*(1), 161–168. Retrieved from https://doi.org/10.1093/schbul/sbt121

Padilla, A., Hogan, R., & Kaiser, R. B. (2007). The toxic triangle: Destructive leaders, susceptible followers, and conducive environments. *The Leadership Quarterly, 18*(3), 176–194. Retrieved from https://doi.org/10.1016/j.leaqua.2007.03.001

Passfield, R. (2018). *Grow Mindfulness – A blog on mindfulness research, practices and benefits.* Retrieved from www.growmindfulness.com

Private Sector Working Group. (2016). *Building the case for mindfulness in the workplace.* Sheffield: The Mindfulness Initiative. Retrieved from http://themindfulnessinitiative.org.uk/publications/building-the-case

Revans, R. (1982). *The origins and growth of action learning.* Bromley: Chartwell-Bratt.

Revans, R. (1991). *Interview with John Mahoney and Denis Loaney, Part 1.* Brisbane, Australia: ALARA. Retrieved from https://www.youtube.com/watch?v=wUfYINYWSdo

Sharot, T. (2017). *The influential mind: What the brain reveals about our power to change others.* London: Little, Brown Book Group.

Sinclair, A. (2016). *Leading mindfully: How to focus on what matters, influence for good, and enjoy leadership more*. Crows Nest: Allen & Unwin.

Trade Union Council (TUC). (2013). *Work and well-being: A trade union resource*. London: TUC.

UK Mindfulness All-Party Parliamentary (MAPP) Group. (2015). *Mindful nation UK*. Sheffield: The Mindfulness Initiative. Retrieved from http://www.themindfulness-initiative.org.uk/images/reports/Mindfulness-APPG-Report_Mindful-Nation-UK_Oct2015.pdf

Vago, D. R., & Silbersweig, D. A. (2012). Self-awareness, self-regulation and self-transcendence (S-ART): A framework for understanding the neurobiological mechanisms of mindfulness. *Frontiers in Human Neuroscience, 6*(296). Retrieved from https://doi.org/10.3389/fnhum.2012.00296

Waddington, R., & Wood, L. (2018). Improving the work climate in a TVET college through changing conversations. *Journal of Further and Higher Education*, 1–28. Retrieved from https://doi.org/10.1080/0309877X.2018.1445829

Chapter 5

Integrating Action Learning with Action Research (ALAR)

Ortrun Zuber-Skerritt

Chapter Outline

This chapter concerns Action Learning and Action Research (ALAR) as an integrated concept and practice. Here I trace its origin, history, development and literature, and discuss the strengths and challenges of this genre. It is important to first understand the philosophical assumptions underpinning action learning: (1) epistemology (how we learn by doing, reflecting on and in action and creating new knowledge), (2) ontology (our assumptions about the nature of being, becoming, existence or reality, as well as the basic categories of being and their relations), (3) paradigm, methodology and methods of addressing and solving a common issue collaboratively and (4) axiology (our values and worldviews that underpin and determine our action). This basic philosophical understanding can be gradually developed through collaborative team work in 'action learning sets' with regular reflections on praxis and learning/project outcomes, before starting the action research cycles in project teams. ALAR is conceived as the basis for other action research genres such as educational action research, systemic action research, action science, appreciative inquiry (AI), critical participatory action research (CPAR) and participatory action learning and action research (PALAR), discussed by world renowned experts in Part II of this book.

Introduction

This chapter serves as a link between Part I on Action Learning (AL) and Part II on Action Research (AR). Before 1990, these two traditions had existed and developed quite separately: AL based on Reg Revans' work (1971, 1980, 1982, 1991; Revans & Pedler, 2011), mainly with managers of coal mines in the UK and with bank managers in Belgium; and AR based on Kurt Lewin's work (1926, 1948, 1951) in Berlin and the US, with a main focus on social and educational issues. Cross-referencing between the two literatures was minimal. In the 1980s,

Action Learning and Action Research: Genres and Approaches, 69–79
Copyright © 2019 by Ortrun Zuber-Skerritt
All rights of reproduction in any form reserved
doi:10.1108/978-1-78769-537-520191008

while I was on a lecture tour at Swedish universities, participants in my work-shops on AR told me repeatedly: "You talk like Reg Revans." I had never heard of him nor read his work. Back in Australia, I searched for his work and was surprised at the similarities between his AL and my AR theory and practice.

In 1990 we brought these two traditions together for the first time in the *First World Congress on Action Learning, Action Research and Process Management* (ALARPM) at Griffith University in Brisbane, Australia, with Reg Revans as one of our keynote speakers. In the following, I tell the story of the origin and develop-ment of AL and AR from my personal experience and involvement. I then discuss the integration of these two concepts and the merger of the two separate tradi-tions and literatures into one as *Action Learning and Action Research* or ALAR as a new genre and the title of a book I published in 2009 (Zuber-Skerritt, 2009). This chapter concludes with reflections on our further development of ALAR into another genre we call participatory action learning and action research (PALAR), presented by Lesley Wood in Chapter 13.

My Story of ALAR

In the 1980s I belonged to three groups of educators, consultants and community leaders interested in AL, AR and PM who met informally and regularly in the various universities, business centres, law firms and even in the Premier's Depart-ment in Queensland, because John Mahoney, Senior Advisor to the Premier, was the leader and newsletter editor of the process management group.

The AL group used action learning as an approach to management educa-tion and development taught in some business schools such as the International Management Centres Association (IMCA), Pacific Region. These AL education programs were mainly for experienced and senior managers who aimed at a pro-fessional Master and/or Doctor of Business Administration (MBA/DBA), and used AL in their organizations in industry, business and government. At the time I was a full-time academic in Higher Education at Griffith University, and a part-time Dean in the IMCA teaching dissertation research and writing by ALAR.

The AR group comprised innovative university academics, school teachers and postgraduate students in various fields in and around Brisbane who met regularly for discussion and sharing of new ideas, practices and processes of AR. These were the days of the 'paradigm wars', when the quantitative, scientific research approach of positivism was dominant in the social sciences and AR was criti-cized as 'unscientific' and so not a valid research approach. My field was 'Higher Education', including academic staff development, course design and evalu-ation of teaching and learning. To study the philosophy, theory and literature of AR in depth, I enrolled in a second PhD at Deakin University, at that time demonstrably the best AR school in Australia, with a young Stephen Kemmis as my supervisor. I would use AR as my research approach and would examine my own professional practice, individually and jointly in collaborative partner-ship with my academic colleagues. I produced one of the first PhD theses using AR in Australia that was accepted by national and international examiners and later published as two books by Kogan Page in London (Zuber-Skerritt, 1992a,

1992b). To some extent this broke the ground; from then it became somewhat easier for postgraduate students to be accepted into higher degrees through AR. But there was still the problem of insufficient examiners who truly understood the AR paradigm and methodology and were willing – or keen – to support its acceptance in the higher education system. Students had to learn to explain their approach in great detail to educate and convince their examiners of the appropriateness of their mainly qualitative research method to provide evidence of their knowledge claims.

The PM group was interested in using process management to explore and practise processes of effective learning, consulting and managing in industry, business and government, as well as in education and higher education. Most in this group were senior practising managers and consultants in many sectors of society. They met regularly in Brisbane to exchange ideas, views, experiences, information, resources and literature, and to change from a focus on 'products', productivity and financial outcomes, to 'processes' of learning, human relationships, team work, collaboration and communication – processes that in the final analysis led to more creative and innovative achievements and even better performance and financial outcomes.

Membership of these three groups overlapped because we shared philosophical assumptions and values in the new, evolving participatory paradigm (explained in Chapters 1, 13 and 14). After the First ALARPM World Congress in 1990, within a year we founded the ALARPM professional network association. When John Mahoney died suddenly of a heart attack (aged 50), the PM group effectively dissolved, but most of its members joined the ALARPM Association. This association was finally renamed Action Learning and Action Research Association (ALARA) in 2007, because the concept of PM had become part of ALAR.

For a more comprehensive story of ALARA, I refer to Zuber-Skerritt and Passfield (2016a, 2016b).[1] Here we trace the origin, history, culture and evolution of ALARA over two and a half decades and its association with like-minded international networks. Examples of these networks include the Participatory Action Research (PAR) Network, the Collaborative Action Research Network (CARN, UK based), the Action Research Network of the Americas (ARNA, North and South America), the Global University for Lifelong Learning (GULL, registered in California, US), the Global Centre for Work-Applied Learning (GCWAL, in Adelaide, Australia), Systematic Participatory Inquiry Research and Action Learning (SPIRAL, Melbourne based) and other collaborative networks of AR and AL, all with international membership (see http://www.alarassociation.org/pages/networks/around-the-world). The number of ALAR centres and institutes in universities and private business schools around the world continues to increase.

Zuber-Skerritt and Passfield (2016a) reflected on ALARA congresses and conferences as 'learning conferences' (further developed in Zuber-Skerritt, 2017) and designed a model for conference organizers and a model for delegates to maximize the opportunities for learning, knowledge creation, collaboration and turning conference papers into publications as journal articles, books or book chapters. We also suggested a new kind of ALAR that has emerged/developed in

ALARA after its close collaboration with the PAR Network: PALAR, the topic of Chapter 13 in this book.

Zuber-Skerritt and Passfield (2016b) reported how the authors suffered severe personal and career disadvantages in the early days when the paradigm of collaborative AL and participatory AR was new and criticized by traditional, positivist researchers in the social sciences. So they joined like-minded interest and support groups. Since then, their goal has been to bring together into the new integrated concept and process of ALAR the closely related concepts of AL and AR, which till then had been developing separately. They have continued to draw together people from all sectors of society to explore ALAR processes, to gradually achieve increasingly higher levels of consciousness, confidence and capabilities in practice and research. Therefore, the aims that have gradually emerged from ALAR include:

- providing an umbrella for the many varieties of ALAR;
- bringing together people from a diverse range of professional disciplines and practices for social change;
- supporting practitioners in addressing the challenges of the twenty-first century through ALAR;
- being relevant to theorists, experienced practitioners and novices;
- networking ALAR scholars and practitioners from local to global levels; and
- complementing, cooperating and collaborating with allied networks and organizations.

The Integration of ALAR

The story above explains how the various approaches to ALAR originated in several places, contexts and organizations, and how cross fertilization occurred gradually in meetings of academics, students, practitioners and professionals from across society locally, nationally and globally. No wonder that boundaries have blurred, extended and integrated in ALAR. I now discuss what I consider the essential characteristics of this integration in terms of theory, practice and processes. I have already discussed the common paradigm of ALAR in Chapter 1.

ALAR Theory

There is not *one* theory of ALAR, but a combination and integration of various aspects of many theories of learning, development and research in this participatory paradigm. So here I talk about theoretical frameworks that may change or vary from person to person or group to group depending on national or local contexts, conditions, situations and/or cultures. I propose that every person conducting ALAR projects or programs should identify and clarify their own theoretical framework of ALAR because it justifies and impacts on the design, implementation and evaluation of an ALAR project. This consciousness may develop gradually and change over time. Examples of my own theoretical frameworks of ALAR include Zuber-Skerritt (1992a, 2011, 2015, 2018).

ALAR Practice

A primary principle in ALAR – and, in fact, in all types of AR – is to practise what we preach. Bob Dick discusses this in Chapter 10 on action science and on Argyris and Schön's (1974) differentiation between 'espoused theory' (what we say we do) and 'theory-in-use' (what we actually do), which can be opposites of intention and action. That is why critical reflection and self-reflection with 'critical friends' in open, trusting and truthful relationships are so important in ALAR.

Another important practice is to start with AL processes before introducing practices, principles and methods of AR, for AL is much simpler and easier to understand because it is natural in our daily lives. For example, we ask fresh questions from childhood on. We communicate, collaborate, compromise and cooperate with each other to play, learn and solve problems together. But what we have to learn anew is to *reflect* individually and collectively – before, in, on and after action – and critically examine the effects of our action and the subsequent implications for future action.

To understand ALAR, participants have to actually do and practise it, rather than reading, being told or lectured about it. They have to personally *experience* and *reflect* on their practices and be encouraged to identify their own and other participants' feelings, emotions, thoughts, views, opinions and reactions, and to the facilitators' processes. These processes enable them to build their own personal constructs (Kelly, 1955; Zuber-Skerritt, 1992c) and grounded theories (Birks & Mills, 2010; Bryant & Charmaz, 2007; Dick, 2007) on the basis of these experiences.

ALAR Processes

The main processes of ALAR can be explained by the three Rs, seven Cs and three Es (Zuber-Skerritt, Wood, & Louw, 2015). Briefly:

The Three Rs. The three Rs refer to relationships, reflection and recognition/ reward. I have discussed the importance of *relationships* in Chapter 1 and *reflection* above. *Recognition* of the ALAR team's effort, achievements and learning outcomes at the end of each project/program is equally important. We always have a 'Celebration Day' when each team in an ALAR program presents their project results and learning outcomes to a large, invited audience of colleagues, students, friends and families. It is always amazing to see how seriously and enthusiastically they appreciate and prepare for this occasion/event (e.g., see Speedy, 2003).

The Seven Cs. Zuber-Skerritt (2012, pp. 217–218) summarized the key values, strategies and behaviour of action learners/researchers, as the 7 Cs:

1. *communication* through relationship, vision and team-building activities at the very start of an ALAR project or program to ensure effective
2. *collaboration* among all members of the group, generating team spirit, symmetrical communication and synergy;
3. *commitment* to the group, to the completion of the project and to positive, sustainable change and development;

4. *coaching* and learning from one another in dialogue, discussion and by asking fresh questions (AL);
5. *critical* and self-critical attitude and reflection on action, being open to feedback from critical friends and to new or different perspectives (AR);
6. *competence* in facilitating ALAR and R&D activities, using effective processes and methods, with a vision of excellence leading to a high level of performance (action leadership); and
7. *character* building as a consequence of the above, characterized by integrity, trust (and being trusted), honesty, respect for others, diversity and difference, resilience and an openness to new perspectives, opportunities and innovations.

The Three Es. Emancipation, empowerment and emergence (of a fairer, more just society) are the three outcomes of a successful ALAR project or program when participants have become (1) *emancipated* from the dictates of what is expected, 'normal' or dominant in social life, (2) *empowered* by the experience and confidence of being able to make positive and sustainable changes to their own life situation and that of others and (3) as a consequence, having realized that these changes have actually contributed towards the gradual *emergence of a fairer and more just community* or society at large.

ALAR Successes

Over the past 30 years I have used, developed and supported others in developing ALAR in theory and practice. My experiences have ranged from the early paradigm struggles and discriminations, through years of striving to provide opportunities, and evidence of what works and what does not, for participants, organizations and communities. My books, articles, videos and other publications were criticized in the early days, as the ALAR paradigm struggled to break ground as a legitimate approach to and basis for scholarship within a higher education system and only gradually were accepted and appreciated as ALAR has developed and spread around the world (see Kearney & Todhunter, 2015).

In 2018 I was awarded an Order of Australia, the nation's highest recognition for "distinguished service to tertiary education *in the field of action research and learning*, as an academic, author and mentor, and to professional bodies." I share this recognition of AR and AL with all my colleagues in this field all over the world, who have struggled and achieved great practical, theoretical and other knowledge outcomes through their R&D projects for the common good and for social justice – like the authors of this volume and in the author index. I rest my case and continue to point out challenges to ALAR that may help less experienced adherents of ALAR overcome problems.

Challenges Facing ALAR and ALAR Networks

As pointed out in Zuber-Skerritt and Passfield (2016a), ALAR faces at least four main challenges. First, ALAR constitutes an alternative paradigm of learning, knowledge creation and research. If positivists read ALAR publications, they are likely to criticize ALAR scholarship because they judge it using the criteria of validity in their scientific paradigm (e.g., generalizability, large samples, control groups, methodological rigour and predominantly quantitative methods and statistics). They fail to understand that the purpose and aims of ALAR are not to conduct large surveys to study national or international trends and predict people's or the economy's future behaviour/outcomes in academic papers. Rather, ALAR practitioners work with small groups of people to understand and help improve their situation, practices and life world, and both learn and create knowledge through these processes. We are therefore proceeding from and with ethical and methodological assumptions and goals that are different from those of positivists, and we are using predominantly qualitative research methods to achieve our goals.

The second challenge is when ALAR projects or programs are run mainly by volunteers working on a low budget, which is often, because adequate funding from outside is still uncommon. ALAR's vision, goals, principles, ethics, values and strategies cannot be adhered to unless all volunteers are well informed, committed and feel engaged and responsible for putting these conceptual aspects into practice (to practise what they preach). As people's lives become increasingly busier, it becomes more difficult to attract members and participants to regular meetings and conferences, especially when conferences in other (inter)disciplinary fields compete for participants.

A third challenge concerns the breadth of the ALAR vision, and ensuring that the activities of ALAR networks and associations contribute to the totality of the vision, rather than focus only on an aspect of the vision or concentrate on the concerns and issues of a particular group. Such narrowing can lead to exclusion of other groups, and can result in disengagement and organizational decline. For example, in ALARA, our initial vision was to bring together diverse sectors and practitioners of all participatory processes, including those engaged in ALAR (of whatever school/modality), and those who focus on processes of genuine engagement (however formulated, originated or conceived). Embracing diversity manifests inclusiveness and presents valuable opportunity for mutual learning, enrichment and growth. This is well argued and demonstrated by Danny Burns in Chapter 9.

A fourth challenge is the growth of electronic media, including social media and the growing dominance of visual media over printed text. ALAR participants have to find ways to embrace these media if they are to stay connected to networks and, specifically, to people who are engaged in participatory ALAR and/or who live in remote areas of the world. In this sense, as well as presenting challenge, electronic media also presents potentially valuable opportunities for extending across the globe both the reach of ALAR and communications/connections between those who use it.

Additional Challenges

Most university academics prefer individual, expert research with/on 'subjects', rather than collaborative and emergent forms of research with 'participants' as co-researchers and co-creators of knowledge. This traditional approach to expert research, which is still dominant, is more standardized, pre-determined and controlled by the researcher who understands his/her position to be an 'objective' observer and analyst of data. And even academics who are at least open to an ALAR approach to research and development, often lack knowledge and experience in the new research paradigm and slide back into their old assumptions or try to comply with the requirements of traditional researchers and their standards, especially to achieve publication in peer-reviewed journals or other publications. Another challenge is that community members often resist the idea of 'doing research'; they feel they are not knowledgeable and competent enough and want to rely on the academic researcher. But an ALAR approach guides them gradually through AL that they usually thrive on, to collaborative, participative AR – an experience they at first find extremely surprising, but in time exciting, enjoyable, satisfying and rewarding.

Finally, it is useful here to refer to Marquardt (1999, p. 13), who identified seven factors that can make AL ineffective for problem solving and organizational learning:

1. choice of inappropriate project;
2. lack of support from top management;
3. lack of time;
4. poor mix of participants;
5. lack of commitment by participants;
6. all action and no learning; and
7. incompetent set advisor.

These factors apply not only to AL for problem solving and organizational learning, but also to ALAR aimed at community engagement. Nevertheless, these pitfalls can be avoided if participants, teams, communities and facilitators:

1. select project topics, issues or concerns that all team members are interested in and passionate about;
2. plan the projects properly in the start-up workshop, including context and stakeholder analysis to have both moral and financial support from stakeholders;
3. allocate sufficient time for critical reflection (Moon, 2006, 2007), for learning during meetings and for project completion;
4. spend time at the beginning of the project on relationship building and SWOT analysis (strengths, weaknesses, opportunities and threats) to form a 'winning team' of participants to cover all necessary attributes and skills;
5. own the problem or project and be committed to its success;
6. emphasize learning, research and evaluation (not just action), and maximize long-term community benefits; and
7. use only experienced facilitators and set advisors.

From this discussion of what makes ALAR programs successful or not, we see how individual participants and teams are instrumental in shaping the process and outcomes of these programs and projects.

Reflections and Conclusions

ALAR participants come from a wide spectrum of fields and contexts: public, private and not-for-profit organizations, business, government and (higher) education, community and environmental sectors. They generate and share a certain learning and research culture, based on humanitarian values true to the ALAR philosophy upholding integration, inclusion, collaboration, community, relationships, critical reflection on action, mutual respect, diversity of multiple perspectives, non-dual dialectics, equality and democratic and ethical principles for social justice, engagement and empowerment of all in a better world. ALAR teams are using action leadership (Zuber-Skerritt, 2011) that is non-hierarchical, shared and distributed among colleagues to achieve social justice, positive change and transformational learning for individuals, groups, whole organizations and communities. These values and worldviews constitute not just 'espoused theories', but 'theories in use' (Argyris & Schön 1974, 1996), practised in the ALAR culture.

To conclude, in this chapter I have explained the origins of ALAR as three roots/traditions (AL, AR and process management) planted in Brisbane in the 1980s that were integrated into the 1989 "First Symposium on Action Research in Higher Education, Industry and Government." This international symposium was, in turn, the catalyst for the "First World Congress on ALARPM" in Brisbane in 1990. As the First World Congress, it constituted the birth of the international association, now called ALARA, and the genesis of further congresses, conferences, workshops, conversations, philosophy cafés, cabarets and informal meetings in the 30-year history of ALARA.

I have discussed the successes, limitations and challenges for ALAR. In the collaborative spirit through which ALAR as a genre has grown, I hope this brief history of ALAR's development and culture may stimulate other action learners and action researchers, especially in developing countries, to start their own projects, networks or branches of existing networks or associations, to consider present and future possibilities of ALAR in its various forms, genres and combinations suitable for their own situations, contexts and needs. ALAR can work for you! Just be open, entrepreneurial, passionate and daring, and believe in yourself, your team and your goals of emancipation, empowerment and the emergence of a fairer, better world.

Topics for Discussion

1. Why would you choose ALAR as a genre of AR?
2. What would be your main aims?
3. How would you go about it initiating an ALAR project?
4. What challenges can you anticipate, and how would you overcome them?

Note

1. I apologize for extensive self-citation in this chapter due to my role as the originator of ALAR and PALAR and hence, this autobiographical narrative about ALAR.

Further Reading

Wood, L. (in press). *Participatory action learning and action research*. Abingdon: Routledge.
Zuber-Skerritt, O. (2009). *Action learning and action research: Songlines through interviews*. Rotterdam, The Netherlands: Sense Publishers.

References

Argyris, C., & Schön, D. (1974). *Theory in practice: Increasing professional effectiveness*. San Francisco, CA: Jossey-Bass.
Argyris, C., & Schön, D. (1996). *Organizational learning II: Theory, method and practice*. Reading, MA: Addison-Wesley.
Birks, M., & Mills, J. (2010). *Grounded theory: A practical guide*. London: Sage.
Bryant, A., & Charmaz, K. (Eds.). (2007). *The Sage handbook of grounded theory*. Thousand Oaks, CA: Sage.
Dick, B. (2007). What can grounded theorists and action researchers learn from each other? In A. Bryant & K. Charmaz (Eds.), *The Sage handbook of grounded theory* (pp. 398–416). Thousand Oaks, CA: Sage.
Kearney, J., & Todhunter, M. (Eds.). (2015). *Lifelong action learning and research: A tribute to the life and pioneering work of Ortrun Zuber-Skerritt*. Rotterdam, The Netherlands: Sense Publishers.
Kelly, G. A. (1955). *The psychology of personal constructs* (Vol. 1–2). New York, NY: Norton.
Lewin, K. (1926). *Vorsatz, Wille und Bedürfnis [Intention, will and need]*. Berlin, Germany: Springer.
Lewin, K. (1948). *Resolving social conflict: Selected papers on group dynamics*. New York, NY: Harper and Brothers.
Lewin, K. (1951). *Field theory in social science: Selected theoretical papers*. New York, NY: Harper & Row.
Marquardt, M. (1999). *Action learning in action: Transforming problems and people for world-class organizational learning*. Palo Alto, CA: Davis-Black.
Moon, J. (2006). *Learning journals: A handbook for reflective practice and professional development* (2nd ed.). London: Routledge.
Moon, J. (2007). *Critical thinking: An exploration of theory and practice*. London: Routledge.
Revans, R. (1971). *Developing effective managers: A new approach to business education*. London: Longmans.
Revans, R. (1980). *Action learning: New techniques for management*. London: Blond and Briggs.
Revans, R. (1982). *The origins and growth of action learning*. Bromley: Chartwell-Bratt.
Revans, R. (1991). Action learning: Reg Revans in Australia [Video program produced by Ortrun Zuber-Skerritt (now on DVD)]. Brisbane: Video Vision, University of Queensland. Retrieved from https://www.alarassociation.org/?q=about-al-and-ar/reg-revans-and-action-learning
Revans, R., & Pedler, M. (2011). *The ABC of action learning*. Farnham: Gower Publishing.
Speedy, S. (Ed.). (2003). *Women using action learning and action research: The South African context*. Lismore, Australia: Southern Cross University Press.
Zuber-Skerritt, O. (1992a). *Professional development in higher education: A theoretical framework for action research*. London: Kogan Page.
Zuber-Skerritt, O. (1992b). *Action research in higher education: Examples and reflections* (1996, 2nd ed.). London: Kogan Page.

Zuber-Skerritt, O. (1992c). Eliciting personal constructs in higher education. In O. Zuber-Skerritt (Ed.), *Action research in higher education: Examples and reflections* (pp. 56–63). London: Kogan Page.

Zuber-Skerritt, O. (2009). *Action learning and action research: Songlines through interviews.* Rotterdam, The Netherlands: Sense Publishers.

Zuber-Skerritt, O. (2011). *Action leadership: Towards a participatory paradigm.* Dordrecht, The Netherlands: Springer.

Zuber-Skerritt, O. (Ed.). (2012). *Action research for sustainable development in a turbulent world.* Bingley: Emerald Publishing.

Zuber-Skerritt, O. (2015). Participatory action learning and action research (PALAR) for community engagement: A theoretical framework. *Educational Research for Social Change, 4*(1), 5–25.

Zuber-Skerritt, O. (Ed.). (2017). *Conferences as sites of learning and development: Using participatory action learning and action research approaches.* Abingdon: Routledge.

Zuber-Skerritt, O. (2018). An educational framework for participatory action learning and action research (PALAR). *Educational Action Research, 26*(4), 513–532.

Zuber-Skerritt, O., & Passfield, R. (2016a). History and culture of ALARA – The action learning and action research association. *Educational Action Research, 24*(1), 65–76.

Zuber-Skerritt, O., & Passfield, R. (2016b). Action learning and action research association (ALARA): History, culture and sustainability. In L. L. Rowell, C. D. Bruce, J. M. Shosh, & M. Riel (Eds.), *Palgrave international handbook of action research* (pp. 419–440). New York, NY: Palgrave Macmillan.

Zuber-Skerritt, O., Wood, L., & Louw, I. (2015). *A participatory paradigm for an engaged scholarship in higher education: Action leadership from a South African perspective.* Rotterdam, The Netherlands: Sense Publishers.

Part II

Action Research (AR)

Part II presents eight specific genres of Action Research (AR) that are used most commonly. Chapter 6 offers a general introduction to AR paradigm, theory, practice and processes, which all kinds of AR have in common. Chapter 7 presents an overview of educational AR conducted by individuals, AR teams and school/faculty wide in higher education institutions. Chapter 8 focuses on the contribution to knowledge creation and knowledge democracy of AR for self-study and living-educational-theories. Systemic AR (SAR), discussed in Chapter 9, is another special genre with an impetus for positive change and development of whole systems, and action science, discussed in Chapter 10, explores and extends the seminal work of Argyris and Schön. Chapter 11 presents Appreciative Inquiry (AI) as strength-based action research for creating positive individual and social change in an organization or community. Chapter 12 discusses the genre of critical AR in the tradition of the Frankfurt and Deakin Schools of critical theory, in combination with recent developments in the participatory paradigm. Chapter 13 presents a fairly new genre, participatory action learning and action research (PALAR), which is likewise in the participatory paradigm.

Chapter 6

Demystifying Action Research

David Coghlan

Chapter Outline

Through the theme of demystification, this chapter takes readers on an experiential journey through the main tenets and practices of action research. The first step is to recognize the familiar structure of human knowing, especially when knowing in a practical mode, and how action research is grounded in a philosophy of practical knowing. The second step explores how action research involves three practices: collaboration with others (second-person processes), the self-reflection of the action researcher (first-person), and the knowledge cogenerated out of the first- and second-person practices (third-person). The third step explores how the term 'action research' is generic, and is used to refer to a family of methods. The chapter provides a basic overview of several modalities and compares them on the basis of their generative insight, distinctive emphasis and use. In a synthesis, the chapter draws on the notion of interiority to provide a framework for engaging in a philosophy of practical knowing in first- and second-person practices across the modalities so as to provide readers with a third-person conceptual framework and a practical tool for navigating their way through action research.

Introduction

There are many questions about action research for the person approaching it for the first time. How can research and action be combined? What does it mean to be a researcher passionately involved in addressing an issue? What kind of knowledge is created through action research? What do the apparently different terms within action research, such as 'action learning', 'action science' or 'cooperative inquiry' mean? In this chapter I seek to demystify action research, by providing an overview of the main tenets and practices of action research, taking you through three steps of demystification. The first step is grasping the structure of human knowing and how you know in different patterns, especially in a practical pattern. The second step explores how in action research you engage in three practices: thinking, valuing, acting and learning; how you work with others in

Action Learning and Action Research: Genres and Approaches, 83–96
Copyright © 2019 by David Coghlan
All rights of reproduction in any form reserved
doi:10.1108/978-1-78769-537-520191010

addressing a practical challenge; and how you generate knowledge that is useful for others. The third step of demystification discusses how action research is a family of approaches or modalities that may often be confusing, and I provide a lens that is useful for working with each of them.

The Structure of Human Knowing

Let us begin by situating ourselves in our world. If you think about your knowing you will notice that human knowing has a familiar and invariant structure (Cronin, 2017). As you move along through life, you have many experiences: what you see, hear, touch, think, feel and imagine, what you do and what is done to you by others. The first step in knowing is to attend to your experience. For example, you hear a noise and wonder what it was and what caused it. You receive an insight (understanding); the noise sounded like breaking glass. You follow that up by checking if glass was broken, and if that checks out then you know you were correct. If it does not check out, that is, you can't find broken glass, then you may pursue other possible answers. In this vein, you can check for yourself how human knowing is a dynamic three-step process: *experience, understanding* and *judgment*. First, you attend to your experience. Then you ask questions about your experience and obtain insight (understanding), and you follow that up by reflecting and weighing up the evidence to determine whether your insight fits the evidence or not (judgment). You may get lots of insights every day, but without judgment they remain mere insights. Judgment is where you say 'yes', 'no', 'maybe' or 'I don't know' or 'I need to find more evidence' in response to your insights. It engages the critical dimension of human knowing, since without being critical of your insights you cannot affirm that you know.

I have begun this chapter with a short account of the familiar process of human knowing. It is familiar as you use it all the time. It is verifiable by attending to any process of knowing, whether you are solving a crossword clue, addressing a problem at work or at home, or engaging in scientific research. Each act of knowing involves experience, understanding and judgment. Human knowing is not any of these operations on their own. Of course, you may not always be attentive to experience. You may not ask questions. Understanding may not flow spontaneously from experience. Your insights may be wrong. You may take short cuts and go with the first answer you come up with or the one that is most convenient. Interpretations of data may be superficial, inaccurate, biased; judgments may be flawed. In engaging with others there may be common misunderstandings, distrust, suspicion and conflict in communities and organizations. You can gain insight into these inaccurate manifestations of knowing by the same threefold process of knowing. As Cronin (2017) describes, learning to appropriate your intellectual activities means to become aware of them, to be able to identify and distinguish them, to grasp how they are related and to be able to make the process explicit. Accordingly, you experience, understand and judge not only the world around you, you also experience, understand and judge your own process of knowing and learning. The cognitional operations of experience, understanding and judgment form a general empirical method, which requires you to be:

- *attentive* to what is going on around you and inside you;
- *intelligent* in envisaging possible explanations of those data;
- *reasonable* in preferring as probable or certain the explanations that provide the best account for the data; and
- *responsible* for your actions.

Being faithful to this general empirical method constitutes not only authenticity in action research but also human authenticity (Coghlan, 2008). You stick close to how you know you can avoid becoming trapped in the multiple philosophical arguments about the nature of knowledge that beset the world of research.

Different Patterns of Knowing

If you continue to think about your knowing, you can notice that you know in different ways in different settings. If you are at a concert or in an art gallery or watching a play or reading a novel or poetry, you are engaging in an *aesthetic* or *presentational* pattern of knowing, where you are appreciating harmonies or colours and shapes, the flow of language or the unfolding of a plot or a character. When you are interacting with other people, whether as friends, work colleagues or customers, you engage in a *relational* form of knowing in how you adapt to different people in different contexts and settings. In other contexts you engage in *propositional or* scientific knowing, as you adopt technical terminology, marshal and weigh evidence, test hypotheses and try to verify statements or propositions. You may also engage in a *spiritual* or *religious* form of knowing, where your knowing is grounded in how religious love shapes experience, understanding and guides living and acting in the world. There is also a *practical* pattern of knowing, from which you perform practical tasks. I elaborate on this form of knowing below. In action research these different patterns of knowing are referred to as an extended epistemology (Bradbury, 2015; Chandler & Torbert, 2003). The form of knowledge that action research aims to produce is practical knowing.

Action Research as Practical Knowing

What you know and how you know in day-to-day living is in the realm of practical knowing. The interests of practical knowing are human living, the successful performance of daily tasks and discovering immediate solutions that will work. Practical knowing differs from scientific knowing in that it is particular and practical, and draws on resources of language, and on support of tone and volume, eloquence and facial expression, pauses, questions, omissions and so on. In an article in 2016, I engaged in a philosophical examination and clarification of the philosophy of practical knowing, to deepen our understanding and practice of action research (Coghlan, 2016). I framed four core characteristics for a framework of a philosophy of practical knowing for action research. I now discuss each characteristic with reference to action research.

- *The everyday concerns of human living*: action research does not pursue knowledge for its own sake. Rather, it pursues worthwhile purposes. Within specific organizational and community settings, there may be concerns about improvement and change. What is deemed to be 'worthwhile' is something that needs to be explored with those who are affected by the situation. As I discuss below, judging something to be 'worthwhile' involves attending to how you make judgments of value.
- *Socially constructed*: human living revolves around meaning, the meaning we attribute to words, to gestures and to actions and the meanings that we create. Accordingly, as an action researcher you need to attend to how you interpret what is real, and learn to critique your interpretations. In your engagement with others, you need to learn to accept how others hold different meanings, and be able to engage in dialogical and collaborative activities to build common understanding and consensual collaborative action (Coghlan, 2017a).
- *Attending to the uniqueness of each situation*: one of the characteristics of practical knowing is that it varies from place to place and from situation to situation. What works in one setting may not work in another. Therefore, practical knowing is always incomplete and can be completed only by attending to figuring out what is needed in the situations that you are in at a given time. No two situations are identical. This is why you reason, reflect and judge in a practical pattern of knowing, in order to move from one setting to another, grasping what modifications are needed and deciding how to act. Action research's emphasis on cycles of action and reflection as they unfold in the present is paramount. Drawing on past experience and previous insights as to what worked and did not work before, you need to inquire into the uniqueness of the present situation and seek insights into the concrete, particular here-and-now situation (Coghlan & Shani, 2017), considering what is relevant to this particular concrete situation and adapting remembered insights in order to choose what to say and do.
- *Values driven and ethical*: practical action is driven by values and is fundamentally ethical in how you decide what is worthwhile to do and make choices and take action. As action research is conducted in the present, attentiveness to values and possible choices and their consequences, and being transparent about them, are significant for considering the quality of action research.

Where does the process of valuing fit into the structure of human knowing described above? Essentially you add the activities of valuing, choosing, deciding and taking action, to the cognitive operations of experiencing, understanding and judging what is known. As you are confronted with concrete choices of what to do, you ask what courses of action are open to you and you review options, weigh choices and decide (Brydon-Miller & Coghlan, 2018). You may reflect on possible value judgments as to what the best option might be, and you decide to follow through and take responsibility for consistency between your knowing and your doing. A judgment that the noise you heard was breaking glass is a judgment of fact. A judgment that an action is good/bad, right/wrong, appropriate/inappropriate, worthwhile or not is a judgment of value. Through enacting the general empirical method of being attentive, intelligent, reasonable and responsible, you can hold the different patterns of knowing in a single process and consolidate how you know how you know in different patterns and settings.

The Theory of Action Research

Now we can step aside and look at the theory of action research in the light of our exploration about human knowing. As I work in the organization development arena in which action research is practised, the definition that I follow, and offer you here, is that by Coghlan and Shani (2018). By this definition, action research is:

> An emergent inquiry process in which applied behavioural science knowledge is integrated with existing organizational knowledge and applied to address real organizational issues. It is simultaneously concerned with bringing about change in organizations, in developing self-help competencies in organizational members, and in adding to scientific knowledge. Finally, it is an evolving process that is undertaken in a spirit of collaboration and co-inquiry. (p. 4)

This definition captures the critical themes of the approach that constitute action research: that as an *emergent inquiry process* it engages in an unfolding story to address a practical issue, where data shift as a consequence of what is said, done or not done, and where it is not possible to predict or to control what takes place. As an emergent process, action research involves researching in the present as Chandler and Torbert (2003) and Coghlan and Shani (2017) elaborate. Much of what we refer to as qualitative research is focused on the past. Action research builds on the past, and takes place in the present, with a view to shaping the future. It focuses on *real organizational issues,* rather than issues created particularly for the purposes of research. It operates in the domain of how people participate in systems (organizations and communities), and so *applied behavioural science knowledge* (i.e., the range of disciplines such as organizational psychology, organization theory, management, teamwork and so on) is both engaged in and drawn upon. Action research's distinctive characteristic is that it addresses the twin tasks of bringing about *change in organizations* and in generating robust, actionable *knowledge*, in an evolving process that is undertaken in a spirit of *collaboration and co-inquiry*, whereby research is constructed *with* people, rather than *on* or *for* them.

From this definition, a comprehensive framework of action research in terms of four factors may be gleaned (Coghlan & Shani, 2018).

- *Context*: action research takes place in a particular context. Understanding that context, such as the sociopolitical and environmental forces that are creating the need or desire for the action research, is critical.
- *Quality of relationships*: the quality of relationship between members of the system and researchers is paramount and evolves during the action research

process. Hence relationships need to be designed for and managed through shared goals, collaborative action, trust building, developing a common language, shared reflection and so on.
- *Quality of the action research process itself:* the quality of the emerging action research process is grounded in the dual focus on both the inquiry process and the action process. As the dual intent is to trigger action and generate new insights, paying attention to how the project is progressing through continuous collaborative cycles is essential.
- *Outcomes:* the dual outcomes of action research are (1) improved organizational practice and the development of self-help competencies; and (2) the creation of actionable theory through the action and inquiry. The outcomes are viewed as an enhanced system of practice and knowledge that impacts human, economic and ecological sustainability.

Hopefully you can now understand that grasping how you know is fundamental to these four factors: (1) your understanding of the context in which the action research takes place; (2) the relationships you build with your co-researchers; (3) how your practical knowing is emergent and developmental as you move from experience, to insight, to value judgment, to action, yielding further experiences, insights and judgments in a continuing pattern of learning and development; and (4) how you engage in collaborative action to achieve desired practical outcomes and to generate knowledge. This completes the first step of demystifying action research.

Three Practices of Action Research

When you engage in action research, three sets of practices run concurrently. These are referred to as first-, second- and third-person practices. These terms mean that engaging in action research involves challenges of self-learning and generates subjective data in the present tense (first-person); working with others to achieve the task, which generates data in the present tense about working together (second-person); and making a contribution to future action by others and to useful knowledge (third-person). Traditional research has focused on creating impersonal knowledge for an impersonal readership. In a more complete vision of research as presented by action research, authentic third-person research integrates first- and second-person practices.

First-person Practice

When you are working as an action researcher in the pattern of practical knowing and engaging in action research cycles with others, and trying to understand and shape what is taking form, you are also engaging in your own experiential learning activities. We call this first-person practice (Marshall, 2016). Here, some of the core skills you need as an action researcher are in the areas of self-awareness and sensitivity to what you observe, supported by the conceptual analytic frameworks on which you base your observations and interpretations. Your inquiry can be focused outward (e.g. what is going on in the organization, in the team?) or inward (e.g. what is going on in you?). When you inquire into what is going on, when you show people your train of thought and put forward ideas to be tested, when you make suggestions for action, you are generating data. People's responses (as organizational team members and fellow researchers) to these interventions generate further data. Accordingly, learning to appropriate your intellectual activities as described above is at the heart of your first-person practice.

Second-person Practice

Second-person practice addresses your engagement in collaborative work in co-inquiry and shared action with others on issues of mutual concern, through face-to-face dialogue, conversation and joint decisions and action. To avoid being pulled into arguments or debates about positions, the common ground in any dialogical conversation is the foundation of how we know. Through drawing out (a) others' experience as to what has happened or is happening; (b) their understanding and judgment as what they think about what has happened or is happening; and (c) possible courses of actions, you may build common ground and enhance collaborative inquiry and action (Coghlan, 2009, 2017a; Schein, 2013).

Third-person Practice

Third-person practice is impersonal, and is actualized through the contribution of the action research to an audience beyond those directly involved, such as through dissemination by reporting and publishing. Action research intentionally merges theory with practice, on the grounds that actionable knowledge can result from the interplay of knowledge with action. Action research demands an explicit concern with theory that is generated from the conceptualization of the particular experience in ways that are intended to be meaningful to others.

Quality in action research may be understood in terms of how, in an evolutionary and developmental process over time, individuals show they have learned the skills of first-person practice and how they have engaged in collaborative work in second-person practice as they enacted cycles of action and reflection. Through these first- and second-person practices, the issue may change, relationships may change, the purpose may change, and what is important may change. Action research aims at an explicit integration of all three practices with action and inquiry. Understanding and becoming skilled in first-, second- and third-person practice is the second step in demystifying action research.

Modalities of Action Research

One of the mystiques of action research is what appears to be a bewildering array of terminology, activities and methods. You find terms like 'action science', 'appreciative inquiry', 'cooperative inquiry' and 'learning history', to name some common ones. The term 'action research' has become generic, and is used to refer to a family of approaches or modalities. I suggest that a way of demystifying action research is to understand how each modality or genre is based on a generative insight that led to the framing of each particular modality by the person or group that first constructed it (Coghlan, 2010). By a generative insight, I mean an insight that was foundational in framing that modality and which led to the development of further insights and methods of working within each modality. Here I provide an introduction to some of the more prominent modalities. Each of these modalities is based on generative insights that give the modality its own distinctive character and emphasis (Table 6.1). Through focusing on generative insights and how the general empirical method may be applied, I hope you will receive your own insight into these action modalities, and thereby discover for yourself how to engage with them.

Action Learning: the generative insight that underpins action learning is found in two statements in Revans (1998): 'There can be no learning without action and no (sober and deliberate) action without learning' (p. 83), and 'Those unable to change themselves cannot change what goes on around them' (p. 85). Grasping this insight is at the heart of understanding what action learning is about, how it works and what it seeks to achieve (Coghlan & Rigg, 2012). Revans (1971) described three processes central to action learning, which he refers to as a *praxeology* of human action.

- A process of inquiry into the issue under consideration – its history, manifestation, what has prevented it from being resolved, and what has previously been attempted. Revans calls this process system *alpha*.
- Action learning is science in progress through rigorous exploration of the resolution of the issue through cycles of action and reflection. Revans calls this system *beta*.
- Action learning is characterized by a quality of group interaction, which enables an individual's critical reflection and ultimately learning. This is the essence of action learning and Revans calls it system *gamma*.

The general empirical method is enacted through subjecting experience to questioning insight in the company of peers and taking action. In this volume, Chapters 2–4 explore action learning in more depth.

Action Science: the generative insight for understanding action science is that we are unaware of the theories-in-use in our heads and how they implicitly guide our behaviour and thereby are likely to contribute to ineffectiveness. Being able to systemically analyse and document patterns of behaviours and the reasoning behind them to identify causal links can produce actionable knowledge, that is, theories for producing desired outcomes (Argyris, Putnam, & Smith, 1985). The general empirical method lies at the heart of action science. The process of inquiry into our theories-in-use requires attention to the operations of knowing and involves testing privately held inferences and attributions and how they lead to ineffective strategies and behaviours. In this volume, Chapter 10 explores action science in more depth.

Appreciative Inquiry: appreciative inquiry is built on the generative insight of inquiry as positive, that is, if people focus on what is valuable in what they do

Table 6.1: Generative Insights and the General Empirical Method across Action Modalities.

	Action Learning	Action Science	Appreciative Inquiry	Clinical Inquiry/ Research	Cooperative Inquiry	Collaborative Developmental Inquiry	Learning History	Participatory Action Research
Generative Insight	There can be no learning without action and no action without learning. Those unable to change themselves cannot change what goes on around them.	People are unaware of their theories-in-use. Analysing reasoning and behaviour to identify causal links enables learning and actionable knowledge.	When people focus on what is valuable in what they do and try to work on how this may be built on, it leverages the capacity for transformational action.	When researchers gain access to organizations by invitation in order to be helpful, richer knowledge of organizations and change is generated.	Each person is a *co-subject* in the experience phases by participating in the activities being researched and a *co-researcher* in the reflection phases.	Learning to inquire and to act in a timely manner contains central and implicit frames that each person acts out of in given periods of time.	By presenting the history through the jointly-told tale readers may learn about organizational change.	People, especially the perceived marginalized and underprivileged, gain critical insight into social structures, and engage in action to liberate themselves from the oppression of these structures.
General Empirical Method	Subjecting experience to questioning insight in the company of peers and taking action.	Testing privately-held inferences and attributions in action.	Attending to insights from power of positive experience, questioning, leading to action.	Helping clients attend to their experience, have insights into that experience, make judgments as to whether the insights fit the evidence and then to take action.	Cycles of shared experiences and inquiry, insights generated, meanings articulated and tested in action, leading to further questions and insights, tested, understood and acted on.	Inquiry-in-action through attending to outcomes, plans, strategies and intentionality.	Attending to and discussing one's questions and insights from reading jointly-told tale.	Attending to shared experience, seeking critical insight into the underlying structures that create and maintain circumstances and mobilizing action to liberate themselves from structures.

Source: Adapted from Coghlan (2010, p. 159).

and try to work on how this may be built upon, then it leverages the generative capacity to facilitate transformational action (Cooperrider, 2017). This insight is itself made up of several insights: that in every organization something works somewhere, what we focus on becomes our reality and the language we use creates our reality. The act of asking questions influences people by getting them to think in new ways, which may lead to them acting in new ways. The appreciative inquiry cycle utilizes four *D*s (*D*iscovery, *D*ream, *D*esign, *D*elivery) to enable researchers and practitioners to move from experience to selected action, and to attend to and receive insights into the power of positive questioning. In this volume, Chapter 11 explores appreciative inquiry in more depth.

Clinical Inquiry/Research: instinctively you may think that clinical inquiry/ research is about healthcare. However, Schein (2008) describes clinical inquiry in terms of trained professionals engaged in helping organizations. His generative insight is that when researchers gain access to an organization at the organization's invitation, in order to be helpful and therefore to intervene to enable change to occur, it is akin to being a sort of organizational therapist, and the researcher receives access to rich data about organizational change. The general empirical method is applied to questioning experience, understanding, judgments, decisions and actions (Coghlan, 2009).

Cooperative Inquiry: Heron and Reason (2008) define cooperative inquiry as "a form of second-person action research in which all participants work together in an inquiry group as co-researchers and co-subjects" (p. 366). The participants research a topic through their own experience of it in order to understand their world, make sense of their life, develop new and creative ways of looking at things, and learn how to act to change things they may want to change and find out how to do things better. The generative insight for understanding cooperative inquiry is how each person is a *co-subject* in the experience phases by participating in the activities being researched, and a *co-researcher* in the reflection phases by participating in generating ideas, designing and managing the project and drawing conclusions. The general empirical method operates in cooperative inquiry as participants' experience is brought to the group and exposed to questioning. So there are continuing cycles of experiences being shared, questions asked, insights generated and meanings articulated and tested in action, leading to further insights tested, understood and acted on. An important element of cooperative inquiry is that it works with the different ways of knowing, so experience and insights may be expressed in different forms.

Collaborative Developmental Action Inquiry: Torbert and Associates (2004) understand developmental action inquiry as an expression of action science, where through insights from developmental psychology, leaders gain insight into their own action-logics as they work to transform their organizations. The generative insight that collaborative developmental action inquiry adds to action science is that learning to inquire and to act in a timely manner contains central and implicit frames that each person acts out of in given periods of time. Torbert adds the developmental dynamic of learning to inquire-in-action by emphasizing that as individuals progress through adulthood, they may intentionally develop new 'action-logics' through stages of ego development (Torbert and Associates, 2004). The general empirical method is applied through a process of inquiry-in-action, through attending to what Torbert calls the four territories of experience in a series of inquiry loops to enable insight into outcomes, plans, strategies and intentionality.

Learning History: Bradbury and Mainmelis (2001) state that "the goal of a learning history is to increase participation in a dialogic reflection on past action for creating desired future practices" (p. 342). The learning history presents the experiences and understandings in the own words of those who have gone through and/or been affected by the change, to help the organization move forward and to contribute to our understanding of the social dynamics of organizational change. Rather than presenting the univocal voice of a single author or group of researchers, the learning history presents concurrent, multiple and often divergent voices in an organizational story. Presenting the jointly told tale is enabled by the format, whereby columns of narrative text are juxtaposed with the interpretative voice of participants (often disagreeing) and the voice of the learning historian. The generative insight underpinning the learning history is that by presenting the history through the jointly told tale, readers may learn about organizational change. Readers of a learning history are encouraged to attend to the questions that arise from their engagement with the text, as they choose which column to read first and how they might switch back and forth from participants' narrative and learning historians' comments, and to the insights they receive from reading multiple voices and perspectives. The general empirical method is enacted through both conversations and written texts (Gearty & Coghlan, 2018). Hearing and reading the multiple voices and perspectives within the process of a learning history enable insight into the insights of others, and through conversation enable the emergence of possibilities for new shared insights, on which judgments may be reached and actions planned and taken.

Participatory Action Research (PAR): PAR is generally understood as the form of action research that is conducted in communities, rather than in organizations. The term describes a variety of community-based approaches to knowledge generation, which combines social investigation, education and action and emphasizes local communities in co-producing knowledge directly relevant to them for an agenda of social change (Chevalier & Buckles, 2013). The generative insight underpinning this approach is that people, especially those who are perceived as marginalized and underprivileged, can be enabled to investigate their circumstances, gain critical insight into the structures that create and maintain those circumstances, and engage in action to liberate themselves from the constrictions, if not the oppression, of these structures. The general empirical method involves being attentive to experience, through shared inquiry, seeking critical insight into the underlying structures that create and maintain circumstances and mobilizing action to liberate themselves from the constrictions. In this volume, Chapters 12 and 13 explore PAR in more depth.

I have made the choice as to the modalities introduced here, primarily due to the limitations of space. There are other modalities, which can be explored in such publications as the successive editions of *The Sage Handbook of Action Research* (Bradbury, 2015; Reason & Bradbury, 2001, 2008). You may also note that modalities are not mutually exclusive and some may be used together. Chapters 5 and 13 in this volume provide such an integration.

Understanding the different modalities of action research is the third step of demystifying action research. Rather than presenting the selection of modalities as a group of approaches to be learned, I have sought to both ground them in the process of human knowing, and show how the adoption of any particular modality is dependent on the questions you are asking out of what experiences, in what context, with whom and the insights through action that you are seeking.

Synthesis through Interiority

Grounding this exploration of the theory and practice of action research in the familiar process of how you know has philosophical implications. The general empirical method encourages you to attend to how you understand and how new experiences and insights change your understanding. In engaging in your knowing you are attending to data of sense (what you see and hear around you) and to data of consciousness (what you think, remember, feel, etc.). Holding both is called 'interiority'. Through its focus on method rather than on formal logic, adopting interiority enables you to avoid getting trapped in the historical philosophical minefields of what constitutes knowing and what objectivity is. You can be attentive to your feelings and mental acts as well as to the sense experiences that are the staple of the empiricists. You can come to reasonable judgments as you probe 'what' and 'why' questions, and affirm definitely or provisionally as appropriate an understanding that fits the evidence. You can come to reasonable judgments about what is good or bad, true or false and act responsibly following such judgments. You can decide how attentive you want to be, whether your understanding is intelligent or biased, whether your judgments are reasonable, and how responsible you are for your actions. As there are always further questions, more evidence to attend to, and more bias to be overcome, your judgments of fact and value will change accordingly. I have provided an example of interiority as I explored the field of organization development research from 24 volumes of *Research in Organizational Change and Development* (Coghlan, 2017b). I describe how my inquiry unfolded as I attended to the contents of the chapters, and how my understanding and judgment developed through my questioning and insights.

Conclusions

In this chapter I have approached demystifying action research experientially. I have invited you to begin with what is familiar, your own knowing and to test your knowing in any situation you choose. Underpinning any example of coming to know is a set of activities of experiencing, understanding and judging, and if you want to take action, making a judgment of value, deciding and acting. By working from what is familiar, I drew you into the world of action research, where your insights on what is worthwhile may lead to action with others and you seek to understand how that action worked (or did not) and what you have learned that can inform others in like situations. When you reflect on your insights, come to judgment and engage with others to address a worthwhile issue, and when you desire to create knowledge for others who were not directly involved, you engage in the practices with your own learning, collaborating with others in knowledge generation. Then you can fit the theory of action research into your knowing and acting, and you have a foundation for dealing with the philosophical debates and with the different modalities.

Topics for Discussion

1. Take an act of knowing that you have engaged in, and track your search for an intelligible answer in the movement from puzzlement to understanding, through insight and how you tested your insight, considered alternative explanations, and came to judgment about the answer that best fitted the evidence.
2. Consider an action research initiative with which you are familiar, and reflect on how the three practices of working with others and your own self-learning through the process led to the articulation of actionable knowledge.
3. Considering a potential action research initiative and how you might approach it, explore how the insights that underpin some or any of the action modalities might inform your design of the initiative.

Acknowledgments

I acknowledge the invaluable help and support of Vivienne Brady and Denise O'Leary of the action research writing group of which I am a member in reviewing a first draft of this chapter. A particular thanks to Ortrun Zuber-Skerritt and Lesley Wood for their editorial encouragement and critique.

Further Reading

Bradbury, H. (Ed.). (2015). *The Sage handbook of action research* (3rd ed.). London: Sage.
Coghlan, D., & Shani, A. B. (Rami) (2018). *Conducting action research for business and management students*. London: Sage.
Cronin, B. (2017). *Phenomenology of human understanding*. Eugene, OR: Pickwick.
Marshall, J. (2016). *First person action research: Living life as inquiry*. London: Sage.

References

Argyris, C., Putnam, R., & Smith, D. (1985). *Action science*. San Francisco, CA: Jossey-Bass.
Bradbury, H. (Ed.). (2015). *The Sage handbook of action research* (3rd ed.). London: Sage.
Bradbury, H., & Mainmelis, C. (2001). Learning history and organizational praxis. *Journal of Management Inquiry*, *10*, 340–357.
Brydon-Miller, M., & Coghlan, D. (2018). First-, second- and third-person values-based ethics in educational action research: Personal resonances, mutual regard and social responsibility. *Educational Action Research*. Retrieved from https://doi.org/10.1080/09650792.2018.1445539.

Chandler, D., & Torbert, W. R. (2003). Transforming inquiry and action: Interweaving 27 flavours of action research. *Action Research, 1*(2), 133–152.

Chevalier, J. M., & Buckles, D. J. (2013). *Participatory action research*. Abingdon: Routledge.

Coghlan, D. (2008). Authenticity as first person practice: An exploration based on Bernard Lonergan. *Action Research, 6*(3), 351–366.

Coghlan, D. (2009). Toward a philosophy of clinical inquiry/research. *Journal of Applied Behavioral Science, 45*(1), 106–121.

Coghlan, D. (2010). Seeking common ground in the diversity and diffusion of action and collaborative management research methodologies: The value of a general empirical method. In W. Pasmore, A. B. (Rami) Shani, & R. Woodman (Eds.), *Research in organizational change and development* (Vol. *18*, pp. 149–181). Bingley: Emerald Publishing.

Coghlan, D. (2016). Retrieving the philosophy of practical knowing for action research. *International Journal of Action Research, 12*(1), 84–107.

Coghlan, D. (2017a). Insight and reflection as key to collaborative engagement. In J. M. Bartunek & J. McKenzie (Eds.), *Academic practitioner research partnerships: Developments, complexities and opportunities* (pp. 36–49). Abingdon: Routledge.

Coghlan, D. (2017b). How might we learn about the philosophy of ODC research from 24 volumes of ROCD? An invitation to interiority. In A. B. (Rami) Shani & D. Noumair (Eds.), *Research in organizational change and development* (Vol. *25*, pp. 335–361). Bingley: Emerald Publishing.

Coghlan, D., & Rigg, C. (2012). Action learning as praxis in learning and changing. In A. B. (Rami) Shani, W. A. Pasmore, & R. W. Woodman (Eds.), *Research in organizational change and development* (Vol. *20*, pp. 59–90). Bingley: Emerald Publishing.

Coghlan, D., & Shani, A. B. (Rami). (2017). Inquiring in the present tense: The dynamic mechanism of action research. *Journal of Change Management, 17*(2), 121–137.

Coghlan, D., & Shani, A. B. (Rami). (2018). *Conducting action research for business and management students*. London: Sage.

Cooperrider, D. (2017). The gift of new eyes: Personal reflections after 30 years of appreciative inquiry in organizational life. In A. B. (Rami) Shani & D. Noumair (Eds.), *Research in organizational change and development* (Vol. *25*, pp. 81–142). Bingley: Emerald Publishing.

Cronin, B. (2017). *Phenomenology of human understanding*. Eugene, OR: Pickwick.

Gearty, M., & Coghlan, D. (2018). The first-, second- and third-person dynamics of learning history. *Systemic Practice & Action Research, 31*(5), 463–478.

Heron, J., & Reason, P. (2008). Extending epistemology within a cooperative inquiry. In P. Reason & H. Bradbury (Eds.), *The Sage handbook of action research* (2nd ed., pp. 366–380). London: Sage.

Marshall, J. (2016). *First person action research: Living life as inquiry*. London: Sage.

Reason, P., & Bradbury, H. (Eds.). (2001). *The handbook of action research*. London: Sage.

Reason, P., & Bradbury, H. (Eds.). (2008). *The Sage handbook of action research* (2nd ed.). London: Sage.

Revans, R. W. (1971). *Developing effective managers*. London: Longmans.

Revans, R. (1998). *ABC of action learning*. London: Lemos & Crane.

Schein, E. H. (2008). Clinical inquiry/research. In P. Reason & H. Bradbury (Eds.), *The Sage handbook of action research* (2nd ed., pp. 266–279). London: Sage.

Schein, E. H. (2013). *Humble inquiry: The gentle art of asking instead of telling*. San Francisco, CA: Berrett-Koehler.

Torbert, W. R. (2004). *Action inquiry*. San Francisco, CA: Jossey-Bass.

Chapter 7

Action Research for Self-study and Living-Educational-Theories

Jack Whitehead

Chapter Outline

This chapter focuses on the contributions to creating and democratizing knowledge that action researchers are making as they engage in self-study and Living Theory research. It focuses on the *what*, *why* and *how* of this particular approach, including challenges to the approach and how these have been overcome. The *what* of the approach is distinguished by evidence of the uniqueness and originality of the researchers' explanations of their educational influence in their own learning, in the learning of others, and in the learning of the social formations that influence the researchers' practice and understandings. The explanations draw insights from the conceptual frameworks and methods of validation of theories from the disciplinary approaches to knowledge. The *why* includes the evidence on the ontological values that are used by Living Theory researchers to give meaning and purpose to their life. These values are clarified and communicated in the course of their emergence in practice, with the help of digital visual data from practice. They are used as explanatory principles in explanations of educational influence and related to the values that carry hope for the flourishing of humanity. The *how* of the approach includes the methodological inventiveness of the practitioner–researcher in creating their own living-theory and living-theory methodology. This includes insights from the methodologies of Phenomenology, Action Research, Living Theory Research, Self-Study Research and Narrative Research.

Introduction

This chapter focuses on the contributions to creating and democratizing knowledge that action researchers are making through their self-studies and living-educational-theories. I first explain my understanding of living-educational-theories,

Action Learning and Action Research: Genres and Approaches, 97–110
Copyright © 2019 by Jack Whitehead
doi:10.1108/978-1-78769-537-520191011

knowledge democracy and action research. I then discuss self-study of teacher education practices and the *what, why* and *how* of a Living Theory approach, including research processes and supervision of masters and doctoral theses, as well as challenges to a Living Theory approach.

Living-Educational-Theories

The idea that individuals could create their own living-educational-theories was developed as an alternative approach to what was known as the 'disciplines' approach to educational theory that was constituted by the philosophy, psychology, sociology and history of education. My main objection to this approach was that the practical principles I used to explain my educational influences in learning were regarded as at best pragmatic maxims having a first crude and superficial justification in practice that in any rationally developed theory would be replaced by principles with more fundamental, theoretical justification (Hirst, 1983, p. 18). I don't want to be misunderstood in developing this alternative. I value insights from the disciplines of education in generating a living-educational-theory. I reject the idea that the disciplines of education taken individually or in any combination can produce a valid explanation for my educational influences in my own learning, in the learning of others, or in the learning of the social formations that influence practice and understandings.

I think it is worth emphasizing that a living-educational-theory can draw insights from the theories of the disciplines of education and other disciplines, but the individual's practical principles are not replaced by principles from the disciplines. They are a necessary component in the individual's explanation of educational influence (Whitehead, 1985, 1989, 2018a, 2018b) in their knowledge-creation. When I use the term "educational influence in learning" I am focusing attention on the idea that what is educational necessarily involves learning, but that the learning, to be educational, must include values that carry hope for the flourishing of humanity.

Glenn, Roche, McDonagh, and Sullivan (2017) have focused on action research for self-study and living-educational-theories in their research on learning communities in educational partnerships, with a focus on action research as transformation. They developed their living-educational-theory of learning communities as each participant evolved their understanding of their practice. They focused on living their values around knowledge creation. Each participant created and articulated their own new learning in relation to their values. Glenn et al. argue that all participants can recognize the potential for knowledge creation in the other, in a merging of ontological, epistemological and methodological values.

The Living Theory approach acknowledges that each group must create the community that best suits their situation. Readers are invited to reveal their passions and enthusiasms for learning together, for our own benefit and the benefit of those with whom we work. We are invited by Glenn et al. (2017) to continue this narrative by sharing our stories on www.eari.ie (p. 164).

Knowledge Creation

One of the distinguishing characteristics of any form of research is that it is concerned with knowledge creation in the form of information gathering and theory generation and testing. At the heart of knowledge creation is making public the data gathering and analysis so that its validity can be publicly tested. In Living Theory research I advocate using two related processes to test and enhance the validity of the knowledge being offered in explanations of educational influence. The first draws on Popper's (1975) insight about the mutual rational control by critical discussion:

> Inter-subjective *testing* is merely a very important aspect of the more general idea of inter-subjective *criticism*, or in other words, of the idea of mutual rational control by critical discussion. (p. 44)

The second draws on Habermas' (1976) four criteria of social validity in reaching an understanding with each other in terms of comprehensibility, evidence, normative influences and authenticity (pp. 1–2). For example, I advocate that the following four questions are included in the responses of a validation group made up of three to eight peers:

- How could the comprehensibility of the explanation be strengthened?
- How could the evidence used to justify assertions be improved?
- How could the normative understandings of socio-historical and sociocultural influences be deepened and extended?
- How could the authenticity of the explanation, in terms of living values as fully as possible, be enhanced?

As well as generating explanations of educational influences in learning, Living Theory researchers create their own living-theory-methodology as they ask, research and answer questions of the kind, "How do I improve what I am doing in living my values as fully as I can?" These contributions to the creation of knowledge are consistent with Dadds and Hart's (2001) idea of 'methodological inventiveness': "To create enquiry approaches that enable new, valid understandings to develop; understandings that empower practitioners to improve their work for the beneficiaries in their care" (p. 169).

Knowledge Democracy

Hall and Tandon (2016) refer to three interrelationships in knowledge democracy: (1) the importance of the existence of multiple epistemologies or ways of knowing; (2) the knowledge both created and represented in multiple forms including text, image, numbers, story, music, drama, poetry, ceremony, meditation and more; and (3) the intentional linking of values of democracy and action to the process of using knowledge.

Rowell (2017) stresses the importance of knowledge mobilization (ARNA, 2017a) in developing such an approach, in supporting seven participatory workshops around the world in preparation for the Action Research Network of the America's (ARNA, 2017b) Conference in Cartagena, Columbia, on "Participation and Democratization of Knowledge: New Convergences for Reconciliation."

Action Research

Corey (1953) produced the first book on action research to improve school practices. Several different forms of research, all claiming to be action research, have developed over the past 70 years through the global spread of action research. I first explicated my use of action–reflection cycles while evaluating the Schools Council Mixed Ability Exercise in Science (Whitehead, 1976). I identified these cycles as insights from Dewey's (1938/1997) ideas on learning from experience. In the 1980s, I used the definition of action research provided by Carr and Kemmis (1986):

> Action research is simply a form of self-reflective enquiry under-taken by participants in social situations in order to improve the rationality and justice of their own practices, their understanding of these practices, and the situations in which the practices are carried out. (p. 162)

Another tradition of action research is "the systematic collection of information that is designed to bring about social change" (Bogdan & Biklen, 1992, p. 223). Bogdan and Biklen claim that action researchers marshal evidence or data to expose unjust practices or environmental dangers and recommend actions for change. This tradition of action research, while exposing unjust practices and recommending actions for change, differs from Living Theory research because it does not place any responsibility on action researchers to account for their own lives and influence as they explore the implications of their recommendations. This responsibility is a characteristic of Living Theory research that also differs from community-based action research as developed by Stringer (1999). In Living Theory research it is not necessary to commence with an interest in the problems of a group, a community, or an organization. It is, however, necessary to ground the Living Theory research in an individual who is living, as fully as possible, their ontological values that they use to give meaning and purpose to their lives.

Kemmis and McTaggart (1988, pp. 5–6) also stress collective and collaborative forms of research in distinguishing action research, while acknowledging the importance of critically examining the actions of individual group members. This approach, unlike Living Theory research, does not stress the importance of the knowledge-creating capacities of individuals to make original contributions to educational knowledge.

The working definition of action research put forward by Altrichter, Kemmis, McTaggart and Zuber-Skerritt (1991) includes both individuals' reflections and inquiries into improving their practice and their own situations and increasing participation and collaboration. This is consistent with Living Theory research.

Like Altrichter et al., Skolimowski (1994) lists some of the main characteristics of a participatory research program and points to love as the deepest form of participation:

> Love is the deepest form of participation.
> Where there is love there is participation.
> Loveless participation is an anaemic involvement.
> To participate is the first step to loving. (p. 159)

The inclusion of love within a research program may be too much for minds trained in the rigors of objectivity. Yet, many of us recognize the importance of love in loving what we are doing. Lohr's (2016) doctoral thesis on "Love at Work" uses Love as an explanatory principle and living standard of judgment.

Participatory action research (PAR) is an approach to research in communities that emphasizes participation and action. It seeks to understand the world by trying to change it, collaboratively. PAR emphasizes collective inquiry and experimentation grounded in experience and social history. Within a PAR process, communities of inquiry and action evolve and address questions and issues that are significant for those who participate as co-researchers.

The Colombian sociologist Orlando Fals Borda and others organized the first explicitly PAR conference in Cartagena, Colombia in 1977. Based on his research with peasant groups in rural Boyaca and with other marginalized groups, Fals Borda and Rahman (1991) called for the 'community action' component to be incorporated into the research plans of traditionally trained researchers. For the work of Rajesh Tandon and others, see Participatory Research in Asia (PRIA) at https://www.pria.org.

Cooperative inquiry, like participatory inquiry and some other forms of action research, defines the research in terms of all participants working together in an inquiry group as co-researchers and as co-subjects. In Heron and Reason's (2008) definition of cooperative inquiry, everyone is engaged in the design and management of the inquiry and is involved in making sense and drawing conclusions.

It isn't that Living Theory researchers deny the value of cooperation. A Living Theory researcher can and does engage in cooperative activities and enquiries, without the necessity of defining their research as participatory or cooperative as understood in the above definitions. Living Theory research, while being grounded in self-study, requires the generation of evidence-based explanations of educational influences in learning.

Self-study of Teacher Education Practices

In 1995, the journal *Teacher Education Quarterly* published a special issue on *Self-Study and Living Educational Theory*. The contributors invited me to respond to their papers. What I focused on (Whitehead, 1995) was what I continue to emphasize. I focused on the importance, in a self-study of a teacher's education practice, of including an evidence-based explanation of the educational influence of the self-study researcher in the learning of students. In *What Counts as*

Evidence in the Self-studies of Teacher Education Practices? (Whitehead, 2004) I focused on the nature of evidence, in an evidence-based explanation of educational influences in learning. I pointed to limitations in purely printed-text of communicating the embodied expressions of meanings of energy-flowing values in explanations of educational influence and have emphasized this point in later writings (Whitehead, 2014).

In responding to a text on *Being Self-Study Researchers in a Digital World* (Whitehead, 2017a), I recognized the importance of the claim to be presenting research on the intersection of self-study research, digital technologies and the development of future-orientated practices in teacher education. The text fulfilled its aim of highlighting how digital technologies can enhance pedagogies and the knowledge-base of teacher education. However, I also pointed out that, as a printed-text communication of self-study and educational action research, its communications are limited by the domination of printed text. I should have also appreciated some engagement with the most advanced social theories of the day, such as the ideas of de Sousa Santos (2014), to explore the possibility that the logic and language used in this book are contributing to what de Sousa Santos has referred to as 'epistemicide' in terms of the killing off of indigenous knowledges (Whitehead, 2016).

The text offers no discernible challenge to the dominance of what de Sousa Santos refers to as the Epistemologies of the North. I know that it is difficult to include digital visual data in solely printed text. However, it is becoming increasingly important to acknowledge the limitations of solely printed text for communicating these explanations, particularly the meanings of embodied expressions of the use of values as explanatory principles.

The *What* of a Living Theory Approach

The *what* of a Living Theory approach is focused on the asking, researching and answering of questions of the kind, "How do I improve what I am doing?," where the question is grounded in the social, cultural and historical context in which the researcher is living and working. The focus on improving practice highlights the importance of clarifying and communicating the meanings of the values that will distinguish something as an improvement. Values can be talked about and written about lexically in the sense that the meanings of value-words are defined in terms of other words rather than by reference to embodied expressions of meaning. Values can also be understood ostensively in the sense that they are clarified in the course of their emergence through practice. Ostensive expressions focus attention on embodied expressions of meaning. We cannot do anything without the expression of energy. The *what* of a Living Theory approach always recognizes the importance of including flows of energy with values that the individual believes carries hope for the flourishing of humanity. The *what* of a Living Theory approach also recognizes that whatever we are doing to improve our practice can include socio-cultural and socio-historical influences. These need to be taken into account if we are to be as effective as possible in improving what we are doing. A Living Theory approach must include the generation and testing of explanations.

Hence, the *what* of the approach is also distinguished by the uniqueness and originality of the action researchers' explanations of their educational influence in their own learning, in the learning of others and in the learning of the social formations that influence their practice and understandings. The explanations draw insights from the conceptual frameworks and methods of validation of theories from the disciplinary approaches to knowledge. I think it is worth repeating that the focus on explanations in Living Theory research is because of a requirement of research that it is focused on data gathering and theory generation and testing.

The *Why* of a Living Theory Approach

I understand the 'why' of Living Theory research in terms of Fromm's (1960) humanistic ethics, with a point from his *Fear of Freedom*. Fromm says that if a person can face the truth without panic, they will realize there is no purpose to life other than that which they create for themselves through their loving relationships and productive work (p. 18). I agree with Fromm that we are faced with the choice of uniting with the world in the spontaneity of love and productive work, or of seeking a kind of security that destroys our integrity and freedom. So, the 'why' of Living Theory research is grounded in exploring the implications of engaging with the world with love and productive work. The 'why' can also be understood in terms of Foucault's reflections on death, cited by Eribon (1989):

> In considering oneself on the point of dying, one can judge each of the acts that one is in the process of committing according to its own worth – "Concerning the moral progress that I shall have been able to make ... I am waiting for the day in which I will become my own judge and I will know if I have virtue on my lips and in my heart." (pp. 331–332)

Living Theory research enables a practitioner–researcher to document the explanations of educational influences in a way that creates an archive of living-theories. This offers the possibility of judging the extent to which one has managed to live a worthwhile life with love and productive work that carries hope for the flourishing of humanity.

The *why* of a Living Theory approach also shares a desire with all researchers to find answers to questions that the individual cares about and to contribute to knowledge. It is distinguished from other forms of research in that, for a Living Theory researcher, the research is a way of life in seeking to live as fully as possible the values that carry hope for the flourishing of humanity (Whitehead, 2018a, 2018b).

Hence, the *why* includes the energy-flowing ontological values used by the Living Theory researcher to give meaning and purpose to their life. These values are clarified and communicated in the course of their emergence in practice with the help of digital visual data from practice. The digital visual data is necessary because it can focus attention on the embodied expressions of these energy-flowing values. The values are used as explanatory principles in explanations of educational influence and related to the values that carry hope for the flourishing of humanity. The epistemological significance of the energy-flowing values is that, as well as providing explanatory principles, they form the living-standards of judgment that can be used to evaluate the validity of the contribution to knowledge.

The *How* of a Living Theory Approach

The *how* of the approach includes the methodological inventiveness (Dadds & Hart, 2001, p. 166) of the Living Theory researcher in creating their own living-theory methodology. This methodology can include insights from Phenomenology, Action Research, Living Theory research, Self-study research and Narrative research (Whitehead, 2018b). For example, Husserl's (1912) insight about the resistance of phenomenology to categorizations by "methodologically devised schemes of constructive symbolism" (p. 12) can be used to understand the importance of methodological inventiveness in making public the educational influences of the embodied expressions of values and personal knowledge (Inoue, 2012, 2015).

The resistance of embodied values and knowledge, to the application of methods in representing their educational influences in learning, highlights the importance of self-study and narrative research in representing and explaining the educational influences of embodied values and knowledge. Laidlaw (1996), for example, used the metaphor of Coleridge's poem *The Ancient Mariner*, to explain in her narrative, her educational influences in a living-theory self-study.

Living Theory researchers can use action-reflection cycles to express values-based concerns, to develop action plans, to act and gather data, to evaluate the effectiveness of the actions, and to modify the concerns, plans and actions in the light of the evaluations. In locating their research as Living Theory research, the researcher is committed to generating and sharing an evidence-based explanation of their educational influences in their own learning, in the learning of others, and in the learning of the social formations that influence their practice and understandings.

In many research programs, especially those being legitimated by universities, practitioner–researchers are often asked, and sometimes required, to specify in a research proposal the methodology that they will be using at the beginning of their research. The recognition that a Living Theory researcher will be creating their living-theory methodology in the course of their inquiry, can create some problems if a research committee requires that the methodology is pre-specified before it is generated through the research. The following processes for Living Theory research in the next section might help Living Theory researchers to emphasize the importance of their methodological inventiveness and to avoid the imposition of inappropriate methods and methodology.

Living Theory Research Processes

In a Living Theory research process it is important to bear in mind the two intentions of improving practice and generating knowledge that contribute to the flourishing of humanity. Improving practice relates to the 'why' by including ontological and relational values, and using them to judge improvements in practice and in generating knowledge. Generating knowledge involves the creation of your own living-theory as an explanation of your educational influences. It includes the generation of your living-theory-methodology. The originality of a Living Theory researcher can be understood epistemologically in that it includes the values-based, living standards of judgment that can be used to judge the validity of the contribution to knowledge.

Masters and Doctoral Programs

I make a distinction between the Living Theory research processes involved in supervising those involved in masters and doctoral research programs. In a master's program there is no requirement to make an original contribution to knowledge. This requirement is part of the award of a doctoral degree. Here are some suggestions and reflections for those involved in the supervision of Living Theory research master's and doctoral programs. For master's programs – see http://www.actionresearch.net/writings/mastermod.shtml.

When supervising Living Theory doctoral students, I usually begin by asking for clarification about the context in which the practitioner–researcher is working and what they would like to focus on in improving their practice. I focus on questions such as "What motivates you?," "What excites you?." I sometimes ask about if or when they experience themselves as 'living contradictions', in the sense of not doing what the person wants to do.

My intention is to help me to understand the ontological and relational values that the researcher uses to give meaning and purpose to their lives and to help them to clarify and to understand these for themselves. I ask them to, for example,

- select an area of practice that they can work on to improve;
- tell me the possible steps they might take to improve their practice and to develop an action plan;
- collect data to make a judgment on their influence; and
- produce an evidence-based explanation of their educational influences in learning, which includes embodied expressions of energy-flowing values as explanatory principles and standards of judgment.

I also ask them to:

- ensure that ethical guidelines are followed;
- ensure that their explanations include evidence of educational influences in learning; and

- use a validation group to strengthen the validity of the explanation in terms of its comprehensibility, evidence, normative understandings and authenticity.

Erica Holley's reflections on her MPhil journey provides an example of how a student has experienced this approach to supervision:

> You offer acceptance of me for what I am and push at the boundaries of what I could become. You accept ideas, puzzlement and confusion from me as part of a process of me coming to understand, but the understanding reached seems always a new understanding for us both. I think I've seen our work as collaborative parallelism. (Personal email)

Jane Spiro's (2008) epilogue to her thesis titled, *Learner and Teacher as Fellow Travellers: A story tribute to Jack Whitehead*, is another example of how a doctoral researcher has experienced this approach to supervision.

What I hope I am communicating in this section on supervising master's and doctoral Living Theory research programs is the importance of a supervisor of Living Theory research trying to understand the unique responses of each individual that enables them to generate their own living-educational-theory and living-theory-methodology. The responses include a concern with scholarship and rigour in engaging creatively and critically with the ideas of others and in subjecting evidence-based explanations to rigorous academic criticism in validation groups. It is important in Living Theory research to show an awareness and response to criticisms of the approach.

Challenges to a Living Theory Approach

I would say that the most helpful criticism of the development of a Living Theory approach is the point made by Noffke (1997) that:

> It seems incapable of addressing social issues in terms of the interconnections between personal identity and the claim of experiential knowledge, as well as power and privilege in society. . . . The process of personal transformation through the examination of practice and self-reflection may be a necessary part of social change, especially in education; it is however, not sufficient. (p. 329)

Evidence that a Living Theory approach is addressing these issues can be seen in the 2018 homepage of living-theory-posters at: http://www.actionresearch.net/writings/posters/homepage020617.pdf and in Coombs et al. (2014).

If you access the 2018 living-poster of Network Educational Action Research Ireland (NEARI), you can access the evidence from Mairin Glenn, Bernie Sullivan, Caitriona McDonagh and Mary Roche that shows how they are addressing social issues in terms of the interconnections between personal identity and the claim of experiential knowledge, as well as power and privilege in society.

Norton's (2009) criticism is that a living-educational-theory is an extreme position on the positivism-interpretivism dimension that does not reflect the capacity of educational action research to embrace the rich middle ground.

The idea of a positivism-interpretivism dimension can be challenged on the grounds that the conceptualization of such a 'dimension' is mistaken. There are epistemological differences between positivism and interpretivism, which mean they should not be placed within a 'dimension'. For example, positivists usually follow the Aristotelean Law of Contradiction, which rejects the idea that mutually exclusive opposites can be true simultaneously, and the Law of Excluded Middle in the sense that everything is either A or Not-A. Interpretivists, influenced by dialectics, include contradiction as the nucleus of correct thought with the acceptance of an Included Middle. The 2,500-year history of battles between these researchers can be illustrated in Popper's (1963, p. 317) rejection of dialectics as being entirely useless as theory, and in Marcuse's (1964, p. 111) point that formal logic masks the dialectical nature of reality (p. 64).

These differences can be transcended in a living-logic for Living Theory research (Whitehead & Rayner, 2009).

Conclusions

In my reviewer's comments to *Conferences as Sites of Learning and Development* (Zuber-Skerritt, 2017), I wrote that:

> The discussion focuses on working and researching together as global citizens to transform the conditions of social life that sustain poverty, oppression and suffering. It does this by focusing on the creation of the conditions that can sustain justice and satisfying forms of human existence .... Shared understandings of present contexts and practices are related to an evaluation of the past contributions of ALARA together with intentions to contribute to the future through participation in conferences as sites of learning and development.

In this present chapter on *Action Research for Self-study and Living-Educational-Theories* I have emphasized the importance of educational learning in the sense that not all learning is educational. I am distinguishing educational learning from learning, with the necessary condition that for the learning to be educational it must include values that carry hope for the flourishing of humanity.

In making explicit a Living Theory research process above, I include an action–reflection cycle while emphasizing the necessity of generating an individual's explanation of their educational influences in their own learning, in the learning of others, and in the learning of the social formations that are influencing and being influenced by the researcher. The explanatory principles in the explanation include the ontological and relational values the researcher uses to give meaning and purpose to their life. The 2018 living-poster homepage (see above) demonstrates how Living Theory researchers can contribute to a global movement of researchers who are clarifying, communicating and responding to each other's inquiries. This movement goes beyond the creation and sharing of individual living-educational-theories in a global process of Living Theory research that is contributing to the enhancement of flows of values and understandings that carry hope for the flourishing of humanity.

Topics for Discussion

1. As you produce an evidence-based explanation of your educational influence, how could you engage with and include your influence in a global social movement to enhance the flow of values and understandings that carry hope for the flourishing of humanity?
2. If you are seeking to gain academic accreditation for your living-theory, how do you analyse the responses of ethics committees, institutional review boards and research committees that have hindered and/or supported your research?
3. As you seek to live your values as fully as possible, how do you understand the power relations that can both hinder and support your inquiries?
4. What problems and possibilities have you encountered with accessing appropriate supervision for the generation of your living-theory?

Further Reading

Coombs, S., Potts, M., & Whitehead, J. (2014). *International educational development and learning through sustainable partnerships: Living global citizenship.* London: Palgrave Macmillan.

Inoue, N. (2012). *Mirrors of the mind: Introduction to mindful ways of thinking education.* New York, NY: Peter Lang.

Inoue, N. (2015). *Beyond actions: Psychology of action research for mindful educational improvement.* New York, NY: Peter Lang.

Whitehead, J. (2016). Review of de Sousa Santos, B. (2014). *Epistemologies of the south: Justice against epistemicide.* London: Paradigm Publishers. *Educational Journal of Living Theories,* 9(2), 87–98. Retrieved from at http://ejolts.net/node/288.

Whitehead, J. (2017b). Review of Sean Warren's and Stephen Bigger's (2017) *Living contradictions: A teacher's examination of tension and disruption in schools, in classrooms and in self.* Carmarthen: Crown House Publishing Limited. *Educational Journal of Living Theories,* 10(2), 105–106. Retrieved from http://ejolts.net/node/312

References

Altrichter, H., Kemmis, S., McTaggart, R., & Zuber-Skerritt, O. (1991). Defining, confining or refining action research? In O. Zuber-Skerritt (Ed.), *Action research for change and development* (pp. 3–9). Aldershot: Gower Publishing Company.

ARNA. (2017a). *Knowledge mobilization.* Retrieved from http://arnawebsite.org/knowledge-mobilization/

ARNA. (2017b). *Participation and democratization of knowledge: New convergences for reconciliation.* Retrieved from http://arnawebsite.org/conferences/cartegena-colombia-2017/

Bogdan, R., & Biklen, S. K. (1992). *Qualitative research for education.* Boston, MA: Allyn & Bacon.

Carr, W., & Kemmis, S. (1986). *Becoming critical: Knowing through action research.* London: Falmer.

Coombs, S., Potts, M., & Whitehead, J. (2014). *International educational development and learning through sustainable partnerships: Living global citizenship.* London: Palgrave Macmillan.

Corey, S. M. (1953). *Action research to improve school practices.* New York, NY: Bureau of Publications, Teachers College, Columbia.

Dadds, M., & Hart, S. (2001). *Doing practitioner research differently.* London: Routledge.

De Sousa Santos, B. (2014). *Epistemologies of the south: Justice against epistemicide.* London: Paradigm Publishers.

Dewey, J. (1938/1997). *Experience and education.* London: Macmillan.

Eribon, D. (1989). *Michel Foucault.* London: Faber and Faber.

Fals Borda, O., & Rahman, M. A. (1991). *Action and knowledge.* Lanham, MD: Rowman & Littlefield.

Fromm, E. (1960). *The fear of freedom.* London: Routledge & Kegan Paul.

Glenn. M., Roche, M., McDonagh, C., & Sullivan, B. (2017). *Learning communities in educational partnerships: Action research as transformation.* London: Bloomsbury.

Habermas, J. (1976). *Communication and the evolution of society.* London: Heinemann.

Hall, B. L., & Tandon, R. (2016). What is knowledge democracy? Retrieved from https://knowledgedemocracy.org/what-is-knowledge-democracy/

Heron, J., & Reason, P. (2008). *Extending epistemology within a co-operative inquiry.* Retrieved from http://www.human-inquiry.com/EECI.htm

Hirst, P. (Ed.). (1983). *Educational theory and its foundation disciplines.* London: RKP.

Husserl, E. (1912). *Ideas: General introduction to phenomenology.* London: Allen & Unwin.

Inoue, N. (2012). *Mirrors of the mind: Introduction to mindful ways of thinking education.* New York, NY: Peter Lang.

Inoue, N. (2015). *Beyond actions: Psychology of action research for mindful educational improvement.* New York, NY: Peter Lang.

Kemmis, S., & McTaggart, R. (1988). *The action research planner.* Victoria: Deakin University Press.

Laidlaw, M. (1996). *How can I create my own living educational theory as I offer you an account of my educational development?* PhD thesis, University of Bath. Retrieved from http://www.actionresearch.net/living/moira2.shtml

Lohr, E. (2016). Teaching with love: How may I continue to improve my practice as I get older? Retrieved from *Educational Journal of Living Theories, 9*(1), 112–130. Retrieved from http://ejolts.net/drupal/node/274

Marcuse, H. (1964). *One dimensional man.* London: Routledge & Kegan Paul.

Noffke, S. (1997). Professional, personal, and political dimensions of action research. In M. Apple (Ed.), *Review of research in education* (pp. 305–343). Washington, DC: AERA.

Norton, L. (2009). *Action research in teaching and learning: A practical guide to conducting pedagogical research in universities.* London: Routledge.

Rowell, L. (2017). *Lonnie Rowell Introducing the First Global Assembly for Knowledge Democracy.* YouTube video retrieved from https://www.youtube.com/watch?v=2sGLGMrrPu0

Popper, K. (1963). *Conjectures and refutations.* Oxford: Oxford University Press.

Popper, K. (1975). *The logic of scientific discovery.* London: Hutchinson & Co.

Spiro. J. (2008). *How I have arrived at a notion of knowledge transformation, through understanding the story of myself as creative writer, creative educator, creative manager, and educational researcher*. PhD thesis, University of Bath. Retrieved from http://www.actionresearch.net/living/janespirophd.shtml

Skolimowski, H. (1994). *The participatory mind: A new theory of knowledge and of the universe*. London: Penguin.

Stringer, E. (1999). *Action research* (2nd ed.). London: Sage.

Whitehead, J. (1976). *Improving learning for 11–14 year olds*. Swindon: Wiltshire Curriculum Development Centre. Retrieved from http://www.actionresearch.net/writings/ilmagall.pdf

Whitehead, J. (1985). An analysis of an individual's educational development: The basis for personally orientated action research. In M. Shipman (Ed.), *Educational research: Principles, policies and practice* (pp. 97–108). London: Falmer.

Whitehead, J. (1989). Creating a living educational theory from questions of the kind, "How do I improve my practice?". *Cambridge Journal of Education, 19*(1), 41–52.

Whitehead, J. (1995). Self-study and living educational theory. *Teacher Education Quarterly, 22*(3), 26–27, 42–43, 62–63, 81–82, 97–98.

Whitehead, J. (2004). What counts as evidence in the self-studies of teacher education practices? In J. J. Loughran, M. L. Hamilton, V. K. LaBoskey, & T. Russell (Eds), *International handbook of self-study of teaching and teacher education practices* (pp. 871–903). Dordrecht: Kluwer Academic Publishers.

Whitehead, J. (2014). A self-study contribution to a history of the self-study of teacher education practices. In D. Garbett & A. Ovens (Eds.), *Changing practices for changing times: Past, present and future possibilities for self-study research*. Proceedings of the Tenth International Conference on Self-Study of Teacher Education Practices (pp. 204–208), Herstmonceaux Castle, East Sussex, UK. Retrieved from http://www.actionresearch.net/writings/sstep2014/whitehej.pdf

Whitehead, J. (2016). *Review of de Sousa Santos, B. (2014) Epistemologies of the south: Justice against epistemicide*. London: Paradigm Publishers. *Educational Journal of Living Theories, 9*(2), 87–98. Retrieved from http://ejolts.net/node/288

Whitehead, J. (2017a). *Jack Whitehead's review of Dawn Garbett & Alan Ovens (Eds.), Being self-study researchers in a digital world*. Retrieved from http://www.actionresearch.net/writings/jack/jwreviewearovensgarbett141117.pdf

Whitehead, J. (2017b). *Review of S. Warren & S. Bigger (Eds.), Living contradictions: A teacher's examination of tension and disruption in schools, in classrooms and in self*. Carmarthen: Crown House Publishing Limited. *Educational Journal of Living Theories, 10*(2), 105–106. Retrieved from http://ejolts.net/node/312

Whitehead, J. (2018a). *Living theory research as a way of life*. Bath: Brown Dog Books. Retrieved from https://amzn.to/2suwR59

Whitehead, J. (2018b). The Action Learning, Action Research Experiences of Professionals. Keynote presentation to the 10th World Congress of the Action Learning Action Research Association on '*The Action Learning and Action Research Legacy for Transforming Social Change: Individuals, Professionals, and Communities' Developments, Organizational Advancements, and Global Initiatives*', Norwich University, USA. Retrieved from http://www.actionresearch.net/writings/jack/jwalarakeynote160618.pdf

Whitehead, J., & Rayner, A. (2009). *From dialectics to inclusionality: A naturally inclusive approach to educational accountability*. Retrieved from http://www.actionresearch.net/writings/jack/arjwdialtoIncl061109.pdf

Zuber-Skerritt, O. (Ed.). (2017). *Conferences as sites of learning and development: Using participatory action learning and action research approaches*. Abingdon: Routledge.

Chapter 8

Educational Action Research

Franz Rauch, Stefan Zehetmeier and Peter Posch

Chapter Outline

In this chapter, we focus on Action Research within the educational realm. After clarifying what we mean by action research, we discuss various forms, possibilities and limitations of action research in classrooms and schools. In particular, we focus on action research that is supported by communities. The chapter provides both theoretical considerations on these issues and practical examples from Austrian large-scale teacher professional development programs based on action research. Finally, we discuss possible implications for both theory and practice of educational action research.

Introduction

Action Research is becoming increasingly known as an approach that encourages practitioners in education to be in control of their own work and contexts. It was first conceived and practised in the USA, and later came to prominence in the UK, in Australia and some European countries, including Austria, in the 1970s and 1980s. Today it makes a significant impact in many professional contexts, particularly in teacher professional education. Its influence is worldwide, and has spread to many areas where personal and professional learning is undertaken.

Action research as originally conceived by Lewin (1948) is oriented to problem solving in social and organizational settings, and has a form that parallels Dewey's (1933) conception of learning from experience. Like any other social research, action research proceeds by exploring problems in a more or less systematic manner – by formulating key questions, planning and designing investigations, gathering, processing and analyzing data, interpreting the data and drawing conclusions, which hopefully provide valid answers to the key questions.

Challenges in education and in the teaching profession through changes in society (e.g., output orientation, quality evaluation and development) have resulted in an increased demand for corresponding professional development and practice-based research. In Austria, teacher professional development programs have

Action Learning and Action Research: Genres and Approaches, 111–126
Copyright © 2019 by Franz Rauch, Stefan Zehetmeier and Peter Posch
doi:10.1108/978-1-78769-537-520191012

been set up since 1982, and they are still running, seeking to respond to changing issues and requirements. This chapter presents examples of two in-service education programs, discussing their action research framework, main objectives and research findings. In this way the chapter provides a complementary perspective on the impact of action-research-based professional development programs for teachers.

Educational Action Research

Educational action research (EAR) applies the concepts and practices of action research to the context of education, so most EARs are teachers. As a genre of action research, EAR recognizes both the uncertainty around the nature and extent of action (that needs to be undertaken in complex situations) and the general precariousness of conceptions of value. Researchers therefore need to engage in ongoing reflection on their actions and understandings, to inform further planning, action and understanding. Through this cyclical process, EARs produce contributions to both conceptual and practical knowledge of education.

Hence, in education as in other contexts, competent, professional action in complex situations requires concomitant learning processes as a *sine qua non*. Inversely, professional learning requires the experience of acting in complex practical situations. Through this lens, professional action and professional learning coincide in one stream of action. As professional learning happens in practical situations, which in turn are seen to require reflection and further development, knowledge and skill development go hand in hand with practical situational development (Altrichter & Posch, 2009). Townsend (2013) distinguishes the following three modes.

First Person Research

Here a person reflects on a situation through careful thought about what has happened, and records their reflections through audio- or video-recording, diary or some similar form. The goal is to understand the self. The person doing the reflection is the only action researcher, for instance, a reflective teacher.

Practitioners' Research

Practitioners investigate their own practice through reflective inquiry. They conduct their research independently, sometimes with outside support, and their goal is to develop their practice. In this case the practitioners are action researchers, for instance a group of teachers who plan to improve their maths instruction and to share their learning materials.

Collaborative Action Research

External facilitators collaborate with a group of people who share a cause. Their goal is to solve a problem or to create innovations. The external facilitators (e.g., university educators) are the outside action researchers, and their partners in participative inquiry (e.g., community activists) are inside co-researchers.

The diversity of the goals and scope of these three modes seems to imply that formulating common criteria for the quality of action research is a complex endeavour. But a close look reveals there are sufficient commonalities to present a list of qualities that apply equally to all three. Based upon the work of Heron and Reason (2008) and others, Stern, Townsend, Rauch, and Schuster (2014) provide four principles of action research as guidelines for EARs:

1. Good action research pursues worthwhile practical purposes by trying to find solutions for authentic problems. It empowers the people concerned to acquire relevant knowledge and to share it with others, leading to actions that are embedded in a humanistic value system.
2. Good action research is collaborative/participatory by involving the people concerned into the research process and agreeing upon ethical rules for the collaboration.
3. Good action research is responsive and developmental, by engaging in a continuous series of research-and-development cycles. It takes into consideration the different perspectives of various stakeholders in search of satisfactory solutions to problems.
4. Good action research connects theory and practice as praxis by balancing action and reflection (reflection can inspire or evaluate actions or uncover the motives behind them, action can prove or disprove theoretical assumptions), and generating theoretical knowledge, delivering problem solutions and promoting practical improvements.

Two important theoretical constructs that help to understand the nature of EAR are constructivism and systems theory. Constructivism tells us that in the field of social systems (and organizations), 'truths' are always mediated socially. Therefore, they are 'constructs' generated by the system (Krainer, 2002; von Glasersfeld, 1987). In systems theory (Luhmann, 1984, 2000), reflection represents a key strategy for gathering system-relevant (both external and internal) data, which allows for the further development of a system's practices. For example, external data may be delivered by feedback from the outside via 'critical friends', internal data may be collected by various methods and instruments of self-evaluation. These data are gathered continuously, they are analysed and returned into the system, with the aim to have system-relevant impact. Erlacher and Ossimitz (2009) argue that "Institutionalized reflection loops [i.e., a system's self-observations] can be used to provide sustained and systemically important information about the system itself" (p. 152).

Teacher Professional Development

EAR is particularly useful for professional development of teachers. Here professional development is reflected between the four dimensions of action and reflection, and autonomy and networking (see Linares & Krainer, 2006).

This perspective is inspired by Krainer (1994, 1998), who suggests a holistic and integrated view of teacher development support in these four dimensions of teachers' professional practice:

- *action*: the attitude towards, and competence in, experimental, constructive and goal-directed work;
- *reflection*: the attitude towards, and competence in, (self-)criticism of one's own actions;
- *autonomy*: the attitude towards, and competence in, self-initiating, self-organized and self-determined work; and
- *networking*: the attitude towards, and competence in, communicative and cooperative work with increasing public relevance.

These dimensions may be used to describe and explain not only teachers' activities but also teachers' learning in in-service courses. Krainer (1998) highlights how "each of the pairs, 'action and reflection' and 'autonomy and networking', express both contrast and unity, and can be seen as complimentary dimensions which have to be kept in a certain balance, depending on the context" (p. 308). In particular, Krainer (2002) highlights the "promotion of reflection and networking as key interventions" (p. 12) in teacher professional development programs. Krainer's four-dimension model can be used to design in-service courses and to explain how teachers' learning is generated. In this sense, the integration of reflection, action research and collaboration and the development of communities of practice (Wenger, 1998) in this model provide holistic tools that can help to enhance knowledge about teachers' learning.

Examples from an Austrian Perspective

In the past 30 years, the teaching profession faces newly emerging challenges, both within the education system (e.g., requirements for output orientation, mandatory quality evaluation and development) and from across society undergoing rapid change. These challenges have resulted in an increased demand for corresponding (new) frameworks of professional competences (Posch, Rauch, & Mayr, 2009). In Austria, some teacher professional development courses have tried to react as effectively as possible to these changes. Starting in 1982, professional development programs have been set up by the IUS (Institut für Unterrichts – und Schulentwicklung: Institute for Teaching and School Development, University of Klagenfurt) and these are still running today. After the first professional development program, each new program or modification has respectively modified and expanded the content and method of the forerunner programs. Thus, the programs' target groups and radius of impact have evolved from teaching and classroom development, over school and district development, up to interventions within the national educational system (Rauch, Zehetmeier & Erlacher, 2014).

Our first example is the university course entitled PFL (Pädagogik und Fachdidaktik für Lehrkräfte: Teacher Education in Subject Areas). We summarize the main characteristics of the PFL course and then consider an application of this course in a primary school in Austria (see Zehetmeier, Grasser, Holzinger, Rauch, Schuster & Wachter, in press), followed by evaluation outcomes across all PFL courses and research findings. The second example is a masters course called Pro-Fil (Professionalität im Lehrberuf: Professionalism in the Teaching Profession) with an example of a secondary school in Austria (see Zehetmeier, Grasser, Holzinger, Rauch, Schuster & Wachter, in press) and an evaluation approach and research findings across all ProFil courses.

The University Course "Teacher Education in Subject Areas" (PFL)

As a professional development program for in-service teachers, PFL is designed for teachers from all types of schools across Austria, including all age groups of students. The focus is on the professional development of teachers in the fields of didactics and pedagogy, with particular emphasis on educational standards, competence-oriented teaching practices, classroom diversity, communication, cooperation and quality evaluation and development. Graduates of this program are also qualified to advise colleagues on the development and implementation of competence-oriented teaching. The program takes two years and is organized in three one-week seminars, with workshops, input, discussions and group work. In addition, five two-day meetings for the regional groups are arranged at participants' schools, with lesson observations, analyses and discussions of the participants' work. The focus, however, is on the individual's own reflective practice (Altrichter & Posch, 2009). By the end of the course, each participant is obliged to write a reflective paper using the data he/she has gathered throughout the process by using qualitative and quantitative research methods (e.g., research diaries, student interviews, classroom observations, etc.). Most of these papers are published in an online database. Participants are supported not only by the PFL team, but also by their colleagues who often take the role of critical friends. The participants' experience is of being a part of a community of practice (Wenger, 1998), since their work is embedded in a structure of mutual assistance and external support. So far, about 1,000 teachers have completed the PFL program. The main characteristics of the program can be summarized as follows:

- *Location of learning is the school:* besides the more distanced learning situations at seminars and regional groups, the individual school situation is the explicit learning site of the course.
- *Starting points are professional challenges:* current professional challenges in the perception of the participants are starting points for the course, and not current issues of the relevant disciplines. The practitioners choose an issue that concerns their own practice, which they consider important for their work.
- *Research and development:* the central task of participants is to plan a developmental project for their own instructional practice, to implement it in the time between the seminars, to do concomitant research assisted by cooperative support and advice in regional groups, and to present experiences and findings in a case study. They reflect on their practical development work using notes in a research diary, student interviews, observations by critical friends and

developing new ideas for action. To date, participating teachers have written more than 300 case studies, which are made public as contributions to professional teacher knowledge.

- *Cooperative learning and exchange:* the participating teacher researchers are invited to offer their experiences in mini-workshops during the seminars, and thereby acquire a qualification in teacher education.
- *Support system and constitution of a 'professional community':* through the seminars and regional groups, individual action research is integrated in a consultancy structure that offers ample opportunities for discussion of problems regarding contents and methods, for critical feedback and assistance (e.g., for student interviews). Partners in this process research their colleagues, and academics support the research process as critical friends.

While the certifications of the PFL program do not carry any formal entitlements in the educational system, course completion is relevant for career advancement (e.g., applying for the position of school principal) and for taking on specific tasks at one's school.

Influenced by the PFL program, an active scene of teacher researchers and didactic development have emerged. The PFL concept and especially its research orientation has inspired several other professional development courses in Austria and abroad, for example, the university course "Education for Sustainable Development Innovations in Teacher Education" (Rauch, Steiner, & Radits, 2010; Steiner, Rauch, & Felbinger, 2010).

A Primary School Participating in PFL

The primary school in St. Veit an der Glan (a town in Austria) took part in the PFL seminar series from 2012 to 2014. The main focus of these seminars was on further developing teaching in the natural sciences.

Through participation, a development process was put in motion to stimulate team building and reflection processes about the participating teachers' own teaching and projects. One of its interventions, the 'analytic discourse', proved especially effective (Feldman, Altrichter, Posch, & Somekh, 2018). With this method, difficulties in natural science instruction were identified. The method allowed a pragmatic approach to these problems. In connection with collegial feedback, problem areas in pedagogical work came to light and raised questions in reference to a research-and-discovery approach in natural science teaching. As a first step at the St. Veit school, the role of communicative processes in research instruction needed to be analysed. Therefore, the following questions were of interest:

- What influence does language have on the development of thinking in science education in primary school children?
- What is the significance of language and communication in the personality development of primary school children?
- How do I implement language-provoking occasions in classroom lessons?

The leading team in the course was experienced, highly professional and respectful, and prepared the participants for designing, managing and evaluating their projects. In particular, assistance was provided with defining goals and refining research questions. The most important basic points of project work were made available in a written guide. The team made it possible for the participants to exchange investigation results and personal experiences through regional group meetings and nationwide meetings. Additionally, individual school sites were visited and linked with particular tasks, such as teacher observation and holding interviews. The subsequent collegial exchange with 'critical friends' had a strong community-building effect. The collegial exchange among participants in the seminar held central importance. The participants' mutual exchange coupled with the seminar team's intensive advice and support promoted deep discussions with respect to the development of their own teaching projects.

After addressing the question "what is good teaching?" which was the focus of the first module, the second module of the course added the aspect of competence. Although the term 'competence orientation' is worn out among teachers, the seminar team and participants agreed that sustainable knowledge acquisition is largely based upon competence-oriented teaching. "What is competence actually?" became the central question posed in the subsequent debate. The intense work on the term 'competence' was carried out in both theory and practice. That sensitized the participants' pedagogical view towards differentiated task assignments, student-activating methods and a positive question-and-answer culture in the classroom. The testing and development of competence-oriented assignments and methods held enduring importance for the participants, as did their acquaintance with external guest lecturers. Joint discussions focused on the following questions: "How do I initiate sustainable learning processes?" and "Which questions stimulate students' intellectual activity, promote their problem-solving capability and facilitate independent learning processes?"

These questions provided the basis for further research plans at the primary school in St. Veit an der Glan. The question regarding student activation methods and communicative processes turned out to be a central theme in the school's natural science courses. The results of the educational research demonstrated that openly formulated research questions stimulated individual and cooperative natural science learning (Holzinger, 2013, p. 5), and along with student activity, the culture of dialogue played a central role in research teaching (Holzinger, 2014, p.10).

The new research plan was supervised by a member of the leading team of the course, and this provided additional support for the participants. In this case, 84 students from the first through fourth classes took part in the research project. Within the specifically designed research classes, competence-oriented assignments dealing with plants were developed and tested. The joint project was carried out over a longer period of time and brought with it an intensive exchange regarding the effects of assignments and methods within lessons. Consequently, not only did the children learn about plants, but also the teacher and the IUS advisor learned about how children in this age group think about plants, which concepts the children bring from their previous experience, how they treat plants, and what knowledge they acquired and were able to apply.

The study used audio and video recording to evaluate the research processes within the teaching sequences. The teaching observation and subsequent analysis promoted the teachers' willingness to step outside their trusted teaching routine. In the normal course of teaching, routine was indeed helpful and afforded security, but it could also hinder openness to new methods in the long term.

In summary, the seminar series promoted a change in perspective in the participating teachers, which brought them to reflect upon their own teaching and their own teaching personality. It provided stimulus for teaching, that in turn expanded to the entire school. As mentioned, on the one hand the seminar program offered plenty of opportunity for collegial exchange and positive feedback, and on the other hand made possible the acquisition of knowledge pertaining to a subject, competences and standards. Additionally, it offered the participants many practical workshops that allowed for the testing of new assignments and methods. The combination of theory and practice invigorated the teaching-related and methodological competences, and, therefore, the self-confidence of the teachers.

At the primary school in St. Veit an der Glan, the teachers' participation in the PFL university courses set sustainable developments in motion. Interested colleagues began to exchange information on natural science teaching. Following the basic ideas of the PFL teaching series, a collegial support program at the school level was developed for teachers who wanted to reflect on their own actions and to try new things. Since the 2016/2017 school year, the team has provided those teachers with a window into natural science teaching by bringing forward their expertise. In the meantime, the initiative at the school has become well-established and is regularly evaluated for quality control.

Evaluation Outcomes and Research Findings across all PFL Courses

The PFL program is continuously evaluated by formative methods at the end of each seminar and at the end of the course. The results of the evaluations are discussed with the participating teachers with the goal of supporting the learning and development of participants and course leaders. Evaluation results point to the program's positive effects on the growth of participants' autonomy and competence, which arises from the relevance of the content, the quality of instruction, the intellectual challenge and the social inclusion of participants. Participants' challenges relate to the examination of relevant literature as well as communication about the professional activities that go beyond the community of a particular PFL group (Posch et al., 2009).

Exemplary results come from a study concerning the 2003–2005 course "PFL: English as a working language" (Erlacher, 2006a), which highlights that teachers understand action research as a useful tool for the development of their own teaching. Moreover, they regard the methods as not only applicable to specific subjects, but also bringing general benefits for the classroom. The concept of 'critical friends' offers further opportunities for individual learning and professional development. The structural and methodological conception of the course provides the opportunity for collegial exchange and collaborative work. Systematic reflection on their own professional practice is emphasized, for example: "For me, the main thing that has always been really missing in the past, quite frankly, was this kind of reflection. The willingness to criticize myself ... needs to be even more extended" (PFL participant; see Erlacher, 2006a, p. 5).

In addition to this evaluation, several external concomitant research projects were conducted (e.g., Müller, Andreitz, & Mayr, 2010). They show that the teachers' self-perceived competencies in different areas increased over time. After the course they assessed themselves as significantly more competent in the domains of 'teaching', "reflection on one's own actions/practice" and "school development."

Another research project investigating the sustainable effects of the PFL program (Zehetmeier, 2014) shows different levels of impact that endured after the program's termination. The main factors that fostered the sustainability of these impacts were networking and personal advantage. These results may be attributed to the overall learning environment of the PFL program, since the PFL concept corresponds with current research on the effectiveness of teacher professional development programs (Zehetmeier, 2014).

The Masters Course "Professionalism in the Teaching Profession" (ProFiL)

The general educational philosophy and organization of this program is in many respects similar to PFL, however, it provides an academic degree ("Master of Arts in Education – Teaching and School Development") for PFL graduates after two years of further study. New in the master's course is the focus on a combination of classroom and school development. To be accepted into the course, participants need a declaration from their school principal to support their work for the course. Participants are required to write three reflective papers and a final thesis on issues that potentially have structural implications for their schools. The case studies written in this course should have produced institutional effects in the schools of some of the participants, such as the institutionalization of project days, and a new form of introducing youngsters to the elementary school.

One-week seminars are held once per semester and collaborative working groups are reserved for sharing good practices, for literature studies and offering practical advice. Elective additional compulsory subjects served to deepen and expand the contents of the mandatory subjects.

A Secondary School Participating in ProFiL

The ProFiL course offers participants both theoretical basics and their application to case studies, and guidance with teaching and school development in practice. The training in the ProFiL Master course combined theory and exercises, along with written reflective papers based upon practical application, with the participation of the EUREGIO Federal Higher Technical School and Test Center in Ferlach (a town in Austria). The school put in place, observed, documented and evaluated arrangements for facilitating individual competence-oriented teaching in subject–theory instruction.

ProFiL supported this work through individual selection of both the training content and the thematic foci to customize, as far as possible, to the participants' specific needs. Additionally, an active exchange between the participants took place that enabled supplemental discussions.

Below we discuss data from both teacher and student levels from the school years 2012/2013 through 2016/2017. The data specifically concern the implementation of project work at the school. At the student level, in 2013 and 2014 the fourth and fifth year cohorts and in 2015 and 2016 the third, fourth and fifth year cohorts were questioned. We focus discussion on three items in the survey: Item 1: Projects help students to better understand and apply subject matter; Item 2: Students enjoy working on projects because they can apply what they have already learned; and Item 3: Are you taking part in a project in this school year?

The survey shows that both teachers and students understand projects as a medium allowing deeper penetration into lesson material through practical application. It also shows that the joy in the projects' execution created positive feedback. The responses demonstrate a clearly positive assessment of the effect of project work on the teaching staff level. While the teacher responses indicate a negative tendency over time on the assessment of project work effectiveness, student responses show a positive tendency.

The results suggest that during the time of their participation in the ProFiL courses, students as well as teachers reacted positively to the use of projects at the school. It can also be determined that about half of the teachers and more than two thirds of the students in the third through fifth year cohorts were involved with projects at the school. The department's feedback is important, especially regarding the professional embedding of projects into the ongoing coursework, in order to support the project realization as well as the enduring effects of the projects.

An important and effective basis for the development of teachers, and therefore also for further long-term development in the school, is the combination of knowledge from theoretical lessons, the exchange of experiences with other teachers within the course, and the implementation in a teacher's own teaching and school routine. That every participant is willing to try something new appears to be an essential fact. Because the course is work-integrated, participants can apply what they have learned directly to their school. For this reason, the accompanying research projects, which are the basis for the reflections, are especially important, so participants can collect their experiences in the area of teaching development during the courses and can then build on them.

Evaluation Outcomes and Research Findings across all ProFiL Courses

Concomitant evaluation and research enables us to draw the following conclusions (Erlacher, 2006b; Krainer, Rauch, & Lesjak, 2002; Posch et al., 2009; Rauch, 2011; Rauch & Krainer, 2002).

Skill building: participants acquired school development design competences in the areas of methodological skills (e.g., using moderating techniques and evaluation instruments), social skills (e.g., addressing fears and resistance) and, above all, reflection skills.

Acting in practice: school development has been described as successful if it is targeted at subject or subject-related teacher groups. Participating teachers stated that launching and implementing comprehensive development projects across the entire school is an endeavour for which schools, as systems, are still poorly prepared and equipped. There is a set of interlinked governing conditions (e.g., the role of the school principal, time, 'mandate' received from fellow teachers, school development mandates, political situation, etc.) that may hamper substantial change. Currently, the mandatory implementation at Austrian schools of development plans as internal tools for quality assurance and development might be a potentially supportive feature of this kind of change.

Problems and Challenges of Action Research

Although action research has proven to be a useful methodology for fostering the professional development of teachers as well as the development of organizations and structures, we have observed at least four challenges.

First, many teachers are deeply skeptical of theories that relate to their professional practice. It has thus been determined that young teachers who begin their professional career enriched with theoretical knowledge quickly adapt to the teaching practice that is prevalent in their school (Korthagen, Kessels, Koster, Lagerwerf, & Wubbels, 2001). Behind the claims of these broadly formulated theories, there is often an idealized view of society and the individual (in our case students), which teachers perceive as representing a task they cannot possibly fulfil. They see such a task as a downright threat, considering the everyday classroom problems at school (Elliott, 1991). They experience the practice as being rather ambiguous, unstable and characterized by conflicts of interest and value, therefore as being more chaotic than the theoretical models suggest. Since they are not alone with this experience, the corresponding offers in the field of teacher training are often felt to be 'too theoretical' and are dismissed as useless, even if they are 'rationally' seen as warranted. This attitude also hinders the teacher's systematic reflection on their own practice if they do not experience the theoretical knowledge they have gained in the training as a context for reflection upon the training experience.

Second, professional communication on substantial issues around their work is a new and unfamiliar challenge for many teachers. In advanced training, the discussions about observations are held largely in the group of persons belonging to the 'professional community'. Only in exceptional cases are discussions of observations held at the schools themselves because there is no real culture of "speaking about teaching" in Austrian schools. An advanced training program has only very limited possibilities to create the conditions at school that are required for this to occur. The initiatives that exist in this direction consist of determining certain acceptance criteria (e.g., teacher applicants need to provide a supporting letter from their school administration to be accepted into the

PROFIL course), the preferred acceptance of teacher teams from a school, and the obligation to provide internships at one's own school within the framework of internal school development measures. This can at least contribute to an awareness of the meaning and purpose of a professional community.

Third, most teachers experience major difficulties when writing up studies and especially when analyzing data within this framework (which is the 'theoretical core' of action research in the narrow sense of the term). The great pressure on teachers to act may be a reason why they have difficulties making the important distinction between a development interest (exactly what do I wish to improve?) and an interest in knowledge (exactly what happened?) and why they are often not aware of the interest in knowledge as an independent category that is fundamental to research. Since research has hardly any significance in teacher training, use of constructive and critical analytical skills (conceptualizing observations, creating and critically examining relationships between observations) is an unusual requirement for many teachers, whether they were trained at a university or (as for teachers in compulsory schools) at an educational academy (Schuster, 2007).

Fourth, the continued low status of the school and teaching practice in scientific research, which is characterized by 'technical rationality' (Schön, 1983, p. 31), continues to be an important inhibiting factor when it comes to spreading action research. Scientific research is based on a substantial division of labor between what is understood to be (high status) science, which is responsible for the creation of theories, and (low status) practice, which is responsible for the implementation of theories. However, dealing with an increasingly complex practice requires not only specialized, subject-related and educational knowledge that is communicated during the training and the advanced training of teachers, but also the ability to generate practical theories through the systematic reflection on one's own practice. Both skills must be provided in teacher training.

Reflections and Conclusions

How can these development processes, research and evaluation results be summarized? What lessons can be learnt? Good practice cannot be cloned, but exchanging experiences on a personal level can foster learning and innovation. With reference to the four functions of networking according to Dalin (1999), such initiatives as the university courses discussed in this chapter may be understood as networks in education that offer goal-oriented exchange processes among teachers (information function). These support teachers' professional development through fresh ideas for classroom teaching and interdisciplinary cooperation among schools (learning function). Networks have the potential to create a culture of trust, with the effect of raising self-esteem of teachers and their willingness to take risks (psychological function) and, as in the PFL course in St. Veit an der Glan school, upgrading science at school (political function).

In the long run, a balance of Krainer's (1998) dimensions of action and reflection (goal-directed planning and evaluation), and autonomy and networking (analysis of one's own situation, but also support by 'critical friends') is paramount to set up a sustainable support system for teachers and schools. Evaluation and research need to be driven by an interactive link between an interest in gaining new knowledge and a developmental interest. These are the circumstances in which an action research culture of self-critical and collective reflection can flourish (Rauch, 2013).

From here we sketch five concrete 'lessons learnt' from our experience in large-scale teacher professional development programs in Austria based on action research. All of these lessons take into account that long-term projects necessitate dealing with conflicting issues and views, and with keeping them in a certain balance. These 'lessons learnt' are based on Krainer and Zehetmeier (2013).

Change Projects Need Both Visible Challenges and Visible Success

To stimulate recognition of the need for change, the key stakeholders of change need a clear rationale. The examples we have discussed in this chapter show that teachers need to receive support, and have opportunities to share their experiences in order to make their success and remaining challenges visible. These new challenges are again a starting point for new innovations. This kind of 'innovation culture' needs challenges that lead to success and success that leads to new questions. Each of the examples reported above can be understood as examples of interplay between challenge and success.

Change Projects Need Both Individual and Organizational Efforts

Change projects need to foster both teachers' autonomy and their networking, supported by knowledgeable others (internal or external experts). However, to raise the likelihood and sustainability of success, their organizations (e.g., schools) need to support these individuals in their efforts to learn and bring about change. This dimension was particularly relevant for the introduction of school development aspects within the PFL courses, as well as for development of the ProFil masters course that focuses on organizational and quality development of the whole school.

Change Projects Need Both Flexible Plans and the Use of Windows of Opportunity

Although the PFL courses had a high reputation in Austria and internationally, it was not at all easy to increase their participant numbers or to establish them more firmly in the Austrian teacher education system. However, in 2004, it was again possible to start a PFL mathematics course (in addition to English, German language and science), and in 2012, the Austrian Ministry of Education supported an increase in the number of PFL courses. Here we see that efforts over the past few decades (in the case of PFL, since 1982) have helped to support recent national initiatives.

Change Projects Need Active Persistence and Resilience as well as Patience

Reform projects need a lot of time and tolerance of frustration by all people concerned. Of course, conflicts of interest arise and need to be solved constructively. Thus, reform projects need a long-term perspective, with recognition that something that is not possible at the moment might be dealt with later on. They also need qualified and dedicated stakeholders, who have lots of creativity, endurance and patience. Larger initiatives open the lens not only for the general and the holistic (e.g., the educational system), but also for the particular and the small (e.g., good ideas by a student in classroom).

Change Projects Need Both Accepting and Allocating Responsibility

Long-term initiatives need to be transferred from short-term status into a stable sustainable project anchored in the educational system. Ideally, a reform project is successful in the long run when it has become unnecessary. The process of accepting responsibility needs to be increasingly accompanied by a process of allocating responsibility to the new institutions that might have been set up in the meanwhile. Collaborations (among colleges for teacher education, universities, local school authorities, etc.) are a central issue of all of the achievements described above. These cooperations are based on negotiated contracts and enable the emergence and development of mutual responsibility and trust.

The overall challenge in the professional development of teachers might be described as keeping up a balance between structures and processes, in other words, between stability and dynamics, to enable sustainable development of learning supported by action research.

Topics for Discussion

1. What makes action research different from other research in education?
2. What is good EAR?
3. What are challenges to implementing good action research in educational settings from your experience/perspective?

Further Reading

Feldman, A., Altrichter, H., Posch, P., & Somekh. B. (2018). *Teachers investigate their work: An introduction to action research across the professions* (3rd ed.). London: Routledge.

Rauch, F., Zehetmeier, S., & Erlacher, W. (2014). Thirty years of educational reform through action research: Traces in the Austrian school system. In T. Stern, A. Townsend, F. Rauch, & A. Schuster (Eds.), *Action research, innovation and change: International perspectives across disciplines* (pp. 27–42). London: Routledge.

Zehetmeier, S., Andreitz, I., Erlacher, W., & Rauch, F. (2015). Researching the impact of teacher professional development programs based on action research, constructivism, and systems theory. *Educational Action Research, 23*(2), 162–177. doi:10.1080/09650792.2014.997261

References

Altrichter, H., & Posch, P. (2009). Action research, professional development and systemic reform. In S. Noffke & B. Somekh (Eds.), *Handbook of educational action research* (pp. 213–225). Los Angeles, CA: Sage.

Dalin, P. (1999). *Theorie und Praxis der Schulenwicklung.* Neuwied: Luchterhand.

Dewey, J. (1933). *How we think: A restatement of the relation of reflective thinking to the educative process* (Rev. ed.), Boston, MA: D.C. Heath.

Elliott, J. (1991). *Action research for educational change.* Philadelphia, PA: Open University Press.

Erlacher, W. (2006a). *PFL Englisch als Arbeitssprache 2003–2005. Endbericht der externen evaluation.* Klagenfurt: Alpen-Adria-University.

Erlacher, W. (2006b). *Bericht über die externe Evaluation des Universitätslehrganges ProFiL.* Klagenfurt: Alpen-Adria-University.

Erlacher, W., & Ossimitz, G. (2009). Reflexion als schulische Notwendigkeit. In K. Krainer, B. Hanfstingl, & S. Zehetmeier (Eds.), *Fragen zur Schule: Antworten aus Theorie und Praxis* (pp. 143–154). Innsbruck: Studienverlag.

Feldman, A., Altrichter, H., Posch, P., & Somekh, B. (2018). *Teachers investigate their work: An introduction to action research across the professions* (3rd ed.). London: Routledge.

Heron, J., & Reason, P. (2008). Extending epistemology within a co-operative inquiry. In P. Reason & H. Bradbury (Eds.), *Handbook of action research: Participative inquiry and practice* (pp. 366–380). London: Sage.

Holzinger, A. (2013). *Kommunikatives Lernen durch Forscherfragen im Sachunterricht der Grundschule.* Sankt Veit an der Glan: Self-published.

Holzinger, A. (2014). *Analyseinstrumente im forschenden Unterricht.* Sankt Veit an der Glan: Self-published.

Korthagen, F., Kessels, J., Koster, B., Lagerwerf, B., & Wubbels, T. (2001). *Linking practice and theory: The pedagogy of realistic teacher education.* Mahwah, NJ: Lawrence Erlbaum.

Krainer, K. (1994). PFL-mathematics: A teacher in-service education course as a contribution to the improvement of professional practice in mathematics instruction. In J. Ponte & F. Matos (Eds.), *Proceedings of the 17th PME International Conference* (Vol. 3, pp. 104–111).

Krainer, K. (1998). Some considerations on problems and perspectives of inservice mathematics teacher education. In C. Alsina et al. (Eds.), *8th International Congress on mathematics education: Selected lectures* (pp. 303–321). Sevilla: S.A.E.M. Thales.

Krainer, K. (2002). Lernen im Aufbruch – Ein Innovationsnetz als chance. In K. Krainer, W. Dörfler, H. Jungwirth, H. Kühnelt, F. Rauch, & T. Stern (Eds.), *Lernen im Aufbruch: Mathematik und Naturwissenschaften* (pp. 13–20). Innsbruck: Studienverlag.

Krainer, K., Rauch, F., & Lesjak, B. (2002). Universitätslehrgang "Professionalität im Lehrberuf" (ProFiL). In G. Knapp (Ed.), *Wissenschaftliche Weiterbildung im Aufbruch? Entwicklungen und Perspektiven* (pp. 312–331). Klagenfurt: Mohorjeva Hermagoras.

Krainer, K., & Zehetmeier, S. (2013). Inquiry-based learning for students, teachers, researchers, and representatives of educational administration and policy: Reflections on a nation-wide initiative fostering educational innovations. *ZDM - The International Journal on Mathematics Education, 45*(6), 875–886.

Lewin, K. (1948) *Resolving social conflicts: Selected papers on group dynamics.* New York, NY: Harper & Row.

Linares, S., & Krainer, K. (2006). Mathematics (student) teachers and teacher educators as learners. In A. Gutiérrez & P. Boero (Eds.), *Handbook of research on the psychology of mathematics education: Past, present and future* (pp. 429–459). Rotterdam: Sense Publishers.

Luhmann, N. (1984). *Soziale Systeme. Grundriss einer allgemeinen Theorie*. Frankfurt: Suhrkamp.

Luhmann, N. (2000). *Organisation und Entscheidung*. Wiesbaden: Opladen.

Müller, F., Andreitz, I., & Mayr, J. (2010). PFL: Pädagogik und Fachdidaktik für Lehrerinnen und Lehrer. Eine Studie zu Wirkungen forschenden Lernens. In F. H. Müller, A. Eichenberger, M. Lüders, & J. Mayr (Eds.), *Lehrerinnen und Lehrer lernen – Konzepte und Befunde zur Lehrerfortbildung* (pp. 177–196). Münster: Waxmann.

Posch, P., Rauch, F., & Mayr, J. (2009). Forschendes Lernen in der Lehrerfortbildung – Die Universitätslehrgänge "Pädagogik und Fachdidaktik für Lehrer/innen" und "Professionalität im Lehrberuf" an der Universität Klagenfurt. In B. Roters, R. Schneider, B. Koch-Priewe, J. Thiele, & J. Wildt (Eds.), *Forschendes Lernen im Lehramtsstudium* (pp. 196–220). Bad Heilbrunn: Klinkhardt.

Rauch, F. (2011). Practitioner research and in-service university courses: Theoretical concepts and evaluation. In M. S. Khine & I. M. Saleh (Eds.), *Practitioner research: Teachers' investigations in classroom teaching* (pp. 51–66). New York, NY: Nova Science Publishers.

Rauch, F. (2013). Regional networks in education: A case study of an Austrian project. *Cambridge Journal of Education, 43*(3), 313–324.

Rauch, F., & Krainer, K. (2002). Grenzgänge zwischen Professionalisierung und Schulentwicklung: Begründungen, Erfahrungen und Reflexionen zum Universitätslehrgang "Professionalität im Lehrberuf" (ProFiL). In K. Eckstein & J. Thonhauser (Eds.), *Einblicke in Prozesse der Forschung und Entwicklung im Bildungsbereich* (pp. 267–282). Innsbruck: Studienverlag.

Rauch, F., Steiner, R., & Radits, F. (2010). Der Universitätslehrgang Bildung für Nachhaltige Entwicklung – Innovationen in der Lehrer/innenbildung (BINE): Ein Instrument zum Aufbau von Forschungskompetenz an Pädagogischen Hochschulen. *Erziehung und Unterricht, 16*(1–2), 92–96.

Rauch, F., Zehetmeier, S., & Erlacher, W. (2014). Thirty years of educational reform through action research: Traces in the Austrian school system. In T. Stern, A. Townsend, F. Rauch, & A. Schuster (Eds.), *Action research, innovation and change: International perspectives across disciplines* (pp. 27–42). London: Routledge.

Schön, D. (1983). *The reflective practitioner*. London: Temple Smith.

Schuster, A. (2007). PFL Science: A turning point in teachers' professional life? In A. Townsend (Ed.), *Differing perceptions of the participative elements of action research* (pp. 72–74). CARN Bulletin 2012.

Steiner, R., Rauch, F., & Felbinger, A. (Eds.) (2010). *Professionalisierung und Forschung in der LehrerInnenbildung: Einblicke in den Universitätslehrgang BINE*. Wien: BMUKK.

Stern, T., Townsend, A., Rauch, F., & Schuster, A. (Eds.) (2014). *Action research, innovation and change: International and interdisciplinary perspectives*. London: Routledge.

Townsend, A. (2013). *Action research: The challenges of understanding and researching practice*. Philadelphia, PA: Open University Press.

von Glasersfeld, E. (1987). *Wissen, Sprache und Wirklichkeit. Arbeiten zum radikalen Konstruktivismus*. Braunschweig: Vieweg.

Wenger, E. (1998). *Communities of practice*. Cambridge: Cambridge University Press.

Zehetmeier, S. (2014). The others' voice. Availing other disciplines' knowledge about sustainable impact of professional development programs. *The Mathematics Enthusiast, 11*(1), 173–196.

Zehetmeier, S., Grasser, M., Holzinger, A., Rauch, F., Schuster, A., & Wachter A. (2015). Teacher Professional Development: Theoretical Considerations and Practical Examples. In T. Janik, I.M. Dalehefte, & S. Zehetmeier (Eds.), *Supporting Teachers: Improving Instruction. Examples of Research-based In-service Teacher Education*. Münster: Waxmann.

Chapter 9

Designing and Facilitating Systemic Action Research at Scale

Danny Burns

Chapter Outline

The chapter explores some ways in which the Action Research process can be designed at scale without diluting its central participatory imperative. It also explores designs that enable the poorest and most marginalized to meaningfully engage. Examples are drawn from a range of large-scale international development processes. These projects have evolved methodologically over time, with a great deal of learning and process modification taking place over nearly 20 years. It is hoped that the examples offer some robust methodological examples of how to develop a systemic approach at scale.

Introduction

Much of my recent work can be described as Systemic Action Research (SAR) (Burns, 2007). There are others who have used this terminology (Coghlan, 2002; Ison, 2010) but who have a different focus, and some who haven't called their work SAR but whose work is profoundly systemic and has been profoundly influential on my work (Wadsworth, 2010). Susan Weil (1998), who I worked with closely and learned a great deal from, often used to talk about Large System Action Research. Others think systemically and build a systemic approach into a different model of Action Research (Flood, 2010), or have drawn on a knowledge of action research but work in other traditions such as Community Operational Research (Midgley, 2000). The work of Robert Flood and many other writers in the journal, *Systemic Practise and Action Research*, shows the extensive use of systems thinking in action research. All of these in some way describe research that takes place across systems and deals with systemic issues. In this chapter I articulate my own approach to SAR, which I also see as a version of Participatory Action Research (PAR).

The aim of this chapter is to help orient the reader in situating this approach within a proliferating body of action research that has sometimes confusing and

Action Learning and Action Research: Genres and Approaches, 127–141
Copyright © 2019 by Danny Burns
All rights of reproduction in any form reserved
doi:10.1108/978-1-78769-537-520191013

contradictory names. I argue that SAR can be characterized by a set of key design and process principles (although inevitably there is an overlap with other forms of action research). I attempt to do this by articulating those core principles, and then I show how these principles are manifest in the research design of a variety of large-scale action research projects.

What is particular to this work is that it is designed to have an impact across whole cities and regions, programs and organizations. Its design is built on multiple parallel and intersecting action research groups that are linked together within a wider learning architecture; it is rooted in the learning and ownership of stakeholders who are often the most marginal – demonstrating their capacity to generate and collectively analyse complex data as well as take action on it.

I start with an explanation of what I mean by systemic in SAR. The chapter then moves on to articulate some key design principles necessary to enable systemic change, and what needs to be done to operationalize these. Finally, I present short case examples that identify the key methodological elements and their sequence in the design and processes of SAR projects.

What is the Systemic in SAR?

I think it is important to be conceptually clear that it is not scale that makes something systemic. For example, systemic family therapy works with the whole family system rather than just the individual, and the rationale for it is that the problems of the individual can be resolved only in the context of changes within the wider family system that they inhabit. At the same time, we need to realize that system dynamics that affect any individual and family typically play out in large systems, which is why we need to engage with them.

Causality is crucial to understanding systems, and it is not necessarily linear (although of course some causalities will be). Causality seen through the lens of complexity means that we need to understand not only how A leads to B, but also how small interventions amplify to create large impacts; how latent change can lead to sudden 'phase change'; how opening up pathways in one part of a system can unlock other pathways, which in turn unlock other pathways, which may allow intractable conflict to be shifted in another part of the system; how feedback loops within systems maintain equilibrium or spiral it out of equilibrium and so on. Combining systems thinking and complexity allows us to understand how change happens through systemic interconnections (Burns, 2014, 2018; Burns & Worsley, 2015).

Causality links factors and explains the relationship between them. A factor is something that happens that is caused by some things and makes other things happen. Research often focuses on factors. Sometimes it focuses on the correlation between factors, but the subject of interest remains the factors. In systemic research, the interest is in the relationship between them, and *how* this relationship is affected by other relationships. Systems thinking then highlights the importance of the inter-relationship between factors, and chains of relationships between people, events, resources and so on. One might, for example, know two people who seem to be bitter and angry. They form a relationship with each other, and this results in them now being warm and loving. We learn very little from knowing that there is a correlation between two bitter people. We learn a great deal from understanding what the nature of the inter-relationship is that changes both them, and what happens between them, and how they then are in the world.

To create transformational and sustainable change for the betterment of society, it is necessary to change negative dynamics. This requires a number of things to be built into our process. The first is that those creating change need to be able to see the dynamics, so they need to build in tools for gathering evidence and then putting it together in ways that reveal the dynamics. The second is that once these are visible, we can see opportunities for small actions but that can have a big impact on system dynamics.

Understanding change is critical to action research. If we don't understand how change happens, then we will generate in action research groups lots of actions that have little or no impact, and our activity may be little different to traditional program activity. Once we have an idea of the system dynamics that create an equilibrium around the problems we are trying to resolve, then we can identify where we need to build action research processes.

The Nature and Scope of Some SAR Projects

Before going on to talk about some of the projects I have been involved in, it might be helpful to be clear about my practice. I have been based in universities for most of the past 20 years. However, I have largely seen them as a base to support action research within communities and organizations. My work has focused on developing participatory methodologies. While I have supervised a number of action research PhDs, this has been only a small part of my action research practice. Most of my practice has involved using action research as a core method in funded research. That research was initially mostly UK-based, but for the past eight years has been entirely internationally based. In this context my role has tended to be that of a methodological advisor and accompanier, someone who helps to design and to model a process, and sometimes to document it. Once the process is underway, it is the local stakeholders in the issue that take on the work. It would take too long to list all of the PAR projects I have been involved with, but it may be helpful for the reader to get a feel of the nature and shape of those that I would call SAR, or which contributed to the development of SAR. The scale of funding of these projects has ranged from a few tens of thousands of pounds to my most recent project that is an £11 million innovation program with an underpinning action research method that is threaded through the whole process. Here I present eight examples of action research projects:

- *An action inquiry into children's initiatives in Bristol* – funded by four Sure Start programs (2002–2005). This involved the facilitation of four parallel action research groups in each of three neighbourhoods, generating a myriad of local actions and pilots (Burns, 2018).
- *Rethinking vulnerability* (2006–2007) – funded by the British Red Cross (BRC). This was an organizational inquiry into the meaning of vulnerability and its implications for this large UK-based charity (Burns, 2018).

- *The role of schools in sustainable development* – funded by the Economic and Social Research Council (2007–2008). In this action research process in four schools across the UK, participants (the children) explored ways to make their schools ecologically sustainable (Percy-Smith & Burns, 2012).
- *Valuing volunteering* (2011–2014) – funded by Voluntary Service Overseas (VSO). This action research process in four countries (the Philippines, Kenya, Nepal and Mozambique) sought to understand the unique contribution of volunteering to international development and to develop practices to amplify the strengths of such volunteering (Burns & Howard, 2015).
- *Applying systemic research to conflict transformation in Myanmar* (2013–2015) – funded by the United States Institute of Peace (USIP) and the United States Agency for International Development (USAID). This program for building peace from the bottom up used action research to generate insight and action across Kachin, a state in the north of Myanmar that had faced civil war for over 50 years (Burns & Worsley, 2015).
- *Vestibule de la paix* (2017–2021) – funded by Humanity United. This program, built on the learning from the Myanmar program, is building a network of action research processes across conflict hotpots in Mali.
- *Modern slavery and bonded labour in Nepal (Eastern Terrain), North India (Bihar and Uttar Pradesh) and South India (Tamil Nadu)* (2015–2020) – funded by the Freedom Fund. The program comprises more than 25 parallel action research groups to tackle slavery in the brick kilns, stone quarries, sex trade, agriculture and cotton mills (Burns, Joseph, & Oosterhoff, in press).
- *Tackling the drivers of modern slavery and child labour: a child-centred approach* (2018–2023) – funded by the UK Department of International Development. This large-scale program involving six consortium partners – the Institute of Development Studies (IDS), Terre des Hommes, Child Hope, the Consortium for Street Children, the Ethical Trading Initiative and the London School of Hygiene and Tropical Medicine – seeks to tackle child labour and modern slavery in Myanmar, Nepal and Bangladesh.

In addition to their intrinsic purpose and value, I see these projects together as a sequenced methodological learning process. Within each project and between each project, there is deep reflection on what has worked and what has not, which has led to new innovations that in turn are reflected upon. I have documented the methodological progression from one project to another in Burns (2018), where I reflect on how the learning from one project contributed to the methodological development of the next.

What these projects have in common is:

- A focus on social or environmental justice, and the full engagement of the most marginal in the process.
- The scale of the programs. They operate across a whole city or region, or a large organization. SAR projects need to operate at a scale that has the potential to challenge the deeper underlying dynamics that perpetuate the injustice they are trying to challenge.

- Each inquiry focus emerges from the process, and is constructed through dialogue, and from evidence, by the participants in the groups. While the participants commit to working on a core problem, when they start the project, it is not clear what the problem is or what they will be working on. These projects tend to have a core focus (e.g., the role of international volunteers, or building peace in Kachin), but within that, in line with an action research tradition and a complexity-aware emergent process, the focus of the action research groups is very open ended and goes where the participants want to take it.

Implications of Systems Thinking for Action Research Design

In my book *Systemic Action Research* (Burns, 2007), I highlighted six key characteristics of SAR. Just over 10 years on, I would like to extend these a bit further. I see the following as critical to a strong SAR process:

- a process for understanding system dynamics;
- an emergent research design with a strong bias towards methodological pluralism;
- multiple inquiry groups across an organizational system;
- multi-stakeholder engagement across the problem domain;
- open groups with changeable membership;
- inquiries kept as unbounded as possible;
- strong, contextually situated evidence;
- embedded processes for collective analysis of data to build ownership for action;
- a networked learning architecture; and
- distributed leadership across the system.

A Process for Understanding System Dynamics

Unless we understand how change happens within the systems that we are operating in, and how new change can be catalysed within these systems, then it is unlikely that we will be able to make any sustainable impact. This means that there needs to be a strong evidence-gathering stage at the beginning of an action research process. Over the past five years, I have developed with colleagues a narrative analysis process that leads to a distillation of system dynamics. The starting point is the collection of open-ended life stories where we ask only questions that prompt, and then questions that seek to clarify and deepen, so that we elicit what people want to tell us rather than what we want or expect to hear. We train the story collectors (peers) how to elicit stories that will surface patterns and causalities.

In North India, bonded labourers with the support of local non-governmental organization (NGO) field workers collected 300 life-story narratives from their peers and others within their geographical communities. We brought a group of around 40 of them together to analyse the stories. We paired one bonded labourer with a field worker from another locality (to minimize the power imbalances). Each pair had 10–15 stories to analyse over 24 hours. The field worker read the story to the illiterate bonded labourer. Both then analysed it. They were asked to identify all of the key factors in the story and the causes and consequences of them. They produced a mini system map for each story. At the end of this process, we used these to create a large system map across the length of a 10-metre wall that depicted the pattern of causalities across all 300 stories. From this we distilled the dominant patterns. These become the subject of intense discussion and debate as participants discuss both the patterns and the potential actions at each point in the complex causal chains that they have surfaced. These chains and 'feedback' loops then become the starting point for the action research groups. The group focus is framed in relation to a set of relationships rather than to a topic or a question. The group task is how to shift the system dynamic. This is not the only method of discerning the system dynamics, and I would encourage action researchers to experiment with different methods, which takes us to the next point.

An Emergent Research Design with a Strong Bias Towards Methodological Pluralism

It is important to hold the possibility of new questions, theories of change, ideas, people, methods at any stage in the process. Plurality is one of the defining features of a systemic approach. As we reach point one in a process, we may discover there is a better way to go to our destination point two, or that it would be better to go to point three. As we change course, we may need different people and different information. We need to use multiple methods to elicit information (in order to see the system) because some people speak more openly (on some or all issues) to NGOs, or to local people they know and trust, or to peers, or to anonymous surveyors. So not only do we need the right method for the questions we are trying to answer, we also typically need more than one method in order to get the full picture. For example, in work I carried out with IDS and international NGO (INGO) colleagues on disability in Bangladesh, we had three inquiry groups. The first two were local groups; one based on a slum in Dhakar; and the other located across poor rural villages in Cox's Bazaar (Burns, Oswald, & Co-researchers, 2015). The third was a group of local NGOs that worked on disability across the country. Many important issues were raised in the stories collected by the local groups, but nothing came up about sexual violence. In contrast, a very high proportion of stories told to the NGOs were about sexual violence. People tell some things more easily to their neighbours and other things to people who are 'professional' and 'anonymous'. This means that to understand a system we need more than one group and more than one method. Similarly, in South India, the issue of alcoholism was writ large in our scoping visits, in our narrative analysis, and later in the group dialogues, but when we tried to triangulate this finding in a large-scale participatory statistics process (whose indicators had been generated by the participatory narrative analysis), it was hardly to be seen. Again, different methods elicit different knowledge.

Multiple Inquiry Groups Across an Organizational System

In our current anti-slavery program in India there are 12 action research groups running in parallel in South India and 10 in North India. We are supporting a further six in Nepal. Building an architecture of multiple parallel action research groups means (a) they are spread across the geographical system so pick up different dynamics; (b) they each create their own innovations so change doesn't become homogenized; (c) a critical mass of groups can lead to contagious action, which spreads to other neighbourhoods and organizations; and (d) the membership of groups engaging with different issues can be developed in a more bespoke fashion.

Multi Stakeholder Engagement across the Problem Domain

Only if multiple stakeholders are engaged in a process is it possible to see the whole system or at least enough of the system to be able to identify the critical system dynamics. All of our work involves multiple stakeholders, although not always at the same time. So, the action research group looking at domestic violence in the Sure Start programs included victims of domestic violence, health visitors, midwives, the police, school teachers and many others. Similarly, the action research group on the impact of drugs on the conflict in Myanmar included drug users, ex drug users, teachers, soldiers from the Kachin Independence Organization, children, drug rehab centre staff, refugees and others.

On the other hand, in the BRC project the groups were segmented and brought together later. For example, there were inquiry groups comprised entirely of local staff, others made up of volunteers. In our work in India we originally started with multi stakeholder groups but found it was much better to start with the slaves themselves until they had built their identity, capacity and ideas. Introducing other stakeholders too early created a power imbalance that quickly rendered the groups useless, as no-one wanted to come and be told what to do by a professional, and no innovation was generated because the professionals already knew the answers!

In situations characterized by conflicting interests, it is often better to build the groups separately. Wadsworth, in her seminal work on mental health in Victoria, Australia, facilitated two strands of work in parallel; one brought together mental health users, and the other brought together institutional staff. At key moments in the processes, she brought them into dialogue and weaved their inquiries together (Wadsworth & Epstein, 1998, 2001). There are two reasons for doing this. The first is that it allows each group to develop their thinking initially uninfluenced by the other. The second is that it prevents the stronger in a power relationship dominating, or two protagonists conflicting. We have found that once there is 'evidence' generated from each side, it is much more productive to dialogue around the evidence rather than across competing views. For example, we found that two groups in the conflict in Kachin were prepared to discuss the system maps but not the life stories. So systemic artefacts help to mediate conflict across systems, as people speak to the map not to (or at, or past) each other. One of most important aspects of systemic work is that the work does not all have to be done in the same room with protagonists who are in conflict. People can work with different groups

in different ways, and impact on the wider system in ways that open up pathways for change that they may not actually travel down. They may never actually have to meet to have an impact.

Open Groups with Changeable Membership

This remains an important distinction between SAR and many other forms of action research. In most action research processes, the core inquiry groups have a relatively fixed membership. Someone may leave and a few may be added in here and there, but generally, the membership of these groups tends to be fairly constant. In the work I have been engaged in, group membership can change radically over time. It changes because there are gaps in knowledge, because new people are motivated to get engaged, because the questions have changed so new people are needed, and so on. This means it is necessary to have processes that allow for this level of fluidity. It places a higher premium on both facilitation and recording to ensure continuity over time.

Inquiries Kept as Unbounded as Possible

Large program donors who focus on addressing 'modern slavery' want to show that their work relates directly to slavery. This drives them systemically towards interventions that have a linear relationship to slavery and child labour. Here the rationale is that if you can keep children in school until they are aged 18, then they won't be child labourers; if you can inform people about their rights (bonded labour is illegal but widespread), then they will find a way out of bondage; if you can 'rescue' children from traffickers, etc., then the children will be 'free'. But often this doesn't take into account the underlying system dynamics. Children may have to work (thus, not go to school) because if they don't earn income the family starves; similarly, 'rescued children' may end up back in exploitative work situations for exactly the same reason, and after these children are rescued, there are hundreds of other children to fill their place and so on. Our analysis highlighted the importance of health as the most critical issue. In North India, up to 60 per cent of high-interest loans were taken in response to a health crisis. This suggested the most impactful interventions might lie in mitigating the health crises (hygiene, sanitation and clear water being crucial); in supporting better access to government health services and so on. But a donor, an action research group, or an NGO, may think that health is something another organization should work on, whereas the focus of their programs should be slavery. The point about a systemic analysis of causes is that you have to go where the problem lies, and this is exactly what these action research groups have done.

Strong Contextually Situated Evidence

Evidence is important because when people generate their own evidence and analyse it, they own it and are more likely to be motivated to take action based on it. Further, it enables learning to travel across the system and innovation to be scaled. Without evidence, it is difficult to see what is happening across the whole system.

As I indicated earlier, it is important first to generate a big-picture understanding of the dominant system dynamics that are at play. Then, once the action research groups have been formed, there is at least one more round of detailed evidence that needs to be collected. For example, in the Bristol Children's Initiatives Action Research Group on domestic violence, because they were unsatisfied with official statistics available from the police and others, the health visitors and midwives in the groups decided to monitor on a monthly basis all the references to domestic violence that appeared in their case load. At the end of this process, they had a much stronger picture of what was going and why, and when this picture was combined with the narratives of victims themselves, the group felt ready to act.

In the South India Action Research group process, the groups collectively established a big-picture pattern through the system mapping. A range of factors emerged – from health crises, to death, to marriage dowry, to loan repayment – that led to people taking high interest loans. People who were unable to pay these loans became locked into bondage relationships. One of the village groups decided they needed more detailed data and went from household to household to talk to people about everything they spent money on. On a day-to-day basis, people have an idea of what they spend money on, but often they have no idea of exactly how much they spend, and what proportion of their income it comprises. The data generated from the action research showed that, from a household income typically around $2 per day, at least 30 per cent was being used to repay old loans. Significantly, roughly 20 per cent was being spent on inter-family gift giving and temple taxes (which are highly traditional), 10 per cent or more on health crises and 10 per cent or more on alcohol – because a vast swathe of the male population has become alcohol addicted, partly in response to their back-breaking work.

The action research group decided to take action on what it could do something about. It organized to close the liquor store and a group of people from the group mobilized the elders, who in turn persuaded the villagers, who in turn were able to negotiate with the Temple committee, to reduce their temple contributions to 50 per cent of what they had traditionally paid. They also decided to radically restrain their expensive practice of mutual gift giving. Some men in the village, realizing that their alcohol consumption was a major factor in their family's poverty, dramatically reduced how much they drank (an example of the point I made above about collective processes leading to personal reflection). Without the detailed evidence that described the wider system dynamics, those who took these actions would have gone nowhere. With it, they were able to challenge decades old practices.

Embedded Processes for Collective Analysis of Data to Build Ownership for Action

Collective analysis is crucial. It enables people from different parts of the system to read (or hear) the evidence and understand it, build ownership around a shared meaning (or understand the diversity of interpretations), and take targeted action as a result. I have used different models of collective analysis. In the section on understanding systems dynamics above, I have already described *local collective analysis of life story analyses*.

Multi stakeholder analysis of data from multiple inquiries is another approach that I have evolved with colleagues. This was introduced to me by Susan Weil in the BRC project. Inquiry groups met across the whole of the organizational system and generated rich data. This included records of dialogues, diagrams and pictures, evidence and stories from the ground, and so on. All of this data was collected, and Susan carried out a first-cut analysis – breaking it up into around 10 broad themes. We then brought around 150 people together from across the BRC including volunteers, beneficiaries, local staff, senior management, the board, and a fairly wide group of critical friends from other organizations. They were divided into mixed groups across tables set up in a cabaret format. Each table had a data pack that contained all of the raw data from the inquiry groups, and people at the tables were asked to read the data, identify the patterns, the things they thought were most significant, and to explore their meaning. This led to the identification of four core findings, which in turn fed into the development of four pilots to be carried out by the organization over the following nine months. We adapted this process for the VSO action research process, where analysis was done at a local level and country level. The core research team identified a set of common themes running across the inquiries in all four countries, and then brought together a team of decision makers from across VSO globally to analyse the data that had been cut up into these broad categories. Like in the BRC work, this collective analysis built ownership strong enough to sustain major changes to the organizational strategy of the whole organization.

A Networked Learning Architecture

In all strong SAR projects, there needs to be a way of linking the learning – vertically, from individual action research groups to the formal organizational system, and horizontally, between inquiry groups. In the Bristol Children's Action Inquiry (which was one of the earliest), I think we missed a great deal of potential because the groups were fairly independent from the professional programs. This was good because these groups generated real innovations, but since they were also a little marginal, the learning wasn't fed through and linked to programming and budget cycles. The story I told above – about how action researchers in an Indian village generated evidence on villagers' spending and then took action in relation to temple contributions and gift giving, did not end there. Within the structure of the process, we planned two cross-learning events, one mid-process and one towards the end. At the first cross-learning event, members of the action research group told this story (in far more detail than I included here) and showed their evidence. Six months later, by the time of the action research review meeting, eight out of twelve of the action research groups had adopted and adapted their innovation and learning from the first group. They were also successful (each in slightly different ways). This process enables innovation to be generated and tested in one action research group, to be spread to others, and then potentially mainstreamed into wider organizational systems if it works in more than one locality. In this context, local NGOs that were part of these learning events and have been supporting the action research groups are working in more than 400 villages and they are now looking at how to scale this innovation into their mainstream practice. This is what Stuart Worsley and I call a process of intentional networking.

Distributed Leadership across the System

Our early training events often have a dual purpose. They are partly to develop capacity in the methods that local action researchers need to know, but they also enable us and local groups to identify who are the local people who show the combination of authority and sensitivity, systemic awareness and facilitation skills that would enable them to be good action researchers. We train these people to be the group facilitators. They in turn are encouraged to give everyone involved specific roles that they feel responsible for. This makes people feel ownership and connection, and it builds long-term leadership. It is important for sustaining formal groups, and for encouraging the sort of 'movement' that allows the innovations from the action research process to grow to scale. Distributed leadership is what enables an action research process to take off, no longer under the 'watch' of external researchers, but largely in the domain of the participants.

These principles have proved to be the most important in generating processes that can deliver social change, but this does not mean that the design of the action research always has to be the same. Broadly, the work I have done falls into two categories: (1) structured large-system action research and (2) movement-based change processes. I illustrate these in the section below.

Designing SAR

Building on these principles, how do you put this all together into the design of a SAR process? What does a SAR project look like? I have approached the design of large-scale change processes in two ways. The first is a highly *structured action research* design across multiple sites and stakeholders. The second is more akin to *movement building*, where ownership of the process spreads horizontally (Burns & Worsley, 2015). In this section, I want to outline the key elements in the design of three large-system action research processes that fit into the first category, and one that is a good example of the second.

Structured Large-system Action Research

Here I discuss, by way of illustration, the key methodological steps that were followed in three large-system projects: 'Re-thinking Vulnerability', 'Valuing Volunteering' and 'Modern Slavery and Bonded Labour'.

The Re-thinking Vulnerability project was commissioned by the BRC. It focused on a large organization in the UK with over 300 staff and 30,000 volunteers. The boundaries of the inquiry in this project were the organization. Stakeholders were not drawn from outside the organization (although if we were to do it again, I think I would broaden the inquiry process to the communities that BRC worked with). They were concerned with a deep strategic question about whether they were really reaching the most vulnerable people through their project work. The early part of the process of course required clarification as to what they meant by 'vulnerability' – a deeply contested concept. Key steps in the process were as follows: (1) 10+ inquiry groups were formed across the organization in different localities and with different groups (e.g., staff and volunteers); (2) evidence was generated in these groups, collated, and built into data packs; (3) a system-wide collective analysis process was conducted, including participants, volunteers, staff, managers, senior managers, critical friends; (4) four system-wide pilots were run over nine months, based on the learning from the first collective analysis; (5) a system-wide collective analysis event was held to assess the impact and implications of the pilot processes; and (6) a new strategy for BRC was created.

The Valuing Volunteering project was commissioned by VSO and focused in four countries, with a view to also generating learning for their global operations. Key steps in the process were: (1) identifying volunteer action researchers; (2) locating action researchers with VSO country offices and other organizations, in the Philippines, Kenya, Mozambique and Nepal; (3) action researchers carrying out generic context analysis and making decisions about where to open up multiple small inquiries engaging local groups and working where there is local enthusiasm; (4) participatory inquiries were opened up, supported, and written up in multiple locations; (5) the participatory inquiries with more traction and local buy-in were extended and developed into action research processes; (6) three to four case studies were written (for each country), as well as a generic report on the learning about what was unique about volunteering as a development intervention; (7) collective analysis of research by decision makers across the global VSO organization; and (8) building the learning into the creation of a new 'relational volunteering' model by VSO globally. In this project we tried to build a continuous learning process at national and global levels, but this was continually thwarted by a seemingly never-ending staff turnover. In the end, the learning from the ground helped to frame a national strategy, but the action generated by the process was local.

The Modern Slavery and Bonded Labour project in India and Nepal was commissioned by the Freedom Fund. It involved working with between eight and twenty local NGOs in three slavery hotspots. In this process we pioneered a number of participatory processes at scale. The key steps were: (1) scoping studies that included interviews, focus groups and group discussions in each hot spot; (2) narrative analysis of around 300 stories by slaves and local NGO field workers in each hot spot, and generation of large system maps from which the system dynamics were distilled; (3) collection of participatory statistics for 3,000+ households across 80 or so villages, to verify some critical insights from the narrative analysis; (4) use of all of the above to help inform the selection of key issues for the action research groups; (5) setting up between six and twelve parallel action research groups in each hotspot with the following stages: (a) a three to four meeting engagement phase; (b) generic action generation in the village to win local support and build local confidence; (c) local evidence gathering and building of local theories of change; (d) action research groups taking action and monitoring the impacts of that action; and (e) cross learning events between action research groups, which supported scale-up of successful interventions across villages. The Freedom Fund modern slavery project was an integrated project where participants' actions had a direct impact at the village level, learning fed into programmatic changes for local NGOs; and these in turn fed into rapid iterative shifts in country-level strategy and the broader strategy of the donor.

Movement-based Action Research Processes

The process in Myanmar, and the process building with colleagues in Mali to support peace processes in those countries, is quite different. One might look at it as an extension, in a more organic direction, of the approach illustrated by the Modern Slavery project discussed above. While the aim of the more structured large-system action research is to systematize the learning and action, and to embed it into structured organizational and community decision-making, the aim of movement-based processes is to create an environment in which innovation is encouraged and learning is spread horizontally, leading to rapid adoption and adaption across a wide geographical and organizational terrain. This is a more complexity-oriented approach, which we (Burns & Worsley, 2015) describe as more akin to tending to the system. We draw an analogy with the way a seed grows into a plant:

> The soil is prepared and needs to be fertile, the seed is planted and needs to be of good quality, the plant is fed with water and nutrients (compost) and needs to interact with its environment – bees need to be encouraged to pollinate it and birds need to be encouraged to eat slugs and so on. Sometimes the seedlings need to be protected and invisible until they are strong enough to survive on their own. Once established they grow and spread quickly. These are all interventions. (p. 113)

In Myanmar this organic movement-based process was an initiative with a more structured action research process that quickly transcended its boundaries. The key steps in the process were: (1) building a strong relationship with an indigenous host organization – in this case the Refugee Action Network for IDP and Refugee (RANIR); (2) carrying out a life-story collection and collective analysis process; (3) training community-based action research facilitators to each facilitate one of the action research groups that emerged on the topics of: (a) conflict between people in the IDP (internally displaced people) camps and the local village communities; (b) resettlement solutions; people had been in camps for over 10 years and wanted to look at various options including going back to their villages (many of which were heavily land-mined), creating new settlements, improving the camps and staying there and migrating across the border in to China; (c) the impact of drugs on the conflict; (4) bringing together multi-stakeholder action research groups to explore the issues and identify actions; and (5) setting up task groups to carry out different actions.

From here the process moved quickly beyond the group. For example, one group identified that most of the conflicts were happening between young people. As a result, the group set up a meeting of young people across the host communities and IDP camps, which resulted in the rapid spread of a series of youth conferences across Kachin. These conferences led to the development of new youth organizations that organized activities and fed their learning into the Kachin Independence Organization. In this kind of process, action research facilitators can lose sight of the many actions that are taking place. But by the end of the process, more than 8,000 people had received land-mine risk education (which had never happened in 50 years of civil war); a curriculum on drugs was built by multiple stakeholders (which was distributed across schools and churches in the region); and youth-dialogue forums resulted in the creation of the Kachin Youth National Network, a representative body that continues to engage in Myanmar's peace process.

Conclusion

What distinguishes SAR from many other forms of action research is that action is designed with a focus on the systemic nature of change, and a multi-stranded participatory architecture is constructed to facilitate learning across the wider system. In SAR, it is necessary to reveal the complex system dynamics, first to understand them and second to take action to shift them. This is important because it is always possible to take action in relation to a problem, and it is sometimes possible to take action that has an impact; however, our goal is to take action that has a transformative and sustainable impact on the deeper pattern that is holding different forms of oppression and injustice in place. As we can see from some of the examples discussed above, significant change that is spread across a wide terrain, with those affected at the core of the process, is achievable.

Topics for Discussion

1. How can a systemic approach to change be reflected in the design of an action research process?
2. What do we need to think about when putting some of the poorest and most marginalized people into the centre of an action research process?
3. What ethical issues are raised by these examples of large-scale SAR?

Acknowledgments

Special thanks to the following for their leadership and co-leadership of these projects: Matthieu Daum (Bristol Children's Initiatives); Susan Weil (British Red Cross); Barry Percy-Smith (Sustainability in Schools); Joanna Wheeler (VSO Valuing Volunteering); Stephen Gray (Myanmar community-based peace project); Pauline Oosterhoff (Modern Slavery and Bonded Labour); and Elise Ford (Mali bottom-up peace process). Thanks also to the many others who took leadership roles in supporting and facilitating these processes, and of course to all who have participated in these powerful transformative processes.

Further Reading

Burns, D. (2007). A strategy for whole system change. *Systemic Action Research, 19*(2), 245–251. doi:10.1080/09650792.2011.569137

Burns, D. (2014). Systemic action research: Changing system dynamics to support sustainable change. *Action Research, 12*(1), 3–18. doi:10.1177/1476750313513910

Burns, D. (2018). Deepening and scaling participatory research with the poorest and most marginalized. *European Journal of Operational Research, 268*(3), 865–874. doi:10.1016/j.ejor.2017.11.025

Burns, D., & Worsley, S. (2015). *Navigating complexity in international development: Facilitating sustainable change at scale.* Rugby: Practical Action Publishing.

References

Burns, D. (2007). A strategy for whole system change. *Systemic Action Research, 19*(2), 245–251. doi:10.1080/09650792.2011.569137

Burns, D. (2014). Systemic action research: Changing system dynamics to support sustainable change. *Action Research, 12*(1), 3–18. doi:10.1177/1476750313513910

Burns, D. (2018). Deepening and scaling participatory research with the poorest and most marginalised. *European Journal of Operational Research, 268*(3), 865–874. doi:10.1016/j.ejor.2017.11.025

Burns, D., & Howard, J. (Eds.). (2015). What is the unique contribution of volunteering to international development [Special issue]. *IDS Bulletin, 46*(5). Retrieved from https://onlinelibrary.wiley.com/doi/abs/10.1111/1759-5436.12170

Burns, D., Joseph, S., & Oosterhoff, P. (in press). *Systemic action research with spinning mill workers in Tamil Nadu.* Brighton: Institute of Development Studies.

Burns, D., Oswald, K., & Co-researchers. (2015). *We can also make change: Piloting participatory research with persons with disabilities and older people in Bangladesh.* Brighton: Institute of Development Studies (IDS). Retrieved from https://www.sightsavers.org/wp-content/uploads/2017/09/VOTM-Summary_WEB.pdf

Burns, D., & Worsley, S. (2015). *Navigating complexity in international development: Facilitating sustainable change at scale.* Rugby: Practical Action Publishing.

Coghlan, D. (2002). Interlevel dynamics in system action research. *Systemic Practice and Action Research, 15*(4), 273–283. doi:10.1023/A:1016392203837

Flood, R. L. (2010). The relationship of systems thinking to action research. *Systemic Practice and Action Research, 23*(4), 269–284. doi:10.1007/s11213-010-9169-1

Ison, R. (2010). *Systems practice: How to act in a climate change world.* London: Springer. doi:0.1007/978-1-84996-125-7

Midgley, G. (2000). *Systemic intervention: Philosophy, methodology and practice.* London: Springer. doi:10.1007/978-1-4615-4201-8

Percy-Smith, B., & Burns, D. (2012). Exploring the role of children and young people as agents of change in sustainable community development. *Local Environment: The International Journal of Justice and Sustainability, 18*(3), 323–339. doi:10.1080/13549839.2012.729565

Wadsworth, Y. (2010). *Building in research and evaluation: Human inquiry for living systems.* Melbourne, Australia: Allen and Unwin.

Wadsworth, Y., & Epstein, M. (1998). Building in dialogue between customers and staff in acute mental health services. *Systemic Practice and Action Research, 11*(4), 353–379. doi:10.1023/A:1022989723259

Wadsworth, Y., & Epstein, M. (Eds.). (2001). *The essential U&I: A one-volume presentation of the findings of a lengthy grounded study of whole systems change towards staff-consumer collaboration for enhancing mental health services.* Melbourne, Australia: Victoria Health Promotion Foundation.

Weil, S. (1998). Rhetorics and realities in public service organizations: Systemic practice and organizational learning as critically reflexive action research (CRAR). *Systemic Practice and Action Research, 11*(1), 37–62. doi:10.1023/A:1022912921692

Chapter 10

Action Science

Bob Dick

Chapter Outline

At the heart of action science are two competing models of human functioning. One of them is the model we espouse not only to others, but also to ourselves. The other is the model that a bystander might deduce from our actual behaviour. We are largely blind to the gap that exists between the two. Action science can surface the gap, providing leverage for change that can be intrapersonal, interpersonal, systemic or very often all three. In all of this, action science provides both the practical methods for intervening in the dynamics of a relationship or an organization, and the concepts and models to assist understanding. Action science can be used as an integrated package. Alternatively, its concepts and processes can be used to enrich other action research interventions. In developing action science, Chris Argyris was motivated in part by a puzzle: how is it that interventions to remedy some interpersonal or system dynamic often actually make it worse? This chapter foregrounds that issue. To do so it explains the central concepts of action science. Key among them is the idea of theories of action, which link actions to outcomes. Also key is the unrecognized gap between our preaching and our practice. The chapter also describes some of the more important conceptual and practical tools that allow that leverage to be applied. Finally, some newer developments and ways forward are identified.

Introduction

Argyris (1985) asked: "Why is it that when a difficult and threatening problem is correctly diagnosed, when a valid implementation plan is designed, when the resources are available, the implementation may fall short of everyone's expectations?" (p. x). The pursuit of that and similar questions led Argyris to wonder why so many attempts to improve a situation made it worse.

Over many decades of research and practice, Argyris developed the elaborate and integrated system now known as action science. Argyris and Schön (1974) at first termed it a 'theory of action approach.' Friedman and Rogers (2008)

Action Learning and Action Research: Genres and Approaches, 143–161
Copyright © 2019 by Bob Dick
All rights of reproduction in any form reserved
doi:10.1108/978-1-78769-537-520191014

explained that they later also adopted the term 'action science' coined by William Torbert (1976). Subsequently *Action Science* became the title for the book (Argyris, Putnam, & Smith, 1985) that gathered together the many different aspects of the approach.

Central to action science is the assumption that *tacit* beliefs can affect interpersonal dynamics – that our actions are driven by unconscious motivations. Those beliefs and actions can then influence the functioning of teams, divisions, organizations and communities. In turn, the whole-system dynamics form the setting in which individual thoughts and actions are shaped. The system impacts at the interpersonal and intrapersonal levels. Action science is thus a system of concepts and processes that explains behaviour at levels ranging from within the person to the whole organization and beyond.

At each scale from intrapersonal to whole system, action science also pursues the goals of most action research. It seeks to help people to take actions to improve their relationships and their situations. It has the typical dual goals of action research – the action goal of improving the situation and the research goal of contributing to understanding. In addition, there are other important elements. It devotes more than the usual effort and attention to building a robust theoretical understanding of each situation and how it can be changed. It makes every effort to develop theory that is practical and actionable. As it does so, it strives to use methods and processes that generate valid findings. As far as possible it builds rigorous research into its diagnostic processes and its interventions.

It can be seen that action science is an ambitious and complex system. There is more to it than can be addressed in any depth in a single book chapter. The early sections in this chapter therefore deal only with some of the central action science concepts in some detail, with particular attention to their practicality. The initial focus is first on interpersonal and then on organizational dynamics, and some tools for improving them. Some current developments in action science are then also examined.

Intrapersonal and Interpersonal Dynamics

To simplify this complex approach, imagine an interaction between two people. A third person observes the interaction. This miniature case study illustrates the apparently simple beginnings of the complexity of a contaminated relationship or a damaged organization.

Suppose that someone – let's call her Alice – observes another person's actions. Let's call him Bill. She assumes that Bill had some reason for his actions. She does not treat her assumptions with the scepticism that assumptions often deserve. She treats them as fact. And that may be all it requires for unhelpful ripples to begin to spread.

Like most people, Alice may act on her assumptions without checking their accuracy. Bill, observing Alice's actions, may form assumptions about Alice's reasons. He, too, is likely to treat his assumptions as fact, and to act on them. Notice what happens if his actions are a repeat or amplification of the very actions of his that started the ripple. A mutual self-fulfilling prophecy is born – in Argyris' terminology, a self-sealing process (e.g., Argyris, 1977). A third person – Carol, let's say – observes the developing drama between Alice and Bill. She says nothing.

Consider a specific example. It describes some of the common patterns in actual interactions I have observed. Alice is a newcomer to a work team. She has been with the team for only a few weeks. Bill is team leader. Carol is another team member. Bill decides that, as team leader, it is about time that he checked to see how Alice is faring. As Alice comes into the office one morning he greets her: "Hello Alice. How are you going? Is everything OK?"

Alice wonders what has prompted Bill's approach. She is not yet fully confident in her new job. Is something wrong, she speculates. She is reluctant to admit her ignorance until she better understands Bill's motivations. To reassure Bill she says, with a bright smile, "Hello Bill. Yes, everything is fine. It's going well."

Bill is not at all reassured. He believes that most newcomers to the team would still be finding their way after only a few weeks. He begins to suspect that he can't trust Alice's reports. The organization will hold him responsible for Alice's performance. He decides he would be wise to attend more to Alice and her progress.

Bill is reluctant to broach this issue directly. He doesn't want to put Alice on the spot. Uncertain how she will respond, he wishes to avoid any conflict or apparent awkwardness. He decides to pay closer attention to her. He will check in with her more often. Reluctant to make this explicit he smiles back and says, "That's good, then. You will let me know any time you need information or help, won't you?"

Alice replies, "Yes, of course. Thank you." However, she wonders if Bill is suspicious or doubtful. She has no intention of asking for help. She does not want to leave herself dependent on Bill's goodwill, which may or may not exist. She will try to avoid Bill's attention. She will be careful not to say anything that might cast doubt on her competence or performance.

Carol, who has observed all this, has her own assumptions about what is happening. She has seen this before in other interactions, and says nothing. She does not even indicate that she has been paying attention. She does not wish to be involved. She doesn't know where involvement might lead.

Theory of Action

Each of them – Alice, Bill and Carol – has chosen to conceal their perceptions. They could have tried to clarify the dynamics of the interaction. They could have initiated a discussion about what is happening. Each is uncertain about what would then happen. Each of them fears that to act might place their control of the situation at risk, leaving them vulnerable to challenge or embarrassment.

In the language of action science, each is guided by a *theory of action*. Such a theory takes the form: "In situation S, if you intend consequence C, do A, given assumptions $a_1 \ldots a_n$" (Argyris & Schön, 1974, p. 29).

The situation may be one where embarrassment or threat or loss of control is possible. Alice, Bill and Carol are each guided by mostly tacit assumptions about how to act in situations like this. They do not realize how highly practised they are at avoiding threat or embarrassment, which they have been doing since childhood. Argyris and Schön (1974) summarized this approach as Model I. They described it as the observance of the following set of governing values (or governing variables, as they are often titled):

> Define goals and try to achieve them.
> Maximise winning and minimise losing.
> Minimise generating or expressing negative feelings.
> Be rational. (pp. 66–67)

Argyris (1990) claimed these are widely held. "Young or old, female or male, minority or majority, wealthy or poor, well-educated or poorly educated – all people use the same theory-in-use." (p. 13) In his many books and papers, Argyris has provided many more detailed examples of similar interactions. His 1976 book (Argyris, 1976a) was a massive case study, reported in detail. Diana Smith (2011) also provided several detailed and in-depth analyses that illustrated how vicious cycles begin and develop. In one example she described how John Sculley and Steve Jobs gradually destroyed their relationship, and very nearly destroyed Apple, through similar dynamics that became progressively more noxious.

Working to evolve action science, Argyris at first struggled to believe that such inadequate interactions could be so common. He thought it unlikely that people would so often persist with behaviour that so often failed. Yet they did. Argyris (2010) inferred:

> Although we say we value openness, honesty, integrity, respect and caring, we act in ways that undercut these values – not just once in a while, on vary rare occasions, but regularly and routinely – whenever we face threatening or otherwise difficult situations. (p. 11)

He finally concluded (Argyris, 1982; Rogers, 2004) that, though widely held, these values are *not* widely acknowledged – to others or to oneself. They guide behaviour tacitly (Argyris, 1999), beyond the user's awareness. Not only that, but people unconsciously conceal them. They act as if there is a taboo against acknowledging their existence. There is also a further taboo against admitting that there is a taboo. Argyris (for instance 1983) called it the cover-up of the cover-up.

Here, then, is what lies at the core of the issue that so puzzled Argyris. In the face of potential threat, people act on unvoiced and untested attributions about each other. In doing so, they worsen the issue they are trying to manage. These Model I values operate as a *theory-in-use*, an implicit theory deduced from the repeated patterns in people's actions.

Each person also holds a second theory of action. It is an *espoused* theory of action, espoused as much to themselves as to others. It is not enacted. If it were, it would usually be more effective in guiding actions constructively. Unlike Model

I, it can vary to some extent from person to person. In its various forms it differs substantially from Model I. As Argyris and Schön (1974) described it, at best it has the following governing values:

> Maximise valid information.
> Maximise free and informed choice.
> Maximise internal commitment to decisions made. (pp. 87–88)

Argyris and Schön (1974) labelled it Model II. They offered a set of action strategies that can be used to implement these values:

> Make designing and managing [the] environment [a] bilateral task.
> Make protection of self or other a joint operation.
> Speak in directly observable categories. (pp. 89–90)

Scattered through Argyris' substantial contributions to the literature there are practical and conceptual tools to assist people in learning to use these strategies. Some of them are briefly discussed later.

Let's return to Bill. If he had been sufficiently aware and skilled, he could have pursued Model II action strategies. Imagine, for instance, that in response to Alice's "Everything is fine," he had said something like this:

> Let me try to be clearer about my intentions. I hope to build a working relationship with you that is productive and satisfying for both of us, and for the team and the organization.
>
> I don't have any reason to be displeased with your progress. Previous occupants have taken some months to become fully proficient in the job. I've learned that regular meetings with them can be of help.
>
> I'd like to know how you would prefer to build a working relationship that benefits both of us, and our employer. I would like to compare notes on how often we wish to meet, how we would like our sessions to proceed, and how I can be of the most help. Is this acceptable to you?

Similarly, Alice or Carol could initiate a change. They could voice their perceptions of the dynamics. They could invite cooperation in improving the situation. They could communicate their perception clearly and specifically.

However, they face a massive obstacle. Almost certainly they are not fully aware of how skilfully they deflect attention and sidestep loss of control. As mentioned, they are not consciously aware of the theory-in-use that guides their behaviour. Argyris, in much of his work, found that most people believe that in fact they follow an espoused theory resembling Model II. This may seem a counter-intuitive conclusion. However, copious support exists in Argyris' work and elsewhere.

At this point I note that there has been a challenge to Argyris' claim of the universality of Model I. Raaijmakers, Bleijenbergh, Fokkinga, and Visser (2018) suggested that there was a high proportion of males in the situations where Argyris developed his theories. If more women had been included, the results might have been different. They believed that the evidence may be less conclusive than Argyris assumed. However, Argyris expressed no such doubts.

For that matter, several other established theories are consistent with Argyris' claim that such interaction patterns are widespread. Consider the attribution of blame. In quality management, Deming (1986) argued that most problems are caused by the system and its poor processes. Yet, more often than not, individuals are blamed. Social psychologists, following Ross (1977), call the same phenomenon the fundamental attribution error. Ross (1977) defined it as a "general tendency to overestimate the importance of personal or dispositional factors relative to environmental influences" (p. 184). Put simply, we blame individuals for what is actually created by the situation.

A related defence mechanism is known within psychology as the self-serving bias. It is defined as a tendency to attribute our successes to our own efforts while blaming our failures on others or the situation (Baumeister & Vohs, 2007). It is strengthened in the presence of threat (Arkin, Appelman, & Burger, 1980). As we have seen, threat increases the likelihood of Model I behaviour.

To improve the situation, Alice or Bill or Carol would have to escape their Model I theory-in-use. But to do so they very probably would need assistance from someone like Argyris – someone who understands the near-universality and near-invisibility of Model I values. Not only are the three colleagues unaware of their Model I assumptions. Their assumptions, being unvoiced, cannot be tested. Concealed Model I assumptions obstruct individual learning.

The wider system – their organization – is the context in which they act. There, other people act similarly, further reinforcing Model I assumptions and behaviour. Thus, there are further obstacles to their learning of Model II skills. The lack of awareness is a further impediment to learning and spreading Model II skills within the organization. Organizational learning, too, is obstructed.

Organizational Learning

If the existence of Model I is as common as Argyris' research attests, it is not surprising that most organizations are afflicted with similar impediments to performance and learning. Model O-I, the organizational equivalent to Model I, has the same governing values as Model I. It differs from Model I primarily in its consideration of the organization-wide consequences of Model I behaviour. Because of the near-ubiquity of Model I, in many organizations the people are immersed in a Model I culture, especially where threat or embarrassment lurk. The Model O-I action strategies, too, are a near-repeat of those of Model I. In the presence of potential threat, interactions become contests in which all are attempting to reach their own desired outcomes. To this end, they strive to control the environment and the task unilaterally. Though mostly done unconsciously, it is skilful and has an appearance of rationality and reasonableness. The same dynamics apply within teams or divisions, and between them. Suppose that Bill has to raise a difficult issue with Dan, from a different division. The same dynamics are likely to exist. They may even be exacerbated because Bill and Dan have fewer work goals in common than do Bill and Alice.

At an organizational level, the collective effect is described by the earlier quote from Argyris. Attempts to remedy threatening situations are more likely to fail than to succeed. Model I assumptions contaminate the culture and management style of the organization. To compound the issue, many organizations are structured as silos, with competition between divisions. To amplify the effect even further, performance management and pay are usually individually based. Individual competes with individual. Team competes with team. Division competes with division. Communication is distorted to support the achievement of local goals.

The literature on high reliability organizations (HROs) provides a telling counterpoint. In HROs, dangerous crises are an ever-present threat. Yet actual errors and crises are rare. As described by Weick and Sutcliffe (2007), examples of HROs include hospital emergency rooms, bush fire-fighting crews, aircraft carrier flight decks and the like. Notice how different the HRO values are to those exhibited by Model O-I. In contrast, HROs:

- try to investigate every error and mistake, without blame;
- acknowledge that in a complex world, 'accidents' are normal;
- pay attention to both operations and strategy;
- take every opportunity to practise the ability to recover from disaster; and
- defer to expertise more than to authority.

Note, particularly, the first and last of these. In HROs, people are *rewarded* for admitting a mistake. The mistake can then be surfaced, analysed, and possibly avoided in future. In any crisis situation, the person best equipped by expertise is expected to provide leadership. Expertise outranks rank. Notice, too, the second point. In HROs, people concur with Charles Perrow's (2007) claim: in complex situations, many 'accidents' (so-called) are natural and to be expected.

The culture of HROs is not easily achieved, as the history of action science implies. In 1974 Argyris and Schön developed a detailed understanding of the way in which interactions between people can be derailed by their unconscious assumptions. They then developed a set of strategies by which the usual reaction to threat or embarrassment – Model I – could be converted to the more constructive Model II. At that stage it seemed that following their prescriptions would yield improvement. In 1978 they gave more attention to whole organizations. They admitted they found *no* examples of Model O-II, as they called their preferred organization model. This was still true when they presented their further development of organizational learning (Argyris & Schön, 1996). By then they acknowledged that Model O-II might be an 'ideal state' (p. 112), seldom if ever achieved. Organizational learning is difficult.

"Organizational learning occurs when individuals within an organization experience a problematic situation and inquire into it on the organization's behalf" (Argyris & Schön, 1996, p. 16). In other words it happens when people can arouse their sense of inquiry to engage honestly with the situation. At such times, curiosity is a valuable mindset. It is less likely to be present when people are defensive.

There are conceptual and practical tools that, applied with persistence and skill, may improve relationships and reduce defensiveness. The action science literature provides many examples. We can hope that in time the tools may help an organization or part of it to begin the difficult journey from Model O-I to Model O-II.

Concepts and Processes for Developing Model II

Below we briefly examine two helpful conceptual tools: double-loop learning and the ladder of inference. A practical tool known as left-hand and right-hand analysis then follows, and a mapping process that can be used to extend the analysis. The fine-grain tactic of balancing advocacy and inquiry concludes the section.

Double-loop Learning

Action science distinguishes between single-loop and double-loop learning (Argyris, 1980, 2004). Fig. 10.1 shows the difference. In single-loop learning only actions are modified. Governing values are left intact. Double-loop learning requires examining and modifying the guiding values.

The double-loop learning tool can be further illustrated using the earlier case study. Alice, Bill and Carol may try to improve their interaction. If they don't achieve their intended outcomes they may decide to adjust their behaviour. Continuing to control the situation unilaterally, they cannot break out of the self-sealing cycle. They can at best achieve only single-loop learning. The Model I values – pursuing their goals, controlling the situation, being (or appearing to be) rational – maintain the existing dynamics. They modify their actions to achieve their tacit guiding values. They leave the values untouched (Argyris, 1976b).

Double-loop learning requires a more profound change. To escape the existing dynamics, they would have to surface and attend to their previously unrecognized assumptions. They would align their approach more closely with their Model II espoused theory. But to do so would require that they re-examine their guiding

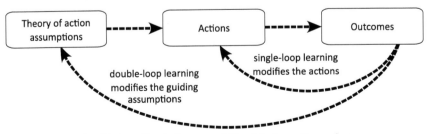

Fig. 10.1:   Single-loop and Double-loop Learning.

values. So far, that hasn't happened. Their tacit theory-in-use protects them, as does their use of hard-to-test generalities. The ladder of inference could help them to become more aware of this, and potentially improve it.

The Ladder of Inference

For Argyris, the ladder of inference had four rungs, or sometimes more (e.g., Argyris, 1982). The ground beneath the ladder represents the many specifics of the actual situation. With our limited consciousness, we are unable to handle such a flood. We must select from it. From our limited selection we form assumptions about what is occurring. I can describe the four rungs as follows:

1. Our selection from the flood of available data constitutes the *first rung*. In the case study, Bill notices Alice's reply.
2. Without conscious thought, we attribute some conventional meaning to this. This is the *second rung*. For Bill it might include the discrepancy between Alice's claim and the usual experience of new team members.
3. The *third rung* is informed by our particular theory-in-use. We draw conclusions about the meanings of the second rung. We often include assumptions about the other person's motives. Bill, for example, suspects that Alice is dishonestly covering up a lack of competence.
4. Finally, we decide what actions will maintain the guiding values of our theory-in-use. That is the *fourth rung*. For Bill, it includes trying to remain in control of the interaction. He plans to feign acceptance of what Alice has said while surreptitiously observing her more closely.

A similar ladder of inference could be constructed for Alice.

By itself, the ladder of inference is unlikely to improve the relationship. Alice and Bill (and Carol) do not realize that their behaviour enacts values contrary to what they espouse. Argyris and Schön (1974 and elsewhere) have provided a powerful tool to assist in surfacing what was previously hidden: left-hand and right-hand analysis.

Left-hand and Right-hand Analysis

As mentioned, achieving double-loop learning is difficult, in part because Model I values are tacit. A tool to help make the tacit values more explicit is variously known as left-hand and right-hand analysis (Argyris, 2010), left-hand column (Noonan, 2007), two-column analysis (Piggot-Irvine, 2015) or sometimes just the analysis of case studies (Argyris & Schön, 1974). By whatever name, it is a process for analysing problematic interactions. Argyris used it widely in his own practice to help clients become aware of their theory-in-use – the values implied by their actions. Copious examples are scattered through much of his writing and that of his colleagues and followers.

Those wishing to understand a problematic interaction divide several pages down the centre. In the right-hand column they record what happened, almost

Table 10.1:   A Partial Two-column Case Analysis.

What Bill Thought and Felt	What Bill and Alice Said and Did
I'll check how well Alice is settling in and performing	*Bill:* Hello Alice. How are you going? Is everything OK?
That's unlikely. I don't believe Alice could possibly be fully competent yet. I don't trust her answer	*Alice:* (With a bright smile) Hello Bill. Yes, everything is fine. It's going well.
I can't trust her. I can't afford poor performance from her – I'll observe her more closely. I'll be subtle, I don't want to upset her	*Bill:* (Smiling) That's good, then. You will let me know any time you need information or help, won't you?

like a play script. They enter their thoughts and feelings in the left-hand column adjacent to each right-hand column entry.

For example, if Bill applied this form of analysis to his interaction (discussed above) with Alice, part of it might look like Table 10.1.

After completing the task, each person re-reads their case analysis. They are invited to describe their underlying assumptions as revealed by the analysis. *What is their implied theory about how to be effective?* Consider Bill's partial example. He might realize that his actions imply that he believes it is better to act covertly than to challenge Alice. But this is not the honesty he usually espouses. The aim of the analysis, as Noonan (2007, p. 130) explained, is for people to "discover the gap" between what they espouse and the theory of action their behaviour implies.

The catalyst for the discovery is usually to be found in left-hand column thoughts and feelings absent from the right-hand column. Their espoused theory, for example, includes being open and honest. Then why do they conceal so much? And if they believe in collaboration, why seek to control the interaction unilaterally?

Following Argyris' common practice, the analysis can then be used within a larger group of people. The analyses, suitably anonymized, are distributed to all group members. In a guided discussion they decide what values the entire group appears to hold. In this way, the individual and interpersonal aspects of behaviour can be related to the shared values in the wider system. Similarly, Bill and Alice might each separately analyse the same interaction. It might then become apparent to them that their assumptions lock them into a mutual self-sealing process. Their unvoiced assumptions about each other generate the unproductive dynamics.

The dynamics can be made even more transparent using a process called mapping. Diana Smith (2011) used it extensively in her own practical work.

Mapping Interaction Patterns

As already mentioned, our untested assumptions about others guide our actions towards them. In turn, they form assumptions about us based on our actions.

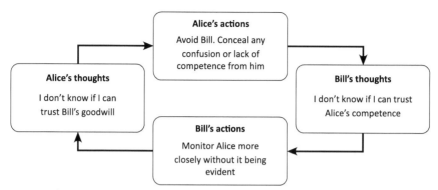

Fig. 10.2:   A Partial Mapping of Alice's and Bill's Interaction.

Mapping can identify and link the two sets of actions and assumptions. Fig. 10.2 depicts a possible partial analysis of the interaction between Alice and Bill.

Alice's and Bill's actions are the source of each other's assumptions. Those assumptions then prompt the very actions that maintain the assumptions. Mapping reveals the unvoiced and untested assumptions, and the resulting mutual self-fulfilling prophecy. It would be most effective for Alice and Bill to do the mapping collaboratively.

Smith (2008, 2011) used the mapping process to track improvement or deterioration in a relationship over time. Mentored by Argyris, she developed his concepts and processes through her own extensive work using action science. Argyris' own writing depicted a style that consciously balances advocacy and inquiry.

In the next major section we explore more of Smith's work, and that of other people who have extended Argyris' own writing and practice. But first, advocacy and inquiry.

Balancing Advocacy and Inquiry

Evident in Argyris' own interventions, illustrated in his many books and papers, is his direct and clear reporting of his own assumptions. At the same time he encouraged those he interacted with to challenge his point of view. He demonstrated the use, in combination, of advocacy and inquiry.

It is not unusual for people to favour either advocacy or inquiry. Some people are more likely to be firm advocates for their own point of view than open to other views. Others are reluctant to argue for their own opinion, while being more willing to listen to what others have to say. Argyris and Schön (1996) advocated aiming for a balance between the two. The more vigorous the advocacy, the greater is the need for strong inquiry.

Other Extensions to Action Science

Several people and teams have extended or modified the Argyris and Schön approach to action science. Victor Friedman (2009), for example, added to the theoretical underpinnings of action science. Peter Senge (2006) and Senge, Kleiner, Roberts, Ross, and Smith (1994) popularized it and added to the tools. Senge, Cambron-McCabe, et al. (2000) applied similar models and processes to school improvement. Viviane Robinson (1993) and Robinson and Lai (2006), in their work in the education sector, simplified elements of action science. For instance, my own clients have found her framework for communicating difficult feedback very learnable and useful.

Here I focus most closely on three practitioners whose enhancements have helped my own understanding. Roger Schwarz (2013, 2016) applied a very accessible form of action science to facilitation and leadership. His sister, Dale Schwarz, extended his approach to coaching, while Diana Smith described how she mapped interactions. She applied action science, including her mapping process, to improving relationships using reflecting and reframing. Discussion of these follows, beginning with Roger Schwarz.

Action Science Applied to Facilitation, Leadership and Coaching

Roger Schwarz's approach to group facilitation has become popular. *The skilled facilitator* (Schwarz, 2016) is in its third edition, with an accompanying field-book (Schwarz, Davidson, Carlson, McKinney, &et al., 2005). Though applied specifically to facilitation, both books observe action science principles. In addition, the language is deliberately accessible. For example, Model I and Model II are rebranded unilateral control and mutual learning respectively (Noonan, 2007, used the same language). Schwarz also used frequent diagrams to aid understanding.

In *Smart leaders, smarter teams*, Schwarz (2013) treated intact work teams as the unit of analysis and intervention. Team leader and team together strive to convert their style of working from unilateral control to mutual learning – from Model I to Model II. This is a timely approach, for a number of reasons. Many of my client organizations struggle to be more responsive to a fast-changing organizational environment. Devolving responsibility to workface teams can improve flexibility and responsiveness. However, it requires a change in style for both team leaders and team members. In addition, some organizations are adopting structures that produce more diverse teams. Team decision-making can then be more difficult unless people are skilled at collaboration, and their relationships are good.

Argyris (1997) stated that successful change depends among other matters on the learning of productive reasoning. Schwarz uses ground rules for this purpose. The teams learn nine ground rules, and practise observing them as they work together. The ground rules encapsulate the principles of action science. Almost all ground rules are expressed clearly enough to be monitored. For example the first two are "1. Test assumptions and inferences" and "2. Share all relevant information." Once learned, the ground rules bring many aspects of action science within easier reach.

In his interventions, Schwarz functions much like a coach. His sister, Dale Schwarz, applied his mutual learning approach to coaching. Schwarz and

Davidson (2009, p. 35) offered specific tools and activities. Five of Roger Schwarz's nine ground rules form part of the foundation for their work:

- test assumptions and inferences;
- share all relevant information;
- explain your reasoning and intent;
- combine advocacy and inquiry; and
- jointly design next steps and ways to test disagreements.

Diana Smith (2008, 2011), too, adopts a coaching role to help teams become more aware of their dynamics.

Reflecting and Reframing

Argyris (1982) regarded some defensiveness as productive. However, Smith (2015) wondered why so many clients responded to Argyris defensively. Was Argyris less Model II in his interventions than he intended? In the interests of research rigour, Argyris taped most of his interactions with clients. When Smith analysed the tapes, they were Model II – Argyris *did* practise what he preached (Smith, 2015). Smith began to explore ways of reducing defensiveness.

She chose not to confront clients directly with the gaps between their espoused theory and their theory-in-action. In a series of practical experiments, she used reflection and reframing to help clients explore their construction of a situation. She adapted the ladder of inference to guide clients through a five-step reframing process. The clients first did this individually, then collaboratively. I can describe the collaborative version as follows:

1. together, collaboratively explore your actions;
2. decide how, together, you create negative results;
3. avoid personalities and motives; focus instead on patterns of behaviour;
4. forecast the effect of these patterns on learning and growth; and
5. devise more effective behaviour to change the undesirable patterns.

She also devoted more attention to building good relationships with her clients (Smith, 2008, 2011). Her 2008 book, *Divide or conquer*, dealt specifically with the resolution of conflict. I return soon to the important issue of relationships.

It is now relevant to assemble some of the threads in the chapter so far, and identify current and possible further developments.

Taking Action Science Further

Peter Pawlowski (2001) has traced the development of action science through three phases. Phase 1 predates the official birth of action science. It concerns the integration of individual and organization, as in Argyris (1964). The collaboration of Argyris and Schön (1974, 1978) instigated the second phase. The third phase sought to overcome organizational defences. It is evident, for example, in Argyris (1990) and Argyris and Schön (1996).

The beginnings of a fourth phase can be seen in the work of other people mentioned in this chapter. It consists of extensions and refinements of the original action science formulation. Threads, some discernable in the earlier work, also suggest possible ways forward. A crucial element that obstructs positive change is the existence of individual and organizational defences. Defensiveness is pervasive. Understanding why may suggest some alternatives.

The point I wish to make is that defensiveness is to be *expected*. It is implicit in the action science of the 1970s. As mentioned several times, when threat or embarrassment looms, people become self-protective and cautious. They try to remain in control of the situation. They form assumptions, often negative, about one another. Surprisingly often they are not consciously aware of doing so.

Unexpressed, the assumptions cannot be tested, but they drive behaviour. Acted out, they often trigger or confirm other peoples' assumptions. Importantly, the people are guided by strategies that are well-practised but tacit. They use strategies inconsistent with how they would like to think they behave. Becoming aware of the inconsistency could generate loss of face, loss of reputation or embarrassment. Defensiveness is a protection.

Defensiveness as a Natural Response

Argyris wrote, often, that Model I thoughts and actions were activated when potential threat or embarrassment loomed. Many action science interventions confront clients with the truth that they don't practise what they preach. They are being asked to recognize that *their own* behaviour triggers the negative outcomes. In addition, action science is a normative approach (Argyris et al., 1985). The consultant is right; the client is wrong, as only Argyris or other action science consultants understand action science. For the clients it is like being an ignorant student.

How then can defensiveness be avoided?

Above, I described Diana Smith adopting a more *client-directed* approach by substituting reframing for the use of Model I and Model II. In coaching clients to use certain ground rules, Roger Schwarz also offers choice to the client, once the ground rules are understood. Smith gives overt attention to relationships. Relationships are important. According to Sedikides, Campbell, Reeder, and Elliot (1998), the attributions and assumptions that people form are less self-serving within trusting relationships. Trusting relations allow more open communication.

There is a parallel here with my own work. I invite clients, if they are genuinely willing, to take part in relationship-building exercises. The exercises I use are designed to legitimize real self-disclosure while allowing substantial choice about what is disclosed. In one such exercise, for example, clients exchange multiple narratives about turning points – people and/or events that were influential in their life or work (Dick, 2018). As trust builds, clients become less defensive. The establishment of trusting relationships provides a valuable foundation for everything that follows. There is much more that could be explained, though I do not have the space to do so here. Robinson (1993) offers some guidance.

I have also had good results by inviting clients first to exchange *positive* attributions that they have made about one another. They are asked to provide evidence for the attributions, in the form of the other person's actions. They also describe their own actions in response. This anchors their less tangible thoughts and feelings to specific and verifiable evidence. I find that, having engaged in this positive activity, clients exchange their less favourable attributions with less defensiveness. The resulting communication is an extension of the information typically surfaced in Smith's mapping activity. Each client describes in turn:

> the other's actions;
> the material consequences for the speaker of those actions;
> the resulting attributions they form about the other's possible motives;
> their emotional response to that;
> possibly, their intended action; and
> their actual action in response.

You will recognize these as the elements of a theory of action. The prior exchange of positive attributions reduces the challenge. Trust is thereby developed, reducing the defensiveness about negative attributions. I use a similar process when overt conflict exists.

Defensiveness can also be reduced by treating Model I and Model II as less binary.

Model I and Model II as Non-binary

If Model I and Model II are binary – that is, you must choose one or the other completely – change is a massive challenge. Though Argyris and Schön (1978) treated them as binary, they did express some doubt. Why not regard Model II as an aspiration rather than as an achievable goal? If the requisite skills and understanding can instead be acquired gradually, the challenge is less. Argyris and Schön (1996) also conceded that Model O-II was rarely if ever achieved. Perhaps steps in the direction of Model II are worthwhile.

To apply this logic, clients choose one behavioural change that achieves two outcomes. It improves their present interactions, however slightly. It is also a useful step towards behaving a little more consistently with their espoused self-image. Again this is their own choice, reducing defensiveness.

Defensiveness can arise when it seems that undiscussable information might be surfaced. The risk of embarrassment or loss of face is substantial. Yet the undiscussability obstructs learning what is really happening. Can the expression of what was previously undiscussable be facilitated?

Discussing the Undiscussable

To judge from the title of his book on action science, Noonan (2007) regarded all action science tools as helping to make the undiscussable discussable. Tim Dalmau and I (Dick & Dalmau, 1999) took a different approach. Instead of asking groups to discuss the undiscussable, we deliberately invite them to be more abstract – to discuss the *nature* of the undiscussables rather than the specific items. We then ask them to identify what they could do to make the undiscussables more discussable.

Here is a brief version of our process:

1. Privately list items that would be productive to discuss, and are presently difficult to surface.
2. Publicly discuss the *nature* of the undiscussables without revealing the exact item. Privately add to your own list any items the discussion suggests to you.
3. Privately categorize your undiscussables into three lists: (A) presently discussable, though only when it is *crucial* to do so; (B) not yet discussable, but potentially discussable if team dynamics were to improve; and (C) likely to remain undiscussable into the future.
4. Privately identify borderline items that are close to being more discussable.
5. Privately identify what changes to team functioning would aid movement of borderline B items to the A list (and perhaps C items to the B list).
6. Publicly discuss the conditions identified at step 5. Identify any of these conditions that the team as a whole might agree to observe.
7. Again consider moving items between lists.
8. Finally, discuss what the team has learned about itself and its communication. Decide any guidelines that the team is now willing to commit to following, to improve team openness.

There is a more detailed version of the process in Dick and Dalmau (1999, pp. 155–168).

We've considered the interactional and systemic dimensions of interpersonal problems, and the various tools to help resolve them. We've also briefly examined some more recent developments. It's time to conclude the chapter.

Conclusion

My engagement with action science began in 1975 when my attention was drawn to the book *Theory in practice* (Argyris & Schön, 1974). I was immediately impressed by its coherence and power. Since then it has influenced my work and life. As other work by Argyris and Schön appeared, I read as much as I could. I continued to learn, to experiment, and to improve my practice. Then and now, I regard action science as an integrated set of theories, concepts and practices that can enhance all or most action research studies.

More recent developments in the action science literature have increased the attention given to relationship building and to the use of more client-directed processes. To my mind, the result is a mutual enhancement of action science and action research. Action science can add to the repertoire of anyone seeking to facilitate individual and organizational change.

Topics for Discussion

1. Recall attempts to improve organizational functioning that you have experienced. How has this chapter enhanced your understanding of them?
2. How can you use the principles and processes of action science to improve your own research – whether or not it is primarily an action research study?
3. What is now your understanding of defensiveness, and its triggers and remedies?

Further Reading

Argyris, C. (2004). *Reasons and rationalizations: The limits to organizational knowledge.* Oxford: Oxford University Press.

Argyris, C. (2010). *Organizational traps: Leadership, culture, organizational design.* Oxford: Oxford University Press.

Argyris, C., & Schön, D. (1996). *Organizational learning II: Theory, method and practice.* Reading, MA: Addison-Wesley.

Noonan, W. R. (2007). *Discussing the undiscussable: A guide to overcoming defensive routines in the workplace.* San Francisco, CA: Jossey-Bass.

Schwarz, R. M. (2013). *Smart leaders, smarter teams: How you and your team get unstuck to get results.* San Francisco, CA: Jossey-Bass.

Smith, D. M. (2015). Action science revisited: Building knowledge out of practice to transform practice. In H. Bradbury (Ed.), *The Sage handbook of action research* (3rd ed., pp. 143–156). London: Sage.

References

Argyris, C. (1964). *Integrating the individual and the organization.* New York, NY: Wiley.

Argyris, C. (1976a). *Increasing leadership effectiveness.* New York, NY: Wiley.

Argyris, C. (1976b). Single-loop and double-loop models in research on decision making. *Administrative Science Quarterly, 21*(3), 363–375. doi:10.2307/2391848

Argyris, C. (1977). Double loop learning in organizations. *Harvard Business Review, 55*(5), 115–125.

Argyris, C. (1980). Making the undiscussable and its undiscussability discussable. *Public Administration Review, 40*(3), 205–213. doi:10.2307/975372

Argyris, C. (1982). *Reasoning, learning and action: Individual and organizational.* San Francisco, CA: Jossey-Bass.

Argyris, C. (1983). Action science and intervention. *Journal of Applied Behavioral Science, 19*(2), 115–140. doi:10.1177/002188638301900204

Argyris, C. (1985). *Strategy, change and defensive routines.* Boston, MA: Pitman.

Argyris, C. (1990). *Overcoming organizational defenses: Facilitating organizational learning.* Boston, MA: Allyn & Bacon.

Argyris, C. (1997). Initiating change that perseveres. *American Behavioural Scientist, 40*(3), 299–309. doi:10.1177/0002764297040003006

Argyris, C. (1999). Tacit knowledge and management. In R. J. Sternberg & J. A. Horvath (Eds.), *Tacit knowledge in professional practice: Researcher and practitioner perspectives* (pp. 123–140). Mahwah, NJ: Lawrence Erlbaum.

Argyris, C. (2004). *Reasons and rationalizations: The limits to organizational knowledge.* Oxford: Oxford University Press.

Argyris, C. (2010). *Organizational traps: Leadership, culture, organizational design.* Oxford: Oxford University Press.

Argyris, C., Putnam, R., & Smith, D. M. (1985). *Action science: Concepts, methods and skills for research and intervention.* San Francisco, CA: Jossey-Bass.

Argyris, C., & Schön, D. (1974). *Theory in practice: Increasing professional effectiveness.* San Francisco, CA: Jossey-Bass.

Argyris, C., & Schön, D. (1978). *Organizational learning: A theory of action perspective.* New York, NY: McGraw-Hill.

Argyris, C., & Schön, D. (1996). *Organizational learning II: Theory, method and practice.* Reading, MA: Addison-Wesley.

Arkin, R. M., Appelman, A. J., & Burger, J. M. (1980). Social anxiety, self-presentation, and the self-serving bias in causal attribution. *Journal of Personality and Social Psychology, 38*(1), 23–35. doi:10.1037/0022-3514.38.1.23

Baumeister, R. F., & Vohs, K. D. (2007). *Encyclopedia of social psychology.* Thousand Oaks, CA: Sage.

Deming, W. E. (1986). *Out of the crisis.* Cambridge, MA: MIT Centre for Advanced Engineering Study.

Dick, B. (2018). "Turning points" activity: An activity for building real relationships in small groups. Retrieved from http://www.aral.com.au/pdfs/02turningpoints.pdf

Dick, B., & Dalmau, T. (1999). *Values in action: Applying the ideas of Argyris and Schön* (2nd ed.). Chapel Hill, Australia: Interchange.

Friedman, V. J. (2009). Metatheory in action research: From field theory to action science. *Ricerche di Psicologia [Psychology Research], 2009*(3–4), 51–66. doi:10.3280/RIP2009-003003

Friedman, V. J., & Rogers, T. (2008). Action science: Linking causal theory and meaning making in action research. In P. Reason & H. Bradbury (Eds.), *The Sage handbook of action research: Participative inquiry and practice* (2nd ed., pp. 252–265). Los Angeles, CA: Sage.

Noonan, W. R. (2007). *Discussing the undiscussable: A guide to overcoming defensive routines in the workplace.* San Francisco, CA: Jossey-Bass.

Pawlowski, P. (2001). The treatment of organizational learning in management science. In M. Dierkes, A. Berthoin-Antal, J. Child, & I. Nonaka (Eds.), *Handbook of organizational learning and knowledge* (pp. 61–88). Oxford: Oxford University Press.

Perrow, C. (2007). *The next catastrophe: Reducing our vulnerabilities to natural, industrial, and terrorist disasters.* Princeton, NJ: Princeton University Press.

Piggot-Irvine, E. (2015). Reflecting on evidence: Leaders use action research to improve their teacher performance reviews. *Canadian Journal of Action Research, 16*(3), 3–26.

Raaijmakers, S., Bleijenbergh, I., Fokkinga, B., & Visser, M. (2018). The gender subtext of organizational learning. *Learning Organization, 25*(1), 19–28. doi:10.1108/TLO-05-2017-0048

Robinson, V. (1993). *Problem-based methodology: Research for the improvement of practice.* Oxford: Pergamon Press.

Robinson, V., & Lai, M. K. (2006). *Practitioner research for educators: A guide to improving classrooms and schools.* Thousand Oaks, CA: Corwin.

Rogers, T. (2004). The doing of a depth-investigation: Implications for the emancipatory aims of critical naturalism. *Journal of Critical Realism, 3*(2), 238–269. doi:10.1163/1572513042692409

Ross, L. (1977). The intuitive psychologist and his shortcomings: Distortions in the attribution process. *Advances in Experimental Social Psychology, 10*, 173–220. doi:10.1016/S0065-2601(08)60357-3

Schwarz, D., & Davidson, A. (2009). *Facilitative coaching: A toolkit for expanding your repertoire and achieving lasting results.* San Francisco, CA: Pfeiffer.

Schwarz, R. M. (2013). *Smart leaders, smarter teams: How you and your team get unstuck to get results*. San Francisco, CA: Jossey-Bass.

Schwarz, R. M. (2016). *The skilled facilitator: A comprehensive resource for consultants, facilitators, managers, trainers, and coaches* (3rd ed.). San Francisco, CA: Jossey-Bass.

Schwarz, R., Davidson, A., Carlson, P., McKinney, S., & contributors (2005). *The skilled facilitator fieldbook: Tips, tools, and tested methods for consultants, facilitators, managers, trainers, and coaches*. San Francisco, CA: Jossey-Bass.

Sedikides, C., Campbell, W. K., Reeder, G. D., & Elliot, A.J. (1998). The self-serving bias in relational context. *Journal of Personality and Social Psychology*, *74*(2), 378–386. doi:10.1037/0022-3514.74.2.378

Senge, P. M. (2006). *The fifth discipline: The art and practice of the learning organization* (revised and updated). New York, NY: Doubleday.

Senge, P. M., Cambron-McCabe, N., Lucas, T., Smith, B., Dutton, J., & Kleiner, A. (Eds.). (2000). *Schools that learn: A fifth discipline fieldbook for educators, parents, and everyone who cares about education*. New York, NY: Doubleday.

Senge, P. M., Kleiner, A., Roberts, C., Ross, R. B., & Smith, B. (Eds.). (1994). *The fifth discipline fieldbook: Strategies and tools for building a learning organization*. New York, NY: Doubleday.

Smith, D. M. (2008). *Divide or conquer: How great teams turn conflict into strength*. New York, NY: Portfolio.

Smith, D. M. (2011). *The elephant in the room: How relationships make or break the success of leaders and organizations*. New York, NY: Jossey-Bass.

Smith, D. M. (2015). Action science revisited: Building knowledge out of practice to transform practice. In H. Bradbury (Ed.), *The Sage handbook of action research* (3rd ed., pp. 143–156). London: Sage.

Torbert, W. R. (1976). *Creating a community of inquiry: Conflict, collaboration, transformation*. New York, NY: Wiley.

Weick, K. E., & Sutcliffe, K. M. (2007). *Managing the unexpected: Resilient performance in an age of uncertainty* (2nd ed.). San Francisco, CA: Jossey Bass.

Chapter 11

Appreciative Inquiry: Positive Action Research

Diana Whitney, Amanda Trosten-Bloom and Maria Giovanna Vianello

Chapter Outline

This chapter provides an overview of Appreciative Inquiry (AI): a high engagement, fully affirmative process for positive organization and community change – in essence, a process of positive Action Research. We describe and demonstrate with case examples three key aspects of AI. (1) It is appreciative, with a positive bias, beginning with a study of what works when the organization or community is at its best, and leading to a profile of a positive core of values and strengths. (2) It is an inclusive, relational process, with the capacity to engage all stakeholders relevant to a specified strategic change agenda. (3) It is a future-focused, world-making process of discovery, dream, design and delivery, with generative potential for large-scale learning, transformation and social innovation. We highlight AI's grounding in social construction theory and its position as a postmodern approach to positive AR.

Introduction

Appreciative Inquiry (AI) is a process for positive change. It is a fully affirmative, high engagement, dialogic process used by organizations and communities, large and small, to create whole system transformation. This chapter locates AI in the field of Action Research.

AI grew from the research and theory building of Srivastva, Fry, Cooperrider, Barrett and others at Case Western University's Weatherhead School of Management in the 1980s. Recognizing that organizations and organizational research at the time was infused with a bias for the negative, they sought to create "a language of the positive" (Srivastva & Cooperrider, 1990). Fry and Barrett (2005), both part of the early conversations at Case, wrote:

> AI emerged in the mid-1980's as an alternative to traditional action research. The impetus for this was the insight that action research

Action Learning and Action Research: Genres and Approaches, 163–177
Copyright © 2019 by Diana Whitney
doi:10.1108/978-1-78769-537-520191015

had not lived up to its potential as an innovative change method, largely because of its reliance on a problem-centered approach to social dynamics. (p. 4)

Watkins and Mohr (2001, p. 15) suggested that AI thus evolved from a theory-building process used primarily by academics, to a process for whole-system organization change. In the past 35 years, AI has grown in scope and significance. It has altered the landscape for how organization development and action research are conducted, creating what David Cooperrider and Diana Whitney (2005) describe as: "a positive revolution in change" (p. viii).

The Positive Bias of AI

Peter Reason and Kate Louise McArdle (2004) describe AI as a variety of action research, suggesting that its positive bias is what differentiates it from other approaches. Indeed, researchers and practitioners describe AI as a fully affirmative process, using phrases such as 'life affirming', 'strength based' and 'capacity building' to describe its positive bias. Below, we highlight three ways in which this positive bias is evident.

Affirmative Change Agenda and Topic Choice

Every AI project is a unique action research process related to issues of relevance to an organization or community. While the design of each process varies to align with the organization or community context, most large-scale AI efforts follow what's known as the AI 4-D cycle. As shown in Fig. 11.1, this cycle flows though

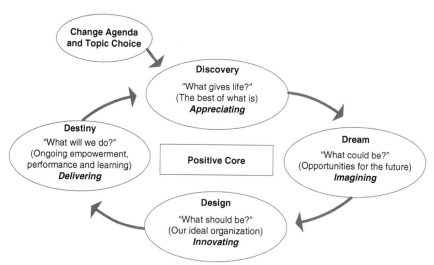

Fig. 11.1:   The AI 4-D Cycle. Adapted with permission from Whitney and Trosten-Bloom (2010, p. 6)

phases of Discovery, Dream, Design and Destiny. Every phase is relational and narrative based, and each has an unconditionally positive bias.[1]

The starting point of the 4-D cycle is articulation of a positive change agenda. It is equivalent to the formulation of a research question. At its best, the change agenda arises from and is linked to a strategic goal of significance. For example, the US Navy conducted a series of AI Summits whose change agenda (desired outcome) was *leadership at all levels*. Similarly, the educational research company, ACT, engaged several hundred employees in an inquiry whose change agenda was creation of a *company-wide career development system*.

Once a positive change agenda has been determined, one or more affirmative topics are selected to guide the AI research process. Topics are sometimes identified by 'flipping' problems. For example, low management credibility might become an inquiry into *inspired leadership*; concerns about staff turnover could lead to an inquiry focused on *workforce retention* or a *magnetic work environment*.

Other times, affirmative topics are expressions of an imagined, desirable state. For example, when the City of Longmont in the state of Colorado launched an 18-month inquiry, the out come of which was a city-wide strategic plan, they inquired into four affirmative topics: *One Giant Front Porch, Prospering Together in Longmont, Enhancing our Environmental Legacy* and *Exciting Living and Business Personality*. Together, inquiry into these topics yielded data and insight into best practices, hopes and dreams: three vital elements of the strategic plan.

The Unconditionally Positive Question

AI involves the art and practice of asking unconditionally positive questions that strengthen a system's capacity to apprehend, anticipate and heighten positive potential. AI questions are fully affirmative. They ask about what is most valued and desired. For example, in an organization seeking enhanced collaboration, an AI protocol might ask: "Think back on your work in the past year and describe a time that you would consider a high point in collaboration – a time when you worked with others, in your department or outside, and the collaboration went well."

As this example illustrates, AI questions seek narrative accounts rather than lists or explanations. They draw upon people's lived experiences. In this way everyone can answer them, and everyone's answer is a right answer. As they explore and respond to these questions, interviewees validate and affirm one another's experience, while gaining insight about the overall change agenda/research question.

The Positive Core of Organizational Life

AI is founded on the simple assumption that human systems move in the direction of what people study. Experience shows that people learn and organizations change most readily when they focus upon and engage in dialogue about strengths, capabilities and patterns of success – what is referred to in AI literature as the 'positive core' of the organization or community. Cooperrider and

Whitney (2005) suggest that the single most important action a group can take to liberate the human spirit and consciously construct a better future is to make the positive core the common and explicit property of all (p. 9). Thus, AI engages large numbers of people in dialogue and deliberation about their individual and collective strengths, hopes and dreams for the future and opportunities and plans for innovative actions.

In the research context, the positive core is the *composite* of strengths, assets and successes identified in the Discovery phase. Following one-on-one conversations, interview partners form groups of 4–10, then share their partners' stories. Group members listen for patterns and outlying insights. Sometimes they conduct a formal "root cause of success" analysis, where they dig into the supportive conditions that enabled the positive experiences they've discussed. They may create a collective image (or positive core map) encapsulating their shared understanding.

AI enables simultaneous discovery and collaborative co-creation of what is known and considered meaningful by those engaged in the process. There is no organizational reality apart from the relational realities brought forth through dialogue. By focusing on accounts of the positive, AI creates resource-full, strengths-based organizations in which people and the environment flourish.

What about Problems?

According to Whitney and Trosten-Bloom (2010), AI's paradox is that it does not aim to change anything. Its focus is on positive potential: the best of what has been, what is and what might be. When people turn their inquiry and conversations to accounts of the positive, things begin to move in the direction of the inquiry.

AI is an alternative to traditional problem solving. It deliberately seeks to discover and leverage the positive core. This shift from problem analysis to positive core analysis is at the heart of 'positive change': a process described as, "any form of organizational change, redesign or planning that involves multiple stakeholders, begins with a comprehensive inquiry, analysis and dialogue of an organization's positive core, and then links this knowledge to the organization's strategic agenda and priorities" (Cooperrider & Whitney, 2005, p. 12).

But – *what about problems*? AI does not suggest we ignore problems. Rather, it posits the most effective way to transform a situation, relationship, organization or community is to focus on strengths. AI has been used in situations fraught with tension and stress such as union–management relations, merger integration and cross-cultural conflict. As it turns people's attention from what is wrong to who they are when they are at their best, conflict turns to cooperation and inspired action.

The organization People Against Sexual Abuse (PASA) shows us how AI 'flips' problems into possibilities. It engaged youth, staff, community members and funders in identifying an affirmative description for their work and organizational identity. In the end, stakeholders renamed PASA "Positive Attitudes,

Solutions and Actions." The director shared, "That name change enabled us to see that leadership (especially youth leadership) prevents violence. So we changed our name to unleash leadership." In short, the organization's new identity focused them on what they were creating, rather than what they were against.

The Inclusive, Relational Stance of AI

In "Research as Relational Practice: Exploring Modes of Inquiry," Professor Sheila McNamee (2014) describes what she and colleagues call "research worlds" – generally accepted practices, conventions and standards that are agreed upon within a particular community of stakeholders (p. 1). She then differentiates quantitative, qualitative and constructionist research worlds and the key characteristics of each describing "relational constructionist research" (p. 6) as co-creating new meaning and new realities, being locally useful, generating possibilities. "Each time we engage with others and our environment," she says, "the possibility of creating new meaning and thus new worldviews is present" (McNamee, 2014, p. 10).

Given this ever-present potential for co-creating new meaning and new ways of doing things, constructionist research poses a number of questions related to inclusion, such as, "Whose future is it that is being studied and talked into being? Who needs to be in the dialogue? How are they to be involved and to participate?"

AI is a radically inclusive, relational approach to action research that is participant-guided and co-creative. It provides new understanding and enables participants to create new meaning and ways of doing things that make sense to them and help them achieve their hopes and dreams. Below we highlight three AI practices that particularly reflect this inclusive, relational approach.

The Core Team

AI is an inclusive, participant-designed and participant-led process, guided by a core team, that is, a small group that is a microcosm of all the stakeholders whose future is at stake. This team is charged with co-designing and collaboratively leading the inquiry.

Reflecting on their own most positive past experiences, core team members select affirmative topics – things they want *more of,* that will enable them to achieve their change agenda. Based on these topics, they craft appreciative interview questions and create an interview protocol.

Next, they design an approach to gathering and making meaning of data that aligns with the change agenda. For example, an organization seeking to enhance its customer service might invite staff members to interview customers and/or other organizations characterized by 'best in class' customer service to learn about times when customer service has been at an all-time high. Similarly, an organization interested in breaking down silos might bring stakeholders together across levels of business units to interview one another about collaborative best practices.

Often, participation in the core team is itself transformative for members of the core team. The act of discussing and selecting affirmative topics and determining strategy strengthens relationships and creates shared understanding.

Inclusive Inquiry

AI can be used to engage a single team or an entire organization or community. At its best, it offers internal and external stakeholders an opportunity to join in dialogue about the future of their work. Over the course of hours, days or perhaps even months, people engage in one- or two-way interviews, one-on-one or in small or large group gatherings. While generally taking place face-to-face, interviews can also be conducted virtually. Regardless of the approach, some significant segment of the affected organization or community participates in a highly relational, narrative-rich interview process that facilitates learning among professionally and culturally diverse groups. Participants in the process own their own research and the stories (data) collected.

AI often involves interviews among 'improbable pairs': members of different stakeholder groups, who do not know one another and do not work regularly together. By inviting people to conduct interviews across boundaries, we can be fairly certain that people will have conversations they have never had before. In the process they will learn, feel validated, discover common values and co-create visions for their shared future.

Novartis' Buddy Site Initiative illustrates this notion of inclusive inquiry. Novartis operates close to 60 manufacturing sites in Europe, USA and Asia. Grouped by a technological platform, the sites face a plethora of regulations impacting production, storage and distribution of medical products. The complexity of these regulations predisposed associates to focus on problems, and production and cultural differences discouraged people from partnering across locations to solve common issues.

The Buddy Site Initiative aimed to encourage cross-site dialogue about root causes of success vs. failure. Inquiry was focused on cross-locational learning, staying curious and daring to dream. Site leaders conducted cross-locational interviews with members of other sites' leadership teams, avoiding travel costs by using videoconferencing software. After the interviews, they reflected in their 'home' teams on what they'd learned (Discovery), defined the future vision of the site (Dream), identified concrete ideas to move towards the future vision (Design) and developed action plans (Destiny, aka Delivery).

Feedback from the sites suggested that the Buddy Site Initiative enabled employees to collaboratively address challenges that had been generated by organizational and operational structures, to learn from other sites' successes and to bridge the deepening divide among people of differing cultures. Participants reported a shift from problem- to solution-focus, and a desire to further include members of the organization in future decisions and activities. In short, the experiment illustrates how AI – a positive action-research process – proactively includes diverse populations in addressing the challenges that affect them.

Co-creative Meaning Making

As organizational consultants grounded in social constructionist theory, we recognize meaning making as an ongoing process. AI interviews and the topics upon which they are based enter an organization or community's ongoing dialogue, thereby changing it – much as a new subject introduced into a meeting changes the direction of the meeting.

While informal and ongoing meaning making occurs throughout the process, AI includes an intentional and structured process for analysing stories and data. Upon completion of interviews, one or more groups of 4–10 people convene to make meaning of what they have heard. They begin by sharing stories they've gathered that best illustrate the interview topics. We call this a 'root cause of success' analysis. (This is analogous to a 'root cause of failure', analysis, traditionally conducted as part of quality improvement efforts.) This analysis identifies interpersonal, team and organizational strengths, as well as conditions that enabled the positive outcomes outlined in the stories.

Having identified contributing strengths and conditions, small groups select what they believe to be the *vital few* (strengths or conditions most compelling or relevant to the ongoing success of their organization or endeavour). They share them with other groups, then cluster and perhaps prioritize them across groups. The composite of these strengths is articulated as the *positive core*. The map or profile of the positive core then serves as an artefact, promoting further dialogue and collaborative meaning making among core team members and throughout the organization.

As organization or community members reflect upon their entity's strengths, values and appreciation resonate and slowly replace vocabularies of problems, deficiencies and blame. Touched by shared narratives and dialogues of success, the organization or community transforms in the direction of its positive core.

What about Confidentiality?

For years, action researchers and organizational change agents have limited the success of organizations and communities by adhering to the positivist research practice of confidentiality. While well intended, confidentiality has rendered people invisible and without voice. It has denied people affirmation and validation for their ideas, and it has created organizations full of people longing to be seen and heard. Organizations do not want their dirty laundry aired publicly; yet they aspire to learn by studying and building upon past successes.

AI privileges transparency over confidentiality. Neither success stories nor strengths are kept in confidence. Thus, AI processes regularly unleash new appreciative dialogue, along with groundbreaking insight into what might be. Having borne witness to one another's stories and insights, participants are often deeply moved, inspired and hopeful. Hearing how others do things well, they gain understanding and capacities to improve their own performance. They then openly share what they have heard and learned with others, thereby engaging and fostering transformation among those not previously involved in the process.

Once again, we turn to Novartis to recognize the power of this transparency. Prior to experiencing AI, confidentiality might have been considered part of the company's DNA. But the inclusive nature of appreciative interviews, combined with the open sharing of stories, fostered trust among employees. It encouraged them to form new connections, to learn from one other and to work together to co-create the future.

The Future Making Focus of AI

In "Action Research and Minority Problems," Kurt Lewin (1946) coined the term 'action research', describing it as, "Comparative research on the conditions and effects of various forms of social action" (p. 35). "Socially, it does not suffice that university organizations produce scientific insight," he said. "It will be necessary to install fact-finding procedures, social eyes and ears, right into social action bodies" (p. 38).

With Lewin leading the way, action research developed as a process that blended social science with social transformation. Shifting from behavioural interventions to systemic efforts, it empowered individuals to transform their own organizations and communities.

Later, social constructionists Ken and Mary Gergen (2004) and others questioned one fundamental assumption of action research: that some 'truth' exists, and that it can be discovered given the right research methodologies and acted upon once the 'right' players are involved. In his award-winning paper, Gergen (2015) wrote:

> [In] conducting research on what exists, we lend inertia to conventional forms of life. We do not readily ask about what does not yet exist, or about ways of life that could be created … [Instead, what if] we closed our eyes and began to imagine the worlds of our hopes? What if we replaced the persistent rush to establish "what is the case" and began to ask, "what kind of world could we build?" (p. 6)

Gergen offered the possibility of research not as a way of 'mirroring' what is, but rather as a means of 'making' or 'forming' what might be.

Founded in social constructionism, AI is a 'future-forming' approach to action research. Following, we provide a brief overview of three practices that embody the future forming thesis of AI.

Questions are Fateful

Contrary to the common belief that organizational change occurs through planned, long-term intervention, AI suggests that even the most innocent question holds potential for changes in awareness, understanding and patterns of interaction. Indeed, given that human systems move in the direction of what they study, the questions we ask are fateful: they set the stage for what we talk about, learn, imagine for the future and become. As such, inquiry can be considered a form of intervention.

AI's unconditionally positive questions enable us to learn about what we want *more of* in our organizations and communities. Generating conversations about the good, the better, and the possible, these questions strengthen people's relationships, build capacity and inspire hope. They prepare people and organizations to go forward by surfacing positive, hopeful stories, conversations and images of the future. As our images of possibility change, so too do our actions.

Inspiring Images of the Future

Whitney and Trosten-Bloom (2010) join academics, educators, athletes and others in suggesting that people's images of the future powerfully influence their present-day actions and performance:

> Fear-based images can incite widespread panic – as in the 1929 run on the American banking system. Conversely, clear, sustaining, and motivating images can mobilize powerful, positive, collective action – as in the 1960s American-Soviet space race ... [Indeed, as] professor and theorist William Berquist contends, "the continuation of any society depends in large part on the presence in the society of a sustaining and motivating image of its own collective future." (p. 61)

In the Dream phase of the AI 4-D cycle, participants consciously and deliberately envision their preferred future. Invited to imagine years into the future, they visualize their organizations' and communities' boldest and best future achievements. They then perform their collectively expressed dreams, thereby – visually, kinesthetically and otherwise – anchoring new compelling images in their mind's eyes and lived experiences. These compelling, positive images serve as magnets, drawing the system forward by inspiring bold, brave, innovative action.

Improvisation and Self-organizing

AI's impact is called by many names: transformation, positive change, future forming and more. It achieves this impact in part by engaging people in study and dialogue about the world they inhabit, and the future they wish to create. Bushe and Kassam (2005) explore what makes AI transformative, or future forming. After reviewing 20 AI initiatives, they concluded that one of AI's distinguishing characteristics – that contributes to transformational outcomes – is the practice of encouraging and nurturing improvised (versus planned) action by system members. As they describe, many AI theorists believe that:

> The first three D's of the [inquiry] ... create a set of images and ideas that are so compelling to system members that they voluntarily find ways to transform their social and work processes.

> By allowing this transformational process to operate from the ground up, creating systems for supporting local initiatives taken without consensual or hierarchical validation, [they] … argue that much more change takes place much faster than can occur from any attempt to control and implement something new. (Bushe & Kassam, 2005, pp. 168–169)

Whitney and Trosten-Bloom Ortrun: Whitney and Trosten-Bloom (2010) reported a similar finding based on their research following a successful AI culture change initiative with Hunter Douglas Window Fashions Division (HDWFD), one of the transformational AI initiatives cited in the Bushe and Kassam article. They conducted appreciative interviews with team members from HDWFD on the heels of a project that the company had described as highly impactful. Their findings suggest that AI succeeds – and is thus future forming – in part because it unleashes the *freedom for people to choose to contribute* and to *act on their dreams with support*.

At its best, AI encourages people to choose their work and learning opportunities and to volunteer based on their interests and passions (rather than job descriptions or plans). They do so, knowing that their actions will be supported, perhaps even 'helped over the wall' by the entire organization. When people act with support in service of what matters most to them, they form new futures that might otherwise not be imagined.

In short, AI initiatives form the future in ways that are sometimes unplanned, perhaps even 'un-managed.' It empowers people to take action to bring that future to life in sometimes surprising ways.

AI as Action Research: The Dahlia Story

Our own experiences and those of colleagues around the world offer an expanding network of successful AI initiatives. To illustrate the three aspects of AI central to this chapter we have chosen to share one story, that of the Dahlia Campus for Health and Well-Being.

Background

Over the course of three years, a state of the art community mental health and wellness facility – the Dahlia Campus for Health and Well-Being – was constructed in a racially charged and economically distressed neighbourhood in Denver, Colorado. Despite initial skepticism and resistance on the part of community members, the facility garnered strong local, regional and national support by the time that it opened in January 2016.

In late 2015 – two months before Dahlia's grand opening – Amanda Trosten-Bloom was introduced to the organization and its history. A long-time AI practitioner and a graduate student in search of a location for her master's thesis research, she was attracted to the organization's commitment to operating from strengths (with both clients and staff). She was also intrigued by the positive story line, and the possibility of studying and learning about a project that had been so successful. She approached Dr. Lydia Prado, Vice President, Mental Health Center of Denver (MHCD) about conducting an AI with staff and community members and was met with enthusiastic support. Prado and her fellow leaders understood that their mission would be better served if they could enhance relationships among Dahlia's management team and key community members.

With this as backdrop, Dahlia launched a three-month AI project. They chose to explore the question: "What enabled community members to move from a position of skepticism to a position of support for the Dahlia Campus?" In the following pages, we provide an overview of the project methodology, highlighting the three elements of the design that distinguish AI as positive action research.

Appreciative Focus

From the moment the project was envisioned, AI was the *only* research methodology that made sense to Prado and Trosten-Bloom. Traditional Participatory Action Research would have engaged the system in studying and deconstructing a problem, but Dahlia's primary interest was in gaining a deeper understanding of *something good* that had happened prior to opening.

In partnership with Prado, Trosten-Bloom designed an appreciative interview protocol that invited people to describe their initial (predominantly negative) impressions of the campus, then focus deeply on what had changed: what they most appreciated about today's campus, the factors that contributed to their shift in perception, and their hopes and dreams for Dahlia's future.

A significant portion of the research was devoted to identifying 'key enablers': the strengths and positive practices that had helped participants shift from skepticism to support for the campus. The strengths (aka positive core) that were identified as having been present in the pre-opening community engagement process included practices such as:

- MHCD leaders listened to, heard and responded to people's concerns;
- communication was transparent and truthful;
- community members were actively engaged in key decisions; and
- local elders and people with particular expertise and interest were actively invited to contribute.

The inquiry's appreciative focus enabled negativity and scepticism to be discussed and validated. But rather than being the sole focus of the inquiry, it became an invitation to share success stories and dreams for the future.

Inclusive, Relational Stance

A primary goal of this research was to enable more Dahlia team members to understand and make decisions based on the positive community engagement practices that had enabled the campus' early success. For this and other reasons, it was vital that these same team members be included in every aspect of the research – from interviews, to analysis, to recommendations. To facilitate this, invitations to participate were sent to both staff and community members.

Once the research team was assembled, project advisors (the Dahlia lead and a local community elder) paired community participants with staff interviewers, taking into consideration who might need to work with one another in the future, who had the most relevant experience or insight to share with whom, etc.

With copies of the interview guide and reflection sheet in hand, staff interviewers contacted their partners and conducted recorded interviews. Rather than gathering responses to tightly scripted questions, they were encouraged to ask clarifying questions, pursue curiosities and probe deeply, as they were moved through conversation. They concluded by sharing with their partners the meaning they had made of the conversation and inviting further input.

The inclusive, relational focus of these interviews forged positive relationships between staff and community participants. It enabled staff members to learn from their leaders' previous successes, and empowered all participants to build upon the 'good' that had already taken place.

Future Making

Once interviews were complete, Trosten-Bloom facilitated a face-to-face 'meaning making' session involving all of the staff interviewers. Here, they shared and interpreted stories and determined the implications of what they had learned. Trosten-Bloom summarized the group's reflections and recommendations in a report, which staff members reviewed, edited and approved prior to distribution.

The project concluded with a celebration luncheon to which staff and community participants were invited. They met one another, exchanged appreciations, discussed what they'd learned and contemplated the future. From this and follow-up meetings with Dahlia's leadership team, several new initiatives were launched, including:

- an 'ambassador' program, allowing community members to more actively engage in the campus' decisions, programs and outreach;
- expanded mentoring programs (parent peers, big brother/sister and elder volunteers in pre-school);
- a job shadowing/internship program enabling community members to learn from and potentially train with campus therapists, teachers, etc.; and
- enhanced efforts to recruit staff and program coordinators from within the community.

Project Outcomes

The Dahlia Campus' AI process built and strengthened staff/community relationships, imprinting the *good* that had taken place prior to the facility's opening. It gave voice to a way of organizing that has since informed how the MHCD goes about implementing new programs and projects. Finally, it contributed to the Dahlia Campus being recognized as Project of the Year by the International Association for Public Participation (2017). The Dahlia case shows that AI's affirmative, inclusive, relational approach has the capacity to generate new and useful knowledge in a manner that transforms the organizations and communities being studied.

Conclusion

AI emerged as a wave of postmodern thought was pushing new ideas to the shores of the social sciences. It began with a query ("How do the questions we ask, as organizational scholars and researchers, influence what we learn and put forth as knowledge?"), and was followed by evocative experiments. By engaging large numbers of stakeholders in conversations about what was working well when they were at their best (rather than what was wrong), AI principles, processes and practices began to evolve. The 4-D cycle, mapping the positive core, the AI Summit, whole system inquiry and more, came to be considered 'the AI way' to create positive change.

From its inception, AI consistently yielded significant practical results including measurable increases in employee engagement and morale, productivity and financial performance. Applied experience was followed by innovative, supportive research and theory building in the fields of positive psychology and social construction. As these gained momentum, so too did academic support for AI as an effective vehicle for participatory action research.

True to Lewin's original intent, AI empowers individuals to make meaning of – and in the process transform – themselves, their organizations and communities. In this chapter, we have highlighted three essential practices that distinguish AI from other approaches to action research: a bias towards the positive; an inclusive, relational orientation; and a future making focus. We have illustrated these three notions with case examples, focusing in particular on the Dahlia Campus for Health and Well-Being's substantive action research process. Finally, we have presented current theory from social constructionism, to locate AI in the academic discussion. In short, we have described AI as a powerful, postmodern, positive approach to action research.

Topics for Discussion

1. How do the questions you ask as a researcher influence what you learn? Is the knowledge you generate life affirming? What questions might you study to generate even more life affirming stories and knowledge?
2. How might you engage your local communities and organizations, large or small, to identify appreciative questions and conduct interviews across stakeholder relationships to foster greater community and organizational wellbeing?
3. How might the AI 4-D process serve your research? How can it help you move from curiosity about a problem, to learning about what works well, to inspired action for a better world?
4. How might you use AI to address the most pressing issues of our time, such as gender inequality, gun violence and climate change?

Note

1. Fig. 11.1 is used with permission of the authors Diana Whitney and Amanda Trosten-Bloom.

Further Reading

Boyd, N., & Bright, D. (2007). Appreciative inquiry as a mode of action research for community psychology. *Journal of Community Psychology*, *35*(8), 1019–1036.

Michael, S. (2005), The promise of appreciative inquiry as an interview tool for field research. *Development in Practice*, *15*(2), 222–230.

Whitney, D., Trosten-Bloom, A., Cooperrider, D., & Kaplin, B. (2013). *Encyclopedia of positive questions: Using appreciative inquiry to bring out the best in your organization* (2nd ed.). Brunswick, OH: Crown Custom Publishing.

References

Boyd, N., & Bright, D. (2007). Appreciative inquiry as a mode of action research for community psychology. *Journal of Community Psychology*, *35*(8), 1019–1036.

Bushe, G. R., & Kassam, A. F. (2005). When is appreciative inquiry transformational? A meta-case analysis. *The Journal of Applied Behavioral Science*, *41*(2), 161–181.

Cooperrider, D. L., & Whitney, D. (2005). *Appreciative inquiry: A positive revolution in change*. San Francisco, CA: Berrett-Koehler Publishers.

Ernst, E. (2017). International core values awards winners announced. Retrieved June 28, 2018 from https://www.iap2.org/news/news.asp?id=370883.

Fry, R., & Barrett, F. (2005). *Appreciative inquiry: A positive approach to building cooperative capacity*. Chagrin Falls, OH: Taos Institute Publications.

Gergen, K. J. (2015). From mirroring to world-making: Research as future forming. *Journal for the Theory of Social Behaviour*, *45*(3), 287–310.

Gergen, K. J., & Gergen, M. (2004). *Social construction: Entering the dialogue*. Chagrin Falls, OH: The Taos Institute.

International Core Values Awards Winners Announced. (2017). Retrieved on June 28, 2018 from https://www.iap2.org/news/news.asp?id=370883

Lewin, K. (1946). Action research and minority problems. *Journal of Social Issues*, *2*(4), 34–46. Retrieved from http://dx.doi.org/10.1111/j.1540-4560.1946.tb02295.x. Accessed on June 28, 2018.

McNamee, S. (2014). Research as relational practice: Exploring modes of inquiry. In G. Simon & A. Chard (Eds.), *Systemic inquiry: Innovations in reflective practice research* (pp. 74–94). London: Everything is Connected Press.

Reason, P., & McArdle, K. (2004). Brief notes on the theory and practice of action research. In S. Becker & A. Bryman (Eds.), *Understanding research methods for social policy and practice*. Bristol: The Polity Press. Retrieved June 28, 2018 from www.peterreason.eu/Papers/Brief_Notes_on_AR.pdf.

Srivastva, S., & Cooperrider, D. L. (1990). *Appreciative management and leadership*. San Francisco, CA: Jossey-Bass.

Watkins, J. M., & Mohr, B. J. (2001). *Appreciative inquiry: Change at the speed of imagination*. San Francisco, CA: Jossey-Bass/Pfeiffer.

Whitney, D., & Trosten-Bloom, A. (2010). *The power of appreciative inquiry: A Practical guide to positive change*. San Francisco, CA: Berrett-Koehler Publishers.

Chapter 12

Critical Participatory Action Research

Stephen Kemmis, Robin McTaggart and Rhonda Nixon

Chapter Outline

In this chapter, we argue that critical participatory action research is one approach to action research that falls within a long standing emancipatory research paradigm (Carr & Kemmis, 1986; Fals Borda, 1979). We define critical participatory action research as a social practice that itself is "a practice changing practice" (Kemmis, McTaggart, & Nixon, 2014, pp. 63–66). We explain how people who share a felt concern about their practices engage in a critical analysis of their *practices* (sayings, doings, relatings) and the conditions that prefigure their practices (*practice architectures*: arrangements that enable or constrain their practices). Such a process requires those involved to simultaneously be in a practice and critically to analyse their practice by seeking to disrupt their existing "ways of doing things around here." Habermas (1984, 1987) referred to this disruptive approach as "communicative action" and Kemmis and McTaggart (2005) contend that taking this stance requires a deliberate commitment by a group to engage in *communicative action* to open up *communicative space* – clarifying their concerns and situations and informing changes in their practices. To practise *communicative action*, people form what Kemmis et al. (2014) describe as a *public sphere* where critical participatory action researchers work together to examine the local history of their practice and the practice traditions of which they are a part, and to document how their practice changes to make the practice less unreasonable or irrational, less unproductive or unsustainable, and less unjust or undemocratic. Participants' analyses of their social practice and their critical participatory action research practice are supported by the theory of *practice architectures*, which asserts that changing a practice also involves changing the practice architectures that make it possible. Critical participatory action research differs from other research traditions, most especially because it supports participants changing "what is happening *here*" in disciplined, prudent and informed ways.

Action Learning and Action Research: Genres and Approaches, 179–192
Copyright © 2019 by Stephen Kemmis, Robin McTaggart and Rhonda Nixon
All rights of reproduction in any form reserved
doi:10.1108/978-1-78769-537-520191016

Introduction

Critical participatory action research is one of a number of approaches to action research. It has been around for quite some time (see e.g., Carr & Kemmis, 1986; Fals Borda, 1979). In our view (e.g. Kemmis, McTaggart & Nixon, 2014), it is *critical* because it aims to make a critical analysis of the nature and consequences of a particular practice, of how people involved and affected understand what is going on in the practice, and of the situation in which the practice is carried out. Critical participatory action researchers entertain the possibility that "the way we do things around here" may be untoward because it is irrational or unreasonable, unproductive or unsustainable, unjust or undemocratic. If critical analysis suggests that a current state of affairs is indeed untoward in one or more of these ways, the researchers acknowledge that they ought to take individual and collective action to transform it, to make it more rational and reasonable, more productive and sustainable and more just and democratic. We now explain why critical participatory action research is participatory, why it concerns action and social practices, and its view of research.

Critical participatory action research is *participatory* because it aims to involve those engaged in and affected by the practice and the situation in both the research, and in the action to transform what is going on in the site. While once (Kemmis & McTaggart, 1988) we regarded it as ideal that as many as possible of the participants *in the action* be involved in the research, more recently (Kemmis et al., 2014) we have come to the conclusion that the 'participants' in critical participatory action research are the people who are willing to be engaged in the analysis of their situation, exploring what might be done to overcome or ameliorate what is untoward about it, and transforming their practices, understandings and situations. Later in this chapter, we will describe these people as those who are willing to be participants in a *public sphere* that comes into existence to do these things. We also take the view that, in critical participatory action research, participants in this public sphere steer the process of analysis, intervention and research, even if they are assisted by a facilitator (e.g., a university researcher skilled in action research processes). Participants are the ones who can together identify a shared legitimate concern about the nature and consequences of their practices, and then work together to address it.

Critical participatory action research is about *action* because it focuses on changing people's individual and collective *social practices*, their understandings and the situations in which they find themselves. Changing people's practices usually also entails changing at least some of the conditions that make these practices possible; we call these conditions of possibility the 'practice architectures' that enable and constrain the way a practice unfolds, thus shaping its nature and consequences. To change practices, critical participatory action researchers argue, it is generally also necessary to change at least some of the practice architectures that enable and constrain practices, channelling them so they form the web of "the ways we do things around here."

Finally, critical participatory action research is *research* because it involves people in making analyses, gathering evidence and reflecting on the nature and consequences of their practices, the way they understand what they are doing, and the situations in which the practices are conducted. It also involves them in trying out possibilities for changing their practices, understandings and situations: that is, in intervening in "the ways we do things around here" to overcome or ameliorate any untoward consequences of the ways things are currently done.

Like other forms of action research, critical participatory action research frequently proceeds through a spiral of individual and collective self-reflective cycles of:

- planning a change;
- acting and observing the process and consequences of the change;
- reflecting on these processes and consequences, and then
- re-planning;
- acting and observing; and
- reflecting and so on...

In practice, however, this process does not always follow a neat spiral of self-contained cycles. Frequently, participants set off in one direction, with one project in mind, and then, after gathering some evidence, find that they want to focus their research efforts on another concern that emerges as more important, so they head off in a different direction, with a redefined project. Sometimes, reflecting on evidence leads to a new analysis of a situation that pushes inquiry in a new direction. Sometimes, the analysis of practice architectures that enable and constrain an existing practice directs efforts towards ways to change, or to work around, existing plans or policies or procedures, rather than changes to the practice itself.

In our view, critical participatory action research is not a 'method' or 'technique' for making change; instead, it involves participants in making a broad social analysis of their situation (exploring the conditions that prefigure their practices) and a collective self-study of their practices to determine whether there is reason to transform the conduct and consequences of their practices through individual and collective efforts. This analysis frequently has a strong historical bent: participants ask themselves questions like "How did we get here?," "How did we come to see things this way?," "What got us into this situation?" and "How did these working conditions come about?" After reflecting on their answers to such questions, participants usually begin to articulate their concerns about "the way we do things around here," and, in particular, begin to explore ways they might be able to change their practices to confront and overcome three kinds of untoward consequences of their practices, identified by Kemmis et al. (2014, p. 5), when their practices are:

1. *irrational* because participants understand the conduct and consequences of their practices as unreasonable, incomprehensible, incoherent or contradictory, or more generally because the practice unreasonably limits the individual and collective self-expression of the people involved and affected by the practice;

2. *unsustainable* because the way the participants conduct their practices is ineffective, unproductive, or non-renewable either immediately or in the long term, or more generally because the practice unreasonably limits the individual and collective self-development of those involved and affected; or
3. *unjust* because the way participants relate to one another in the practice, and to others affected by their practice, serves the interests of some at the expense of others, or causes unreasonable conflict or suffering among them, or more generally because the practice unreasonably limits the individual and collective self-determination of those involved and affected.

We now explain in more detail the 'communicative action' in 'public spheres' and critical participatory action research as 'social practice'.

Communicative Action in Public Spheres

First we turn to the notion of communicative action, before outlining the meaning and characteristics of public spheres.

German philosopher Jürgen Habermas (1984, 1987) drew a distinction between *strategic action* and *communicative action*. Strategic (or instrumental) action is what people do when they deploy particular means (usually already known) to attain a purpose or end or goal (also usually known in advance). Examples are building a fence, teaching an algorithm and cooking a meal. These things produce 'external outcomes' – things in the real world. Communicative action is rather different. In communicative action, people interrupt what they are doing (frequently, a strategic action) to stop and think about what they are doing and why. They ask questions like "What is going on here?," "How did we get into this situation?," "Are things going as we hoped and expected?" and "How is this practice turning out for us, and for others involved and affected?"

People frequently decide to undertake critical participatory action research prompted by a shared concern about how things are going in the situation in which they find themselves. They may have noticed that something is amiss: for example, that their practices are producing unanticipated or unintended outcomes (like dissatisfactions felt by clients, or concerns about unsatisfactory working conditions for practitioners). Under such circumstances, they may want to discuss their concerns collectively, to try to understand how the situation they are in enables or constrains their practices in untoward ways, and to change their practices, their situation and the ways they understand both, towards collectively agreed outcomes. When they open a space to engage with each other in a genuine discussion about how things are going, they can agree to proceed through *communicative action*. According to Kemmis and McTaggart (2005), people engage in *communicative action* when they consciously and deliberately aim to reach:

1. *intersubjective agreement* about the language they are using to understand what is going on, as a basis for
2. *mutual understanding* about their points of view and perspectives (although they may mutually agree to continue seeing things differently), in order to achieve

3. an *unforced consensus about what to do* in the particular practical situation in which they find themselves.

They do so by interrupting what they are doing, to ask four particular kinds of questions (the four validity claims) about whether their understandings of what they are doing are:

a. *comprehensible* (and make sense);
b. *true* (in the sense of being accurate);
c. *sincerely held* (not deceptive) *and stated*; and
d. *morally right and appropriate* in the circumstances.

When they engage one another in communicative action, participants open up *communicative space*, a space in which they can freely play any of the roles of speaker, listener and observer, or freely leave the space. In the space, they identify and respond to shared concerns and decide on actions that could be taken to address their concerns, which might include changing their practices, their understandings of their practices, or the situations in which they find themselves. Through conversation in the mode of communicative action, participants generate *communicative power* (the power to act and to speak out together) and typically strengthen their *solidarity* with one another. Following Habermas (1996), we describe the kind of space created in such conversations as a *public sphere* (Kemmis et al., 2014). In our view, communicative action, constituted in public spheres, is at the heart of the social practice of critical participatory action research.

Based on our reading of Habermas (1996), Kemmis and McTaggart (2005) formulated ten key features of public spheres. We think that people collaborating in critical collaborative action research initiatives can use these ten features as guides to the ways they could relate to one another within the public sphere, as well as to others involved in or affected by their practices.

1. *Public spheres are constituted as actual networks of communication among actual participants.*
   This means that public spheres are made up of people who are in fact in conversation with one another; they are not just spaces of possibility, where people could perhaps, or in theory, meet one another. A public sphere could be conducted in virtual space (e.g., via a blog or chat room), but, in critical participatory action research, participants frequently meet face-to-face. In everyday life, and in organizations, most people are involved in many public spheres composed of friends, community members, colleagues or other individuals or groups.
2. *Public spheres are self-constituted, voluntary and autonomous.*
   Public spheres are not the creatures of organizations. They are self-constituted – they are constituted by the people who participate in them, not by bosses in an organization, for example. Voluntarism is an important feature of public spheres: people join them, and can leave them, voluntarily. Public spheres

are relatively autonomous in the sense that they are outside (or marginal or peripheral to) formal systems like the formal administrative systems of the state or organization, and outside formal systems of influence (like political parties, the press or lobby groups). When people get together voluntarily to explore and act on a particular problem or issue, they form a public sphere – public spheres usually form around a theme or felt concern.

3. *Public spheres come into existence in response to legitimation deficits.*
   Often, public spheres come into existence when people have doubts or concerns about how things are going, or when they perceive problems or unresolved issues about the legitimacy of particular ideas or perspectives, or about the legitimacy of plans, proposals, policies or laws, or particular practices or working conditions. These are examples of *legitimation deficits* – where people feel that things are "not quite right."

4. *Public spheres are constituted for communicative action and for public discourse.*
   Communication in public spheres is usually through face-to-face communication, but it can also include communications between or among participants who are unknown to one another or anonymous from the perspective of any one individual – digitally or via email, for example. The aim of communicative action in public spheres is to ensure that participants give themselves the best possible opportunity to recognize and acknowledge one another's understandings of the language they use, and their different perspectives on the situation at hand, so they can do their best to reach unforced consensus about what they should do in this moment, in the particular historical situation in which they find themselves.

5. *Public spheres are inclusive and permeable.*
   Public spheres are attempts to create communicative spaces that include not only the parties most obviously interested in and affected by decisions, but also other people who are involved or affected but sometimes excluded from discussion and decisions taken. When a communicative space deliberately excludes people, doubt arises as to whether it is in fact a *public* sphere. Public spheres thus tend to have weak and permeable boundaries between 'insiders' and 'outsiders'.

6. *In public spheres, people usually communicate in ordinary language.*
   People opening a communicative space that is intended to be a public sphere often aim to break down the barriers and hierarchies created when people use specialist discourses and bureaucratic and hierarchical modes of address. Because public spheres aim to be inclusive, conversation in them is frequently conducted in ordinary language.

7. *Public spheres presuppose communicative freedom.*
   In public spheres, people are free to occupy (or not occupy) the particular communicative roles of speaker, listener and observer, and they are free to withdraw from the communicative space of the discussion. This freedom, grounded in voluntary participation, gives public spheres a powerful kind of legitimacy.

8. *Public spheres generate communicative power.*
   Because they are voluntary and presuppose communicative freedom, public spheres constituted for public discourse generate communicative power – that is, because participants arrive at particular positions and viewpoints through communicative action and unforced consensus, the positions they arrive at command respect, and they also command respect of participants and of others who are not participants in the public sphere (even though these outsiders' respect is sometimes grudging). Agreements reached through public discourse in public spheres command respect not by virtue of obligation, but by intersubjective agreement, mutual understanding and unforced consensus about what to do – consensus reached by the force of better argument alone, without coercion. Communication in public spheres thus creates legitimacy in the strongest sense – the shared belief among participants that they can and do freely and authentically consent to the decisions, positions or viewpoints arrived at through their own participation in public discourse.

9. *Public spheres generally have an indirect, not direct, impact on social systems.*
   Since public spheres are self-constituted, voluntary and autonomous, they form 'alongside' the formal social structures of a community or the formal structures of an organization (even when they are entirely composed of people within the organization). Sometimes, however, participants in the public sphere find it difficult to escape the responsibilities they have in their roles within the organization. Since public spheres depend on communicative action, as distinct from the strategic action ordinarily associated with an organization as a system, however, participants must temporarily 'suspend' their system responsibilities if they are genuinely to participate in an open conversation about what is going on or how things are going in the organization. As a consequence of their standing 'alongside' the community or organization, public spheres thus have their influence *indirectly* rather than directly through social or organizational functions, roles, rules and hierarchies. Like voluntary groups and associations in civil society, they affect communities and organizations indirectly by changing the climate of debate, the ways things are thought about, and/or how situations are understood. They frequently suggest that alternative ways of doing things are possible and feasible, and show how to resolve problems, overcome dissatisfactions or address issues.

10. *Public spheres are often associated with social movements.*
    In practice, public spheres frequently arise in relation to the themes and issues addressed by wider social movements – like social movements responding to climate change, or abuses of human and civil rights, or domestic violence, or sexual harassment, or workplace conditions and relations. Frequently, a group within a community or an organization takes up such a theme, to explore how people within the organization, and the organization itself, might respond to it. As already indicated, in such cases, voluntary groupings of participants emerge in response to a legitimation deficit, or a shared sense that a problem has arisen and needs to be addressed.

Critical Participatory Action Research as a Social Practice

In this section we discuss the issues of participation in a public sphere, changing practices and practice architectures, critical participatory action research as a practice-changing practice, and as research within practice traditions.

Participating in a Public Sphere

There are three elements to 'participation' in critical participatory action research:

1. participation in the life and work of a local community or organization;
2. participation in the research process by which people identify and analyse problems, issues and shared concerns, collect evidence about how things are going, and reflect on the nature and consequences of their practices, understandings and situations; and
3. participation in public discourse in the public spheres in which these matters are explored, in the mode of communicative action, in which people strive for intersubjective agreement about the ideas and the language they use, mutual understanding of one another's perspectives, and unforced consensus about what to do.

Once a public sphere has formed around a shared felt concern, participants are in a position to engage in critical participatory action research. Establishing a public sphere is a necessary precondition for critical participatory action research. In public spheres, people establish relationships intended to allow them to think openly, respectfully and critically in open conversations that allow them to explore whether "the way we do things around here" (existing social practices) is (are) in fact rational and reasonable, productive and sustainable, and just and democratic. Such a communicative space enables those involved to explore whether there might be better ways to do things. Because "the ways we do things around here" are practices held in place by familiar forms of talking, thinking, doing and relating, participants in critical participatory action research are aware that they may need to change the ways their current practices are constituted if they are to reconstitute their practices and thus avoid reproducing the world as they currently know it.

Changing Practices and Practice Architectures

Kemmis, McTaggart et al. (2014), following Kemmis and Grootenboer (2008) and Kemmis, Wiulkinson et al. (2014), describe how practices are held in place by *practice architectures*: combinations of cultural-discursive, material-economic and social–political arrangements that enable and constrain how a practice can unfold. Practice architectures prefigure social practices, channelling them in their course in the way that the bed and banks of a river channel its flow. Changing a practice, these authors contend, generally also requires disrupting or changing the practice architectures that prefigure it: changing the cultural-discursive arrangements that shape how the practice unfolds in semantic space, the material-economic arrangements that shape how it unfolds in physical space-time and the social–political arrangements that shape how it unfolds in social space.

Recently, Kemmis (2018) defined a practice as:

> a form of human action in history, in which particular activities (doings) are comprehensible in terms of particular ideas and talk (sayings), and when the people involved are distributed in particular kinds of relationships (relatings), and when this combination of sayings, doings and relatings 'hangs together' in the project of the practice (the ends and purposes that motivate the practice). (pp. 2–3)

This definition of practice encompasses practices at a variety of scales, from large-scale phenomena, through medium-level cases of the conduct of practices, to the moment-by-moment talk and interaction that unfold in practices as they are performed. Examples of large scales of practices are: medicine, history, education or automobility. Below that scale are things like: administering chemotherapy, consulting primary sources in an archive, teaching physics to high schoolers or driving from home to work. And at a still more granular level, there are performances like checking the dosage, making a photocopy of a document, answering a question in a high-school physics class and applying the brake before approaching a corner. We should note that critical participatory action research is itself a practice within this definition, and that it embodies within it a variety of other practices at a variety of scales (like proposing an initial design for a project, collecting evidence, using a GoPro camera to record a class at work, analysing a transcript and answering a question about an interpretation of the evidence).

As already intimated, the sayings, doings and relatings that compose a practice, hanging together in the project of a practice, are made possible by practice architectures – conditions (arrangements) that make the practice possible. These conditions are not entirely *subjective*, at the disposal of the individuals who participate in a practice, but *intersubjective*. By this we mean that:

1. the *sayings* that occur in a practice are made possible by *cultural-discursive arrangements* found in or brought to a site, in the shared medium of *language*, and in a *semantic space* in which people encounter one another as *interlocutors*;
2. the *doings* that occur in a practice are made possible by *material-economic arrangements* found in or brought to a site, in the shared medium of *activity* or *work*, and in *physical space-time* in which people encounter one another as *embodied beings*; and
3. the *relatings* that occur in a practice are made possible by *social-political arrangements* found in or brought to a site, in the shared medium of *solidarity* and *power*, and in a *social space* in which people encounter one another as *social beings*.

For example, if we observe the practices that unfold after dinner and bath, as two-and-a-half-year-old Giles prepares – and is prepared – for bed, we see him ask (*sayings*) for a bedtime story, approximating or using words (*cultural-discursive arrangements* in the medium of *language*) that his parents recognize as appropriate to the situation, in a shared communicative space (*semantic space*) in which Giles and his parents encounter one another as *interlocutors*. We see Giles going to the bookshelf and taking down four books (*doings*); the book-shelf, the books, the fleecy rug on the floor that Giles and his parents occupy, and the time taken for this activity (among the *material-economic arrangements* in the medium of *activity*) help compose the space and time as a bedtime read-ing session (in *physical space-time*), in which Giles climbs onto Mother's lap as Father sits close alongside, and – if things go well – all are keenly aware of the warmth of their mutual encounter as *embodied beings* as all their eyes fall on the current page. Repeated with variations (sometimes successful, sometimes not) each evening, Giles and his parents now enter the special relationship (*relat-ings*) of the bedtime reading space, one which is especially charged by the reas-surance of *solidarity* (which may be replaced, should things go awry, with an exercise of parental *power*) that is the precursor to Giles's being put into bed and making the transition from the conviviality of family to feeling secure in a cosy bed while Mum and Dad return to the living room (a transition from one *social space* to another) – a moment in which all participants are acutely aware that they exist not as atomistic individuals but as *social beings* and as creatures existentially bound together in this family.

Like the practice architectures of Giles's bedtime story, practice architectures *prefigure* (Schatzki, 2002) practices without determining them. As the practice of bedtime reading suggests, however, practices and the practice architectures that enable and constrain them vary from occasion to occasion, so people adjust their practices to meet changed conditions, and as conditions themselves change. Rivers slowly erode their beds and banks; a fallen tree or boulder may also change the flow of the river. Similarly practices and practice architectures change, both in relation to one another, and as practitioners and conditions change. Chang-ing practices requires more than changing participants' knowledge about prac-tices; it also requires changing the conditions – the practice architectures – that make their practices possible. To have new practices, with new sayings, doings and relatings, we must also have new practice architectures to support them: new cultural-discursive arrangements, new material-economic arrangements and new social–political arrangements. Only when new practice architectures are in place can new practices survive.

Critical Participatory Action Research As a Practice-Changing Practice

Critical participatory action research is a practice whose aim is to change other practices that compose work and lives in communities and organizations – such as practices of social work, primary health care, management, banking, farm-ing, fishing, automobility, consumption of power, preservation of biodiversity and helping babies get to sleep. In this sense, Kemmis (2009) described it as 'a practice-changing practice.'

Critical participatory action research aims to change not only practitioners' practices, but also their understandings of their practices, and the situations in which they practise (including the practice architectures that shape them). None of these three is prior to the others; all are constantly in interplay with one another. Thus, critical participatory action research aims to create conditions in which participants can engage in communicative action in public discourse in public spheres to explore the ways that local practices (the ways we do things around here), participants' local understandings and the local conditions of practice shape and reshape one another.

Thus, through critical participatory action research, participants in a public sphere aim to analyse, explore, and, where appropriate, transform:

1. the particular *sayings* (and ideas, and narratives, and perspectives) that inform their practice, and the ways these are made possible by the particular, local *cultural-discursive arrangements* (or new ways of thinking) found in or brought to their site, in their shared medium of *language*, and in the *semantic spaces* in which participants and others affected by the practice encounter one another as *interlocutors* here in this site;
2. the particular *doings* (and activities, and patterns of work and life) that animate their practice, and the ways these are made possible by the particular, local *material-economic arrangements* (or new ways of doing things) found in or brought to their site, in their shared medium of *activity* or *work*, and in *physical space-time* in which people encounter one another as *embodied beings* here in this site; and
3. the particular *relatings* that are enacted in their practice, and the ways these are made possible by the particular, local *social-political arrangements* (or new ways of relating to others) found in or brought to their site, in their shared medium of *solidarity* and *power*, and in the *social spaces* in which people encounter one another as *social beings* here in this site.

The point of these transformations, it will be recalled, is not change for change's sake. On the contrary, when participants in a public sphere respond in the form of critical participatory action research to a shared concern, a felt dissatisfaction or a legitimation deficit, it is usually in order to overcome or ameliorate the unreasonableness or irrationality, the unproductiveness or unsustainability or the injustices or undemocratic character of the conduct and consequences of practices as they are currently enacted in the setting. It is for reasons of these kinds that critical participatory action research is a practice-changing practice.

The 'research' part of critical participatory action research consists in gathering *evidence* of whether and how our practices, our understandings of our practices, and the conditions under which we practise are becoming more rational and reasonable, more productive and sustainable and more just and democratic – as we consider whether we may need to change, as we begin to make the change and observe its effects, and when we come to the conclusion that the change has overcome or ameliorated the problems or issues we set out to address.

Critical Participatory Action Research as Research Within Practice Traditions

We have proposed (Kemmis, McTaggart et al., 2014), that critical participatory action researchers study practices from 'within a practice tradition'. Researching a practice from within a practice tradition means standing alongside (other) practitioners to make or remake the practice by doing it differently. These authors then suggest that doing critical participatory action research is unlike other traditions of social science in which the researcher stands outside the practice and the tradition that informs it, in a third-person ('them') or even second-person ('you') relationship with those whose work constitutes the practice and the tradition.

Rather, the critical participatory action researcher stands within the tradition – formed through the history of the practice – in the first-person singular ('I', 'me') and plural ('we') location of the practitioner who is part of the community of practitioners of the practice. Further, we argue, the critical participatory action researcher works less like many conventional social science researchers who seek an 'objective' and 'external' perspective on the social worlds they study, and they work more like a *historian*, to write the local history of the practice and the tradition of which they are part, and to document how it changes in the light of the efforts of the public sphere of participants working to make the practice less unreasonable or irrational, less unproductive or unsustainable or less unjust or undemocratic. The particular kind of historian we have in mind is one who aims to write a critical history of what needed changing, how people worked to make changes they thought might be for the better, and how things turned out, and to write this history from the perspective of a participant who stands among and alongside other participants also committed to making changes in their practices, their understandings of their practices and the situations in which they practise.

Conclusion

We have argued that critical participatory action research is a social practice, guided by particular views of participation, the nature of social practice and the relationship between research and practice. It arises when potential participants sense a lack of legitimacy in their work and lives. Participants come together with shared concerns in public spheres with the aim of communicative action – conducting critical participatory research and contesting irrationality, unsustainability and injustice — towards mutually agreed goals and in pursuit of their common good.

Topics for Discussion

1. What are the features that make *critical* participatory action research different from participatory action research?

2. The authors have re-defined what 'participation' means in critical participatory action research, from "participation in the action being studied" to
   "participation in a public sphere which is exploring what is going on in the
   action, and what the consequences are." What do you think might be gained
   or lost from this shift of focus?
3. The authors take a more theoretical perspective on what is the 'action' in
   'action research', seeing it instead in terms of 'practice'. From your perspective, and your understanding, is this view of practice helpful?
4. The authors take a particular view on the kind of 'research' they have in mind
   in critical participatory action research. Is their view of research too narrow,
   or is it more liberating, in terms of what action researchers can or should do
   in action research?

Further reading

Kemmis, S., & McTaggart, R. (2005). Participatory action research: Communicative action
    and the public sphere. In N. Denzin & Y. Lincoln (Eds.), *Handbook of qualitative
    research* (3rd ed., pp. 559–604). Thousand Oaks, CA: Sage.
Kemmis, S., McTaggart, R., & Nixon, R. (2014). *The action research planner: Doing critical
    participatory action research*. Singapore: Springer.
McTaggart, R. (Ed.). (1997). *Participatory action research: International contexts and
    consequences*. Albany, NY: State University of New York Press.

References

Carr, W., & Kemmis, S. (1986). *Becoming critical: Education, knowledge and action research*.
    London: Falmer.
Fals Borda, O. (1979). Investigating reality in order to transform it: The Colombian experi-
    ence. *Dialectical Anthropology*, *4*, 33–55.
Habermas, J. (1984). *Theory of communicative action, Volume I: Reason and the rationaliza-
    tion of society* (Trans. T. McCarthy). Cambridge, Polity.
Habermas, J. (1987). *Theory of communicative action, Volume II: Lifeworld and system:
    A critique of functionalist reason* (Trans. T. McCarthy). Boston, MA: Beacon.
Habermas, J. (1996). *Between facts and norms: Contributions to discourse theory of law and
    democracy* (Trans. W. Rehg). Boston, MA: MIT Press.
Kemmis, S. (2009). Action research: A practice-changing practice. *Educational Action
    Research Journal*, *17*(3), 463–474.
Kemmis, S. (2018). Educational research and the good for humankind: Changing education
    to secure a sustainable world. Keynote address at the *Seminar 'Education, Fatherland
    and Humanity'* held on the occasion of the fiftieth anniversary of the foundation of
    the Finnish Institute for Educational Research, University of Jyväskylä, Finland,
    June 7. Retrieved from https://ktl.jyu.fi/en/current/news/180524-ed-research-and-
    the-good_23.pdf
Kemmis, S., & Grootenboer P. (2008). *Developing praxis: Challenges for education*.
    Rotterdam: Sense.
Kemmis, S., & McTaggart, R. (Eds.). (1988). *The action research planner* (3rd ed., substan-
    tially revised). Geelong: Deakin University Press.

Kemmis, S., & McTaggart, R. (2005). Participatory action research: Communicative action and the public sphere. In N. Denzin & Y. Lincoln (Eds.), *Handbook of qualitative research* (3rd ed., pp. 559–604). Thousand Oaks, CA: Sage.

Kemmis, S., McTaggart, R., & Nixon, R. (2014). *The action research planner: Doing critical participatory action research*. Singapore: Springer.

Kemmis, S., Wilkinson, J., Edwards-Groves, C., Hardy, I., Grootenboer, P., & Bristol, L. (2014). *Changing practices, changing education*. Singapore: Springer.

Schatzki, T. R. (2002). *The site of the social: A philosophical account of the constitution of social life and change*. University Park, PA: University of Pennsylvania Press.

Chapter 13

PALAR: Participatory Action Learning and Action Research for Community Engagement

Lesley Wood

Chapter Outline

This chapter provides a rationale for participatory Action Learning and Action Research (PALAR) as my preferred approach for achieving sustainable social change in communities with complex needs. Findings from PALAR projects continue to show how learning and action, when embedded within a participatory action research paradigm, lead to co-creation of knowledge and practical outcomes that are beneficial for communities. At the same time, use of PALAR in community contexts enables universities to advance an engaged scholarship agenda that contributes to a common good. In this chapter, I illustrate how a PALAR approach has been applied in community–university partnerships in the context of a developing country, South Africa. In sharing these examples, I demonstrate key features of PALAR, which both align with and distinguish it from other genres of action research. I discuss both the benefits and challenges of implementing a PALAR approach.

Introduction

There is no denying that we live in a fast-changing world on all levels. How we communicate, how we travel, how we work, how we define social institutions such as the family, how we understand health and wellbeing, how we learn – all these have changed dramatically over recent years and naturally will continue to change going forward. Yet, the way we do education, particularly schooling and higher education, does not seem to have undergone the same rapid transformation. We are still doing education and educational research within a system that was developed to supply the nineteenth century industrialized societies with the human resources to make meaningful contributions to a tightly controlled

Action Learning and Action Research: Genres and Approaches, 193–206
Copyright © 2019 by Lesley Wood
All rights of reproduction in any form reserved
doi:10.1108/978-1-78769-537-520191017

capitalist economy. We are no longer living in such times, and the challenges we face as a human race have become increasingly complex and 'wicked', requiring us, as educators (in all senses), to think, teach and work differently. But although our research speaks to the need to transform, substantive changes seem difficult to attain.

However, recent years have seen universities, as publicly funded institutions, beginning to embrace the challenge of responding to the lived needs of the communities they serve (Fitzgerald, Bruns, Sonka, Furco, & Swanson, 2016). Community education is becoming an increasingly popular area of research (Purcell & Beck, 2010; Reid, Gill, & Sears, 2010; Rogers, 2007; Schutz, 2010; Schutz & Sandy, 2011; Tett & Fife, 2010). Worldwide, research institutions are investigating how community mobilization can lead to deep learning (Cammarota & Fine, 2008; Ginwright, Noguera, & Cammarota, 2006; Kgobe, Baatjes, & Sotuku, 2012; Warren & Mapp, 2011) about community problems and solutions through the use of participatory and community-based Action Research. The primary purpose of community education is to respond to people's own concerns and to create a shared, active and political space for learning and development (Tett & Fyfe, 2010). For such spaces to be created, particularly in societies where people have been colonized and oppressed, requires a research approach that works to restore participants' feelings of worth, foregrounds their previously silenced voices, and helps them to develop both personal and technical skills. However, not only community participants are in need of transforming their thinking; university-based researchers also need to learn how to create authentic, educative and mutually beneficial relationships to generate learning and development at both theoretical and practical levels (Wood, 2017). I have found participatory action learning and action research (PALAR) to be a useful research approach to attain such outcomes.

PALAR: More Than Just a Methodology

Zuber-Skerritt (2018), the originator of the PALAR concept, refers to participatory action learning and action research as "a special kind of action research that integrates various concepts and processes, including lifelong learning, collaborative action learning, participatory action research, and action leadership" (p. 3). In previous chapters of this book, she and other authors have provided succinct explanations of lifelong learning (Chapter 3); action learning (Chapter 2); action research (Chapter 6); action learning and action research (Chapter 5) and participatory action research (PAR) (Chapter 12). I will not reiterate these explanations, but focus here on what features of PALAR make it my preferred genre of action research for community–university engagement. Although PALAR is discussed in this chapter as a conceptual framework for community-based research, it is an equally powerful and successful approach for professional development in organizational and institutional settings (see, e.g., Zuber-Skerritt, Fletcher, & Kearney, 2015; Zuber-Skerritt & Louw, 2014; Zuber-Skerritt, Wood, & Louw, 2015) and for student learning (Cameron, 2013; Cameron & Allen, 2013; Schiller, Jaffray, Ridley, & Du Plessis, 2018).

As leader of an entity for community-based educational research in my institution in South Africa, I was influenced by the thinking of Odora-Hoppers and Richards (2012) who suggest we need to rethink schooling, higher education, research and community-based learning to enable multi-paradigmatic, multi-epistemic, place-relevant learning and knowledge generation. Community-based research and education, which embodies these characteristics, is thus an important component of an engaged scholarship (Zuber-Skerritt, Wood, & Louw, 2015) where teaching, research and community-engagement all inform each other, rather than being approached as separate projects.

However, community education has to be community-driven, meaning that those at whom it is aimed should be the determiners of what they want to learn and why (Baatjes & Chaka, 2012). Programs should be socially driven and linked to actual local issues, rather than a centralized and standardized curriculum. Community-based research, approached in this way, can address social justice issues that impede learning and development. Baatjes and Chaka (2012) argue that "active participatory citizenship" (p. 12) enables people to participate in social, economic and civic learning – in other words, participation in itself is educative. Seen in this light, participation is a process of empowerment and development.

Policy in South Africa (e.g., Department of Arts, Culture, Science and Technology (DACST), 1996; Medium Term Strategic Framework (MTSF), 2009) stresses the need to increase scientific and technical expertise in the country. While this is an admirable aim, it is unrealistic given the South African context. Millions of people lack access to quality basic education, not to mention further and higher education, and so require foundational skills as well as guidance on developing personal viability (Teare, 2013). Training in technical skills is of course needed, but without simultaneous development of personal characteristics (e.g., integrity, social conscience, moral framework, intrinsic motivation, self-directed learning, self-discipline), people are unlikely to sustain change or use the skills to benefit themselves, their families and the community in the long term. I agree with Teare (Chapter 3) that what is needed is a conceptual framework to enable universities to partner with governmental and/or non-governmental agencies and communities, to initiate and sustain a learning system that enables people, and specifically those living in economic and social adversity, to discover and develop their talents together with like-minded people, become self-confident, self-directed and self-sufficient, and then cascade what they have learned to help others.

It is no longer enough for people to learn to know: they have to learn how to live in relation to others in this fast-changing world, in a way that promotes the good of all. The ability to think like an entrepreneur is a twenty-first century skill that everyone needs, whether in formal employment or self-employment (Bridgstock, 2009). This requires individuals to develop social, emotional, moral, spiritual, cognitive and behavioural competences to help them adapt to the needs of a changing and challenging environment, in addition to learning technical skills. This approach to education is echoed by the emerging ideas on how we can educate to prepare people for the fourth industrial revolution (Industrie 4.0), where lifelong learning and learning to play a better role in society will become the most important skills to master (Fisk, 2017). We need to develop Education 4.0

to match the advances in technology, and some of the key features of such an education are learning to learn with and from other people, being able to determine what you need to learn to improve your life (rather than following standardized curricula), and finding mentors to support you. Community education thus has to move away from an 'intervention' approach, where a project is envisaged, implemented and evaluated by 'experts'; the project inevitably comes to an end, and often the change stops there too when the university researchers have generated enough data to write their research outputs. We need an approach to research that brings about ontological and epistemological change, not only for community participants, but just as importantly, for academia itself.

I am not advocating that everyone should adopt PALAR as a methodology, but rather that we have to be open to alternative approaches to learning and development and value their worth as educative processes and sources of knowledge generation fit for our twenty-first century world. PALAR is not just a methodology that can be applied by any researcher. It requires personal acceptance of, and commitment to living out, all the principles, values and paradigms that underpin it. As Zuber-Skerritt (2015) explains, "PALAR is conceived as a philosophy, a methodology, a theory of learning, and as a facilitation process for community engagement" (p. 5). The complexity of the PALAR process renders it an apt conceptual framework for thinking about the complex and multi-faceted business of community engagement in contexts of severe social, psychological, historical and economic adversity. Of course, these different features of PALAR all overlap to some extent, but I discuss them below separately for purposes of clarity.

PALAR As a Philosophy or Paradigm

As Kuhn (1970) pointed out, how we understand the world is determined by what knowledge we are exposed to and at certain times scientific thinking undergoes what he termed 'paradigm shifts'. As argued earlier in this chapter, the time is ripe for such a shift in education and educational research, to align it with current educational paradigms. Futurists tell us that the prevalent political, social and economic paradigms of the world are changing, requiring us to find ways of generating theory through research that takes the complexity of the world into account. Paradigm shifts occur continually – for example, the world now refutes colonial practices (at least from a geographical perspective), that at one time were accepted as 'right' and 'just' by the majority of Western countries.

PALAR, like critical PAR (Chapter 12) is grounded in a transformative paradigm. According to Jackson et al. (2018), "The transformative paradigm is a research framework that centres the experiences of marginalized communities, includes analysis of power differentials that have led to marginalization, and links research findings to actions intended to mitigate disparities" (p. 111). PAR is grounded in this quest for social justice and improving the quality of life for all (Kemmis, McTaggart, & Nixon, 2013; Torre, Fine, Stoudt, & Fox, 2012), as we now realize we share a world with shrinking resources. Rather than viewing academic, 'scientific' knowledge as the only knowledge that is valid and valuable,

PALAR is concerned with the relations between people and their social environments and thus it values local knowledge. Through the promotion of critical consciousness (Freire, 1970) and inclusion, people are more likely to participate and learn how to improve their own lives through developing capabilities (Sen, 2017) and personal integrity, as well as acquiring technical skills and knowledge (Teare, 2013). As Wood (forthcoming) says:

> In PALAR we ask questions about *why* it is important to involve people in improving their own circumstances; *how* this can be done in ways that result in sustainable outcomes, and *who* should be involved in establishing collaborative partnerships and processes; *what* impact does the application of PALAR have on quality of life in contexts of learning and development, in addition to generating theory about specific issues?

PALAR, as a paradigm, is based on the understanding that sustainable learning and development should be transformative (Strand, 2000) to facilitate social change at systemic and structural levels. A transformative paradigm promotes preventative action towards social justice by viewing structural and intersectional disadvantage as the problem (Aziz, Shams, & Khan, 2011; Burns, Harvey, & Ortiz Aragón, 2013), rather than viewing the individual or group as deficient in some way. This requires a radical paradigm shift by most academic researchers who have been 'trained' to believe that research needs to be objective, value-free and controlled in order to be valid. Excerpts like the following from a doctoral candidate's reflections are common at the start of a PALAR journey, as researchers trained in more traditional approaches struggle to change their paradigms:

> PALAR process is so different from the research that I read about, even the more post-positivist methodology experts still expect conformity to the existing research protocols. I definitely want to do the PhD research and I am so grateful to have a PALAR researcher as my promoter, but do I have the strength to convince the experts that this alternative way is empirically valid? I foresee so many questions and challenges when interacting with the experienced researchers. I just want to do my thing and not need to keep justifying it along the way to people who just would not want to understand anyway. (RS, 9/2014)

The paradigm shift needs to happen not only on the part of the researcher, but also among community members who generally have been colonized into thinking their knowledge is inferior to that of university researchers. In a country like South Africa, this sense of inferiority has been ingrained over centuries, first with colonialism and then with Apartheid, and profound, systemic problems have meant power relations are deeply entrenched in race, class, gender and language hierarchies (Nhamo, 2012). For this reason, the methodological process of PALAR is especially apt as it foregrounds action learning within the PAR process to create dialogical spaces where power relations can be minimized through the development of trusting *relationships*, critical *reflection* on on-going interaction and *recognition* of all levels and forms of learning and development.

PALAR As a Theory of Learning

The question then becomes: How can people in the most disadvantaged communities learn how to improve their lives in a way that is sustainable? Community education should be organic; what it is and how it is done should stem from the community and not be imposed on it by external experts. Communities hold within themselves vast repositories of local knowledge – they know what the issues are, which responses are likely to work and which will not; they are in tune with local values, cultures, practices and politics. To ensure the necessary participation of people in their own learning, we have to create democratic spaces for learning; use pedagogies that foster action learning; and be open to multiple views. Through democratic learning (Allman, 2001) we can enable people to develop activism and agency to improve their own lives. A concise explanation of action learning has been given elsewhere in this book (e.g., Chapters 2 and 5).

Within PALAR, the formation of a core research team as an action learning set is fundamental to enable a collaborative and iterative approach to solving real-life problems by those involved, with a view to implementing change and reflecting upon the results to inform future actions. The action learning set is at the heart of the PALAR process, and it is in this safe, democratic and inclusive space that all participants learn many important skills to not only improve the practical problems they are addressing, but also to foster personal development on many levels. As with all action research, the intent is not only to effect practical change, but also to emancipate participants, both community and university-based, from imposed and self-imposed thinking that blinds them to other possibilities, paradigms and opportunities, while generating useful theories about the issue under investigation (Ledwith, 2017). Formal education at all levels tends to develop content knowledge and technical skills, rather than foster lifelong, self-directed learning. It is only when people master this skill that they can decide what learning is relevant to them and learn how to flourish as individuals and in community with others (Walker, 2006).

To break the vicious circle created by poverty, unemployment and inequality, people need to develop holistically. Many community skills-training programs have provided contract work and stipends for people in South Africa, but the money they receive helps only in the short-term. Without knowledge of how to best use their new-found skills to improve their circumstances, any long-term improvement in quality of life is unlikely. PALAR is based on the assumption that community education has to start from participatory understandings of life-long learning and development and it is designed to cultivate this.

PALAR As a Methodology

There appear to be different understandings of the concept of methodology in the literature (Swain, 2016). I understand it as being synonymous with research design, which encompasses how participants are recruited, how data is generated and analysed, and what methods are in place to ensure validity of the findings. Research textbooks argue that the research question determines the choice of design, but the type of questions we ask is influenced by our paradigmatic assumptions. With PALAR, the transformative and participatory paradigm cannot be separated from the design, as perhaps is the case in more objective, traditional forms of research. Zuber-Skerritt (2015) states, "PALAR is not static; it is an on-going, emergent genre in the large family of action research" (p. 3). This dynamic nature means that the design can be adapted for different contexts, as long as it remains true to the foundational principles and values of critical action research. The PALAR research design was originally conceived by Zuber-Skerritt within the context of higher education and also for organizational development purposes. She, with others, then began to apply it within the field of community engagement. Over the last few years, myself and colleagues have adapted it slightly to suit our specific South African context. The next sections explain briefly the PALAR design, as we have been using it as a form of community-based research.

Developing Partnerships. The PALAR process encourages democratic, mutually rewarding partnerships between members of the academy and external communities (Wood & Zuber-Skerritt, 2013). However, given the context in which we work, where the social, educational and economic gap between the university researchers and the community participants is perhaps wider than in the global north, I have found that gaining entry into the community can be a long and intricate process. Many protocols have to be observed before a project is allowed to commence. For example, in rural communities the tribal hierarchy means that the chief has to approve the project, and often he, or his officers, will decide who may join the core project team. In more urban communities, there are politically affiliated ward councillors who may have to approve the project and their goodwill and support are essential to the success of any partnership. I have also partnered with agencies that are registered with the government but lack the leadership and capacity to carry out their intended programs, and time has to be spent in first helping them to establish functionality. The forming of the action learning set is thus complicated and can take considerable time and energy.

Developing Working Relationships and a Shared Focus. Once the action learning set is formed, then its members can start crafting their vision for the project, building relationships, relating their vision to the context, deciding on roles and responsibilities and how to work together, setting broad research goals and negotiating an ethical contract. This process is outlined in Fig. 13.1. Although the process remains the same, we changed the language from a business to an education discourse.

Although the process may seem straightforward, we have to constantly reflect on the question of how our ascribed positions of power and (white) middle-class privilege may hamper the participation of people who do not usually self-identify as knowledge producers. We have to work hard to ensure that issues such as language (often three or more different languages are represented) and lack of confidence do not hamper the forming of trusting, inclusive relationships. Where Zuber-Skerritt (2011) recommends doing this work in a five-day start-up workshop,

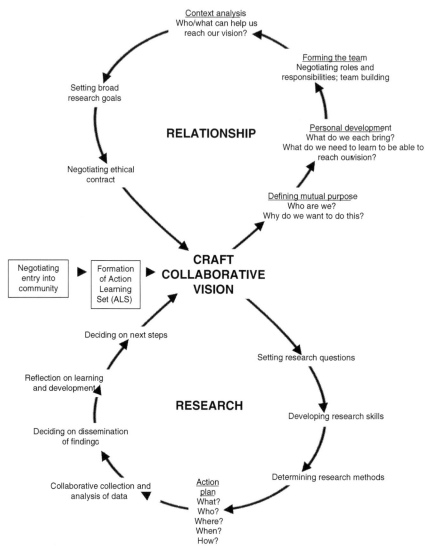

Fig. 13.1:   The PALAR Process.

in a location away from participants' normal environment, in practice it is difficult for participants to take five days out of their family commitments. We therefore have to spread the start-up workshop over several sessions, meaning that we often have to repeat aspects as people may not be able to attend all the sessions.

We have also found that it is crucial to spend time on negotiating ethical expectancies. The usual, and in my opinion inadequate, ethical procedures do not require exploration of the expectations of community members, but merely that we (researchers) inform them what we expect of them. For example, in one project, community members of the action learning set decided that, since the knowledge generated belonged to them also, they wanted to be paid for sharing their learning with the academic researchers during project evaluation. They had previously signed an ethical consent form consenting to sharing of information, but we had not envisioned this request and so could not accommodate it. I learnt that we need to spend considerable time discussing ethical issues, both at the beginning of the project and throughout, as people develop the ability to think critically and become more aware of their choices – which is the aim of PALAR after all.

Conducting the Research. Fig. 13.1 is akin to an infinity sign; it is continuous, meaning that the work contained in the upper circle never ceases, as members shift their focus to the cycles of reflection and action in the practice phase. The community members learn experientially how to conduct research as the group sets research questions, determines methods of data generation and implements the action plan. The methods used in PALAR projects are predominantly qualitative, but quantitative data generation strategies can be used to triangulate findings or provide evidence of change (Kearney, Wood, & Zuber-Skerritt, 2013). Data is analysed within the group to find answers to the research questions, but the university-based researchers can also analyse it from a theoretical perspective for their purposes. The base primary criterion for quality and reliability is 'authenticity', meaning that research results are valid if they are confirmed by the participants as being of benefit (Herr & Anderson, 2005). For this design to be effective, the quality of facilitation in the action learning set is paramount.

PALAR As a Facilitation Process

The centrality of the action learning set to the success of a PALAR project makes it imperative that university-based researchers are able to facilitate to create democratic, inclusive and productive spaces for dialogue. This is one of the main challenges of PALAR, particularly outside of fields like psychology, social work or community-development, because researchers, in general, have never been required to learn how to conduct effective group facilitation and to reflect on their influence within the group. To assist my postgraduate students in learning how to do this, I used the characteristics of PALAR, identified by Zuber-Skerritt (2009) as the 'seven Cs and three Rs' as a means of reflecting on their facilitation of a PALAR process (see Table 13.1).

For most who embark on a PALAR study, learning how to engage in dialogue with people from different backgrounds and life experiences is a valuable and life-changing experience. In South Africa there still are clear divisions along racial and gender lines. Under Apartheid, race was ranked in strict order, with Black on the lowest rung, followed by Coloured, Indian, Asian and White at the top and status was ascribed accordingly (Wood & McAteer, 2017). In both Afrikaner and non-Western cultures, women are ascribed a lesser status and younger people are not accorded the same respect as elders (Wamba, 2016). Although the South African

Table 13.1: An Example of a Template to Guide Critical Reflection on the PALAR Process.

The 7 Cs of PALAR for character building	Consider the following questions: "How well am I living out these characteristics in my project?," "What successes/challenges do I encounter?," "What do I need to change in my thinking and acting?" and "How can I improve these aspects?"
Communication	*How dialogical, how symmetrical and how inclusive is my communication?*
Commitment	*How committed am I to the project, the participants and the outcome?*
Competence	*As facilitator of the process, and as researcher, what do I need to learn?*
Compromise	*How willing am I to listen to other points of view and reach mutual agreement?*
Critical reflection	*How do my feelings, thoughts, motives and values impact the research process?*
Collaboration	*How collaborative is the process? What role do I and the participants play? Who holds the power at each stage?*
Coaching	*How directive am I? How can I improve my mentoring/facilitation skills?*
3 Rs	
Reflection	*How can I foster critical reflection on our own learning?*
Relationships	*How can I improve the research relationships?*
Recognition	*How do I recognize and value participants' achievements and learning?*

Source: Adapted from Wood, Seobi, Setlhare-Meltor, and Waddington (2015).

constitution no longer upholds such divisions, society is slow in transforming and many university-based researchers have never engaged on such an equal footing with people from our so-called townships and rural settings – and vice versa. Learning how to encourage the formation of a democratic and humanizing space for collaboration towards shared goals is of benefit to all, and is well worth the effort it takes to set up and sustain the action learning set through effective facilitation strategies.

Conclusion

This chapter has presented an argument for why PALAR is a suitable genre of action research for conducting community-based research in a developing country context. I have argued that PALAR is more than just a methodology: like all action research that operates from a transformative paradigm, it has a strong emancipatory and social justice intent. What makes it so suitable for enhancing university–community research partnerships is the foregrounding of action learning within an action learning set, which creates the space for explicit reflection on learning. Given the historical, economic and social divides due to our colonial history in South Africa, this learning is a necessary precursor to, and sustainer of, authentic participation of all in the design, implementation and evaluation of the project, as well as dissemination of the knowledge generated through the project. The key features of PALAR make it suitable for both community education and transforming the mindsets of university–based researchers to enhance the formation of mutually beneficial relationships for the common good. I hinted at some of the challenges emanating from trying to create authentic research partnerships between community participants who live in contexts of adversity and the relatively privileged academics who operate within rigid ethical and bureaucratic systems. Based on learning from the examples presented in the chapter, I conclude that more research is needed to: (1) address the need for capacity development for those who wish to embark on a PALAR project; (2) develop more appropriate ethical procedures for PALAR projects; and (3) find ways to recognize and certify the learning of community members without whose local knowledge such projects would not exist.

Topics for Discussion

1. What concerns do you have about conducting research using PALAR?
2. What skills/characteristics do you think you would need to improve in order to be able to conduct a PALAR project?
3. What ethical barriers exist in your institution to conducting participatory forms of research?
4. What ideas do you have for improving university procedures and processes to make it easier to conduct authentic, participatory research?

Further Reading

Kearney, J., Wood, L., & Zuber-Skerritt, O. (2013). Community-university partnerships using participatory action learning and action research (PALAR). *Gateways: International Journal of Community Research and Engagement*, 6(1), 113–130.

Wood, L., & Zuber-Skerritt, O. (2013). PALAR as a methodology for community engagement by faculties of education. *South African Journal of Education*, 33(4), 1–15.

Zuber-Skerritt, O. (2015). Participatory action learning and action research (PALAR) for community engagement: A theoretical framework. *Educational Research for Social Change*, 4(1), 5–25.

Zuber-Skerritt, O. (2018). An educational framework for participatory action learning and action research (PALAR). *Educational Action Research*, 26(4). Retrieved from https://doi.org/10.1080/09650792.2018.1464939

Zuber-Skerritt, O., & Teare, R. (2013). *Lifelong action learning for community development: Learning and development for a better world.* Rotterdam: Sense Publishers.

References

Allman, P. (2001). *Critical education against global capitalism: Karl Marx and revolutionary critical education.* Westport, CT: Greenwood Publishing Group.

Aziz, A., Shams, M., & Khan, K. (2011). Participatory action research as the approach for women's empowerment. *Action Research, 9*(3), 303–323.

Baatjes, I., & Chaka, T. (2012). *Imagining community and education training centres.* Retrieved from http://www.dhet.gov.za/Adult%20Education%20and%20Training%20Programs/CETC%20report%20-%20ANNEXURE%20C%20-%20Community%20Research.pdf

Bridgstock, R. (2009). The graduate attributes we've overlooked: Enhancing graduate employability through career management skills. *Higher Education Research & Development, 28*(1), 31–44.

Burns, D., Harvey, B., & Ortiz Aragón, A. O. (2013). Introduction: Action research for development and social change. *IDS Bulletin, 43*(3), 1–7.

Cameron, L. (2013, August). Participative action learning and action research (PALAR): Blending teaching and research. Paper presented at *Learning & Teaching Week: Blended learning: An agile response to a dynamic world,* University of the Sunshine Coast, Australia. Retrieved from https://www.usc.edu.au/media/1324188/LT_Program_2013.pdf

Cameron, L., & Allen, B. (2013). Achieving educational sustainability: A PALAR reflection of success. *ALAR: Action Learning and Action Research Journal, 19*(1), 135–162.

Cammarota, J., & Fine, M. (2008). *Revolutionizing education: Youth participatory action research in motion.* New York, NY: Routledge.

Department of Arts, Culture, Science and Technology (DACST). (1996). *White paper on science and technology: Preparing for the 21st century.* Pretoria: Government Printers.

Fisk, P. (2017). *Education 4.0 … the future of learning will be dramatically different, in school and throughout life.* Retrieved from https://www.thegeniusworks.com/2017/01/future-education-young-everyone-taught-together/

Fitzgerald, H. E., Bruns, K., Sonka, S. T., Furco, A., & Swanson, L. (2016). The centrality of engagement in higher education. *Journal of Higher Education Outreach and Engagement, 20*(1), 223–244.

Freire, P. (1970). *Pedagogy of the oppressed.* New York, NY: Continuum International Publishing.

Ginwright, S., Noguera, P., & Cammarota, J. (2006). *Beyond resistance! Youth activism and community change: New democratic possibilities for practice and policy.* New York, NY: Routledge.

Herr, K. G., & Anderson, G. L. (2005). *The action research dissertation: A guide for students and faculty.* New York, NY: Sage.

Jackson, K. M., Pukys, S., Castro, A., Hermosura, L., Mendez, J., Vohra-Gupta, S., … Morales, G. (2018). Using the transformative paradigm to conduct a mixed methods needs assessment of a marginalized community: Methodological lessons and implications. *Evaluation and Program Planning, 66,* 111–119.

Kearney, J., Wood, L., & Zuber-Skerritt, O. (2013). Community-university partnerships using participatory action learning and action research (PALAR). *Gateways: International Journal of Community Research and Engagement, 6,* 113–130.

Kemmis, S., McTaggart, R., & Nixon, R. (2013). *The action research planner: Doing critical participatory action research.* Singapore: Springer Science & Business Media.

Kgobe, M., Baatjes, I., & Sotuku, N. (2012). *Report of the community literacy and numeracy group project: 3Rs consortium.* Johannesburg: Centre for Education Policy Development.

Kuhn, T. (1970). Reflections on my critics. In I. Lakatos & A. Musgrave (Eds.), *Criticism and the growth of knowledge: Proceedings of the International Colloquium in the Philosophy of Science, London* (1965, Vol. *4*. pp. 231–278). Cambridge: Cambridge University Press.

Ledwith, M. (2017). Emancipatory action research as a critical living praxis: From dominant narratives to counter narrative. In L. Rowell, C. Bruce, J. Shosh, & M. Riel (Eds.), *The Palgrave international handbook of action research* (pp. 49–62). New York, NY: Palgrave Macmillan.

Medium-Term Strategic Framework (MTSF). (2009). *Guide to Government's Program for the Electoral Mandate Period 2009–2014*. Pretoria: Treasury.

Nhamo, G. (2012). Participatory action research as platform for community engagement in higher education. *Journal of Higher Education in Africa, 10*(1), 1–21.

Odora-Hoppers, C. A., & Richards, H. (2012). *Rethinking thinking: Modernity's "other" and the transformation of the university*. Pretoria: University of South Africa Press.

Purcell, R., & Beck, D. (2010). *Popular education practice for youth and community development work*. Exeter: Learning Matters.

Reid, A., Gill, J., & Sears, A. (2010). The forming of citizens in a globalizing world. In A. Reid, J. Gill, & A. Sears (Eds.), *Globalization, the nation-state and the citizen: Dilemmas and directions for civics and citizenship education* (pp. 3–16). New York, NY: Routledge.

Rogers, A. (2007). *Non-formal education: Flexible schooling or participatory education?* (Vol. 15). New York, NY: Springer Science & Business Media.

Schiller, U., Jaffray, P., Ridley, T., & Du Plessis, C. (2018). Facilitating a participatory action learning and action research process in a higher educational context. *Action Research, 33*(4), 1–15.

Schutz, A. (2010). *Social class, social action, and education: The failure of progressive democracy*. New York, NY: Palgrave Macmillan.

Schutz, A., & Sandy, M. (2011). *Collective action for social change: An introduction to community organizing*. New York, NY: Palgrave Macmillan.

Sen, A. (2017). Elements of a theory of human rights. In T. Brooks (Ed.), *Justice and the capabilities approach* (pp. 221–262). London: Routledge.

Strand, K. J. (2000). Community-based research as pedagogy. *Michigan Journal of Community Service Learning, 7*, 85–96.

Swain, J. (Ed.). (2016). *Designing research in education: Concepts and methodologies*. Thousand Oaks, CA: Sage.

Teare, R. (2013). Personal viability: The journey to self-reliance and financial independence. In O. Zuber-Skerritt & R. Teare (Eds.), *Lifelong action learning for community development: Learning and development for a better world* (pp. 99–132). Rotterdam: Sense Publishers.

Tett, L., & Fyfe, I. (2010). *Community education, learning and development* (3rd ed.). Edinburgh: Dunedin Academic Press.

Torre, M. E., Fine, M., Stoudt, B. G., & Fox, M. (2012). Critical participatory action research as public science. In H. Cooper, P. M. Camic, D. L. Long, A. T. Panter, D. Rindskopf, & K. J. Sher (Eds.), *APA handbook of research methods in psychology, Vol. 2. Research designs: Quantitative, qualitative, neuropsychological, and biological* (pp. 171–184). Washington, DC: American Psychological Association.

Walker, M. (2006). Towards a capability-based theory of social justice for education policy-making. *Journal of Education Policy, 21*(2), 163–185.

Wamba, N. G. (2016). The challenges of participation in doing community-based participatory action research: Lessons from the Kwithu Project. *Action Research, 15*(2), 198–213.

Warren, M. R., & Mapp, K. L. (2011). *A match on dry grass: Community organizing as a catalyst for school reform.* New York, NY: Oxford University Press.

Wood, L. (2017). Community development in higher education: How do academics ensure their community-based research makes a difference? *Journal of Community Development, 52*(4), 685–701.

Wood, L. (forthcoming). *Participatory action learning and action research:* Abingdon, Routledge.

Wood, L., & McAteer, M. (2017). Levelling the playing fields in PAR: The intricacies of power, privilege, and participation in a university–community–school partnership. *Adult Education Quarterly, 67*(4), 251–264.

Wood, L., Seobi, A., Setlhare-Meltor, R., & Waddington, R. (2015). Reflecting on reflecting: Fostering student capacity for critical reflection in an action research project. *Educational Research for Social Change, 4*(1), 79–93.

Wood, L., & Zuber-Skerritt, O. (2013). PALAR as a methodology for community engagement by faculties of education. *South African Journal of Education, 33*(4), 1–15.

Zuber-Skerritt, O. (2009). *Action learning and action research: Songlines through interviews.* Rotterdam: Sense Publishers.

Zuber-Skerritt, O. (2011). *Action leadership: Towards a participatory paradigm.* London: Springer Science & Business Media.

Zuber-Skerritt, O. (2015). Participatory action learning and action research (PALAR) for community engagement: A theoretical framework. *Educational Research for Social Change, 4*(1), 5–25.

Zuber-Skerritt, O. (2018). An educational framework for participatory action learning and action research (PALAR). *Educational Action Research, 26*(4), 514–532.

Zuber-Skerritt, O., Fletcher, M., & Kearney, J. (2015). *Professional learning in higher education and communities: Towards a new vision for action research.* London: Palgrave.

Zuber-Skerritt, O., & Louw, I. (2014). Academic leadership development programs: A model for sustained institutional change. *Journal of Organizational Change Management, 27*(6), 1008–1024.

Zuber-Skerritt, O., & Teare, R. (2013). *Lifelong action learning for community development: Learning and development for a better world.* Rotterdam: Sense Publishers.

Zuber-Skerritt, O., Wood, L., & Louw, I. (2015). *A participatory paradigm for an engaged scholarship in higher education.* Rotterdam: Sense Publishers.

Conclusion

Chapter 14

Reflections and Conclusions

Ortrun Zuber-Skerritt and Lesley Wood

Chapter Outline

This chapter reflects on and draws conclusions from the foregoing chapters. It affirms the book's main argument, introduced in the first chapter and illustrated throughout, that the Action Learning (AL) and Action Research (AR) paradigm is by its very nature evolutionary. The application of its core principles to most effectively identify and sustainably address shared concerns – through cycles of inclusive collaboration, planning, action and reflection – has inevitably given birth to the AL/AR family. The main genres discussed in this book illustrate this argument and highlight how the utility of the transformative participatory AL/AR paradigm for approaching large-scale as well as small-scale concerns will see the continuing creation of new genres. Because the evolution of many genres in the AL/AR family has led to some confusion and misuse of AL/AR as a methodology, this book has aimed to demystify the AL/AR paradigm. We therefore consider how the chapters speak collectively to the non-negotiables of this paradigm, and illustrate how, as long as the basic principles are adhered to, it can be usefully adapted and developed to facilitate the collaborative learning and shared democratic leadership required for contemporary research and development. We also present our critical self-reflections on preparing this book and insights into the AL/AR paradigm, with a model of the main principles and processes of AL/AR that all its genres share. We conclude with discussion of the book's contributions to knowledge.

Introduction

In true Action Learning (AL) and Action Research (AR) style, this concluding chapter reflects on this book – its content, its preparation and its contributions to knowledge. As editors, we return to the aims of this book as set out in our introductory Chapter 1, and consider whether and how these aims – primarily to demystify the AL/AR paradigm – have been achieved across the preceding chapters. We consider how the main genres discussed in this book illustrate our

Action Learning and Action Research: Genres and Approaches, 209–221
Copyright © 2019 by Ortrun Zuber-Skerritt and Lesley Wood
All rights of reproduction in any form reserved
doi:10.1108/978-1-78769-537-520191019

argument that the AL/AR paradigm is by its very nature evolutionary. The application of its core principles to most effectively identify and sustainably address shared concerns has inevitably given birth to the AL/AR family. We highlight how the utility of the AL/AR paradigm for approaching large and small concerns will see the continuing creation of new genres. By keeping to the basic principles of AL/AR, the paradigm can be usefully adapted and developed to facilitate the collaborative learning and shared democratic leadership required for contemporary research and development whatever its scale. On the basis of this discussion, we present our critical self-reflections on preparing this book, with a model of the main principles and processes shared by all the AL/AR genres. We share the insights we have developed into the AL/AR paradigm through meta-reflection on these reflections. We then conclude with discussion of the book's contributions to knowledge.

Meeting the Aims of This Book: Demystifying the AL/AR Paradigm

As we stated in Chapter 1, our main aim in preparing this book is to demystify AL and AR, not just by shedding light on the genres they have inspired, but also, particularly, by explaining their common paradigm. The AL/AR paradigm has emerged over the last few decades in many countries across the world as a challenge to prevailing paradigms in the social sciences. Those paradigms are generally informed by worldviews that see people as competing individuals rather than, or more than, cooperative/collaborative groupings or communities. These paradigms generally assess through measurement (of quantity) rather than evaluation (of quality). They usually depersonalize both what is to be researched/learned and the role of the researcher/learner, hence circumscribing, unselfconsciously, the type of knowledge these paradigms can be used to create or acquire. The worldview of the AL/AR paradigm sees through a different lens. It is phenomenological and so relies heavily on personal experience. Its understanding that people can live and work, learn and research *with* each other, and awareness that our role as researchers/learners inevitably shapes what we research/learn positions AL/AR outside these dominant paradigms.

Here lies a core problem for AL/AR, which often forces its advocates and users into defensive mode – and strengthens the imperative for us to create this 'demystifying' explanatory volume as a general guide to AL/AR's 'action' family and paradigm! Many in mainstream scholarship see the AL/AR family of learning and research as not just different, or even as an alternative approach well suited to particular learning/research tasks. They see it through a competitive lens, casting it as a threat to the dominant paradigms and therefore to be discredited or dismissed. AL/AR is indeed alternative to mainstream thinking. But when explained and illustrated it is not a mystery or necessarily a threat. To the contrary, when the principles of the paradigm are understood, AL/AR is easy to use, highly adaptable, and open to creative, developmental learning and research as the chapters in this volume make clear.

We understand the most effective way to demystify AL and AR is through a unified collection of primary works directly from the main originators, rather than producing secondary literature ourselves. That is why we have presented this inclusive overview of the most common genres by leaders in their fields explaining their ideas, personal theories, arguments, methods, processes and experiences themselves, so readers can hear these stories "from the horse's mouth." The chapters bring to light not only the distinctive features of each of the AL/AR genres discussed here. They also highlight what the genres share, that is, their roots in and adherence to the basic AL and AR principles that are epistemological (concerning knowledge), ontological (concerning being) and axiological (concerning value). In this way the chapters identify the paradigm's non-negotiable features: inclusion, participation, democratic processes, relationships, collaboration, action and reflection. We present in Table 14.1 the responses of chapter authors to our initial questions about key features of each genre. The table helpfully summarizes what each genre is and is not, its purposes, context and processes (See Table 14.1 on pp. 212–215).

The types of contemporary AL and AR discussed in this volume are different from traditional technical forms of action research conducted some decades back, which were influenced by the philosophical assumptions underpinning most research in the social sciences at the time. The epistemological, ontological and methodological assumptions shared by the AL/AR genres of today have evolved over time through experience, discussion and collaboration by practitioners as participants and co-researchers. Discussion of how AL/AR and its genres have continued to evolve over time attests to the evolutionary nature of the AL/AR paradigm.

Reaffirming the Argument: The Evolutionary Nature of the AL/AR Paradigm

Adaptability and development of the AL/AR paradigm takes us to this book's main argument about AL/AR, illustrated across the preceding chapters. It is that the AL/AR paradigm is by its very nature evolutionary. Application of its core principles to most effectively identify and sustainably address shared concerns – through cycles of inclusive collaboration, planning, action and reflection – has inevitably given birth to the AL/AR family. The main genres discussed in this book illustrate this argument well. They have revealed how visionary learners/researchers have responded to the paradigm's relative flexibility and encouragement to collaborate and discover, and in the process have extended AL/AR thinking (concepts) and action (practices) in new directions.

Consistent with these developments, the evolutionary nature of the AL/AR paradigm has also spurred the evolution of publications and organizations that further cultivate the AL/AR family of learning and research. Publications include not just books but importantly journals, such as *Action Research* and *Educational Action Research*. Network organizations include Action Learning and Action Research Association (ALARA) based in Australia, Collaborative Action Research Network (CARN), UK based, Action Research Network of the Americas (ARNA) and Network for Educational Action Research in Ireland (NEARI).

This book's chapters have illustrated how the various genres of ALAR and approaches to personal, professional, organizational and community development bring people together to think and act in various configurations:

Table 14.1:   Main Features of AL/AR Genres.

Genre	What It Is	What It Is Not	Purpose	Context	Processes
Action Learning	Learning from experience, by doing, reflecting and learning from and with others to address a 'wicked' problem.	Rote learning, learning by heart.	To address a major problem that is of common concern in an AL set.	In an organization, community, government department, university or school.	Relationship/team building; collaborative project planning; and conducting, discussing, evaluating and reflecting on the data, and project and learning outcomes.
Lifelong Action Learning	Action learning that is for life and enduring, but conscious, deliberate, purposeful and systematic, as in the GULL programs.	Formal education conducted in registered institutions with a set curriculum.	Holistic development for the many who would like to develop themselves but face barriers in accessing traditional forms of education.	In communities where people struggle to access formal education due to lack of income and/or prior qualifications.	Using a narrative format with tools for personal planning, reflection and for recording outcomes in the participants' LAL learning journey.
Action Learning and Mindfulness	AL and mindfulness are complementary and mutually reinforcing, sharing the goals of 'self-awareness' and building 'agency' for managers and non-managerial employees.	Self-deception by not admitting what we don't know; fear and sense of being out of control.	To provide a framework/model for organizational interventions designed to address toxic work environments.	Mental health in the workplace.	Developing self-awareness and agency through AL and mindfulness.

Action Learning and Action Research (ALAR)	An integrated concept and practice of ALAR based on a shared paradigm. It is the basis for other action research genres.	A learning/research method in the social sciences that aims only at knowledge creation, and not improving or changing practice.	To improve a situation through collaboration for the common good and to advance knowledge in the field.	Personal and professional development, organizational and community development.	Practising what we preach; personal experience; critical and self-critical reflection on action and experience.
Action Research	A generic term used to refer to a family of methods and modalities; human knowing in a practical mode.	A learning/research method in the social sciences that aims only at knowledge creation and theory building and not on improving/changing practice.	To provide a third-person framework for engaging in a philosophy of practical knowing in first- and second-person practices so as to provide readers with a practical tool for finding their way through AR.	Personal and professional development, organizational and community development.	The action researcher's self-reflection (first person); collaboration with others (second-person processes) in cycles of action and reflection; and knowledge co-generated out of the first- and second-person practices (third person).
Action Research for Self-Study and Living-Educational Theory	An individual's explanation of their educational influences in their own learning, in the learning of others and in the learning of the social formations that are influencing and being influenced by the researcher.	A 'disciplines' approach to educational theory constituted by the philosophy, sociology and history of education.	To focus on the what, why and how of this particular living theory approach.	Personal and professional development, individually and in learning communities in educational partnerships.	Systematic enquiry to find answers to the following: What is my concern? Why am I concerned? What can I do about it? How can I make sure the data I generate is reasonably accurate? What have I learnt? What is the significance of my learning?

Table 14.1: *(Continued)*

Genre	What It Is	What It Is Not	Purpose	Context	Processes
Educational Action Research	AR within the educational realm and supported by communities.	A 'disciplines' approach to educational theory constituted by the philosophy, sociology and history of education.	To provide both theoretical considerations and practical examples from Austrian large-scale teacher professional development programs.	Primary and secondary schools; universities and colleges of teacher education.	Systematic cycles of inquiry and action in communities of practice.
Systemic Action Research	A systemic approach to AR that can be applied at scale (but could also be used to explore localized systemic change, e.g., within a school); PAR research that takes place across systems and deals with systemic issues to attain social and environmental justice.	Large-scale traditional research that focuses on trends and quantitative surveys to make generalizations and predict future directions.	To attain institutional, organization or community change on a wider scale than most small AR projects.	Across whole cities and regions, programs and organizations.	Understanding systems dynamics; methodological pluralism; open groups with changeable membership; strong contextually situated evidence; collective analysis of data; and distributed leadership across the system.
Action Science	Theories of action (espoused and in use) that link actions to outcomes.	Traditional science that focuses on trends and quantitative surveys to make generalizations and predict future directions.	To improve human relationships and situations.	Interpersonal and team relationships; coaching; organizations and other social systems.	Intrapersonal and interpersonal dynamics; defining goals and trying to achieve them; maximizing winning and minimizing losing; minimizing negative feelings; discussing the undiscussable; and process facilitation, leadership and coaching.

Appreciative Inquiry as Positive Action Research	An inclusive, relational, fully affirmative process, enabling the co-creation of new meaning that generates positive organization and community change.	A problem-centred approach to AR.	Large-scale learning, transformation and social innovation.	Social innovation; organizational and community transformation.	Positive change agenda and affirmative topics; unconditionally positive questions about what is most valued and desired; and structured conversations about individual and collective strengths, hopes and future dreams.
Critical Participatory Action Research	A social practice that itself is 'a practice changing practice'. People share a felt concern about their practices and their practice architecture. They engage in communicative action in a public sphere and document how their practice changes.	Technical, traditional AR.	To change practices to make them more reasonable, rational, productive, sustainable, just and democratic.	Educational institutions, teacher education and community engagement in any discipline.	AR spiral of cycles of planning, acting, observing and reflecting; and critical and self-critical reflection on and in action.
Participatory Action Learning and Action Research for Community Engagement	An integrated concept and practice of AL and AR in a participatory paradigm.	Technical, traditional AR in a positivist paradigm.	To achieve sustainable social change in communities with complex needs.	Community development; community–university partnerships.	Developing working relationships and a shared focus; conducting and facilitating the research; and critical and self-critical reflection, appraisal and evaluation.

informal groups, formal organizations or communities locally, nationally and globally. These sites of collective thinking and action to respond to complex issues have been fertile for continually extending the utility of the AL/AR paradigm. They have also enriched scholarship, contributed to conceptual and practical knowledge, and further extended the range of AL/AR genres. The AL/AR paradigm clearly has transformative capacity as all the chapters have illustrated. This quality equips it well for learning, research and development in the twenty-first century, whether large-scale or small.

Why the AL/AR Paradigm is Particularly Useful in Today's World

The world today is marked by significant transformations as we move towards the end of the second decade of the twenty-first century. These are days of complexity, uncertainty and conflict for many. It appears that climate change and its deracinating consequences are already becoming evident and set to create unprecedented upheaval across much or all of the globe. Power transitions between nations at the international level contribute to this upheaval. Millions of refugees are fleeing ravages of war and other life-threatening circumstances, and are joined by some who recognize an opportunity to escape deep poverty in their homeland. War, violence, crime and atrocities against women, children, migrants and disadvantaged minority groups still imperil the lives of many. Greater inequality in distribution of wealth sees poverty markedly on the rise, even in countries that have long known relative wealth.

Today neoliberalism is the dominant paradigm, setting people against each other in much of the world. Its mindset of competitive individualism, with value determined exclusively by 'the market', entrenches problems practically and conceptually. To help address these problems, now is a time for knowledge sharing, through collaboration and cooperation. It is a time to approach difficulties by engaging all stakeholders as participants, in projects informed by AL/AR principles to pursue creative solutions for the common good. The state of the world today is such that AL/AR is well positioned to contribute to positive transformational change.

The mindset of the various genres in the participatory paradigm of AL/AR favours and sustains mutually supportive collaboration in pursuit of shared interests, to improve conditions for present and future generations through collective effort. This book's discussion of the AL/AR genres well illustrates how in keeping to the basic principles of AL/AR, the paradigm can be usefully adapted and developed to facilitate the collaborative learning and shared democratic leadership required for contemporary research and development, to achieve self-change, organizational and community development and 'human flourishing' – especially needed in this turbulent world of the twenty-first century.

Editors' Reflections: Preparing this Book and Insights into the AL/AR Paradigm

As practitioners and advocates of AL and AR, we could not end this book without critical reflection. Our reflections on preparing this book have enabled us to prepare a model of the main principles and processes of AL/AR that all the genres have in common. And through meta-reflection, we have identified how the process of preparing this book has further deepened our insights into the AL/AR paradigm.

Preparing this Book

Reflecting on the whole process of preparing this book, we recognize that at all stages from initial idea to final copyediting it has been truly a collaborative, creative and productive experience. As co-editors we have consulted with and supported each other at all steps – from recognizing the need for this book, through approaching publishers and authors, designing content, reviewing, editing, evaluating and accepting chapters; and all the editorial and administrative tasks beyond that transform 12 electronic draft chapters into a completed, indexed volume of work. The volume is one we believe has been very much needed as the first collection of writings on ALAR genres that identifies their shared and distinctive features to demystify the AL/AR paradigm. We believe this collection will help to make AL and AR in all their forms more comprehensible and accessible to those who are interested in further exploring and adapting it for their own learning and research, especially since AL/AR is so well suited for application to contemporary concerns. As true to the ALAR experience, we learnt a great deal from and with each other throughout the preparation process. Through reflection we appreciate that in preparing this book we have practised what we preach. We have done so intuitively because we have no other way; for us the ALAR paradigm is our way of living.

When times became tough for either one of us, the other took over the reins without any problem. Through reflection, we recognize this is because we have developed trust in each other over the last few years of working together. Just as we preach in the PALAR process, a strong, purposeful relationship is the key to attaining our shared goals for our research; the compilation of this edited book is another example of how AL can be applied in many different contexts. We planned this book collaboratively; we asked outside critical friends for their opinion; we adjusted our proposal based on their feedback; we planned how to edit/write the book – who would do what, by when and how; we kept in frequent contact to reflect on how we were progressing and what needed to change in order to stay on track. We supported each other where possible in dealing with personal issues, and so we continued until we produced the final product that is this book. Just like participants in any AR project, we had to be flexible, creative, patient, daring and committed.

Through reflection we also recognize the importance of other relationships, beyond our own as editors. Here we have been fortunate to work with the 'giants' of AR, our co-authors of the chapters in this book. We are all, without exception, passionate about promoting AR for positive change in the world. Without this passion, AL and AR could not have come so far as an alternative paradigm in the social sciences. With this passion, we do our best to uphold ALAR principles, learn from and with each other and pursue collaborative inquiry towards improved wellbeing for others and ourselves.

We appreciate here that we have also considered other important relationships. These concern how the members of the ALAR family – the genres that the ALAR giants have helped to inspire – relate to each other. In this chapter we have highlighted the features of the AL/AR paradigm to which all the genres hold true. This book cannot be exhaustive in the genres it presents to readers, but we believe the chapters included here present a constructive overview that interested readers will find illuminating at least for their own conceptual and practical work. We have prepared Fig. 14.1 to capture the principles and processes of ALAR as revealed across the chapters in this book.

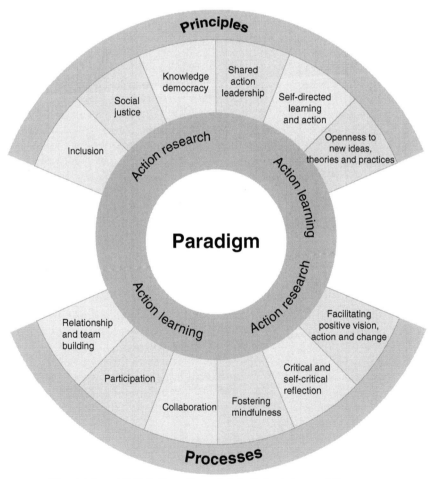

Fig. 14.1:   AL/AR Paradigm, Main Principles and Processes.

Insights into AL/AR Paradigm

Preparing this book – particularly identifying its argument – has brought us to articulate not just the evolutionary nature of AL and AR but also *how* their evolutionary nature has both enabled and fostered the flourish of AL/AR genres over time. Through this lens the birth of multiple genres is an inevitable outcome of AL/AR thinking and action. The genres have been created *because* the AL/AR paradigm encourages learning/research participants to think and act creatively, to collaborate mutually, to accommodate differences among themselves, to adapt and adjust their thinking and actions, and importantly to critically self-reflect for deeper understanding of processes, possibilities and their own agency at all turns. The genres' emergence is therefore testament to how AL/AR practitioners practise what they preach, and in creating new ideas, appreciations and applications they help to further develop a paradigm that is transformative and emancipatory. This observation of AL/AR's evolutionary nature also speaks to the utility and potential appeal of AL/AR, particularly as people search for ways to address 'wicked problems' that can only be addressed collectively.

That observation draws our critical thinking to the primary place in AL and AR of sharing, holding in common and acting collectively rather than as individuals. Sharing and unity apply to interest in the concern at hand as well as to the way of responding to that shared concern. This perspective creates the space for pursuing interest in human wellbeing, for caring and for drawing on the strengths and abilities of all participants. Basically, and perhaps most importantly, it recognizes our humanity – that we are sentient creatures who perceive and feel, and that we are interdependent; we can live well only through mindful, collaborative coexistence.

This critical reflection returns our thoughts to the paradigm struggle that AL/AR has faced continuously. As we noted earlier in this chapter, the dominant paradigms in the social sciences are rooted in worldviews and values different from those of AL/AR and that generally disregard human sentience as an aspect of learning and research. Here we recognize that the current pervasiveness of neoliberalism not only has entrenched competitive individualism in ethos and practice, but it has done so through a process to which many people are inured. This process has continued to erode discourses of equality, shared interest and the common good. It seeks to blind us to the broader contexts of democracy, social justice and communities small and large. It is intrinsic to the paradigm struggle in which opponents of AL/AR seek to delegitimize it.

This, too, is inevitable. Paradigms are vehicles that subliminally but powerfully shape how and what knowledge is created. They shape what worldviews are formed, what values are embedded in society and what desires are mobilized. ALAR is antithetical to competitive individualism. Not only does it explicitly uphold pursuit of common interest and shared wellbeing, it encourages us to think critically, to reflect and to take collective action to address shared concerns. It cultivates passion, compassion and active imagination. It accepts and appreciates that there is not just one kind of conventional knowledge, namely scientific, theoretical knowledge, but many kinds such as local and shared knowledge, intuitive knowledge based on feelings and intuition, indigenous and spiritual knowledges and knowledge created through democratic, distributed action leadership. AL/AR advocates and practitioners recognize that ALAR is an alternative rather than a mainstream paradigm. But even as such it is a way that we can at least to some extent influence what knowledge is created, what worldviews are cultivated and what outcomes are supported by collective, caring action.

Contributions to Knowledge

This is a seminal work on the AL and AR paradigm. It has shed light on the evolution of the paradigm, particularly through gradual development of its main genres and its utility for transformational and emancipatory research. In recent years especially, we have observed how serious interest in trying to gain a firmer handle on this field of scholarship has generated some confusion about the paradigm and genres, especially among newly emerging scholars/researchers. That is why we have produced this book, with contributions directly from AL and AR luminaries to strengthen and help expand our field and the learning and research that it creates. Throughout, this book offers readers deeper understanding about most of the main genres stemming from the AL/AR paradigm. Especially in this chapter, it explains how and why the paradigm has usefully enabled this genre-building process, but also why the AL/AR paradigm remains 'an alternative' in mainstream scholarship that has long sought to subvert it. This book has explained the particular utility of AL/AR for responding to contemporary concerns in ways that yield sustainable positive outcomes for shared benefit. We believe this utility will see continued growth of interest in this paradigm and use of it for transformational and emancipatory outcomes wherever in the world AL/AR is used.

Conclusions

Since in AL/AR we are swimming against the stream so much of the time, we have to really believe in what we are doing to survive the cynicism and patronizing remarks we so often encounter from colleagues who advocate a more traditional approach to research. Perhaps many of us who use the AL/AR paradigm have been accused of being idealistic in wanting to "change the world." But because we care about humankind, we have to start somewhere, and if we want to make a difference, we have to start with ourselves. Margaret Mead is so often quoted as saying, "Never doubt that a small group of thoughtful, committed citizens can change the world; indeed, it's the only thing that ever has." (https://www.brainyquote.com/quotes/margaret_mead_100502). Reflecting on the future directions of AR, we understand that it is this passion for wanting our research to contribute to changing human lives and the planet for the better that will keep us going. We hope that this book will inspire other younger, emerging researchers to embrace AR as their preferred paradigm and methodology. We hope that they will continue to evolve it and find ways to make the world a better place for all.

Topics for Discussion

1. What are your conclusions and reflections on this book?
2. Would you recommend it? To whom and why?
3. What genre(s) do you favour most and why?

Acknowledgments

As co-editors of this book, we had drafted this concluding chapter in our shared voice. Copy-editor, Maureen Todhunter, substantially contributed to the discussion, conceptualization and revision of this chapter. At her request, rather than acknowledge her as co-author we acknowledge her valuable contribution – with deep thanks.

Further Reading

McNiff, J. (2017). *Jean McNiff discusses action research*. SAGE Research Methods Video, Sage, London. Retrieved from https://methods.sagepub.com/video/srmpromo/0jCBqH/jean-mcniff-discusses-action-research

Revans, R. (2006). *Reg Revans and action learning*. DVD, based on the video program produced by Ortrun Zuber-Skerritt in 1991. Brisbane: Video Vision, ITS, University of Queensland. Retrieved from https://www.alarassociation.org/?q=about-al-and-ar/reg-revans-and-action-learning

Zuber-Skerritt, O. (2011). *Action leadership: Towards a participatory paradigm*. Dordrecht: Springer.

Author Index

Subject Index

VOYAGES AND TRAVELS TO INDIA, CEYLON, THE RED SEA, ABYSSINIA, AND EGYPT

VOYAGES AND TRAVELS TO INDIA, CEYLON, THE RED SEA, ABYSSINIA, AND EGYPT

George Annesley Mountnorris

A General Books LLC Publication.

CONTENTS

1

SECTION 1

CHAPTER I.

Motives for voyage to the Red Sea.|Departure from Mango- lore.|Cape Guarda- fui.|Cape Aden.|Passage through the Straitt of Bab-el-mandeb.|Arrival at Mocha.|Reception there.|Departure for the African Coast.|Ras Beiloul.|Island of Rackmah.|Saiel Abaiel.|Amphila.|, Misfras.|Island of Valentin.|Arrival at the Island of Dha- lc.|Visit to the Dola.|Mr. Salt's Journey to Dhalac-el- kibeer.|Departure for Mansowah.|Arrival thtre.

IT had always appeared to me an extraordinary circumstance, that if the western coast of the Red Sea were really as dangerous as the moderns have uniformly repre- sented it, the ancients should invariably have navigated it in preference to the eastern coast; nor could any suspicions that a western passage existed be removed by the silence of the British officers, after a long continuance of our fleet in that sea. The evils which they had experienced from the want of water, fresh provisions, and fuel, pointed out indeed most strongly the importance of ascertaining, whether these articles were not attainable at Massowah, Dhalac, or the adjacent islands, where in former times, the Egyptian and Roman merchants were induced to fix their residence for the purpose of carrying on the trade with Abyssinia, and the interior of Africa. At Dhalac Mr, Vol. 11. B

Bruce has asserted, that three hundred and sixty tanks, which had been erected by the munificence of the Ptolemies, were still in a state of preservation to afford,- with care, a supply of water, more than sufficient for any fleet which the British could ever have occasion to send into that sea.

The commercial advantages which might attend the opening of a communication with Abyssinia, appeared also worthy of attention; and a more favourable time for making the attempt could never be expected, than immediately after the British naval power had been so fully displayed on the shores of Arabia and Egypt, and when the trade with the interior of Africa had been interrupted in its usual channel through the latter country, first by the conquest of the French, and afterwards by the civil war between the Porte and the Beys, which had caused a perfect separation between the upper and lower provinces.

I confess also that I felt it as a national reflection, that a coast which had afforded a profitable and extensive trade in gold, ivory, and pearls, to the sovereigns of Egypt, should be a perfect blank in our charts, and that while new islands, and even continents were discovered by the abilities of our seamen, we should have become so ignorant of the eastern shore of Africa, as to be unable to ascertain many of the harbours and islands described by an ancient navigator in the Periplus of the Erythrean Sea.

During my stay at Calcutta I had the honour of frequently conversing with the Marquis Wellesley on the subject of the Red Sea, and of stating to him my ideas and feelings; in which I had the happiness of finding that he fully concurred. At length I proposed to his Excellency, that he should order one of the Bombay cruizers to be preparedfor a voyage to the Red Sea; and I offered my gratuitous services to endeavour to remove our disgraceful ignorance, by embarking in her, for the purpose of investigating the eastern shore of Africa, and making the necessary inquiries into the present state of Abyssinia, and the neighbouring countries. His Excellency approved of the plan, and it was determined in order to obviate any difficulties which might arise, from the commanding officer differing with me in opinion, with respect to the eligibility of going to particular places, that he should be placed under my orders. The necessary instructions were immediately transmitted to Bombay, and I hastened my departure for Columbo, as it was desirable to reach the Red Sea as early in the year as possible.

When I arrived at Tanjore I received dispatches from Bombay, acquainting me that the Antelope cruizer would be at Mangalore ready to receive me, and convey me to the Red Sea iq the beginning of February; at the same time I lad letters from Mr. Lumsden, Chief Secretary a Calcutta, inclosing, under a flying seal, the proper orders to Captain Keys, to consider himself as under my command. A t Madras I heard that he was actually arrived; yet from my servant's indisposition there, and the previous delay at Columbo, I was unable to reach Mangalore before the 8th of March. This was particularly unfortunate, as it precluded the possibility of my reaching Suez, previously to the change of the monsoon in the Arabian Gulf. It was however some consolation to know that the very heavy gales in that quarter rarely set in before June, by which time I hoped to be safe on land, and that the sailing in unknown seas was probably safer when beating up, than when going briskly before the wind. As far as Mocha, wewere certain of having the N. E. monsoon, though probably, 011 account of the lateness of the season, it would be only light, and we should be much baffled with calms, and for the remainder of the voyage we knew we could take shelter in an harbour, and wait for finer weather, should a gale overtake us. Admiral Rainier, whom I had the good fortune to find at Mangalore, visited me the morning after my arrival, with several of his officers, some of whom had been in the Red Sea; from them I had the pleasure of learning many circumstances, which tended to diminish alarms that might have been excited by the accounts of former travellers; and they confirmed me in my determination of surveying the Abyssinian shore, by the admission of the fact, that, during the whole time our fleets were in the Red Sea, not one vessel had quitted the Arabian coast.

With Captain Keys of the Antelope, I was much pleased, and the concern he expressed at the smallness of his,vessel, and the consequent difficulty of accommodating me to his wish, induced me to suppose that I should find him inclined to do every thing in his power to make my voyage comfortable. I determined to go on board the Antelope immediately: I found her to be a brig, quite as large as I expected, about one hundred and fifty tons, mounting twelve eighteen pound carronades, and having on board forty- one Europeans, including officers, sixteen marines, and thirty lascars and servants. For these they had on board six month's rice and salt meat, with forty days water; of course there could be little room left for my baggage. The cabin was of a tolerable size: rather more than one third had been partitioned *off* for me; the remainder served as a dining-room, in which the Captain and Mr. Saltwere obliged to swing their cots at night. For myself, I was perfectly satisfied, but determined to lessen my baggage by sending part of my linen to England from Bombay. Captain Keys accompanied me on board the flag-ship to visit the Admiral, who paid me the honour of a salute : I undertook to convey dispatches for him to England.

On returning to Mr. Ravenshaw's, I instantly began my preparations for departure: these were soon completed, as well as circumstances would permit; and Mr. Salt having arrived we got on board the Antelope by eleven o'clock at night on the 13th of March. By twelve every thing was embarked, and we weighed anchor for the Red Sea, bidding a farewell to India, after a residence of fifteen months. According to the power with which I was invested, I directed the Captain to proceed to Aden.

Our little vessel sailed ill, which was probably owing to the bad condition of her bottom, which was perfectly covered with barnacles, being also deep in the water: she rolled and pitched much, but had one good quality|she obeyed her helm, and wore with facility. The wind was directly against us. The shore that we passed was a bold one; the mountains which I beheld in crossing the table-land,were completely visible. We passed several islands of a rocky nature, and among others one strongly fortified by Tippoo, but for what purpose it would be difficult to conjecture as it affords no protection to shipping.

Till the 26th we had the wind inclining to the west,; and consequently made little way. The calms had been frequent, yet the heat had never been unpleasant, and the sea had been as smooth as glass. We were on that day in long. 68 40' 15" and had at length got hold of the N. E. monsoon.

Our latitude was much the same as when we sailed, viz. 12 1' 37". When it is so late in the season, it would be better to sail from Bombay, as the monsoon at that time still keeps close to the shore. As the vessel was lightened by consumption of stock, she sailed better. The delay was the less disagreeable, as it gave me time to prepare charts of the Red Sea from the logs we had procured.

The men caught a dolphin, a most beautiful fish, generally from two to three feet long. When in the water it appears of a rich dark blue, or green, or golden yellow colour, according to the point of view in which it is beheld. On being caught, it changes rapidly. The body at first is chiefly orange, spotted with the brightest blue: the fins are green, and then blue. The dorsal fin, when the fish is dying, is of a dark green throughout. The ventral fins lie close to the body, where there is a hollow that partly receives them: these are of a bright gold-coloured orange on the outside; on the inside, when alive, bright blue; when nearly dead, a dark green. The anal fin, during life, is blue and light gold colour; at death, lighter, and silvery: the caudal the same. The pupil of the eye dark: the iris yellowish gold colour. It has three rows of small teeth, separated by a grove in the centre. When dying, the blue tint, for a few seconds, sometimes covers the whole fish, and then settles in the blue spots only. Linnasus's description, as far as it goes, is accurate. It follows the ship in company. In its belly was found the flying fish. The Coryphaena hippuris is also called a dolphin by the sailors.

The dolphins on the 31st were about the ship in shoals. The men killed eight. We had one for dinner, and it was as good as an albicore. On the 30th we saw many sharks, one of which, seven feet long, the men caught. The following day the dolphins were still more numerous, and every mess had one.

Coryphaena equisetalis.

The wind for the last five days had been extremely light, but we had been favoured by a current to the S. W. which enabled us to make a degree a day. The sea perfectly smooth. On the 1st of April the men killed nine dolphins. Long. *61'59'*, lat. 11 92'.

The current deserted us on the 2nd, and the breezes became extremely light. We had plenty of dolphins; and several very singular species of sea-blubber floated by. One was a large scarlet mass, about seven feet long and two or three wide, a part of which was got on board; it consisted of a great number of distinct living substances, adhering to each other. Each was about four inches diameter, tubular, and closed at the ends. A circular thread of scarlet spots was twined in circles amidst the gelatinous substance. Another was about two inches long by one in diameter; partly hollow. It had a dark yellow spot and one red, close to each other, at the lower extremity. It was covered with fine prickles externally, which, produced no smart on being touched.

As we approached the land, the breezes became more light; the fish, less afraid of the ship's foul bottom than they would have been of a clean one, were in great abundance. With the bait of a cockroach, my servant caught a small fish of the genus Diodon, but not of the species described by Linnaeus, though I think it is the one mentioned in Chambers's Dictionary under the name of Gua- majacu atinga, and for which he quotes Piso's Nat. Hist. lib. V. cap. 16. The description perfectly corresponds, but the drawing; given has no resemblance. Mr. Salt drew it and I stuffed its skin, which was thick and glutinous. It is covered with prickles, which it has the power of expanding when it blows out its body; the cavity of which is filled with a very large air-bladder, and a liver disproportioned to its size. Its length is about four inches: as we caught several, I conclude this to be its full growth. No injury follows the puncture of one of its prickles, though a juice exudes from the base, of a bright yellow colour, that permanently stains paper and other substances. It puts out two small tentacula from its mouth as it swims, and lives a considerable time out of water. Towards evening the wind began to come round to the southward.

On the 12th at day-light the African coast was in view, bearing N. W. distant about eleven leagues. As we approached it most rapidly, by twelve we were only about three miles from Cape Guardafui. The Cape itself is not very high, but the land behind it is extremely lofty. It consists of rocky beds, one over the other, with gullies apparently formed by the rain. Not a vestige of vegetation was seen. We made it in 51 10' E. and 11 50' N. There was a considerable cross swell as we rounded the land, Our little vessel was going seven knots, which I did not expect from her. We had during trie whole of the last day a strong set to the south, which took us thirty miles. We coasted the land during the whole time. Mount Felix is united to the main land by a low sand; it is conspicuous, and cannot be mistaken. We were opposite to it after it was dark.

On the 13th a very pleasant breeze came on from the north of east. We steered W. and by N.Straight for Aden, and passed the high land behind Cape St. Peter. The coast is very high and barren: it was still in sight at night, though a haze, which extended across the whole sea, concealed the base. The stars near the horizon were hardly visible. Several meteors, called falling stars, shot occasionally across the sky; but no aurora borealis had appeared during the whole voyage. A heavy dew fell all night. The sea was smooth, though we went at the rate of six knots an hour.

We had a very fine breeze during the whole night of the 13th, but no land was visible on the following morning. The sky was clear, and the water smooth. At twelve o'clock we had run one hundred and twenty miles in twenty-four hours.

At eight in the morning of the 15th a part of the African shore was insight, distant about eleven leagues, which was as high as that on the opposite side. At one, Cape Aden bore right a-head W by N -l: N. distant eleven leagues. We went on till night, when it was so near, that we determined to come to an anchor. We passed the head land, and anchored at nine o'clock on the other side, close as we supposed to the town; but could not be certain, as no one on board had ever been there, and we had no directions respecting making it. The land sheltered us, and we had little motion.

At day light on the 16th we found no town was visible, and thought we had not got far enough; and that it lay beyond another head land, nearly W, accordingly we weighed anchor at six, and steered .along shore. Cape Aden is a very lofty rock, on the top of which are several ruined towers. The bay we anchored in, was a fine one, about six miles wide, and as many deep. Onproceeding we found our mistake: that in which we anchored was Back Bay, and Aden itself was on the eastern side of the head-land. The bottom of every bay was a sandy beach ; beyond that ran a chain of mountains at a distance. I never beheld a more dreary scene; nor one that less accorded with the idea that might be formed of the country from the beautiful description of Milton: no " Sabasan odours" came off to gratify our senses, from the shore, nor did they ever exist there, but in the mind of the poet, as a more wretched country does not exist; for the myrrh and frankincense come from the opposite coast, though the Arabs were, and are still the medium of conveyance to Europe.

It would have been a serious loss of time to have beaten back, and therefore I determined to go on, though much vexed at a mistake, which prevented our having excellent water, instead of that which is to be obtained higher up, and is invariably brackish. Back Bay is the best watering-place, though it is five miles from the town: the only expence is three dollars demanded by the Dola, as I learned from Lieutenant Powell of the Wasp, who was there in 1803. In East Bay it is pur- chaseable, but at a high price. On the western side is a range of rocks extending out nearly as far south as the hill of Aden itself. The tops of these are singularly broken, and rise into Gothic spires in several parts : two of these have got the names of Ass's Ears. Another bay is west of them, in size and appearance exactly like the former. Its western boundary is a range of rocks, one of which so perfectly resembles a funnel as to deserve that name: it can never be mistaken. The coast is shelving to the south of west. Before sunset the Cape itself was perfectly visible like a gunner's

quoin, Cape St. Anthony being Ob our bow. This is not very high land. We kept at the distance of three or four leagues to avoid a shoal that extends out from it. The breeze continued from the eastward, and freshened as we advanced. At ten the island of Perim was in sight, and soon afterwards we entered the smaller straits which run between it and the land. We kept nearer the island than the main, with from eleven to six fathom water. The breeze was assisted by the tide, and soon brought us under shelter of the promontory. We anchored by twelve in.smooth water, in defiance of a very strong breeze.

Before day on the 17th the small boat was hoisted out. My servant and Mr. Hall were sent on shore with their guns and dogs, in hopes of killing us some game. After an early breakfast Mr. Salt and I, attended by Mr. Hurst the midshipman, and four sepoys, went on shore to see the country, and collect shells. We landed on the beach, on which nothing grows but a species of sa- licornia. A ridge of broken hills, detached from the Cape, rises about a mile from the shore : this we determined to ascend. The way up was craggy, but the heat of the sun was tempered by the strong breeze, and the fatigue was relieved by discovering several curious plants, and some mineral specimens. From the summit we had an excellent view of Cape Bab-el-mandeb and the island of Perim. A bay to the eastward of the Cape extends inwards a considerable way: the land between that and the westernmost, in which the ship lay, is perfectly flat, and a dry salt sand: if the sea were to rise only a very few feet it would cover it. Already part of it is a lake of salt water. Accidents have occurred from mistaking this east bay for the strait; a circumstance that can never happen, if itshould be only observed that Perim is perfectly flat, which ought to be kept close on the larboard side; whereas Bab-el-mandeb hill is the loftiest land in the neighbourhood. The hill on which we were, rises suddenly out of a plain of sand; no others are near it.

The shooting party were at the bottom of the hill, from which we soon descended, and joined them. They had seen several antelopes, and had wounded one, but itescaped. They had killed some partridges, and also purchased some milch goats very cheap, and remarkably fine. On reaching the seashore we found a great many Arab fishermen, with a profusion of mullets, and other fish. These we purchased and sent on board, to procure, in return, a supply of water, none of which was to be obtained on the land. The boys went in amongst the coral rocks, and procured a few shell-fish, that were fine of their kind. It was still early, and as the breeze continued, we determined to walk along the shore to point Bab-el-mandeb. Between us was a small creek communicating with the salt-water lake, now nearly dry, over which we were obliged to pass in the boat. As we advanced, it was less pleasant, from the air being frequently heated by the sand over which it passed, which gave it all the effect of the hot winds of India in scorching the skin, and producing intense drought. Dr. Macgie, who had accompanied us, and Mr. Salt bathed, from which they suffered considerably, but not so much as the two officers of the ship, who, from being more exposed, were soon of a perfectly red colour.

On the beach is the tomb of a Mussulmaun saint, which, though a heap of ruins, is much visited. The extreme point is low, but rocky. We procured from its sides several shells, but none of value. Itwas now three o'clock, and we were all heartily fatigued. We took to our boat, but the breeze had so freshened that nothing but the shelter of the land prevented its being difficult to get on board. I am convinced that the Straits are not above three miles wide. We all took the precaution of anointing our faces; those who had had their bodies exposed, suffered severely; we, who were more prudent, escaped with losing the skin off our noses. The bay in which we had anchored was most excellently defended by the island and promontory, and is much frequented by vessels that are too late to reach Mocha by day-light. Behind the hill, on which we were, is a wood of stunted mimosas, which seems of considerable extent, but would soon be exhausted, were Perim to be inhabited. We were too far out, and not land-locked, for some mountainous islands were visible through the Straits, composing part of the cluster called the Seven Brothers. The high land of Africa could be seen over the island, reaching up towards the north. This is, according to Bruce, the myrrh and frankincense country.

On the 18th before day, the anchor was up, and we set sail. At sun-rise we could perceive a ship enter the Straits and follow us. We had no doubt that this was the Fox frigate. Captain Vashon, as no other was likely to be in these seas, and Admiral Rainier had informed me that we should meet her here, as, at the request of the Bombay government, he had directed her to proceed to Mocha, to convoy to India the trade from that place. The breeze continued extremely fresh, as we sailed along the Arabian shore: the coast itself is low land, but the chain of mountains was seen, though with difficulty, from the haze, extending N. at about thirty miles from the shore. At ten, Mocha Was visible: we were obliged to keep out, to avoid*t*

a dangerous shoal, till the great mosque bore E, by S. when we stood right in for the town. We anchored at a distance of about four miles, in little more than four fathoms. The wind was very fresh, and the swell, though broken by the shoal, was considerable. We saluted the town with three guns, which were answered by one. The Fox soon afterwards came in, and anchored about a mile to the N. W.; she could not get more to the S. on account of the wind. A fishing boat came off with fish; it was small and narrow, and the people nearly naked; the sail was cloth, and held by the hand. It went with great velocity, and very close to the wind. The fish was excellent.

Captain Keys wrote to Mr. Pringle, acting Agent to the East India Company, to inform him of my arrival. Mr. Pringle came off, while we were at dinner, to invite me to the Factory. He told me that he had notified my arrival to the Dola, or Governor, and had enquired, in case I visited him, how he would receive me. To this he answered, that he was not well, and would not move from his seat. Mr. Pringle added, that as the meeting him at the door had been insisted on by General Baird, and had been complied with, he could, on no account, advise me to visit him in any other manner. I assured him that I should be entirely guided by him, as my only wish was to act in the manner that would be most conducive to the advantage of the English character; and that I considered him as the best judge on such an occasion.

After dinner, attended by Mr. Pringle, Captain Keys, and Mr. Salt, I quitted the Antelope, and was saluted with seventeen guns. These the Dola chose to take as a compliment to himself, and returned it with one. We were so conveniently anchored, that the S. W. wind was a side one, both.

for embarking and disembarking. We were soon at the pier, and proceeded imme- diately to the fac- - tory. I took care to let the Dola know, that the seventeen guns were not intended as any compliment to him, or the state, as the Antelope would certainly never again salute the town, till the former guns had been returned : to this I received no answer. This circumstance, trifling in itself, very strongly marks the Arab character.

More than a month having been consumed in the voyage from Mangalore, it was thought advisable to lay in a sufficient supply of water and provisions, before we proceeded to a coast of which we had no positive information. This was not completed till the 8th of May, when the Antelope was reported by Captain Keys to be ready for sea. During my stay at Mocha, I resided at the British Factory, where Mr. Pringle did every thing in his power to make me comfortable. He had filled this situation, since the departure of the British armament, to the satisfaction of the Bombay Government, and was very well acquainted with the Arab character, and the trade of the Red Sea.

I was painfully surprised at learning from Mr. Pringle, that the idea of examining the western side was so disagreeable to Captain Keys, that he had applied to him to allow him a room at the factory, till he could procure a passage back to Bombay, as he was determined, in consequence of ill health, to give up the command to his first officer. Mr. Pringle, at my request, pointed out to him in such strong colours the consequences that would ensue, that he abandoned his intentions ; but an impression of anxiety was left on my mind, which by no means diminished the evils necessarily attendant on a voyage of discovery. I, however, determined to execute the business I had undertaken,

in defiance of any surmountable obstacle, and therefore began to make every necessary enquiry respecting my intended route.

I discovered that a regular communication existed between Mocha and Massowah, and between this latter place and Suakin; that Massowah was by no means the unsafe place which Mr. Bruce represented it to be in his time; and that pilots could be procured for the whole way. As, however, the upper part of the voyage was to be performed through very narrow straits, and at a time when the N. W. winds were blowing strong down the gulf, I thought it would add greatly to our safety, to hire a country vessel, called a Dow, to go a head, and show the way. This would also enable me to visit many islands which the Antelope might not be able to approach. A dow was therefore hired for four hundred dollars, to go to Dhalac, Massowah, Suakin, and up to the latitude of the river Farat, where we meant to end our observations, and make the best of our way to Cosseir. I hired also an Arab boy of the name of Hyder, as an interpreter till the Antelope returned. He spoke English tolerably well, and bore an excellent character. I intended to have sailed on this day, and I dined on board the Fox, on my way to the Antelope, but a proposal from Captain Vashon made me alter my intention. This was, that if I would stay till the morrow, he would accompany us to Jibbel Teir and Dhalac. The pleasure of his society, and the use of his boats, were inducements too powerful to be resisted; the agreement was therefore made.

It being tolerably calm by six o'clock, I quitted the Fox, where I had slept, and went on board the Antelope. To my very great surprise, I now leajned, through the medium of Hyder, that .thepilot knew nothing of the passage from Jibbel Teir to Massowah; that the usual way was stretching across to the Abyssinian coast, and working up it to Dhalac. Captain Keys felt himself incapable of conducting the vessel through an unknown and intricate sea, and consequently all idea of Jibbel Teir was abandoned. The only inconvenience was respecting Captain Vashon. As we were under weigh, I could not go on board the Fox with any comfort, owing to the heavy swell. We however ran the brig so close to her, that our main top sail caught in her yard, and was rent. I told him where we were going, and our reasons. He answered he should go the old way by Jibbel Zeig- hur. We could say no more, and separated. He waited a little for a shore boat, and then made sail to the northward, whilst we stretched right across rather to the south of west. The wind was very fresh, as usual, from the S. E. with a considerable swell. The Abyssinian shore was soon in sight right a-head, which the pilot said was Ras Beiloul. This, according to Niebuhr, is the name of a town and district.

Our pilot seemed a sensible old fellow, and I was happy to find that he was an inhabitant of Dhalac. He expressed great pleasure at meeting Mr. Mac- gic, the surgeon, whom he had known before. He had been much employed by the English, when at Perim, and had purchased a boat with the money which he had obtained from them. He gave his directions clearly; and when they heaved the log, told them that it was not necessary, as he knew where he was, and there was plenty of water. We did not however choose to trust him. As we got nearer the African coast the wind became more moderate. We now perceived a lower point, stretching from Ras Beiloul, which the pilot said was Ras

Vol, n. C

Firmah. It is the most easterly point. Nearly south of it, and close to it, is an island, Saiel Bei- loul. At three we closed in with the land, and anchored about three miles west of a head-land, which the pilot called Ras Bunder Beiloul. Like a true pilot of Mr. Bruce's description, he gave orders to anchor so suddenly, that it was impossible to obey, and, consequently, we were carried farther from the shore than we meant; however, at a mile and a half from it we had a sand and mud bottom at thirteen fathom. A chain of islands and rocks had continued the whole way to the north of us, the largest of which the pilot called Jibbel Anish, but which must be the Jibbel Azroe of the charts.

The bay we now entered is of very great extent, and excellently defended from the south winds. The water was smooth, though strong gusts came over the hill. The width of the channel, opposite to Mocha, proved to be less than I conjectured from the view of the Abyssinian land when there. I did not lose any time in sending off my servants in the pilot's boat to the shore to look for shells. The people bear a bad character ; but probably the accounts of their ferocity are exaggerated. Our pilot offered to go to the village, which he said was beyond the hills.. The whole coast had a black, barren appearance, except where it was broken by white sand. ;

After dinner Mr. Salt and Captain Keys went on shore in the boat, and took with them the lead line. They found, contrary to Mr. Bruce's assertions, " that there was no anchoring ground on the Abyssinian shore, and that you might have your bowsprit over the land without any bottom astern," that the land gradually shallowed to seven fathom within a quarter of a mile of the shore. They found an inner bay perfectly defended, except to thenorth. A strong gust of wind prevented their entering to sound it. It was about five miles round. Under a stone were lying a net and iron head of an harpoon, but they saw no native. A few mimosas and herbaceous plants were all the vegetation; but as yet I had not been able to discover Mr. Bruce's Absinthium. My servant procured some beautiful specimens of the Neritas. Many dead shells showed the riches beneath the sea, but, as I had no diver, I could only wish for them. The seamen caught several cat-fish, as they call them.

We got under weigh at six next day, and steered N. N. W. directly across the Bay, which, as it was clear, appeared of a magnificent extent. It could not be less than twelve miles deep, and about thirty from one head-land to a large island, which formed the other extremity. In the bottom, the land had a very singular appearance; large masses being perfectly flat, and others of a conical figure. It blew fresh with a considerable swell. By twelve we were across, and discovered an archipelago of islands and rocks around the island above mentioned, which the pilot called Rackmah. He informed us that there was a river, and very civil people, where every article was to be procured. As this was to me a very interesting assertion, I was greatly pleased by Captain Keys proposing that we should bear up and examine into the truth of it. At half after twelve we did so; and with regular soundings as we approached the land; at length we cast anchor under the lee of the island, in four and a half fathom, with a hard sandy bottom. I asked the pilot if he could persuade the natives to come down to us, and I would make them some presents. He said, no, they would meet us on the beach, but would never come on board. This suspicion could not have originated without cause, and I fear that they,or their neighbours, have experienced ill treatment from European vessels. We saw several groves of trees, which made us hope the pilot had not deceived us.

Mr. Salt wished to go to the village, which was at some miles distance up a bay. He was accompanied byMr. Hurst, the midshipman, and Hyder as an interpreter. I went in the boat to the island to examine it, and was attended in another boat by a Naig and three sepoys, my servant, and some lascars. We found an excellent landing-place about a mile and a half from the ship. No shells, that were new, met our notice; we therefore ascended the hill, which was composed of a blackish brown stone that looked as if it had been burnt. Vegetation was nearly annihilated. I saw a Sali-cornia, an unknown shrub, and a species of Indi- gofera, of which I collected seeds. On descending to the opposite shore, I found the green trees I had observed, to be a species of Rhizophora that covered the beach. Some flamingos were seen, but too distant to be reached with the gun. Two natives, who lived on the island, were brought to us by the report of a shot: they seemed not to be afraid, and were very civil. They understood a little Arabic, and had not the woolly head. My people went to their hut, and procured some turtle. They seemed to be there merely for the purpose of catching them : and they had no boat. Not expecting that I should meet with any inhabitants, I had nothing with me to give them; but being unwilling they should go unrequited, I wrapped my handkerchief round the young boy's head, which was shaved all over, except a tuft above the forehead. We found that a sandy bar extended from the island to the main, and formed one side of the bay; the other islands above mentioned were beyond it, and, at a distance, they looked as if in a line with it. The passage is about two miles across, with shallow water.

After coasting a rocky head-land, which at first we had supposed an island, we proceeded to a third, which was likewise connected by a sandy bar, and formed altogether a most excellent bay for small vessels. We here procured a few good shells, and discovered the tomb of a native chief, around which had been set up a circle of stones. At one end were the bones and shells of several turtles, half burnt. In the middle were several drinking vessels : one was an English China sugar bason. We found a second tomb nearly similar, and were again informed by some of the boatmen, that this belonged to a chief. As these islands have no names among the pilots, I gave it that of Burial Island. I did my best to procure the native names, as it might be of use to future navigators; and wherever I succeeded, I have, as accurately as I could, preserved them. On the northern side were some excellent oysters fastened to the rock: their shells were of a fine purple at the edges, and by no means inelegant. Soon after it was dark, I got to the ship: there was a considerable swell, which rendered it by no means pleasant, and the wind was right against us. Tht island we first went to is by far the largest in the group, and forms the north-eastern point of the bay. It consists of two hills divided by a low sandy plain; the highest is to the N. W. In no part is it more than two miles and a half wide. Its latitude 13 50" N. Long. 42!(/' E. To the eastward every thing is clear, and it may be approached very close. Mr. Salt had, as we perceived from the ship, gone several miles up the gulf between Burial Island, and another to the northward of it.As the wind was right against him, we did not expect him to return soon; but our anxiety was removed by perceiving his boat before it was quite dark. He arrived at ten completely fatigued, and without having been much gratified. The river had vanished, though certainly in the rainy season torrents had run to the sea, of which he perceived visible marks. At present there were only two wells about sixty yards from the sea : the water of the nearest was as bad as the Mocha water; that of the farthest was better, and in tolerable quantity. He met with no village, but saw three men, with a numerous troop of camels, and two flocks of sheep: the natives were extremely civil, offered him water, and willingly exchanged a fine sheep for some tobacco, refusing a dollar that was offered. They had driven their animals down to the water, and were returning to their habitations at some distance in the interior, but they objected to the party's going thither. They wore crooked knives, like the Arabs, by their side, and had spears lying at the wells. They knew the old pilot, and shook the whole party by the hand, without expressing the least fear. They had curling black hair, drawn out into points in every direction. There was plenty of *tr&* mimosa close to the water side. The svvelf continued all night, and the heat was most oppressive.

We were under sail by six, our dow preceding us. We continued coasting along the land, which receded considerably to the west. At first we had soundings, but afterwards none with 15 fathom. We kept about twelve miles from land: a great many islands and rocks were seen, none of them so far out as we were. At twelve we were opposite to one which the pilot called Saiel Abaiel. Its long, is 42 10" E. lat. 13 50" N. It is impossible to sail along a safer coast than this: not a sand-bank appeared, and the rocks were all close to the land. The wind became light from the eastward : during a part of the night it was calm. We cast the lead, and had bottom at 37 fathom, with a current carrying us somewhat to the north. We kept all night nearly the same distance from the land, with regular soundings from 37 to 40 fathom.

On the 13th we had variable winds.|At twelve a pleasant breeze: we were then 14 miles from shore, with 21 fathom water; the country hilly and barren; lat. 14 26", long. 41 38" 30'. We continued coasting along shore till evening, when we came so near as three miles and a half to a low point that advanced beyond the mountains. It shoaled gradually till we anchored in seven fathom, with a sandy bottom. It was uncommonly sultry in the night: the wind for a short time at south. We discovered that we had anchored off a low cape called Ras Kussa, whence the land runs rapidly to the westward; we make-it by computation in lat. 14 34" N. long. 41 23" E.

We weighed anchor at five with a light breeze directly in our teeth, so that we were obliged to tack off and on. In the morning we saw two dows, which met us. The bank from the headland continued a considerable way out. At eleven o'clock we had 21 fathom 9 miles from shore; but the tack before, when six miles from shore, we had only 6 fathom. The immediate beach was low land, and a great haze hid the mountain from our sight. At twelve we were in long. 41 13", lat. 14 41". At six we anchored in six and a half fathom, sand, off a low black rocky point, near which the pilot affirmed there was a well of fresh water. He also said that these rocks extended to the depth of 5 fathom. A low island bore by compass NW f W. The night was extremely sultry, and the water smooth. The coast was low, and the haze continued so great -that we could only see the tops of the hills beyond.it.

We weighed anchor at four, the wind right ahead, but it soon came round. We anchored at twelve in seven fathom, to give the pilot an opportunity of getting some articles he wanted from a village which he said was near us. Further oh there is a bay, formed by the main-land, and a chain of islands to the N. and W. They called them Ras Amphila, Bunder Amphila, and the Islands of Amphila. Mr. Salt and Captain Keys went on shoYe on the island, which is uninhabited: Mr. Salt brought me back some seeds, one of which was of a very beautiful purple icosandrous plant, with succulent leaves. He found the island to be about a mile broad, by three loug, perfectly flat and sandy. It was thickly covered with a low shrub and herbaceous plants, among which was the Portulaca officinalis in abundance. They saw several snakes, which the Abyssinians wanted to catch. The dow's people brought me some shells of the same kind as I had procured at Mocha. The pilot boat did not return all night. We saw a dow round the island, and enter the strait beyond the point. The night was rather cooler.

After we had weighed anchor on the 16th, the pilot arrived, and brought us some sheep. He asserted this to be a place of some trade, which was confirmed by the appearance of several dows. We kept without all the five Amphila islands, which were equally flat and sandy, raised only about ten feet above the water, and without a single tree on them. The shore stretches out rapidly to the westward, is low, but backed by lofty hills, of fantastical forms. Some high trees

That nearest us they called Kuddo; but I believe they often gave us false names.

frew on the water's edge. As we coasted along, y the assistance of a kind of sea breeze, it was , extremely pleasant. At twelve our lat. was 14 52", long 40 58" 45'. We passed Ras Ratta, which is a very conspicuous piece of land, and of a singular form. We found all the charts of the coast extremely incorrect. At three or four leagues distance, when without every island, it is impossible to have a coast more free from danger. This day we had from about ten to fourteen fathom. Late in the evening we passed two remarkable headlands, which extend considerably from the shore, and which I conceived were islands. Several rocks were between them, and the usual line of the main: The pilot called them Ras Sarbo and Ras Rorah. A lofty island ahead appeared faintly at sun set. The pilot cast anchor oft' an island which lay in the bay formed by the head-land. It was low, and perfectly flat. The soundings were unequal, from sixteen fathom suddenly shoaling to ten; but as they afterwards continued regular at fourteen till we anchored, 1 conceived there was some error. The night was immoderately sultry. On the 17th we did not weigh till six; as there was not a breath of air till the sea breeze set in, which had hitherto invariably been the case about nine. We passed the island looked for by the pilot; he called it Howakel. It is lofty, rugged, and about nine miles in length. Off the north of it are three low sandy islands. The coast here again began to approach them, from which at one time it had apparently been three leagues distant. In the evening we saw four small islands to the eastward, distant five leagues: the pilot called them

Miseras ; of which the curious name of the Great and Little Miseries, as laid down in Mr. Apres de Menonville's chart is probably a corruption. We came to anchor about six o'clock between the main and an island, which, from the pilot's considering it as an important mark, we called Pilot's Island. The sky to the N. W. was cloudy, and the sun set behind a dense body of clouds. This the pilot said denoted a S. W. wind; and he was right. It blew rather fresh till ten o'clock, when it came round to the E. of N. and was extremely sultry.

On the 18th we were not under sail till six, when, for the first time, we kept within the islands. As the channel was narrow, and the wind against us, our tacks were but short. The channel is not above a mile wide, but the water is ten fathom and 'upwards. Pilot's Island is small and woody, has two spits of sand extending parallel to the shore for a considerable distance, one at each end ; it is distant from the main three miles, and every danger Ils visible. The sea breeze changed the northwest monsoon a little in our favour, so that for some 'time we ran along shore. However, we could not get a sight of Dhalac in the latitude, and nearly in longitude in which Mr. Bruce placed it, viz. lat, 1 S 29", long. 40 1,5" 30'; yet he says it is visible at the distance of nine leagues, which is in itself impossible, as he admits that the land is low. I began to fear that he had invented much in his travels, The soundings were regular the whole day. We passed within several islands, keeping close to the shore, which was flat, with gentle acclivities beyond, covered with wood; and farther off, the lofty mountains of Abyssinia appeared nearly hidden in the haze. At four we came to anchor within a mile and a half of the

land. In fishing from the ship, the hooks caught on some dark brown pieces of coral, from the holes of which issued a profusion of living animalculas: each was nearly brown, about a quarter of an inch long, with a black head. I put a specimen several times in water, and they extended themselves directly: when out of the water they did not retire, but hung close to the sides, one over the other. We also caught a very large specimen of the pearl muscle, with a piece of madrapore growing on it. The night was as sultry as ever. We passed a vessel this day.

On the 18th we sailed at four: the north-west wind still continued sufficiently strong to be pleasant. We had to work between an island that was ahead of us, and the main, in a passage about three miles wide. The channel was nearly as broad, as it was deep water close to the main land. We were not through till eleven, when we bore away along the Abyssinian shore. We passed another vessel this day.

A great deal of trade seems to be carried on at Massowah. The coast also seemed tolerably full of inhabitants. Last night there was a fire on the shore. Our pilot declared he could not reach Dhalac this day: he wished to anchor off an island to the west of us, which forms a bay, where he said large vessels may anchor in safety. The people, he declared to be very good friends of his, and very civil. We entered it in a S. S. W. direction, and anchored off a very picturesque island. The bay fully answered the pilot's description: it is eight or nine miles deep and about seven miles wide. A sand bank, which runs off from the island forms its N.W. defence. Behind that is another bay. The water is deep. We anchored in seventeen fathom, and at only three quarters of a mile from the shore. As no description of the island has ever been given, and we were, probably, the first Europeans that had visited it, we called it Valentia. Mr. Salt went on shore to take the different bearings, from which we formed a plan of the harbour, &c.; my servant .went with Hyder in the dow's boat to procure shells. The men did not choose to assist, so that I got very few, but from these I was convinced that with proper assistance, it was the best spot for the purpose at which I had hitherto touched. Mr. Salt was accompanied by two of the inhabitants to the summit of the hill: they were very civil. The water we got from a tank was good, and we procured a few sheep, which belonged to the Nayib of Massowah. The high hills of Habesh were in full view: and in one part, a ridge appeared between us and them, which terminates a point said to form the bay of Massowah, and is called Ras Gidden. The night was as sultry as usual.

On the 20th we heaved anchor at five. Our pilot seemed to be less acquainted than usual with the islands. We made a direct N.E. course, but tacked incessantly. The distance we ran was about twenty-two miles, when we anchored in another bay, the extremities of the land extending from N.W. by W. to S. by E. It was very deep and a village was situated on the bank at the bottom of it. This, he said, was Dhalac, but it agreed so little with the description I had met with, that I had considerable doubts on the subject. I enquired for Dhalac-el-Kibeer, which he told me was at some distance, but that the port was not safe for vessels of our size; nor would he dare to take us there without permission from the IJola.

A native soon came along side, on a catamaran, formed of four pieces of wood, about ten feet long, and six inches in diameter. On this he floatednearly naked. On recognising our pilot, he came on board, but seemed considerably alarmed. He was a fine muscular figure, with a large black beard, not woolly. He afterwards proved to be the son of the Dola, who commanded the whole island on the part of the Nayib of Massowah. He pressed us to land, which I determined to do. He then begged leave to accompany me. By an unfortunate fatality, I consented to our pilot's being of the party. As from the appearance of the young man, who was perfectly naked, except a cloth wrapped round his waist, I had no very high idea of the Dola's dignity, I consulted the former what present I should take on shore. Money, cloth, rice, tobacco, &c. &c. were mentioned ; in short I found any thing would be acceptable. I dressed myself in an Asiatic dress, as did Mr. Salt. Hyder went with us as interpreter. The water on this shore is shallow, and has undermined the madrapore rocks, of which the beach is composed, in such a manner, as to render a landing in most parts impracticable. At length we entered a strait, formed by an island called Nokhara, and the mainland of Dhalac. Here is a very excellent but small landing place.

The pilot and native went on to announce our arrival, while we reclined in the shade of a rock, and caused our people to collect some oysters, that grew in large clusters, suspended from the roof of the caverns, formed by the beating of the sea. At length more natives arrived, who begged us to advance to the village. We were met by a tall native, almost naked, with a cast of the wool in his hair, who, my pilot said was the Dola, and to whom the present was to be given. He accompanied us till I was met by another man, in the Arab dress, with a cap; his beard white as snow,and he had a more respectable appearance than the former. I immediately conceived this to be the Dola, but the old pilot would not admit it. We were conducted into a house, built like all the others in the place, of inadrapore, drawn from the sea, squared, and raised about twelve feet from the ground. It was thatched with a species of grass, and had one door, but no window. The bare earth formed the floor, and there was no furniture except five beds, made of wood, with cords drawn across and raised about three feet from the ground. These were covered with matting made of the leaves of the doom-tree. I seated myself on one, Mr. Salt on another, the rest were occupied by natives and my lascars, who were sitting together in amicable equality.

No one was armed even with a knife. I again urged that I thought the man in the Arab dress ought to have the present, but was over-ruled. The native therefore received a piece of blue Surat cloth and ten dollars, while the other had only a -piece of blue cloth. Coffee was immediately ordered, and our conversation commenced. I stated that we wished to procure water and sheep, for which we would willingly pay. They assured us they would supply us: a specimen of the former was produced, and was excellent. I could not state the quantity wanted, but referred them to Captain Keys. They spoke in the highest terms of their master, the Nayib of Massuah, or, as they pronounce it, Massowah. They said, he was a good man, and if I wanted one pilot would give me two. There were plenty on the island, who could pilot Hie to Suakin, whither I told them I was going. The old man was now recognised as being the Nayib's representative, and Governor ofall the island, and our young visitor on board as his son. I more particularly engaged him to attend me during my stay, by a promise of a present on my departure. They told me that the place I was on was an island called Nokhara, and the constant residence of the Dola, who had sub- dolas at every other station; that Dhalac-el-Kibeer had formerly been the principal residence, that now the port was bad, and could not admit our ship, but that we were very well situated where we were.

A species of palm tree.

In defiance of the heat, I determined to visit the wells or tanks, where the water was kept, conceiving they were probably near the village. My young Dola accompanied me. We passed through the narrow passages that separated the houses from each other, without seeing a female, or being importuned by a beggar. There was a small unorna- mented oblong building on the road side, which I learnt was a mosque; near it were a few tombstones and two doom-trees. We ascended nearly a mile along a small foot-path tracked in the rock, on which nothing grew except a few stunted plants of the mimosa. Here the channel which separates Nokhara from the larger island of Dhalac, became visible, and below us in the valley, the site of the water was distinctly marked by a kind of meadow, and several plantations of doom-trees. It was distant another mile, but as I had advanced so far, I determined to proceed. On my arrival I was much surprized to find that the well was a natural one, formed by a chasm in the rock, which was covered for several feet with good soil, and occasionally produced excellent herbage. It was about seven feet from the water, which presented a clear surface of about ten feet long, by three wide, irregular in its shape, from the rocks protruding sides.

As it never fails in the driest season, and supplies the whole island, the reservoir probably extends under a great part of the plain. Its superincumbent bed prevents the heat from having any effect on it. At the distance of forty or fifty yards they had sunk a well, and at the same depth had found water. The Dola told me, that at Dhalac-el-Ki- beer, you could not search three feet deep without obtaining it. On returning to our boat we found the Dola there, who assured us, that water and fresh provisions should be ready in the morning, when I intended to proceed to the opposite island with my tent, and view the port of Dobelew, where Mr. Bruce had anchored.

When I returned on board, I stated my plan to Captain Keys; and observed to him, that as every thing hitherto had appeared so totally different from what we had been led to expect from Mr. Bruce's statement, I conceived it to be of the greatest public advantage to ascertain the real situation and shape of the islands; that for this purpose, I requested the use of one of the boats on the morrow, to attend me till my return, which would probably be in the course of two days. To this I received a positive refusal; with the information, that it was contrary to the regulations of their ship, that any of their boats should be out all night. These regulations were singularly urged by a person, who had kept his boat two nights on shore at Mocha, merely because he preferred sleeping on land; though in consequence he was not on board the Antelope to receive me on my return from the Fox.

I was awakened early the next morning by a violent dispute between Mr. Salt and the pilot, who, although he had the evening before consented to our arrangement, declared that he would not go, nor should his boat go, unless he received ten dollars; a demand which was positively refused. By the interference of Captain Keys he was induced to proceed, but returned under some other pretence ; when the Captain ordered the cutter to be prepared. On this he instantly departed, fearing to lose an opportunity of plundering the party. I staid on board: Keys went on shore to the Dola. He found a large collection of skins filled with water, lying on the beach, covered with mats to protect them from the sun. These were sent on board in the boat, which made three trips, and nearly completed our supply. The Dola demanded only a dollar for twenty-seven skins, which is much cheaper than at Mocha, and the water was far better. The goats we procured were excellent, and not inferior to the mutton we before got. I obtained some shells, but none equal to what I expected. Several of the natives came off in the course of the day. At night I received a note from Mr. Salt, informing me that he had reached Dhalac-el-Ki- beer, but that the Dola of the place would not permit him to move without an order from the Chief Dola at Nokhara. He requested me to procure this, and send him a piece of Surat blue cloth. All this was complied with, and I endeavoured to com pose myself to rest.

Captain Keys went the following morning on shore. At night Mr. Salt returned with a view of Dhalac-el-Kibeer, and made a report of his tour, which led to the following observations. Standing in shore at half a mile from the ship, there were soundings at 3,*1* and 2 fathom, at two hundred yards from the shore. The ship bore W. by S. S. the extremities of the bay from S. by E. to W. by N. N. They proceeded along shore till the ship bore W. N. W. § N. when a sand ap-

Vol. ir. D

peared equidistant from them, about three miles, bearing W. S. W. Close to a plantation of doom - trees, about two miles from the place where they landed, were sixteen wells like those at Nokhara, but the water was not more than two feet below the surface. Here two shepherds were tending, and drawing water for, several camels with their young, a great herd of asses, a few fine goats, and two sheep. As soon as the camels were supplied and driven off, some water was placed in the stone for the birds, which arrived in vast flights, particularly doves. A plantation of date-trees had been lately formed here; which at present did not bear fruit. They hired two asses for a dollar, but they were low and unmanageable.

About four miles and a half from the wells they passed a creek, where they met with a great number of pelicans, plenty of madrapore, and sea-weed, but no shells. On the right was a salt-marsh, which probably, at high spring tides, is connected with one more distant. They rested under the shade of a mimosa, till Hyder, and old Hassan, the boat-man, joined them. The pilot had constantly kept up with them. A native came down from a hill with some milk and water ; he was very civil, but objected to their going to the place from which he came; to avoid affronting him, they did not press it. He got ready two asses, and went on, "with them. The road was rocky and uneven, and in several places the earth had divided, and formed clefts, about three feet across, where widest, and several hundred yards in length. They were of considerable depth; and the splashing of the stones thrown down, proved that there was water at the bottom.

After a fatiguing journey of five miles from their resting place, they got to Dhalac-el-Kibeer by twoo'clock. A pleasant breeze had enabled them to bear the heat. At a little distance from the town they were met by several of the inhabitants, and among others by the priest; he differed in appearance from the rest in nothing except his having a string of beads round his neck. Mr. Salt and his companions were conducted to the Serai, had couches prepared for them, obtained milk and water to drink, and soon afterwards coffee. Their visitors were numerous, as the curiosity of the whole place was excited to view the first Europeans that ever had, in their time, visited them. Mr. Maxfield's uniform in particular excited much curiosity. On their expressing a wish to go out with their books and papers, the priest informed them, that without an order from Nokhara he could not allow it, but that he would, if they pleased, send off a messenger instantly, who might be able to return in the course of the night. This was done, and, as I have before observed, the letter to me was faithfully delivered. Upon expressing a wish to be left to themselves, every body retired, and some very good cakes with milk and water were sent them: these, with the articles they had brought with them, afforded a very tolerable meal, after which they again had coffee. In the evening, under pretence of bathing, they visited the harbour, and, in consequence of what the priest had said, made some observations. They slept on couches in the open air, but were very much disturbed by the rats, which, in the course of the night, seized and carried off from under Mr. Salt's bed, a napkin laid in a basket, which contained all their provisions. Before they were up, the messenger arrived with all the articles sent for, and the necessary permission from the Dola at Nokhara. The. piece of blue Surat cloth was immediately presented to the priest of

the place, and seemed very acceptable. After breakfast, they set off to make their observations.

A little way to the south of the town is the tomb of a most holy Mussulmaun prophet and saint, Abou-el-Heimen. A light is kept constantly burning: to support which, they assured Mr. Salt, it was customary for all travellers to give half a dollar. He would not be the first to break so laudable a custom, and therefore gave the money. Near this place are the ruins of a tank; it was 28 feet long, by 12 broad, and about 18 feet deep. It appeared to have been originally arched at top, and resembled another at some distance ; the form of which was a regular oval, flat at the bottom, of great breadth, and 20 feet deep; the sides also arched at top, leaving a circular opening in the centre about three feet diameter, towards which large gutters were formed in the rock to bring in the water. Near the sea were four others: one was much larger, two others smaller than those above described, and circular. The one in ruins was cut out of the solid rock, then lined with stone and chunamed. There was no water in any of them, but a sediment appeared at the bottom; and on stooping down to look into them, the air was found extremely sultry. All these, they heard, were built by the Parsees, of whom nothing is known except from tradition; from the same source, they have an account of 316 tanks, similar to those above mentioned ; but they admit that they never saw or heard of any one who had seen more than twelve or fourteen: they added, there were none at Do- belew.

Dhalac-el-Kibeer was formerly the principal port of the island. The town is about half a mile from the sea, with a sloping beach of sand between. The harbour is nearly inclosed by a chain of nine

islands that lie off at the distance of about two miles. Beyond these the island of Chumma was visible, bearing from S. "W. § S. to S. -I W. while the extremities of the land bore from S. E. to W. S. W. At present there is scarcely water enough for a dow to approach the shore: till near the islands, it is seldom more than three or four feet deep. Only two vessels were there, one belonging to the place, the other to Massowah. The port still exhibits many vestiges of its former consequence. On the northern side are the ruins of two small mosques built of stone, with round cupolas at top, but of a rude workmanship. In the one towards the sea is an Arabic inscription cut on a stone placed in a recess. Around the mosque a great number of monumental stones are placed upright in the ground, at the heads of the persons whom they commemorate: many are well carved, and beautifully adorned with flowers, and other ornaments: some in Cufic, some in Arabic characters. As the stones are in general of a portable size, Mr. Salt was desirous of taking one away; but, as he was assured by the priest that this could not be done without express permission from the Nayib of Massowah, he contented himself with taking a copy of one inscription, which seemed to be held in the highest veneration, although externally it had nothing to recommend it, being indifferently carved, andx having a corner broken. The priest informed him that it belonged to the Sheik or Sultaun, (he is called both), who built the tanks. It is immediately opposite to the principal mosque, and by the natives constantly kept moist with oil. Among the ruins were several pieces of brick and glass, some of which were perfectly clear. The women seemed to be kept out of the way, as they never appeared except at adistance, and the men objected to their being approached by strangers. The men had not the curling head of the Negroes. There are no trees near the town except two doom-trees and some Acacias. In spite of the opposition of the old pilot, who assured him that there were Bedowees, &c. in the place, Mr. Salt determined to go up a small ascent, whence he had hopes of seeing the Antelope. He set off alone, but finding that he persevered, several of the natives soon followed. He ascended without the least molestation, and had the good fortune to ascertain the following bearings. The Antelope N. 35 W. the mosque nearest the sea S. -I W. the other end of the town S. b. E. distant a mile and three quarters; the extremes of Chumma S. % W. and S. W. b. S.; a sand S. W. b. W.

Leaving the hills, Mr. Salt proceeded about half a mile north to a creek, which they said is the same that separates Dhalac from Nokhara, and ends here; a small boat may come up it. Dobelew is reckoned two days journey distant; Nokhara one; so that their day's journey is about nine miles. About four o'clock the party set off on its return. When they got to the wells, the baggage, with old Hassan, was not come up. They waited some time, and at length sent the pilot to look for him. It was nearly two hours before he made his appearance, with a pitiful story that he had fallen asleep on the road, during which all the things had been stolen. The pilot soon came back by a different way. This old rascal had made so many attempts to cheat them, though in most he had been frustrated by Hyder, that Mr. Salt had not the least doubt that this was another plan to extort money, by re-obtaining the articles lost; he was the more confirmed in his idea, from the pilot's extremeanxiety to have them intrusted to old Hassan, as being honest, instead of a younger man, who could have kept up with the party. The only important article was Mr. Salt's drawing book; he therefore threatened the severest vengeance if the book, &c. were not produced by morning. They returned to, the vessel, and by day light the next morning the old rogue brought every thing, pretending they were obtained with difficulty from a person to whom he had given two dollars, which he desired might be repaid him. This was positively refused, and he only got the four dollars that were originally given for his boat.

I had many observations to make respecting Mr. Bruce's account of these islands, but resolved to defer them till I could fully enter on the subject. In the morning the Dola came off iu the boat: he breakfasted with us on coffee and sweetmeats, and seemed much pleased. I gave him a few pounds of coffee. In the course of the day, his son brought several baskets of shells, among which were some very excellent. I learnt nothing more respecting the place, as the boats were employed in bringing water. At night, however, Mr. Hall, the first Lieutenant, was permitted by Captain Keys to go to a reef, whence he procured some very fine sea eggs (Echini); one species had spines a foot long, and sharp as a needle; the other vvas of a larger kind, and when cleaned, very beautiful. The madrapore was not remarkable. Of coral or coraline I saw no specimen.

I had given notice to the yaptain that I wished to proceed to Massowah. The old Dola came on board in his catamaran, (rather an undignified conveyance,) with his son, who requested a passage" to Massowah: this was willingly granted. His father sent a letter by Keys to the Nayib, praising, as I heard, our good behaviour while at his island. He received the money due to him, and having expressed a wish to hear one of the great guns, as he called them, fired, he was saluted him with one, as his catamaran left the side of the ship. We weighed anchor between ten and eleven, and with a tolerable breeze bore away for Ras Gid- den, which, since we had left Valentia, had never been out of sight. The pilot kept us so much to windward, that at three o'clock we were opposite to Massowah, though distant about three leagues. The wind was very light, and we were not able to get completely into the bay, but anchored without. We were alarmed during this day's sailing by a man calling out that there were shoals right a-head; but they proved only masses of floating fishes spawn, which had so defined an outline, and were so extensive, as to have the complete appearance of shoals. In the night we heard several guns from the shore.

CHAPTER II.

'*Arrival at Massowah.\Reception there.\Visits to the Nayib. \Preparations for the continuation of the voyage.\Disputes with the Captain of the Antelope, and consequent determination to return to Mocha.\Transactions at Massowah, and price of articles there.\Visit to the island of Valentia.\Return to Mocha.\Desertions from the ship.\Encouragement given by the Arab government to European seamen to become Mussulmauns.\Departure of Mr. Salt for India in the Antelope.\Voyage in the Fox friga te to Aden.\Transactions there.\Return to Mocha.\Transactions there.\Voyage to Bombay.*

.A.T six, on May 24, we were under weigh, but were obliged soon to come to an anchor, as the land-wind was against us, and there was no room to work. Mr. Maxfield had been sent off in the jolly boat to the shore, where we saw a considerable crowd collected close to a mud building, which we presumed to be the castle. On his return he informed us, that the natives had perceived our approach, and had taken us for the Wa- habees, in consequence of which the Nayib had come over from Arkeko, and they had been all 'night under arms. Mr. Maxfield informed themthat a great man was on board, going to Suez, who would probably pay the Nayib a visit; that we wished for permission to enter the port, and obtain water and provisions; that we were willing to salute the fort with three, five, or seven guns, whichever the Nayib would return. He was at the head of his troops, and replied, that he should be happy to see the great man; that the island and every thing it afforded was his, and that he would return five guns, but did not wish for more, as it would alarm the Bedowees of the surrounding country, and make them hasten down to protect him. Mr. Maxfield said the natives were extremely civil, and told him, he might stay if he pleased, and send away the boat. This he thought suspicious, for which we laughed at him, and compared him to Mr. Bruce, who thought the man near Crab Island must be a villain from his smiling.

We so strongly suspected our old pilot, that we would not permit him to leave the ship till *I* had gone on shore and secured a good reception. During the whole voyage he had been threatening the Naqueda, or native master, of the dow, that he would, on his arrival here, complain to the Nayib of his injustice in giving him only fifteen dollars for piloting the ship to Massowah, when he himself received so large a sum as four hundred. When he saw the dow's boat going on shore without him, he thought they might make their story good, and his rage exceeded all bounds: he called to them, on their peril, not to proceed, and, when they went on, continued muttering to himself, and told the Captain he was so angry, that if his head shpuld be cut off, it would not prevent his complaining.

Several Banians came off in a boat, the end of which was covered with green and red silk. They brought an additional invitation to me from theNayib. Our salute of five guns was immediately fired, and was answered, first by two guns near the castle. These were loaded with ball, the whizzing of which, though the guns were pointed wide of us, we could plainly hear, and from such bad marksmen was by no means pleasant: the third from the same place missed fire. At length two more were fired from the same place, and, half an hour afterwards, a fifth from the other side of the town, all loaded with ball. I had a letter from Devage, the India Company's broker at Mocha, to one of the Banians, which I delivered. I consulted him on the subject, and then determined to go on shore. I put on a plain Indian dress of muslin, with a shawl round my middle, in which I stuck my tulwah, or Indian sword. Mr. Salt and my servant had also dresses of that country, and Hy- der went as interpreter.

We set off in the boat, under a salute from the ship, followed by all the Banians. We landed close to the town. There were three brass cannon there, much injured by time: with these they attempted a salute, but as the first missed fire, and I advanced, I cannot tell with how many they intended to honour me. I landed at a pier, with a small open space, that led to an ancient gateway, on one side of which was a large building. In one of its balconies I perceived several well dressed people. There was a considerable crowd, but they behaved very well. I entered by the gateway, and turning to the left, passed through several ruined rooms, and ascended a slope of rubbish to a large apartment, the end of which was covered with mats, on which was seated a very numerous assemblage of half clad natives. On the left side, in the balcony, was the Nayib, and several well dressed men. Opposite to them were two old fashioned English elbow chairs with high backs.

On entering, I made my salaam to the Nayib, who pointed to the chairs. Mr. Salt and I immediately seated ourselves, my servant and Hyder standing by. The Nayib was in one corner; he was dressed in white muslin with a shawl of scarlet for a turban, precisely similar to the one I wore round my waist. Next him, (as I have since learned,) was his brother, the Sirdar of the forces, in a large Janissary turban of scarlet: the others were his sons and secretary, &c. The crowd followed us in, and were now crouched on their haunches, over the whole surface to the door, completely filling the room, like Milton's devils in Pan- dsemonium; but in no other respect would the comparison hold, for their countenances were generally pleasing and intelligent, free from the traces of violent passions. I delivered a message to Hyder, expressive of my thanks for the answer the Nayib had returned me in the morning. Hyder interpreted this to the Banian, who went stooping, and in a low voice communicated it to the Nayib. Our whole conversation passed in the same way, and was merely complimentary : as I had been informed it would be wrong to enter on any business at my public audience. He told me that the island was mine, and begged I would make what use I pleased of it; that a house was prepared for me, and that he hoped I would continue in it during my stay. To this I assented. Coffee was brought, after the Arab fashion, in very small china cups, without milk or sugar: these were placed in larger ones of gilt filagree, to prevent the fingers from being burnt. Afterwards a caftan of red silk was thrown over my shoulders. They enquired who Mr. Salt was; and, on being informed he was my Secretary, there was some confusion, and a man went out. I now wished to take my leave, but was desired to stay till myhouse would be ready. I suspected what afterwards proved to be the case. A man entered, and immediately a caftan of blue cloth with yellow silk facing was thrown over Mr. Salt.

I now made my salaam, and the Nayib rose to attend me. We went down together. The troops in the gateway got up from their couches to make their salaams, which he returned by a wave of the hand. He attended me a considerable distance, but without saying a word. At a sharp turning he departed one way, and directed some of his people to shew me another. At length I reached a small house by the sea-side, nearly opposite to the Antelope. Here, in a stone built room, several couches were prepared, some with carpets and some with blankets thrown over them; it was however comparatively cool, from the thickness of the walls, and the many openings which admitted the sea-breeze. The Banians attended me, and I was soon overpowered by visitors. After obtaining some sherbet, I sent off Mr. Salt to inform the Captain of what had passed, and to invite him on shore. I then told my visitors I wished to go to sleep, and they immediately retired.

The next day I was informed by the Banian that the Nayib intended to visit me in the evening, when I should have an opportunity of delivering my present. About four o'clock he sent for Hyder, and told him to acquaint me that he had no such intentions; that if he came he must have all his people and troops with him, who would all expect presents from him; and added, what have I to give them? He wished that when it was quite dark, I would come alone to his house, when he would give me a private audience. As I was assured that the reason assigned was a realone, I consented to his request, without hesitation.

Accordingly, about eight o'clock, the Banian, and another person, arrived to conduct me. I did not even take Mr. Salt with me. Hyder carried my present concealed, which consisted of a handsome pair of shawls, a gold tissue dress, complete, but not made up, and a piece of kincaub. He received me in an undress, sitting on a bed of the country, out of doors, in one of the yards of his house: the only light was from two small Ian- thorns, the one suspended, the other on the ground. He made his salaams in return to mine, by placing his hand on his breast, and pointed to a seat placed close to his, at right angles. Perceiving Mr. Salt was not with me, he sent for him, and he soon arrived, accompanied by my landlord.

We had a long conversation, in which I represented that *Jny* motive for coming was to ascertain, whether our ships could with safety pass up this coast to Suez, and obtain water and provisions on the way. I pointed out the great advantage that would consequently ensue to his people, and expressed my satisfaction at having hitherto met with so much civility from his subjects, and in having succeeded in ascertaining what I wished. He replied that the island was mine, and that I might do what I pleased. That if our ships came, they should have every thing he could supply them with. That here they were very civil, good people; but, that, on the main, though they belonged to him, he could not equally answer for them. He offered sherbet in a silver cup, which the person who brought it, tasted in my presence.

I now produced my present, prefacing it by saying, that I was not a merchant, but a man of rank in my own country, travelling for amusement, andreturning thither after a long absence; that I therefore had no merchandize, nor any thing worthy his acceptance; nevertheless, I wished him to accept a part of what I had, as a mark of my respect and gratitude, for his attentions since my arrival. He received my present, but said, What is this for? Have you not every thing? what do you ask from me ? I replied, that through his kindness, I had every thing I wished for, and I hoped he would continue it to me and mine. I mentioned the pilots; he said they had been sent for. I asked permission for my people to look for shells, and to shoot. He begged me to apply to the Banian whenever I wished them to go out, and I should have some of his people to attend : but said there was a contagious disorder on the islands and therefore he wished us not to visit them lest we should bring it back. He assured me the ship should have every supply she wanted. He gave Hyder five dollars3 and, after coffee, we took our leave much pleased with his behaviour.

He was rather a small man, of a grave countenance, and about forty years of age. His name was Edris; he had been nine years Nayib, and bore a most excellent character. He was the son of the late Nayib Hannes or Othman, who was the son of Achmed, of whom Mr. Bruce speaks so well, and who was nephew and heir of Hassan the then Nayib, but did not survive him.

The heat was very great; the thermometer at 96, and less air than usual. I was for a day or two exceedingly unwell.

The Nayib sent frequently to enquire after me. His brother and sons were all here. A great number of the natives visited the ship: by the Captain's orders they had coffee and raisins, with

S

which they were much pleased. My room was, as pleasant as could be in this climate. I viewed from my window the island of Valentia, distant about five leagues, Ras Gidden, and the chain of mountains that lines the coast of the Red Sea from this place to the plains of Egypt. Behind these the summit of Taranta peeps out, which gives credit, by its height, to Mr. Bruce's account of the diffi culty he had in ascending it. The island of Shiek Said is pleasingly covered with trees, and seems to be nearly in the middle of this unruffled bason.

When I became a convalescent my visitors were numerous, and my host proved extremely intelligent. I gathered from him the following information. Dhalac is considered as a profitable government for the person who holds it. The Nayib receives from him only sixty dollars in money, and also obtains some camels, goats, and asses. If any thing should throw a large sum into the hands of the Dola, the Nayib would send to him and claim it; but if as in our case, it amounted to no more than thirty or forty dollars, he would let him keep all. The Nayib lives generally at Arkeko, where he has a very good house, and one wife, although the place is not so pleasant as Massowah ; but in this he finds his interest, because the greater part of his dominions lie there, and his people have an easy access to him.

On the hills of Jibbel Gidden, and those behind Arkeko, are elephants, the teeth of which are exported: from Habesh they send gee, hides, gold dust, civet, sheep, and slaves. Of the latter the number is lately much lessened : a very satisfactory circumstance, and a proof of the increasing civilization of that country. The Suakin trade inslaves is, they say, proportionably augmenting. In return, they send up British broad-cloth, arms, ammunition, and the different manufactures of India: a little grain is also brought down from Abyssinia. They have, in their own country, plenty of goats and oxen; the sea supplies them with an inexhaustible variety of fish of the finest kinds; so that their living is by no means bad: game also seems in the greatest plenty. Water at Arkeko is not very good, but abundant. On the island of Massowah are about thirty tanks, which are filled in the rainy season : these are kept closed, and are, I believe, private property. They are not sufficient for the supply of the place, and much water is brought every morning by the boats from Arkeko.

The houses are each surrounded by a fence of reeds: the rooms are detached, and built of the same: within, they are lined with mats. The common people are extremely civil, and no oihe carries any arms, except the immediate family of the Nayib. My Ascar had no weapon except a stick. The natives did not seem jealous of their women, who came down to bathe, and perform their ablutions close to the place where I sat, without any appearance of shame. The slaves of the neighbours had, I believe, been found not over coy by the Europeans on shore. My next door neighbour was the Sirdar of the Ascarri, and I suspected, the intercourse was permitted by him, and that he shared in the profit. I satf only one deformed person, a female dwarf with bandy legs, who bathed before us regularly every day. The men and women are naturally well made, but child birth destroys the figures of the latter.

The Ascarri are completely under the influence
Vol. *u,* E
of the Nayib, who pays them out of the duties which ought to be remitted to Constantinople. They still recognise the Sultaun as their master, but it is a mere form. The Nayib pays nothing to the King of Abyssinia, but they are, I understand, on very good terms.

The Banians here are very comfortable: they say they have ever been the same, and some of them were those mentioned by Mr. Bruce. They are allowed wives, if they please, which is not the case at Mocha; and they seem less oppressed. They amount to eighteen in number, and carry on a considerable trade. The Nayib receives ten per cent, ad valorem on all goods exported and imported, and one dollar for each individual who enters the country to trade. The pearl fishery is renewed to a certain degree by the people of Dha- lac, but although the best banks belong to the Nayib, he receives no share of the profit.

We were still delayed here, though the dow was ready for sea. The pilot arrived from Dhalac, but went back immediately to procure two more, who he said were absolutely necessary for so large a vessel. If the passage above should prove as clear as that below, this delay will never be necessary hereafter: I had indeed to regret that we did not do more; but Captain Keys threw every difficulty in our way, prevented Mr. Maxfield from making many observations that he wished, and, as we were all convinced, endeavoured even to mislead us by false longitude. Latterly he concealed it entirely, and then he declared his time-keeper was out of order, and that he should take Mr. Bruce's longitude, and begin a new rate. We determined not to follow him, but (as we should anchor every night,) to endeavour to carry on a chain of bearings the whole way to Suakin. Mr, Maxfield had finished a chart of tire harbour, and proved Mr. Bruce's to be erroneous. It seems indeed that his was a copy from that of a Portuguese, corrected by a bird's eye view.

I sent to the Nayib for permission for Mr. Salt and my servant to go out on a shooting party on the main-land. To this he willingly assented; and said he would send to Arkeko for mules and people to attend them. The Sirdar procured me some good shells, but begged Hyder would desire me to remember, and take care of him ; adding, he wanted dollars. I told Hyder to say I had only sufficient for my expences, as we never travelled with much money, and that I could procure no more till I got to Egypt; but that of what I had, I had given him a part. He, however, seemed to hope for something, as he was very active in procuring shells.

The shooting party returned by ten o'clock, with seven birds of the pheasant kind, with mottled black, or rather brown and white feathers, the neck bare, and yellow underneath, red and bare about the eyes: they also killed a hare, and two small deer, which tasted exactly like the roebuck. Fortunately for the sportsmen, it was cloudy the whole of the morning, who, however, were heartily fatigued and sore in the feet. Thermometer 98. The Sirdar brought me another collection of shells, which contained only one worth having. I explained what I wished, and he sent the men off again. Hyder privately promised them a present, if they exerted themselves, which should not be mentioned to their master. My servant bore the climate well: he went out on a catamaran like a native, and brought me from the reef a considerable variety of madrapores, some very beautiful.

The most desirable article to the natives iscutlery. They asked for some pencils and paper, and every kind of nick-knack. They had scarcely seen any of our European conveniences, and were much delighted with them. They learned their names, and pronounced them with great facility. The Nayib's son asked for powder and ball, to kill me an elephant. One of the pilots arrived from Dhalac: he seemed doubtful whether he could take the ship to Suakin, but wished to wait for his brother's opinion, who had been sent for.

The Banian came to me to say, that he was my servant, and would do whatever I pleased; that if I did not choose to let him manage the Captain's business, he would never go near him. I told him, I had no such wish, but desired he would prevent any underhand dealings with the pilots, to induce them to declare the voyage to Suakin impracticable. He assured me that he would. This visit gave me great satisfaction, as it assured me I possessed a sufficient influence with the pilots to induce them to speak the truth. I had been not a little astonished by an observation Captain Keys made to Mr. Macgie, that if we could not go to Suakin, we must return back to Hodeida, there being no passage between the islands above Dhalac. How this could be known to him, except from the accurate Mr. Bruce, I know not; I therefore suspected a plan to prevent our continuing our researches. Indeed, Hyder told me that the Na- queda was constantly desiring the Captain's interpreter to persuade his master that the winds were too strong for the ship to venture among the rocks of Suakin. He naturally wished his voyage should end here, that he might pocket his four hundred dollars, without any farther trouble. I was afraid our old pilot might corrupt the new ones, and therefore requested the Nayib to send him offbefore their arrival, which he did. I found, however, that I only got rid of half the evil.

The Nayib sent to request I would come to him, to meet C'aptain Keys and the pilots. I sent in answer, that I would with pleasure obey his commands, but that I did not wish, on this occasion, to meet Captain Keys, as he had nothing to do with my arrangement. They came a second time to request, that if I did not choose to come myself, I would send Mr. Salt. I now entered with them into a full explanation of my situation; that I was at liberty to go wherever I thought proper; that my wish was to go to Suakin ; but before I could decide, I must consult the pilots. That I should then inform Captain Keys what my plans were; and it remained for him to settle with the men, with which matter I had no concern. That in consequence our meeting would be useless, or the attendance of any one on my part, when he waited on the Nayib. They were themselves perfectly satisfied (my landlord and the Banian), and immediately went to the Nayib. In a short time they returned with both the pilots, and a very kind message from the Nayib, in the true Asiatic style, " that he only wished to know my will to obey it; and that he had sent the people for me to do what I pleased with them."

I found the brothers equally well behaved, and intelligent. They informed me that the first part of the voyage was open sea, through which they could conduct the ship night and day, if I were not afraid. I asked if, at this time of the year, they could steer a dow day and night; they said, yes. Then I said, we should not be afraid to go on. They continued, " that at a place called Ageeg, the passage became narrow, between rocks aad islands, but that the former were all abovewater; that it was sufficiently deep, and about a mile wide; that there was a place where we could, anchor, and that a fair wind of one day would take us to Suakin." I asked, if we should find any difficulty in getting from Ageeg to Suakin, and whether they would carry us to Jidda. They said they would not go themselves, but that they would take us on the outside of a very large island, where we should be in the main sea, and could run ourselves easily to that place without assistance." I was now perfectly satisfied, and told the Nayib's messengers, that I should write to-morrow to the Captain, to inform him of my plans, and require him to make the proper arrangements with the pilots. I begged them again to express to their master how very grateful I felt for his numerous attentions to me, which I should take care to represent to all my countrymen, who might visit the Red Sea.

I sent to require a boat to carry my servant to a reef opposite the town to search for shells, which was complied with. He had not much success. The natives, in the course of the day, brought me some new species. There was a great variety of dead shells thrown on shore of a species, of which I was not able to procure living specimens : they probably came from some of the opposite islands. Money will hardly induce the natives to exert themselves. I found our landlord's name was Abou Yusuff, or Father Joseph, and he well became the title, for he had all the appearance of a jolly, good natured, Benedictine monk.

On the 8th I wrote officially to Captain Keys, informing him of my intention to go to Suakin, but that if the winds should prove too strong, I might probably go only to Ageeg, and then roceed for Jidda. He afterwards saw the Nayib. pilots and Naqueda of the dow were there.The Captain required the Naqueda to hire both the pilots, which he refused. He then demanded that he should give back the four hundred dollars. The Naqueda offered one hundred, or said he would hire one pilot. The Captain said that one must then go in his ship, and the dow go ahead without one. This the man positively refused, and said he would not go to Suakin. The Nayib told him, if he did not do what the Captain desired, he would put him in prison ; and so the conference ended. I had this from the Banian, who was present, and was sent by the Nayib to communicate it to me. Mr. Salt and my servant caught some very beautiful small fish; they also procured a few shells.

The Captain was again sent for by the Nayib in the evening, who wished him to pay one pilot, and the Naqueda the other, but nothing definitive was settled. I had a most extraordinary answer from the Captain at night, stating, that there had been much delay by taking this passage, that we should not be able to reach Suez, and most probably not even Tor; and notifying to me that the Antelope must leave the Red Sea by the middle of August, in order to save her passage for the season. The pilot informed Hyder, that the Captain's interpreter had been talking with him, and telling him that if he went with us, he would be starved, for there was no rice on board.

I wrote a reply to Captain Keys, stating that I considered his letter as a declaration, that he would not obey the Governor General's orders, and requiring that he would communicate to me his instructions from the Bombay Government, and give me a definitive answer in regard to his intentions of obeying the Governor General, with respect to my future voyage.

About four o'clock my landlord came to mefrom the Nayib, to say that the pilots were ready it to go to Suakin, as I and the Captain had desired. *i* That the Captain had been with him and refused 3 to give two hundred dollars, (which the pilots si asked, and the Nayib desired they might receive,) n saying he would give but one hundred and sixty, u and that if the Nayib did not make them accept i] this offer, that he would go back immediately to *n* Bombay. The Nayib desired him to express to u me, that the Captain, neither last night nor that 5 day, had behaved civilly to him : that he staid a there merely to assist me; that he wished to return to Arkeko, and desired to know my intentions, and when I meant to depart; and added, that he wished to have my commands to go to Arkeko. He also used an Asiatic expression, that the Nayib said " the Captain had two tongues." I expressed my extreme regret that such a circumstance should have occurred. I stated that the Captain was no servant of mine, but of great people of rny country in India, who had ordered him to carry me to Suez ; that I could therefore only represent to them his misconduct, when I had no doubt he would be punished. That I wished as much as possible to be gone, but that my departure in some degree depended on the Captain ; that, however, I would myself with pleasure visit the Nayib, and take my leave of him in the evening, and hoped he would not stay a moment longer there to be insulted.

As soon as he retired, the Banian arrived, who confirmed what had passed at the interview, but knew nothing of the Nayib's message to me. He advised me to give something to the Nayib that night, and promise something more when I went on board the ship. I went about eight o'clock, and had merely a conference of civility. He wishedto know whether I should want pilots or not. I told him I was going to write to the Captain, and his answer would decide me, and that I would positively let him know the next day. I found the Nayib, dressed in a dark India muslin, in the same place, with the same attendants, and without any arms. He confirmed all the Banian had said. J made apologies, and pleaded that all the English were not like Captain Keys. He positively refused returning to Arkeko till I departed.

I received an answer from Keys. He expressed his concern that I should suppose it possible he could intend to disobey the Governor General's orders, that he conceived they were issuetf under the idea that our voyage would be over long before the fifteenth of August, and that, therefore, on that day, he should positively depart on his return to India. However astonished I might be at his thus placing his conjectures in opposition to his Excellency's most positive orders, 1 had no. means of preventing his carrying his resolution into effect; as he, however, professed his resolution to comply with any request of mine till that period, it remained for me to decide what I should do.

To continue my voyage, for the purpose of surveying the coast or visiting Suakin, was totally out of the question, as nine weeks were evidently insufficient for that purpose; I had therefore only to consider, whether, by abandoning all my plans of discovery, I could reach Suez within the time he was pleased to allow me. He had in his letter declared that it was highly improbable, and upon calculation we found it impossible. The average passage of the ships during the Egyptian expedi tion, was six weeks from Mocha to Cosseir, a fortnight of which took them to Jidda, as the wind is

fair to Jibbel Teir. Our pilots told us we should be more than that time in getting there, and we should be obliged to stop to take in water, of which the ship could not carry a quantity more than sufficient for forty days; and also provisions of every kind, of which they did not pretend she had above two months stock on board: of bread she had not one month's. These articles are not to be procured in Egypt. The Antelope's bottom was alse in a state that prevented her sailing quick. The Captain was evidently alarmed, and would not carry much sail; I could not therefore calculate on getting to Cosseir in less than eight weeks. If I staid there, I had only a week to write to Mr. Rosette, to receive his answer, to prepare a guard of camels, to pass to Kenne, and thence to secure boats to go down the Nile. This would have taken up at least six weeks; and for my safety it was necessary that the ship should still wait till I could send back intelligence of my safe arrival. Unless, therefore, I meant to deliver myself into the hands of the greatest thieves and robbers in the world, without any protection; my stay at Cosseir was out of the question; to get in a week to Suez from Cosseir was impossible; and indeed in all probability it would have been three weeks. My stay there, to make the necessary preparations, would have been at least a fortnight, and the subsequent delay about a week. Unwilling, therefore, as I, of course, was, to measure back my way, and submit to the confinement of a ship for four months, I was compelled to do so, and I determined -to write in the morning to Captain Keys, directing him to go to Mocha, where I could consult with Mr. Pringle; and wait there for Captain Vashon, who would probably give me a passage to Bombay, where he would arrive with the coffee in time for me to take my pas-

sage in one of the Chinamen. By these means I should be certain of getting to England in January. The moment I quitted the Antelope she came under Captain Vashon's command.

I therefore wrote fully to Captain Keys pointing out the impracticability of my getting up to Suez, within the period he had prescribed, and the absurdity of my wandering about till that time in a rough sea. I concluded by giving him notice, that in a few days I should return to Mocha. I sent to the Nayib to say I should not want the pilots, and gave them ten dollars, as a compensation for the trouble they had in coming over. The Dola of Dhalac arrived, and paid me a visit: I suspected he brought over presents to the different men, for our landlord got two goats, one of which he gave to Mr. Salt, and the other to the Doctor. The latter had plenty of patients, but in general they were cases of debility from intermittent fevers.

Captain Keys went on board in the morning. I wrote to him, and requested two of the Europeans might assist my servant in collecting shells and madrapores, as I should have no future place to touch at, where they would be found in such variety. This was complied with immediately. In short, the Captain seemed to be in high glee at having escaped the dangers of the voyage; an idea that superseded every other; or else he expected that he should, by his politeness in future, prevent me from exercising that retaliation which was so completely in my power. The Nayib wished to persuade us to pursue our original plan of going to Suakin. The fact was, he would have got at least one hundred dollars out of the two hundred which the pilots were to have received, and he did not like to lose the money.

My servant and the men brought some very finespecimens of madrapore, and the natives some new shells. At night we heard a most terrible uproar of women, screaming and crying: on enquiry we found that a dow had arrived from Jidda, and brought intelligence of the death of the master of one of the neighbouring houses, whose brother was in the service of the Nayib. On going out, we found the street crowded with people, all crying, as well as the women within the habitation. The tom-toms soon set them a dancing; and this continued to our great annoyance all night, with only occasional intermissions. They told us this would be continued every morning for two years; but as the town has been free from this nuisance since our arrival, and probably several people have died within the last two years, I did not give credit to their assertions.

We learned from the dow that Captain Vashon arrived at Jidda about ten days before she sailed ; I hoped, therefore, he would soon get down to Mocha. The Nayib in the evening sent to request some vinegar, and something to smell to for the head-ach. I sent some Chili vinegar, and one of my silver stopper bottles, filled with volatile alkali, which were acceptable.

Early in the morning, all the women in the town were down at the water side in their best clothes, to wash themselves and the widow in the sea, after having assisted her all night in her lamentations. At the end of four months she may marry again. None of them attempted to keep their faces covered. Their dress consisted of two pieces of the striped cloths of Arabia, one worn round their middle, and another over their shoulders. Their hair was plaited, whether woolly or not: the pains taken with these plaits, when the former is the case, conquers nature, and gives a length of several inches to the hair. They wore ornaments of beads, small hoop ear-rings of gold or silver, and sequins. The dress of the men is nearly similar. The higher order wear the Arab dress, or a plain shirt and drawers of the same: the common people, a single wrapper round the middle. They use sandals, as drawn by Niebuhr. My servant and the men went off with the catamaran for the islands. The boys brought a great many shells: some were good.

Nothing particular occurred during five days; we had been chiefly employed in packing the ma- drapore. The air till the 18th had been much hotter, the wind rather southerly. The clouds hung over the Habesh hills, and rain on the 16th fell so near as Arkeko. It lightened much, and thunder was heard at a distance: dappled clouds covered the horizon every morning. The thermometer was never above 96, yet the want of the usual breeze made us suffer more than if it had been 100. The Nayib left Massowah on the 16th, and the next day sent to say he would come back, which I requested he would not. A man who was ill of the small-pox died. No wonder the disease is so fatal, as the natives confine the patients, as soon as they are seized, to a warm room. After the Nayib's departure I had no water nor any thing else sent me, and was consequently obliged to buy, which we considered as a hint that they wished us gone; the seamen were allowed water only from Arkeko, of which they complained bitterly, as having a mixture of the sea water, no more of the water of the place being allowed to be sold, except to me. I this day notified to the Captain my intention of going on board in the morning.

The day was a busy one, and I was pestered with visitors. Mr. Macgie and the sailors went on board at six, and Abou Yusuff watched me very closely lest I also should make my escape The Banian brought me a piece of Habesh cloth, and Mr. Salt a pair of horns. We were told the Nayib had been at the wars against the Bedowees, and had driven them away, having taken one prisoner, and retaken the cattle they had driven off. He threatened to return before 1 went. I was very much vexed at discovering that I had lost my thermometer, a thing which could be of no value to any native. My servant was quite as much so on missing a shawl and several shirts of his own. I found living here by no means cheap, though the necessaries of life are not dear. The following is a list of several articles with their prices. A few rhinoceros horns are to be had at *1* dollars

per frassel. Gold per Massowah wakea, llf dollars. N. B.

The Mocha wakea is to the Massowah as *5* to

6; 10 wakea yield one of silver, as they say. Civet, 3l- dollars per wakea. Rhinoceros horns, ?§ dollars per wakea. Elephants teeth, 22 dollars per frassel. A good female slave, 60 dollars. A good male ditto, according to his age, from 40

to 80 dollars.

Rice per bag of 105lb. *5* dollars,

A rotol of gee, 2 dollars.

Fowls, 12 for a dollar.

Goats, 2 for ditto.

Sheep, 2 for ditto.

Cow, 1 for 5 dollars.

Camels, 4 to 5 dollars.

Horses, 100 dollars.

Mules, 15 to 50 dollars.

Asses, 3 for 4 dollars.

Water, 23 skins for a dollar.

Fire wood, a man's load for 3 dahab or harf (360

beads.)

Sequins do not pass current; dollars and Venetian glass beads are the only money in use; 2760 of the latter make a dollar. The subdivision is into 23 dahabs of 120 beads each. The whole charge of the Nayib, for water, wood, and fresh provisions during our stay for the use of the ship, was sixty dollars. The people are extremely civil, and seem perfectly happy. The soldiers have each three dollars per month, which proves that that sum is adequate to maintaining a family. Many fruits and vegetables, I have no doubt, would grow here. I saw none of the former, and of the latter only a species of Solanum. From the highest to the lowest they are importunate beggars, and, from my experience I can add, occasionally thieves. The usual price of a house is one dollar per month; yet my landlord was ever asking for something, and seemed hardly satisfied with the ten dollars which I gave him for the tAventy-six days I had occupied his house. I saw several Abyssinians, and had much conversation with them respecting their country. The account that they gave me was found afterwards by Mr. Salt to be in many respects inaccurate, and must be uninteresting to the public, as I have given, in another part of my travels, the observations which were made by him and two other gentlemen during a residence of several months with the Ras Welleta Selasse, in the province of

At five in the morning I escaped in the Captain's boat from all my beggars, except from Abou Yusuff, and the Banian, who determined to attend me to the ship, which had already quitted the harbour. The land breeze was fresher than usual, and a considerable swell came from the northward, but the Captain continued his course, and it was two hours before we overtook him, when the sun was already extremely powerful. I gave the Banian a shawl, in return for many little presents he had made me, though I knew that he had handsomely profited by purchasing every article I wanted for my table. He had been extremely attentive, and deserved a reward. He had some difference with the Captain before he left the vessel, but 1 did not enquire into the cause. I sent a sword by him to the Nayib, as a last proof of my regard, with many wishes for his health and prosperity. He and Abou Yusuff at length departed, I believe, well satisfied with the presents made them. We had already stretched out a considerable distance from Massowah. The breeze was pleasant, and after rounding the point of the shoal, we anchored in Antelope bay, within a quarter of a mile of Va- lentia Island, by four o'clock. The Captain wished Mr. Maxfield to survey it, and I consented to stay two days for that purpose. Mr. Salt and he went out in the evening to measure a base. It was so sultry that I slept on the deck.

The next day Mr. Maxfield was top ill to go out; Mr. Salt went to take some bearings, and I obtained a boat and some sailors to attend my servant in collecting shells. The heat was very great, and my situation extremely unpleasant. As Mr. Maxfield was too unwell to continue the survey of the island, I determined to depart the next day. A great quantity of biscuit was this day condemned and thrown overboard. I heard that the salt provisions were in an equally bad state, and that there was only a small quantity of spirits on board, it was therefore fortunate that we did not continue our voyage; yet the Antelope was reported to me as being ready for sea.

We weighed anchor with a pleasant breeze from the W. N. W. The dow went a-head after clearing Antelope bay she kept farther out from the land. The man at the mast head, about half after nine, called out that there was shoal water a-head: no notice was taken by the officer of the watch, and we passed over the identical shoal, which we had in going up observed and laid down Fortunately for us there were three fathom and a quarter on it, so we passed in safety. It is only a few hundred yards in extent. Our dow was of much use. We sailed all night; light airs and pleasant. I slept on the deck.

We continued along shore till night, confirming our chart by new bearings. We found it as accurate as we could expect. A light breeze ; little sail carried. At night still less.

June 23. | At day-light Jibbel Zeigur was ES. ; the Abyssinian land hardly visible through the haze. At nine Jibbel Aroe bore from E|S. to

We passed it before dark, leaving on our right the white rocks, which we had seen from Bunder Baileul. We found that instead of a cluster of small rocks, the Aroes consisted of one large island, with five or six to E. and S. of it of different sizes ; the passage was seven miles wide at least, and there was apparently deep water close to the shore and rocks. We then made with a freshening breeze for the Arabian coast, which was visible, but did not reach it till near twelve, when we cast anchor. There was a considerable swell.

June 24. | At six we were again under sail and coasting down ; by seven saw the town of Mocha : before twelve came to an anchor, closer in than we were before. The swell was much less than when the wind blew from the south. We were much surprised at the colours not being hoisted on the factory, but a boat coming on board, we learned that

Vol. n. f

Mr. Pringle was well. I requested the boat to go on shore, which was ordered, and I landed about two o'clock. Mr. Pringle was excessively astonished to see me, believing me dead, from my flag not being hoisted, and there being no salute. I soon explained to him the cause, and took possession of the upper apartments at the factory. We found here an American ship which came from Salem near Boston, for a cargo of coffee.

To my great astonishment I was informed this morning that two English boys belonging to the Antelope, who had been left here in consequence of illness, had deserted to the Dola. I immediately sent my servant to them to enquire the reason, and to try to persuade them to return. Their answer was, that the evening before they had been sent for by Captain Keys, who asked them if they were not quite well; they replied, nearly so. He then said he supposed they were tired of being idle on shore, and would be glad to return to the ship. They said they had not been idle, and that they liked best to be on shore, because they got plenty to at. " Very well, gentlemen," he replied, " you will be pleased to go on board tomorrow morning, and I will give you a note to Mr. Hall, who shall punish you for this." This, they said, decided them, and in the night they got over the wall. One fell, and was severely hurt. Both had the liver disease, and must inevitably perish in this climate; I therefore consulted with Mr. Pringle, and we determined to do all we could to get them back. Captain Keys sent for my ship servant, and gave him a lecture for presuming to obey me in going to the boys without his permission. He also declared his resolution of visiting the Dola himself. We were sorry for this, but conceived we had no right to interfere: as histhreats had driven them away, it was not very likely that any declaration of his would bring them back. They could have no confidence in the promise of a Captain of the Bombay marine, after a transaction that took place during the expedition to Egypt. A man was delivered up by the Arabs to the Captain of the Crui.zer, on his pledging his honour that he should not be punished; yet, as soon as he had him in his power, he tied him up, and flogged him in the presence of the very people to whom he had made the engagement. A promise is by the Arabs considered as most sacred, and the laws of hospitality bound them to protect the man; their indignation, therefore, was excited beyond all bounds. The Banian, who attended Captain Keys, informed me that the boys Repeated this story, and told him they would never go back.

When I applied to the Dola to let me and Mr. Pringle see them, it was positively refused, though in the morning it had been acceded to; he pretended, that as the Captain had seen them, it was unnecessary that any one else should. As a last resource, I wrote to Mr. Pringle's interpreter, the Hadgi, who was at Sanna, to make the strongest remonstrances to the Vizier, to claim them as my servants, and to represent that the offence was greatly aggravated by their being taken from the factory which was more immediately under the protection, of the Imaum. I likewise desired that he would obtain for me a definitive answer, whether they were determined to persevere in their present system of encouraging our sailors to desert, that 1 might, on my return, be able to represent the case properly to the India Government. The extent of this evil calls loudly for remedy, and nothing can in my ttiind be easier, as a single ship would oblige, them

to restore every renegado. Some years ago the French bombarded the town, in consequence of the Dola's not paying a debt of seventy thousand dollars. They first fired on his house, where they killed several persons; and afterwards on a Friday (the sabbath of the Mussulmauns), threw a shell into the great mosque. This brought the Dola to his senses, and the cash was paid. He even grew so polite as to lower the duties from three to two and a half per cent. Our character certainly suffers very considerably in the eyes of the native powers for having so long submitted to the insult.

The system of decoying away seamen in a Mussulmaun port, which is so very serious an inconvenience to all Christian ships, is not done from any religious motive, but from an idea that all Christians understand the working of great guns, and to this office they are all destined. In the time of Niebuhr the pay of a renegado was one dollar and a half per month ; it was then raised to two dollars and a half: and within the last ten months has been sncreased to four dollars, in consideration of the high price of every article. The Captain of the renegadoes is an Italian, who, thirty years ago, came here in the command of a native vessel from India : he turned Mussulmaun sold the vessel and cargo, and shared the profits of his villainy with the Dola of that time. He is now the active instrument in inducing others to desert their religion; he watches for them on the pier, and invites them to the Jew's town, where spirits are to be purchased. If intoxication follow, they are carried in that state to the Dola's, whence it is not easy to make a retreat. A shew of liberality is kept up by permitting their friends to see them for the first three days, during which time they

never circumcised, but the most liberal offers are made; and the temptation of free access to the women can seldom be resisted by the sailor. Repentance soon overtakes them from poverty, and the deprivation of their usual comforts.

They are not much troubled on the score of their new religion, though at first they are obliged to learn the necessary prayers, and the forms of prostration and ablution. These are acquired at Moosa, a town about thirty miles up the country. On their return to Mocha no compulsion is used to make them attend the mosque. At present there are only four white renegadoes, though numbers deserted from our fleet during their stay here. It was then thought necessary to conciliate the Yemen Government; and consequently, though threats were used by several officers, whose men deserted, yet nothing was done, and the Arabs were confirmed in their insolence by our forbearance. One man deserted from Captain Vashon during the time he was here. He was immediately demanded from the Dola, who in *very* haughty terms refused to deliver him up, advising the Lieutenant, who delivered the message, to keep his men on board, if he wished them not to turn Mussulmauns. He was permitted to see the man, who on being asked why he took such a step, turned away without condescending to give any answer. Captain Vashon, though extremely indignant, did not feel himself justified in resorting to violence, and very properly avoided using any threat, which he did not mean to carry into effect. I wish every officer had done the same, and our character would have been more respected in Yemen.

I heard there had been great confusion on board the Antelope since our arrival; yet Captain Keys tranquilly staid on shore: on the 2d, indeed, he

on board to punish two men, one of whom he immediately sent on board an American vessel which came in after our arrival. By what authority he did this it would be difficult to discover, as I can hardly conceive that a power is vested in the officers of the Company's marine to transport his Majesty's subjects. The man came to me, and informed me that he was a deserter from the Lancaster, Sir Roger Curtis. Another of the Company's apprentices escaped, a;S I learned, on board the American. The Captain of which said, very properly, that he believed he was there, but without his knowledge or consent, and that he wished the Antelope's people would find him. They searched the ship, but without success. She sailed on the 4th of July, and with her two of his Majesty's subjects.

. Another of the seamen, also a deserter from a King's ship, fled to the Dola, and became a Mus- sulmaun. He, and the one who sailed in the American, were the two that were on shore with me at Massowah. Mr. Hall went to see him, but was only abused.

The heat of the weather was more oppressive than I had hitherto experienced"; the'winds were northerly, and extremely warm, though the thermometer was only 92 and 94. I could bear no covering at night, and was so completely relaxed, that I was obliged to take a few glasses of wine. The swell in the road is much less than when the southerly winds prevail. The rains fell every day to the northward, and on the mountains of the interior, but not a drop reached Mocha. We obtained grapes, which were tolerable, and some very indifferent figs and peaches. .

Since my arrival here my suspicions at Massowah were fully confirmed. The masters of the dow,en being interrogated by Mr. Pringle, declared that Abdulcauder was sent to them by the Captain to advise them not to procure a pilot, to represent that if they did not, I should be obliged to go back to Mocha, and that they would get their four hundred dollars for nothing; on the contrary, if they went on, they would not only have to pay one hundred for a pilot, but would incur the danger and expence of a long voyage with a contrary wind. Abdul cauder admitted that he was sent, and that he did deliver the message. I found also from them, that he declared his objections to the voyage before he left Mocha, saying, all he wanted was to go straight to Suez. The dow's bargain was to hire only one pilot at Massowah; consequently Captain Keys' demand of hiring two, was unjust.

I was again informed that two more boys had run away from the Antelope. They were two of the youngest apprentices, and swam away in the night. This was the more astonishing, as two sentinels were mounted every night. Mr. Pringle represented in the strongest terms to Captain Keys the shameful degree of negligence that must have taken place, to enable those boys to escape ; and advised him, at any rate, to punish the sentinels, if he did not choose to go on board and look after his ship himself. He said that he had done all he could by ordering an officer's watch; that he conld not punish the sentinels, as he should then be obliged to put the officer of the watch under an arrest. There was no replying to so military and conclusive an argument. Mr. Hall came on shore early, and, on receiving the Captain's instructions, went to the Dola. He saw one - of the boys, and asked him if he had turned Mussulmaun. He said, yes; on which Mr. Hall drew forth a pistol and attempted to shoot him. Fortunately it was not primed. The guards rushed on him and poorDevagee, who was frightened out of his life, and secured them. The Dola only said, " Carry that madman to Mr. Pringle." Had he wounded the boy, his own death would probably have instantly followed; and even the factory might have been in danger, as we had no intimation of his intention, and the gates were left open.

To our very great delight the Fox frigate came in sight early in the morning, and towards noon was at anchor in the roads. I wrote to Captain Vashon, merely stating that Captain Keys's conduct had been such as to oblige me to abandon my voyage; that I would explain to him the whole if he would send off a boat, and ended, by requesting him to give me a passage to Bombay. The boat immediately arrived, with a very kind note, offering me every accommodation the Fox could afford, and saying he should wait dinner for me. He requested to see Mr. Pringle on business, who therefore accompanied me on board. I found that he had come down from Jidda, in consequence of the Wahabees successes. They had taken Yam bo, and were besieging Medina, which must soon be starved into a surrender. The Sheriffe, much alarmed for Mecca and Jidda, the only two places remaining in his possession, came down to the latter place to see Captain Vashon, to whom he bad applied for assistance; and particularly requested, that the Fox would accompany his fleet to retake Yambo. Adversity had lowered his pride, and he was all politeness and attention; yet, during the Egyptian expedition, he had treated Admiral Blanket with the greatest insolence, and no Englishman could land there without being insulted.

Captain Vashon did not conceive it prudent to comply with any of his requests, but said he would with the utmost expedition communicate them tothe Government of India. The application had at his desire been made in writing, signed by the Sheriffe and Pacha, who were, I believe, not a little disconcerted by his answer. The delay will, I suspect, be fatal to them. Provisions were already so scarce at Jidda, that the Sheriffe could not supply the Fox; and as the Wahabees were in possession of the whole country, they could only be procured by sea. The Janisaries from Yambo and Cosseir had come down thither, the latter of which places the Mamelukes had seized, who prudently sent away the Turkish soldiers; for if the enemy intended starving them out, this increase of force will only hasten their ruin. Captain Vashon brought down a man to buy rice, but the quantity to be procured at Mocha is but small. I proposed to Captain Vashon to let the Antelope return to India with his dispatches, as she was of no farther use to me; and I thought the sooner she was gone the better, as she was daily losing her men. He approved of my plan, and it was decided that I should resign my nominal command the next day, and that she should be ordered off as soon as our letters were finished.

Captain Vashon came on shore in the morning, to whom I communicated all that had passed. I wrote officially to give up the vessel, and notified the same to Captain Keys, at the same time requiring the assistance of the apprentice Thomas Smith, who had acted as my servant during the voyage. This he complied with ; and here ended all my connections with the Antelope. As I had much to represent to the Government at Bombay, which could not be done by letter, and, as I thought it advisable that no misrepresentations should go abroad previously to my arrival there, I requested Captain Vashon would order Captain Keys to giveMr. Salt, a passage, in order to deliver safely my dispatches to Mr. Duncan, and forward those for his Excellency the Governor General. With this he complied.

A singular circumstance occurred that evening. The Italian renegado came to Mr. Pringle, and earnestly requested that he would try to induce the two last boys not to stay at the Dola's, as their situation would be wretched. This he would have never dared to do without the Dola's consent; and it seems an additional proof of the idea I entertained, that religion had nothing to do with their receiving deserters. These boys were too young to be of any use, and he would be glad not to pay them the four dollars each per month for doing nothing. The Dola seemed considerably alarmed that day: during our dinner all the guns on the batteries were shotted. A portion of his fears may be attributed to the Fox's having moved this morning much closer to the northern fort.

One of Captain Vashon's Maltese marines deserted to the Dola. He was perfectly drunk, and refused to return with the officer. Captain Vashon applied to Mr. Pringle, as Resident, for his opinion respecting the effect it might have on the India Company's trade, if he should deem it eligible to support the dignity of the British flag, by recurring to force to obtain the whole of the renegadoes. The reply was indefinite: that he thought after the ships were loaded it would be of little consequence, so far as the coffee trade went, as that only amounted to 1700 and odd bales per annum at an average of the last ten years, and it might be procured elsewhere; but that a very large import of India goods took place annually; and how far that might be injured he could not venture to say. Surely Mr. Pringle might have recollectedthat the Imaum or his subjects procured the money to pay for the articles, only by the sale of their coffee, and that, consequently, the one trade would follow the other, whether to Loheia, Hodeida, or Aden. Captain Vashon sent on board the Antelope, and took out four men whom the officers pointed out as being suspected by them to have deserted from King's ships. One fellow who has turned Mussulmaun, broke out of the hospital, and, as it is said by himself, a man was killed in the affray. He however sent to me to beg a Bible. I complied, and thought it my duty to write to him, warning him of the criminality of his conduct. I received a long answer, in which he told me he could now be as good a Christian as before, and indeed that he had more time to pay his respects to God Almighty. The two unfortunate boys, that were left here, are recovered from the effects of their change, and removed into the Dola's house, where they are particularly well treated. They are to be put into the cavalry: but when this Dola departs, his successor will probably use them like the rest, and wretched will be their fate. I hope Government will take some steps to assert the dignity of the British flag, and recover to their country those, whose youth may, in some degree, palliate their desertion.

The man above mentioned had been up at Moosa, and came down, without leave, to beg some medicine from me. He had applied to the Dola of the place, who told him, that if he prayed as often as he did, he would not be ill. The man looked wretchedly, and told me he was afraid I was right in saying he should soon repent it. One of the boys who fled from the factory was very ill with the liver complaint, and extremely low spirited, constantly reproaching his companion forhaving persuaded him to take such a step. They were all to set off in a few days for Sana to be shewn to the Imaum. The change of climate, with bad food, will probably soon end them. Sana ia;&tremely unhealthy to Europeans and natives of the Tehama. It was probably their residence there, and journey through the mountains, that laid the foundation of those diseases that carried Mr. Niebuhr's companions to the grave.

Mr. Salt sailed,on the 9th in the Antelope, for Bombay, with a strong breeze from the N. W. He took with him letters for Mr. Duncan, in which I officially forwarded to him charges against Captain Keys. I also sent a detail of all that had passed, together with copies of the correspondence between me and Keys, to Major Shawe, to be laid before his Excellency the Governor General.

Captain Vashon proposed to go down to Aden for a fortnight, and, as I felt myself extremely relaxed, I wished to try the air of the more open sea, and accepted his invitation to accompany him.

On the 15th I went on board the Fox to breakfast. It was however calm, and we did not sail till noon. We passed the straits at seven, and found a most pleasing difference in the climate. It was cool, except when a strong gust of wind came off from the promontory. In the night it became nearly calm.

We were off Cape St. Anthony. A brig was in sight at day light, to which we gave chase. She proved to be an American from Salem, but last from the Isle of France. The calm continued most part of the day, with a heavy swell from Jhe eastward of south. Still the air. was cooler than at Mocha, and I felt myself most sensibly relieved.

July 18.|With variable winds we got by fouro'clock to an anchor in Aden roads, distant from Fortified Island about a mile. The swell was much more considerable than I could have expected, as the wind came right over the land. The town of Aden has a most miserable appearance from the sea. It is nearly a heap of ruins, out of which two minarets and two mosques rear their whitewashed heads. The rocky peninsula, on which the town is situated, has all the appearance of the half of a volcano, the crater of which is covered by the sea, and on the edge of which lies the town; the rocks rise to a very considerable height. On the summits are numerous small square forts; and a second ridge towards the bay is covered with the ruins of lines and forts. Fortified Island was also covered with works, so as to resemble the hill forts of India. It must have been impregnable; and a very little trouble would render it so again.

That the trade of Arabia should at present have quitted Aden with its excellent harbour, for Mocha, an open road, liable to very heavy gales of wind, can only be attributed to the sovereign of Mocha having been till lately in possession of the whole of the coffee country ; but as his kingdom is torn in pieces by the Wahabees, Aden will probably recover its former importance, and again become the mart of an extensive trade, as it was in the time of the author of Periplus; who most certainly designated it under the name of Eudaimon. It is the only good sea-port in Arabia Felix, and has the great advantage over every harbour, within the straits, that it can be quitted at all seasons, while it is almost impossible to repass Bab-el-Mandeb during the S. W. monsoon. The present heaps of ruins and solitary minarets, give but little idea of the splendour which Marco Polodescribes it as possessing in the thirteenth century;

any more than the humble Sultaun of a little territory will bear a comparison with the Mussulmaun chieftain who could bring into the field 30,000 horse.

Aden must then have been at its highest state of prosperity, and was, probably, from the commercial convenience it afforded, the capital of Arabia Felix. Its decline seems to have been gradual, for in 1513, Don Alphonso Albuquerque found the fortifications sufficiently strong to twice resist his attack, although trade had in a great degree fled to Mocha and Loheia.

Aden appears to have tranquilly remainedunder its Arabian masters till this period, when hostilities between the Soldan of Egypt and the Portuguese, having induced the former to bring ships across the desert, and embark them on the Red Sea, a naval war took place between the twp powers, and its excellent harbour rendered Aden an object of great importance to each party. In 1516 it was attacked by the fleet of Selim, who had conquered the Soldan of Egypt; but without success: however, in 1539 Soolimaun fiasha, when proceeding to attack the Portuguese in India, treacherously seized the sovereign of Aden, and got possession of the place. The fortifications were greatly increased by the Turks, and some of their enormous pieces of cannon were mounted on the walls. It was considered as a place of such importance, that so late as 1610, when Sir Henry Middleton was there, it had a Basha, as Governor, and the walls were still very strong.

As the power of the Turks gradually declined, the Arabians, by degrees, threw off their yolce; and in 1708 Aden was found by the French jn the possession of an Arab prince. The fortificationswere in ruins, and the baths were the only places which, by their rich marbles, bore any marks of ancient magnificence. These have now totally disappeared, and not a single piece of cannon defends the walls. The Sultaun has a small tract of country belonging to him, which he has hitherto defended from the Wahabees. He is much attached to the English, and offered to hold his country under them; at the same time giving a proof of his sincerity, by admitting the whole army of Colonel Murray within his walls.

Banians from Mocha reside here, to carry on the trade with Berbera, and purchase the myrrh and gum arabic, which is still brought hither by the Samaulies, and pays to the Sultaun a duty of three per cent.

An American was in the harbour, on board of which 3 son of the Honourable Mr. Goodhues, a senator of the United States, was supercargo. Mr. Prngle had written to him by me; I forwarded the letter, with an invitation to come on board the Fox.

By day-break I went with Captain Vashon on shore, to look out for a place to pitch our tents. We found a tolerable one on the ruins of the houses near one of the rocks. The Sultaun's house is a very wretched one externally; all the others seemed of basket-work and matting. The wind freshened very much as the sun rose, and by eleven it blew so strong that we were obliged to let go another anchor. It was fortunately right off the land, but the hills formed eddies, and caused the gusts to be very violent. Mr. Goodhues came early and staid the whole day. In the evening it lulled, and the tents were pitched on shore.

July 20.IThe wind was very hot, but at night I returned on shore to sleep. It was extremelyunpleasant from the heat. The Sultaun came in at noon. He always comes down for some time at this season; for what purpose I know not.

On the morning of the 21st I left the shore for the ship. The wind freshened every morning from the W. or S. and blowed all day hot like an oven. At night it lulled, but too late to enable us to go on shore. The nights were cool and pleasant, but there was a considerable swell. At this season, Aden is altogether a most unpleasant place. Grapes and pomegranates are to be had in plenty, but no vegetables. The beef had hitherto been bad, but we were promised some good bullocks, that had been sent for by the Sultaun.

The wind continued as usual; except that on the night of the 22d, so violent a gale commenced all at once, that every body expected our anchors would have been brought home. The heat and dust were insufferable. The swell also was very great during the day. As, therefore, living on shore was impossible, and we had no particular business at this place, it was determined that we should return on the 27th to Mocha. A very great variety of dead shells were thrown upon the beach: but there are no shoals, and we were unable to procure live specimens. I purchased some from the crew of the Fox, which they got at Jidda, and had several given me by Captain Vashon and Lieutenant Flint. The boats were sent out every morning when the weather would permit, but with very little success. At first, for some reason, the natives sent us offbad water; but on strong remonstrances we procured as good as could be wished.

The pier does not extend far enough out, for the boats to reach it at low water: this is extremely inconvenient. The Sultaun procured us excellentbullocks; he was himself the sole dealer in these articles. He was extremely civil, sent Captain Vashon and me a present of a cow, two sheep, and seven goats, and invited us on shore, saying, he had horses, &c. at our service. The limes were excellent, and in profusion. Fire wood is to be obtained. The climate is healthy, and I suspect we were particularly unfortunate in having it so unpleasant. Our tents were blown down and torn to pieces.

July 27.|Yesterday the wind was so violent that no boat put off after the early part of the morning. One that went on shore was nearly swamped in returning. My servant went out on an ass, and procured me another plant of the balsam of Mecca, and some seeds. At seven in the evening it suddenly fell calm, and a light sea breeze sprung up. Last night it began to blow at half past one; but, fortunately, this morning it became moderate, which enabled us to get off our tents, bullocks, fruit and water. Towards evening it again blew so fresh that we left our anchor behind us when we weighed for sea.

July 28.|A ship was in sight early, bearing from the Straits: we gave chace, and neared her considerably, till it fell calm. We suspected her to be a French privateer, and cleared for action. She hoisted American colours, but immediately took them down ugaiu. At night she was out of sight.

August 2.|The vessel we chased steered in so strange a way that we did not wish to leave her, and, consequently, were considerably delayed. On the 29th she was visible in the morning, but astern. On our firing a gun to leeward, and hoisting our colours, she took no notice, but continued her way. The winds were extremely light from the south, with frequent calms. The moment we

VOL. II. G

passed the straits, the change in the atmosphere was most singular: the heat became so great that the cabin was insupportable: and the prickly heat came out in one night with more violence than I ever before experienced. The chace for these two last days lias been ahead, and this morning we perceived she had run to the N. of Mocha roads. We got into an excellent birth off the north fort at six this evening. The heat had been so oppressive that I determined to go on shore, though the gates were shut, and therefore landing at the pier was out of the question. We got as near the beach as possible, to the south of the town. The water is so shallow that the men were obliged to carry me a considerable distance. We got in at a little wicket, which is kept open till eleven. Mr. Prin- gle had given over expecting me, but my old comfortable quarters had been prepared for my reception.

At length the ship came into harbour, and proved to be an American, last from the Isle of France.

I found that, on our coming in sight, all the boys that had run away from the Antelope had been sent up to Moosa, lest we should persuade them to desert back again. They were in a wretched state, and sorely repented the steps they had taken. They had not the indulgences of other Mussulmauns, but were considered as slaves, and'obliged to do as they were ordered for their four dollars a month, a pittance scarcely sufficient to keep them alive ; yet were the Dola who converted them to be recalled, even this would be diminished. I received the following reply to my application to the Imaum: " That old customs could not be altered ; that no man had ever been given up who had applied to the Dola; that heknew the English were very powerful, and wished to do every where just as they pleased; but that, with the blessing of God, nothing would happen."

By the American that came last, a letter was received from the Banian, who went down to the Isle of France, to obtain the repayment of the money he had advanced for several years as rent of the French factory. He took with him two Arabs, and I strongly suspect that they were sent to make application to the French Government there, for assistance against the English. The above speech of the Imaum seems to confirm it.

I learned that several applications were made at the American's ship for the letter, and that they expressed the greatest alarm lest Devagee should get hold of it. The letter of course could not be procured by us, but the contents were published in part; highly extolling the French power, and stating that they had taken sixteen sail of our China fleet, and brought them into the Isle of France. This could only have been said to encourage his employers. The report was contradicted by all the Americans, to the great displeasure of the Dola.

Another circumstance confirmed my suspicions respecting the application to the Isle of France. The Americans have been supposed by the Arabs to be friends of the French, and have been frequently spoken to as such, asking them if they were not so, and assuring them that the Arabs all were, and wished to see the French back again.

Some very fine specimens of the shells of this shore were procured by Abdullah, a servant of Mr. Pringle, and two boys that went out with him. I employed myself in sorting and packingmy shells, and other curiosities, for Europe. Botanising was out of the question, from the intense heat of the climate: rarely is the thermometer under 90 day or night, and generally it was 92 or 94. The wind was frequently southerly, more especially towards the middle of August, when the sun became vertical; at other times it was calm for hours together.

Mr. Pringle requested me to visit a Seid called Sidi Mahomed Akil, a man of very considerable property, who had the best house in Mocha. He was a Wahabee, and much hated by the Dola, Though occasionally there, he was a native of Morabat, where his wives lived: he had also houses at Jidda, Muscat, and somewhere on the Malabar coast. He had married a relation of the Imaum, but not liking her, sent her back the next morning, with her dowry. As I wished much to see an Arab house, I complied with Mr. Pringle's request to visit the Seid. The house was lighted up; and as he had notice of my visit, every thing1 was in the best possible order. He met me at the door, and hurried me from one flight of narrow steps to another, till at length we reached two very pleasant wooden rooms on the summit of the house, the sides of which were composed of Venetian blinds: they were carpeted, anil had English elbow chairs covered with cushions.

Ve were served with sherbet spiced wiih nutmegs, and afterwards with coffee, scented with cloves. We abused the Dola most cordially; and as the Seid had just come from Jidda, we after- wards fell on the Sheriffe. He seemed to think, that however the Sheriffe might resist for a time, nothing but a strong external assistance could prevent his being ultimately starved into a surrender. The force of the Turks was estimated at about

1,000; these are superior to any Arabs, and would be quite sufficient to defend him from the Waha- bees. The Seid mentioned that he was going to Bombay, and hoped I would there assist him in obtaining some favour he wished from Government. I told him I had no such power; but as I should be at Mr. Duncan's, I would willingly obtain him an opportunity of making his own application.

The conversation became more free than I expected from an Arab. He laughed about the women, and asked me if I wished to become acquainted with all the secrets of the harem. I said, certainly. He then said he would give me a book which would answer that purpose. From what he afterwards said, it must much resemble a work of Peter Aretin, well known in Europe. He however forgot his promise: other things intervened, and I never got the book. The next morning, he sent me a history, and a collection of fables. He had a library of some hundred volumes, chiefly polemical, and among others, a most beautiful Koran in Persian and Arabic characters, written on vellum. The pages that faced each other, had the same sentences in each language; the whole was richly ornamented. He valued it at two hundred and fifty dollars. The rooms below, that I saw, were of a good size, and were filled with many nick-knacks which he had picked up in his different voyages. On my taking leave, we had rose water thrown on our handkerchiefs. He conducted me back to the door. There cannot be a stronger instance of the timidity of this Government, than its permitting such a man to live in the town; he is in avowed correspondence with the Sheriffe of Abou Arish, and, through him, with the Wahabee Chif, Jund. Possibly, however, the Dola mayhave been making terms for himself. He was only continued in his office because his successor was sent to Beit-el-Tahih, where the Wahabees were making rapid encroachments. He found, however, that he could not resist them, and has returned to Sanna, saying, " that as there were many outgoings and few comings in, it was useless to stay." He may now resume his appointment to the Government of Mocha.

On the 14th of August, the Banian of theNayib of Massowah arrived on his own affairs. As he was in perfect safety, it was more easy to make him speak freely. He spoke of the Nayib as a most excellent man, but allowed that he was much controlled by his brothers, and those about them, who were very great rascals; and he confirmed what I had before heard, that, immediately after my departure, they had obliged him to give up to them a great proportion of the presents I had made him. The poor Banian gave a melancholy account of his distress after he quitted the vessel to return to Massowah. He had no water with him, and could not drink any which was contaminated by having passed through the hands of Christians.

He informed me that since my departure, the Aboona of Abyssinia had died, and that fifty people had arrived thence, on their way to Egypt, to fetch another; a circumstance extremely agreeable to every body at Massowah, as they were respectable people, and spent a great deal of money. The Nayib receives one hundred ounces of gold; but the Janisaries, not existing, cannot receive forty ounces, as Mr. Bruce asserts, though they possibly did so, in much more ancient times, when the power of the Porte was unbroken. The Ascarri, who may be considered as their successors, receive nothing, as the Banian most solemnly declared.

The Nayib also claims, and receives, all the horses and mules belonging to the messengers. I was much gratified by finding that the Abyssinians had desired the Banian to enquire if there were any English vessel at Mocha that would undertake, for a handsome reward, to convey them to Suez, and bring back the Aboona. It shews a flattering opinion of our national character.

In a conversation at Massowah with my landlord, Abou Yusuff, the assertion of Mr. Bruce, that no one would be permitted to enter Abyssinia by that place, had been confirmed. I asked the Banian his opinion, and was surprised to find that he positively asserted the contrary, and that, to his knowledge, the Nayib would have no objection. I enquired if there would be any danger in the journey. He said not the least; that he would be answerable that the Nayib should place any one in the King's presence at Gondar in perfect safety. I then asked what the Nayib would take to do so, finding horses, mules, guards, &c. from Massowah to Gondar ? He said, four hundred dollars ; and, on my repeating the question, said, he would himself be responsible for it, and would, if I pleased, give it me under his hand. I had no reason to doubt his assertions, yet I could not help suspecting, that the brothers of the Nayib would attempt to extort presents from any unprotected traveller.

My friend Seid Mahommed Akil got into an unfortunate dispute with Captain Vashon, to whom he had applied to permit two native vessels, bound for Cannanore, to sail without delay. He declared they were both his, and gave a certificate under his hand that they were so. They were ac- s cordingly permitted to depart. He next applied for leave to sail in his own dow, which was also complied with, on his pledging himself that he had no specie on board except his own. The very

morning of his departure several Banians went to Mr. Pringle, and informed him that all the Surat merchants' agents had sent specie by him, and even brought a list of the bags with their private marks, and to whom they belonged. Of this Mr. Pringle sent instant notice to Captain Vashon. The dow had actually quitted the harbour, but boats were sent after her, and a shot fired. She took no notice of this, but a second went right over her, and brought her to. People from the ship were sent on board her, but the wind and current rendered it impossible to get her along side of the Fox. The Seid went on board to Captain Vashon, and complained greatly, declaring he had no cash but his own, (the money was in two bags, the outer one with his name, the inner with the true direction). The information received was too positive for Captain Vashon to mind what he said; the dow was therefore ordered along side with him on board her. By the negligence of the warrant officer on board her, the dow got among the others in the harbour, and the Seid escaped to the shore. He immediately applied to the Dola for assistance to protect the vessel, and complained heavily of the British Captain's conduct. The Council met, and sent to request Mr. Pringle would come to them, which he did. The Seid stood out that he had no money but his ow n ; and Mr. Pringle declared he would prove the contrary. He produced the list, and the tables were completely turned. The Dola said the money must be relanded, as it had not paid him the half per cent, duty on the export. Mr. Pringle said he had no idea that Captain Vashon would permit this. The Dola remonstrated and said she had been detained in the port, which was an insult to the Imaum. This Mr. Priagto denied. The Dola said the whole sea from Perimto Camaran belonged to the Imaum. This Mr. Pringle ridiculed in the strongest terms, and warned him that he had better take care what he was about, as it might lead to hostilities between the two countries.

A circumstance which I had omitted to mention in its proper place, led however to a different determination. The Fox, a few days before, had been driven on shore in consequence of her anchor coming home, but fortunately the ground was soft. It lulled immediately afterwards, and the tide was rising; she therefore escaped with the loss of her rudder only, and was in safe anchorage by night. The rudder was found the next day with only the iron work damaged. A forge was erected on shore to repair this, and it was in part completed when- the dispute took place. An officer and some Europeans were on shore to superintend it. Captain Vashon fully perceived, the moment the (low got close to the shore, that he could not without open hostilities secure her ic- moval. From the unprotected state of the Europeans on shore, and the incapacity of his ship to go to sea, he was induced to abandon her, and accordingly withdrew all his men by signal. As soon as the Dola learnt this, he became extremely valiant, and ordered twenty soldiers and an officer on board the dow. These received two dollars each from .the Seid. and the officer ten. On enquiring what fee was to do if the English soldiers resisted, (they rery well knew that all had been withdrawn two hoars before this time) he was told gravely, he was to- fire on them, and use the power put into hw hands.

Mr. Prrogle then interfered in the name of the Honourable Company, and demanded that the treasure might be landed and examined. This wasdone: and, of coarse the bags he had described were found. Captain Vashon had mentioned to Mr. Pringle the certificate respecting the Cana- nore ships belonging to the Seid, and was assured it was a gross falsity, accordingly he gave the paper to Mr. Pringle to shew the Council, thereby to prove what a rascal the Seid was. On its being produced, his confusion was very great, and he attempted to deny his hand writing, his signature being in English characters; Mr. Pringle, however, proved it, by producing a great many other papers signed by him in the same manner, with his signature in Arabic underneath. He was now completely convicted, and received a severe reprimand from the Bas Kateb and

Kadi, the other two members in Council. Since this transaction the Seid declares he will not go to Bombay, and has been proposing to the Americans to take him to the Isle of France. I presume he is now so angry with the English, that he wishes to get assistance against them from that place. The Americans having asked him one thousand rupees for his passage, which he would not pay, I afterwards heard that he determined upon sailing in his own dow for Muscat.

When the Fox was aground, application was made to the Imaum's minister for their boats, which was positively refused; and we were subsequently informed that he expressed his hopes she would not get off, as then he should obtain her guns and powder. This expectation was in consequence of a claim made here, that all wrecks belong to the Imaum. The Forte" frigate was, on a similar occasion, given to the Sheriffe of Mecca by Admiral Blanket: this they consider as a precedent. In this, however, he would have been mistaken. She would not have gone to pieces; and abattery with *two* hundred men would have commanded the town, and secured a safe depot for her stores. She was ready for sea before the 24th, the day fixed by the merchants for the departure of their vessels ; nor did she make any more water in the twenty four hours, than before the accident.

On the 23d I went on board, with my servants, and was received by Captain Vashon with the usual salute. For several days past I had been extremely indisposed, which I believe was chiefly owing to drinking some French claret brought by the last American. The heat of the weather too had been very oppressive, and I was rejoiced to try a change of air. Mr. Pringle dined with us, and took his leave.

We did not sail till the 25th. We passed the Straits that night, and were the next day overtaken by a severe squall. Not one ship had put herself under convoy, or received a single order. However, the ship, the brig, and the two dows laden with coffee for Mr. Forbes, sailed at' the same time, and Captain Vashon determined to see them safe, at least, beyond Cape Aden, where alone it was probable a French vessel might lie to intercept them. This had been the case once during the last war, when there was no convoy, by which the native merchants lost nine lac of dollars. Had it not been for this, we should have taken advantage of the squall, and got far on our way; as it was, we lay to. We had constantly light breezes to the end of the month, with a current, sometimes to the northward, and sometimes to the southward of E.

On the 1st of September we were carried by a strong southerly current within sight of Mount Felix, and, to our great mortification, instead of having to look out for the land of India, we hadnot yet got clear of Africa; an extraordinary circumstance for the season.

It was so fresh a monsoon that Captain Vasbon did not think it safe to venture into Surat roads, which are totally unprotected; we therefore directed our course for Bombay. By three o'clock on the 12th Malabar Point was in sight, but we were not close in with it until the evening, when an officer came on board us from a Company's cruizer, anchored at the mouth of the harbour, and immediately took us in. It was dusk, but the scenery was still sufficiently visible to be admired. The islands that separate it into several parts are covered with wood to the top; beyond them the main land rises into a chain of mountains of the wildest and most picturesque forms imaginable, to which the Island of Bombay, covered with cocoa- nut trees, forms a contrast by its flat figure. It was dark when we came to an anchor: no King's ship was there. I immediately sent a note on shore to Mr. Salt, to request that he would notify my arrival to Mr. Duncan, and would come on board in the morning.

2

SECTION 2

CHAPTER III.

Residence at Bombay.|Departure for Poonah.|Harbour of Bombay.|Panwell.|Campaly.|Tillege at the British Residency near Poonah.|Account of the Dusserah. |Visit to the Paishwa.|Dreadful famine.|Dinner at the Paishwa's country house.|Dinner given by the Dtwan of the Empire.|Paishwa's character,|Political observations on the Mahratta Empire,

MR. SALT came onboard, accompanied by Major Green the Town Major of Bombay, bearing the Governor's invitation to me to reside at his house during my stay. I left the Fox soon afterwards under the usual salute, and on landing received a similar compliment from the fort. Mr. Duncan's palanquin conveyed me to the Government-house, where I was met by himself, and most kindly congratulated on my arrival. After breakfast he expressed his extreme regret at the misconduct of Captain Keys, who, he informed me, had been under an arrest since his arrival. He also kindly assured me that, whatever were my future plans, I should have his best assistance, and that if I should determine to go to Suez or Bussorah, he trusted he could find me a better vessel thanthe Antelope, and a better commander than Captain Keys.

The kindness that I invariably experienced from Mr. Duncan, and the information of which I found him possessed, made me almost rejoice that I had been obliged to return from the Red Sea. The anxiety which I had experienced during my voyage was.

fully compensated by the discovery, that the western shore was navigable, and that it could supply provisions. I lost no time in communicating to the Marquis Wellesley the result of my voyage, and urgently represented the eligibility of a small vessel's being dispatched to Massowah, to continue the survey from that island to Cosseir. I at the same time stated to his Excellency my intention of returning to Europe by the Persian Gulf, and requested he would have the goodness to send me letters of recommendation to the Pacha of Bagdad. I expected that this Chief would afford me every assistance in crossing the Desert, as he was anxiously looking for assistance from India to resist the incursions of the Wahabees, and had actually an Embassador in Bengal, who had been received with every attention, having all his expences paid, and the crazy vessel in which he had arrived, repaired by the public. I therefore preferred throwing myself on his protection, to again braving the adverse winds of the Red Sea. As the answer could not be received from Calcutta in less than six weeks, I thought the interval would be very satisfactorily filled up, by paying a visit to Poonah; I therefore wrote to Col. Close, the British Resident with the Paishwa, to enquire whether he conceived it would be politically advisable; and if he did, to request that he would state to his highness my wish to pay my respects to him. I was obligingly favoured with an immediate answer, expressing the satisfaction it would give him to receive me at the Residency, and informing me that the Paishwa was much pleased at the idea of my visit, which he wished should take place at the approaching festival of the Dus- serah, which would commence on the 13th of October; a wish with which I most readily complied.

On the 6th of October every preparation, as I understood, had been made for my departure by the orders of the Governor: tents had been sent on to the different stations at which I should stop; forty bearers had been procured for our three palanquins, and the Governor's gold sticks had been ordered to attend me. Captain Young, who was stationed at the first post in the Mahratta country, as Commissary of stores for the army in the field, had orders to provide every thing, and attend me himself to Poonah. Above the gauts Colonel Close had undertaken to form arrangements for my conveyance.

The river, on which Panwell is situated, is in the dry season only an inlet of the sea, and navigable to that place at high water; we were therefore obliged to consult the tide. It turned at eight, and we set off with it, under a salute of fifteen guns from the fort. The Governor's Aides-decamp, and Major Green, attended me to the water side. The balloon boat, from its drawing less water, was preferred to the yacht; it had a cabin, and held us very well. The harbour improved in beauty as we advanced. The islands are, in general, covered with wood; but Butcher's Island is clear, except at the northern side, where several buildings are erected close to an old Mahratta fort. Among the lofty hills, which formed a back ground to the scene, Funnel Hill was most con-

96

spicuous from the singularity of its shape: the summit has all the appearance of a vast pillar, elevated in the centre of a flat, on the top of a rock. The whole range of hills is singular in iti appearance, and continually afforded subjects for Mr. Salt's pencil. We passed between the islands of Salsette and Elephanta, where the bay begins to contract in its dimensions. The sea breeze here overtook us. The entrance to the river Pan is defended by a small fort, which was built by the English, and formed into a depot during the old Mahratta war: it is now nearly in ruins. The river was full; the trees being actually half covered by the water. The paddy fields presented a cheering prospect by their healthy state, and eveu the mountains were covered with verdure, except where their smooth surface was broken by rocky pinnacles rising to a great height. The cloud floated around them, and occasionally, in part concealed them from our view, which greatly improved the scene. High cultivation and picturesque scenery have no where in India been so perfectly united.

The tide had just turned as we reached the landing-place near the village of Pan well. I was extremely shocked at discovering the vultures and Paria dogs disputing over the body of a poor wretch, whom the recent famine had hurried to a better world. Captain Young employed twelve men to bury the bodies, at an expence of forty -five rupees per month. They have sometimes performed this office to thirty in a day; during the rainy monsoon, the average was twenty.five. The want of rain had caused a scarcity, which had been heightened into a famine by the devastations of the Mahratta war. Holcar and Scindiah laid waste whole provinces, and through a vast extentof country left neither tree nor habitation. The British power has hitherto protected the Guzerat, Cokan, and the neighbouring poor of Bombay. It has even gone farther, and has daily fed twelve thousand people from the stores of rice procured from Bengal.

They were now reaping the first crops, but poverty still rendered numbers the victims of famine. Captain Young was hardly settled, and his habitation was new; it is situated on a rock, which in the rains, is an island. His business was to forward all the stores for our garrison at Poonah, which would otherwise have been almost starving. These proceedings have been fortunate for the poor, as nearly five thousand people have been employed, who have had provisions from the stores; one hundred and fifty people have also been charitably fed every day at the kitchen on rice; yet the deaths for six months were estimated by Captain Young at four thousand. Rice being procurable here, the poor wretches exerted themselves to crawl down, and perished even in sight of the house.

The Aumildar of the district came to wait on me with presents of fruit. He was a handsome Brahmin, but was very troublesome, and wished to tax even the Bombay people, that were here on public service. In consequence of a reprimand, he was obliged to desist. I therefore paid him little attention. The village seems populous, and is prettily situated on the banks of the river, in a plain surrounded by lofty mountains, one of which much resembles the table-land of the Cape. The priest of the tomb of Kurrun Ali Khan also waited on me. It is a neat building, with a dome, and two small pinnacles, that peep out from a grove of mango trees. Kurrun, he informed me, was a

Vol. 41. H

native of Lucknow, who lived here for six years; There are twenty-five readers of the Koran attached to the tomb.

I was much mortified to find that the tents had not been carried on, and that the superintendantof our stores was not even arrived. The bullocks could not carry the tents, and we were obliged to apply to the Aumildar for cooleys. These were not obtained till night, so that all removal was impracticable. We found Lieutenant Smith at this place, a complete invalid; and as Dr. Murray, who attended me in a medical capacity,'thought that the journey up the Gauts might render him essential service, I persuaded him to join our party. Dr. Murray's and Captain Young's palanquins and bearers had not made their appearance.

October 7.|Our Italian superintendant arrived early this morning, and by ten we got his baggage, as well as our tents, safe on the way. The widow of the famous Nana Furnese sent me some breakfast, with her salaams. She is a young girl of sixteen, and is said to be pretty ; he married her when an infant; she resided here with her. uncle. Our Mussulmaun priest sent us some excellent rice pancakes; as lie had also the credit of being a good curry maker, we persuaded him to go on with us. Before breakfast we walked through the village to visit a pagoda. It was dedicated to Mahadeo, and had nothing to recommend it, the pillars being wood, except a good tank in front of it. The building was filled with poor, who live there, and begin the town. Some children among them were living skeletons, with scarcely a muscle to be seen. As we returned we were shocked by one of Captain Young's charnel-men dragging a dead body in a state of putrefaction. The Mus- suhnuuu tomb has also a tank covered with the

red and white nymphaea in high beauty. We dined early in order to get off in time; when it came to the point, our Mussulmaun friend would not go, and the Italian was left behind, as his horse was not arrived. The part of the village that we now passed through, is extensive, and we were happy in not beholding so many wretched objects as on the other side. The paddy fields, as we proceeded, had in many places interrupted the road, and rendered it difficult to pass. We winded among the hills, and at half-after seven, reached oifr tents, close to the village of Choke or Chouke, a distance of thirteen miles. We had only one large tent, so that some of us slept within, and the others, in their palanquins, under the outer fly. In consequence of the tents not being sent forward a day before, we were obliged to wait there till after breakfast: and indeed with difficulty we procured men sufficient to carry them on. The Aumil of the district came and brought fruit, fowls, and kids, which we accepted. It was the middle of the day when we set off: we passed through a country like that of yesterday: the crops very fine, and nearly ripe. The hills preserve their strata perfectly horizontal. We passed several m)- serable wretches hardly alive, and an occasional stench too often informed us of the vicinity of dead bodies. We reached Campaly, a stage of twelve miles, by day-light: it is close to the foot of the pass, surrounded by hills covered with jungle, and has a very fine tank, and a neat pagoda. Several small streams were descending from the table-land, and a rivulet ran through the village. All ideas of pleasure were however banished by the sight of several wretches who were too weak to raise themselves up, to receive the charity that was offered them. Close to the choultry werebodies in every state of decay; some with their cloaths on, that could not have been dead above a day or two; others with only a small portion of flesh left on their bones, by the vultures and jackals. The vale was so small, that the tents could not be pitched at a sufficient distance from the effluvia, to prevent its occasionally reaching us.

October 9.|We set off at half past five. For a great part of the Gaut we were obliged to walk, though it was by far easier than the Bessely Gaut, nor was it half its length. The village of Can- dalla being just at the top, we had sent our breakfast to it. There is a very large tank, and below it a plain, which exhibited a more horrid spectacle than

Campaly : above one hundred dead bodies lay upon it, on which the vultures and Paria dogs were feeding : famine was in every face, several houses were uninhabited, and the last victims had never been removed from the places where they perished. We assembled all the poor that were alive, and gave them several pice each. The harvest is now so near that it may be hoped not many more will perish. We had but little appetite for breakfast, and hastened from this scene of horror. The country was fine and well cultivated. Our bearers were in high spirits; the air was cool, and we reached a spot near the celebrated caves of Carli by half after eleven, a distance of fifteen miles, where Colonel Close had pitched his tents for our reception, which were excellent, and provided with every proper convenience. The Killadar of the Esapoor fort eame to pay his compliments; he had a guard of native soldiers, and told me his garrison consisted of two thousand. A messenger bearing excellent butter. Military Governor.

and a profusion of fruit, arrived from Colonel Close, who sent to say, that we need not reach Poonah till the 12th. For the first time we had the good fortune to be at a distance from any village, and its melancholy accompaniments; a mango tope formed a screen to the south, and a pellucid tank was in our front. A very heavy thunder storm discomposed us a little, as the rain beat partially through the tent. The crashes of thunder were the most tremendous I ever heard, and were so close as to give reasonable ground of alarm. The Esapoor Killadar came again in the evening with fowls, sheep, &c. It rained in the night.

The want of cooleys obliged us to stay breakfast where we were, and make our own people assist in carrying the baggage. It was as cool as in England during summer, and consequently the men got on well. The whole way was through a valley covered with pieces of agate, onyx, and cornelian. The hills were green to the top, and the paddy fields frequent. We halted two miles from Tillegam, the Rajah of which place sent his servant, who spoke English, to congratulate me on my arrival. Our stage was twelve miles.

The cooleys came, but too late for us to set off before breakfast. The road lay through a level country, without cultivation or trees, except near the village. The Rajah of Tillegam had sent his head man early in the morning, to invite me to visit him as I passed through. I excused myself, as I had not yet seen the Paishwa. The truth was. I did not know the proper etiquette, and wished to consult Colonel Close. I however expressed a hope that I should be able to see him on my return. I passed to the right of Tillegam, between it and a fine tank. I saw no very wretched objects. I reached the tents a little beyond Chin- ehoor, a distance of twelve miles, by half after twelve, having passed through a populous town, and forded a river. Captain Frissel arrived from Colonel Close to attend me to Poouah.

At day-light I entered my palanquin : the gentlemen rode, except Mr. Salt and Lieutenant Smith. The country had been devastated by Holcar, and the village of Ound, situated on the bank of the river Moota, was nearly in ruins. On the opposite shore I was met by Lieutenant Colonel Close, the Resident at Poonah, and the officers of the British detachment at that place. The Colonel had elephants, camels, and a very well dressed suwarry. We alighted and mutually paid our compliments, afterwards forming one party. A little to the westward of the village of Gunnais Coondah, so called from an adjacent temple dedicated to Gunnais, the deputation from the Durbar of his Highness the Paishwa was waiting to receive me, close to a small pagoda which commanded a view of Poonah, distant two miles. The chiefs were on elephants in covered houdahs. A large body of horse was drawn up: the officers made their salaams, as I passed along the line. At a little distance I halted, and the Colonel went on. A carpet was spread on the plain : the deputation alighted, and after a few minutes, I advanced. We met on the carpet. Each person was presented separately to me by the Colonel, and embraced; we then seated ourselves without chairs or cushions. The chief person was Abbah Pooruu- dery, the Jaghirdar of Sapoor, a handsome young man, with an expressive countenance, and pleasing manners. He wore several ornaments of pearls and jewels. He was accompanied by Anund Row, the Paishwa's Minister for the British affairs; Kist-

nagie Rowannie, the assistant Dewah of the state; and Seedogie Row Nepawnkur, who commanded a body of horse, along with General Wellesley, during the late campaign in the Decan. There were also several Maunkarries, officers whose duty it is to attend the Paishwa on all visits of ceremony: these were seated behind. Anund Row delivered the congratulatory compliments of his Highness on my arrival near his capital. He expressed his satisfaction that it had taken place at so propitious a season as the Dusserah, and hoped it was an omen of the continuance of friendship between the two nations. Colonel Close replied in my name, with the general Asiatic expressions of regard for his Highness, and my conviction that the friendship would be lasting. As they were considered to be my guests, I presented to the Chiefs

fawn and attar with my own hand. Colonel Hose's Dewan gave pawn only to the Maunkarries. We all then arose, and having made our salaams, departed; they towards the town, we to Colonel Close's residence at some little distance from it.

After the hurry of a march, and the inconvenience of a tent, I found myself most pleasantly situated under Colonel Close's hospitable roof. His gardens are on the banks of the Moota, where it joins the Moola, and forms the Mootamoola river. This runs into the Beema, which again falls into the Kistna. It is singular that by these means a person, when not forty miles distant from the western shore of the Peninsula, might proceed by water to the Eastern Sea. It is a charming spot, adorned with cypress and fruit trees. At the point a very handsome bungelow is erected, where breakfast and dinner are served; at one end is a billiard table for the idlers. The Colonel keeps a veryexcellent table; beef, however, out of respect to the prejudices of the natives, is never used. Holcar, when here, had so little control over hia Patan troops, that the sacred animal was frequently slaughtered. Sir Charles Mallet, when he first came as Resident to Poonah, was obliged to live in a wretched house in the town, which had been provided for him : finding this extremely unpleasant, he pitched his tents during the summer on the banks of the river, but on the commencement of the rains was forced to return to town. He remonstrated very much, and at length obtained permission to erect a temporary house in this garden. One night it was burnt down, and Sir Charles being then enabled to complain with effect, was allowed to build the bungelow, which now is used as the Resident's office. Still not a fence was permitted; and even the present Resident had great difficulty in obtaining permission to erect a gateway and several additional buildings. The large bungelow on the banks of the river was built for a festival, at which his Highness assisted, in commemoration of the conclusion of the Mahratta war. On the opposite bank the natives burn the dead bodies, and afterwards commit the remains to the stream.

October 13th was the day of the celebrated Hindoo festival of the Dusserah. The Paishwa was to attend, and perform a principal part. As I had not been presented to him, it was contrary to etiquette that I should fall in his way; I was therefore obliged to observe the festival at a small distance. As soon as his Highness quitted the palace, Colonel Close and I mounted our elephant, and attended by the horse guard and suwarry, proceeded across the river to the British lines, where all the troops were drawn out in line, with theartillery on the left. We retired behind them, by way of being incognito. His Highness passed obliquely along the line to a spot where a branch of a .tree had been stuck in the ground. Here he descended from his elephant, and performed the proper ceremonies', which we could not observe. On their being concluded a royal salute was fired. His Highness then mounted, and passed in front of the line from right to left, being received with presented arms. The regimental colours were lowered, but not the King's; and as he passed the artillery, another royal salute was fired. He was mounted in a howdah of looking glass, and had but a little suwarry. The only interesting part of the sight was the British troops, now for the first time assisting at this holy ceremony at the capital of the Hindoo empire. Formerly Holcar, Sciudiah, and the other chiefs, used to attend, and their prodigious bodies of horse covered the surrounding plains. Whole fields were then devastated, the Paishwa himself setting the example; but now his attendants only gathered a few heads of grain. After celebrating together this festival, they were accustomed to set out on their predatory excursions into the neighbouring countries; but these excursions are now probably terminated for ever. It was considered a fortunate day to begin a war, after a celebration of the victory obtained by Ram over the giant Rawan.

As I could see but little, I applied for information, through Colonel Close, to the most intelligent Brahmins, who gave me the following account. " When Ram was on his way to attack the giant Rawan, who had carried off his wife Seeta, he arrived at a place called Kiskinda, which was governed by an ape or monkey named Walee, Wa-lee had seized the wife of his brother Soogreoo, and expelled him from the town. Soogreoo, attended by four other monkeys, viz. Hunooman, Nul, Neel, and Jamoowunt, took up their abode on a mountain six coss from Kiskinda. Ram happened to pass over the same mountain. As soon as he was seen by Soogreoo at a distance, the latter sent Hunooman to ascertain who he was. Hunooman. explained to Ram the case of Soogreoo, and prevailed on him to espouse his cause; and he then introduced them to each other. In a short time Ram destroyed Walee, restored the wife of Soogreoo, and gave him the government of Kiskinda. Ram, attended by Hunooman, on whose back indeed he rode, moved from Kiskinda to attack Ra- wan on the 10th of the moon As win, which is celebrated as the Veejya Dasmee, or the 10th of victory, generally called the Dusserah. The first night Ram baited under the shade of. a tree called Go- kurnee, which derives its name from the resemblance of its blossom in shape to a cow's ear; go, in Shanscrit, signifying cow, and kuru, ear. Ram then performed his devotions under the tree, which was itself one of the objects of them. When the devotions were finished, the monkeys by whom he was attended brought him leaves of theGokur- Tiee, as the only offerings then in their power to make. In a short time, however, all the leaves of the tree were expended. They then brought the leaves of another tree, that was at hand, called Ap- tah; and, when they were all expended, the leaves of a third tree, called Shummee, were brought. Ram then ordained, that, if he should be successful in his expedition against Rawan, devotion should for ever be paid to those trees on the VeejyaDusmee, that is, to one at a time; to the Gokur- nee, if procurable; if not, to the Aptah, or last, to the Shummee. After the monkeys had made their offerings to Ram they interchanged the leaves among themselves."

This was brought me at Chinchoor; I think it is a Cassia. The sbummee was also brought: it is a Mimosa.

This is the history of the origin of the festival, as given to me by a learned Brahmin, who consulted his friends on the subject. The Aptah was the tree used here: I saw the leaves; it is a species of Bauhinia. When a tree is not in a convenient situation, a branch of it is procured, as was now the case. The ceremony is described in the Shanscrit books, that treat on the ceremonies of the Hindoos to be observed each month throughout the year. The same Brahmin gave me the following account. " The devotion paid to the tree on the Dusserah, may be performed by every Hindoo of every cast, without the assistance of a Brahmin; neither is it necessary that any part of the person's clothes should be taken off. First, he throws a little water over the tree or branch. He then throws on a few grains of rice. He next rubs on a little powdered sandal wood mixed in water. He then ornaments it with flowers. A little sugar, or any sweetmeat, and some betel nut, prepared in the usual manner, are then laid before the tree as offerings, and some is given to a poor Brahmin, who also takes the money laid before the tree. This concludes the ceremony, which is celebrated throughout the Hindoo governments. At Poonah, however, an addition is made, which is not ordered by any of their books. The Paishwa receives a number of leaves from the bough, which he gives to his followers, and which they interchange, in imitation of the monkeys. His Highness afterwards holds a durbar, where nazurs of from two to five gold mohura are presented, and in return he gives each a leaf.

He also sends Khelauts and leaves to the Rajah of Sattarah, and Scindiah. The Brahmin could not say that there was any motive for, or effect assigned to, the exchange of leaves. I should suppose it was a kind of compact that they would assist each other in their approaching warfare. It took place in the evening, and it was nearly dark when we got home.

His Highness had fixed the following day to receive my visit of ceremony. The fortunate hour was about four o'clock; when, having received intelligence that the deputation from the durbar was on the opposite side of the river, we set off. I was attended by the Colonel and suite, my own suite, and our suwarries. A salute announced my departure. The Paishwa's minister for British affairs, and the assistant Dewan of the state after paying their compliments, put themselves at the head of the procession, to show me the way to the palace. They were attended by a large body of horse, and some soldiers; an escort of British infantry waited also on the opposite shore, and joined my suwarry. On entering the place before the palace we found his Highness's cavalry and guard of infantry drawn out, with his elephants and suwarry: they were by no means splendid. As we passed under the Nobit Kanah the kettle drums beat. Within the walls the servants were all at their posts, and the crowd considerable. In the windows were numbers of the higher orders. We quitted our palanquins at the foot of the stairs, which we mounted, attended only by our Chubdars and Ausubadars. A small . anti-room led to the durbar. At the door I waited a few seconds, till I saw that the Dewan of the state, Sadasheo Maunkesor, was sufficiently near; when, having quitted my slippers, I stepped on the white cloth with which the whole room was co-

vered, Colonel Close supporting my left arm. I embraced the Dewan, and presented the officers of my suite. At that moment the Paishwa entered the room, and stepped on his guddy or throne. I hastened towards him, supported as before, by the Colonel, with the Dewan on my right. His Highness continued standing, and slightly embraced with his right hand, I doing the same. His brother was on his right, to whom I was next presented, and who also embraced me. I then returned and presented to the Paishwa the gentlemen of my suite, who were also embraced. We then sat down. The Dewan was next his Highness on the left, but rather behind: I was close to him; next to me was the Colonel, and then the other European gentlemen. We had no chairs or cushions, and were not permitted to put out our feet, as showing the sole of the foot is considered as disrespectful. His Highness had no slippers on. The etiquette of the court is silence : and when any thing is said, it is in a low whisper. I spoke to the Colonel, who translated it to the Dewan, who stretching himself out towards his Highness on his knees with his hands closed and raised up, in a low voice reported what I had said. The answer was returned by the same conveyance. By the direction of Colonel Close I first enquired after his Highness's health, and was answered that he was well, and hoped I arrived in good health at Poonah. I then asked'after the health of his brother. The message was carried across the room, in front of the guddy, by Anund Row. The answer was complimentary. His Highness now expressed a wish, through the Dewan, that we might retire into a more private place, that the conversation might be more free. This originated solely from himself, and was as unexpected, as it was flattering. Indeed, the

whole of his Highness's conduct had evinced a wish to pay me every attention. The deputations sent to meet me were the highest honours he could bestow. I immediately arose and followed him into a very neat small room, attended by Colonel Close, the Dewan of the state, the sub-Dewan, and the minister for British affairs. His Highness seated himself on a small turkey carpet in the corner of the room. He placed me next him on his left, and the rest formed a part of a circle in face of him, He now began a very interesting conversation, in which he considerably relaxed from his etiquette, smiled, and frequently spoke immediately from, himself to me and Colonel Close. With all the disadvantages of interpretation, I could frequently perceive that he gave a very elegant turn to the expressions he used. Among many other compliments, he expressed a wish to give me a fete at his country-house, to which I with pleasure assented. This had been previously arranged, and was to take place after he had honoured me with a visit. On political subjects he spoke fully, and clearly, and seemed much better informed than I had reason to expect. After about an hour we returned to the Durbar. I was so extremely tired with my position, that it was with some difficulty I could rise, and for a few minutes was obliged to rest against the. wall. No conversation passed after he was seated on the guddy. Pawn was placed before him in a large gold plate; on the top was a gold box, containing a parcel of the same; attar, rose water, and spices were in the same line. Anund ttow, the minister for British affairs, gave rose water, pawn and attar with spices to all the party, except the Colonel and me. He began at the lowest, contrary to the etiquette of the other Asiatic courts that I have visited. The Dewan gave pawn, rose

water, attar, and spices to the Colonel; to me he gave attar and rose water. We then arose, and his Highness presented me with the gold box, filled with pawn from his own hand. As I was to visit him at his country-house, the giving of presents was deferred till that time. We made our salaams and retired, the Dewans attending us to the door. We then returned as we came; but the sun being set, there was no salute.

His Highness and his brother were in plain white muslin dresses, without a single jewel. The Dewan of the empire had some handsome flat diamonds in his turban, a necklace of emeralds, and large pearls, and ear-rings of gold, suspending the finest pearls I ever beheld. They were perfectly round and clear, and were as large as the pupil of the human eye. The palace is a tolerable handsome building, and was very clean. The Durbar room is large; it is supported by wooden pillars handsomely carved. His guddy was of white muslin, richly embroidered in gold and coloured silk. His attendants stood round without the pillars, except a few with silver sticks. Holkar did not much injure the palace, but he carried away every thing moveable; a small armoury and the elephant-houdahs did not escape. The town is indifferent; several houses are large, and built with square blocks of granite, to about fourteen feet from the ground; the upper part is a frame work of timber, with slight walls merely to keep out the wet and air. The lime, bricks, and tiles are so bad in this country, that the rain washes away any building that does not depend on timber for support. A great plenty of this useful article is brought from the gauts and the westward; it is not much dearer than at Madras. Holcar's stay did not improve the town. He

pulled down several large houses in search of treasure, and they say found a great deal. We forded the river both going and returning; the foundations of a granite bridge rise above the water ; but they were laid in misfortune, and superstition will not permit their superstructure to be completed. A bridge of boats had been laid across by General Wellesley, but it has not been kept up.

The spectacle of dead bodies on the banks of the river, in every state of putrefaction, was truly distressing. During the famine, many were murdered for the rice they had just received from British charity, which,. I am proud to say, extended to this place, whither a very handsome subscription, amounting to 40,000 rupees, was sent, which had been collected at Bombay under the patronage of Lady Mackintosh. Colonel Close had the distribution of it: he had previously fed fifteen hundred people daily with boiled rice ; but the sight of the food rendered them nearly frantic; confusion ensued, and numbers lost their share, particularly the more helpless. The Colonel therefore determined that this contribution should be distributed in money, each person to receive sufficient to purchase one good meal in the four and twenty hours. Eight pice were adequate to this ; children had a smaller sum, who, with the women, had the preference. About five thousand daily were relieved, and it sustained them till the new crops were gathered in, so that their lives were actually saved to society. The money operated less on their feelings, than the food :'the confusion was consequently less. It was regularly the business of an officer, with a guard of sepoys, to superintend the distribution. The sending up rice from the coast was considered as ineligible,from the expence of conveyance. Indian wheat and juwarry had already been got in; rice was expected to be so in about a fortnight. The officer commanding the garrison was particularly careful in protecting the fields around the town ; the English name was therefore very popular among the lower orders. The guard of one hundred sea- poys was not more than sufficient for these purposes. Several Brahmins, who were no objects of charity, mixed with the beggars and tried to obtain a share: when detected, they were instantly punished with four dozen lashes, in defiance of the holiness of their character; nor has this been since objected to. His Highness feeds a great number of his own cast, but his charity has not extended further.

It is impossible to teach a native Prince the duty of protecting his subjects. During the scarcity, the number of lives saved by the Residency were many, not only by food, but by attendance and wine, when necessary. The poor wretches, during the rains, perished by hundreds, even in sight of the house. General relief was impossible. Not only would they have sold their children, but they would have been grateful to any one who would have accepted them. Now the evil is over. Leasing is allowed in India, which at this moment feeds many. Any person may earn sufficient to maintain him by going to the fields and working, or even bringing in a bundle of grass. The camp sustains many hands. In no country are the means of life procurable with greater facility than in the Mahratta states; it is a garden, which would produce crop after crop as fast as they could be sown. Tanks might every where be

Vol, n. I

formed, so as to render a supply of water certain, at all seasons.

I had intended, on the 16th, to receive the Vakeels of the native powers, who might be at Poonah; but the Vakeel of Scindiah being on the eve of his departure, obtained permission to pay his compliments this day. His name is Juswunt Rao Goreporah; his family is very respectable ; one of his relations, Morari Row, heldGooty from the Poonah Government, and was one of its Generals : he is mentioned by Orme. From the respectability of the family, the British on the conquest of Mysore, gave to them the little district of Sondoor, a beautiful valley, situated between Chittledroog and Neydroog, and completely surrounded by the British territory. Juswunt Rao Goreporah himself was high in Scindiah's confidence, and was the Vakeel appointed by him to negotiate the latet reaty of peace with General Welles- ley. His other Vakeel, Naroo Hurry, also waited upon me : the former alone spoke. The conversation was merely complimentary; but they expressed great anxiety for the arrival of General Wel- lesley. They received pawn and attar on their departure.

The other Vakeels paid me a visit next morning. Among them was the Vakeel of Imrut Rao, the adopted brother of the Paishwa. Ragonaut Rao had no hopes of children at the time he adopted him; but afterwards, the present Paishwa and his brother were born. The disappointment of Imrut Rao's hopes has prevented his being on good terms with his Highness; they are now, however, apparently reconciled, through the mediation of Colonel Close. Imrut Rao is on his way to Benares, to perform his ablutions. He is the first of his family that ever did so, and he is, I learn, highly gratified by the circumstance.

A nephew of Colonel Close arrived from Hydra- bad, three hundred and seventy miles, which he had rode in twelve days. He describes the Nizam's country as being as much devastated by famine as this. Several villages had not a living creature in them, and the dead bodies were lying at the doors, and in the houses. He had been himself nearly starved, having procured only native grain since he left Hydrabad, with now and then some milk. This must be owing to the want of rain, for Holcar and Scindiah caused no devastations in that country. Mr. Salt has taken a few views: one very beautiful is from the gardens, taking in the junction of the rivers, and the pagodas built on the opposite side, a very favourite spot among the Hindoos. Mahadeo is the deity chiefly worshipped. The pagoda is beyond dedicated to his wife, Parbuttee, who, with her son Gunnais, share in the adoration. This pagoda has a pretty effect, as it crowns the top of a sugar loaf-hill, and behind it is the flat mountain on which is situated the fort of Saoghur. Holcar never took this place, nor could his offers tempt the fidelity of the Killadar. It seems strong, but does not cover the whole surface of the hill, so that on one side it is accessible. On the whole I think Poonah well situated, and when it has a little enjoyed the blessings of tranquillity, will be a handsom capital.

His Highness having fixed a day to return my visit, Colonel Close had a very large tent pitched in front of the house; two others were joined to it without their sides, so as to form one large apartment: the guddy was sent forward, and placed in the centre, as at his own Durbar. On nis coming in sight. Colonel Close mounted anelephant, and advanced to meet him. At the door of the tent I awaited his approach. He came close up, but did not dismount till the Dewan of the state, the Sub-dewan, and the Dewan for British affairs had paid their compliments, and had presented to me the different Sirdars and Maunkarries who attended him. They made their salaams, and passed by into the tent. His Highness then descended from his elephant, with his brother, who rode behind him. I made my compliments, and leaving a space on my right hand for him to walk in, moved into the tent. We all seated ourselves as at the Durbar. A few compliments passed, while the nautch girls were singing and dancing. As his Highness was considered as master of the house, the pawn and attar were placed on the ground before him, and he ordered it to be given to the Sirdars, and other attendants. I then requested his Highness to permit me to attire him, and his brothers; which being acceded to, the trays were brought forward, and laid before them. I got up, and crossing the musnud, began with his brother. The jewels were first placed in his head dress, consisting of a serpaish, jigger, and toorrah.f I then put the mala J round his neck: a person stood behind who fastened the strings. The same ceremonies were then gone through with his Highness, but in addition he had bracelets of diamonds. A telescope, and bonbon box, ornamented with a beautiful picture of the goddess Gunja, were also given to his Highness.His brother had a bon-bon box,vithlndra painted oa it. The figures were appropriate to their character. I then gave them pawn and attar, as he did to me, except that the attar was poured into my hands, and I gently rubbed it down both his shoulders. This was done at his particular request, and is the highest possible compliment. His Highness was in such excellent humour, that although it was a public visit of ceremony, he frequently addressed himself with smiles to me and the Colonel.

Ornaments for the head of diamonds and coloured precious stones.

t Mahratta ornament of several strings of pearls fastened together and suspended on one side of the turban. : *I* A necklace of pearl with a jewel of coloured precious, stones suspended from the centre.

The ministers did not receive attar, as it wa my wish they should stay till the rest were gone. There is a great jealousy between these officers and the Maunkarries, so that to have made them any presents in the company of the latter, would have been an insult to their dignity. We mentioned to the Dewan that a horse and elephant were at the gate, as presents to his Highness. These are always given on state occasions, but vithout being habited, as up the country. It was nearly dark before the Paishwa departed. The nautch-girls had sung some very interesting Mahratta, or, as they called them, Deckany songs which we now made them repeat, as a relaxation from the fatigue of a state visit. I afterwards learned that on this day there was a great religious festival, at which his Highness ought to have assisted, and that he was fined several hundred rupees for his absence. This provided a handsome feast for the Brahmins. Parbuttee pagoda was illuminated all over at night.

The presents were provided by the India Company. His Highness's were worth about twelve thousand rupees. The others altogether nearly eight. .

At a little after four we set off with the usual suwarry to pay a visit to the Paishwa at his country-house, the Hora Baug. The road for a considerable distance was covered by his Highness's suwarry, chiefly horsemen, so that it was rather difficult to get to the gate; fortunately 1 had a party of sepoys from the lines, who joined on the opposite bank of the river, and made way for me. It is prettily situated on the bank of a very large tank, perfectly irregular in its shape. In the centre is a small island with a pagoda. The opposite bank rises gradually into a sugar loaf hill, the summit of which is capped by the white buildings of the pagoda dedicated to Parbuttee. The house itself is insignificant, and has never been finished. The garden is fine, and is ornamented with several noble mango trees, and a great number of cocoa- nut trees, which I had seen no where else above the Gauts, and which several people told me would not grow there. The guddy was placed in a verandah, opening to a bason of water, with fountains, and covered by a trellis of vines. We had the pleasure to announce to his Highness the surrender of Chandore to the united army of the British and the Paishwa, under Colonel Wallace, who was rapidly conquering the hill forts of Holcar, that extend towards the Guzerat, in hopes of preventing his making an incursion into that fertile province or into the territories of the Paishwa, to maintain his predatory bands. His Highness was in great spirits, and observed, that his father always wished for the friendship of the English, but that it remained for him first to reap the blessings of it. He had said in a former conversa- tion, that he would mention another circumstance on a future occasion; it turned out to be a reqnest, that I would procure him an Arab mare. The Colonel of course assured him that I would do my best; but unfortunately I knew it was impossible, as the Arabs never will part with their mares.

We soon had notice to move up stairs; the Paishwa passing through a back door, while we mounted, by a narrow stair case, to a platform with two verandahs, one at each end. In the farther a white cloth was spread, on which were plantain leaves equal in number to the English gentlemen present. On each was a Brahmin's dinner, consisting of rice, plain and sweet, pastry thin as paper, and rolled up, paslrycakes, bread, and pea&e pudding. Along one side was a range of sweetmeats, laid in a row, having the appearance of paints on a pallet; on the other were seven different kinds of curried vegetables. On one side of the leaf were rice milk, gee, and some other liquids, m small pans of plantain leaf, which were all excellent of their kinds. We had taken the precaution to bring spoons, knives, and forks, which we wsed actively out of respect to our host, who soon joined the party by seating himself on the guddy, a little on the outside of the verandah. Of course, he could not contaminate himself by eating in our presence.

On giving notice that we had finished, he retired, and we soon followed. After seating ourselves below, the betel was laid at his feet and served round. My servant had placed himself at the bottom of the line, by a hint from Captain Fris- sel, and was consequently served first. They proceeded upwards till they reached me, where they stopped. The presents were then brought in, again beginning with my servant. These were better

than had ever been given on a former occasion, the shawls being new, and good ones for this part of India. A horse and elephant were at the door : the former was a fine animal, and in good condition : a most unusual circumstance at Poonah.

After this was concluded, a sword was given into his hands, and by him presented to me: it was handsomely mounted in green and gold, and had a very fine blade: it was not part of the present of ceremony, and I therefore valued it the more. I assured him I would hand it down to my son, and my son's son; and kept it by me, instead of delivering it to my servants, as I had done the trays. The nautch-girls were the same as onthePaishwa's visit to me. A few compliments passed at taking leave, and he paid the usual one of requesting to hear of my welfare. The Dewan attended to the end of the carpet, and then took his leave. We returned through the town, which is much larger than I expected, and the bazar much finer. There are several large houses three stories high ; the pagodas are insignificant.

A deputation arrived from the Dewan of the empire, requesting I would honour him with my company to a party at the Paishwa's garden. This was merely a matter of form, as I had previously consented, his Highness having expressed a wish that it should be so, as a proper close to the attentions I had received at Poonah. The party set *off* at the usual hour. We were received at the entrance by the Dewan, who walked by my side to a carpet divided in two by a single pillow, and spread where his Highness's guddy had been yesterday placed. He sat on the right hand of it, I on the left; my party next me, in a line down the room; his, on the opposite side. We soon adjourned up stairs, where a dinner, as before, was laid.out. The Dewan sat close to us, and conversed the whole time. 1 praised some of the sweet things, and requested he would send me some for my journey, which he took as a compliment, and immediately promised to do. I begged him for the last time most anxiously to preserve, by his endeavours, the alliance between the two states, and to represent to his Highness that this was the last wish I had to express. He replied, that the Mahrattas now depended upon the English for protection. I requested Colonel Close to enforce, in the strongest terms, my denial of this: that the dependence was mutual, and only that of one friend on another. Though he had made the remark, he seemed pleased at the denial, and assured me nothing should be wanting on his part, but that he was only what his master pleased; on which I concluded with my personal wishes for his continuance in office.

Colonel Close had been so kind as to permit the Assistant Resident, Captain Frissel, to attend me to Bombay, and meant to go himself as far as Chinchoor. The following was the day fixed for our journey. I had procured several old figures of Hindoo deities, and some of considerable merit; my people had picked up a large collection of agates, which are here in profusion. Many of my people were ill of fevers and colds, a very common complaint among the inhabitants of the Cokan, when they ascend the Gauts. It is also the case with Europeans, a circumstance that I cannot avoid considering as extraordinary, though the same took place in the Tehama of Arabia.

The empire of the Mahrattas, which had once been sufficiently powerful to contest the possession of India with the Mussulmauns, though weakened by the total overthrow they experienced at Pani- put, was yet in a very flourishing state; and was prevented only by its internal dissensions from carrying its victorious arms through the greater part of cthe Peninsula. The treaty of Bassein, however, has, in fact, annihilated this empire, and has, in its stead, established the relatively independent states of the Berar Rajah, the Paishwa, Scindiah, Guikwar, and, if he should not be conquered in the present war, Holcar. An incalculable degree of security has been by these means acquired for the British provinces, which, after the conquests of Tippoo, had only to fear an union of the Hindoo Princes of India.

In the preparatory steps to the attainment of the important objects of an union between the Paishwa and the British, the greatest difficulty was the wavering and uncertain character of his Highness, who wanted sufficient firmness to adopt those de- cisive measures, of which he could not avoid perceiving the necessity, surrounded as he was by open and concealed enemies, and only nominally in possession of his legal power. Lord Wellesley gave way to his timidity, indulged him in his caprices and delays, and, at length, most perfectly acquired h:s confidence. In my private conference with his Highness, which I have before mentioned, he expressed his great satisfaction at the arrangements that had taken place; he spoke in the warmest manner of the comfort and security he enjoyed since his alliance with the English, and seemed extremely anxious to impress me with the idea that the friendship of our nation had been sought by his father previously to his time, and consequently was not a new measure. He spoke f the benefits as mutual; and declared his conviction, that, as it was both their interests,-he had no

doubt the two nations would continue united. He expressed great anxiety for the arrival of General Wellesley, when, he said, every thing would go on well, and the disturbers of the tranquillity of India would soon be annihilated. He then turned the conversation to myself; declared that he considered my arrival at so propitious a season as a very good omen, and rejoiced that my stay in his Capital, and the manner in which we associated together, would prove to the public the real friendship between the two countries. He particularly wished that I would, in England, make known that these were his feelings. In reply, I in general assured him of the regard which the English nation had for him and his family, and my conviction that the empires united were invincible. I told him that I would certainly make known his favourable sentiments towards my countrymen on my return; that, however, it would be unnecessary, as Lord Wellesley undoubtedly had already done so. I then declared the high character his Excellency bore among his countrymen, and the confidence we had in his talents and integrity. If, however, any troublesome people should in England pretend, that Lord Wellesley's friendship had induced him to give too favourable an account of the Paishwa's sentiments, I should, with the greatest satisfaction, step forward to contradict them. I afterwards expressed my gratitude for the honours he conferred on me, which I considered as a proof of his friendship for my country.

Colonel Close was highly gratified with the result of the conference, and assured me he had no doubt of the Paishwa's being sincere in what he had said. He had never seen him so evidently pleased, or heard him more unequivocally declare his sentiments, His heart is excellent, which isproved by the intimacy that subsists between him and his brother Chimnajee; they live in the same house, and seem to have only one purse and one opinion ; yet this brother might be viewed with some jealousy, as having been himself installed Paishwa during the troubles which followed the death of Mahdoo Rao Narain. His Highness is like the majority of his countrymen, superstitious to a high degree: he however relaxes from the strictness of his moral obligations in one respect, having had three wives and several mistresses. His brother's conduct is more' strict, and is, in every respect, so steady, that when seated at the Durbar he moves neither hand nor foot, and seems a candidate for the office of Swamie.

His Highness at the festival of Gunnais has a large party of ladies to dance before the deity, on which occasion he is accused of dressing himself out to the greatest advantage. Although this is according to precedent, yet his brother thought it might appear not sufficiently dignified in his present situation, and he accordingly sent a private friend to Colonel Close, who began by stating the Prince's high satisfaction at the British.conduct, and the conviction of their extreme anxiety for his brother's prosperity. He then mentioned the dancing, and his fears concerning it, asking if Colonel Close could not give a hint to his Highness on the subject, which, coming from him, might have great weight. Colonel Close in reply observed, that he saw no possible means by which he could with delicacy interfere in a business, which related solely to their religious policy, but that if he would point out any means that occurred to him, the Colonel would try to use them. The Prince then sent to say, that if no means occurred to the superior understanding of Colonel Close,
there were no hopes that he should discover any - and here the matter ended.

A perfect degree of cordiality subsists between the Mahratta durbar and the British Resident, yet frequently it is almost impossible to transact business from the inter-ference of their superstitions. The waiting for a fortunate day may put off the most important concerns ; and if a member of the minister's family dies, he is shut up for a month, and all business is at a stand. Formerly these difficulties were purposely brought forward, but even now we cannot quite get rid of them.

Our influence has hitherto been used to conciliate the minds of all. The brother of the widow of Nana Furnese had been put in prison during some former disturbances: we obtained his release. Im- rut Row, his Highness's brother by adoption, was also essentially served by us. A friendship will probably never exist between them, but in the arrangements at a peace with Holcar, he may have a provision, and be kept on terms with his brother, without the power of doing him mischief. Imrut Row's absence, on a pilgrimage to Benares, will give time for the Paishwa's resentment to wear out, and his religious prejudices will be gratified by the benefits to be derived therefrom by the whole family.

Imrut Row was certainly the chief cause of the Paishwa's misfortunes, having invited Holcar down to Poonah, and corresponded with him the whole time. This was ungrateful and unjustifiable, his Highness having ever been an affectionate brother to him. It seems to have been their plan to place a son of his on the throne, in whose name the father would have governed. If they had seized the Paishwa, he would have been kept a prisoner. Imrut Row has thoroughly repentedof his misconduct, abandoned all his evil connections, and thrown himself upon the protection of the English. His allowance is at present from them, and their interest is employed in his favour, with' his justly irritated brother. His son is with him, and is a very fine boy. Nana Furnese's family were implicated in the conspiracy, but we induced his Highness to pardon them. He did it a little unwillingly, and has not restored their property.

When two Frenchmen landed on this coast, and made their way for Poonah, his Highness was on a religious journey to the source of the Kistna. On their overtaking him, he never admitted them to his presence, but sent them prisoners to Poonah. Colonel Close was not here, but, as soon as he heard of it, sent to desire they might be given up as our enemies. The Colonel was very much alarmed lest they should escape from the town, where they were slightly guarded, or be liberated by any of his Highness's enemies, when it would have been difficult, nay almost impossible, to prove that he had not connived at it. The Paishwa immediately gave them up, but put in a plea, that as we wished to imprison our enemies, we should not wish to liberate his; and this seems to have been his only motive for not sending them immediately to the Resident. 1 understand, they were much surprised to find his Highness so attached to the English. Bonaparte had probably calculated on a very different reception. They were intelligent men, who certainly had before been in the country, and their escape might, in many ways, have been disadvantageous.

The Paishwa is extremely exact in the performance of all the duties of his religion. is supposed to be increased by some anxiety about the present state of his father's soul. Suspicions respecting the death of Sewai Mahdoo Rao Narain, who died by a fall from the terrace of the palace, were entertained by many. Some thought Ragonaut Rao had been instrumental to his fall, but Colonel Close believes him to have been innocent. He conceives that the Paishwa threw himself down in a fit of spleen, in consequence of a severe lecture he received from Nana, who treated him as a child. This happened when the Dewan discovered, that he had been carrying on a correspondence with the present Paishwa and his brother, the object of which was to liberate themselves from the severe tutorage of the old gentleman. They were all young men, and what they did was very natural, but the event proved fatal. The death of Narain Rao bears still heavier on Ragonaut Rao; though he was killed in an insurrection of his guards, yet it was generally supposed they were instigated by his uncle, who would have instantly reaped the profit of the crime by becoming Paishwa, had not the Brahmins declared, that one of his wives was wilh child, and that that child would be a son. It turned out so; and though on the boy's death, Ragonaut Rao had the power of the state for some time in his hands, yet for the want of a few forms he was never actually Paishwa. His son Chimnagee is reckoned as the sixth, and the present as the seventh, as will appear from the pedigree of the family, which will be given in the Appendix. His Highness's filial piety in endeavouring to liberate his father's soul from the stain of these crimes, by his own works of supererogation, is worthy of praise, however we may pity the ignorance that gives rise to an expectation of success.

The satisfaction expressed by his Highness at the result of his alliance with the British, and which every part of his conduct has shown to be unfeigned, will be easily accounted for by an examination of his situation prior to its taking place, and a comparison of it with his present ameliorated condition. Although the Paishwa was recognised as the representative of the sovereign, by the great feudatories of the Mahratta states, Scindiah, Holcar, and Guikwar, and by the Rajah of Berar, yet the control which he could exercise over princes, who each independently possessed revenues and forces equal to his own, must at all times have been trifling; but latterly Scindiah had, in fact, reduced him to a state of subjection, and merely used his name as a cloak to his ambitious plan of uniting in himself the whole power of the Mahratta empire. In this attempt he met with resistance from Holcar, who was defeated by him, but whom he imprudently permitted to retire unmolested to Chandore, where having rapidly increased his forces, he attacked the troops of Scindiah and the Paishwa forty miles from Poonah, in turn defeated them completely, and got possession of the capital.

The Paishwa took this occasion to escape, though he was so hurried as to be obliged to leave his family behind him. Thus driven from his rights and territories by the successive attacks of these feudatory chiefs, it was natural that he should seek for assistance against them, where alone it could be procured. He accepted therefore the offer of offensive and defensive alliance made to him by the British Government in India, and ultimately concluded with them the treaty of Bassein on the 31st of December 1802. The most active preparations were immediately commenced

for the re-establishment of his Highness in his just rights. Major General Wellesley proceeded at the head of an army from the southward, and obliged the troops of Holcar to evacuate Poonah, having saved that place from being plundered by a rapid march of sixty miles in thirty-two hours. His Highness made his public entry into his capital on the 13th of May 1803, since which period he has, by the assistance of his allies, gradually got possession of his territories, the prosperity of which has been greatly increased by the uninterrupted state of tranquillity which has followed the successes of the British arms.

In another respect, his Highness has been essentially benefited by his connection with the British Government; *I* mean in the improvement of his finances, by the arrangements which have been adopted according to the plan recommended by Colonel Close. Formerly every Sirdar retained, with impunity, whatever part of the revenue he pleased, and in many of the provinces no part of it found its way to the treasury of the Paishwa. This was the case in Bundelcund, which was estimated at sixty lac of rupees per annum, and in the districts ceded by Tippoo, which were estimated at forty-one lac. The former has been given up to the British by a treaty, subsequent to that of Bassein, and now nets forty-four lac, of which thirty six are retained for the payment of the subsidiary force, and his Highness receives the other eight. The latter was originally ceded to the British, and, though given up on receiving Bundelcund, the system of collection had been so far improved, that his Highness now obtains from it above twenty-one lac. .The provinces nearer to the seat of government were of course more productive; but even these were liable to all the

VOL. *II.* K

peculations which naturally existed under a weak government, and were too frequently devastated by the hostile presence of the contending chieftains, or by the more amicable but not much less dreadful, annual assemblage of undisciplined cavalry of the Dusserah. These evils are put an end to by the British victories; and it seems probable that the territories above the Gauts will be rendered secure from any future hostile incursions, by Colonel Wallace's conquest of the hill forts that belong to Holcar, and which command the passes between the two countries. The presence of a subsidiary force ready to enforce obedience, has also operated in causing the payments to be regularly made.

His Highness's gross revenue may be fairly estimated as follows:

Rupees.

rAhmood - - 2,00,000
In Guzerat - - Jumbooseer - 5,00,000
CDuboy- - - 1,25,000
Cokan - - - 0,00,000
Sevendroog,&c. 2,00,000
Above the Gauts, N. 5 Juneer IJ
-Ahmednuggur 4,0
Added by the treaty r Savanore - - 8,72,838
of Seringapatam, Bankapore - 7,51,278
1792- - - - CDarwar - - 4,15,608
Bundelcund - 8,00,OOO
R. 71,64,724

Were the above revenue realised, it would be more than sufficient for the maintenance of the Paishwa, as chief of the Mahratta empire; but this is far from being the case, though it is impossibleto know exactly what portion of it reaches his treasury. The actual expence of collection is very great; the hill forts are numerous, and the garrisons large, which must be regularly paid; provisions are sent in kind for the use of his family; and what is a still greater expence, he is obliged to connive at many abuses to conciliate the chief natives who are about his person. Yet there is no doubt that he receives double the sum he ever did before: and it is probable, that by following the suggestions of the able and upright officer who manages the British affairs at his court, he will shortly be in affluence, and have a full treasury, to which he may recur in cases of emergency. At present, should only a lac or two of rupees be wanting, he must borrow it, or procure it by harsher means. This is entirely owing to mismanagement, for were the above provinces under the British Government, they would yield twice the sum at which they are estimated, without any additional burthen to the inhabitants.

Nothing can have been more prudent and conciliatory, than the conduct of the British since the connection between the two powers. No object has been pressed hastily or warmly, and every opportunity has been seized to oblige his Highness. By the treaty of Bassein he had been induced, at the particular request of the Company, to accommodate them by a grant of a small slip of sea- coast in Guzerat, valued at ten lac per annum; yet on a representation being made that the district of Olpar had formerly been in the possession of a Sirdar, to whom he was particularly attached, it was immediately exchanged with his Highness for a district of equal value in Bundel-cund, although Olpar was particularly desirableon account of its vicinity to Surat. It would be an object of the greatest importance to the British Government, to obtain a cession of the tract of land below the Gauts from Damaun to Carwar, as it would complete the security of the sea coast from the Gulf of Cambay to the Indus; but unfortunately the greater part of this, was a grant of the Mogul to Bajee Rao, the first Paishwa, as a. jaghire, and being therefore considered by them as a private property of the family, they are extremely unwilling to alienate it. This reason was candidly admitted, and the subject dropt. Any alarm which might have been excited in the Paishwa's mind, (a mind timid from a deficient education, having been brought up by Brahmins in complete seclusion, where he was taught nothing but their religious ceremonies, of which he is a perfect master,) by the idea that the British wished to grasp at every thing, and merely to employ him as an instrument of their ambition, has been done away by the free gift of the strong fort of Ahmednuggur and the district around it, which was conquered by Major General Wellesley, and to which he had no claim; and still more strongly since, by their having engaged in a war with Holcar, on terms so beneficial to him, and so triflingly advantageous to themselves, even if complete success should attend their arms.

The friendship which the Paishwa evidently feels for the British, must in a great degree, be attributed to the able conduct of Colonel Close, the Resident, but still more so to the confidence he places in the military and civil talents of General Wellesley, to whose active exertions he owes his re-establishment at Poonah, an event that might never have taken place, had the servicebeen entrusted to a less able officer. Rapidity of movement was in this, as in every other Indian war, of the first importance, and to render this practicable, a regular supply of provisions was absolutely necessary. Of this branch of the military art, General Wellesley has shown himself a perfect master; and has added to it a decision in council, and a spirit in action, which have rarely appeared in India. The provinces which his arms have conquered, have been conciliated by the protection he has invariably afforded them from all military oppression ; and a personal confidence has been excited by the suavity of his manners, and an invariable attention to their religious prejudices. Uniform success attended him in the Mahratta war; but since the disturbances excited by Holcar, he has not commanded, and events have been less prosperous. It is natural therefore that the Paishwa should wish anxiously for his return, with a firm conviction that the tide of victory will again attend him.

Holcar, who is an active and able man, had very wisely employed the time, while his rival Scindiah was engaged in a destructive war, to occupy all the estates of his family, to replenish his coffers and recruit his forces. Had he been satisfied with this, he might have tranquilly retained the possession, although an illegitimate son of the late Holcar, and consequently not the representative of the family; but, instead of this, he made the most unreasonable demands of property beyond Delhi, which, he said, had been held prior to the battle of Paniput; and, on being refused, com- . menced actual hostilities by levying contributions on the Jeypoor Rajah, an ally of the British. Colonel Monson entered his country, and tookRampoora; but unfortunately despising his enemy too much, had his supplies of provisions cut off, and was obliged to make a retreat, in which he was pursued by Holcar, and lost a great number of men, and all his ammunition and cannon. It is probably in some respects fortunate, that Holcar has been thus drawn to the northward, where he can make no impression against General Lake's army, as he might otherwise have plundered the plains of Guzerat, and done incalculable mischief to the Guikwar, an evil that is now prevented by the success of Colonel Wallace.

The original Mahratta system of warfare had, been greatly changed by Scindiah: instead of vast bodies of cavalry, which by forced marches would attack an unsuspecting province, and retire with their booty before a sufficient force could be assembled to resist them, he attempted to establish an army of infantry, disciplined after the European system, and commanded by European officers. As these increased in numbers, he diminished the other, but fortunately was seduced by his vanity into a war with the British, before his plans had been matured. Warned by his fate, Holcar ban, in a great degree, depended on his cavalry, of which he has eighteen thousand, independent of twelve thousand Pindanis, or undisciplined free hooters, while his infantry does not amount to above ten thousand men. Such a force can make little resistance to the army opposed to him, when under General Wellesley, whose appearance will give confidence to all. This is one great advantage in employing an officer, in whom the Supreme Government can place unlimited confidence. Much may be done at the moment of victory, which would be impracticable were an application necessary to the seat of Government; more particularly in a war with a Mahratta power, whose whole system of policy is delay. Had not General Wellesley been authorised to treat after the battle of Assaye, without referring to Calcutta, the enemy would have had time to recover their panic, recruit their forces, and prepare for another war.

3

SECTION 3

CHAPTER IV.

Departure from Peonah. | Arrival at Chinchoor. | Visit to a supposed Incarnation of Gunputty. | History of the Founder of his Family. | Visit to the Rajah of Tillegam Account of the excavated Pagodas at Carli, | Visit to the Hill Fort of Low Ghur. | Return to and Observations on Bombay. Fortifications | Town | Dock-yards. | Marine. | Trade. | Insalubrity of Climate. | Country Residences in the vicinity. | Manner of living: | Establishment of the Bombay Literary Society. | Evils attendant on the cheapness of spirits. | Character of the Persees. | Embassies to Persia. | Visit to the Pagodas at Salsette and Elephanta.

sunrise, on the 22nd October, I departed from the hospitable mansion of Col. Close, where I had spent ten most pleasant days. Soon afterwards the village of Ound was pointed out to me, as a remarkable instance of the manner in which the possessions of the different Chieftains of the Mahratta empire were separated from each other. This little district, though surrounded on every side by the territories of the Paishwa, is the property of Scindiah, while, at the other extremity of the empire, Culpee belongs to his Highness. In the same mannerWaufgorn, though only twenty-four miles north of Poonah, gave birth to the family of Holcar, to whom also belongs Kooch, on the banks of the Jumna. This intermixture of estates was formerly considered beneficial, as preventing a separation of interests; but now that the union of these independent Princes is at an end, it has been proposed to exchange such detached possessions, and consolidate the territories of each.

My palanquin bearers were very lazy, so that I did not reach the encampment at Chinchoor till nine o'clock. I found there Colonel Chalmers and my other friends, who had kindly attended me thus far, that we might together visit the extraordinary personage, described by Captain Edward Moore, in the seventh volume of the Asiatic Researches, and who is believed, by a large proportion of the Mahratta nation, to be an incarnation of their favourite deity Gunputty. Immediately on my arrival I sent a messenger to Chintau-mun-Deo, who is the present reigning Deity, with the usual compliments, notifying my intention of paying him a visit in the evening, and requesting that he would, in the mean time, send some learned Brahmins, who could give me an account of his family. A most gracious answer was returned; and with the most learned of his Brahmins, came one of his own relations.

Colonel Close undertook most kindly to make every inquiry that I wished, and by his assistance, and that of Captain Frissell, I collected the following history of the Deo's ancestors.

Mooraba Gosseyn was a native of Beder, and a Mahratta or country Brahmin. In his youth he would attend to no business, but used to run up and down the country collecting flowers, and offering them to the deities. His father, finding he could make nothing of him, turned him out of doors. In passing Moraishwer, near Baramutty, he was struck with the deity Gunputty, and determined to pay him regular devotion. He however went on to Chinchoor, which had then but two houses, and no name: pleased with the spot, he took up his residence there. In the morning he regularly performed the ablutions in the river, and then set oft for Moraishwer, distant twenty-five coss, where lie performed his devotions to Gun- putty, and at night returned to Chinchoor. The Pingli family of Mahratta Brahmins were at that time in great power at Moraishwer, and performed the Pooja. On the first grand festival of Gunnais Chout, Mooraba, having prepared his necessary offerings and flowers, conceived great hopes of his being able to perform the ceremony, which he thought would be particularly meritorious. The Pingli Brahmins being in possession of the civil power, performed the ceremonies with great splendour. Mooraba, being poor, could not approach for the crowd of richer suppliants. At this he was severely mortified, but at length retired to the foot of a Naipte tree, which still exists there, performed his Pooja, and left his offerings. In the evening he, as usual, returned to Chinchoor. In the course of the night the offerings were transposed, Moora- ba's being placed before the Deity, while the Pingli's were found at the foot of the tree. The Poojanie Brahmins, astonished and alarmed, inquired to whom the accepted offerings belonged, and learned that a Cokan Brahmin had been there the day before, had performed his devotion at the foot of the tree, and had since disappeared.

On Mooraba's appearance the following day, the event was instantly communicated to the Pingli, who ordered him to be brought before them. On their interrogating him respecting the whole business, he simply related what had passed. They then demanded where he lived; he replied "below the Gauts, but the place has no name : you may come along, and see where it is, if you please.' Believing this to be impossible from the distance, unless he were a sorcerer, they immediately ordered him to be driven across the river, and forbad his return under pain of punishment.

Mooraba was now completely heart-broken. He laid himself down at the foot of a Mimosa, and humbling himself before the Deity, deprecated his wrath; and declared his willingness to give up his life to him, which he conceived necessary, as he could not eat till he had performed his devotions, and he was now completely debarred from the possibility of doing so. On looking up he perceived a Brahmin standing before him, who was, in reality, Gunputty. He inquired the cause of his grief, and after hearing his whole story, comforted him, offered him utensils and provisions, and added that he would himself conduct him to the Deity. To this arrangement Mooraba objected, stating, that if the sacrifice were made of things not procured by himself, he should have no merit. Mooraba therefore requested that the Brahmin would advance him the money necessary to purchase the offerings, and would, as a security, keep his lota, or small vessel in which he was accustomed to dress his provisions. To this the Brahmin replied, that without his lota he could not mix up the offering ; that therefore he should first procure the articles, and, after the ceremony was over, and the lota washed, it might be given as a pledge. To tins proposal Mooraba assented, and, attended by the Brahmin, went into the town, no where meeting with any obstruction. After the devotionswere over, they returned to the foot of the tree, and eat together. Mooraba then went down to the river to wash his lota, that he might give it to the Brahmin, but on his return he could no where see him. Mooraba now feared the shopman might have been cheated, and therefore returned to him for the purpose of lodging his lota in pledge; but, finding that the Brahmin had paid for every thing, returned to Chinchoor with his lota.

That night Gunputty appeared in a dream to the Pingli Brahmins, and other magistrates, and told them he was extremely offended at their ill usage of the poor Brahmin, who had shown so much devotion to him by his daily pilgrimages, and so much zeal by his offerings, and that therefore he was determined to be served by him, and to quit them. Mooraba arrived, as usual, in the morning at the foot of the tree, but dared not to approach any farther without his friendly Brahmin. As soon as his arrival was notified to the Pingli, they set out to visit him, attended by the magistrates and other Brahmins. Poor Mooraba, extremely alarmed after the ill usage he had already received, retreated as they advanced. They however at length induced him to stop, by assurances that they only came to pay their respects to him. They then told him the dream they had had, and requested he would stay at Moraishwer. This he positively refused. They then demanded where he lived. He said they might send a man with him who would see. This they did, but the man could only keep up with him for ten coss. He then lost him, and returned to the Pingli. Mooraba himself returned in the morning to his devotions. The Pingli again sent a person with him, who again returned, having got only ten coss, as before. This continued for some time; at length Gunputty appeared in a dream to Mooraba, still preserving the form of the friendly Brahmin, and told him that he had too much trouble to go every day to Moraishwer to perform his devotions; that, the next morning he, Gunputty, would visit him at his own habitation, and take up his abode with him. The morning ablutions of Mooraba were performed up to his middle in the river: he, as usual, dipped his hands, joined together, and his head at the same time, under the water; when he raised them up again, he was equally surprised and delighted, to discover in his hands the image of Gunputty, as worshipped at Moraishwer. On recognising this, he took it home, smeared it with red paint, prepared a shrine for it, and ever afterwards performed his pooja to it, without thinking it necessary to visit Moraishwer. The fame of the Deity's taking up his residence at Chinchoor brought thither a great number of Brahmins, and one of great respectability offered his daughter to Mooraba. They were married, and after a certain time the God appeared in a dream to Mooraba, and told him his wife was with child, that he would have one son only, and that that son would be himself, " woh humara avatar howega." He therefore directed him to call his name " Chintau-mun-Deo," which was one of the titles of Gunputty.

The event of course fulfilled the prophecy of the Deity, and Chintau-mun-Deo received the adorations of the surrounding country. He, in his turn, had a son, who was called Narain Deo, and from that time they have taken this name, and that of Chintau-mun-Deo alternately; the seventh in descent being the present Deo, and who goes by the latter name. Major Moore calls him Bawa, and his father Gabajee, but these are only familiar appellatives, like Baba, Appa, Nana, so commonamong the Mahrattas, and so puzzling to strangers. Each Deity at his death has been burnt, and invariably a small image of Gunputty has miraculously arisen from the ashes, which is placed in a tomb and worshipped.

I asked my informers whether Chintau-mun- Deo, who was himself an avatar, performed pooja to his other self as taken out of the water; they replied, certainly, for that the statue was greatest, nor was his power diminished by the avatar. I then wished to know how it was clear that the descendants of Chintau-mun-Deo were avatars. They replied that when Gunputty first took up his residence with Mooraba Gosseyn, he was asked by him how long he would stay with him, and was assured it should be for twenty-one generations. As Captain Moore had stated that it was only for seven generations, I repeated my inquiries, but they were positive it was for twenty-one. I suggested the possibility of a failure of the male line, which they would by no means admit, declaring that Gun- putty had made the promise, and he would take care to fulfil it. I think however they have not acted with their usual prudence, for the present Deo has no son, and his wife is still a child: were any accident to happen to him before she is old enough to have children, I think the Brahmins, *m*- genious as they are, would have some difficulty in carrying on the imposture.

Captain Moore mentions the constant miracle of the Deo's expences being so much greater than his income: this might easily be accounted for by the secret contributions of other Brahmins, who are essentially interested in the imposture, or by the supposition of a secret treasure having fallen into their hands, by no means a singular circumstance in a country, where perpetual danger induces every body to bury a large part of their property, without intrusting the secret to any one. Of this some conjecture may be drawn from an event, that has lately taken place at Bisnagur. A man has appeared there, who declares that he is sent by heaven to rebuild that ancient city: he has actually laid out the plan of the new town in a regular manner, with gardens to each house, and goes on building rapidly. Whenever he wants money, he goes to the top of a hill, where he declares he receives it from heaven, but probably he has discovered some secret treasure, from which he draws such ample resources. -..'-"

The Deo resides on the opposite side of the river, in a very excellent house for the country, part of which was built by old Nana Furnese, and part by Hurry Punt. We went over in a boat, and landed at the place where the former Deos were buried: they were burnt, and their ashes deposited in small stone pagodas. In each is the Gunputty that appeared on the occasion; they are of different sizes, without any merit. The temple of the first deity is the largest, and is of stone without ornaments; the walls very thick, with strong doors, and bolts on the inside. Our Brahmin friends accompanied us, and pointed out every object. We did not enter the little buildings, but approached close to the doors. When we reached the habitation of the Deo, we were seated in the verandah described by Captain Moore; the small door was open, which communicated with the room where the Deo was seated, on a small elevation ; but as the room was dark, he was hardly discernible. I presented a nazur, as did the Colonel. The money was given into the hands of a Brahmin; who laid it at his feet. He looked at it attentively, and then motioned to have it taken away.

After a compliment, the people enquired if there were not a medical gentleman with us. On being informed that there was, the Brahmin said, the Deo wanted his assistance. A window had been opened, which gave us a full view of him; he was a heavy looking man, with very weak eyes ; it was to relieve these that he now applied for assistance. Mr. Murray said he wished to examine them. The Deo accordingly moved forward on his seat, close to the light, and Mr. Murray was admitted into the sanctum sanctorum. His Godship was too anxious about his eyes to recollect his dignity; he expln- ed his case himself, and answered pertinently to all questions. A film had grown completely over both eyes, so that little assistance could be afforded without constant attendance, and that it was impossible to give. He would not permit Mr. Murray to touch his eyes, as he said he had then performed his ablutions for the day. In the morning there would have been no such objection, as he could have been purified; but now he was only waiting for our departure to have a large party of Brahmins dine with him, and there was no time for purification. Almonds were brought to him, of which he took a handful, and emptied them into mine, which I held underneath to receive them. I entered the inner apartment, as did the other gentlemen in their turns. He took care that no one touched him. He also gave me a pan full of rice, which he said was of a very fine sort, and particularly holy.

We now took leave, and Mr. Murray told him he would send him something for his eyes. He said, if I had any enquiries to make, he would answer them. I merely asked if I should reach my home in safety. The reply of course was, that every thing prosperous would attend me. The

vot. ii. L

Brahmins returned with us, but before their departure took occasion to observe, that they worshiped him, but he worshipped Gunputty. This brah- minieai imposture has been of great use to the country during Holcar's invasion. It was never plundered, which was probably owing to the Chief's superstition; but the Brahmins attribute it to a miracle. They told us several stories : as that, when some Patans attempted to approach the town, they saw a guard of supernatural horse drawn up to protect it; and that another party that came even to the tope in which we were encamped, close to the river, and directly opposite the holy burial place, were seized with such violent pains in their bowels, that they were obliged to retire in dismay. On our return we were pestered with several beggars.

At day light we took leave of our hospitable friends, and with ease reached Tillegam to breakfast. I was met, about a mile from the town, by the Rajah's cousin, who attended me to the tents, where he and the minister paid their compliments, and delivered an invitation from the Rajala to visit hjrn: which I promised, as I found, by enquiries at Poonah, that he was a respectable man, a Mahrat ta, holding under that government, on the tenure of military service only. He was formerly powerful, but at present, like many others, is much reduced. As his territories lie between Poonah, where the British subsidiary force is generally star tioned, and the presidency of Bombay, it is advisar ble to be on good terms with him. One anecdote does him great credit: be fed nearly the whole of his village during the late famine.

Four o'clock was the time settled for our visit, as he wished us to take a repast with him, and had sent for our table, knives, forks, and spoons : theMinisters came to attend us. The town was larger than I supposed, and seemed thriving; his own residence bore the marks of ancient splendor. He received us in a small verandah on the ground floor, covered with a piece of velvet carpeting. Several decently dressed people were around him. He was rather a young man, with a good-natured open, countenance. To our enquiries after his health, he answered in English, that he was very well. His English interpreter then said, he was there to teach him that language. Mr. Frissel found that he also spoke Persian tolerably : a very remarkable proof in a Mahratta of a desire to acquire information. We adjourned to the repast up stairs, where we found some good meat curries, and a bottle of brandy, a liquor I did not expect in a Rajah's house, but to which he has the character of being considerably attached.

On returning down stairs, it was whispered to Mr. Frissel that there were more gentlemen present than he expected, and that therefore he had not prepared presents for all of them. It was settled that a distinction would be indecorous, and that he should offer them only to me. They consisted of a dress, a part of which he wished to put on, but Mr. Frissel told him it could not be permitted : he tied a small serpaish round my hat. The minister inundated me with plain water instead of rose water, which was,not very agreeable. I had however the pleasure of afterwards seeing all the rest of the party undergo the same punishment. Pawn and attar were served round, and we took our leave. We had a party of Bazeegurs or Nats, who are described by Captain Richardson in the seventh volume of the Asiatic Researches, to amuse us at our tents. The women tumbled very actively, and were remarkably robust figures. Theirsmall tents were pitched without the town, and were in size like those of our gypsies. Captain Richardson has, in the work above quoted, pointed out other circumstances of resemblance, that certainly justify, in a very great degree, his conjecture of their having a common origin. The similarity of language is almost a conclusive argument.

In order to visit the Caves of Cadi to more advantage, we had the tents pitched at the foot of the hill, which contains these interesting antiquities. It is nearly opposite to the fort of LowGhur, distant about four miles, directly across the vale. The chain of hills here runs nearly east and west, but this protrudes from them at right angles.

The chief cave fronts due west. There are also a few in a bluff point at the southern extremity, the entrances to which are visible from the bottom. The whole road was covered with small agates, of which I collected a few. It was a long stage, and I did not reach the ground till eleven. The Killadar of Esapoor paid me a visit, and informed me that he had received orders to show me the fort of Low Ghur. In the evening, Hurry Punt Bow, deputy to Cundeh Row Rastieh, Ser Soobah of the Cokan, who was on his road to the country below the Gauts, came also to wait on me, and brought presents of fruit, $c. Cundeh Row, being supreme head of Low Ghur, Esapoor, and most other forts in the country, had sent Hurry Punt to represent him, and receive my visit. He was a fine old man, with a white beard, and smiling countenance. I gave him notice of my intention to be there on the 26th, to breakfast, and desired guides to be sent.

Breakfast was sent up to the caves, and we went there before the sun became hot. The ascent was steep, but rendered easy by steps which had been cut in the rock. The whole brow of the hill was

covered with jungle, which concealed the caves till we came to an open space of about one hundred feet, which had been levelled by the cutting away of the sloping hill, till a perpendicular surface of about fifty feet had been found in the solid rock. Here a line of caverns had been excavated, the principal of which struck me with the greatest astonishment from its size, and the peculiarity of its form. It consisted of a vestibule of an oblong square shape, divided from the temple itself, which was arched, and supported by pillars. The accompanying view will give a better idea than words can, of its internal appearance. The length of the whole is one hundred and twenty six feet, the breadth forty six feet. No figures of any deities are to be found within the pagoda, but the walls of the vestibule are covered with carvings in alto- relievo of elephants, of human figures of both sexes, and of Boodh, who is represented in some places as sitting cross legged, with his hands in the posture common among the Cingalese ; in others he is erect, but in all he is attended by figures in the act of adoration ; and in one place two figures standing on the lotus are fanning him with chou- ries, while two others are suspending a rich crown over his head. I think it therefore beyond dispute, that the whole was dedicated to Boodh. The detail of the different ornaments and figures, with drawings of them, I sent to the Bombay Literary- Society, in whose works they will appear; it is therefore unnecessary to repeat them here. The inscriptions are numerous in different parts, and are all in the same unknown character which is found at the Seven Pagodas, and is described in the fifth volume of the Asiatic Researches. We copied all that we could discover, and chalked over the letters for the benefit of any traveller that might

come after us. There may be others concealed under the coat of chunam which still covers a great part of the wall; where it is broken off, the marks of the chissel are perfectly visible.

The ribs on the roof, which are seen in the drawing, are of wood, and are very difficult to be accounted for. They cannot be supposed to be of an equal age with the excavation, yet who would have been at the expence of replacing them ? The followers of Boodh no longer worship here ; the country is in possession of their great enemies, the Brahmins, and the pagoda itself is considered as haunted by evil spirits, in defiance of the vicinity of the holy goddess Bowannie; so much so, that the native draftsman who drew the cave at Ellora for Sir Charles Mallet, could not be induced to accompany us by any persuasion of Colonel Close, declaring that if he did, the evil spirit would injure him.

Without the vestibule stands a pillar twenty four feet high, and eight feet in diameter, on which is a single line in the unknown characters. On the Capital are four lions, much resembling the Chinese. Opposite to it was another pillar, but it was removed about forty years ago, to make room for the insignificant temple of Bowannie, which now occupies its place. A view of the whole front, which was too large to be introduced iti this work, 'is given by Mr. Salt in his Indian Views.

The Paishwa has settled a revenue on Bowan- nie's pagoda, and there is a regular establishment of Brahmins to attend her, while the splendid abode of Boodh is completely neglected.

A line of caves extends from about one hundred and fifty yards to the north of the great one. These are all flat-roofed, of a square form, and appear to have been destined for the attendants Obthe pagoda. In the last is a figure of Boodh, and in another is an inscription. They evidently were never finished.

A veil at present is suspended over the relative antiquity of the Boodhistsand the Brahmins, which may possibly be hereafter removed; but these hopes are lessened by the recollection, that all the learning that has yet been found in India, has been in the possession of the Brahmins, who seem to have completely triumphed over their dangerous rivals, the Boodhists, who profanely gave precedence to the Royal Cast, above the holy face of the Priesthood.

Lieutenant Ambrose joined us. I was sorry *to* find that he had lain the preceding night under a inango tree, in the tope where we had encamped in going up, without any thing to cover him. He was a lively, pleasing young man, who had been in the navy during the Egyptian expedition, and afforded us great assistance in copying the itiscriptions. Before night I Was happy to find, that we were possessed of every inscription and necessary admeasurement. Mr. Salt's work was more extensive; he therefore determined not to accompany us to Low Ghur, but again to visit the caves on the morrow, and join us at the mango tope, whither we meant to remove our encampment. To th Brahmins who attended the small pagoda, dedicated to Jftowannie, and to others who lived in the great cave, we gave some rupees, as they had been civil and useful.

Very early on the next day all the party, except Messrs. Salt asnd Smith, set off for Low Ghur. The road across the valley was good, but when we began to ascend, the palanquins were of little use. We saw a line of caves facing due West on our left under the hill, oaf the sumwift of whichis the fort of Esapoor. My servant visited them by iny orders, to examine if there were any thing worthy of inspection. He reported that there was a small arched temple, similar in plan to that at Carli, but that the pillars were plain, and there was not any inscription or figure of Boodh, and that smaller flat caves were on each side, but uninteresting ; we did not therefore take the trouble of climbing to them. Hurry Punt had taken great pains to render our ascent easy. The bushes were cut away on both sides, and in many parts, the road had been levelled. The mount we ascended was part of Esapoor ; we left the fort rather to the left, and as we came close to it, we were hailed from it. The walls were covered with men, and on the reply that it was the Lord Sahib, they sounded the trumpets, and gave a cheer.

At the top we were met by the acting Killadar of Esapoor, who conducted us to the village at the bottom of the rock, on which Low Ghur is built. Here we left the palanquins, which had only been of use the last half mile. We mounted by a very steep path that led in a zig-zag direction to the top. There are five gates with parapets and loop holes for musquetry : these were far from adding to the strength of the place, as in many parts they afford lodgements for a storming party. At every gateway was a guard. In the open space before the hall of audience, Hurry Punt was ready to receive me. He conducted me to the durbar, where a guddy was placed with one pillow. He sat down on the left of it; I seated myself in state upon it: my party on my right hand ; his, beyond him on the left. After a few compliments, we adjourned to a breakfast prepared for us in a verandah, near at hand, and afterwards, in defiance of the heat, walked round the fort.

On the north side is a range of decayed cannon which were always ust.less, as the height of the perpendicular rock is too great on every side, to be stormed. Towards the west, a very extraordinary ledge extends several hundred yards in length, by about twenty wide. A wall is built along, on each side, to prevent accidents : at small distances are houses, inhabited by the guard, which we found drawn out to receive us. Though this ledge is lower than the main body of the fort, yet it is of sufficient height to prevent any attack, the rock being perfectly bare, and perpendicular. The whole in shape considerably resembles a tadpole, the fort representing the body, and this ledge the tail. From the summit the view was very extensive : the sea beyond Bombay appeared to the west; inland a chain of hills was visible in every direction, whose tops frequently rose into fortified summits, with rocky sides, as perpendicular as Low Ghur, The most extraordinary circumstance was the regularity of the strata, and the equal height of the rocky sides : were the line continued from one hill to another, it would touch the corresponding parts of similar strata. The summits were mostly green, and capable of cultivation. Low Ghur has numerous tanks, and several small streams from the springs above were falling down the rocks. Esa- poor is higher, and only a musquet-shot from Low Ghur. Were the former, however, in the hands of an enemy, it could do but little harm, as this place is very extensive, and is protected from shot by rocks in almost every direction. Lieutenant Ambrose had been here before, when it was surrendered to the British arms. He told us that the .quantity of ammunition and stores of all kinds was prodigious. . ; ',... . .,.,.

Dondoe Punt was the person who had been intrusted with the custody of the fort by Nana Fur- nese, and refused, after his death, to give it up. Here Nana had deposited all his treasures, the plunder of the treasury at Poonah, and the savings of his administration. Here also resided his widow. Dondoe at first demanded the restoration of Nana's adherents to their offices under the state, which of course, the Paishwa could never consent to, they having all been rebellious, both under Nana, and afterwards under Imrut Row. At length he gave up this point, and only required permission for himself and the widow to retire with their private property. He always denied that there was any of Nana's there, but the Paishwa thought otherwise, and conceived that when, he had concluded the treaty With the English, they would take it for him by force. General Wellesley negociated for him, and on Dondoe's promising to behave as a faithful subject of the Paishwa, he was permitted to hold the fort. When, however, has Highness went, as he annually does, to bathe in. the Kistna, the garrison of another fort, held by the same man, fired on him, and would not permit him to pass to a pagoda. This the General took up, and threatened to storm Low Ghur. At length terms were agreed upon : Dondoe gave up the place, retired with his personal poperty to Tanna, ad the widow to Panwell. Their petsonal safety was guaranteed by the British, and JSyOdO rupees, per ana. were secured to the widow. She ha& also one of Nana's houses to *setive* to at Poottab, whenever she pleases.

The garrison'geeflisBmeroasi but itbe fe-Ucw- ers of Hurry Punt afld the KiHadar of Esapoor were there, I cannot gwess the amcwwit: t© have asked, would have been useless. The buildings are miserable. The old gentleman, when I tookmy leave, presented a handsome pair of shawls, a piece of kincaub, and a piece of cloth. We examined the gateways as we came down, and I am quite convinced that the whole of the artificial works much lessen the natural strength of the place. Each high side of the way forms a sheltering place, secure against all attacks from the top, whether of musquetry, or their more usual weapons, large stones rolled down from above. The gateways and parapets have the same effect. Had the whole been scalped off, and only a strong work at the top, I believe no earthly power could have taken it. It is considered as the strongest fort in the Paishwa's possession, and an order from him was necessary to see it. The magazines are cut in the rock, but are now nearly empty ; however, as the state grows richer, they will probably be replenished.

We set off next morning for the top of the Gaut. Candalla had presented too melancholy a spectacle for as to wish to stay there again ; we therefore went on to the point, about a mile beyond. The scene was magnificent. The small plain which served for our encampment was on the extremity of a tongue of the table land. On one side the sea was visible ; on the other Low Ghur, and the other hills : close to us, between these objects, was a woody glen, with impass-able rocky sides, the depth of the whole gatit, at one extremity of which a cascade fell two or three hundred feet. In the rainy season it must be tremendous.. Mr. Salt took a view of it as it was, but the scale reduced the stream to insignificance. Captain Young is Com- arissary for the supplying of the British subsidiary force with rice ; and by contracting on moderate terras, and to be paid only for what he actually delivered, put an end to one of the most enormousabuses that existed. We here met several of his bullocks loaded with rice, which he stopped, and humanely gave two seer to each person who came to us from the village. It is an almost incredible circumstance, but which strongly marks the patient forbearance, the resignation of the Hindoo, that during the whole of the late dreadful famine, grain has passed up to Poonah through villages, where the inhabitants were perishing themselves, and, what is still more dreadful, seeingtheir nearest relatives perishing for want, without a single tumult having taken place, or a single convoy having been intercepted!

As we walked down the Gauts, the change in, the climate was very evident. The heat was most oppressive, with not a breath of air. We encamped at Colapore, which we had left on the right as we went up, where we found in the Choultry an old woman dead, a lad nearly so, and a young woman much reduced. We first gave some congee to the boy, which his stomach bore, and afterwards some rice. The old woman was buried, and the young one went off gaily with a sufficient sum to keep her till provisions should he again in plenty. We had fowls and eggs from the Patale of the village. Our people were all better, though some were still obliged to be carried.

The next morning before day-light I was in my palanquin. By eight I reached Panwell. I received the compliment of sweet cakes from Nana's widow, and learned that her brother Pur- seram Punt had arrived four days before from Poonah to assist in receiving me. He had been confined by the Paishwa, together with the other connections of the Nana, till the British interest obtained his release, when he became a constant visitor to the Residency. He is a modest, well- behaved young man, and in great favour with the Colonel. When presented to me, I expressed a wish to see his sister on my return, and asked whether it was against the Mahratta custom, that no purdah should he between us? He allowed that, by their own principles, there would be no impropriety in my seeing her, but that they had adopted from the Mussulmauns, since they had been so powerful in India, the custom of keeping their women concealed. He, however, promised to do his best for me, if I would visit her on my return to Panwell; to which I consented. He did not appear in the morning, nor Dondoe Punt, the late Governor of Low Ghur, who had come down on a visit to the widow, probably also to assist in receiving the visit. As I suspected that their absence was meant as a mark of dignity, in stealing the compliment of the first visit, Mr. Frissel sent to them to say, that he expected they would come here. The answer was, they were coming immediately, which they did.

Dondoe is a laughing old man, and talks a great deal. He soon began with Mr. Frissel about his own merits in giving up the fort to us, and his claims to compensation. To this but little was replied. We asked him respecting some steps down into the rock at the narrow end of the fort. He said it was intended by one of the Sattera Rajahs, who visited the fort, to have made another outlet at that end, but it had never been completed. He allowed he had only three months provisions when he capitulated. The garrison, in his time, varied from one to three thousand men, according to circumstances. He had lived there thirty years without ever descending, and complained that the climate below did not agree with

him, but supposed he should soon get accustomed to it. He said that several hundred horses, which he had brought down with him, had all perished. Captain Young said in English, it was a great blessing to Panwell, where most of them were kept, for his followers had plundered the whole country to maintain them. We did not after this . observation, express much pity for his loss. Four o'clock was the hour fixed for visiting the lady. He said he heard I meant to visit Salsette, and he should be happy to entertain me. If I did not go to Tannah, where he lived, he would meet me at the caves; to which proposal I assented.

At four the whole party set off with my suwar- ry. The little widow's house is not large, and most of the people in it are Brahmins. We were introduced into a small court, and seated on carpets covered with a white cloth, in a verandah, at the end of which was a door with a purdah of rushes, through which it would have been easy to distinguish any object, had not the room beyond been darkened. As I took no notice of the widow not being visible, the attendants began the subject by repeating the observations her. brother had made at Poonah about the Mussulmaun women. It was evident they meant me to see her, from their having fixed, up a liuen curtain to conceal her from the people in the court of the house, I therefore wished to hasten them on, and replied, that it was very well, they might do as they pleased, and that I was satisfied. They knew I Was not, and wished me to go nearer the purdah, which I refused. The brother then began to observe that, as I M'as going to England, he hoped, Bow that I knew Ins sister, I would be a friend to her there. I told him that I knew nothing of his sister; *I* only knew a purdah that was hungbefore her, and to that only I could be a friend. Uf laughed, and went again to speak to his sister. I and Mr. Frissel approached close to the purdah, and he spokq directly to her, and she replied.

After innumerable difficulties we were gratified with a sight of her : she was really a very pretty girl, fair, round faced, with beautiful eyes, and apparently about seventeen years of age. By the customs of India she can never marry. She is considered as the representative of the family of Nana, and as such is much looked up to by all his numerous dependants. She wishes to adopt a son, who would in that case succeed to the claims of the old man. These were too many, and too important, for the Paishwa to wish to see them revived; she will consequently never obtain her wish. She made several requests to us: first, that she might obtain some of her personal jewels, which the Paishwa had in his possession: and secondly, a garden-house near Poonalj, which belonged to Nana. These requests Mr. Frissel assured her Colonel Close would employ his interest to procure for her. She will probably succeed. After some more conversation I received a dress, and Purseram Punt tied a serpaish on my hat. It was with difficulty I saved my coat from having the attar rubbed down the sleeves, but I begged to wave the honour, and, with Mr. Frissel's assistance, succeeded.

The tide served at ten on the following day, when we embarked in the balloon, and reached Bombay about four. Bombay, as a place of consequence, owes its origin entirely to the Portuguese; for in 1530, when, it was ceded to them, it was merely adependance on the chief residing atTannah, in the island of Salsette. Its favourable position at the entrance of the finest harbour on the western shore of India, soon excited the attention of its new masters, and a fort was erected by them to defend the anchorage. Nevertheless, the vicinity to Goa, the capital of all the eastern possessions of the Portuguese, prevented it from becoming a place of any great importance during the time it continued in their hands ; but, on being ceded to the English in 1662 as part of the portion of Queen Catherine of Portugal, it rapidly rose into consequence, and ultimately became the great naval arsenal of that nation, and an independent Presidency, though certainly only the third in rank.

The fortifications of Bombay have been, improved as it has increased in trade and importance : and lately a very considerable addition was made to their strength by including Dungaree Hill within the fort. This place previously commanded the town; it is however doubtful whether it would not have been more advisable to level the hill, as the lines of defence were before too extensive, requiring a garrison of several tlvousand men to defend them, while there were rarely as many hundreds in the place. Towards the sea Bombay is extremely strong, and battery above battery completely commands the harbour: to the land side it by no means offers the same resistance; but this is of little consequence, as, at present, were an enemy once landed, and capable of making regular approaches, the town must surrender. The houses, which are lofty and combustible, approach so close to the walls, that were they once in flames, it would be impossible for any troops to stand on the ramparts. A bombardmentwould lay the whole town in ashes in a few hours, and even the magazines themselves would probably share the same fate.

If Bombay and the valuable arsenals and naval stores which it contains, are to be rendered secure against an enemy, a large proportion of the town ought to be destroyed, and the fortifications brought nearer to the dock-yard, and within a much narrower compass. Accident has rendered this a much easier and cheaper work than it formerly would have been ; for a most dreadful fire has reduced one third of the town to ashes, in the very division which would, were the above plan adopted, be thrown without the walls. It was with the utmost difficulty that the rest of the town was saved from destruction by the exertions of the Governor and the military. The old Government-house, which is within the old fort, was frequently on fire by the flakes that were carried towards it: had they been unable to extinguish it, the magazine must have shared the same fate, from its being close to it, and the unfortunate 'town would have been carried to all the points of the compass by the explosion of several thousand barrels of gun-powder.

. -To complete the plan of reducing the size of the fort, many houses must still be purchased, and pulled down ; and the destroying of the old fortifications, and the erection of new, would carry the expence to a great height. It is hardly reasonable to expect that this should be defrayed by the East India Company, who can only be considered as tenants under a short lease; but that it should be done by some arrangement with the Supreme Government at home, cannot for a moment be doubted, when it is considered, that our

VOL. II. .M

most implacable enemy has all his attention turned towards our Indian possessions, and that in no place are we so vulnerable as at Bombay, from the smallnes of the surrounding territory, and the distance from which all supplies must be drawn. If any hostile spirit does remain in the breasts of the Mahratta chieftains, and of which I fear there can be no doubt, Bombay affords to the French the only means of communication; and a brilliant success in an attack on that place would give spirits to every secret enemy, and induce them at once to throw off the mask. Of the ultimate result I should still have no fear; but the mischief of such a war would be incalculable, and the ex- pence would be far greater than the alteration of the fort of Bombay, which the Governor seems to have some hopes will take place, for he has, for the present, refused permission to the inhabitants to rebuild their houses, which were consumed by the fire.

Many other alterations seem necessary to render Bombay as secure from surprise as it is from an open attack. The public landing place is, at present, in the dock-yard, and free access is allowed to this important spot during the whole of the day. At night centinels prohibit the approach ; but the guard in the harbour is hardly sufficient to prevent boats from reaching it, without exciting suspicion; and so large is the bay, that an enemy might enter it at night, without being discovered by the solitary guard-ship, which is frequently its only protection. The expence that would attend the necessary precautions against this danger would be trifling, and cannot therefore be an impediment; but there seems to be a want of active zeal in those to whom thesuperintendence of the dock-yard is committed, that leaves it thus open to inspection, and possibly to injury.

It is in the light of a marine arsenal that Bombay appears of the greatest importance, and its value has been hitherto little diminished by the conquest of Trincomalee, which, at present, affords only a scanty and precarious supply of fresh provisions for a fleet. Here are established docks for the repair of the King's ships, as well as of the vessels belonging to the East India Company's marine, an establishment that seems, at present, -of little use, and of which the expence is incalculable. Most of the situations in it seem to have sunk into sinecure employments, and its very existence must have been doubted by its former enemies, the Pirates. If the East India Company are really in embarrassed circumstances, it appears to me that in no part of their establishment can they more easily oeconomise than in the marine of Bombay ; even if they do not think it advisable to abolish it at once. Were a new system adopted, and a reform carried into the higher and lower orders, I believe the marine might become a respectable and useful establishment. As far as the exertions of an individual can go to the completion of this, I have no doubt that success will attend on Captain Money, the present Superintendent of the marine; but it will require the power and the perseverance of a Hercules to cleanse this Augean stable.

Some of the present arrangements of the marine seem to have been ingeniously formed for the sole purpose of acting contrary to the system of the King's navy. Instead of an officer who is appointed to a vessel, continuing for a length of time in her, till he is acquainted with the characters of those under him, it is a very unusual circumstance for an officer to command the same vessel for two successive voyages; and if, by accident, he should do so, it is probable that he may lose every officer under him. I have known a' Lieutenant appointed to three different vessels in four days; and the Panther cruizer had three different commanders in one week. This system of perpetual change, annihilates that pride which a Captain in the King's navy feels in the neatness and good condition of his ship, and leaves to the Bombay marine commander, no motive for exerting himself to bring his vessel to the highest possible state of improvement. It has indeed no one advantage, and can only enable the Superintendent to provide whenever he pleases for a new favourite, and to keep in implicit obedience to his caprice the officers, who must be conscious that if they offend him, they can instantly be removed to the most disagreeable situalions.

If the East India Company determine to make their marine a respectable body, this evil must be rectified as well as many others; they must increase the number of their officers, which, at present, bears so little proportion to the size and number of their vessels, that the Mornington of twenty-four guns, and the Ternate of sixteeu, when they sailed from the Persian Gulf, had each only one Midshipman. They must enforce the proper regulations in their vessels, and make the officers amenable to a strict judicature; and, above all things, they must avoid exercising that most mischievous of all privileges, the reinstating such officers as have been dismissed by a court of inquiry. They must also arrange with his Majesty's Government the real situation of their marine officers, who, at present, claim, under their directions,

a relative rank with the officers of the King's navy which is not recognised by them, owing to which, disputes often occur, and more serious consequences have frequently been expected to follow. The respectable officers of the marine would rejoice in every reformation, and would be fully repaid by the benefit which would accrue to the service, for any losses that they themselves might sustain. That there are some men of high honour and unimpeached bravery in the marine, I can vouch from my own knowledge, and I cannot have the least doubt that there exist many others, whom it was not my good fortune to meet during my short stay at Bombay.

The establishment of the dock-yard is almost entirely composed of Persees, a people of whom I shall have much to say hereafter. It has been attempted to appoint an European master-builder, but the new comer has seldom long survived his arrival, and the only builders are now Persees. They are certainly fully equal to the business; but the absolute monopoly they possess has given rise to many abuses. The person who contracts to supply the timber, and the person M'ho examines it on its receipt, are both Persees; consequently the articles are frequently of inferior quality. The master-builder has only people of his own persuasion under him; no complaint therefore is ever made of neglect of work on the one part, or of overcharges on the other. A still greater evil arises from the local circumstances of the dockyard, which is a perfect thoroughfare, nay more, a fashionable lounging place for all the idlers of the town. The consequence is, that instead of working the whole day, many of the artificers only make their appearance to answer to their name at the hour of calling the roll, and if they, please,depart immediately afterwards, without any possibility of their being convicted of the neglect of work; for the dock-yard is open to the town, and they may pass and repass as often as they choose. The frauds which must arise from the same cause are incalculable, and call aloud for reform; than which nothing could be more easy, by the shutting up of the yard fronv all but the workmen and Officers, and the introducti6n of the regulations of his Majesty's docks at Portsmouth, Plymouth, and Chatham. The Bombay Government have, to a certain degree, felt themselves obliged to submit to these abuses, from the dread of the Persees giving up the ship-building business, of which they are the only possessors. I caniot believe that such would be the result of an attempt to reform abuses, though it might take place if they conceived their monopoly was in danger, as they are a rich and independent people, With caution, every necessary arrangement might be formed, and the workmen be retained in a situation, for which, by their talents and experience, they are now so well adapted.

The Presidency of Bombay has sunk into political insignificance since the supreme authority of Calcutta has undertaken all the arrangements with the Mahratta empire and its other neighbours ; but in the late war, and indeed at this moment, it has a load thrown on it which it finds very difficult to bear; the supplying of the armies on this side India with provisions and money : in consequence of which, the outgoings per month are above fifteen lac of rupees, independent of the civil establishment; although its whole revenue, including the ceded districts hi Guzerat, does not amount to above forty lac. The deficiency is provided for by bills on Bengal, and it shows avery favourable state of trade at Bombay, that so large a sum is procurable at no very high premium.

The trade of Bombay is at present, however, very inferior to what it was in former times, which is chiefly owing to the indulgences given to the Arabs, particularly to the Imaum of Muscat, whose flag being recognised as neutral, his vessels sail to and from the Isle of France, carrying there provisions, and taking back prize goods, which they purchase at half their prime cost. The navigation-act with respect to them seems to be totally suspended in India: they enter their vessels at Bombay as English, and navigate from one part of the Peninsula to the other without having an. European in the ship, or one rupee of the property in them belonging to a British subject. They have frequently a French protection also: so that they enjoy every privilege, and are French or English, as it suits their convenience. No wonder that their navy is rapidly increasing, while the English builders can hardly find sufficient employment to keep their gangs together.

Bombay has been said to receive its name from the Portuguese words bon bain, or good bay ; but this, I believe, is a mistake, as it was the original name of the island before the Portuguese possessed it, and was probably called after a Goddess Bornba, who is, as I am informed by Mr. Duncan, at present worshipped there. The town within the walls was commenced by the Portuguese, and even those that have been since built, are of a similar construction, with wooden pillars supporting wooden verandahs. The consequence is that Bombay bears no external resemblance to either of the other Presidencies. The Government-house is a handsome building, with several good apartments, but it hasthe great inconvenience of the largest apartment on both floors being a passage room to the others. Mr. Duncan, from system, avoids all parade ; and even admitting that the general principle were right, which, I have before observed, I believe not to be the case, it is here certainly carried to too great an extreme, for a more ragged, dirty set of beings than the Government peons I never beheld.

The view from the fort is extremely beautiful towards the bay, whose smooth expanse is here and there broken by the islands that are, many of them, covered with wood, while the lofty and whimsically shaped hills of the table land, form a striking back ground to the landscape. The sea is on three sides of it, and on the fourth an esplanade, at the extremity of which is the black town, embosomed in a grove of cocoa-nut trees. The situation ought to be healthy, but unfortunately experience proves that it is not so.

The fever is at present making most alarming ravages, and the liver complaint is more frequent and more fatal here, than in any part of India. Mr. Duncan and Dr. Scott assure me, that this season is more than usually unhealthy ; but they both admit the general insalubrity of the place, and particularly, that exposure to the land breeze, which sets in every evening, is generally followed by a fever, and frequently by a loss of the use of the limbs. This breeze is chillingly cold at present, and its deleterious effects may probably be attributed nqt only to this, but to the noxious vapours that it brings with it from passing over the rank .vegetation which springs up in the marshy boundaries of the bay immediately after the rains are over. The Island of Salsette is still more unhealthy Bombay, the jungle being closer, and thevalleys more closed in. The young cadets that came out this year were sent to the new establishment at Varsova, when the fever immediately attacked them. They were instantly removed to Bombay, but many fell victims to the violence of the disease. Moderate living, cautiously avoiding opposite extremes, is found most conducive to health. Here, as in other parts of India, gentlemen are to be met with, who have enjoyed their health in defiance of intemperance, or with great abstemiousness, and both recommend their own example ; yet, in my mind, both are exceptions to a general rule : hundreds certainly perish from intemperance ; and the abstemious life of the native by no means shelters him from fevers, and their result with him is more frequently fatal, from the impossibility of lowering his temperament when attacked.

The rage for country houses prevails at Bombay as generally as at Madras, and the same inconveniences attend it; for as all business is carried on in the fort, every person is obliged to come in the morning, and return at night. The Governor is almost singular in living constantly in town, having lent his country house at Perelle to Sir James Mackintosh. This place was the property of the Jesuits, and is the handsomest in the island. The apartments and verandahs are extremely handsome, and the former chapel on the ground floor is now a magnificent and lofty dining room. It has, however, the inconvenience of not being open to the sea breeze, and appears to be far from healthy, for Sir James and Lady Mackintosh, with a great proportion of their family, had been attacked by an intermittent fever. The generality of the country houses are comfortable and elegant; and if they have not the splendid Grecian porticos of Calcuttaand Madras, they are probably better adapted ta the climate, and have most unquestionably the advantage of charming views; for even the Island of Bombay itself is broken by several beautiful hilU either covered with cocoa-nut tree groves, or villas of the inhabitants.

It cannot be expected that the third Presidency in point of rank, should vie with the others in splendor or expence. The society is less numerous, and the salaries are smaller ; economy is consequently more attended to by a kind of tacit compact ; the style of living is however frequently elegant, and always comfortable and abundant. I confess, that having so lately quitted my native country, I preferred it to the splendid profusion of Calcutta. The necessaries of life are here dearer than in the other parts of India ; the wages of servants are consequently much higher. Rice, the chief food of the lower orders, is imported from Bengal even in favourable years ; at present the famine has raised it to an alarming price. Grateful, however, must the inhabitants be to Providence, for having, at such an eventful period, placed them under the British protection, and relieved them from those sufferings, which afflict the nations around them. The subscriptions, which were entered into to extend this benefit beyond the limits of their territory, do honour to the gentlemen of the settlement. Hospitals were opened for the gradual administering of relief to such as were too much exhausted to feed themselves, and hir- carrahs were placed on the confines to bring in those whose strength had failed them before they could reach the fostering aid, that was held out to them by the hands of British benevolence. The preservation of several hundreds of thousands on the Malabar coast may be attributed to the overflowing supplies which Bengal was able to pour out for their support, in consequence of the fifty years tranquillity which she has enjoyed under her present masters. India, under one supreme controul, can never expect to feel the effects of famine; for a season which causes a scarcity in one part, generally produces an increase of produce in another; and the devastations of hostile armies will be at an end, which can alone counteract this beneficent arrangement of Providence. For the sake of the population of sixty millions, as well as for our own sake, we may therefore wish that the British influence in India may remain unshaken by external force, or internal dissatisfaction.

A Society has been established at Bombay on a plan somewhat similar to the Bengal Asiatic Society, but it intends to limit itself to the present state of manners among the inhabitants, rather than to launch into ancient mythology, or the history of the country. Much I think may be expected from the active superintendence of Sir James Mackintosh, whose talents would throw a lustre on any society, and whose discourse on the first day of their meeting would have been heard with satisfaction by the father of Asiatic literature, Sir William Jones himself. Sir James is ably supported by Mr. Duncan, who is, I believe, as learned as any European in the wild fancies of the Hindoo mythology, and was the writer of those papers, on the singular Hindoo customs at Benares, and the two fakeers that resided there, which were communicated by Sir John Shore to the Asiatic Society, but without stating from whom he had received the intelligence. To these are added the ftames of many other gentlemen, whose long resilience in India, and known acquirements, may fairly justify an expectation in the public, that without rivalling their prototype at Calcutta, they may- communicate much interesting information respecting that part of India which has come under their immediate observation.

One of the greatest evils in India is the cheapness of spirituous liquors, which leads to a dreadful mortality among the European soldiers, particularly on their first arrival. The quantity allowed by Government is too great, if not totally useless. In the field, it is a gallon for every twenty men, or two drams each: at other times Only half the quantity. This might probably do no harm, were it not that the soldier is able, at his own expence, to procure as much as he pleases, in addition, from the camp followers, who are licensed by Government, and pay a duty on all they sell. This plan has been adopted in preference to allowing the profits to be received by the commanding officers, which had led to the greatest abuses. To deprive the soldier of an injurious quantity of spirits is impossible in a country, where an execrable kind is sold at a low rate in every village; it has been therefore considered as more advantageous, to secure him a supply of a less deleterious kind. Could the quantity allowed by the Government be reduced one half, a diminution would no doubt take place in the deaths; and every exertion ought unquestionably to be made, to preserve the lives of persons, so valuable to their country, as the soldiers employed in India.

The greater proportion of the inhabitants of Bombay are Persees, descendants of the ancient Persians, who fled from the persecution of Shah Abbas, who in the sixteenth century destroyed the temples which had till then remained in the mountain Albend, and drove the worshippers of fire to seek an asylum in other countries. Bombay they have almost entirely made their own, for hardly a house or a foot of land in the island belongs to any other. They form a body of people totally dissimilar to any in India, and seem to have perfectly domesticated themselves in their new abode, where they receive a protection, for which they are very grateful. I asked a very respectable Per- see why they built such splendid habitations, and purchased land at a price, that yielded only four per cent, when they could so easily make eight or twelve. His answer, I believe, conveyed the real sentiments of his nation. " This is our native country, where we are also to die : we have now no other home to look to, and therefore like to have some certain property for our children to inherit: you English are only here for a short time, and therefore wish to make as much of your money as possible, that you may return to your country, where I suppose you act, as we do here." They are a very rich, active, and loyal body of men, greatly increasing the prosperity of the settlement by their residence in it. There is not an European house of trade in which one of them has not a share, and generally indeed it is the Persee that produces the largest part of the capital. Their influence is consequently very great, and the kind of brotherly connection that subsists among them, enables them to act with the force of an united family. The conduct of the Government towards them has been indulgent and wise. They openly avow their obligations, and express their conviction, that they could in no other part of the East obtain the same advantages. I consider them as a most valuable body of subjects, and am convinced that, unless from mismanagement, they will ever continue so, and form an important barrier against the more powerful casts of India.

From the length of time which Bombay has been under the control of Europeans, the Persees, since their residence there, have adopted little of the Asiatic manners. They indeed wear the dress, which they informed me had been adopted on their arrival, but they eat and drink like the English. Ardiseer Dady, one of their richest members, gave me a most magnificent entertainment. The table for the Europeans was chiefly covered with English cookery, but they sent me from their own, several dishes, which were very highly seasoned, and good. The wines were excellent; but when I adjourned to their table, I was not a little astonished to find liqueurs placed opposite each Persee, which they drank in glasses as freely as wine, and which, though they sat late, seemed to have no effect upon them. Their houses are furnished with a profusion of English looking-glasses, prints, and paintings. They always light them up remarkably well; but on this occasion the whole gardens were illuminated with torches and lamps, which had a most brilliant effect. The band playing in the verandah, and the crowd of differently dressed people, had the semblance of an English masquerade. Coffee and tea, pawn and attar, lavender water, and other perfumes, completed the melange of this Anglo-Asiatic entertainment, from which we departed about midnight.

To the credit of the Persee humanity, they provide for all their poor : and to the credit of their private morals, there is not a single prostitute, or mistress to a gentleman, of their cast, in the settlement. They are generous and splendid in the higher orders; and in the lower, active and intelligent, far surpassing as servants the Mussulmauns or Hindoos. They mostly speak English with propriety. In their persons they are a handsome race,fairer than the natives, though not possessing the clear skin of the Europeans. In their manners they are uniformly conciliatory and mild. I confess that I infinitely prefer them to any race of people in the East, subject to the British control. They have numerous temples to Fire, but their priests seem to have no authority in temporal concerns, nor much spiritual control. Their religion is tolerant, and, as far as it throws no impediment in the way of the public service, must be considered politically a good one. Sir William Jones petulantly attacked the authenticity of their sacred code, the Zend Avesta, as translated by Monsieur Anquetil de Perron; but he himself, before his death, was convinced of his error. Sir James Mackintosh is studying the language, and will probably favour the world with some additional information on the subject;

but from the accounts that I have received, I have no doubt of the authenticity of the original, or of the fidelity of Monsieur Anquetil de Perron's translation.

The beauty of the esplanade, every morning and evening, is greatly heightened by the votaries of the Sun, who crowd there in their white flowing garments, and.coloured turbans, to hail his rising, or pay respect, by their humble prostration, to his parting rays. On this occasion the females do not appear, but they still go to the wells for water, as did the wives of the ancient patriarchs. Many of those in a higher line of life, retire from the city to their country residences early in the evening, in which case they assemble in their one-horse chaises at a beautiful spot called the Breach, where a former Governor built a noble causeway at an expence of 10,000 rupees, thereby saving a considerable tract of country from the gradual incroach- ments of the sea, which had nearly made its wayacross the island. It is a work of great merit, and has stood firm against all the violence of the S. W. monsoon. The India Company were however offended at the expence, and the poor Governor lost his place. The tract that was recovered has hitherto been marshy and useless, but some gentlemen have undertaken to drain it, and, apparently, are likely to succeed.

The strict attention that is paid in Bengal to the conduct of the Cadets on their arrival, unfortunately does not exist at Bombay, and the consequence of the neglect is melancholy. On their landing they too often are obliged to live at the tavern, not having any fixed place of abode, where they not only run in debt, frequently to the blasting of their future prospects, but by the facility of access to wine and women, sow the seeds of those complaints, which afterwards carry them prematurely to the grave. Varsovah had been chosen as a residence for the Cadets, but in 1804 the fever broke out there, and they were obliged to be removed to Mehum, but not before numbers had perished from the unhealthiness of the climate, and, it is said, from the want of proper regulation in the establishment, the young men having been permitted to bathe when they pleased, and expose themselves to the effect of the night air.

It was at one of the country houses in the vici- nity of Bombay, that the unfortunate accident of the death of Hadjefi Khaleb Khan took place in July 1802. He had arrived only a few days before as Ambassador from the Persian Court to the Government of India, when a dispute arose between some of his Excellency's followers and the sepoys who guarded the house, in consequence of one of the former's insisting on entering a part of the garden, which the Ambassador had ordered to be kept

private. The centinel, in obedience to his orders, refused to permit him, when the Persian, who was drunk, at length drew his sword, and, being joined by his countrymen, a regular battle ensued. The Ambassador, who had retired to his couch after having himself too freely indulged in the pleasures of the table, arose on hearing the tumult, and rushed out to separate the combatants. In the confusion he was not known, and a chance shot in a moment put an end to his life. Several of his followers also perished, but they deserved their fate; for they had irritated the sepoys by the most insulting language, and the severest ridicule of their religious prejudices. The Ambassador's nephew, though severely wounded, recovered, and received the kindest attentions from the officers of the Bombay Government, who were fully exculpated in his mind, from any blame respecting the untimely fate of his uncle.

The Marquis Wellesley learned, soon after his arrival in India, that attempts were making by Tip- poo to form a close alliance with Zemaun Shan, Sultaun of Cabul, and to induce him to attack the British in the North, at the time when he should occupy their attention by hostilities in the Peninsula. To render the projects of Tippoo abortive, his Lordship sent a respectable native, Mindi Affi Khan, to the Court of Ispahan, to open a communication with the present sovereign, who was at that time engaged in hostilities with Zemaun Shah. He was directed to urge the King to approach the frontiers of Korasan, as soon as his enemy should move towards the Indies; and, if he should find a favourable reception, Mindi Alii Khan was to announce the Governor General's intention of sending a public embassy to arrange a commercial treaty, and cement a close alliance between the

VOL. II. N

two countries. The King of Persia was fully aware of the importance of the British alliance, and complied with the request made to him. Zemaun Shah, who had advanced as far as Lahore, immediately returned back, and his brother, taking advantage of his unpopularity, deposed him, and, with the barbarity so common in Asia, put out his eyes. India having been thus relieved from immediate alarm, Major Malcolm was, in 1799, sent to the Court of Ispahan, where he completely conciliated the sovereign and his ministers, and induced them to refuse to receive a person deputed with the most conciliatory propositions from Bonaparte' in Egypt. Commercial arrangements were also entered into, and every required security was granted to the British for more freely carrying on their trade.

The unfortunate fate of the Ambassador, who was sent to repay the compliment of Major Malcolm's mission, has been before observed; but there was no reason to suppose that it would have any effect in diminishing the friendship between Persia and India; since the Governor General immediately sent off an explanation of the trans-action by a Mr. Loveit, who was directed to carry the letter to Persia. Unfortunately for the East India Company, he became alarmed at Busheir, and delivered the letter to Mr. Manesty, who immediately raised himself into an Ambassador, and departed for Ispahan, determined to rival Major Malcolm in importance. He had already drawn for a lac and forty thousand rupees, which would not pay half his expences. Lord Wellesley, at first, ordered the bill to be refused payment, but on considering that it might affect our credit in Persia, he altered his intention, but directed that Mr. Manesty should be made responsible for the amount.

The King of Persia, engaged as he was in a difficult, and rather disastrous war with Russia, rejoiced to hear that another embassy had arrived from India, and hastened to meet it at Balk, where he received the Ambassador with the highest honours. It was immediately urged by the King, that we should afford him assistance against his enemy; and he was not a little mortified to find that the affair of Hadjee Khaleb Khan's death, about which he was perfectly indifferent, was the only subject on which the new ambassador could speak. Had a simple messenger, like Mr. Loveit, carried the letter, this inconvenience would have been prevented, and the Company would have saved three lac of rupees, that is, if they should please to allow Mr. Manesty his expences, a point which will be referred to them by Lord Wellesley. With prudent management, I think a close connection might be cemented bet ween the two countries, as the trade between them would be beneficial to both ; and the only difficulty, the impracticability of our assisting one ally against another, might be obviated by a friendly mediation at St. Petersburgh. At present our respectability is not great in the Persian Gulf, where we have submitted to have our merchant vessels plundered, and our cruizers insulted, by the piratical states on its shores. Of these the most powerful are the Johesserm Arabs, whose coast extends from Cape Mus- sendom to Bahrein. Their chief ports are Rossel- keim, about forty leagues S. S. W. of the Cape, and Egmaum, about twenty-four miles further on. Through the systematic forbearance of the Bombay Government they have risen to a great maritime power, and possess at least thirty-five dows of different sizes, carrying from fifty to three hundred men each. They have few guns, but, being braveand fierce, chiefly attack by boarding, with their crooked daggers stabbing every one who resists. They have taken two large vessels belonging to Mr. Manesty, and had even the impudence to attack the Mornington frigate; but were beaten off. The Honourable Company's cruizers have positive orders to treat these pirates with civility, never to attack them, but only to act on the defensive: the consequence is, that they only look at the stronger vessels, but take every one that has not the power of resistance.

Independently of the real loss, which the native merchants suffer from the value of the captured cargoes, this mean submission ought to be ended, from the conviction of the degradation we suffer in the eye of Persia, by permitting it. A dignified independence, a visible power of supporting the honour of our flag, of protecting our friends, and punishing our enemies, are necessary for the acquirement of the confidence of an Eastern sovereign. Persia herself neither is, nor can be, a great naval power. Were we to protect her coast from the depredations of these pirates, who even extend their devastations to the villages on the sea shore, she would be gratefully attached to us, arid would be bound by the strong tie of interest to protect the northern frontier of our dominion, by being prepared to enter the territories of the Abdalli, ishould he leave them unguarded to attack us. To ascertain the real value of a close connection with Persia is impossible; but some idea may be entertained of it, by a reference to the splendour with which the barren island of Ormus shone forth under the Portuguese, when they monopolized the trade of the Gulf, and secured it from the attack of pirates by a marine, as pre-eminent in those days, as ours is now in every part of the globe, except in the Eastern seas.

I had been so highly gratified by the pagoda at Carli, that I determined to visit others in the Island of Salsette, which, according to the accounts I had received, were formed on a, similar plan. Accordingly I set off early on the morning of the 22nd of November, accompanied by Mr. Salt, and some of the Governor's family. We breakfasted at a small village of Ambola, where we were received by the Portuguese Cure, and afterwards we turned out of our way to examine an extensive excavation, which Monsieur Anquetil du Perron has described in his introduction to the translation of the Zend Avesta, and has given a plan of it, under the. name of Djegueseri. All the apartments were square, and the roof was flat, throughout; in the centre was a smaller building with a lingam ; the whole -was therefore probably dedicated to Maha- deo. Several groups of figures in basso relievo, adorned the walls. They were much decayed, and the whole had a very unpleasant appearance. The floor, being lower than the surrounding country, was extremely damp, and the light, admitted at the three entrances, was nothing better than darkness visible. They run north and south, passing through a small hill that, in parts, is covered with jungle. There was no appearance of attendant Brahmins, but the lingam had been newly ornamented.

We went on to dinner to Mont Pesier, where our tents were pitched for us. Here are the ruins of a very handsome church and monastery, which, I understand, formerly belonged to the Jesuits : Monsieur Anquetil du Perron says, to the Franciscans ; but I am inclined to consider my information correct, from there being the remains of an observatory on a small hill in the neighbourhood, which was more probably the work of the intelligent followers of Ignatius Loyola, than of the lazy monks of St. Francis. The church was originally lined with pannel-work of wood, disposed in compartments, and richly ornamented with carving. In the centre of each was the head of a saint, tolerably executed, surrounded by wreaths of flowers, and other fanciful sculpture, in a very excellent taste. The whole is in ruins, the roof having fallen in. The author, whom I have before mentioned, attributes this to the devastations of the Mahrattas, who, he says, carried away the wood work to Tan- nah ? but this appears improbable. Timber is not scarce: and if they had carried away the more solid work, they would hardly have left behind them the parts that were richly ornamented. Under the church a small pagoda has been formed out of the rock; it is square, and flat roofed, with a few deities, and other figures, in basso-relievo. These the good priests had covered up with a smooth coat of plaister, and had converted the whole into a.chapel. At present the original proprietors have been uncovered, and have again become objects of adoration to the ignorant native.

Early on the morning of the 23d we departed for the Caves of Kenneri, which are the most important in the island, and are formed out of a high knowl, in the middle of the range of hills which divides the island nearly into two equal parts. I soon found that, limited as I was for time, it would be impossible to investigate the whole of the caves, I therefore gave my chief attention to the great cavern, which resembles the one at Carli, in being oblong, and having a coved roof, though it is inferior to it in size, in elegance of design, and in beauty of execution. It has the same singular building at the upper end, and the vestibule is equally adorned with figures. Its peculiar ornaments are *two* gigantic figures of Boodh, nearly twenty feet high, each filling one side of the vestibule. They are exactly alike, and are in perfect preservation, in consequence of their having been christened and painted red by the Portuguese, who left them as an appendage to a Christian church, for such this temple of Boodh became under their transforming hands. I have given a view of the front of the temple, and an etching of the gigantic figure of the presiding deity, whose image, in all the usual attitudes, embellishes several other parts of the vestibule; and one in particular is ornamented with the conical cap worn by the Chinese Fo. The entrance, on which there are several inscriptions in the unknown character, faces the west. It is worthy observation, that these two circumstances, and the coved roof, seem to be peculiar to the temples dedicated to Boodh ; at least it is so in the two I have seen, and in the one at Ellora described by Sir Charles Mallet in the Asiatic Researches. In one of the large square caves which adjoin that above described, are many figures, and one that is very remarkable, as it shows Vishnou himself in the act of fanning Boodh

with the chourie : a superior deity may, however, be supposed to reside in the circular temples, for within them is no image, unless the circular building called by the natives the Dhagope, can be considered as a prodigious lingam. I ought to add, that in the cave of Ellora there does appear a statue annexed to the Dhagope, which, from the manner of holding the finger of one hand

between the finger and thumb of the other, is probably designed for Boodh.

The innumerable caves, which have been formed in every part of the hill, are square, and flat roofed. I cannot but consider them as meant for the habitations of the attendant Brahmins. A very curious tradition is mentioned by Monsieur Anquetil du. Perron, as having been recorded by a Jesuit in a history of the Indies, printed in Portugal; it is, that the whole of these caves were the work of a Gentoo king, some thousand years ago, to secure his only son from the attempts of another nation to gain him over to their religion. This must probably refer to some disputes between the Brahmins and the Boodhists, and might, if it could be traced, throw some light on the relative antiquity of the two religions. The most perplexing circumstance, that the character used by the latter is now no longer understood, while that of the former is in constant use, makes it difficult to believe that the Brahmins are justified in their claim to superior antiquity. It is a subject, however, on which I cannot presume to give an opinion.

It is not only the numerous caves, that give an idea of what the population of this barren rock must once have been, but the tanks, the terraces, and the flights of steps which lead from one part to another; yet now not a human footstep is to be heard, except when the curiosity of a traveller leads him to pay a hasty visit to the ruined habitation of those, whose very name has passed away, and whose cultivated fields are become an almost impassable jungle, the haunt of tigers, and the seat of pestilence and desolation. After copying the inscriptions and taking views of the most interesting objects, we with difficulty made ourway through the jungle to ati open space, oa the verge of the cultivated tracts, where our tents were pitched out of the way of fever and tigers.

We reached Tannah, the capital of the Island of Salsette, to breakfast, and were hospitably received by Mr. Spencer the Resident. A small fort commands the passage between the island and the Mahratta country, but is otherwise of little use. Confined as the settlement of Bombay formerly was, the acquisition of Salsette was an incalculable advantage, from the ceiv tainty which is afforded of a constant supply of fresh provision for the town and fleet. Little however has hitherto been done to increase its produce, and the greater part remains an useless jungle, instead of being converted into fields of rice, and plantations of sugar ; even wood itself is only procured at a very high price, chiefly for want of arrangement. If no better use is to be made of the island, it might certainly supply this article at half the price that is now paid for it. Dr. Scott has set a good example of enter- prize, by establishing a very valuable sugar plantation. On the 25th we returned to Bombay in the Government boat.

I was afterwards tempted by the verdant appearance of the Island of Elephanta, which rears its woody head nearly in the centre of the bay, as much as by the report of its celebrated cave, to pay it a visit. The accurate Niebuhr has given so good an account of it, that a description i& unnecessary. I have only to observe, that I do not think either his drawing, or the etching in the Asiatic Researches, have given the character of the triune deity. Brahmah's countenance admirably expresses the undisturbed composure of the creator of the world; Vishnou's, on the left, has every feature of benevolence, while the lotus which he holds in his hand seems to be expanding under the genial ray of his eye. Seva's, on the contrary, has a ghastly and dire scowl, that well accords with the objects that he holds before him, two of the most venomous of serpents, the covra copel. I was much surprised at the ingenuity of the conception, and the merit of the execution, of these figures. How superior must they have appeared when in a state of perfection!

It was pleasing to me to find, that the great cave of Elephanta, which opens to the north, and has a flat roof, had no inscription in the unknown character, nor any figure of Boodh. Of the numerous deities of the Hindoo mythology, many have been honoured with a place; but the most curious figure, and which has been noted by every traveller, is that of a female amazon, which, from having four arms, most probably represents some super-human personage. Did the romance of' the Amazons reach Greece from India, or were there ever such personages in the Eastern world, are interesting questions, but at present incapable of solution. There is no appearance of any great violence having been used to injure the figures. Had cannon been employed by the Portuguese for that purpose, the marks of the balls would have been visible, and the destruction would have been among the figures. As it is, the pillars are more rapidly decaying than any other part. The water is permitted during the rains to lodge in the cave, and the stone, being a soft one, moulders perceptibly away in the vicinity of the open air. The scene,from the little level space in front, is extremely beautiful, and a cool breeze tempers the heat in the most sultry day of summer. The beauty of the place has however been considerably diminished by a wall, which has been erected across the front, to prevent cattle from getting in, and, as I hear, to prevent curious visitors also from treacherously carrying *off* the legs, heads, and arms of these helpless deities.

4

SECTION 4

CHAPTER V.

Departure from Bombay.|Arrival at Mocha.|Vint to the Dola, and Has Kateb.|Preparations for continuing the Voyage.|Departure from Mocha.|Aroe Islands.|Sir H. Popham's Chart of the Red Sea.|Howakel.|Arrival at Dhalat,|Mr. Maxfield's Report of his Voyage.|Reasons for supposing Howakel Bay to lie Opsian Bay f tht Periplus.|Mr. Salt's Report of his Visit to Dhalac-el-Ki- betr, Girbeshid, and Dobelew.| Captain Court's Survey of Dhalac.|Observations on Mr. Bruce's Account.|Arrival at Massowah.|Commercial arrangements.|Dispute with the Dola of Arkeko.|Departure from Massowah.

MR. DUNCAN had most obligingly ordered one of the Company's vessels, the Mornington, to be prepared to convey:me to Bussorah, whither I had determined to proceed, when all my plans were changed by the arrival of dispatches from the Governor General, recommending a continuation of the survey of the Red Sea, and at the same time delicately hinting, that I might possibly be induced to make an attempt to complete what 'I "had so well begun. On receiving from Mr. Dim- can assurances that every arrangement should bemade for the immediate departure of the vessel, and that I should be permitted to select the officers I determined to comply with his Excellency's intimation. The Panther cruizer, being a smaller vessel than the Mornington, was considered as more suitable to the service of surveying, and was therefore ordered to be got ready. Lieutenant Charles Court was appointed to command her, in consequence of the very high character which he bore, as a seaman, and a man of science.

Lieutenant Maxfield, who had been second Lieutenant of the Antelope, received the appointment of the Assaye, a small French schooner, which had been taken by a King's ship, and had been purchased by the Bombay Government, ou the recommendation of the Marine board, as being a capital sailer. She was intended to accompany us as a tender in the more difficult navigation which we had reason to expect above Massowah.

Mr. Macgie was, at my particular request, nomi- . nated as Surgeon, although not in the East India Company's service, in consequence of the experience I had in my former voyage had of his abilities, and his great attention to the health of the men.

Two time-keepers, and the instruments requisite for nautical observations and land surveying, were

B'ovided by the Bombay Government; and Mr. uncan completed his kind attentions to my comfort by directing Captain Court to keep a table for me at the expence of the East India Company.

Captain Rudland of the Bombay army having expressed a wish to join our party, instead of returning to England by sea, I rejoiced in obtaining for him the necessary permission from the Governor, and the Commander in Chief, as an additional European gentleman would be a great satisfaction in crossing the desert from Suez to Cairo. Nothing could be more favourable than the season, as the monsoon was N. E. 'to the straits of Bab-el-mandeb, and S. E. from the Red Sea to Suez; we were therefore impatient to depart, and the 1st of December was fixed for that purpose. It was however not till the 3d, that Captain Court received his final orders, which were in every respect to obey the instructions that he should receive from me. I parted with Mr. Duncan, whose amiable and benevolent character must conciliate the esteem of all who know him, with great, and I flatter myself, with mutual, regret. He paid a last attention to me by sending his Aid de-camp and the Town Major to attend me to the sea shore, and saluting me on my departure.

We set sail at four in the morning of Dec. 4th, with a very pleasant breeze, and before night the land was completely out of sight. The Panther had been considered as a bad sailer, and we were led to suppose that the Assaye would constantly keep ahead; we however found the contrary, with a fair wind. The Panther sailed tolerably well, and we were obliged to shorten sail for the Assaye.

On the sixth I experienced the deleterious effect of a land breeze in Bombay harbour. I had unfortunately forgotten on the night of the third, that I was still within its reach, and the port-hole of my cabin had been left open: in consequence of which a severe attack of fever came on, but without a cold fit: and, as I was at sea, which is generally prescribed as a certain cure, I hoped not to suffer long.

I had no return of inv fever on the 14th. On the15th we saw the Arab shore. It was the high land of Kisseen, distant about eighteen miles. As there was now no danger of the Assaye's not making her passage, I determined to make the best of our way to Mocha: accordingly Mr. Maxfield was sent for, and directed to stop at Aden, and enquire if Mr. Pringle was there, a circumstance by no means impossible; and if he was, to bring him up with him. We made sail in the evening.

We coasted along with pleasant land and sea breezes; passed Aden early in the morning of the] 8th; through the Straits of Bab-el-mandeb, with a stiff gale from theS.E. during the same night; and at seven anchored considerably to the northward of the north fort of Mocha. It blew so heavy a gale that we were not able to make the roads. The Panther was extremely crank, and totally unable to make any way when close to the wind. This defect was in some measure compensated by our discovering that though the swell was very great, she rode well at anchor. Besides, she was very comfortable, drew little water, and went well before a wind. She had however a very considerable heel to starboard, that was much against us, and for which we could not account. It will hardly be believed, that in a vessel reported ready for sea, there was not a single buoy; yet such was the fact, and we were daily in the habit of discovering similar deficiencies. Two .fishermen, 'who, in consequence of their supplying the British squadron in the Red Sea, had been named Admiral Blanket, and Lord Bombay, came off in one of the native boats, by whom I sent a short note to Mr. Pringle, and received an answer, .saying he would be with me as soon as the weather would permit. We were a little alarmed on getting into sight of the roads to perceive three large ships there. They hoisted American colours as weapproached, and we soon found that they were of that nation, two from Salem, and one from Baltimore.

We made an attempt on the 20th, with the tide in our favour, to reach the roads, but without success; and had the misfortune, in heaving our anchor, to injure the capstern. On examination it appeared, that though newly put together, for the Panther had lately been in dock, it had been made of old wood/partly consumed by the dry rot. However vexatious the delay might be, it was impossible to proceed till this injury should be repaired. We had also here to procure money for the expences of the ship, and for my own private expenditure, by drawing bills on Bombay, which had been recommended to us as more advantageous than bringing cash from that place. Captain Court also required an interpreter, and I wished to get a servant who spoke English and Arabic ; a communication with the shore became therefore absolutely necessary ; but as I could not venture during the violence of the gale, in our small boat, I wrote to Mr. Pringle, stating all our wants, and requesting, if possible, he would come off in an American long boat, which would be a much better sea-boat than ours.

I received in the course of the next day letters in abundance from Mr. Pringle, but he did not come off, though he certainly might have done so in the American boats, which went several times to their ships. Surprised at this neglect, I accepted Mr. Salt's offer to go on shore in a native boat, and return in the morning either with or without Mr. Pringle. I also desired him to wait on the Dola, and request, in my name, permission for a servant and interpreter to accompany me up the Red Sea.

VOL. II. O

Early in the morning Mr. Salt returned, and with him Mr. Pringle, in an American cutter. Mr. Salt had, according to my request, seen the Dola, who had behaved with the utmost politeness, not only permitting the servant I applied for to accompany me, but also giving me leave to hire any one I pleased for an interpreter. He at the same time assured Mr. Salt, that he was extremely concerned he was not properly acquainted with my rank when I was last at Mocha, in consequence of which he did not pay me the requisite attention, but that now, if I chose to land, his horses and people should meet me; and, if I visited him, I should be saluted with four guns on my arrival, and on my leaving him. I was not a little asto- uished at this ridiculous change in his behaviour, being certain that he was perfectly informed of every particular respecting me, before I landed from trie Antelope; however, I determined to go on shore, and treat him with equal politeness. It was usually calmer in the morning, but we had delayed till it blew very fresh. We attempted to make the shore opposite, but found rocks at some distance, and were obliged to beat four miles to windward, which took us up several hours. It was extremely unpleasant, the boat making more water on one tack, than we could bale: but on the other we were able to get her dry. She sailed well, or it would have been impossible for us to reach the shore.

After much difficulty and some danger we landed, and found horses waiting for us. Captain Crowninshield and the other Americans who were on shore met us without the town, as did Devage, and many others; at the gate the Dola's horses and tom-toms were waiting, which preceded me with their incessant din to his house. I was permittedto ride to the steps of the door, a very unusual condescension at the present day, though formerly it was allowed to all Europeans who visited the Dola. It was the fast of Ramadan, when the Arabs eat nothing from the rising of the sun to the setting; to make which as easy as possible, they turn night into day, carousing during the whole of the former, and dedicating the latter to sleep. The Dola was not awake, so that he could not receive me, and I was kept waiting a few minutes; however to compensate this neglect he rose up to pay his compliments to each of the gentlemen of my party, who were successively presented to him. The usual compliments passed. Rose water was presented, and our chins perfumed with frankincense. To a bearded Arab this must be a pleasant ceremony; but to us I always thought it had a ridiculous appearance, and smiled when my friends underwent the operation. The Americans were very sensible and intelligent men, particularly Captain Crowninshield, who belonged to the very ' respectable house of that name, and Captain Bancroft, who was originally educated for the bar, but obliged by ill health to give it up. Abdallah, whom I wished to take with me as my servant, agreed to go, and immediately began to procure us the necessaries wanted. We urged Devage to get us a dow without delay, and immediately procured from him the money we required.

We hired a dow for three hundred dollars to go the voyage to above Suakin. I paid the Dola an evening visit, Mr. Pringle having previously sent him presents, in my name, to the amount of five hundred dollars, and to the Bas Kateb two hundred. Nothing particular passed, except his saying that he begged I would consider Mocha as my house, and that the gates should be open for meat any hour. He expressed a wish to have some private conversation with me before my departure. I said, I would wait on him the evening before I embarked. Mr. Criddle, our youngest Midshipman, was with us; the Dola wanted to know if he was my son, whence arose a conversation respecting our sons. He showed me his, and told jne he had one more, an infant. He then asked after mine. His manners were bad and his whole appearance mean. The apartment was small, and the staircases, as usual in Arab houses, narrow and inconvenient, with numerous doors at the landing places; probably meant as a defence against a sudden attack.

The Americans kindly lent us their boats and carpenters to repair our capstern. The wind rendered all communication with the vessel extremely difficult. We spent a very pleasant Christmas day at the factory, being fourteen in number, a large party of white faces for so distant a part of the globe.

Our dow met with an accident in being launched, in consequence of which we were still delayed. We therefore determined to send off Mr. Maxfield in the Assaye direct to Massowah, with letters for the Nayib, informing him of my intention to visit him, and requesting that two pilots might be procured to conduct the ship to Suakin, assuring him that the two hundred dollars should be paid for them, being the price he had previously demanded. Mr. Maxfield had instructions to meet us at Dhalac, where we intended to water. I wrote at the same time to the Banian, to de- . sire he would expedite the procuring of the pilots.

Mr. Maxfield sailed on the 27th; but there was o much sea that he parted his cable, and left hisanchor behind him, nor were we able to recover it. We lived very pleasantly at the factory : all the officers that could be spared coming on shore. The Americans exerted themselves to please and serve us. The weather was very pleasant, and the nights perfectly cool.

We were fortunate in procuring a pilot, who bore a most excellent character, and had been for thirty years sailing between Mocha and Suakin. He was brother to the Naqueda of the dow. He asked one hundred and fifty dollars for the trip, and I gave them to him, lest there should be any delay at Massowah. It rendered us completely independent of the Nayib. On the evening of the 30th I visited the Dola, to request the gates might be opened for me at four o'clock in the morning, that 1 might be gone before the wind freshened. He said it could not be, and began to argue about it. I was very angry, and told him, that if he had not offered it, I should never have made the application. He wanted me to go out at the sally port, which I positively refused, and desired that the servants might be turned out of the room that we might speak in private. This was done; and Mr. Pringle pointedly reprobated his caprice about the gates. He then said they should be open.

We had now a very singular political conversation of about two hours. It began by his observing that old customs should be preserved. This I denied, and said they ought to change with the times: that in India we had become masters by the will of God, and that many customs existed before that period, which must now be laid aside. He replied, " I know very well that is the case in India; but what do you English mean to do with Yemen?" I replied, laughing, " nothing, but to get as much coffee from it as we can," He said,he believed we were all Wababees. I told him I knew but one Wahabee, and that was Sidi Mohammed Akil. He laughed, and asked how I knew him to be one. I replied, he told me so.

He now asked Mr. Pringle's permission to say something to me, which being of course granted, he began a regular complaint against that gentleman ; " that without his knowledge he had written to the Sheriffe of Abou Arish, who was making war against the Imaum, and taking his country from him." The fact certainly was so ; but it was merely commercial, respecting coffee to be purchased at Loheia. This I represented ;

but he seemed by no means satisfied. I assured him in the most solemn manner, that I knew it was the determination of the Bombay Government not to assist the Wahabees against the Imaum of Sana; and that had such been their intention, they would have sent a direct intimation, and not through the medium of Mr. Pringle, who was only a civil servant employed for the purposes of trade. He could not, for some time, be convinced. He said, " Why was not the letter shewn ?" And asked me explicitly, if the carrying on such a correspondence was not criminal. I replied, that if Mr. Pringle wrote to any enemy of the Imaum, in a way that could be injurious to that Prince, while living under his protection, he would certainly act criminally, and deserve to be punished; but if it was merely about coffee, he must not blame Mr. Pringle, but that Providence which had placed the coffee country under the control of the Sheriffe ; that where the articles were to be had, there the merchant would go. He said it had never been so, and that the Imaum would not permit coffee to be exported from Loheia. I asked how he would hinder it. He laughed, and said, ' well, if youare determined, you must send ships to Loheia, but the Imaum will not like it."

He enquired where the Assaye was gone, and where I was going. 1 told him, to Massowah, as he might know by the pilots I had hired. He was evidently uneasy, and under an impression that I had some hostile intentions. I again repeated all I had said; and added, that had I received any instructions from India inimical to him, I should have proceeded directly to Loheia, and not visited him and drank coffee with him. He at length declared he was satisfied, and that I had removed a heavy load from his mind. When I arose up to take my leave,' I requested to put his hand into Mr. Pringle's, to which he consented ; and I left them professedly friends. He conducted me the whole length of the room quite to the door, a compliment he never before paid to any one.

The whole conversation gave me a much better opinion of his understanding than I had before. He certainly had reason for his alarms ; and the manner in which he pushed forward the enquiry was decorous, yet able. The Wahabees were assembling a very large force at Loheia and Hodeida. They had collected the revenue of Beit-il-Fakih and the surrounding country, and sent to Mocha to say they would be there as soon as Ramadan is over. They have many friends in the town, and I see nothing that can resist them. To add to the Dola's alarms, I arrived in a vessel, which, instead of anchoring in the roads near the fort, kept aloof to the north; and instead of landing, I only sent off letters to the Resident. To his fears, therefore, I attribute his civility ; and in this idea I am confirmed by Nathaniel Pierce, one of the men, who, from fear of Captain Keys, ran away from the Antelope, and turned Mussulmaun; this man, throughmy servant, applied to me, stating the wretched situation he was in, declaring his sincere repentance, and beseeching me to permit him to attend me, even as a slave, to Europe. I consented to receive him, and he came *off* in the boat last night. He tells me that the Dola has been alarmed ever since my departure, suspecting that I was gone to the Wahabees, and would return with them. He frequently asked Pierce if I was as great a man as Sir Home Popham, and whether he thought I should come back. Pierce assured him I should not; yet here I was, at the moment the Wahabees were expected.

I confess I felt very great pleasure in depriving the Dola of this man at so critical a moment. All the old renegadoes had gone *off* with a party of fifty Turks belonging to dows, who marched them down to the pier in the middle of the day, and the Dok's askaris dared not attempt to prevent them. They became Wahabees, and are now at Loheia, jready to march against Mocha, every foot of which they are perfectly acquainted with. They know the proper place for the attack, and even sent word to Pierce not to be near the middle fort, as they should enter there. This may be done with the utmost facility, as the ports are only a few feet from the ground. The Dola is so much alarmed that, on about one hundred Wahabees coming to one of the gates, and offering to inlist with him, he gave them a dollar each, and sent them away; afraid to take them, and yet afraid to refuse. It is singular, that the very act of procuring converts, on which the Dola so much prided himself, should now conduce to his ruin. His violation of the law of nations recoiled on his own head. One of the two boys, who escaped from the factory, was dead; the other was to be married this Ede. The littleboys were very ill. I sent them some medicine which they took secretly; the bigotry of the Mus- sulmauns will not allow them to do it openly. Some laudanum I gave Pierce was taken from him; they said it was sheitan, and that prayers were better. AH the remaining renegadoes meant to try to get off in the three American ships: when we went on shore they were at Moosa, so that our people did not see them.

Early in the morning of January 2, our little dow was along side, and we received from the shore our last stock of vegetables. At eight we weighed anchor and steered for the Aroe Islands, so called in the charts, but probably a corruption of Jibbel Arish, the name of the largest island. We had a very stiff breeze, and a strong current to the northward. The swell lessened as we approached the African shore. This was the case during our last voyage, and it was satisfactory to find it the same at this season. Our vessel was so crank that we were obliged to carry only close- reefed topsails on the cap. We passed between the white rocks, which the pilot called the Children of Arish, and the islands, as on our return from Massowah, and were extremely surprised to find how incorrectly they were laid down in Sir Home Popham's chart of the Red Sea; the Great Aroe having been left out, while the others were none of them in their true position. Captain Court expressed his surprise, that Mr. Maxfield had been able to lay the places down so accurately in his chart, from the little assistance he received. We went close to Rackmah, and upon the credit of Mr. Maxfield's chart, sailed all night. It blew very fresh, and there was a considerable following sea. The Panther was so light, that we could not make her go less than seven knots with adouble reefed fore-topsail close to the cap. We kept rather without the line of the Antelope's course, and had deeper water, with sometimes ne soundings.

Ras Kussar was in sight next morning, and the weather more moderate, with a smooth sea. We found that our dow had left us in the night, having probably run in shore for shelter. We coasted along, going as near the shore as possible. Captain Court was indefatigable in taking bearings. We did not think it safe to pass betwen Pilot's Island and the African shore in the dark, and therefore in the evening came to an anchor in ten fathom, under shelter of a small island called Ad- juice, a little to the north of Howakil. There were several fishing boats, and some dows, which ran away on our approach. Our pilot seemed well acquainted with the coast, and was on the whole a much more intelligent man than the one we had in the Antelope. He expressed great astonishment during the day at our knowing the names of the capes and islands.

In the morning one of the dows came along side. They were only fishing, and belonged to the eastern coast of Arabia. They said that the island, though inhabited, had no water; but that there was some on the main land behind Howakil. The former part of this account was certainly true at this time, as they begged some water from us, which we .willingly gave them ; but it is impossible to suppose that this can be always the case, or the inhabitants would remove to the main land. Don Juan de Castro, who anchored here in 1540, with the Portuguese fleet under Don Stefano de Gama, says that there was water on the great island, called from its figure Whale Island, by which he undoubtedly meant Howakil. They describe the Bay as not deep, nor fit for large vessels, having an entrance for dows at the southern extremity. As I considered this as probably the Op- sian Bay of the Periplus, I had given Mr. Maxfield directions to examine it in the Assaye.

We sailed at day-break. Our pilot took us without Pilot's Island, through a new and good channel, but no soundings. We had baffling winds as we approached Dhalac, and did not get to an anchor till dark. We were nearly in the old spot. Our friend the Dola came off on his catamaran, and was rejoiced to see us. We told him we came for water. He said we should have it, and every thing else we .wished for. He received a present of tobacco and rice : the people all wanted some of the latter. There has been no rain since I was here, and the island is nearly burnt up. Many of their cattle and goats have died in consequence. It was determined that Captain Court should go on shore to settle every thing to-morrow. During the night we had a fresh gale from south.

Captain Court, Mr. Salt, and Captain Rudland went on shore on the 5th, and arranged every thing with the Dola for surveying the island: he himself consented for forty dollars to accompany them. They had a camel for their baggage, and asses for themselves, two Europeans as servants, and Mr. Criddle, the youngest midshipman, as assistant observer. They took with them a week's provisions; on the 6th they went on shore and departed. The Dola left a request that our people would not wander about the island, nor fire *off* guns in the interior, as it would alarm the inhabitants : this I faithfully promised to prevent.

The situation of the ship made it absolutely necessary to examine the state of the hold. We found that she had not sufficient ballast by several tons ; that all the fire-wood had been placed under the ground tier of water-barrels, thereby raising the centre of gravity above a foot; and that the casks which were sent on board as new, had leaked out nearly the whole of their contents, being made of old worm-eaten ship timber; another instance of the neglect in every department of the marine at Bombay. Would any one believe that these vessels were received into store as new, and issued again as such ! Every thing was removed, and new stowed. The water was put at the bottom, and ve took in six hundred and eighty-seven skins full. The Assaye received two hundred and eighteen. The water on the island near Nokhara was exhausted the second day ; the rest was procured from the wells on Dhalac, near the doom-trees, where Mr. Salt formerly landed. When they shall have been more accustomed to water ships, it will be done more expeditiously. After the 6th the wind from the S. changed to light variable airs, with a land and sea breeze. When it blew freshest there was no swell, nor can there be, as on every side, at thirty miles, this anchorage is land-locked. The ground is mud and sand, without coral.

On the 6th Mr. Maxfield was in sight, and late at night anchored close to us. On the 7th he came on board with a letter from the Nayib of Massowah, couched in the most friendly terms. He sent one pilot, and had hired another, who was to be ready on my reaching that place. He sent a man to procure me every thing I wished for at Dhalac, whom I dispatched immediately to Captain Court.

Mr. Maxfield informed me, that on leaving Mocha roads he had not been able to weather the Aroe Islands, but had been carried to the northward by the strength of the current, where he had found a free passage, which is laid down in the charts. Agreeably to the instructions he had received, he steered for Howakil, and came to an anchor among the Sarbo Zeghir Islands, forming a very safe bay, which he named Assaye Bay. He attempted to enter the harbour behind Howakil, but was driven back by a very strong current, which he could not stem with his sweeps, as the wind was adverse. The only passage that appeared practicable was extremely narrow, and had two shoals extending from the points of entrance. The natives' account, that it is passable only for dows, seems therefore to be true; and Howakil Bay can be an object of curiosity only to ascertain whether the Opsian stone is found in it; for I think the description of the Periplus so exactly accords with what we have seen, that there can be no doubt of its being the Opsian Bay.

The vast accumulation or sand, that existed in the time of the Egyptian traveller, is now. become a cluster of low sandy islands, nearly level with the sea, which are designated in the chart as the Arenah Islands; and the bay itself most admirably answers the description of l3Sh/raTor; for it is the deepest on the whole western coast of the Red Sea, except Foul Bay in lat. 23, which cannot, from its position, be the one described. The distance from Aduli to the Opsian Bay, as stated in the Periplus, is eight hundred stadia, or, according to Dr. Vincent, eighty miles, which it ought to be, if the stadium used was the Roman, of ten to a mile; but I confess I am inclined to suppose that it was the Egyptian, of fifteen to a mile, which will make the distance a little more than fifty- three miles. This is, in fact, the real distance from the Arenah islands to the sea shore near Massowah;

at twenty stadia, or about a mile and a half, from which, stood the town of Aduli. It is highly improbable, in stating the distance between this town and the bay, that the author should have meant to carry his admeasurement to the cape at the farther extremity, instead of the one at the entrance; yet Dr. Vincent has been obliged to measure the distance to Cape Sarbo in order to make it seventy- five miles, which is still short of the eight hundred stadia mentioned in the Periplus. This difficulty, as well as many others that still encumber the work, may be removed, by supposing that the Egyptian stadium was the one meant by the author; and nothing seems to me more rational than the idea, that an Egyptian merchant sailing from Egypt would use the stadium of that country. It is, however, with the greatest hesitation that I venture to differ from Dr. Vincent, whose perfect knowledge and laborious investigation of ancient geography, entitle him to the highest deference in $very point connected with it.

During Mr. Maxfield's stay at Massowah, the Nayib had given a very strong proof of his friendly regard: two of the lascars belonging to the As- saye ran away from the vessel, but were caught by some Arabs, belonging to a dow, before they could reach the shore, and carried before the Nayib, who immediately sent them to Mr. Maxfield, with a request that they might not be punished, which was promised and faithfully performed. The evils that attend the trading with Mocha from the Arab spirit of proselyting, will not therefore be extended to Massowah. On the 8th, another complimentary letter arrived from the Nayib, with a present of sheep, vegetables, limes, and water.

I dispatched the dow with her people to Valen- tia Island to look for shells, and employed my serVant and another European in the same pursuit. They procured a few fine specimens of Cyprsea, but the others that they brought were of little value.

I sent Alii Nohri on shore to procure sheep: he brought off twenty goats, for which he said they demanded fourteen dollars; and if I did not like them at that price, I must send them back. Astonished at conduct so different from what I had before experienced, I instantly did so, being convinced that it was a contrivance of this rascally Arab, who wanted to purchase every thing here, as he did at Mocha, and have cent, per cent, profit. I was convinced of his knavery by another incident. The dow brought a heifer to sell, and asked four dollars: we objected, and they would have taken three; but Alii Nohri prevented them by saying in Arabic, it was cheap at four: this they afterwards owned to my servant and Pierce.

January 14.|Captain Court, Mr. Salt, and the party, all returned, having surveyed the southern and eastern parts of the island. Mr. Salt made the following report of their proceedings during their absence.

" We left Nokhara at seven in the morning, and crossed the creek to Dhalac ; but not finding the asses ready, walked to the wells on the sea shore, marked by the doom-trees, and whence latterly the water was procured for the ship. The distance was about one mile and three quarters. The country was dried up, as not a drop of rain had fallen since our last visit to the island, yet the wells were as full as ever, the water being within two feet of the surface, and good. Near the wells were some bulbs, apparently Frittilaria, of which specimens were sent on board, and also a small knotty root of a species of grass of an aromatic flavour, which is eaten by the natives. We were 9

obliged to wait till twelve, when Captain Court took the meridian altitude, and also a set of bearings. This is a more convenient place for a vessel to water at than Nokhara, as the water is near the shore, and it is well marked by the doom trees. At the wells was a small flock of sheep, ten or twelve in number. The date trees seemed not to have thriven since we were here, yet the soil is far better than at Mocha: a flight of small birds; not unlike averdavats, came and settled among their branches; and two vultures, of different species, that had fled, like ourselves, for shelter from the wind and sun, remained stationary under their shade. The number of goats that we this day met with is worthy of observation, considering that there was scarcely a blade of grass to be seen; but the mimosa, that braves the most burning heat, seems to afford sufficient nourishment to these as well as to the camels that roam at large- about the island. The asses at length arrived, and were more steady than usual; but the ride was unpleasant from the heat of the sun, and the force of the wind.

" After passing by the salt marsh, we stopped a few minutes, and endeavoured to procure milk or water, at a place where I had' formerly obtained both, but in vain. We went up to the building where I had before been requested not to go, and found that it was only a shelter for their kids. On our arrival at Dhalac-el-Kibeer, we experienced a most welcome reception from the inhabitants. My friend the priest, who was acting as, Dola when I was here with Mr. Maxfield, now presented to me the real Dola, a venerable old man, who had then been confined by indisposition. I was glad to see that they had not forgotten me, and that they expressed pleasure at our arrival.Captain Court made an observation, and after the sun had set we took a short walk, and then laid ourselves down, well satisfied, on the humble couches prepared for us. Thermometer at Dhalac 80 in the morning, 87 at noon.

" January 8.lAfter breakfast we set out with all our implements of surveying, and, while the two Europeans were measuring a base from Sheik Abou-el-Heimen's tomb, made a circuit to the southward to examine the tanks. We found twelve all nearly of the same construction, though some were much larger than others, and one was uncovered and square. Captain Court thought the largest would hold one hundred and fifty tons. They were cut out of the solid rock, and chunamed, but not lined with stone. Thence we went round to the eminence, which Captain Court had fixed upon for the other extreme of his base, at about a mile from the mausoleum. While he was engaged in taking bearings, I rode off to the point whence I had before seen the Antelope, but wandered about for a considerable time in vain, then mounted a tree, but with as little success; at length I got upon the top of a large upright stone, that stands, like a land-mark, in the middle of the plain, when I was gladdened with a sight of the Panther, which I kept steadily in view, retreating until I came into the line of the measured base, at about one mile from the stone. Captain Court took bearings from this spot, and a meridian altitude, with an artificial horizon. We afterwards returned by the north mosque, and, on our way, examined three more of the cisterns, all similar to those we had seen in the morning.

" We had fixed with the Dola to depart at noon, but it was already past that hour, and we had not nearly finished our observations; so we

Vol. ir. P

dined at two ; at half past three Captain Court took sights, and at four went down to the mausoleum, to take a set of bearings from its summit, while in the mean time I examined the inside, in the centre of which was the tomb, covered by two pieces of coloured Indian chintz spread on a wooden frame. We extended our walk, by going round to the southern mosque, in which is a rough inscription. The architecture is tolerably regular, and the arch of the dome well formed. We then looked into five more cisterns, one of which differed from all the others, in having the roof supported by five pillars, though it was not so large as some we had seen in the morning. Its dimensions, which were taken by a man we let down by the log-line, were as follows; its longest diameter twenty-four feet, its shortest twenty-two; the pillars six feet in circumference, and six feet distant from each other, but at unequal distances from the wall, some two feet, some four feet; they were somewhat thicker at top, but had no regular capitals. The depth of the tank was thirteen feet, and the whole was covered with chunam. The birds seen this day were white- breasted crows, vultures, kites, pelicans, small birds of the sparrow kind, water-wagtails, the abou hannes of Bruce, and which are called so by the natives here, ring-doves, and a bird of an iron brown colour, about the size of a pigeon. Thermometer as yesterday.

"jJanuary 9.IWe departed early in the morning froiii Dhalac-el-Kibeer, having procured asses for all our people, and camels for the baggage. On parting we gave a piece of blue cloth to the Sheik- el-Belled, a dollar to Abouel-Heimen's tomb, and another to my friend the Sheik of the mosque, and distributed some tobacco to the people who hadassisted us in onr excursions. As there was scarcely a breath of air, the heat was intolerably oppressive. The road lay at first south-easterly, over a stony plain, on which not a blade of grass was discernible. After marching about three miles, a large bird, that was passing to the left, induced us to stop until the musquets were brought up; it was of a brown colour, and appeared not unlike a cassowary; the people said it was good to eat; on firing at it, it ran away, expanding its wings, but did not attempt to fly. Soon after we had recommenced our march, the road began to incline about N. E. by E. over a low sandy plain, about half a mile wide, and nearly four miles in extent, with ridges of rock on either side, that gave it somewhat the appearance of a river's bed. The rocks on the left rise into a remarkable cliff, not less, I imagine, than thirty feet above the

Elain; the strata lie horizontally, and are so regu- ir that when near us, they resembled the walls of an ancient castle.

" At a little before twelve we turned off the plain, and ascended the rocky ground to the right; when our guides pointed out to us the village of Gerbeschid, about a mile in front, which was easily distinguished, (as are all other villages or towns on the island,) by the doom-trees rising above the Mimosas, with which this part of the island more particularly abounds. We reached it soon after twelve, and took possession of a tenement, in every respect like what we had at Nok- hara and Dhalac. From the last place Gerbeschid is by the road about nine miles distant. It is *a.* most wretched assemblage of about twenty huts, and is distant three miles from the sea. It is difficult to conceive how its inhabitants manage to preserve their existence, as the drought has killedgreat part of their goats, on which they depend chiefly for their support, a considerable quantity of cheese being annually exported from this place to Loheia. The putrid carcases of the dead goats still lie around the town in every direction, and send forth most pestilential effluvia. The few that survive are too ill fed to give milk, and too lean to afford substantial nourishment if killed, so that th'ese poor people are obliged to live almost entirely upon fish, of which there is also but a scanty supply; their water, which is drawn from wells, is indeed tolerably good, but very muddy. During the most favourable seasons, this place produces few even of the necessaries of life; the additional deprivation is therefore more severely felt than it would be, probably, in most parts of the globe.

" Captain Court took observations for the latitude, and a lunar observation for the longitude; and after dinner walked towards the sea in an easterly direction. Hence the land is seen at a very considerable distance to the south, forming a creek or bay, which Captain Court afterwards ascertained to be a part of the main land of Dhalac. I learned

from the Sheik-el-Belled that there were forty or fifty men living here, about eighty
women, and only about ten children in the whole place; which I have reason to believe
true, from the very few we saw, both then, and on our return. He added the following
particulars; that they had lost between two and three hundred goats and kids ; that
they have but eight wells, and no tanks of any description; that from Ras Shoke to Ras
Antalou is four days journey; that their principal employment is making mats, and
that some of their people are engaged in the sea-faring line at Loheia. Thermometer
at day light 80, at night 90.

" January 10.|*We* rose at day light, and in the
course of an hour had all ready for departure, but were detained, much against our
inclinations, by the loss of a bunch of keys, for which we ransacked the house and
baggage in vain; it was past seven, when finding, probably, that we were determined
not to go without them, a boy belonging to the village brought them to us, pretending
that he had found them on the road. The track this day led over a plain, quite level,
but not so stony as on the west side of the island. The wind was blowing light from
the N. W. The direction of our march lay to the N. E. on our setting out; the sea
was three miles distant on our right, and two miles out lay the island of Irwee, its
extremes bearing from S. E. to east. Off its northern extremity are two trees on the
edge of the water, which appeared, at the distance we were, like rocks. We continued
a direct course for about two miles and a half, when we saw the high trees about
Dobelew, bearing from us due north ; we could likewise just distinguish to our right
on the horizon the island of Dalcoos. We soon after passed on our left a miserable
kind of edifice, which they called Sheik Othman's tomb. The country here made some
slight approach towards vegetation. I observed a few trees of a different species of
mimosa from what we had hitherto seen, as also a parasitical plant entwining round
its branches. We arrived at Dobelew at nine, and computed it to be four miles and a
half from Gerbeschid. It appeared to be full as large as Dhalac-el-Kibeer, had a white
tomb at the east and west .ends, and two smaller ones on the north.

" They conducted us at first to a wretched hovel, from which they had just driven
their goats; but, on our expressing dissatisfaction, they found us another somewhat
more decent, and, to compensate for their rudeness, turned a family out of the next
habitation, and gave it to us for a cook- room. This was, however, after having been
severely reprimanded by the Nayib's servant; who had evidently received very strict
orders to proviue for our accommodation; he had throughout been of the greatest use
to us, and had uniformly paid attention to all our wishes. There was no milk to be
procured here, but we got a kid, with some little trouble, and three fowls.

" The weather was so cloudy, that the sun was not visible at twelve; but Captain
Court afterwards took a double altitude, to ascertain the latitude. In the evening he
went and measured a base from the north-western mosque to a goat-shed half a mile
distant, and at the latter station took a set of bearings, having in sight the islands of
Irwee, Dalcoos, and Saiel Sezan, and to the west, the village of Saied-el-Ait. We used
our utmost endeavours to procure a boat to go over to Irwee, but in vain. We were
informed that there is only a small village on the island, visited by a few fishermen on
catamarans; that its coast is low, with here and there a tree upon it; and that the water
between it and the nearest point of the coast to Dobelew, is shallow, and full of shoals.

We now proposed to the Dola going up to Ras Antalou; but he assured us, that the only practicable means of doing so, would be to go by water from Nokhara, since, on the road from this place, there were neither asses nor camels to be procured, nor people to afford us accommodations of any kind. It was determined, therefore, that we should walk in the morning to a rocky eminence, called Jissoom, which is the highest land in the neighbourhood of Dobelew. Abdallah and the two seamen went down to the sea side in the morning to look for shells; but the few that they were able to procure were of little value. I urged the Seid tosend out some of the fishermen on the same pursuit, and promised to pay them handsomely; but the inhabitants of this village seemed to be as idle as they wtre poor, and in consequence nothing could be done.

" January 11.|We set out on our proposed expedition at half past six, marching in a direct line for Jissoom, which bore from us N. 35 E. We had advanced about three miles, when we came to a creek of salt water that crossed our road at right angles, which we passed over, the water being shallow. As we proceeded a herd of deer galloped by us on our right, at no great distance. Having reached Jissoom, Captain Court 6xed his theodolite, and took the bearings of all the islands, and principal objects around us, as follows, Dobelew from S. 31 W. to S. 27 West. Irwee from S. 37, | E. to S. 3 W. Saiel Arabic S. 64 E. Dalcoos from S. 86 E to N. 86$ E. Saiel Sezan from N. 59 E. to N. 52 E. a distant island from N. 55 to N. 45 E. Dalhedeia N. 21.| E, Delgammon or Derghiman, of which there are two, Kibeer and Zeguir from N. 19 E. to N. 30 W. Saiel-el-Ait, the village we had before seen, S. 79 W. We found that the creek we had passed completely insulates Jissoom hill, and the low land around it, forming nearly a circular island about two miles in circumference. On the point of Dhalac bearing N. 38 W. is a village called Ebaru. All around us there appeared to be shoal water as far as the eye could reach.

" Here we measured the distance back to the northern mosque, and arrived at half past ten. The weather cloudy, and thermometer only 82 at noon day. Captain Court took a meridian altitude, and at four p. m. he went out, and, proceeding from the northern mosque, measured a base to the water's edge, in a line with the northern point of Irwee. He found the space between Ras-el-Shoel and Irwee, which forms what Bruce calls the harbour of Dobelew, filled up with sandy shoals, and small islets, excepting close to Irwee, where there appears to be a channel sufficiently deep for boats of small burthen. Hence the south end of Irwee makes in one, and seems almost connected, with the main land of Dhalac. Seied-el- Arabie and Seied-el-Sezan were both in sight, but, from some particular effect in the atmosphere, they were not able to distinguish Dalcoos. As far as this chain of islands extends outwards, Captain Court is satisfied that the water is shoally, and that no vessel would be safe in attempting a passage within them, except small craft; and it is only a few days ago that two dows were lost on the outside of Irwee, driven in by stress of weather. During Captain Court's absence I endeavoured to get as much information as possible concerning the place, and, for this purpose, one of the elder inhabitants, who had spent his life in pilotting vessels to and fro, was brought to me by the Na- yib's man. He confirmed to me the names of all the islands we had seen in the morning, which agree most perfectly with what Bruce has called them. He recognized every island, excepting two, mentioned by Bruce, as I named them from the book. Abdel Gaffar's tomb, however, they assured me was on the island of Noorah, off Ras Antalou, where is a small village, and not on Dahalottum, as asserted by Bruce. They say, thre are two islands of el-Surat, the largest of which had once wells and inhabitants, but the latter have removed, and the former have been all filled up.

" January 12.lAbout two o'clock in the morning a heavy shower of rain fell, which obliged usto remove our cots, on vhich we had hitherto slept in the open air, into the house for shelter; but the covering of these habitations is so little adapted for keeping out the inclemency of the rainy season, that we could not find even one "snug corner." Captain Court went out at dawn of day, and took a set of bearings from the top of the northern mosque. The water, which we this morning procured, was filled with so thick a sediment, that we were obliged to give up our tea. The well itself we found, on measuring it, to be seven fathom deep, and with only three feet water. This is, I think, the most inhospitable place we have visited. The men were by no means obliging, and seemed to be jealous, or the women were extremely shy, for they evidently kept out of our way as much as possible. The character of the people is probably, in no small degree, affected by their intercourse with Arabia. The shell of a turtle was lying in the yard, about two feet and a half diameter; they speak of them as being very common; by a small piece of the shell which remained, it appeared to be of that species which yields the true tortoise shell. The stench of dead goats was as unpleasant to us here, as at Gerbeschid. There are more doom trees than at the other villages, besides many other species of tree.

" At half past nine we quitted this miserable place. Captain Court took an exact account of our bearings, and found Gerbeschid to be, as we computed, only four miles and a half from Dobe- lew. We saw a covey of partridges on the road, and got to our journey's end by half past ten. Immediately on our arrival at Gerbeschid, we looked out for an eminence, from which we might see some one of the points which Captain Court hadtaken, and thus connect the line of bearings: but, after mounting walls and houses in vain, we almost despaired of success, the situation of this village being extremely low, and no rising ground in the neighbourhood. At last we resorted to the old expedient of ascending to the top of the mosque, an indignity which we found might be always compensated by the gift of a dollar, and here, after piling a triple story of couches, one upon the other, which were procured from the owner of the adjacent house, we gained, most fortunately, a good bearing of a goat-shed, whence Captain Court had taken his last bearings. Hence we likewise saw the cliff, and the high land of the Abyssinian coast, somewhere near Hurtoo. The day was unluckily too cloudy to get any solar observation, which made it the more important that we should get a point of bearing between Gerbes- chid and Dhalac-el-Kibeer; we therefore determined to wait until morning, and proceed at daylight, when we expected to attain our object, by mounting the cliff. I learned to day, that there were at this time seventeen trankies, from near Muscat, looking out among the islands for pearls, tortoise-shell, wood, or indeed whateverkthey could pick up; many of these we saw lying off the coast in different directions. Thermometer 82$. " January 13.lLeft Gerbeschid at half past seven, and reached the cliff in about half an hour, having more spirited asses than usual. We computed the distance to be two miles and an half. Leaving our animals at the bottom, we ascended to the highest point, on which stand the two trees, which were set from Gerbeschid. This cliff is nearly perpendicular, except in one or two places, where loose fragments of rock, that have fallen, form stepping-places, which render the ascent easy. In some parts of the rock are deep chasms, that appeared almost the work of art. The view from the top fully answered our expectations, and discovered to us, somewhat unexpectedly, a sight of the Panther, an object most particularly interesting to our purposes; it appeared over the point of Dhalac, nearest to Nokhara, on the opposite side of a large salt-water lake, which was distant about three quarters of a mile, and which apparently is deep enough for the largest vessels. We could also just distinguish one of the mausoleums at Nokhara, distant between six and seven miles. We had at the same time in sight Cape Sarbo, and the island of Howakil, the high peak behind Hurtoo, and the village of Gerbeschid.

" As the surest way of ascertaining the sites of these objects. Captain Court measured a base of eight hundred paces, and took bearings at each end. The land descends, in a sloping line, hence to the lake, round which is a sandy beach. On coming down we observed a few deer, which were very wild, and speedily bounded over the rocks out of sight. The valley, formed by the cliffs, which we passed through a second time to day, seems by far the richest part of the island ; it is well sheltered, the soil is good, and there was, even still, a little verdure covering the greater part of it. I also observed three species of shrubs, different from what I had before noted. It is probable that even the small quantity of rain which had fallen, occasioned, in a great degree, the more luxuriant appearance of this valley, or it might be the difference of our feelings, at the times that we passed through it. Two or three species of birds, the plumage of one of which was very beautiful, were seen flying from bush to bush. We arrived at Dhalac-el-Kibeer at half past one. Thermometer 84. 5'. -

" January 14. IAt day-light I went with Abdal- lah and the two Europeans to the northern mosque, for the purpose of getting possession of some of the monumental stones, mentioned in my former account. The best finished inscriptions were engraved on stones, which were too heavy to carry away. I therefore made choice of two of the most perfect, carved in different characters, that were portable, and wrapping them up very carefully, proceeded back to our lodgings, not quite satisfied, I own, with the propriety of what I was about. Our proceedings having been observed, by the time we reached the house a crowd had assembled, among which were several principal inhabitants. I immediately perceived that they were acquainted with what we had been doing, and that they wished to examine the contents of our bags, which we evaded, and got our plunder safe into the yard. The crowd now began to increase, and I heard them debating the matter rather warmly on the outside. Soon afterwards they came into the yard, in a body, with Seied Yusuff and the Nayib's messenger at their head ; there were also, among the foremost, the Sheik-el- Belled and the Sheik of the mosque. Abdallah being called, they began a most lamentable complaint against our proceedings, said these stones were sacred to the dead, and that the Nayib had positively forbidden that any of them should be removed. The Nayib's man, however, who was spokesman, said nothing as from himself, but premised every sentence with, " thus do they infer." The Seied Yusuff also (having been previously bribed) kept a becoming silence; so I cut the matter short by telling them, that they might rest assured that I should do nothing except what the Nayib approved; and that I should not think of arguing with them upon the subject, (whom it did not at all concern,) but would settle the matter with their superior, when we arrived at Massowah. This, I told them, was my determination, and forbad Abdallah to interpret another word on the subject. The only fear now was, that we should not get any animal to carry them away. As soon therefore as tranquillity was a little restored, we took an opportunity of making rather a larger present than we had intended, to the two Sheiks, and distributed the remainder of our tobacco among the lower order. This completely removed their scruples, and they immediately assisted,1 most cordially, in repacking the sacred spoils, and in fastening them on the back of a camel. It was eleven o'clock before we got away : we saw many deer on the road, and, by accident, caught a doe big with young, that had been previously wounded. She was large, of a light-dun colour, white on the belly and rump, with small black horns, which were circled with rings. Captain Court stopped at the wells to take the meridian altitude, and, at half past one, we were welcomed on board the Panther by all our friends."

This second tour of Mr. Salt through Dhalac, has completely proved that the account of it, as given by Mr. Bruce, is in a great degree erroneous; and leaves it extremely probable, that he never landed on the Island. " The three hundred and seventy cisterns, all hewn out of the solid rock," have, after the most minute investigation, been reduced to less than twenty ; and of these not one is to be found at Dobelew, where he asserts, as an eyewitness, " that they are neglected, and open to every sort of animal, and half full of the filth that they leave there after drinking and washing in them." If the plan of the island of Dhalac, the harbour of Dobelew, and the surrounding islands, as laid down by that excellent hydrographer Captain Court, and now given to the public in my chart, be compared with the description of Mr. Bruce, hardly one point of resemblance will be found between the two ; and I trust there will be no doubt in the public mind to which the credit ought to be given.

The round harbour of Dobelew, with its narrow entrance, is no where discoverable, and the 'town itself, instead of being, as Bruce states, three miles S. W. of the harbour, is, in fact, on a parallel with the northern extremity of Irwee, which forms the harbour, and is an island ; a circumstance which ought to have been known to him had he actually been on the spot. It is not however with Captain Court only that Mr. Bruce diifers ; his bearings, as given by himself, are irreconcileable, and, after several attempts, it was found impossible to lay down the islands between Jibbel Teir and Dhalac from his account, which is much to be regretted, as it is improbable that any other traveller will venture through the shoals on the eastern side of the island, when a passage so much safer is afforded on the western.

The account given by Mr. Bruce of the animals drinking out of the cisterns, and washing in them, is evidently untrue, from the construction of them, as described by iMr. Salt, they being arched over, with a hole in the centre.

The impudence ascribed by Mr. Bruce to the women of Dobelew makes me still more doubtful of his having been at that place; since it is hardlyprobable that they would have totally changed their habits in a period of thirty years, during which time it is evident that their poverty had not diminished.

The errors in Mr. Bruce's account of Dhalac-el- Kibeer, its harbour, and the numerous tanks on the island, might have been excused, had he stated the circumstances less positively, and given them only as he received them by the report of the inhabitants. In Mr. Salt's first visit to Dhalac-el- Kibeer, he heard from several, that there was a tradition among them of three hundred and sixteen tanks: and this tradition was probably mentioned to Mr. Bruce, and, if given by him as such, would have been justifiable. The same observation will hold good respecting the harbour, which, from his journal, it is evident he could not have seen, and te which he only transfers the information that was given him respecting Nokhara. I can by no means extend the same indulgence to his account of the islands, and their relative bearings. When a person attempts to give geographical information to the public, it is necessary that this information should be accurate; and that he should not advance, as certain, a single circumstance, of which he has not positively informed himself. That Mr. Bruce, on the contrary, has erred in many points, and falsified in others, must be clear by a comparison of his own bearings with each other, and of the whole with the chart of Captain Court. I feel him to be the less justifiable on this"occasion, as he had it in his power to give a true account of the island, and its dependencies; for his having been at anchor somewhere near Dobelew is proved by his knowledge of the names of the numerous islands in its vicinity, and by his having stated its latitude as15 42' 22", which is within two miles of its true position, 15 44'.

I dispatched Mr. Maxfield at night with a message to the Nayib, saying that we should be at Massowah the next day. We took a cordial leave of the Dola, and, in consideration of his good con- duct during the survey, gave him several presents, and left a letter, certifying how well he had behaved. The Nayib's man demanded the money for the water in his master's name, and the forty dollars were delivered to him. There had been one thousand skins put on board the boats ; we paid for the whole, though some had burst. The water was not quite so good as on our last visit, which was owing to the drought. It was, however, as good as the best at Mocha.

By four o'clock next morning it began to blow very fresh from the south. It was full moon, and the tide rose by the lead line near nine feet. We attempted to get up our anchor, but it came home, and we were obliged to let go another, which brought us up. It moderated towards evening ; and the wind coming round to the eastward, we got under weigh, and in five hours, were within soundings. After four hours sail we fired a gun, and burnt a blue light as a signal to Mr. Maxfield, and in half an hour a second, which was answered. We stood on till we were met by him in a boat. He brought us safe into harbour, about eleven, to the great astonishment of our pilots. The sea was perfectly smooth as we approached the main land.

Our anchor dragged in the night, and a strong breeze from the N. drove us close to the shoal on. the N. E. extremity of Massowah. We had all our anchors out, and the weight of them alonesaved us, as the ground was too hard for them to lay hold of. It grew more moderate at noon, and before night, the vessel was warped into a place of safety. By agreement we saluted the fort with three guns, which were returned. The Banian came on board, and I gave him a commission from Mr. Pringle to act as broker of the India Company at Massowah. He informed me the Nayib would be happy to see me, and would receive me at his durbar, but did not wish to return the visit on board the Panther, which, of course, I did not press. There was some mention of the political situation of Massowah, which I did not perfectly understand. Captain

Court declined leaving the ship, our party therefore on shore consisted of Mr. Salt, Captain Rudland, and myself. We were received precisely as on my former visit. I had a similar kelaut; Mr. Salt one that was old, and tarnished. I went to Abou Yusuffs house, where several of the natives paid me visits, whom I treated with coffee and sweetmeats. I was assured of every supply that I wanted.

Determining on the following evening to visit the Nayib, I ordered two barrels of gunpowder to be brought on shore, one of which I sent to him, as a present in the name of the Bombay Government, the other in my own ; at the same time the Banian presented my salaams, and requested that he would permit some of our party to shoot on the morrow, attended by some of his people. The answer I received was, that when he saw me, we would talk over that and other circumstances. Surprised at this equivocal answer, I called the Banian aside, and desired to know what was the meaning of it. He at last told me, that it was to see what present I meant to make him, before he

VOL. II. Q

gave his orders. I expressed myself extremely displeased, and told him to inform the Nayi.b, that I did not consider myself as bound to give him any thing; that I was willing to pay for every thing I had, and wished, out of friendship to him, to induce English ships to come here for provision and water, by which he would reap a very considerable advantage; that even had a present been necessary, the gunpowder in the morning was more than sufficient, as I knew they valued it at five hundred dollars. I desired him to mention this to the Nayib, and add, that as I did not understand the Arabic language, the business had better be settled through the medium of himself, and my Arab servant Abdallah, and that therefore I would decline visiting him in the evening.

The answer was long, turning much on the attentions I had received from the Nayib, on his wishes to serve me, on his wanting money, as his brothers were importunate to get a portion of what they believed he received, and urging, as a conclusive argument, Captain Keys having given two hundred dollars. This put me into a worse humour. I told the Banian that Captain Keys had in this, as in other things, behaved extremely ill; that it was an act his Government highly disapproved of, and which therefore I could never follow. He said the Nayib knew two hundred dollars would be no object, and that if I requested the Captain to give it, he would comply in a moment. I told him it was out of the question ; that I was determined not to give a dollar, nor would the Captain; that some presents I had prepared, which I thought would be acceptable to the Nayib, but that I neither would deliver them, or visit him, till all idea of a present of money was abandoned. He tookAbdallah with him, and brought back an answer in the evening, that the Nayib considered me as one of his best friends; that he ever wished to oblige me ; that the horses should be ready for the shooting party ; but he hoped I would fill his belly. I laughed, and desired to know what would do this. The answer was, two hundred dollars. I asked if this was insisted on; he said, no, I was to do just as I pleased. On this I dismissed him. Alii Nohri was sent on shore in the course of the day to return to Mocha, as I did not consider it safe to take him with us, after his misconduct at Dhalac. Captain Rudland, Mr. Salt, and Mr. Maxfield, slept at the old residence of Captain Keys ; Mr. Macgie, and all our servants, staid with me at

Abou Yusuff's. Captain Court, from the difference of conduct in the Nayib, thought it advisable to send six marines on shore as a guard. The air was cool and pleasant the whole night.

Captain Rudland, Mr. Salt, Mr. Macgie, my servant, and Pierce, were out by break of day on a shooting excursion : the Nayib's son went with them: Captain Court came on shore to breakfast with me. Soon afterwards the Nayib's servant, who attended Mr. Salt at Dhalac, came with the Banian, and represented, that Alii Nohri had been saying, that I had given him two hundred dollars for the tomb stones mentioned in Mr. Salt's account, and as much to the Dola of Dhalac ; that the Nayib was very angry with them, and he begged I would take all the blame on myself. I told Jiim I not only would, but that I considered myself as at liberty to keep them on the sole condition of the Nayib giving his permission; and that if he wished it, I would restore them. This I desired the Banian to tell the Nayib. He also informed me, that Alii Nohri had declared I came to build a fort, and conquer the island, and that other ships were coming.

I felt heartily vexed at having let this fellow go on shore, who had probably excited suspicion and alarm in the breasts of the natives, which it would be almost impossible for me to eradicate, and which would disappoint my well founded hopes, that every thing would go on in the usual amicable way, and that a permanent commercial arrangement would be formed with the Government of Massowah. I told the Banian I was astonished at the Nayib's giving any credit to such a rascal; and that after my former visit, he ought to have known me better, than to suppose me capable of meditating any thing hostile to him. On the Ba- tiian's return, he declared the Nayib did not believe a word that Alii Nohri said, and was perfectly convinced of my friendship; that, however, the stones were not his property, but belonged to the Sultaun of Rome; and consequently he could not give them to me. I replied, I knew too well his connection with Rome, not to laugh at this reason, but he should have them; at the same time I took it very ill, as I could not forget that he offered them to me when I was last here.

Soon afterwards a respectable man made his appearance, and was introduced to me as Vizier of the Nayib. When last here I had heard nothing of such a personage, and now suspected he was an instrument to procure money through another ch&nnel. He said he had been to the Nayib, arid represented, that it would be a discredit to him, if, after I had bought these stones, I should be obliged to give them up : and that on his advice the Nayib had consented to let me keep them, and I might give him what I pleased, I said I wouldnot, on any preten.ce, give a single dollar. He replied, the Nayib did not wish it; that he gave up all claims to it, and hoped we were now as good friends as ever. I assured him we were, and that I would visit him on the morrow ; in the mean time, as he had acted like a friend, I begged his acceptance of a shawl. I now spoke about trade. He said the Nayib would arrange the duties, and no anchorage should be demanded for any English ship. It was settled that he should come in the evening.

The eldest son of the Nayib, after he returned from the chace, wished to go on board the ship; I therefore went with him. Captain Court showed him the whole, and gave him a few pounds of powder and some balls. I also presented him with a rich piece of kincaub, sufficient for a dress. He was highly pleased, and sent us some fowls in the evening. He was about eighteen years eld. His manners were gentle, his figure tall and well proportioned, and his countenance expressive of good nature. His younger brother was to go on board at some other time. He had asked for somepowder and ball, saying, that, when last here, I had given him nothing. I told him he should have a shawl, as well as the'powder and ball; we were consequently excellent friends. He begged me not to say any thing about it to his brother. I employed myself in cleaning and packing sea shells, which I procured from the children of the town, who collected them in every direction. My European servants and the people belonging to the dow were active in the same pursuit, but, except Cypraea, few of any value are to be had in the harbour. Our sportsmen had great success, and brought home a variety of fine game.

We enjoyed some pheasants and a chevreuil, fordinner, with some French claret purchased from the Americans. Our Dhalac friend, the Nayib's servant, drank several glasses of Madeira, and was perfectly intoxicated. Abou Yusuff would not taste it: he said the other was a soldier, and that all soldiers were allowed wine, but that he was a Sheik, and could not. We laughed most immoderately at his claim to this title, which he had never before mentioned ; and declared he was Sheik Sheitan or Sheik Affrit; a joke which, though coming from Christians, he bore with the greatest good humour. Soon afterwards the Vizier came in, when we instantly cleared the table, took coffee with him, and entered on the subject of the duties. I have given in the Appendix a list of the article's on which the Nayib demands a duty, and the sum demanded, which is in general moderate, though graduated by no regular principle of trade.

Abou Yusuff told me at night that he was in great want of a pair of shawls to give to a friend. I told him I was very happy to hear it, as I was precisely in the same predicament. He and others had advised Pierce not to stir out at night, as Alii Nohri had been trying to excite the people to use him ill for having again turned Christian., We thought it a wise precaution, and he kept close. This day a dow arrived from Jidda belonging to Mocha.

Very early in the morning the Nayib's two sons, attended by the Banian, came to me to request, in their father's name, that I would go on board the ship; representing that the Dola of Arkeko, Emir Moosa, who, though a younger brother of the Nayib, was more powerful from his influence with the soldiers, had come over to Massowah to make the Nayib demand money from us for anchorage ; that the Nayib was determined not to do it, andthat therefore it might probably end in fighting; that if I was safely out of the way, he might do his worst; but that till then, the Nayib would be miserable, lest any thing should happen to me. I assured them I had not the least fear; that I was fully able to defend myself, if their uncle attacked me, which I hardly conceived he would dare to do; and that if the Nayib wished it, I would guard him also. An answer was returned strongly expressive of anxiety for my safety, and begging as a favour that I would go on board; adding, that every thing I wished should be done for me. On consideration I determined to comply ; at the same time stating that it was merely to oblige him, and not out of any fear of the Dola of Ar- keko, whose power I heartily despised.

In the course of the day we frequently heard that the Nayib and Dola were disputing violently. As the interference of a subject, however powerful, was fatal to all idea of trade, I determined to bring the business to an issue one way or other; I therefore sent Abdallah to the Dola, with my salaams, adding that I had been given to understand he came over to Massowah with purposes hostile to me; that I had left the shore not out of fear of him, but to oblige the Nayib; that if he had any thing to say to me, he might come on board the ship, or I would send a person to converse with him on shore. Abdallah soon came back with an answer, that he came here for money, and demanded a thousand dollars for the anchorage of the two vessels; that he desired I would send him an answer by the Banian, whether I would pay it or not; for if I did not, he would get it from him. I learned from Abdallah, that on his saying this, there had been a considerable altercation.

the Nayib declaring that the Banian had no obligation to pay, and that he had never made nor would ever make, such a demand from us. The Dola continued, that he would not come on board the ship, nor did he want to see any body from me. The Nayib had called Abdallah on one side, and desired him to say to me, that he wished the English ships of war would take in what they wanted at Dhalac, where he could take care they should have every thing, and not come here, as it made disputes between him and his brother.

I learned from the Banian, that by an agreement with these turbulent relations he paid them half of the duties on merchandize; that when our vessels arrived, the Dola had supposed the Nayib made much money, and demanded a share; nor would he believe, at first, that we gave no money; that the Askari at Arkeko gained nothing by us, and were therefore equally vexed, and determined to try the experiment whether they could not bully us out of payment for anchorage. The Banian added, that though the Dola had but seventeen armed men with him, he had completely intimidated the Nayib, and had possession of all his power.

I considered the demand of the Dola, that I should pay anchorage, after I had but the evening before settled with the Sovereign of the country that no English ships should ever pay any, as a gross insult, much heightened by the manner in which it was made; I therefore determined to take it up in a strong way. I asked the Banian if he was afraid to deliver any answer I might wish to send: he said, no; and I then directed him to assure the Nayib of my esteem and regard, and itty wish to'do every thing to serve and obligehim; that his brother had treated me with insolence in making a demand, which he only could have a right to make, and that therefore I was determined to resent it, I sent word to the Dola, that the English ships of war never paid anchorage here or any where else; that at any rate he had no right to demand it j and that if he did not immediately send a man to make an excuse for his insolence, I would sail in the morning for his town of Arkeko, and burn it down to the ground.

The Banian took this threat and brought back for answer, that he would send to Arkeko, to report that the English never paid anchorage, and would inform us in the morning what was their determination. I sent again to say, I would not wait till morning; that I would have an immediate answer, or would be at Arkeko myself in the morning to settle the business. Soon after the Naqueda of the Dow, Unus Barilla, came on board laughing, and said there had been a violent quarrel between the Nayib and Dola; that the Askari of Massowah had taken part with the former, declaring the English were very good, and ought not to have any demands made on them. It had nearly ended in blows; but at length the whole town being in an uproar, and the very boys taking up stones to pelt the Dola's soldiers, they had retired to their boats on the opposite side of the town, and slipt off unperceived by us.

The Banian soon afterwards arrived, and confirmed the fact. He brought a message from the Dola, that he did not require any money for the anchorage, nor had he the least wish to offend the English. The Nayib sent to say, he had gone to Arkeko to settle every thing; that he would return the next day, and come on board the Panther ; till when he begged I would not move. The transaction had now taken the turn I wished; they had tried the experiment of threats, to establish a dangerous precedent, and had failed. I therefore agreed to wait till morning. I was much pleased by a visit from the Nayib's youngest son, which shewed great confidence in us at such a moment. After-having been served with sweetmeats and coffee, I gave him a piece of kincaub, and several little articles which he admired. He then asked for some soap, which was of course given to him, and a box to keep his things in. Captain Court also presented him with some powder, which is always a most acceptable gift. Abou Yusuff and his brother both came on board in the evening.

The Banian came off in the morning of January 20, and informed me he had received a letter from the Nayib, declaring that he and the Dola solemnly agreed no anchorage should ever be demanded from English ships; that the English had ever behaved well; that Massowah was theirs to come to whenever they pleased ; and that they begged every thing might be friendly between us. The Nayib would come to Massowah when I pleased, and would come on board and settle the duties. I had much conversation with the Banian respecting the political situation of this country, and the probability of danger to any vessel that might come loaded to it. He assured me from himself, that they would certainly be satisfied with the duties, and would do her no injury. He informed me that the Dola was not dependent on his breather, but shared the power with him, though the latter was first in rank'; that they divided the duties between them; and that the real cause of the late disputes was a suspicion on the part of the Dola, that the Nayib had concealed the cash he ha$ received from us. Dhalac and other places are the Nayib's private property, in which his brother does not share. The third brother is Sirdar of the Askari. They are first paid out of the duties: the amount is one thousand five hundred dollars per month, and when there is a deficiency the Dola first is obliged to make it good, and then the Nayib; and about this there are frequent hostilities.

The Nayib used to receive his khelaut from Jidda, and still nominally owns the Sultaun of Rome as sovereign. He is therefore certainly the sovereign of the country, though controlled by the influence of his brother. Something of this kind seems to have been the case in Bruce's time. Achmet, whom he mentions as the Nayib's uephew and heir, certainly exercised a power in some parts of the country, while his uncle had it in others, and the duties seem to have been shared between them. At the death of Edris, Emir Moosa, his brother, will, by the laws of the country, be Nayib, but the sons of the former will then succeed, in preference to those of the latter. This custom, which I am told prevails in the other tribes, must frequently give rise to revolutions.

The number of soldiers is very inconvenient, as the duties often do not amount to the sum of one thousand five hundred dollars, required for their monthly pay : they are, however, so connected by marriage with the Nayib and his family that it is impossible to reduce them. The Nayib calls them all brothers. The Sirdarship of them is always in the family. The two last years the trade, they 5

say, has decreased, yet we had a constant succession of dows coming in, and going out during the whole time we were here. I assured the Banian that I wished to see the Mayib, and that I was as much his friend as ever. He brought me a present from himself of Abyssinian cloth, and honey; the latter was put up with the wax, was very white, and remarkably good.

The Vizier came off between three and four, to say that he had written for the Nayib, and to procure me a letter from the Dola, declaring that he would make no claims for anchorage of English ships, and that he wished to be at friendship with them. I made, of course, the same professions in reply, and gave him coffee and sweetmeats, as we did to all our guests. He then requested we would give him two pieces of plank.; as they were small, he requested a third, which was complied with, and the old gentleman left us well pleased, We tried the whole day, but without success, to procure fowls; they are chiefly at Arkeko, and as the Banian will not buy them, there is a difficulty in finding others to do it. The Banian came again in the evening, about eight, to say the Nayib was come, and wished me to go and see him : this I most peremptorily refused. He then requested that Abdallah might go, to which I consented, and sent by him to the Nayib eight china dishes, which I heard would be acceptable. After settling our accounts, he gave me another piece of Habesh cloth, and I gave him a shawl. I wrote a letter to Mr. Pringle, stating my ideas respecting the trade of Massowah, and requesting he would never employ Alii Nohri. Abdallah, on his return, brought a letter to me from the Nayib, and another for the Dola of Suakin. My servant and fierce were out a great part of the day, so also were the dow-boys; they procured a few good Cyprasa, but no others.

At four next morning, we began to unmoor: at half after six the Nayib's elder son, his brother the Sirdar, the Vizier, Abou Yusuff, and the Banian came on board, as they said, to express the Nayib's anxious desire that I should go away in friendship with him. A question was added, which betrayed their real motive, which was, whether I meant to give any thing else to the Nayib. At first I determined to do so, knowing that he really was tormented for money; but I afterwards considered that it would be better, to express some feeling of disapprobation at my difference of treatment on this my second visit. I therefore called the son and Vizier into the cabin, and assured them that I parted a sincere friend, but that I must feel mortified at being obliged to leave the shore, and could not therefore send a present as a proof of satisfaction; that I would only send an ivory box of castor, an article here of great value, as a mark of friendship. I gave one, also, to each person of the party. The land breeze and our boats soon cleared us of the harbour, and delivered us from our visitors. .The young Hammed (the Nayib's son') seemed to part with regret. Captain Rudlaml .gave him a pair of pistols. His brother got some powder by a private hand.

On maturely considering all that had passed I was inclined to consider these circumstances as increasing instead of lessening, the security of Mas- sowah for

British ships. They are convinced we not be imposed upon, and yet ate willing topay well for every thing. The Banian assured me the Dola is now of the Nayib's opinion, that it is better to secure a moderate profit, than to lose all by preventing ships from coming there. It is possible that the Nayib had in reality no objection to his brother's trying the experiment of bullying us out of the thousand dollars, while he should still profess to be our friend, and become a mediator in case of hostility. I learned that the threat of going to Arkeko terrified them beyond measure ; so that whatever they meant, the result has been equally good. I warned them that a King's ship came every year to Mocha, and that, if an unprotected vessel should be injured, she would make them repent it. The Ascari of Arkeko were gaining nothing by us, and therefore cared nothing for us; but there was hardly a family at Massowah who did not derive advantage from our stay, either by collecting shells, bringing fish, &c. for the ship, by labour, or by the presents of the gentlemen. They therefore took our part: and I am convinced that they would never willingly permit an Englishman to be injured.

The two little Abyssinians whom Captain Keys had purchased at Massowah, and taken to Bombay, had been repurchased by the Government, and sent back by the Panther, to be returned to their native country, if the Nayib should desire it, as a proof that the British would not violate the laws while in his dominions. On communicating these circumstances to the Nayib, he replied, that this could be settled at our first interview. Affairs took another turn, and the boys were left in our hands; at their own wish they were now entered on the ship's books, and instead of theslavish names of Sidi and Pompey, assumed the more Christian designations of George Habesh, and Harry Gondar. Christians they were born, but of the doctrines of Christianity, or indeed those of any other religion, they had no idea; I therefore placed them under Pierce, to teach them to read and say their prayers.

5

SECTION 5

CHAPTER VI.

Observations on the PeripMi.|Massowah Bay the Bay of Aiiuli.|Valtntia Island, Orine.|Monsieur Gosselin's Theory erroneous.| Asseez, Ptolemais Theron.|Berenice in Foul Bay.|Departure from Massowah.|Arrival at Port Mor- nington and Wellesley's Islands.|Ras Asseez.|Bother'em Bay.|Arrival at Suakin.|Transactions with the Natives.| Departure from Suakin.

THE true position of Myos Hormus, at the upper end of the Red Sea, being very doubtful, it seems to me that it would be a more clear method of ascertaining the places mentioned by the author of the Periplus, to measure his distances from Aduli, which, I think, has been fixed near Massowah, by Dr. Vincent, in a most incontrovertible manner.

I most fully agree with this able and learned elucidator of the Periplus, that the an- cient positions are much more accurately to be ascertained by existing circumstances, than by the astronomical observations, which were originally made with very imper- fect instruments, and have come down to us with numerous errors and imperfections; and it is for this reason, that I consider the position of Aduli as ascertained; for not a circumstance i mentioned in the Peri-

Vol. n. R

pltis, as belonging to it, which cannot be discovered in the Bay of Massowah. The Island of Dio- dorus, which was separated from the main-land by so narrow a channel as to be fordable at low water, is easily referred to Toualout; while the Orine, to which the merchants retired, on their being plundered in their former residence by the Barbarians, is now satisfactorily asscertained to be Valentia Island, whose numerous hills well intitle it to its ancient kname, whose distance of seventeen miles from the coast of Aduli accords with the two hundred stadia mentioned in the Periplus, and whose embosomed situation in Annesley Bay, explains the hitherto incomprehensible description of the Periplus, that the continent was adjacent to it on both sides; and the assertion of Cosmas, that it was but two miles distant from the main land ; an assertion that Dr. Vincent could not reconcile with the two hundred stadia of the Periplus. The islands called Alalaiou, many in number, small and sandy, still remain a memorial of the accuracy of the original describer, and may be found in Captain Court's chart, surrounding the island of Dhalac. Were any additional evidence necessary to prove that Aduli was situated in the Bay of Massowah, a very strong presumptive argument might be drawn from the fact, that the great export trade of Abyssinia in ivory and rhinoceros' horns, and the imports in European and Indian articles, still continue to find their way through the same passes of the mountains to Massowah, and that the elephants still are, occasionally, but rarely, seen in the neighbourhood of Ras Gedam.

Since my return to England I have been very much astonished by the singular theory which Monsieur Gosselinhas advanced, in his Recherches sur la Geographic des Anciens, and by which he

OBSERVATIONS ON THE PERIPLUS. 243

has carried the Bay of Aduli to Assab, where the whole coast is covered with low, sandy islands, and reefs of coral, without a single point of resemblance to the description of the Periplus. M. Gosselin might have been aware that, as it was a journey of only eight days from Aduli to Axum, the latter place could never have been at Assab, a distance of above three hundred miles; neither was it probable that the Romans would have passed so excellent an harbour as Massowah, where a ready communication existed with their chief mart at Axum, by a journey of little more than one hundred miles, and proceed three hundred miles farther, by sea, to a bad harbour, whence their land journey would also be extended to treble the distance.

The strange assertion of Monsieur Gosselin, that the author of the Periplus reckoned only eight hundred stadia, from Aduli to the straits of Bab-el-Mandeb, has been properly taken notice of by Dr. Vincent. It is indeed difficult to conjecture what could have given rise to the mistake ; a mistake, however, which became- necessary, when his argument had carried Aduli to Assab, which is within fifty miles of the Straits.

Dr. Vincent conceives that, it was the difference of one hundred and twenty-one miles between the distances of seven thousand stadia or seven hundred miles, as given in the Periplus, and the real distance of five hundred and seventy-nine miles from Berenice to Aduli, that induced Monsieur Gosselin to carry the latter to Assab; and he himself seems to feel a difficulty in reconciling them. It however appears to me, that this may be done by admitting that an Egyptian merchant used Egyptian stadia, and that he calculated the distances

from the difference of latitude alone, without
bringing to account the longitude, which was run
down at the same time, as I think will appear by
the following calculations.
From Aduli to Ptolemais Theron is 3000 stadia ;
From Ptolemais Theron to Berenice 4000 stadia ;
which, at the Egyptian stadium of fifteen to a
mile, will make the distance from Aduli to Ptolemais Theron two hundred miles ; from Ptolemais
Theron to Berenice two hundred and sixty-six
miles.

If therefore Aduli be in 15 36',
Ptolemais Theron will be 18 *5ff,*
And Berenice - 23 22'.

The position of Berenice has been laid down from local circumstances with as
much certainty as that of Aduli. It is described by Strabo as situated in the bottom
of a bay, which, on account of its numerous shoals and rocks, had been designated
W6afTof, immundus, and, as being at the extremity of the Thebais or Upper Egypt.
The latter observation limits our conjectures to within 23" 30' and 24, and the former
fixes us in the bottom of a bay which has preserved its name, and among modern
navigators is called Foul Bay. According to D'Anville this is in 23 15',
    Gosselin - - 23 28',
    an English chart 23 19'.
Though the distances in the Periplus deserve a greater degree of credit than usual
from their being given in words at full length, instead of figures, yet I cannot receive
them without some degree of caution, from their being evidently given in round
numbers, without any fractional parts, and from a knowledge of the difficulty of
measuring distances at sea, without a nicer degree of observation than was probably
employed by Egyptian merchants, or is now used by those of our own nation.
I should therefore consider the relative distances between Aduli, Berenice, and
Ptolemais Theron, as a more certain guide to the discovery of the latter. The whole
distance is five hundred and seventy-nine miles, three sevenths of which, or two
hundred forty-six miles, if measured from Aduli on the chart, will exactly reach a
peninsula in latitude 18 24', of which I shall hereafter have occasion to speak, and
where the more valuable data of local circumstances seem to point out the Ptolemais
Theron of the Periplus.
I am well aware that it is impossible to reconcile this conclusion with the positive
assertion of the ancients, that Ptolemais Theron was in the same parallel as Meroe;
but I have before observed, that little credit can be given to the accuracy of their
admeasurements; and I feel less alarm in differing from them, and in my placing
Ptolemais Theron where I have done, from having the sanction of D'Anville, who has,
in defiance of all difficulties, conjectured that it lay between 18 and 18 30' N.

We kept about ten miles distant from the shore, which, as we sailed along with a land breeze from the N. W. and afterwards with the sea breeze N. E. by E. appeared low, sandy, and without trees, but was backed by lofty mouritains covered with clouds, the soundings gradually deepening from eleven to thirty-five fathom, the bottom mud the whole way. The course of the shore was nearly N. then N. by W. To the eastward was a chain of low islands, with doom-trees on them, distant about five or six miles, leaving a noble andclear channel of fifteen miles. On two of these the pilot informed us that water and goats could be procured. The sea was as smooth as glass. The pilot said we might go on all night, and run in as close as six fathom with safety ; as however, it was our wish to examine the whole coast, we determined to anchor, and about seven steered W. right in for the coast. We were astonished, when in twenty-two fathom, with the white appearance of breakers; when the Captain immediately let go the anchor. The pilots declared that it was only fish, and so it proved ; for soon afterwards, they approached and passed under the vessel. It is singular, that the same circumstance should have been observed by Don Juan de Castro and should have had the same effect, of inducing him to let go his anchor. He does not account for it, because it happened in the night, but he mentions, that it cast flames like fire; which confirms the conjecture, that the brilliant appearance of the sea is owing to fish-spawn and animalcula. Don Juan passed this spot on the 20th of February, one month later than I did, but the spawning may probably continue for that period. It was nearly oelm the whole night, so that we lost but little by anchoring.

January 22.'IWe were under sail as soon as Captain Court had taken a set of bearings. The breezes were light, and there was a tide against us. The coast was low, with the lofty mountains at a distance ; between them and the sea were occasionally hillocks, some of which might have been thought hills, had it not been for their more lofty neighbours. The coast still kept a northerly direction with very little westing ; in sixty miles N. only seventeen west. The soundings as usual, and the chain of islands to the eastward, low, witha few trees, that often had the appearance of ships under sail. We had anchored in seven fathom, with a good bottom. About half a mile nearer was a chain of madrapore rocks, with four fathom and a half on them, as Mr. Hardy reported, who was sent with our boat to examine it. A little to the southward was a small port, called by the pilot Mirsa Mombarrick : two dows were in it; a small island is at the entrance. Our pilots say there is no village, but that the natives come down from a little way inland, and that there are water and provisions. A calm, as usual, at night.

In the morning I perceived that immediately on the beach, the whole way we could see, was a strip of bright verdure, though beyond it, all was as barren as usual. The boat was out early to examine the reef. We weighed at seven, but it soon fell calm, and obliged us again to come to an anchor. The boat was sent again to survey the beach beyond the reef. The officers reported it was hard sand, and it shoaled to two fathom water within half a mile of the shore, when the rocks again began. They were followed by a great number of sharks, some very large. They brought a branch of the tree, which proved to be Mr. Bruce's Rack ; it had fruit on it, which Mr. Salt drew. The breeze sprang up about eleven; but our boat was not back till twelve, when we weighed. We again anchored at night) after having made twenty- seven miles, with a strong sea breeze. There was some swell from the N. E. probably owing to the sea being open to the main channel, where the monsoon prevails in all its force. At least there were now no islands in sight to the eastward from the mast head. The coast had changed its appearance ; the smaller range of hills are near to theshore. The soundings were this day irregular, but there was always plenty of water.

January 24.IThe sea breeze sprang up earlier, and we were under sail by nine. Our friend Unus Barilla brought us some very finev fish. Inland we could distinguish large groves of trees, and others to the north, on the sea shore. These the pilot said are doom-trees, and that there are also great quantities of the common mimosa. He described the country as inhabited by Bedowee, and as being a part of the sovereign of Sennaar's dominions. Lions, panthers, and elephants are in great numbers ; this may therefore be considered as a part of the great forest, from which Ptolemy Philadelphus procured the latter animals, and for the convenience of hunting in which, he established the port of Ptolemais Theron. We were at twelve o'clock in latitude 17 12', where Mr. Bruce has placed a deep bay, near which, on the projecting point of a head-land, Dr. Vincent conjectures Ptolemais Theron was built. 1 watched the coast as we passed along, and can positively assert that it was, as usual, low, and free from headlands, without a single projection that could justify Mr. Bruce's chart, or give weight to the consequent conjecture of Dr. Vincent. Towards evening the coast began to run off more to the west, and the soundings were very irregular, from nineteen to thirty-six fathom in a cast, with a bottom, sometimes of mud, and sometimes of coral rock. The swell was greater, and from the S. E. in the same direction as the monsoon on the opposite shore. We anchored about eight in thirteen fathom, mud, but rocky near us. Lest we should drive, we let go our best bower anchor.

It rained a short time the next morning,when we were within two miles of the shore, which began to have a bolder appearance. The hillocks were near the shore; beyond them a number of detached conical mountains; and in the back ground the same lofty range that had beerr constantly visible. On one of the hillocks was a small white Mussulmaun tomb ; another was visible seven miles north, close to the sea. Our pilot said they were Turkish, but that at present no inhabitants were there. He called it Mundalow. I did not wish to examine it, as the buildings were evidently modern. On the tops of some of the other hillocks were protuberances, which were either watch-towers in ruins, or rocks; which at our distance it was impossible to distinguish. At ten a remarkable range of hills was in sight, making four pointed tops. At eleven it was clearly seen, N. 55 W. over a low point of land, covered with trees. At half after eleven another tomb was visible on the shore, the skirting of trees having ended. Near the land were several reefs. At twelve the wood again began. The hills abovementioned ended in a very conspicuous point, off which was a detached sugar-loaf hill, and no high land visible to the northward. The northernmost extremity of the land, the pilots say, is a Ras ; but as they have changed the name several times, I shall not record it. We had during the day a brisk monsoon at S. S. E. which carried us at the rate of seven knots an hour, with a heavy following swell. By five we came to an anchor in eight fathom, mud and sand, in a very fine bay, among a cluster of low islands. We had excellent soundings the whole way in, after we had passed the low point of land abovementioned, which is called Aveed, and off which ran a reef .about three miles, in a N. E. direction. It formsthe south-eastern point of a bay that seems full of shoals, the N. W. side of which is formed by the islands among which we anchored. Here the Assaye led the way; and as we approached the shore, Mr. Maxfield hailed, and told us that his pilots said there was no passage with safety. Our pilots denied this, and went on. There are several passages leading to land-locked bays, from the bay we are in. Many dows were on the outside, when we came in sight, which fled immediately into one of the inner bays, whither I believe our pilot meant to conduct us, had not the point been too far to windward.

Very early in the morning many of the dows got out, and passed close by us, having, I suppose, recovered from their fright. Our cutter went off with Abdallah and the pilot to make our compliments to the Dola, and invite him on board; he had also directions to purchase for us fowls, eggs, and any other articles of provision, and to learn what he could respecting the place. He did not return till twelve, when the Dola came with him, a Bedowee; the Sub-dola, a decent well-dressed Arab; and the Sheik, a respectable old Bedowee, with the curls of his hair incrusted with fat, who brought me a present of three fowls. Their coming at once on board, without any scruple or fear, gave me a favourable impression of their own upright intentions, and showed a strong degree of confidence in us, and a liberal judgment of our motives for visiting this unfrequented shore. No European ship has been here since the time of the Portuguese. We gave them coffee to drink, a present of tobacco, and a frassel of raw coffee. Captain Court obtained from them the names of the hills in sight, and of some of the islands. There are several of these, each under a separate Sheik, but all under a Dola, who is sent from Suakih, not from Massowah, as we were there given to understand. Badour is the name of the village where the Dola resides; it is a miserable little place, one small mosque being the only stone building; the rest are grass huts. It is on a small island, close to the water. There is no trade, except an export of ghee, and some tortoise shells. The dows now come this way from Suakin, Jidda, and Massowah, from fear of the Wahabee. We saw a large drove of cattle on the shore, and learned that there were plenty, as there must be when ghee becomes an article of exportation ; but these unfortunately belonged to a Sheik who was absent, and were therefore not to be procured. Our civil Sheik, who visited us, had his cattle at some short distance ; we were consequently obliged to wait till next day. Sheep are also in abundance, and poultry : the prices demanded were, however, high; for a bullock they asked seven dollars, but came down to five; fowls were only eight for a dollar; sheep were more reasonable, a fine fat one being procurable for a dollar. We got some eggs in return for a little tobacco. I should, however, observe, that the Dola said money was little known here, and that Surat cloth would be much more valuable. Unfortunately they chose none but white, and we, on the credit of Mr. Bruce, had laid in blue. We asked what quantity of white cloth would procure a bullock. He said two pieces, which are each worth only a dollar. Had we therefore been in possession of this article, wt should have purchased every thing reasonably. There is not a fisherman on the island, and they say, there are no fish near it; a singular fact, which seems corroborated by the bad success of our people, who have hitherto caught only one.Captain Court lost no time in sending Mr. Max- field with the Assaye into the harbour, directing him to begin the survey of it, and, for the sake of expedition, allowed Mr. Crawford to accompany hjrh.

On the 28th and 29th Captain Court and Mr. Maxfield were actively employed in completing the survey of the harbour, and surrounding land, while Mr. Salt made an accurate drawing of the hills; which, after having from Massowah kept at a distance from the coast, here approach the sea, and rising one above the other, as they retire inland, form a mass of a most irregular out-line. The islands which form the north-eastern side of the harbour, and the peninsula which protects it on the north-western side, are chiefly of madrapore rocks. The head land, formed by the peninsula and islands, is by the natives called Ras Akeek ; but they use the word generally, without applying it to any particular spot. It is the Ras Ahehaz of D'Anville. The only entrance for large vessels is at the northern extremity of the harbour, though dows enter at the southern. The passage is rather narrow, but the whole navy of Europe might lie within as in a bason, protected from every wind, in from five to seven fathom, with a bottom free from every danger. The town, which is situated on a larger island within the harbour than any of those that protect it from the sea, is a still more wretched place than Dhalac-el-Kibeer. Water is to be had, which, though not very good, is equal to that at Mocha ; and our eyes convinced us that fresh provision might have been obtained, had we possessed the articles necessary for barter.

The harbour itself I immediately determined to name after the Governor-General of India, through whose assistance alone I had been able to pursue my plan of ascertaining the real situation of this unknown part of the coast; I therefore named it Port Morning-ton, and the islands, which form its barrier against the waves to the north-eastward, Wellesley's Islands. The bay in which we anchored we called Panther Bay.

When it is considered that Port Mornington lies on a most dangerous coast, off which are numerous shoals, low islands, and rocks that render the navigation danger-ous, the discovery of it must be allowed to be of great importance. As high as 17 north it appears from the Portuguese, and Sir Home Popham's chart, that the range of coral rocks and sand banks, which run to the eastward of Dhalac, are not at an end ; but beyond that degree the sea appears open till 19 north, where the shoals again commence. Port Mornington is therefore accessible without danger at any season of the year, and will afford to any ships not only a secure asylum, but a supply of water and fresh provisions. I cannot help expressing my astonishment, that, during the continuance of our fleet in this sea, no attempt was made to examine a coast which offered no impediment, and where the Victor's track had plainly demonstrated that a safe passage existed among the islands.

The neglect with which all ancient authors have passed over this, though the best harbour in the Red Sea, is so extraordinary that I know not how to account for it. It is certainly very near the place where the Astaboras is said by Strabo, to mingle a small proportion of its waters with the sea, but from the most accurate inquiries we could trace no vestige of any such circumstance ; nor is it probable, that a stream could make its way through the lofty chain of mountains which binds

Lu...

the western shore of the Red Sea. I think that Wellesley's Islands are the six Latomian islands of Strabo, and possibly the harbour itself may be the Sabaiticon

Stoma of the same author, since in his description they immediately follow Ptolemais Theron.

On our first arrival we were assured, that no trade was carried on here; but this appeared to be so contradictory to the fact of a great number of dows resorting to it, that we determined to be more particular in our inquiries. We soon perceived that the boats belonging to the dows left their vessels early every morning, went to the main land, and returned at night; but we could discover nothing large that they either took with them, or brought back. At length an old Naqueda paid Mr. Maxfield a visit, and produced a certificate from Admiral Blanket, that he had been employed by him. This led to a more intimate acquaintance, and a more free conversation, but on the subject of trade it was difficult to get any answer from him. On being asked what so many dows did there, he said they were all Wahabee. On Captain Court's objecting to this, and saying, that they would then have molested him ; he only replied, "God is great!" On being pressed, he owned that there was a trade carried on with the Bedowee, and that it was intirely by barter. I know tortoise-shell is obtained here, and I should suspect that gold is the chief article received in return for India goods. Mr. Maxfield wished to go to the main land, but the Naqueda advised him on no account to do so without a juard, as there were several wandering tribes of Arabs in the vicinity. I wished to stay long enough to conciliate them, and a open communication ; but

this was impossible ; and I therefore did not permit Mr. Maxfield to hazard the inconveniences that might attend such an expedition.

Our people liberated Port Mornington from the opprobrium of having no fish in it, for, with a net, they caught an abundance. I was less fortunate in my conchological pursuits, not having procured a single shell during my stay. The Assaye came out of the harbour early in the morning, Jan. 29th, and soon after twelve we were under weigh, with a moderate breeze. Immediately on clearing the peninsula we saw three small islands, but the main land retired and formed a deep bay. Our course lay W. N. W. the coast here running off much more westward than usual.

About four o'clock we came up with a headland, which ran a long way into the sea, and which the pilot called Has Asseez. It at first appeared as an island, from the lowness of the spit of sand which united it to the continent. As I had been induced by D'Anville's arguments to suppose that Ptolemais Theron lay somewhere near the latitude we now were in, I inquired of the pilot whether he had ever been on shore there, and he assured me he had, but that there were no inhabitants, though the Parsees once possessed the place, an4 that there was one large tank still remaining. He also said, that though it was not an island, yet that it was cut off from the main land by a ditch, which, at high water, was sometimes nearly full. These circumstances so strongly convinced me that this was Ptolemais Theron, that I should have stopped and landed, had not the vessel, during the time we were conversing, past it for someway. Captain Court was however particularly careful in taking its bearings, that its shape might be correctly laid down.

Asseez is in '18 24' N. lat. and in 38 18', longA east of Greenwich, and therefore its position agrees with that I have attributed to Ptolemais Theron, in the beginning of this Chapter. I consider, however, the circumstances I have mentioned as forming a much stronger proof of its actually being that place ; and I can venture to assert, that no other place exists on the whole coast that will answer the description given us by the ancients, which in many respects is more minute than usual. The peninsula of Port Mornington could alone create a doubt, as it is in nearly the same latitude, and at a distance of only seventeen miles ; but this peninsula is much more uniformly elevated above the sea, and has even rocks, which would have been a work of infinite labour to cut through, and could not have been done privately, as we are informed by Strabo the works of Eu- medes were executed at Ptolemais Theron. It is also ascertained from the Periplus, that the settlement of Ptolemy was not a port, and was only approachable by boats, a circumstance that is still the case at AsseeZ, but which is contrary to fact at Port Mornington. It seems probable to me that Ptolemy would fix his station for hunting elephants, not at the farthest extremity of the Shumeta or Nubran forest, where elephants were procurable, but at the place nearest his own dominions, within the limits of the forest; and this would certainly be at Asseez, which gave him an opportunity of hastily, and privately, securing his settlement from any hostile assaults of the people, among whom he was settling himself without their consent. This might indeed induce him to prefer Asseez to Port Mornington ; but that he should pass so fine a harbour to go down still further on tiie coast to a more inconvenient position, seems

to be improbable. Port Mornington may have afforded protection to his vessels, though the military station was at Asseez: and it is not impossible, that the latter place may have afforded facilities of embarking the elephants, which the former did not.

Our pilots mentioned as a fact that Cushtan, the district most abounding in elephants, was directly behind Asseez, which if true, (and as they could not possibly conjecture what answers I wished them to make to my questions, I think there is no reason to doubt it) affords a very sufficient argument why Ptolemy fixed his hunting station there in preference to any other place. I have only to add, that he could not do it much higher up, as elephants are never seen at Suakin. Asseez is, undoubtedly, the long point of sand which is mentioned by Don Juan de Castro, and is laid down by him in 18 30', a trifling error in latitude. It is a singular circumstance, that Pliny states Ptolemais The- ron as being five days sail from Aduli, and we were exactly that period in reaching Port Mornington, and might have easily gone on to Asseez. The ancients probably anchored every night as we did. We anchored as soon as it was dark in ten fathom, mud.

January 30.lAs soon as Captain Court had taken his observations we set sail. By ten Ras Howie was in sight. Here a very fine bay opened between it and the main. The Ras is a low spit of sand, partly above water; beyond was a chain of islands. The wind was from the north of east, and without tacking we could not weather it. Our pilots much wished us to anchor, and wait for a fair wind, as, they said, there was no anchoring ground after we left this, till we reached Suakin, which we could not do in one day, unless

VOL. II. S

we sailed early in the morning. We, however, remonstrated, and asked if we could not go within the chain of sands and islands. They both said they could not venture to take the ship, as, in one part, there was not above two fathom and a half of water. We then persuaded them to let us tack, and weather the point. This was agreed to ;

and by twelve we tacked back, being sufficiently to windward. Here we crossed the Assaye. Mr. Maxfield hailed us to say, that his pilot assured him the passage was very safe, having fine anchorage the whole way, and three fathom and a half in the deepest part; that on the outside of the island there was no anchorage, but deep water : that it was impossible to reach Suakin by night; and that even a whole day would hardly be sufficient. On this Captain Court replied, that in consideration of the anchorage he would try the passage ; and directed Mr. Maxfield to go ahead, and sound.

Mr. Maxfield had received signals for the purpose of communicating to us every occurrence, such as what water he found, any approaching, or any actual danger : we sailed accordingly for nearly two hours in a most noble passage, which gradually narrowed and shoaled. Mr. Maxfield made no signal, and we went on till we were in four fathom, when we made a signal to him to inform us in what water he was ; but before he could answer we were in three fathom, with islands close to us on each side. No signal appeared from the Assaye, but we perceived that, on a sudden, all her sails were lowered in evident confusion. We were ourselves in but two and a half fathom, and therefore, as soon as we had cleared one of the islands, let go our anchor. The ship instantly swung round against a rock, with only one and ahalf fathom, and there struck. At this moment our dow, which had been crowding all sail behind us, came up, and Unus leaped overboard and came to us. He then dived, and ascertained the situation of the vessel's bottom, and of the anchor. Our boat sounded around, and we found that we were in a cul-de-sac, with rocks in every direction, even that in which we entered. To add to our alarm, it was apparently high water, and how much the tide might fall we knew not. The only thing in our favour was the perfect smoothness of this salt water lake, which no wind could possibly ruffle. The Captain was active and collected. He instantly began to lighten the vessel by pumping out the salt water which was in the casks ; Unus brought his dow along side to take in our guns ; our yards and top masts were lowered, and an anchor was carried astern to warp us out. At the earnest request of Captain Court, I and the other gentlemen removed to the Assaye, that he might be more at liberty. My European and other servants staid on board, and assisted the ship's company.

To our good fortune, the tide did not fall quite a foot; the wind was light; the ship was therefore perfectly manageable, and wore round as she was towed. She with great difficulty cleared another rock; but by four, I had the satisfaction to be hailed, and told that she was safe in a quarter less two fathom, being more than she now drew. By night she was warped further out, and safely anchored in two and a half fathom. Ireturned at seven to the Panther. Mr. Maxfield had our boats to bring him close to us. Our crew, the Captain assured me, had acted wonderfully well, much better than he could have expected ; but of Unus Barilla he spoke in the highestterms of praise. He had rendered every personal service, with a cordiality and friendship that surprised him. He had, without scruple, received the loaded cannon on board his dow, and had come to cook his provisions in ours. He had headed the workmen, had cheered them with singing, and had put up a prayer of thanksgiving when we were in safety. He, in consequence, obtained handsome presents from me, Captain Court, and Captain Kuril and. To him in a great measure the safety of the vessel was owing, although probably she might have been saved by sending the guns to the island. This, however, would have been a work of time as well as difficulty, for the water round the island was shallow.

Very early in the morning we began our warping, and brought the vessel free of all danger. We then sent off Mr. Maxfield to examine a passage, which all the pilots declared to be the true one, but which Mr. Maxfield's pilot had quitted for the cul-de-sac, where we had so nearly been lost. Mr. Salt visited the island near which we grounded : he procured a species of Orobanche, with a very large yellow bloom, a Stapelia, a Com- melina, and a syngenesious plant that eat well as a salad. Several grasses also grew there. It was singular to find such a variety of plants on a little spot of arid sand. A curious nest, three or four feet in diameter, composed of sticks and madra- pore, was found on the ground ; it belongs to a very large species of bird that was seen by my servant on another island. Four large eggs were brought me of a fine blue colour.

Mr. Maxfield on his return informed us, that the passage for a very considerable distance was good, with from seven to ten fathom ; we therefore determined to try it. The wind continued to the N".of *E:* which made tacking necessary; we, however, got into the true channel before night, and anchored in good ground. The mountains were visible in the evening, which here again come near to the shore. The hills above Suakin were pointed out to us by the pilots.

We were under weigh about seven; the wind was fresh from the N. E. so that we could only just lie our course ; the sea was perfectly smooth, and it rained a little. The channel was extremely narrow, in some parts not more than a cable's length from shoal to shoal. Mr. Maxfield kept ahead, making signals of eight and ten fathom. About five miles from our anchoring ground we bore up round a point of sand. Unus Barilla had gone on, and sagaciously anchored his dow at the entrance of the narrows, where there is said to be only three fathom : we could not however reach him for the wind ; and the pilots determined to keep on for another passage ahead, Mr. Maxfield still leading. He soon came to an anchor, as we did instantly, and when he bore up for us, we learned, that though he was in ten fathom, he found the passage so narrow that he did not like to enter it. It was fortunate he came up to us, for though his anchor had been down not more than a quarter of an hour, yet it was nearly worn through by the rocks, while we were in strong clay. We now determined to send the boats to examine the passage to windward : Mr. Hardy went in the cutter, Mr. Maxfield in the dow. When they returned, their reports were rather favourable; but as they penetrated only about five miles to windward, and the pilots were positive they could not take the vessel through, with the wind that now blew, and as they said it might continue these twenty days, we were for some time uncertain how to act. Wewere unwilling to return to Ras Howie, and beat round the outside of the shoals, as we should leave it undecided whether a passage existed within them or not; yet to stay here was impracticable, as we were pressed for time, and had only twenty days water on board. At length Mr. Hardy proposed that he should go off with the dow and cutter, and ascertain the passage the whole way to Suakin. This was approved, and we beat up to the windward extremity of the land-locked harbour, in which we were lying, and which, had it proper and safe entrances, would be one of the finest in the world, being in size about six miles every way, with generally ten fathom and a good bottom. The passage is, however, unfortunately so complicated, and the sand islands are so alike, that no ship could venture through it without a pilot. We passed right over one shoal not many yards wide, on which there was only three fathom, and another of the same size, which had five. The sea was as smooth as glass, and the weather fine with us ; but it rained hard over the lofty mountains of Africa, which, according to Mr. Bruce and D'Anville are of porphyry. I do not know what authority either had for the assertion.

Mr. Hardy returned, and reported that he had found no passage through which the Panther could possibly be taken. He had been atSuakin, and had seen the Turkish Do] a, from whom he brought as presents to me two bullocks, ten sheep, ten fowls, and a basket of vegetables, which were most acceptable, as our live stock was reduced to a few fowls. A Dola of the Bedowee also resides there, who was considerably alarmed at the report of an English ship's coming, under an idea that she meant to attack the island. He therefore proposed to seize the boat and crew. This indeedwould have been a more difficult matter than he supposed, as the seven sailors with Mr. Hardy had musquets and plenty of ball cartridge. The Turkish Dola, however, prevented any thing unpleasant. He assured the Bedowee that he knew the English well, that he had frequently seen their ships at Jidda, and that they never did any harm to any one. They, however, were still uneasy, and said, the English never came before, why should they do so now ? At length they swore Unus on the Koran, that all the people in the Panther were good people, and meant no harm to Suakin. This he did willingly, and instantly all was friendship. Mr. Hardy stated our situation, and the Dola sent us two pilots to bring us clear of the dangers. He sent a very civil message to me, that he would prepare a house for me on shore, and would fire every gun he had in compliment to me, as he knew that the English and the Sultaun of Rome were always friends. They confirmed the circumstance of Jidda being besieged, which accounts for their civility. My servant went to look for shells; he procured a few, and one most beautiful fish.

During the night two of the Lascars ran away, with the jolly boat; they took with themthe sails and rudder of the cutter, which, to prevent pursuit, they also cut adrift. Most fortunately it was not far off, and was soon secured by Mr. Maxfield's small boat. The fellows were out of sight from the mast head. We sent Unus direct to Suakin to represent the circumstance, and offer a reward for the boat, which is a serious loss. Our new pilots were most respectable men, and as Mr. Hardy declared that they were perfectly acquainted with every shoal they passed, we had sufficient confidence in them to return by a new route. Anisland and a shoal formed in one place a very narrow passage, which we had to work through right in the wind's eye, but fortunately we cleared it. k The rest of the passage was broad enough for the ship to work tolerably well. It was far preferable to the one by which we entered. The pilots expressed their astonishment at any body's having been able to bring a vessel like the Panther into such a place, where a large dow could hardly enter with safety. In the time of the Egyptian trade, this port seems to have been as little known as Port Mornington : it may, however, be the Euangelion Limen of Ptolemy ; but without some better authority than his tables, it would be absurd to speak positively on the subject. Don Juan de Castro passed through the bay, and by the narrow passage, which MrHardy examined in going in the cutter to Suakin. His Marale and Shaback may be sought for in vain, among the windings and mazes of this singular harbour, which presents on the charts such a mass of confusion, that at my request Captain Court called it Bother'em Bay. The Aveather was fine, the wind light, and the sea as- smooth as glass : we had eight, nine, and ten fathom till we got into the channel by which we had entered, at about three o'clock, and soon afterwards we came to an anchor.

February 7. We weighed anchor about six, with a favourable wind to quit the straits, but directly contrary when we had to bear up for Suakin. We continued to tack till three o'clock, when we came to an anchor about four miles E. by N. of Has Howie, in eleven fathoms, mud and sand : we did this from the goodness of the bottom, lest we should be obliged to let go in a worse, for the wind was fresh, with a considerable degree of svell. We had overfalls during the day, butnever less than five fathom. It rained in the evening.

The next day it blew so fresh, with rain, that -we could not attempt to stir, the wind being right in our teeth. Mr. Maxfield's cable parted ; we sent our cutter to heave the anchor by the buoy, but the rope was so rotten that it immediately broke. He let go two small anchors, but they would not hold ; we were therefore obliged to give him a hawser, and let him hang to our stern. It moderated in the afternoon, after several heavy showers, when the swell went gradually down, till at night it was perfectly calm.

We weighed at daylight in hopes of a fair wind. It freshened gradually till one, when we were nearly opposite two islands, which the pilot named something so like Hurroo Riot, that I could not help being amused with the resemblance. These islands, they said, were half way from our anchoring ground, yet we had not made above nine miles, and we understood Suakin was a good day's run. There is here good anchorage, and they wanted us to stop; but as there was a favourable breeze, we represented to them the probability of our reaching Suakin, to which they acceded. The clouds hung over the high hills, and perfectly concealed them from our view during the greater part of the day; the pilots therefore were very anxious to come to an anchor about four o'clock, with which we complied, as the water was gradually deepening. We had a good bottom in twenty-four fathom ; the Assaye was fastened to us.

At seven we weighed anchor, and made sail with a light air from the southward. We passed between some islands, and found good soundings, but with overfalls at very short distances; the water as smooth as glass. We were, in fact, sailing in a channel, formed by a reef and a chain of sand banks ; there were also shoals between us and the shore. We were not a little surprised to find excellent anchoring ground within six miles of Sua- kin, when the water became too deep. We went too quick to get soundings till *off* the entrance of the passage, which is not sixty fathom wide, but leads to a wider reach, where the pilots insisted on our casting anchor, though at above a mile distance from the town. As they confessed that they had received orders to do it from the Dola, we submitted, and let go an anchor in sixteen fathom, the deepest part of the land-locked bason being nineteen fathom, perfectly free from rock. A small fort was building on a little island to the northward. We sent Abdallah in the evening with compliments to the two Dolas.

In the night a strong gale came on from the north-westward, and overset our anchor into the deepest water. It however, struck there, and held us at a few yards distance from the S. easternmost shoal, in not a very pleasant situation. Captain Court and I were both on deck, and I was just returning to my cot when we saw a boat coming down the harbour. It nearly ran foul of us; on being hailed, Abdallah answered, and we found that he had brought us off a bullock as a present from the Dola, and numerous compliments. It blew very fresh all night, and the sea beat very heavy on the outside of the reef and shoal. In the morning the haze was so great, we could hardly distinguish the town; the mountains were perfectly covered.

Two boats came to us at breakfast; one with the pilots; the other contained the son of the Be- dowee Dola, who brought a present of sheep and vegetables. This visit gave me great pleasure, asit proved a total change of opinion in our favour, and showed a great confidence in our hospitality, as his father had been the person who proposed detaining Mr. Hardy and the boat's crew. He was a good-looking young man, and handsomely dressed. He assured us of every assistance from his father, who was, he said, the chief of the most considerable tribe of Bedovvee in the vicinity. He informed me, that the letter I brought from the Nayib of Massowah was for himself. It was immediately delivered. He read, or pretended to read it, and said it was very well. He sat down to breakfast, and used his spoon properly: he tasted the tea, and liked it very much. Abdallah returned with him to the shore, but came back soon. He brought me word the Turkish Dola was very angry with the young Dola for having visited me first, who had pleaded, that he only came to get the Nayib's letter, which he had learned I had for him, from a dow of the Nayib's, that had quitted Massowah since I did. The Turkish Dola sent me word not to receive presents from any body; that he was master here, and would supply the ship with every thing she wanted.

I had sent a message by the young Dola, that I intended to go on shore the next morning to visit the Chiefs, but the Turkish Dola now sent word by Abdallah, that he desired I would not; that the people would all be wanting to give me presents, and to obtain others in return ; seeking under that pretence to sell their articles at a higher price than they would otherwise bring ; but that he would himself pay me a visit in the evening. I suspected the fact was, that he wished to secure all the presents himself. At night another message came off, that the Bedowee Dola had insisted on coming with him, and that therefore he wouldnot come; but if I chose to pay him a visit 'on shore, he should be happy to see me. I sefit word I certainly would. We gave a salute to the town of three guns in the morning, which was returned. I, Mr. Salt, and Captain Rudland went on the little island. We found no shells. A Salicornia, a Statice. and a species of grass, were the only plants. A few fishermen were at the fort. We procured some fine mullets for a handful of tobacco. The wind was very unpleasant all day, but our anchor held fast. We got several boatloads of stone from the vicinity of the fort, which we distributed in the hold as additional ballast.

The Bedowee Dola's son, Emir Mohammed, came off early in the morning to attend me on shore, and brought us two bullocks as a present from his uncle, who, (and not his father, as I before understood,) is Emir of the Chief Bedowee tribe in the neighbourhood. Captain Rudland, Mr. Salt, and myself, wore Asiatic dresses ; Captain Court was in his uniform. We departed soon after breakfast, under a salute 'of seventeen guns. On landing, one gun was fired, which shook the mortar from the gateway under which we were passing. Two Janisaries in decent red dresses conducted us to a little plain room, at the upper end of which was placed a common couch of the country, covered with a carpet and two cushions ; on the right of this were three chairs, a fourth was soon brought. Opposite was a low stone bench covered with carpet; behind us was the same, both extending the whole length of the building. A reverend Arab of sixty, tall, and thin, was presented to us by Emir Mohammed, as his father. The usual compliments passed. After being seated a little time, the Turkish Dola entered, and making a general salaam, seated himself. We paid our compliments through Abdallah, and returned thanks for the pilots he had sent us, and the provisions. He said he was happy to assist the English, who were ever friends of the Sultaun of Rome. Coffee was brought, and nothing interesting passed, till I asked if he had any late news from Misr. He said, yes, very late. That all was now quiet there ; that the Turks had got possession of the whole country, having an army of 60,000 men. That the English had entered the Port of Iscandaria with sixty vessels of different descriptions, and had landed soldiers there. He added, that the Beys were quiet, and that there were five Turkish Pachas there. On asking about Jidda, he assured me that 10,000 Turks had liberated Mecca from the Wahabee, and were on their march to Jidda. Yambo also was under a Turkish Pacha. I made many inquiries, if possible, to detect him in an error, but he answered so correctly as to induce us to believe the account, so far as related to a British force being at Alexandria, and Egypt's being quiet; two most important objects to us, as securing our safe passage through Egypt, and a speedy departure from Alexandria for Europe. It much increased our impatience to reach Cosseir.

After sitting an hour, sherbet, made with honey, was handed about. Afterwards a khelaut was put over my shoulders, which, to my great surprise, was of the most holy colour, green. Such a gift would never have been permitted in Turkey a few years ago. Even the wearing a bit of that colour would have been dangerous to a Christian, It was handsomely lined with ermine. I asked Emir Ma- hommed where these skins were procured : he said they were not of this country, but that the dresses were sent from Constantinople to be given on public occasions, and that the Dola brought them from Jidda. Captain Court, who sat next me, had a yellow khelaut, lined also with ermine, but old and discoloured. I was surprised at their being so good. The Dola was a dignified man, with good manners. He wore a scarlet cloth dress, lined with blue silk ; his attendant officers were in similar dresses; and this uniformity gave an appearance of respectability to the little divan we were seated in. Around the room were hung sabres, matchlocks, European guns, and blunderbusses. Before our departure, he promised to come on board the Panther the next day. His servants escorted us to the water side, and kept off the crowd.

The town is nearly in ruins : two miuars give it a handsome appearance at a distance, and the buildings, being white-washed, and on an elevation, look much better than they really are. It covers the whole of a small island, as it did in the days of De Castro, but the extensive trade, which, according to his account, had rendered it superior to every city he had seen, except Lisbon, has nearly vanished, and instead of numerous ships, unloading their cargoes on every side of the island, into the houses of merchants, I could only perceive a few miserable dows anchored along side of a few wretched houses. The port however still retains all its advantages, and vessels larger than the Panther might anchor close to the island, where there is seven fathom. D'Anville's chart is accurate as to the outline, but he has erred greatly with respect to the depth of water, which is from fifteen to nineteen fathoms the whole way to the town. He has likewise been mistaken in the relative size of the two islands, which isnearly equal, and in its latitude, which, after the Portuguese, he has stated as 19 20' N. instead of 19 4' 8".

I believe D'Anville is correct in his supposition, that this was the Soter Limen of Diodorus, the Theon Soter of Ptolemy, but I think it ill deserves the description he has given of it, as the safest asylum for navigators on this coast. The reefs and shoals that lie off it, in every direction, render an approach to it extremely dangerous, and the narrowness of the mouth makes it almost impracticable to enter it with any, but a leading wind. It is difficult to account for a narrow passage between two lines of coral rock having continued for so long a period free for vessels, without having been filled up, either by a sea constantly breaking on its mouth, after having passed over sand banks, or by the clouds of sand which at one season of the year are borne towards it from the desert. Since the Turks have ceased to have a fleet in the Red Sea, and have sunk into political insignificance in Arabia, Suakin has been kept from total ruin only by the caravans, which still comeannually from the interior of Africa, by Sennaar, to that place, in their way to Mecca. The town itself is all that belongs to the Sublime Porte, and their Dola, or Aga, dares not put his foot on the main land, which belongs to a powerful tribe of Be- dowee, who take their name from the town, and call themselves Suakini. To them, as I have before observed, belongs the country around Port Mornington, and their influence must extend to Macowar, as Emir Mohammed has offered to send a man with us to that place, who, he says, will procure us provisions the whole way, but he at the same time warns us on no account to land ourselves. As we returned to the ship it blew fresh,but as the passage was marked out by buoys, fixed on the sand heads, we met with no accident; what a convenience it would be at Mocha, if the same precaution had been taken by the Government !

February 13.lThe weather was much more moderate and cool. The Dola paid us an early visit, and was in high good humour, talking much of his friendship for the English, and claiming an acquaintance with Captain Court, whom, he said, he had seen at Jidda. This, though a mistake, was acquiesced in from prudential motives. I enquired how long he had been at Suakin. He replied, two years ; that the appointment was annual, but that frequently the same person was allowed to stay ten years in officell presume, if he contrives to bribe the Pacha atJidda, in whose hands is the appointment. I learned from him, that the caravan will set off to-morrow for Sennaar, and will be about twenty-five days on the journey. He said all was quiet there, that the King was dead, and no one had succeeded, but that the Vizier managed every thing. As he had several people with him, I again asked, if there was any river on any part of this coast. They all positively assured me that there was not, though there was plenty of fresh water at several places. I also enquired respecting ruins on the coast; particularly if any pillars existed: they equally denied knowledge of either ; and the Bedowee declared, that if there were any they could not be ignorant of them. The Turkish Dola drank coffee; the old Bedowee eat some sweetmeats, but only just tasted the coffee.

Some of the followers had sat down on one of the couches. The Turk asked why I permitted it; I replied that I could not presume to give any orders to his people, when he was *by*. He however did not order them to remove, nor do I think the)7 would have obeyed ; but he said laughing, " they are like the animals I send you on board, goats and sheep, ignorant and stupid, they know no better." He requested permission to have his hookah, which was granted. He declined sherbet, and after a visit of several hours said he wished to have his present, and take his leave. Abdallah put on him a shawl of gold tissue, which is worn as a scarf over the right shoulder, and under the left arm. I also presented him with a turban of the same materials. The Bedowee Dola had a scarf of an inferior quality. He took his leave in much good humour, and was saluted with three guns, as he was on his arrival. We had brought off several loads of stone from the island to use as ballast, but the Dola objected to this, saying he wanted it to finish the fort, as he wished to make the place strong against the Wahabee; the fact was he wanted to be paid for them. We applied to the young Dola, Emir Mohammed, who said he would send us one thousand stones.

My servant killed a beautiful flamingo : the under feathers of the wing, black ; the rest gradually shading from a fine scarlet to a pure white. It was four feet from the tip of the beak to the extremity of the toe, and about the same from wing's end to wing's end. Abdallah procured us from the town a good vegetable, a Chenopodium, that tasted exactly like spinach. This, the Hibiscus esculentus, and green pumpkins, Avere all that were procurable.

The people themselves seemed civil and good natured; none of them were armed : they wear a piece of white cloth wrapped round their middle, and thrown ovej the shoulder. In general their

VOL. II. T

figures are very fine, and the expression of their countenances good. They are of a dark copper colour, their hair is somewhat woolly drawn out into points, and dressed with fat, occasionally powdered with red; a piece of wood is stuck through it, nearly horizontally, which they frequently use to disturb any animalcula that bite too hard. It is in shape like a porcupine's quill, and of course polished by the grease. They also use it to separate the hair into ringlets and turn it round the finger. Many had the long hair behind separated by a narrow shaved passage, from the front curly division, which was formed into an oval. They certainly are on the whole a well looking race of people. Their skins are perfectly clear from eruptions of any sort, but are much marked where actual cautery has been applied as a remedy for local disease. We saw great numbers during our stay, as every day strangers came off in the water-boat to view the ship. I have given an etching of a man, who was above six feet high, and had a most singular expression of countenance. The likeness is admirably preserved. It is impossible not to be struck by the resemblance between them and the South Sea islanders, as drawn in Captain Cook's voyages. Their teeth, which are beautifully white and regular, they constantly clean with a piece of the rack-wood. They wear nothing on the head, which is sufficiently protected from the sun by the mass of wool and grease that covers it.

We got fifteen barrels of water a day, good, and tolerably clear. They have both wells and tanks. Fish in abundance and cheap; the mullets are particularly fine. Mr. Maxfield's pilot made his escape on shore. We had detained him lest he shpuld breed any more mischief. I recollectedthat I had two letters given me by Devage" when I was coming hither in the Antelope. I looked them out, and sent them to the people, who immediately came off, and proved to be very respectable men; merchants of course. I learned from them that nothing was brought from the inter.ior of Africa to this place, except slaves, horses, gold, and ivory : in which articles, however, a very considerable trade is carried on.

Abdallah, who had been sent on shore for provisions, returned with the water-boat. He brought me word, that there had been vehement disputes on shore ; that Emir Mohammed told him, he had learned we gave five hundred dollars to the Nayib of Massowah, and that the Bedowee Emirs wanted to come off, with presents, and ask for the same sum. That both Unus and he had inquired whether this was in his letter, and defied him to produce it. He said, no, it was not, but he had been told so; no doubt by Mr. Maxfield's rascally pilot. They declared it was an absolute falshood; that the English never gave presents of that sort, that they only came here for provisions, and would pay for what they got, but would receive no presents or make returns. The two Dolas and the Emir took Ouf part, and the whole business was amicably adjusted. Three sheep were sent off, but Abdallah told me the Emir said they would be one dollar and a half each. This was evidently an imposition, though they were worth double the price of those we obtained at Massowah. One of the merchants to whom I had letters, was on board; I spoke to him, and he admitted the price was too high, for that a dollar was sufficient for the best, three-fourths for a middling one, and half a dollar for a small one. I said that, at that rate, I would buy for the crew; but if the other price wascharged, I should not want half the quantity, as I should only buy for myself. He said, he was a friend of Emir Mohammed, and would speak to him. A brother of Emir Mohammed was on board, to consult Mr. Macgie, who also promised to do the same. Abdallah brought a message from the Emir, that his brother was that day to be married, and requested that when the town guns were fired, we would fire three, which was promised. He also requested a few pounds of sugar-candy, and two candles: the former we sent, the latter we could not spare. Abdallah went on shore. The boys went a shell-hunting on the reefs, and procured some very good ones. The wind varied much in the course of the day. It was once E. The weather was moderate and pleasant.

February 15.|The water-boat and Abdallah came off as usual. He brought two large sheep for a dollar each, and some vegetables, but not sufficient for the ship's company. On enquiring respecting grain, we learned that none was to be had here, except juwarry, and for a hundred weight of that they asked three dollars, no very pleasant intelligence, as we were short of rice, and other articles; the cock-roaches having eaten much and wasted more. The weather, as usual; wind from the N. E. and N. W. We took on board more stones, having received the requisite permission, on paying seven dollars. I had a letter from the Dola, saying that the pilots who brought us in had in the first instance been promised thirty-five dollars. We had paid them twenty, with which they departed extremely well satisfied; this therefore was too barefaced an imposition to succeed. We laughed at the demand, and refused to pay it.

February 16.|The water came off at eight, and

Abdallah brought two large sheep, with a request from the Dola, that we would give him some tobacco. We sent him ten pounds. Unus came off for his letter, and to take his leave, his bargain extending only to this place. We gave him from the

Company thirty dollars for his exertions in saving the Panther when aground, with which he was the more delighted, as he had no expectations beyond the presents we had given him that night. We asked if he would hire himself to accompany us as far as Jibbel Macowar, to which place we meant to have pilots; their knowledge of the coast extending no further, as they there strike off for Jidda. He said he had no objection, but that he must consult his crew, who were only hired to Suakin. Many of the men of the water-boat had been very pressing every day for drams. This morning they again made their representations to me, through Abdallah. I told them, that I had been informed Mussulmauns did not drink any thing of that sort, and consequently had not provided myself with a sufficient stock ; but that in future, now I had found out my mistake, I would take care to have plenty. This excited a laugh against the petitioners, and their friends continued to ridicule them till they left the vessel. I should recommend to every person, who means to touch on this coast, to have spirits to spare: all soldiers drink publicly, and many others in private. I need not observe, that, to those who like it, no present is so acceptable. Common white cloth is another useful article for barter. Our tobacco has been of the greatest service, our sweetmeats have also been acceptable to all visitors. We sent Abdallah on shore to procure fowls, even at only four for a dollar, our stock of them being completely exhausted. It isa bad precedent, but they really seem to be scarce. At each place we were told there were plenty at the next, but, on our arrival, we only experienced disappointment. The air was pleasant and cool.

February 18.|It rained hard till ten, when the young Dola came offwith several of his friends, and his sick brother, who was rather better. We had a long conversation about Jibbel Macowar, which by Bruce is placed in 24 N. and by others in 21 and a half. They talk of its. being as far from hence as Massowah. We cannot ascertain precisely where it is, which we are anxious to do, that we may know what price to pay the pilot. The Emirs offered to hire us one on shore, but we thought it more advisable to have him sent to us, that we might make the bargain ourselves.

The young Dola informed me, that he had frequently be.en with the caravan to Sennaar, since his father had thought him old enough to have the care of it. I asked him, if the Vizier continued to collect the revenue from the inhabitants of the southern country, as they passed up into the sands ; he said he knew of no such thing. I made every possible inquiry, but in vain, he still persevering in his assertion, that no such thing ever took place. I made Abdallah translate to him Bruce's history of the Zimb or Tsaltsalya, but he positively asserted that he had never heard of the animal. As he was extremely free in his communications on every other subject, and had no motive for concealment on this, I cannot attribute to him a wanton and deliberate falshood, merely because Mr. Bruce has asserted the contrary, on whose veracity, I confess, 1 have lost all dependence. These declarations of Emir Mohammed are confirmed by the testimony of Mr. Brown, who assures me, that, when travelling in Africa,he made the same inquiries of people who had visited Sennaar, and with the same success. I can declare from my own knowledge, that there is no foundation for his assertion that the same migration takes place from Cape Gardafuito the Straits, any more than there is for the idea, that the chain of mountains, which runs parallel to the Red Sea, divides the seasons equally, and that it is fair on one side, while the torrents of rain pour down on the other. This is certainly the case in the peninsula of India, from which, probably, Mr. Bruce caught the idea. His own travels gave him no opportunity of ascertaining the fact.

The young Dola requested a letter from me to show at Mocha, which he frequently visits in the way of trade. He also hoped we would give him a present, when we settled accounts, for the trouble he had taken. He again drank tea, and praised it.

After his departure the Steward informed the first Lieutenant that there was not a single day's rice on board, although, when we sailed from Bombay on the 1st of December, it was understood that we had a sufficiency for five months. Upon examining the accounts, we found there ought to be one hundred and thirty-three maund, supposing every man had had his full allowance since our departure, which had not been the case. It was too large a quantity to have been consumed or wasted; we therefore must have owed the inconvenience to a fraud. The hurry in which the Panther was sent to sea rendered it impossible for Captain Court to look to the stores. We immediately sent to the town to buy all the juwarry that could be got.

We now thought it advisable to examine our other stores, and the result was a discovery thatwe had only a sufficient quantity of flour left for one week, the cockroaches having devoured the rest. Fortunately our crew had been served with biscuit for a period ending the 1st of March. This deficiency fell on the white men, and was really alarming. The Captain called them all aft, and stated the" discovery : he told them that any grain that could be purchased here, should be bought at any price; that at Cosseir they should have wheat,- but that they must make their present allowance of biscuit last till the 15th of March, by which time he had every reason to hope he should reach that place. To the Lascars he promised juwarry, and fresh meat. The whole were in perfect good humour, and assured him they were satisfied.

We have every reason to rejoice that we made Suakin the day we did: ever since, the wind had been so steady to the northward, that we could not have quitted Bother'em Bay, and our distress there for water and provisions would have been greatindeed. It was also fortunate that the northerly winds had blown only at a period when, by our having a complete stock of water to take in, they caused no delay. Their continuance however excited an unpleasant suspicion in my mind, that the monsoon had changed; which Mr. Macgie increased by the information, that he once sailed on the 1st of March from Jidda, and was six weeks in reaching Suez. The delay, however, was in getting through the Straits of Jubal. The natives consoled me by saying, that this is always a rainy month with them.

The cutter's crew, with my servant and Pierce, went to collect shells, and brought a good many, some new, but chiefly Cypraea; handsome, butcommon. In the evening of Feb. 20th, the Emir, the old pilot, and Unus came *off*. The Emir agreed to let us have a boat of his ; and the old pilot said, if we would pay him the fifteen dollars, he was ready to engage. Before we would promise this, we demanded what he asked for pilotage : he said one hundred and sixty dollars; adding, that he received thirty or forty for a dow. We were amused by the argument, though provoked by the impudence of the demand. The Emir told him he was a fool, and I observed it was so totally out of the question, that I would say nothing more. At length he wished to know what I would give ; observing that it was a very large vessel, and a very dangerous passage.

I replied, that he seemed to have forgotten his telling me that the way was good to Macowar, and that the size of the vessel was nothing to him, as we did not want him to be answerable for it. That I considered it as worth one-third as much as the pilotage from Mocha; and that I would therefore give fifty dollars, and no more ; that on the same principle I would give one hundred for a dow. If they did not choose to take that, I would sail without either. The argument lasted a long time: the Emir wished me to give sixty, which I refused, and they went away without any thing being settled ; but Unus said apart, that he would settle every thing.

The next day Captain Court took bearings for a plan of Suakin harbour.

As I had several letters to write, I requested the other gentlemen to pay their visit to the Dola without me. They set off soon after breakfast. On their return, I found that, after visiting Emir Mohammed, they had gone to pay their compliments to the Turkish Dola. He was at first in avery ill humour. The pHot had positively refused to go with us for less than sixty.five dollars ; they therefore applied to the Dola to know if he could assist us. He now brake forth, and represented, that we could not expect to hire another pilot, when we had not paid the last all his wages. The Captain repeated to him our reasons ; but he positively declared, he had himself hired them for thirty-five dollars. Captain Court assured him, that had the men claimed five hundred on his word, we would have paid them, and that the money should be sent to him on the morrow.

Emir Mohammed came on board in the evening with the merchants ; all our accounts were settled, which were not very exorbitant. For his own boat he would charge nothing, only the men's hire who came in her. The water was twenty-five skins for a dollar; the bullocks six and seven dollars each; the sheep a dollar each, and sometimes a little less. All the vegetables were only two dollars. Captain Court and I gave, each of us, letters of recommendation to him, and to Unus. I also wrote to Mr. Pringle in favour of the latter.

Captain Court and I, on mature consideration, determined to submit to their demands, and pay the hundred dollars for the dow, and sixty-five for the pilot; since, if we did not, it would be out of our power to examine the coast as far as Macowar, which I was extremely anxious to do, both from personal inclination, and a sense of duty. The dangerous state of the Assay e also made a boat desirable ; besides that we were unacquainted with the passage among the shoals into the open sea. We therefore notified our change of sentiment to the Dola, who promised that every thing should be ready by to-morrow evening. We were impatient to be gone, as the weather was very fine, and the wind in the middle of the day came round to the east.

February 22.|The pilot and Emir Mohammed came *off* in the morning with two nephews of the Turkish Dola. They would not drink coffee, which is not permitted till they are fifteen, but they took sweetmeats. I gave the Emir fifty dollars, a turban, and cummurbund, for his exertions. We sent the old Dola a little oil of cinnamon, and fifty pounds of powder. The old pilot agreed to go, and received his money. Unus took his leave with sorrow. He begged a flag, and wanted other articles, which, being unreasonable, were refused. The Emir obtained from us a half- hour sand-glass. On his departure we saluted him with two guns. A dow arrived yesterday from Jidda. I was happy to hear from the Turkish Dola, that she brought a confirmation of the

Egyptian news, and that there was a Pacha waiting to pass from Suez to Jidda with a large army. The weather was very mild, and at twelve the wind came round to the eastward, and gave us hopes of a favourable change.

February 23.|The dow came off early in the morning. From the narrowness of the harbour we were obliged to warp, and made but little way; our crew not being sufficient, and our boats scarcely strong enough to sustain the weight of a large cable. It blew fresher than yesterday, from the N. and N. E.

In the night the wind gradually increased to a gale, and we were nearly driven on the southern shoal, by our anchor's falling into the deepest part of the channel: there, however, it held fast. When more moderate, we warped farther, but dragged back, the wind being fresh, and right intothe mouth of the harbour. We kept quiet the whole of the afternoon.

February '25.|It blew fresh and adverse in the night, and till the sun rose, when the swell and wind went down. We again began to warp out, but our anchor fell into deep water, and we were within ten feet of the southern shoal. We found, to our cost, that in northerly winds this harbour is a prison. It is too narrow to work in, and too deep to warp out of, with facility. When the winds are from the south, there is a regular land breeze every morning, which obviates all difficulties. The old pilot says, that southerly winds blow here eight months out of the twelve, but never for any length of time without intermission. From all I can learn from different people, who have been in the Red Sea, I believe that there is no season in which the winds blow from one point without changing for a few days; and, in the middle part of the gulf, they may almost be called variable, at least as much so as in the British Channel, where, for nine months in the j'ear, the wind blows from the westward. We for five weeks had N. E. winds, yet the monsoons of this sea are said to be N. W. and S. E. After a hard day's labour we regained the spot from which we were driven. It was fortunate for us that we procured at Mocha some native hawsers made of grass, with which we cleared the harbour, by fastening them to the beacons raised at the points of the shoals by the pilots of the place. These hawsers are much lighter than the European, and a less boat will consequently carry them out. If Suakin was in the hands of an European power, rings might easily be fixed in these rocks, and the warping out would be no longer difficult. As it is in the hands of the Turks, more has been donethan could be expected. On getting out we found anchorage at twenty-five fathom, when in entering we could find no bottom, from the rapidity with which we moved. This is of great importance, as the passage into the harbour is so extremely narrow.

6

SECTION 6

CHAPTER VII.

Departure from Suakin. | Lent Bay.|Sheik Baroud.| Daroor.|Danger of the Panther among the rocks.|Loss of anchors|Recovery of them.|Salaku.|Mousetrap Bay.| Gale of wind.|Obliged to return to Mocha.|Observations en Macowar, probably the Berenice Pancrysos of the Ancients.|Observations on Mr. Bruce's supposed Voyage from Cosseir to Macowar.|Conjectures respecting Myos Hormot. |Arrival at Massowah.|Visit to the Island of Valentin.| Return to Mocha.

IT was moderate in the morning, February 26th, with a fine land breeze, when all the dows left the harbour. Unus passed us, making his salaams, with his English colours flying. By nine we were under weigh, accompanied by Mr. Maxfield, the dow, and a smaller boat. The sea breeze did not set in favourably, but held to the N. of N. E.; we, of course, made but little way. The channel was very narrow, and our tacks short. About twelve it freshened considerably, and continued to do so till four, when it was due north. The pilot pointed out an anchoring ground, for which we stood : but he changed his mind, and pushed on foranother, which we soon found it impossible to reach ; and indeed his account of it was not very pleasant: he said it was near the shore, and in forty fathom. It blew very fresh, and the sky promised a gale. Captain Court therefore returned to the first. We had only our stay-sail and mizen set, yet were going five knots an hour. As we neared the shore there were no soundings, till the man in the chains called out four fathom rocks. Exceedingly alarmed, we instantly tried to let go the stream anchor with the chain, but it would not run ; we then let go the bower, which went. The next heave was ten fathom, mud, and then fourteen, in which we let go the stream anchor. We now found ourselves in a perfect bason formed by a circle of rocks, over a part of which we had passed. The pilot knew what he was about; hut being rather alarmed, and anxious, he had omitted giving us notice that we should pass such a shallow spot. The entrance is narrow, as not half a cable's length to larboard we found a quarter less one. Mr. Maxfield kept to starboard under bare poles, but came in very fast. He had. nothing to fear where we had passed. It blew a gale all night; and we had reason to be thankful that we had safely entered this bason. We were sufficiently protected from the swell, and had excellent holding ground, a fine blue clay; yet never did we run a greater risk than in entering. Not knowing the place, we were obliged to trust to a pilot with whom we could have no communication, except through an interpreter. He was alarmed; the ship was going at the rate of five knots an hour, and the evening was dark ; yet, with all this, we were to pass a strait where a mistake of half a cable would have carried us to destruction. It blew too fresh in the morning to heave ouranchors. Perceiving that the shore next to us was formed of a parcel of islands covered with trees, a party was sent .off to cut some wood. Mr. Salt and my servant went in the boat; they returned at nine. Mr. Salt could find no plants; and he reported that these islands, at low water, are connected with the main land, and that they are only a kind of sunderbunds, composed of the rack tree, with a reef of rocks towards the sea protecting the whole line. My servant shot one of the very large grey birds, that we have often mistaken for natives; it stands nearly six feet upright. By the meridian altitude we made the day before but seven miles. Though the Panther sailed better for the ballast we took in, yet, from her great height above the water, she made hardly any way against a foul wind. Had the monsoon set in from the northward, I know not what we should have done. On the next day was to be a new moon, from which we had considerable hopes, as the day had been moderate, and the sky clear.

It blew however too fresh to stir with safety, as we found by experience ; for in trying to get under weigh, our anchor dragged, and we were obliged to let go another. We therefore continued in statu quo, hoping that the change of the moon would yet bring a change of weather.

It blew a gale in the night from the N. N. W., so as to oblige us to let go a third anchor, by which we rode safely. It lulled towards morning, and we attempted to get under weigh, though there was a considerable swell. In doing this we drifted to within a quarter of a cable's length of the rock, that has but a quarter less one on it. In the course of the morning we contrived to get an anchor down farther from it. It blew very fresh;

voi. It. U

but the sky was clear. .A fishing boat from Sua- kin brought us fish. The fishermen promised to follow us as far as possible; our custom was too valuable to be given up easily.

It blew very fresh again in the night: the As- saye dragged, and then parted her anchor. Mr. Maxfield let go his last when only in three fathom, rock, at which time there was a very heavy swell from the northward. His situation being dangerous, he fired signal guns of distress. We immediately sent off our cutter with a hawser, and fortunately his vessel rode safe till it was fastened ; we then warped her astern of us. It was extremely alarming for us also, since, if the wind had come round two points to the westward, we should in all probability have been driven on the dangerous rock that was so near us. We had three anchors down, and a fourth ready to let go : fortunately the wind continued in the same point. It was cold all day, and the motion was considerable. Mr. Maxfield came on board to report, that his ship made much more water, and that the whole of her was, he believed, rotten. The pilot also added his share of comfort, by positively as- 'serting that the N. W. monsoon had set in, and that we should have no change of wind. This would have been bad news, as we should have been obliged to go to Jidda to obtain a supply of provisions, and abandon the survey of the coast to Macowar, which I find Bruce positively asserts is in 24' N. and that he was there.

March 3.|It was more moderate during the night, and towards morning quite calm. We took advantage of it to get up two of our anchors, putting down one at a sufficient distance to secure us from the rock, before mentioned. At twelve the wind was from the eastward, but toolight for us to venture out at so late an hour. The Captain and Mr. Hardy went to examine the As- saye, and found her quite as bad as reported, her timbers being perfectly rotten. They thought that she might be trusted in fine weather, but were satisfied that whenever we met with a change of the monsoon, she must be abandoned. Yet but four months since she was purchased by the East India Company's marine officers at Bombay, after having been, as they said, regularly inspected, and reported fit for service.

March 4.|The breeze came off from the land, and we got safe out by seven from our unpleasant station, which we called Lent Bay, having passed the reef in two fathom and a half; soon afterwards we had no soundings. At twelve, we found no bottom with eighty fathom. The shore was as usual protected by a reef of rocks, and was composed of small islands covered with the rack-tree. There was another reef to the eastward, leaving a channel about three miles wide. In the evening we had soundings of twenty-seven fathom, mud. We cast anchor, as we supposed, in a similar bottom, but, on sounding, found fourteen fathom, rocks. If a vessel carried very little sail, she might find out a good anchorage ; but the ground is so unequal that, when moving fast, there is no certainty that the next throw of the lead may not differ several fathom in depth, and more essentially in the quality of the bottom. The night was moderate.

Our stream anchor was entangled among the rocks, and we were obliged to leave it there, after having used every exertion, but in vain, to raise it. The breeze was fine, but hung too much to the northward ; the channel was from 2 to 3 miles wide. A whole fleet of dows was in sight,steering northward. We hailed one, and found it was from Mocha, laden with coffee. The pilot intended to have anchored between two of the shoals to the E. where he said there was good bottom, and moderate water, but the breeze came round to the eastward, and freshened; he therefore determined to run for a harbour he pointed out, sanctified by the tomb of Sheik Baroud, who has kindly chosen to be buried on a rising hillock, that marks the northern extremity of a narrow peninsula. Behind this lies a very excellent harbour, free from rocks, in which every danger is visible, and where a vessel may lie perfectly landlocked from every wind. We got in just as it was dark,to our very great satisfaction, as thewindfreshened considerably. The reefs on the outside are visible, and the space between perfectly sufficient for a vessel to pass with safety. The pilot said that five miles north of the harbour there is a communication with the open sea, which appears probable from the great increase of swell.

In the morning it blew very fresh, so as to make us rejoice on being so snug. I felt too weak from illness to go on shore, but the Captain and Mr. Salt went to the tomb. It is composed of mats only. Should the British ever form any arrangements for the Red Sea, a tomb might be built of white stone, Avhich would conciliate the natives, and answer as an excellent sea mark. A few plants grow on the peninsula, among these was an Asclepias without any leaves. I procured several very fine shells of the genus Conus, and a Murex, which I have since found to be a new species.

A dow was in the harbour, the master of which our pilot wished to visit, as he said he was a friend, 'and would procure us provisions from the natives,

to whom he was well known. He accordingly Went, but brought back word, that the Bedowee were gone up the mountains, and he was therefore unable to procure what he wanted for his own dow, which was filled with Abyssinian slaves for the Jidda market. Suspecting a little the truth of this *story,* and thinking it possible that he might wish to prevent our having any communication with the natives, lest we should interfere with his market, or raise the price of the necessary supplies, we watched him with a telescope, and at length saw several loaded camels coming to the beach. As the pilot concurred with us in opinion, and thought this friend might get us fresh provision if he pleased, we determined to try what a little threatening would do. Abdallah was therefore dispatched to him, with the pilot, to say, if that he did not procure us some fresh meat, we would take all the provisions he had in his vessel, and leave him to get a supply with the money we would pay him. Abdallah returned with an answer that the camels were going from Suakin to Macowar, and had brought nothing for him ; that there really were no animals to be purchased near; but that he had sent off a person to a village at a small distance, to try and purchase sheep. If he was successful, he would bring them to the point opposite the ship in the morning. He said if we wanted water there was plenty to be had, but that we must send our own vessels to fetch it, for the inhabitants had no skins.

Mirza Sheik Baroud appears to be a modern appellation of this harbour, for it is undoubtedly the Tradate of Don Juan de Castro, though he has kid it down in *195tf,* instead of 19 35' 42",. which is its true position. I have before observed that there was a mistake in the latitude of Suakin asgiven by D'Anville of about ten miles; he has made an equal error here, by placing his Dradate in 19 45". Though he certainly took his information from De Castro, he corrected the latitude five miles, but he has not done it sufficiently. The narrow passage in which we were sailing, and which, the pilot said, reaches to Macowar, would be impassable for any vessels, if it were not for the numerous small harbours, into which a vessel can run in bad weather. As the sea is perfectly smooth, in consequence of the reef to the eastward keeping off the swell, vessels with oars could always make their way against the strongest monsoon, when the force of the wind in the open channel would be irresistible. If the ancient navigators kept along the shore, which seems probable from the list of promontories, and other land marks, given in Ptolemy's tables, it is singular that no notice has been taken by Strabo, the author of the Periplus, or by Pliny, of the many harbours which are laid down by D'Anville between Myos Hormos and Ptolemais Theron. There is no ancient name which can with any degree of probability be affixed to Mirza Sheik J3ardud. . ;

We set 'sail by day-light March 7th, with the land breeze, which soon afterwards freshened considerably, and at length set in with a considerable swell from the N. N. E. As the land lay nearly in this direction, we made but little way, having to tack every twenty minutes, and generally missing stays. The pilot told us there was no anchoring, except in rocks, till we reached another harbour, distant twenty miles. At twelve the wind continued steady, and convinced us we could not reach it; we therefore turned about, and got safely into our old birth at Sheik Baroud. We in-

stantly sent Abdallah to the dow to learn if any Bedowee were in the vicinity, and to offer the Naqueda ten dollars as a present, if he would procure us a sufficient supply of sheep or goats, over and above any profit he might make in the purchase ; he brought us word that none were to be had here, but if we would send a person with money to Torateit, where our dow, and several 'others, were at anchor, we might the next day have goats and sheep in r.eturn. He undertook to

fo with our messenger, but we preferred trusting im with the money, having his dow as a security ; and accordingly sent him forty dollars. Two men who had seen us at Suakin brought off some rock cod as a present, for which we gave them two dollars, to their great satisfaction. They promised to procure us a supply of fish.

Mr. Maxfield's vessel has made much more water by the exertion of beating to windward. I got some fine shells, and our men caught some rock cod and several sharks.

We did not attempt to move on the 8th. The Captain and the other gentlemen went in the cutter up the bay, which extends considerably inwards, with deep water. The dow man brought us two bullocks, for which he declared he had paid twenty dollars, and seven sheep for eight dollars; the other twelve he wished to keep, as a security for the present; but said, that if we would send him more money, he would procure more provisions. This we did, but desired him not to send it away, as we must have it back if we sailed in the morning.

"... It blew from the west of north, and we got un- derweigh by day-light, as did the dow. We sent the cutter on board, and got back our dollars. The wind gradually came round to the N. E. so

that we lay well up shore, and by four o'clock la anchored in an open bay, behind which was a iol harbour called Daroor. We were in ten fa- jw thorn, mud and clay, but had the reefs very close 1 Is to us on both sides. The Assaye was at our stern. : 31 In the night it blew fresh, but moderating to- ;t! wards morning, we attempted to get under weigh, j tl After getting up one anchor, the other dragged, - t and obliged us to let go the first again. It came . c on to blow very fresh from the northward, veer- j ing in the middle of the day to the N. E. The M swell was great, and we were as much exposed to it as if we had been in the open sea. Captain i Court, the other gentlemen, Abdallah, my servant, and the pilot, went up the harbour, and landed on the shore: they spoke to several natives, who were very civiL They gave them tobacco, and to oblige them, cut some buttons off their coats, which were greatly prized. The Bedowee wished them to go up to a village at some distance; but this was not thought prudent. The pilot asked them to get us some sheep. One man said he would try, and bring them to the beach if he succeeded. They saw some bullocks and a great number of camels. My servant killed three flamingoes. We roasted one, and found the breast very good. The harbour is of considerable extent, when the narrow entrance is once passed. This is very short, and lies nearly E. andW., so that the land breeze in the morning will always carry a ship out. It is perfectly land-locked, and has from two to four fathom water, with a mud bottom. Had we been aware of its excellence, we should have run in at first, and not lain tumbling on the outside; but unfortunately the sun was right in our faces, and made it difficult, when we arrived, to distinguish the reefs. This, by its re-

d lative latitude with Suakin, should be the Dorho s *i* of D'Anville ; but the latitude is, as usual, errone- ia ous, being 19 50'; only five miles more than the os(latitude he gives to Dradate. Its longitude is To 37 33'. The hills are still extremely high, and line to the coast regularly at the distance of a few miles; ll the intermediate space is flat sand, with a few eJ, trees. The beach itself is frequently a sunderbund mil of rack trees. Some islands in the harbour are a] completely covered with it. Plenty of dry wood k might be picked up along the beach. to The night was nearly calm ; and in the morn- inj ing a light breeze from the land made us hasten to get under weigh. It however took from four Id to six to raise one anchor. On trying to get up o the other, the wind headed us, and the anchor dragged. We again let it go, but the weather being extremely fine, we soon after again set to work. Unfortunately one anchor caught hold of the other, and we got close to the southern reef; so close that we could distinguish the beautiful coral of the rocks that threatened us with destruction. The anchors prevented the ship from wearing round into a channel which opened to the southward, and exposed us to the most imminent danger, as there was not a foot between the vessel's bottom and the rocks, which were there so steep, that had she struck, she would probably have gone over. Captain Court instantly cut both cables, and by the blessing of God the ship wore clear of danger, though without an inch to spare. Had a squall then come off, such as we had experienced just before, the ship and every thing in her must have been lost; and though our lives might have been saved, we should have been left on an inhospitable shore, with no assistance but from the Assaye, who had not three days provisions for us on board.

When recovered from our alarm, we found reason sufficient to make us uneasy, as we had only our sheet anchor left. We therefore determined to return into Daroor, and endeavour with the Assaye to recover our two bower anchors : fortunately a buoy was left to one, and a considerable quantity of cable to the other. The wind freshened very considerably, and the Panther was as crank as ever; we therefore determined not to trust to our sheet anchor in a heavy swell, but to run into the harbour. This we did, and found it as smooth as glass. We let go in two fathom, mud, but dropped into three. It blew a gale from the E. of north, so that the mountains were, as usual on such occasions, concealed from our view by clouds of sand. Mr. Maxfield had cast anchor on the outside to be ready to assist in getting up the anchors. Mr. Hardy went off to him with cables, &c. but after ascertaining their position, found it blew too fresh to do any thing, and returned.

We perceived a native on the shore, and sent off for him. He proved to be one of our dow's crew, who informed us, that Emir Mohammed had been up to Torateit, and conceiving that the monsoon (Shamaul) had set in, and would prevent the dow's coming on, had sent him by land to procure here what provisions we might want. This conduct of Emir Mohammed gave me great pleasure ; it was attentive and friendly, and argued well for a future connexion between the natives of the African coast, and the English, if cultivated by those who follow us, and not violated by caprice or tyranny, as has too often been the case. We have done the best we could to leave behind us a good impression of the British character, and, so far as we can judge, have succeeded. I sent the Suakin

man on shore, with instructions to persuade, if possible, one of the chief natives to pay us a visit. Mr. Hurst, in the boat of the Assaye, was driven on the reef as he was returning to the vessel, from having fastened a warp to the buoy of our anchor. Fortunately he landed safe with his men. We sent a boat with people to their assistance, who brought them clear of the surf. Mr. Hardy, with the cutter and crew, went to pass the night with the Assaye, to assist her in case of accident, as Mr. Maxfield had imprudently anchored her close to the reef. They got down an anchor for her farther to windward. It blew a perfect gale from the W. of N. in the night,

March 12.lIt blew too fresh for Mr. Hardy to do any thing with the anchors ; he therefore returned on board. We got the Assaye's boat on board, and repaired her. Two natives appeared on the beach; we sent a boat, and one came off. He brought a basket of broiled fish to sell. We requested him to procure some raw, which he said he would do. He was the same man that our gentlemen had seen when they went on shore. He said he had brought down two sheep yesterday, but as nobody came from the ship, he had taken them back. He expressed no fear or surprize ; he told us there was water, but that they had no vessels to bring it in, We gave him a dollar for his fish, and he went off to get more. Captain Rudland and my servant went on the northern shoal in pursuit of a large flight of birds, which were gone before they could land. They walked a considerable way, and saw several natives spearing fish, who retired as they approached. Captain Court went on shore to-take the meridian altitude. He made the latitude 19 48' 30". N. The refraction was so great, that it is almost impossible to take a true observation.

The Emir Mohammed's man came on board in the afternoon, with the Sheik of the village, who rode to the water's edge on a very fine camel. A man came down with four sheep to sell, but it was impossible to purchase them, as he even refused two dollars each. The Sheik brought me one as a present. He was a decent looking man, and was armed with a sword. I gave him two dollars and some tobacco, with which he was well satisfied, though they seem to have little knowledge of the value of money. It was extremely vexatious that Mr. Bruce's assertion of blue cloth being preferred by the Be- dowee, should have prevented our bringing any white, which would have insured us a ready supply of all we wished. The fisherman came with some very fine mullet. We gave him a dollar, which he asked ; he then wanted more : we offered half a dollar, which he objected to, and at length would not have the dollar. The Sheik scolded, but he took it patiently, and insisted on more, saying, " what would you do if I did not bring you fish? you would starve !" We assured him he was under a mistake, though a very natural one for a native of a country, where fish constitutes their chief food, and where it is caught in profusion, and with facility. They have no grain of any kind : milk, and goats, and sheep, are their other provisions. The Sheik promised to assist our native in procuring sheep: the fellow wanted more money, but we objected to giving it till he had procured us something in return. It was rather calmer in the evening, and Mr. Hardy went again on board the Assaye with the boat's crew.

Early in the morning the cutter and Assaye set to work with one of the anchors, it being very moderate. One of the Europeans dived in five fathom, and fastened a hawser to the junk of the

cable. It was got up with great ease, and the Assaye brought it into the bay, when we had again the pleasure of fastening it to our bows. We saw the fisherman on shore. Pierce went *off,* and found him at breakfast on broiled fish, with his wife and family. He said he would go and catch us some, as soon as that was over. He sent a sting ray, another species, and four of the ray saw fish. Abdallah caught three new species of fish, the day being very calm. In the evening the Assaye went out again, and returned with our other anchor, which had fallen from among the rocks into the sand, and was got up with the same ease as the first; and before night we had the satisfaction to be in a safe station, with our lost anchors at our bows, and in every respect ready for sea. The man brought us some fish, for which we gave him two dollars. He begged to choose two shining ones, an evident proof of his ignorance of their value as money. Our man came from the village with two sheep, for which he had given four dollars. He restored the rest, saying that he could procure no more for money, as the natives did not want it; but that with white cloth, we might have procured plenty. I made him take a piece of Lucknow chintz as a present to the Sheik, and desired him to request he would assist us in the purchase of some cattle. The weather was much warmer.

The next was so fine a morning that we began at four to weigh our sheet anchor, but it stuck so fast that we were not off till seven, leaving our man and money behind. The weather was pleasant, but we were still confined by reefs to the E. and obliged to make short tacks. We were alarmed near one of them by finding ourselves within twenty yards of a sunken rock, with which ourpilot was unacquainted. We hove to, and sent an officer in the cutter to sound, who reported that there was only three and four feet of water on it. It was not above twice the size of the boat, and no bottom close to it. We accurately ascertained its position, as it is the most dangerous spot we have discovered in the Red Sea. The shore runs N. and even a little easterly. As the wind was from N. by W. to N. E.: we did not make much way. We passed a small anchorage among the reefs close to the shore, which the pilot called Aroos, and another which he called Fadja. This is a good harbour, by his account, and lies in 20 3' N. It is evidently the Fusha of D'Anville, though with the usual error of latitude, as he has placed it in 20 15'. The wind towards evening was more favourable, and we ran on in hopes to reach a good harbour called Howie-terie. This is not mentioned by D'Anville, nor by the Portuguese, from whom he copies; which is owing to their having gone on to Arekea, a mile further north, which Don Juan de Castro describes as the most defensible harbour he had entered, and as being above two miles long and one wide. Nothing can be more accurate than their description of the coast, as rising into hills and tumuli, with the mountains behind. These elevations are of most singular forms, and rise out of the level Te- hama in an abrupt manner. During the former part of the day the country was a little wooded, but afterwards it had a most barren appearance. At sun-set the pilot could distinguish none of his marks by which to enter the harbour; we were therefore obliged to make the best choice among evils, and work all night, as there was no possibility of anchoring. By his watch Captain Court regulated the tacks, and we were assisted by a fine

moon, and by the calmness of the night. We stood off and on, till twelve, when we lay to, lest we should reach a part of the channel where the pilot said there were sunken rocks. Providentially it was moderate all night, and we met with no accident. In a channel unknown to us, only three miles wide, of which by night the pilot was equally ignorant, with rocks and shoals around us, as far as we could see, our situation was certainly alarming. We all felt it so, and Captain Court never quitted the deck till we lay to, and then only for short intervals. All the crew were kept on deck the whole night.

We had, as usual, the morning breeze from the land, but towards nine it fell calm. We were among the shoals and rocks, of which the pilot was last night afraid. We passed by a sunken one as bad as that of yesterday : on others, there was sufficient water, and close to them sixteen fathom, hard sand ; the next cast, no bottom, seventy fathom. At twelve we were in latitude 20 11' 23" ; we could see Howie-terie, and by our bearings ascertained that it was in 20 10' 38". Arekea was also in sight, which is erroneously stated by D'Anville to be in 20 32', though its real latitude is $0 11'; a greater mistake than he has yet made, and for which he cannot blame the original Portuguese authors, who have not given its latitude, but only mentioned its distance from Suakin. Beyond was a lofty mountain which we named Tridactylos, from having at first mistaken it for the Pentadactylos of Pliny : hitherto, however, only three peaks had appeared. It continued calm till two, when a light breeze sprung up from the southward of east. We experienced during the calm, a current against us, of about a mile an, hour; the breeze gradually freshened, and cameround to the southward. The passage continued narrow, and very dangerous, from the numerous shoals. We had once soundings in ten fathom, mud, with the shoals so narrow and close, that we clewed up to let go our anchor; but the pilot persuaded us to go on for the anchorage of Salaka which we reached by five, after passing a bar of rocks in 2-$ fathom, with less on either side. When in, we had ten fathom mud, but not sufficient room to swing with safety. The anchorage was open to the southward, but protected by a spit of low sand on the other sides. It was far more dangerous than Lent Bay; but we had no remedy. It blew fresh, with a little rain in the evening from the south.

In the night it blew a gale from the south for a short time, and obliged us to let go our sheet anchor. Towards morning the wind came round to the west of south, and we hove up two anchors ; but before we could get out, the wind came round to the S. E. and prevented our moving It was so truly vexatious to see four dows sail by us about eleven, with a fair wind, while we were fast in a pound, that in a splenetic fit I gave it the name of Mousetrap Bay. Salaka lies in lat. 20 28', which differs from D'Anville about the same number of miles as usual. In the evening the wind came round off shore. I got some dead specimens of very fine shells.

It was moderate all night. We swung round with our stern over the rocks in three fathom, and not a hundred yards from us had a quarter less one. It was cloudy and hazy. The old pilot, as well as ourselves, expected from the appearance that we should have a fresh wind; but our situation was so dangerous, from not being able to give the ship a sufficient scope of cable, that CaptainCourt determined to try to beat to Macowar which appeared from the mast head to be a fine harbour, distant about ten miles. We had not cleared the rocks half an hour before the gale began to freshen, and by eight blew so hard, as to put an end to all hopes of our reaching Macowar. The shoals were so numerous around us, that we were in danger every tack, and once were obliged to wear ship to save us from a reef that was but a few yards ahead. To return to Salaka was impossible, and would have been madness had it not been so, as we could expect nothing there but to be driven on the rocks. Captain Court was therefore under the necessity of trying to make Howie-terie, which the pilot said was an excellent port. We had double-reefed topsails close to the cap, yet went six knots, with a very heavy swell. Our old pilot very ably conducted us through a labyrinth of shoals, and by nine we were in a safe channel.

It was a most mortifying circumstance to be driven back, so near the completion of our labours ; for at Macowar the open sea commences, and we. should have had only the usual difficulties of navigation to contend with. Providence had singularly interfered in confining us at Salaka while the wind was fair. Had we been less impatient, and rested at Arekea, we should the preceding day have run the whole way with ease. However, I was resigned and satisfied. We had been deterred by no dangers, or inconveniencies however great from prosecuting the voyage: we had been for some time without bread ; we had not two days flour or rice, and eould procure no live stock except sheep, which will not live long on ship board with the provisions we could give them. Our seamen had nothing but juwarry and salt meat, and of the former

VOL. II. X

scarcely sufficient for sixteen days ; the spirits were very likely to be out before a fresh supply could be obtained; and, owing to the leaking of Cue casks, there was not more than three weeks' water on board. The delay of being driven back eighteen miles, with almost a certainty of the She- maul's continuing to blow against us for some days, made it necessary to consider what place we should look to for supplies. Captain Court suggested that the water and juwarry could be replaced at Suakin, and that we could then go out into the main channel at Howie; but, on considering the deficit of other articles for the crew; that no rice, flour, poultry, or vegetables, could be procured for ourselves : articles, which the shattered state of my own health rendered not luxuries, but necessaries ; considering also that the ship was deficient in ballast; and though better from having put her guns in the hold, yet still crank ; I determined to return to Mocha, where every thing could be had that she required, and then try to beat up to Cosseir. I was also inclined to this decision, by the dangers we had expe- riencedin Suakin harbour, and the probability, that now the northerly winds were certainly set in, we might be detailed there on wretched food, as long as we should be by the additional voyage to Mocha. I therefore gave the necessaiy directions to Captain Court. Our dow had come into Salaka the night before : by her we learned that the boy we left at Sheik Baroud had gone on to Macowar. We knew that he would be disappointed, but he had ten dollars to console himself. Our dow did not attempt to move. It blew a very fresh gale, and we reached Sheik Baroud before dark.

It was a very great mortification to me to be thus obliged to abandon myi voyage of discovery, at *the*moment when our difficulties were so nearly ended; for had we once got out into the open sea, we should have been able to run over to Jidda, where supplies could be procured: for this, the Shemaul would have been a fair wind. Every important object had, however, been attained respecting the passage within the shoals, from Suakin to Macowar, a passage which no vessel will probably again attempt, till an extensive trade shall have taken place in the Red Sea, when, probably, the advantages it holds forth of smooth water and occasional land and sea breezes, may cause it to be navigated by small vessels in the adverse monsoon. I think that a vessel with oars would, at such seasons, find it infinitely preferable to the open sea, as was the case with the fleet of Don Stephano de Gama, to the account of whose voyage by Don Juan de Castro I have so frequently had occasion to refer. Had there been any doubt of there being a free communication from this passage to the open sea near to Salaka, after the account of the Portuguese navigators, it would be removed by the track of Captain Court in the Panther cruizer in the year 1795, who approached sufficiently near to the island of Macowar to ascertain its position, and to perceive that the sea was free in its vicinity; thus confirming the assertions which had been made to us by our friends at Massowah and Suakin. During our unfortunate confinement in Mouse-trap Bay, frequent visits were paid to the mast head, and numerous bearings were taken of the rocky Island of Macowar, and its adjacent harbour. All these so perfectly agreed with the observations made by Captain Court on his former voyage, that I cannot but consider their identity, and consequently their actual position, as sufficiently established. If, hereafter, navigators should use thispassage, which among the moderns was first navigated by the Portuguese, and next by myself, they will receive important assistance from the chart of my amiable and able friend Captain Charles Court, to whose indefatigable exertions during a voyage of considerable danger, and perpetual anxiety, in taking bearings, and making every useful nautical observation, the public is indebted for the accurate chart of the Western Coast of the Red Sea, which I have the pleasure of laying before them. As a tribute of that esteem which 1 entertained for his private character, and professional abilities, I have called the narrow passage between the shoals from Suakin to Macowar, Court's Passage.

It would have given me particular satisfaction to have examined the port of Ma-cowar, on account of the advantages, which it has over any of those in Court's Passage, from its being accessible to vessels without their entering the shoals. It was invariably represented by the pilots as being an excellent harbour ; and that it is one, is confirmed by Don Juan de Castro, who speaks of it under the name of Salaka, for Mouse-trap Bay could never be meant by a port which received the Portuguese fleet. Water is undoubtedly to be procured there, though, in very dry seasons, it is not very good, and fresh provisions are in abundance. An amicable intercourse with the Bedowee might be established through Emir Mohammed, and the Suakini tribe, by which means, not only supplies might be obtained for any ship without the risk of entering the dangerous harbour of Jidda, but probably a very considerable trade might be carried on direct with the neighbouring Arab tribes, who are at present supplied with the coarse Indian cloths, which compose their dress, at a very high price, through Suakin, or Jidda.

t

Macowar becomes a place, of much more importance, if Monsieur D'Anville is right in his conjecture of its being near the Alaki of Abulfeda, and the Ollaki of Edresi, described by these authors as a mountain rich in mines of gold and silver. The conjecture seems more than probable from the evidence adduced by D'Anville of the concurrence of the bearings and distance between Assuan and Salaka, and Assuan and Ollaki, and of the agreement between the position of Salaka, and the mountains which, in the time of the Ptolemies, yielded such great abundance of the precious metals. The similarity of the name must also be considered as no trifling support to his conjecture, since the modern Arabian names are so frequently only corruptions of the classical names given by their authors. If D'Anville is right in his conjecture, and even an unsupported conjecture ought to be received with the greatest deference from such authority, he has also satisfactorily ascertained the position of the Berenice Pancrysos of the Egyptians as being the present Macowar or Salaka of the Arabs. I can in some degree confirm the conjecture of D'Anville by the evidence of the pilots, at a time when they fully expected we should reach Macowar, and should therefore be able to detect any falsity they might advance, that at a little distance from the village in the harbour, were some ruins, and large tanks, that bespoke ancient magnificence. I can also assert that the mountains which, from Port Mornington, have kept at a considerable distance from the shore, here again approach it, a circumstance which confirms the description of the Arabian au-

In my edition of Edresi, by Hartman, I find the name written Alalaki.

thors, and the statement of Diodorus, that the mines were situated on the confines of Egypt, and near to Arabia and Ethiopia, consequently on the shore of the Arabian Gulf.

To the question, why are these valuable mines no longer worked ? it would be difficult to give any positive answer. We find by the account of Diodorus, that it was only by the most violent exertions that the Ptolemies were able to work them; and that so dreadful was the slavery of those, whom force alone had driven to the employment, that death was considered as preferable to such a life. He also represents the veins of gold as running in an irregular manner between the strata of rock. It is probable, therefore, that the difficulty of procuring it increased; and that the heavy hand of power being removed, no people were found who would voluntarily undertake so dreadfully laborious an employment. These mines may however be again worked in some future period, since the science of modern times has so much improved and facilitated the operations of mining; but whether this is a " consummation devoutly to be wished," for the sake of the inhabitants, is, I think, a matter of considerable uncertainty.

Although I was not so fortunate as to reach Macowar, yet I was sufficiently near it to convince myself, that the accounts I had received at Mas- sowah and Suakin of its actual position, were perfectly true, and that Mr. Bruce's adventures at, and near it, were complete romances. I confess that I always had some doubts in my mind respecting his voyage from Cosseir, from the absurdity of the account he gives of his taking a prodigious mat sail, distended by the wind, then blowing a gale, in his arms, and yet having one hand at liberty to cut it in pieces with a knife. Norcould I more easiiy credit his finding at Jibbel Zumrud or Sibergeit, the pits still remaining, " five in number, none of them four feet in diameter, from which the ancients were said to have drawn the emeralds." That five wells should now exist, which have not been worked since the days of the Romans' holding Egypt, a period of thirteen centuries, in a country where the sand is driven about by incessant gales ; that he should find a man who had twice before visited these unworked mines situated in a desert country ; and, above all, that he should there have found, " nozzles, and some fragments of lamps," still lying on the brink of these wells, which would have been covered with sand by one single Shamaul, or north wester, are circumstances of such extreme improbability, that nothing but the highest character for veracity could induce me to believe the person who narrated them.

Had these been all the objections, Mr. Bruce's friends might have pleaded that there was no positive proof against him. He has however convicted himself,, by pretending to give us latitudes. He declares that, by his own observations, Jibbel Zumrud is in lat. 25 3'N. when, in fact, it is a place as well known as any part of the Red Sea, and is in 23" 48'. It might be supposed that this is an error of the press, were it not that he has placed the island in the same latitude in his extraordinary chart, of which I shall have to speak hereafter; and also that the account of his voyage renders a lower latitude impossible. He says, that he sailed from Cosseir with a light air on the 14th of March, and, about twelve on the 15th, was three miles from Jibbel Zumrud, For these twenty-seven hours it is impossible, with a light air, to allow him more than a degree of latitude, which, with the addition of the longitude, would amount to seventy miles.Besides, on his return, with a strong gale, Jibbel Zumrud was on his lee bow at day light, and he arrived before sun-set "at Cosseir, having run the same distance in eleven hours, which occupied twenty-seven hours with a light air: consequently the distance could not be more than seventy miles. D'Anville seems to have led him into the mistake, who places, not the Island of Emeralds, but Maa- den-el-Zumrud, or the emerald mines, in $445'.

Mr. Bruce departed from Jibbel Zumrud on the 16th at three in the afternoon, and on the 17th at twelve he *vtas,* as he says, four miles north of an island called Macowar, which he found to be in latitude 24 2' N. The asserted position of this island cannot be owing to any error of the press, not only for the same reason, of his having given the run of a degree in the twenty-one hours, but also from his stating, that it lies off the celebrated Ras-d-Anf, or Cape of the Nose, where he rightly observes, that " the land, after running in a direction nearly N. W. and S. E. turns round in the shape of a large promontory, and changes its direction to N. E. and S. W". It is evident that there is an island in the position he has given to Macowar, which is by mistake called Emerald Island in Sir Home Popham's chart, but is in fact the Kornaka of Don Juan de Castro, while the real Jibbel Zumrud is placed in its proper position, but is called St. John's island. Mr. Bruce says, that Macowar is the place, " to which the coasting vessels from Massowah and Suakin, which are bound to Jidda during the strength of the summer monsoon, stand close in shore down the coast of Abyssinia." He adds, " that arrived at this island, they set their prow towards the oppo-. site shore, and cross the channel in one night to the coast of Arabia, being nearly before the wind;" and he finishes the paragraph by the modest assertion, that " the track of this extraordinary navigation is marked on the map, and is so well verified, that no ship-master need doubt it." Not one word of this narrative can be made to agree with the islands actually in the vicinity of Ras-el- Anf; nor could any thing be more absurd than to suppose, that the dows would beat against a contrary monsoon as high as 24 2' N.; when they would have a fair wind for the port they were bound to, Jidda, when in lat. 20 38' N. That the entire description of the island, and the plan of starting from it for Jidda, is perfectly true, when referred to the real Macowar, I can, from my own information, and the evidence of the pilots, most positively assert; and the declarations of the natives are strongly corroborated by their total ignorance of the western coast above Macowar. No pilot could be found at Massowah, or Suakin, who would undertake to carry the Panther into Foul Bay, where 1 was particularly anxious to go, and look for Berenice, though they all knew the way as far as lat. 20 38'.

I think it clear from the above observations, that Mr. Bruce has represented himself, in the first place, as visiting an island called Jibbel Zum- rud, in lat. 25 3' N. though in fact, that island toes in 23 48', and afterwards as reaching another island, Macowar, in 24 2.' N. which, in fact, lies in 20 38'.

A. I think it appears equally clear that it was in possible for him to have made a voyage from Cosseir to the real Macowar, a distance of nearly four hundred miles, in the period he allows himself, from the 14th of March to the 17th, and consequently that he never did see that place, although his de-. scription of it, and also his assertion that the Arabs there quit the coast of Africa to strike off for Jidda, are both accurate.

I think it impossible to account for these errors in any other way than by considering the whole voyage as an episodical fiction compiled from the accounts of other navigators, and the information he might pick up at Jidda respecting the course of the Arab navigation; an idea which I strongly entertained on the spot, and which has been confirmed, since my return, by the observation first made by an ingenious but anonymous writer in the Monthly Magazine, that of twenty charts or drawings taken by Mr. Bruce's assistant, Luigi Ba- lugani, in the Red Sea, not one relates to the pretended voyage from Cosseir to Jibbel Zumrud. I am surprised that the same writer did not take notice of the equally remarkable circumstance, that not a single observation of latitude is to be found in Mr. Bruce's list, as taken either at Jibbel Zumrud, or Macowar, or even the island which he named after himself, though he has asserted in his voyage, that he ascertained the position of these places by the meridian altitude, and has actually given observations made at Cosseir, both before his departure, and immediately after his return to that place.

The only celebrated port of antiquity, that remains to be ascertained on the western shore of the Red Sea, is Myos Hormos, which is mentioned by the Periplus, as being one thousand eight hundred staclia, from Berenice. These, if considered as Egyptian stadia, will make one hundred and twenty miles.

Berenice is nearly in latitude 2Se'2,'J N. If therefore we calculate, as in the former case, by latitude alone, Myos Hormos must be in 25 23 N. which brings us to that part of the coast where Don Juan de Castro has laid down two ports, close to each, other, which he calls Gualibo, and Tuna; but if we measure the distance on the chart, weshall find that, owing to the promontory of Ras-el- Anf extending so far to the east, the one hundred and twenty miles will only bring us to about latitude 25 N. I have before had occasion to observe that less dependance can be placed on the distances, as given in round numbers in the Periplus, than on local circumstances mentioned in that work, or in the works of others, on the same subject. De Castro is the only modern, who has visited and described the coast from Foul Bay to Cosseir, and we must therefore refer to him, to see if there is any place, within a few miles of the latitude, that probably belongs to Myos Hormos, which will answer to the description given by the ancients of that place. It is stated by the author of the Periplus, as being *Xtpw,* a port, and not an open road, and as being on the extreme border of Egypt. Strabo calls it " *Kiva. piy^{TM},* "1 a large port, with a winding entrance, and having three islands lying off it. Diodorus speaks or a port, which he calls Aphrodites, but which seems to be the same as Myos Hormos, from the description of its being a port with a winding entrance, and as being placed at the foot of a mountain of red rock, which shone so as to hurt the eyes ; a circumstance which, by Agafharchides, is attributed to Myos Hormos, who positively declares, that they are the same port, though differently named at different times.

Such are the accounts we have received of the ancient port of Myos Hormos; and it is a coincidence of circumstances that could hardly have been expected to be noted by a traveller who did not direct his attention particularly to a comparison of what was before his eyes, with the description of former navigators, that Don Juan De Castro describes a port called Shakara as encompassed by a very red hill, and near to it another" very capacious and noted harbour, called Shawna, where, according to the report of the Moors and inhabitants, there stood formerly a famous city of the gentiles." The latter place is laid down by De la Rochette in 24.53', and the former in 25 8', either! of which would sufficiently agree with the distance from Berenice as given in the. Periplus. As the red hill is represented as beinga very large one, it might be supposed to reach sufficiently near to Shawna to have been described by the ancients, as a mark of that port, where are probably existing the remains of ancient magnificence which have have given rise to the Moorish account. But if this difficulty were removed, the circumstance of the three islands is still remaining to cause a doubt of Shawna being Myos Hormos. I can only observe, that at present there is no proof that three §mall islands do not 'exist, opposite to their harbours, and that we know of no other that will answer the description given. Strabo and Diodorus both observe, that two of these islands were covered with olive trees, and the third was frequented by sea birds. This description is so positive that I cannot admit the supposition that there might be other islands which were over-looked; yet this would be the case were Myos Hormos placed opposite to the Jaffateen Islands. A still stronger objection to this conjecture is that the coast there is perfectly open, and cannot therefore be considered as a port with a winding entrance. There is indeed a harbour formed by the cluster of the Jaffateen Islands, but the word *uiripxsivTw* of Diodorus, and TTfoxsio.Oai of Strabo, evidently prove, that these islands lay off the harbour, and were not a component part of it.

As the coast from Ras-el-Anf to Cosseir is perfectly free from hidden dangers, it is to be hoped that some future navigator will find leisure to examinethe numerous harbours which, according to Don Juan de Castro, lie within that space. If an ancient town actually exists, water must no doubt be found near it; and it is probable that there is a passage through the mountains, from the name of one of the ports, Sharm-el-Kiman, which is translated " the opening of the mountain." If so, how valuable would a port be, to which vessels could resort, for such supplies as the Bedowee can afford, instead of being obliged to lie in a miserable roadstead at Cosseir, unprotected from the S. E. monsoon, and even where water itself is unattainable, except of a brackish quality !

I submit the preceding observations, on the ancient geography of the Red Sea, to the public, with some diffidence, because the view I have been induced to take of the subject, chiefly from observations made on the spot, differs, on some points, from the judgment formed by Dr. Vincent, after a mature consideration of the information handed down to us by ancient authors ; but as in the position of the Opsian Bay, I have been already flattered by the sanction of this candid and learned anno- tator on the Periplus, I feel perfectly convinced that I am affording the highest gratification to his mind, in endeavouring, by local observations, to elucidate the work he has investigated with so much acuteness, although my conclusions may, on some points, differ from his. . ... . .

We were clear of Mirza Sheik Baroud early in the morning of March 18th. The wind was more moderate, but a great swell followed us. At twelve we were off Suakin, and sent our old pilot pn shore in the cutter. We gave him ten dollars, and three pieces of Surat cloth, being satisfied of his merit, and of his having served us faithfully. Now that we knew the dangers of the navigation, his demand of sixty-five dollars did not appear sounreasonable. Before dark we got a sight of Hurroo Riot Island, which ends the narrow passage between the shoals. We took a new departure from it, and sailed on all night.

March 19.|At daylight we were *off* Akeek. The wind was more moderate, with a land breeze in the morning, and a sea breeze after twelve o'clock.

March 20.|A continuation of moderate breezes and pleasant weather during the whole day.

March 21.|We lay to after nine o'clock last night, as we were by our reckoning ten miles from Massowah; but a current carried us beyond it. The morning was fine, but at eight it began to rain, with a strong gale from the N. W. It cleared up about ten, and we got into Massowah harbour. I sent Abdallah on shore to make my salaams to the Nayib, and to bring off the Banian. The Nayib returned civil messages, and the Banian came on board. In the course of the day we procured some fowls, but no goats, sheep, or bullocks were to be had without delay, as, the rains having failed, the scarcity was great, and the remaining stock had been sent up the country; the tanks were completely exhausted, and the inhabitants were obliged to drink the Arkeko water, which is brackish.

The Nayib sent at night a present of Habesh cotton cloth, and honey, with a message that his daughter was going to be married, who was also my daughter, as he and I were one. This was a broad hint for a present, which I could not evade; I therefore sent the bride a piece of gold tissue, and some Lucknow chintz. The native pilots so positively assured us that the N. W. monsoon had set in, and our own experience gave such weight to their report, that we were induced to abandon our intention of trying to reach Suez during thepresent season, and adopted in its stead a determination to open a communication with the Court of Abyssinia, and if possible, to send some of our party up into the country. The Banian had frequently mentioned to me that the Ras Welleta Selasse was anxious to hear from me ; I therefore delivered him a message for that chief, expressive of my wishes, which I requested him to put on paper, and send up by a special messenger to Tigr6, for which I agreed to pay him fourteen dollars, he covenanting that the man should be back at Massowah with the answer in fifteen days. He now spoke less cautiously of the political situation of Massowah, and acknowledged that it lies at the mercy of the King of Abyssinia, and could offer no resistance were he to choose to attack it, as his most forcible instrument would be starvation, by cutting off the supplies from the upper country. In fact, Massowah is only of importance from being the port of Abyssinia, and were the trade to be turned into any other channel, it would sink into insignificance. I found that my friend the Nayib had, after my departure, made Currumchund pay sixty dollars for the cattle and sheep, which he had sent me as presents during my stay: he, of course, was repaid the whole, as it was not dearer than they would have cost had they been supposed to be purchased instead of given. We were told that there were accounts in the neighbourhood, of our boat having been broken on the shore, between this place and Akeek, but that the Lascars had escaped. We could not learn the truth of this. The natives sold us fish for empty bottles. My servant went a shooting on the point which covers the north side of the harbour, and in a few hours killed six antelopes, and three hares. The night was sultry.

The Banian came again in the morning to take his leave. -We sailed for Mocha at seven, but the wind was so fresh from the E. that we could not weather the N. extreme of Valentia shoal; we therefore kept to the W. of it, in a very fine bay, about five miles wide from the Island to Ras Ge- dam. The soundings the whole way were from thirty to forty fathom, mud. Captain Court gave it the name of Annesley Bay. At half after eight we anchored close to the western side of the island in twelve fathom. An officer in the boat went out to sound, and discovered close to us a reef of rocks, which run off from the shore: fortunately the wind kept to the E. and we were safe till morning. The Assaye had gone up the bay, close to the main land, and was not in sight.

At five we weighed to get into safer anchorage. We found soundings and good bottom as we went S. along shore. We tried to pass through the channel, made by the S. extremity of the island and the main land, intending to anchor off the village, as the Antelope had done. The passage is free from all hidden danger, and sufficiently wide: two rocks are in the centre, but rise considerably above water. The wind was so fresh from the N. E. that we could make no way, and therefore came to an anchor under shelter of the S. W. point of the island. Soon afterwards Mr. Maxfield joined us. He reported that he had been nearly to the extremity of the western part of Annesley Bay; that the water gradually shoaled to four fathom, mud, when he had come to an anchor. It is certainly a noble bay from its size, from the goodness of its bottom, and from its being perfectly protected from every wind that blows in this sea. It is not surprising that the ancients preferred anchoring in it to the narrow harbour of Massowah,

where the ground *is* hard. Though the channel between the island and the mainland is sufficiently deep to prevent its being forded, yet it is so narrow, that a communication is kept up with the greatest ease. The trade that comes down from Abyssinia might easily be brought to the bottom of the bay at the southern extremity of Gedam, instead of passing along the side of that mountain. The distance would be less, as Dixan, the first town of Abyssinia, lies nearly due south of Mas- sowah, and the facilities of embarkation would be equally good. I have no doubt that the trading inhabitants of Orine brought all their goods by this road after they had removed from Massowah or Toualout; and independently of the security from the attacks of the barbarians, they might be very probably induced to remove their station by the facilities which Annesley Bay afforded them, in embarking their elephants' and rhinocefos' teeth.

At ten o'clock all the passengers, with Mr. Macgie and the boys sent to collect snells, landed on Valentia Island, to walk to the village, while the two vessels beat round to the anchorage. Captain Rudland, and my servant took their guns, and soon parted from the botanisers. We had tolerable success, as the herbaceous plants were many of them, in seed. The only trees were of the genus Mimosa, except one which I had never before seen. The southern part of the island is a cluster of small hills sprinkled with trees and herbs. We were obliged frequently to ascend by narrow winding paths, made by the natives. The rock *is* visible in every part, and is dissimilar from that of the other islands near, not having any marine productions in its composition. Water seems plentiful, from the verdure of the little valleys stretching

VOL. II. Y

between the hills to the sea shore, forming a remarkable contrast to the burnt appearance of the neighbouring country. In one place the shooters actually found a spring. Two years have now passed without a fall of rain, consequently it may be safely asserted that water is always to be procured here. The goats were numerous on all the hills. The most lofty of these overhangs the village, and its base forms a rocky protuberance within high-water mark. We named it Mount Norris, out of respect to my father, as being the highest place in the island. It was fortunately low water, and we were able to pass round it. The village then came in view, consisting of about forty round and square basket-work huts. The hills here became less, and the plain much larger, being a mile in length, with a grove of Mimosas at the end : beyond this, my servant had shot several very fine wild geese. The Dola and inhabitants of the village gave us a very civil reception, the former appropriating a great part of his house to our use, having couches in it covered with mats, as- at Dhalac. The day had fortunately been over cast, and there was a pleasant breeze ; yet a walk of four miles, continually ascending and descending, had completely fatigued me, and worn out the shoes of the whole party. We had seen a large heap of the saw-fish's saws in one of the vales ; these we sent for, and purchased for a dollar. They kill the fish for the fins, which is a large article of export to India : it finds a market in China with those of the shark, where they are used, like the birds nests, to give a glutinous richness to the soups.

I now applied for sheep and bullocks for the Panther, but was extremely disconcerted by the discovery that German crowns alone were current here,and we had only Spanish dollars. However, the Dola very kindly took my word, that I would pay for them as soon as the ship anchored. There were no sheep, but the goats were excellent, though dear; one large, or two small, for a dollar. A drove of cattle was brought for me to choose out of: they were by far the finest and fattest I had seen in the Red Sea ; for one I paid ten, for the other six dollars. As it would not have been safe to send the largest on board alive, I wished to have him killed. The owner hesitated a little, and desired to be first paid; but the Dola passed his word for me, and he was led to the slaughter. This was performed in a most unbutcherlike manner, with an old sword. They were several minutes in cutting through his neck till they reached the arteries.

As the Panther was at two o'clock too far off to give us any hopes of dining on board, we applied to our friendly Dola, who readily undertook to give us the best the island would afford. A fine young kid was killed, and delivered to his wife, who performed the office of cook, in an inner room, where we were not permitted to enter : a goose was also delivered over to her. In about two hours the whole was served up in very clean bowls of wood, and instead of a table cloth we had new mats. The good lady had also made us some excellent cakes with juwarry and ghee; pepper and salt were laid beside them. The only desiderata were knives and forks : of the former they had but one, which had killed the kid, and now was employed to cut it in pieces. It was excellently roasted ; and I do not know that I ever enjoyed a dinner more. It was nearly dark before the Panther anchored. I procured the German crowns, paid all my debts, gave my good landlady, and every one who had assisted us, presents, and returned on board after it was dark. We procured" here some ghee, which the officers assured me was better than any to be had at Massowah or Mocha. It gives me great pleasure to be able to speak so favourably of a little island, to which I must now naturally be attached. If ever a trade is carried on with Habesh, it will again rise into importance. Supplies could constantly be procured from the main land, where we saw with our glasses numerous droves of cattle, and flocks of sheep. The abundance of water renders it preferable to Massowah, and its vicinity to that place makes it better than Dhalac, while the bays are superior in anchorage to either.

It was nearly dark when we got sight of the Aroes, or Anish Islands on March 26th. The rocks, between which'and the high land is the channel, were not visible, yet, as it blew fresh, Captain Court took the bearings, and determined to stand on. We went under our topsails, Captain Court himself keeping a look out. The risk was considerable from the sunken rock, and breakers of Anish ; however, we providentially passed safe between them at eleven o'clock, when Captain Court declared he would not again venture it on any consideration. We lay to part of the night, that we might not pass Mocha, the wind being still fresh from the north.

At daylight we stood on, having had a current against us in the night. The airs were become light, and there was every symptom of a change of wind. At two we were nearly in theRoads, when it began to blow very fresh from the south. The guns had been got up, and loaded, to salute, when the first squall took us; one gun got loose and ran out, so that the port could not be shut. The ship was so crank that we were obliged instantly to take inmost of our sails; we, however, fortunately reach ed a tolerable birth. We set off in the cutter as soon as possible, and got safe ashore at some dis" tance above the north fort. We were met by Mr Pringle, Mr. Bancroft, and a new party of Americans, arrived since our departure, who all resided at the British factory, were I once again took up my residence. It blew very fresh all night, and made us rejoice that we had ventured through the Aroes, as otherwise we should have been driven back to Rackmah.

7

SECTION 7

CHAPTER VIII.

Description of Mocha.|Construction of the houses.|Fortifications.| Garrison. | Cavalry and Infantry exercise.|Jews town.|Arabian women.|Appearance of the Arabs and their food. | Government of Mocha.|Police.| Character of the Arabs resident in towns and Sedowee Arabs.|Arabian horses.|Climate of Mocha.|Mr. Salt's Tour to Moosa.| Observations on the formation of the Tehama.|Measures pursued in sinking a well at Mocha.|Foundation of Mocha.| Establishment of European Factories.|Account of the Iradt in Coffee, Gum Arabic, Myrrh, Frankincense, Gold, Ivoryt and India Goods.|The Fair of Berbera. |Possibility of penetrating into Africa.|Government of Yemen.|Account of the Imaum and Family.|Account of Sana.|Polygamy.| Kite and present state of the Wahabee power.

THE appearance of Mocha from the sea is tolerably handsome, as all the buildings are whitewashed, and the three minarets of the mosques rise to a considerable height. The uniform line of the flat-roofed houses is also broken by several tombs, which are called Kobas, after a celebrated mosque at that place, which was consecrated by Mohammed himself, and was similar to them in its construction, being a square edifice coveredwith a circular dome. On landing at a pier, which has been constructed for the convenience of trade, the effect is improved, by the battlements of the walls, and a lofty tower on which cannon are mounted, which advances before the town, and is meant to protect the sea gate. The moment however that the traveller passes the gates, these pleasing ideas are put to flight by the filth that abounds in every street, and more particularly in the open spaces, which are left within the walls, by the gradual decay of the deserted habitations which once filled them. The principal building in the town is the residence of the Dola, which is large and lofty, having one front to the sea, and another to a square, where, on a Friday, he and his chief officers amuse themselves in throwing the jerid in the manner described by Niebuhr. Another side of the square, which is the only regular place in the town, is filled up by the official residence of theBas Kateb, or Secretary of State ; and an extensive serai built by the Turkish Pacha during the time Mocha was tributary to the Grand Seignior. These buildings externally have no pretensions to architectural elegance, yet are by no means ugly objects, from their tutretled tops, and fantastic ornaments in white stucco. The windows are in general small, stuck into the wall jn an irregular manner, closed with lattices, and sometimes opening into a wooden, crved-work balcony. In the upper apartments there is generally a range of circular windows above the others, filled by thin strata of a transparent stone, which is found in veins in a mountain near Sana. None of these can be opened, and only a few of the lower ones, in consequence of which a thorough air is rare in their houses ; yet the people of rank do not seem oppressed by the heat, which is frejuently almost insupportable to an European. The floors, as well as the roofs of the larger houses, are made of chunam, which is sustained by beams, with pieces of plank, or thin sticks of wood, laid across, and close to each other. As they never use a level, the floors are extremely uneven ; but this is a trifling inconvenience to people who never use chairs or tables, but are always reclining on couches, supported on every side by cushions. The internal construction of their houses is uniformly bad. The passages are long and narrow, and the staircases so steep that it is frequently difficult to niount them. At the Dola's, numerous doors are well secured on the landing places, to prevent any sudden hostile attack. Little lime is used in any of their buildings ; a constant care is therefore necessary to prevent the introduction of moisture; but with caution they last for many years. If however a house is neglected, it speedily becomes a heap of rubbish; the walls returning to their original state of mud, from which they had been formed into bricks by the heat of the sun alone. The wooden materials very soon vanish in a country, where firing is extremely scarce, so that even the ruins of cities, which were celebrated for their magnificence in former times, may now be sought for in vain.

The best houses are all facing the sea, and chiefly to the north of the sea gate. The British factory is a large and lofty building, but has most of the inconveniencies of an Arab house. It is however far superior to the French or Danish factories, which are rapidly falling to decay. The lower order of Arabs live in huts, composed of wicker-work, covered on the inside with mats, and sometimes on the outside with a little clay. The roofs arc uniformly thatched. A small yard i\$fenced off in front of each house; but this is too small to admit a circulation of air. It is singular that these habitations should be crowded close together, while a large part of the space within the walls is left unoccupied.

The town of Mocha is surrounded by a wall, which towards the sea is not above sixteen feet high, though on the land side it may, in some places be thirty. In every part it is too thin to resist a cannon ball, and the batteries along shore are ett able to bear the shock of firing the cannon that are upon them. Two forts are erected, for the protection of the harbour, on two points of land which project considerably into the sea, at about a mile and a half from each other. An English .man of war would level either to the ground with a single broadside. There are two other batteries within the town, but they are in a still more defenceless state. The guns on all these places are useless, except to return a salute. The Arabs, when they purchased them from infidels, considered them as Sheitan, or belonging to the devil, and therefore immediately set to work to make them holy. To effect this, they with the mo'st perfect ignorance enlarge the touch-hole, till nearly the whole of the gunpowder explodes by it, which is also the way by which it very frequently enters. As, however, they have never had occasion to use these guns hostilely, they are not aware of the mischief they have done. The walls on the land side are a sufficient defence against the Wahabee, who always storm a town by means of their cavalry, and the numerous round towers have a very imposing effect on people who are totally ignorant of the use of artillery. Although under constant alarm from the Wahabee, they have neglected to repair the fortifications, and seem to consider the many small doors, nearlyon the level of the ground, as affording no facility of entrance to an enemy. Near the sea gate a part of the wall has actually fallen down, and has been repaired with a few boards and matting. The town runs, for about half a mile, in nearly a straight line facing the sea, but afterwards the walls take a circular direction inland. The space thus included is in part not built upon, and, I should suppose, does not contain a population of above five thousand souls.

The garrison, in general, consists of about eighty horse, and two hundred matchlock-men, who receive a regular pay of two dollars and a half per month, for which they provide their own arms, and powder and ball for exercise; but when they quit Mocha, they are supplied with every thing, and have four dollars in advance. There is not a vestige of discipline among them, but they are by no means bad marks-men, though they are a long time in taking aim. When on guard at the different gates, they recline on couches, with their matchlocks lying neglected by their sides; while the right hand is occupied, either in sustaining the pipe, or a cup of coffee. Their matchlocks are good, and richly ornamented with silver. This, and their crooked dagger or jambea, are their chief pride; and it requires the most rigid economy for several years, to enable a young Arab to provide himself with them. The troops attend the Dola every Friday to the great mosque, and afterwards exercise in the front of his house. I was present several times to see the infantry fire three vollies, which they do with ball cartridge, or at least ought to do, though I suspect economy induces them frequently to leave out the ball. Before they fire, they throw themselves into loose disorder ; a plan which the Dola strongly justified to Mr. Pringle,

when he waited on him to announce the late glorious victories of the British in the east. On that occasion he fairly told him, that he was very much surprised our soldiers ever gained a victory, disciplined as they were, " Why," said he, " your men are all drawn up in a row, so that any man may be distinguished by a person who has an enmity to him, and be shot immediately; whereas my men, by standing in disorder, and continually changing place, cannot be known." The ball that they use is small, and ill formed, so that, at the respectful distance they keep from each other, a wound is seldom received. As the chief Mussul- maun inhabitants attend the Dola on the Friday, as well as the soldiers, the procession is handsome, several gay streamers being carried by the horsemen, and before the Dola the green and red flags of the Imaum ; on the former of which is figured, in white, the double-bladed sword of Mohammed, which has a much greater resemblance to the figure of an European, with his head, feet, and hands cut off. The Arab dress looks well on horseback, and is composed of the richest satins and kincaubs of India. The flowing scarf, and the turban with the ends hanging low on the back, add greatly to the elegance of the dress.

Without the walls of the town are two extensive villages embosomed in groves of date trees ; the one is occupied by the Samaulies, the other by the Jews, who here carry on an extensive but disgraceful trade, in a spirit which is extracted from the date tree ; although fiery and unwholesome, it is drunk by the Mussulmauns in private. A more profitable trade is carried on by their females with the seamen; a certain degree of mystery is pretended to, but in reality the fact is known and (Connived at by the Dola, not only for the sake ofthe profits which he receives, but as being an additional inducement to the Europeans to desert and become Mussulmauns. Ostensibly any connection between a Christian and an Arab woman is severely reprobated, and, if detected, the female suffers a ludicrous punishment; her head is shaved and blackened, she is led round the town on a jackass, exposed to the insults of the populace, and at length, is driven from the place. At night, however, a dollar or two will induce one of the Dola's soldiers to conduct a Christian to those females, who exist in abundance at Mocha for the use of the Mussulmauns, and he will stay quietly at the door to protect them from intrusion. These villages are not more cleanly than the town ; and the gully, in which the river of Moosa has occasionally reached the sea, is filled with an accumulation of filth which, in a more moist country, would certainly breed a pestilence, through here it has no ill effect.

The Arabs are in general a healthy race of people, fevers being very unusual, though severe colds are common during the cooler months. Ulcers are so prevalent, that it is rare to see a person without a mark from them on the legs : this is chiefly owing to their bad treatment; they only apply a piece of wax to the wound, which is never changed till it falls off; cleanliness is indeed no quality of an Arab, either in his person or habitation. The part of his dress, which is concealed, is rarely changed till it is worn out; and it was a work of the greatest difficulty to force the servants to keep even the British factory, free from accumulations of nuisances in every part. The form is gone through, every morning, of sweeping a path across the square from the Dola's house to his stables;yet, at the same time, a dunghill is formed under his windows by the filth thrown out from his Zenana, so extremely offensive, as often to induce the Europeans to take a circuit to avoid it.

The Arabs, when very young, have an expressive, but mild countenance, and a pleasing eye. As they become men, the change is very disadvantageous : their figures are not good, and the beard is generally scanty; but, in advanced age, their appearance is truly venerable. The fine dark eye is then admirably contrasted by the long white beard, and the loose drapery prevents the meagre figure from being observed. The few women, who were visible, had rather pretty countenances, but in contrast to the males, their legs were of an astonishing thickness.

The food of the Arabians of inferior rank is a coarse grain raised in the country, juwarry, ghee, dates, and, on the sea coast, fish, which is procurable, in any quantity, with very little trouble. The higher orders occasionally had some mutton or beef, boiled to rags, and on festivals, a little pilau. The cavva made from the husk of the coffee berry, is drank by most of them several times a day, and the pipe is rarely out of the hands of the men. At the factory a very excellent table was kept by Mr. Pringle. The beef and mutton, which are procured from the coast of Berbera, and particularly from Zeila, where the Imaum has a garrison, are excellent. Poultry is in great abundance, and cheap. Sweet potatoes, chilies, onions, and water melons, are cultivated in the small gardens without the town, wherever water is procurable from wells.

Mocha, as well as the other towns belonging to the Imaum, is governed by a Dola. Formerly an Arab of high rank Was appointed to this office, but now that the authority of the sovereign is greatly weakened, it has been considered as more prudent to give the situation to a slave, who can always be removed, and from whom it is more safe to take the profits of his government. The Sheriffe of Abou Arish is an instance of the danger of appointing an Arab of the Prophet's family, who are, in fact, an hereditary nobility, that still consider themselves as intitled to all power among the Mussulmauns. He was appointed to Loheia by the present Imaum, and no sooner reached his government than he prepared to rebel, and with very little difficulty resisted all attempts to drive him out. He has now become a Wahabee, and perfectly secured his independence. The second officer in the town is the Bas Kateb, or Secretary of State. This office is always held by an Arab, who is considered as a licensed spy over the Dola. The third is the Cadi, or Judge ; and these three compose the Divan, where all public business is conducted, and where the Dola has only a vote.

The Government of Mocha is the best in the gift of the Imaum; not from the salary, which is trifling, but from the large sums which he is able to squeeze from the Banians, and foreign merchants. The present Dola was a slave of the Vizier, but in consideration of his good conduct, he has received a title from the Imaum, and, with it, his freedom. He is avaricious and tyrannical; but he has realised a considerable revenue for the Imaum, as well as secured a great treasure for himself. He invented a new method of extorting money from the Banians, by confining them in a room, and fumigating them with sulphur, till they complied with his demands. Mr. Pringle has frequently been obliged to complain at Sana of the obstructions he has put in the way of commerce, and probably he will soon be recalled, and obliged to disgorge his plunder. The Arabs have a whimsical apologue on the subject. They say, that when a Dola is appointed, he weighs nothing; that on going out of the gates of Sana he weighs a frasel; that on arriving at his government he weighs two; and goes on growing heavier and heavier, during his stay; but that he dwindles and dwindles as he returns, till the gates of Sana reduce him to his primitive leanness.

The present Cadi is a most respectable character, and I am assured that he would consider it as an insult were a fee to be offered him. The consequence is, that Mocha is in general a peaceable town, and, during my whole residence there, no act of violence took place. The police is strict at night; and if any person should be found out of his house after the Dola has retired to rest, a period that is marked by the drums beating before his door, he would be conducted to prison. Opposite to the British factory is a collection of thatched huts, which answer this purpose, where a prisoner lives as comfortably as he can do in any part of the town. At present a large number of people are confined there, who quarrelled with the vizier at Sana about religion, broke his windows, and committed several other outrages. They were originally confined in the island of Zeila, but the Dola there, finding that the violent heat of the climate injured their health, humanely sent them back to Mocha, where they still remain, without a hope of release. They are fanatics, and regularly chant their evening prayers in a plaintive, and by no means unpleasing manner.

The Arabs, in general, seem to care very little about their religion. Friday is no otherwise dislinguished, than by the flag of the Imaum being hoisted on the forts, and the troops being paraded in the square, whilst the lower order carry on their usual occupations. Money will at any time, induce an Arab to wave his prejudices, of which a curious instance occurred during my first residence at the British factory. Captain Keys had given a pig to Mr. Pringle, which the Lascars of the Antelope refused to bring on shore. Some fishermen were however easily procured, who, for the usual fee of a dollar, brought it safe to the factory. Admiral Blanket, the chief of the fishermen, attended it himself, in a state of perfect intoxication; but this was probably done to diminish his scruples in touching so unclean an animal.

A longer residence among the Arabs settled in towns, has only increased the dislike and contempt, with which I behold them. They have all the vices of civilized society, without having quitted those o? a savage state. Scarcely possessed of a single good quality, they believe themselves superior to every other nation ; and, though inveterate cowards, they are cruel and revengeful. Superstitious followers of Mohammed, they do not obey one moral precept of the Koran; and though they perform the prescribed ablutions with strict regularity, yet I never heard of a vice, natural or unnatural, which they do not practise and avow; and, though they pray at regulated times to the Deity, yet they also address their prayers to more saints, than are to be found in the Romish calendar. Hyprocrisy and deceit are so natural to them, that they prefer telling a lie, to speaking the truth, even when not urged to do so by any motive of interest. To this they are trained from their youth, and it forms a principal part of their educa- ion. As a government, they are extortioners and

VOL. II. Z

tyrants; as traders, they are fraudulent and corrupt; as individuals, they are sunk into the lowest atate of ignorance and debauchery ; and, in short, require jto be civilized than the inhabitants more of the South Seas.

The difference between this character of the Arabs, and that given by Mr. Niebuhr, may at first sight appear extraordinary ; but the difference is more in appearance than reality, as it is evident that he takes his opinion from the reception he had met with among the wandering tribes. He seems, however, to have imbibed a partiality for the nation in general, which the conduct of the Dola of Mocha, m particular, by no means justified; and he has attributed virtues to them, which I cannot admit them to possess. Whatever his reception might have been among the tented tribes in Yemen, it was neither hospitable nor generous. Many, even in that country, are charitable, but it is an outward duty of religion ; and never extends beyond their own sect. I'am perfectly ready jto concur with him in his character of the wandering tribes, who I believe, are less civilized, and have fewer vices. The virtue of hospitality, so necessary in the barren deserts which they occupy, is completely theirs; and their bravery, and strict sense of honour, elevate them far above their countrymen, who reside in cities. I should feel happy in supposing that this was owing to their Jblood being less contaminated by the mixture of slaves from every nation, a degradation from which they are preserved by their poverty; a poverty, however, that is invaluable, as it secures their freedom.

The Arabs have essentially altered their conduct towards Christians, who may now walk about the streets of their towns without being liable to in-

ault. The different events which have taken place in India, and have so conspicuously elevated the Cross above the Crescent, have struck a panic to the heart of the Mussulmaun throughout the East. It cannot be supposed that he has beheld the change without repining; but it has forced upon his mind a conviction of the superior power of the Christian, whom he hates as he ever did; but now fears instead of despising. The English have been the chief instruments in producing this change, and are therefore less popular in Arabia than their rivals, the French. Arabia was for a long time too remote from the scene of action to form any idea of the British power ; the veil was removed by the expedition to Egypt, when they were supported by the firmaun of the Grand Seignior, ordering them to destroy any of the ports in the Red Sea that did not afford them protection ; and when it was evident that they had the power to put the order into execution. Still, the neglect, or timid caution of our officers, in submitting to the insult of having their seamen stolen from them, and circumcised, in defiance of their remonstrances, prevented the Arabs from feeling our real power; and this was heightened into contempt, by the not resenting the affronts which were heaped on Sir Home Popham, who endeavoured to make his way to Sana as an Ambassador, but was obliged to return, as I have been informed by Mr. Pringle, in no very pleasant manner: though attended, when he set out, by a guard of one hundred marines, which he ought either not to have taken, or to have employed in protecting him from insult. The defeated soldiers of Scindiah at length returned in hundreds, and, after great difficulty, convinced the Dola, and the inhabitants of Mocha, that the English actually

could, and would fight: a fact which Mr. Pringle had found it impossible to make them credit.

A calm and moderate firmness would, I have no doubt, easily procure, for Christians in Arabia, every immunity and privilege which, as strangers, they could require. A single ship of war could at any time stop, not only the whole trade of Mocha, but also the necessary supplies of provisions from Berbera. This would force a compliance with the reasonable demand, that the deserters should be given up; and this, once accomplished the idea of impunity would be done away, and not a seaman would ever afterwards place any confidence in their threats. A disgraceful prohibition also ought to be removed ; a Christian is not permitted to go out at the Mecca gate, although the Jews and Banians are. This is the more singular, as the two latter are considered by Mussulmauns as inferior in character to the former, the Jews not believing in

Christ, nor the Banians in Moses or Christ, who are both revered by the followers of Mohammed.

The British factory, though one of the best houses in the town, has many inconveniencies, independently of its construction, the chief of which is its vicinity to the Dola's stables, where the asses keep up an incessant braying, particularly if any noise in the night excite their attention. The horses are, in the day time, brought out into the streets, where they are fastened by their hind legs with chains to the ground, and by the head to the wall, so that it requires some precaution to pass between them, and still more to enter the gates of the factory, from the crowd of children belonging to the stable-keepers, who demand, rather than petition for, charity. The horses of Arabia are celebrated for their superior qualities, and certainly I saw some at Mocha of uncommon beauty, particularly about the head and neck. The Imaum is the only horse-dealer in his dominions, and these were his property, being sent down to Mocha for sale. The price rarely exceeds one thousand dollars. The Arab system of riding totally destroys a horse in a very short time. He is taught only to walk, canter, or gallop, as at the menage; and when at full speed is made to stop short by means of a strong bit, which ruins his mouth in a year or two, while the force employed throws him on his haunches, and very frequently founders him at an early age. The asses are of two species; the one has a stripe.of black down the shoulders, and cross bands of black on the legs ; the other is like the Spanish, and as fine a breed; the mules are consequently very handsome.

The climate of Mocha is more sultry than any I have yet experienced, in consequence of its vicinity to the arid sands of Africa, over which the S. E. wind blows for so long a continuance, as not to be cooled in its short passage over the sea below the straits of Bab-el-mandeb. This monsoon continues above eight months in the year with such force, as frequently to render all communication between the vessels in the road, and the shore, impossible. For the three or four months that the opposite monsoon from the N. W. blows, the heat is much greater, and the airs are light. These winds extend only to Jibbel Teir; from which place to above Jidda, they may be considered as variable for the whole year, though the prevailing one is generally from the same point in which the monsoon blows in the lower part of the Gulf. Above Cosseir an extraordinary change takes place, for, thence to Suez the wind blows for rather more than eight months from the N. W. At Mocha, during the prevalence of the S. E. wind, a thick haze covers the opposite coast, but the moment the north-wester commences, the opposite mountains and islands gradually appear. The high land of Assab is visible from Mocha, as given in the drawing, although its distance was ascertained to be seventy miles, by a set of cross bearings taken from the island of Perim. This proves that there is a great degree of refraction in the atmosphere, of which indeed ve had still more positive proof, by the appearance of several other headlands at the same time, and which we knew were much too low to' be seen directly at the distance they actually were: a very singular phenomenon also occurred, which has been taken notice of by the ancients|the sun set like a pillar of fire, having totally lost its usual round form, a splendid testimony in favour of Agatharchides, who says, the sun rose iike a pillar of fire.

The country, in the vicinity of Mocha, is more dreary than can well be conceived : to the foot of the mountains it is an arid sand, covered with a saline efflorescence, and producing in abundance the common Mimosa, and a species of Salicornia, whose embrowned leaves, and burnt appearance, gives little idea of vegetation. Near the tow.n the date trees are in profusion; but their stunted growth shows the difference between the soil of Arabia, and the fertile plains of India: even where a brackish well has given an opportunity of raising a few vegetables, the scene is still cheerless, from the fence of dried reeds, which is alone visible. Mr. Salt, by the permission of the Dola, paid a visit to Moosa, and intended to have gone on to Beit-el-Fakih, but was recalled in consequence of the disputes running high respecting the renega- does. He describes the country, even there, asuninteresting, though the mountains were fine, and there were fields of grain, and other appearances of cultivation. This is owing to the river, which rises in the hills, and at one season is full of water, though it, in general, loses itself in the Tehama, without reaching the sea. Once, indeed, it found its way to Mocha, where it carried away a considerable part of the Jews' town, which is built in its usually unfrequented bed. Had Mocha not existed, and had a vessel by accident approached the coast at that time, the mariners might justly have reported, that a river of fresh water there emptied itself into the sea. Future navigators would have positively contradicted them ; and they would have been accused as liars, without having merited the title. I think it probable that the accounts of the river Charles above Jidda, and the river Frat opposite to it, have originated in a similar circumstance. By the influence of money Mr. Salt experienced a civil reception: he drew the town, of which I have given an engraving ; and also the Dola's son, who did the honours of the place, his father being absent.

The singular appearance of the flat Tehama of barren sand, extending from the mountains to the sea, has given rise to the supposition, that it has been formed by gradual incroachments on that element; a supposition which is greatly confirmed by the strata that Mr. Pringle passed through in sinking a well, within the walls of the factory, and which are as follows:

1. Rubbish of buildings, - - 8 feet,
the level of high water.
2. Clay ... - 2 ditto.
3. Sea mud and wreck, - 1 ditto. 4- Broken madrapore and shells 6 ditto. 5. Sea sand and shells, - 11 ditto.

In this measure he still persists, though the water oozes in so fast, that he has been obliged to sink a frame of wood, to keep it out. In the third measure the water was mephitic, and extremely offensive. As the depth increases it becomes less brackish, and at present one hundred pounds of water yields about one pound of salt. It is evident therefore that, at Mocha, the Tehama, to the depth of twenty-eight feet, is composed of marine productions, except indeed the clay, the position of which seems to me most extraordinary. The harbour of Mocha, formed by the two forts, and the spits of land on which they are built, is still gradually filling up. Dows cannot now lie in it; and the sea, which once washed the walls, is now at some little distance. A longer period has shown this gradual incroachment still more in the ancient harbour of Okelis, close to the straits of Bab-eKmandeb, where the Egyptian fleet could once lie, but where there is at present little more than a foot of water.

The celebrated ancient mart of Moosa was probably at Mocha, from the appropriate description handed down to us of its excellent anchorage on a sandy bottom. But if so, it ceased to exist for many generations, till the accidental residence of a hermit, and the discovery of the coffee, again brought it into notice. The history of the accidental landing of the crew of a ship, bound from India to Jidda, of the visit paid by the Captain to Sheik Shadelei, and the consequent sale of his cargo to the Arabs, who were followers df the Sheik, was narrated to me by the Hadje Abdallah, and confirmed by the Bas Kateb, to whom I applied for information: Mocha, according to these learned natives, was not in existence four hundred years ago; from which period we know no-

thing of it, till the discoveries and conquests of the Portuguese in India opened the Red Sea to the navies of Europe. The first entered it in 1513, under Don Alphonso Albuquerque, with an intention of uniting themselves with the Ahyssinians against their common enemy the Mussulmauns, but returned without having reaped any advantage. In 1538, Soolirnaun Basha, commanding the fleet of the Soldan of Egypt, stopped at Mocha, on his return from his disgraceful expedition against Diu. It is only mentioned in his voyage as a castle, and was therefore probably a place of little importance, and had a Turk for its governor. In 1609, when the Red Sea was first visited by the English under Alexander Sharpey, Mocha had greatly risen in importance, and had become the great mart for the trade between India and Egypt. The Turkish governor was, at that time, a man of prudence and liberality, so that the English traded without any injury ; but his successor, in the following year, had very different ideas, as Sir Henry Middleton experienced to his cost, who was betrayed, and kept a prisoner for some time. These circumstances were too inimical to trade to admit of its continuance, and there was only a Dutch factory at Mocha, when Monsieur de la Marveille visited it in 1708, and established a factory for his countrymen. Between that period and 1738 the English must have arrived, as, according to Niebuhr, they were there when the French bombarded the town, and obliged the Dola to pay his debts, and reduce the duties from three to two and a half per cent. Mocha was probably then at its highest state of prosperity, when the English, the French, and the Dutch carried on a regular trade with it, and by means of the navigation round the Cape of Good of Hope the expence of the freight

of coffee was math lessened, and the consumption of it in Europe began proportionably to increase. Coffee is the only article of trade produced in Arabia, and formerly the whole of this was carried from Loheia, by dows, to Jidda, and thence, either by the caravan of pilgrims to Constantinople, or, in large Turkish vessels by sea to Suez, and across Egypt to Alexandria; whence it found its way to every part of Europe. As early however as the beginning of the last century, the large European vessels began to carry the coffee round the Cape of Good Hope; which so much reduced the duties in Egypt, that the Porte sent an embassy to Sana to complain of this new system of trade, and to request that no coffee might be exported except through Egypt. The average quantity, that annually went up to Jidda, was about sixteen thousand bales till the year 1803, when a single American ship appeared, and by the great profit of her voyage, induced so many others to follow her example, that the quantity sent to Egypt was reduced nearly one half. Previously to this event, the Porle seems to have had little cause of complaint against the European merchants, as will appear from the following account of the quantity of coffee exported by them during the eight years prior to 1803.

Bales.

In 1795, 2154 ; 2100 for the India Company.

1796, 2000 for the India Company.

1797, 130 for a private merchant.

1798, 72 for a private merchant.

1799, 1866 for a private merchant.

1800, 6441; 1000 for the India Company.

1801, 1340; 716 for the India Company.

1803, -I-

The FrtAcl *vei* ift Egypt.

The Company have, according to the above statement, which was given me by their broker, taken in the eight years not quite six thousand bales of coffee, a circumstance that seems, at first sight, unaccountable, as the Americans not having then made their way to Mocha, the market remained free from competition, and coffee was at its usual price of from thirty-six to forty dollars the bale of 305lbs. net. At present a competition having arisen, by the Company's broker and the Americans bidding against each other, the price has been raised to fifty dollars ; but, at that price, above eight thousand bales have been exported direct for America, and two thousand bales for Bombay, for the use of the Company.

The actual expence at which this has been brought to market, will appear in the calculations No. I. and II. That the subject of the coffee trade might be brought into one view, I have added in No. III. a calculation of the expence of bringing coffee direct from Mocha, by sea, to England ; in No. IV. of bringing it, in dows, by the way of Egypt, to Alexandria ; and in No. V. of bringing it the same way in a vessel, hired at Bombay for the purpose.

No. I.

Calculation of the Cost and Expences of 2,000 Bales of Mocha Coffee brought to England by the way of Bombay, as at present practised by the Honourable the East India Company.

Dollars.

Dollars.

2,000 bales of 305lbs. each, at 50 dollars per bale 100,000

Commission to the purchaser,)

5 per.ct.f

Duty - - - 3 perct.r12Perct.

Cleaning, shipping, &c. 4 perct.)

Freight from Mocha to Bombay - - 22,477

Insurance on 141,500 ds. at *5l.* per cent. 7,0/5

Interest on 141,500ds.for4months,at9perct. 4,245
Cooley and boat hire, 1 per cent, on the

amount insured 1,415
Damage and waste, estimated at 2I per cent
on ditto 3,537I
Cooley and boat hire on board the vessel at
Bombay, 1 per cent. ... 1,415 52,164I
Cost on board, and ready for sea at Bombay - 152,164I
At 5s. per dollar, the local value of the dollar .$38,041 2 6 Freight on 2,000 bales
from Bombay to
England, reckoning on 382 tons for
cwt. 5,730 gross weight, at 15l. per $
ton - - - . 5,730
Insurance on 42,500l. at 10 per cent. 4,250
Interest on 42.500l. for 1 year, at 9 per ct. 3,825
Loss in weight, estimated at 7. 2d. per

cent, on sum insured - - 3,187 10 Landing charges, at 1 per cent, on ditto 425 17,417 10
Cost to the Company, when warehoused - $55,458 12 6 Or 10l. 3s. Sd. per cwt. –
The above would be the cost to the East India Company, were they to purchase the coffee themselves at Mocha ; but as they frequently prefer to enter into a contract for the delivery at Bombay, they in fact, must pay a profit to the contracting merchant.
No. II.
Calculation of the Cost and Expences of 2,000 Bales of Mocha Coffee from Mocha to America, according to the present practice of carrying on that Trade by the Americans.
Dollars.
2,000 bales of 305 Ibs. each, at 60 dollars per bale 100,000
Commission to the supercargo, 5 per et.)
t Duty - - 3 per ct. I2perct. 12,000

t Packing, shipping, &c. 4 per ct.)
Insurance on 110,000 ds. at 10 per cent. - 11,000
Freight —— 19,000
Interest on 100,000 ds. for 1 year, at 6 per cent. 6,000
Supercargoes expences on shore - - say 400
t Loss in weight, damage, &c. 10 percent on the sum
insured —— 11,000
t Landing expences, &c. 1 per cent - - 1,100
Duty in America 4 per cent on the value, which is
estimated at 93 ds. per bale, and makes 186,000 ds. 7,440
At 4,s. 6d. per dollar 167,90
.$37,786 10 Or 6l. 18. 9rf. per cwt.

The above estimate was given me by a very respectable American captain, excepting the articles marked t, which, however, must fall upon the American traders, and every other exporter of coffee from Arabia.

No. III.

Calculation of the Cost and Expences of 2,000 Bales of Mocha Coffee brought to England direct from Mocha, by Sea.

Dollars.

2,000 bales of 305 Ibs. each, at 50 dollars per bale 100,000 Commission of purchase, 5 per c t.)

Duty - 3 per ct. 12 per cent. - 12,OOO

Cleaning, shipping, &c. 4 per ct.*)*

Cost on board at Mocha, at 4. *6d.* per dollar - 112,000

$.$25,200

Freight on 382 tons, at 15*l.* per ton - 5,730

Insurance on 28.000*l.* at 10 per cent - 2,800

Policy duty on 28.000*l.* at I per cent. - 70

Interest on 25,200*l.* for 9 months, at 5 per ct. 945

Loss in weight, 10 per cent on sum insured 2,800

Landing and charges, 1 per cent, on ditto 280 12,625

Cost when warehoused in England $37,825

Or 6*l.* 185. 1()d. per cwt.

The above quantity being 5446cwt. 1 q. 20lbs.

if sold at the present price of 380s. per cwt.

would produce the sum of - - ,$103,482 2 10

I suppose this article imported for re-exportation, and not subject to any duty at our own Custom-house.

No. IV.

Calculation of the Cost and Expences of 2,000 Bales of Mocha Coffee conveyed by the Red Sea, and across the Isthmus to Alexandria.

Dollars. 100,000

16,000

8,000 bales of 305 Ibs. each, at 50 dollars per bale

Commission to the purchaser, 5 per ct.

Duty to Egypt 7 per ct. 16 per cent

Cleaning, shipping, &c. - 4 per ct.*)*

Freight by a dow to Jidda on 1,564 bales of 390 Ibs.

each being equivalent to 2,000 bales of 305 Ibs.

each, at 2l ds. per bale ... 3,910

Duty to the sheriffe, 3 dollars per bale - - 4,692

Transhipment at Jidda for Suez, 1 per cent. - 1,000

Freight by a dow from Jidda to Suez, at 2 ds. per bale 3,128

Paras. Patacs. Paras.

Landing at Suez, and por-
terage at
Factorage at Suez
Camel hire from Suez to

Cairo -
Fee of the leader of the

caravan
Weigher's fee and housing

at Cairo
Duty at Cairo
Factorage at Cairo
Porterage and weighing on

departure
Canvas wrappers, and

packing - - - Carriage to Boulac, and
Janissary
Custom-heuse dues
Boat hire to Rosetta
Landing and re-shipping

for Alexandria T
Factorage at Rosetta -
Boat hire to Alexandria
Landing and housing at

Alexandria Itt ditto 173 70
90 paras per patac, at 160 per dollar 56,981 66 32,052
Dollars 1&,782
10 per bale 173 45 ditto 78270270ditto4,692l21ditto364843 2,475 30ditto ditto
ditto52 43,010 521IS8010ditto17370X2Qditto2,0853040 120 60ditto ditto ditto695
2,085 1,04219306020 30 15ditto ditto ditto347 521 26050 30 60No.V.
Calculation of the Cost and Expences of 2,000 Bales of Mocha Coffee conveyed
from Mocha, in a Vessel hired for the Purpose, to Suez, and thence to Alexandria.
Dollars.
2,000 bales of 305 Ibs. each, at 50 dollars per bale 100,600 Commission to the
purchaser, 5 perct.')
Duty to Egypt - 7 per ct. 16 per cent. 16,000
Cleaning, shipping, &c. - 4perct. J
Freight of a vessel from Mocha to Suez and back, for

5 months, at 3,000 dollars per month - - J 0,000 Insurance on 125,000 dollars, at 7 per cent, to and fro 8,750 Expences to Alexandria, as per calculation No. IV. 7,857 Duty at Cairo 3 per cent, on the value there, 120 dollars per bale - - - - 7,200 Interest on 100,000 dollars, for 5 months, at 9 per ct. 3,750

At 4. *6d.* each Dollars 153,557

$34,550 6 6

In the estimate No. IV. no allowance is made for the risks by land or sea, or the wastage of 1Q per cent, by the drying of coffee. The Arab merchants cover this by the price, which, when 50 dollars per bale at Mocha, is at Suez 90 dollars, at Cairo 120, and at Alexandria 137.

Although three per cent, be the duty levied by the Imaum en all coffee exported beyond the Straits, yet he demands seven per cent, on all that is sent up the Red Sea, even by Europeans.

From the foregoing calculations we learn the following very important facts. That the Mocha coffee which the East India Company brings into the English market for sale, costs *$0. 3s. 8d.* per cwt.; that the Americans do actually take it to America, where it costs them only *$6. 18. 9d.* per cwt.; and that they are therefore enabled greatly to undersell the East India Company iu the markets of the Mediterranean, where the actual consumption is: but that it may be brought direct to England, in British vessels, and only cost *$6. 1Ss. Wd.* per cwt.; which being only one penny per cwt. more than it costs in America, it is evident, that it might be re-sold by the British in the Mediterranean, at a less price than it can be by the Americans, and consequently that the trade mrght be completely recovered out of their hands, were it not for the insuperable impediment of the Red Sea being within the charter of the East India Company.

It may also be considered as worthy of remark, that, with respect to the produce of Arabia, the discovery of the passage round the Cape of Good Hope seems to have been of little use : since the articles, according to the present system of trade, as carried on by the East India Company, can be delivered equally cheap at Alexandria by the old route.

Independently of coffee, the export trade of Mocha is very considerable in Gum Arabic, Myrrh, and Frankincense; which is imported from the opposite coast of Africa, but chiefly from Berbera, without the Straits, where a great fair is annually held, which begins in October, and continues till April. The first caravan is always the largest. It brings down about fifteen thousand babar of gum arabic, each 320 Ibs.: also all the

Vol. n. A A

myrrh that is consumed, about two thousand bahar. The former produces on the spot about fifteen dollars, the latter twenty-two dollars per bahar. The Frankincense is chiefly cultivated near to Cape Gardafui, and is exported from a harbour of the Samaulies, called Bunder Cassim, near to Jibbel Feel, called by the English Cape Felix, and is usually sold at about twelve dollars per bahar. A small quantity of these articles, at present, finds its way to Bombay, and thence to Europe, while the larger proportion goes up to the Red Sea to Egypt, and some is consumed in Arabia and Persia.

The Samaulies, who inhabit the coast from the Straits to Cape Gardafui, have a kind of navigation act, by which they exclude the Arab vessels from their ports, and bring the produce of their country either to Aden, or Mocha, in their own dows. Aden is so much better situated for trade with Berbera, in consequence of both monsoons being favourable for passing and repassing, that the greater part of the myrrh and gum arabic is carried to that place, where the Banians of Mocha have each a partner established, to conduct their business. By these means a monopoly is established, and the trade is loaded by them with the most enormous profits, though they profess to clear only fifty per cent. As the Samaulies claim only half a dollar freight per bahar, the expence of bringing these articles to market will be shown by the following calculations.

GUM ARABIC'.

15,000 bahars of 320 Ibs. each, at 16 dollars

per bahar, are 240,000 ds. at 4. *6d.* each .$54,000 0 0 Expences of unpacking, repacking, sorting, and

delivery, at 4 per cent. ... 2,160 0 0

Agency 5 per cent. - 2,700 0 0

Duties to the Sultaun of Aden, 3 per cent. - 1,6"20 0 0

Cost on board at Aden o$6o,4bO 0 O

Freight on 3,000 tons, at 15/. per ton.

Insurance on 6"7,200/. at *10l.* per cent.

Policy duty on ditto, at *j,* per cent.

Interest of money on actual disbursements

45,000

6,720

0 0 0 0 0 0

Aden *9* months on the sum of 60,4SO/.

the rate of 5 per cent. Duty on 42,857 cwt. at 4. 2rf. per cwt. 27-f per cent, and 8. *3d.* per cent.

Landing charges, housing, &c. &c. 1 per cent.

nts aO

0l. at

2,268 0 0

12,127

604

18 6

16" 0

Cost in the warehouse at London 0$'127,368 14 6

Said 15,000 bahars or 42,857 cwt. if sold here at the low price of 10/. per cwt. would produce

Or ...

Whereas the cost is only about
Which leaves a profit of
o$'428,570 0 0
28

8

115 per bahar.
9 9 Per bahar.

$20 1 8 per bahar.

In the above estimate I have taken the price of gum arabic, as it was in the beginning of September 1808, when the continental markets were shut. It has frequently been sold in London at 30?. per cwt.

GUM MYRRH.

2,000 bahars of 320 Ibs. each at 22 dollars per
bahar 44,000 dollars at 4. *6d.* Expences of unpacking, repacking, sorting, and delivery on board, 4 per cent. Agency 5 per cent, ...

Duties to the Sultaun of Aden, 3 per cent.

,$9,900 0 0
396

495
297

O 0 0 0 0 0

Cost on board at Aden $ 1,088 O 0 Freight on 400 tons measureme/it, each bahar measuring 8 cubic feet, at *151.* per ton - 6,000 0 0

Insurance on 12.320/. at 10 per cent. - 1,232 0 0

Policy duty on 12,400 at I per cent. - 31 O 0 Interest on 11,088/. cost on board for 9 months,

at, 5 per cent. - - 415 16 0 Duty on 640,000 Ibs. at *8d.* per Ib. 27I per ct.

and *8s. 3d.* per cent. - - 28,977 15 6

Landing charges, housing, &c. 1 percent. - 110 17 6

Cost in the warehouse at London ,$47,855 9 0 Said 2,000 bahars, or 5,714 cwt. sold at 25/.

per cwt. would produce ,$142,850, or =$"71 8 6 per bahar.

Whereas the cost is only - 23 18 6 per bahar.

Which leaves an apparent profit of

$47 10 0 per bahar.

Myrrh is frequently sold at 40/. per cwt., and I was informed by a most respectable broker that the 2,000 bahars would find a market at that price if there were no competition ; which would be impossible, as the above quantity is all that is produced. I have taken the price of September 1808.

FRANKINCENSE.

10 bahars of 320 Ibs. each at 12 dollars per bahar
are 120 dollars, at 4. *6d.* each - - $27 00

Expences of unpacking, repacking, sorting, and
delivery on board to 4 per cent. - - 117
Agency 5 per cent. - - - - 170
Duties to the Sultaun of Aden 3 per cent. - 0 1(J 2
Cost on board at Aden $ZQ 4 9
Freight on 2 tons at 15/. per ton - - 30 0 0
Insurance on 35/. at *101.* per cent. - - 3 10 0
Policy duty - - - . 050
Interest on *301.* for nine months, at 5 per cent. - 126 Duty on 28 cwt. 2 qrs. 8 Ib.
at *6s. Zd.* per cwt. 27f
per cent, and *8s. 3d.* per cent. - . 11193
Charges of landing, housing, &c. 1 per cent. 0 6 0
=$"77 7 6
Said 10 bahars or 28 cwt. 2 qrs. 8 Ib. sold
at5/. cwt. would produce 142/. 17. or $"14 5 8 per bahar. Whereas the cost is
only about - 7149 per bahar.

Which leaves an apparent profit of *$6* 1011 per bahar.

The quantity of incense to be procured being unlimited, I have only made the estimate per 10 bahars. A great quantity is consumed in Catholic countries.

The prices, at which the gum arabic, myrrh, and frankincense are stated to be purchased, were the actual prices at Berbera in 1805; but the competition raised at Mocha by the arrival of the Americans affected these articles in as great a degree, as it did the coffee, and raised the price to a ruinous height. I have not however any hesitation in asserting, that the British may, with the utmost facility, secure the trade to themselves : but if Arabia should in future be as much neglected as it has hitherto been, the trade will again fall into the hands of the Americans, who will undersell us in every market in Europe, and justly laugh at our remissness and folly.

From the fair of Berbera, Arabia draws her supplies of ghee, and a great number of slaves, camels, horses, mules, and asses; but the profit on these articles is much less than on the sale of India goods, which is the return made to the inhabitants of Africa, for the whole produce of the country thus brought to Berbera. Many chiefs of the interior, and particularly the sovereign of Hanim, who lives twenty days journey west of Berbera, send down caravans of their own, to purchase, with gold and ivory, the manufactures of India. It is much to be regretted, that the sale is at present clogged by the unreasonable profits of the Banians, which of course, greatly diminish the consumption. Were a regular trade carried on at Aden, whose sovereign would rejoice at the adoption of any plan likely to increase his small revenue, and were the profit reduced to about forty or fifty percent, the consumption would probably increase ten fold, for, at present, the Africans have no limits to their purchases of these articles, except the amount of their sales of ivory, gold, $c. The profits of the Banians would indeed be diminished, but thehonest manufacturer would be a gainer in an equal proportion.

It is a well known fact, that even in India, the muslins of British manufacture find a considerable market; and a few pieces of a checked pattern, vhich I had in Arabia, were universally admired. It is probable, therefore, that, if these were sent out to Aden, they would find a ready sale; as would, I have no doubt, our printed and quilled callicoes. The different articles of hard-ware, which are much wanted by every uncivilized nation, at present, only reach the eastern coast of Africa by the way of Bombay and Mocha, though the estimates, that I have before made, respecting the return of Arabian articles to Europe, show equally, that British manufactures could be carried to Mocha, at a little more than half the price they at present obtain.

The Samaulies, through whose territories the whole produce of the interior of Africa must consequently reach Arabia, have been represented by Mr. Bruce, and many others, as a savage race, with whom it would be dangerous to have connection. I think that this is an unjust accusation, and sufficiently disproved by the extent of their inland trade, their great fairs, and their large exports in their own vessels. A great number of them live close to Mocha, and are a peaceable inoffensive race. Some Indian vessels were wrecked on the coast between Mount Felix and Zeila; the chief immediately seized all the property, but he not only saved the lives of the crews, but maintained them till they were sent to Mocha. This might have led to a closer intercourse, had it not been for the misconduct of the commander of a small vessel, who during the Egyptian expedition, stopped at the same place, and tried to force the chief to bring water on board, without being paid for it. On receiving a civil refusal to this unreasonable request, he sent his people on shore to storm the town. The inhabitants laid an ambush, and cut them all off. The chief immediately wrote a letter to Mr. Pringle, which I saw ; in it he professed his good will towards the English, and cited his conduct towards the wrecked mariners as a proof of his not wishing to injure that nation, but stated, that it was out of his power to oblige his people to comply with the unreasonable request of the Captain, and that the destruction of the assailants was only owing to their own misconduct. I fear that this is not a solitary instance, and that on every side of Africa, the natives have occasionally had reason to consider a stranger and an enemy as the same thing.

In their persons the Samaulies are neither Negroes nor Arabs. They have woolly hair, drawn out into points, in every direction, but their noses are not flat. They are finely limbed, with a very dark skin, and beautifully white teeth. The expression of their countenance is neither fierce nor unpleasing. I consulted several of the respectable merchants of Aden and Mocha, respecting the possibility of penetrating into the interior of Africa, by the caravans, which return from Berbera, and they uniformly agreed that, by securing the friendship of one of the Samauli chiefs, and learning the language, an European might, in his own character, make the journey in safety. It would certainly however be more wise that he should pass for a Mussulmaun, but not for an Arab, a nation whom they detest. I think it probable that a trade is carried on westward from Hanim, bywhich a communication exists with the nations in the vicinity of the mountains of Komri. If so, a traveller might at length reach the sources of the Nile, by departing from Berbera, which is the position nearest to them, that is accessible to Europeans.

The riches of Yemen may be considered as solely owing to its coffee, for it is from the sale of that article, that its merchants receive the dollars in Egypt, with which they purchase the manufactures and spices of India. In former times the balance of bullion, which was remitted to this latter country; amounted to twelve lac of dollars per annum. This year it will not be above two lac, a falling off, which is chiefly owing to the increase of the Muscat merchant vessels, which, under the protection of the neutral flag, carry rice to the isle of France, and bring thence prize goods, which they purchase at half their original cost; by these means, not only injuring the regular trade of Surat and Bombay, but greatly encouraging the privateering of the Isle of France, whose inhabitants would otherwise have no means of disposing of the property they capture. It is even believed, that frequently the Muscat flag is only a cover, and the foods thus exported to Arabia, are bona fide, 'rench property. Arabia itself consumes only a small proportion of its imports, the residue, after paying a duty of three per cent, on the import, and seven on the export, is sent, by dows, to Masso- wah, Jidda, and Aden, for the fair of Berbera. On the returns of gold, and ivory, a very considerable profit is also made by the Banians, who nearly monopolise the whole trade.

The number of these Gentoo merchants, at present resident at Mocha, is about two hundred and fifty ; there are also about thirty at Beit-el-Fakih,and fifty at Zebeid. Most of them come from Jeygat, a piratical state at the entrance of the Gulf of Cutch ; they come young, and stay till they have made a sufficient property to live comfortably at home. They never bring their wives with them, from a dread of their being insulted by the Arabs. Nothing but the great profits attending their trade, could induce a person of any property to live so wretched a life; yet Devage, the Company's broker, is considered as sufficiently rich to command three or four lacs of dollars at a moment's notice. The Arabs are perfectly aware of their riches, and frequently extort money from them, particularly when about to return to India. Devage's brother, who, was, before his departure, the head of the house, escaped on board an English vessel, without having undergone the last squeeze which the Dola intended to give him. Devage, to avoid punishment, was obliged to prove, that he had been carried on board against his will. The Gentoos live according to their own laws, and show a great obedience to the chief Banian, who acts for them in all public concerns. In private life they are inoffensive and timid ; and even their religious prejudice, which prevents their destroying any thing that has life in it, is amiable. As traders, however, it is impossible to speak well of them, for no tie of honesty binds them. One merchant boasted to Mr. Pringle that, in a sale of silk, he had made ten frassels turn out twelve and a half. This, however, was after that gentleman had detected their frauds, and had procured proper weights for the use of the factory.

A very large kind of dow, which is called a Trankey, is employed in the trade between India and Mocha. These vessels have the privilege of not paying any duty to the Imaum, while a shipthat lands any part of her cargo, is obliged to pay five hundred dollars, and a brig three hundred. This prevents the vessels that come for coffee, from bringing any articles for sale, as a whole cargo would not be sold under some months, and the profits upon a few pieces of muslin or cloth, would not equal the five hundred dollars. It is however " an old custom, and cannot be changed." Yemen has probably reached its greatest prosperity, and may indeed be considered as on the decline. The coffee country is gradually falling into the hands of the Sheriffe of Abou Arish, who has become a follower of Abdul Waheb, and has opened the port of Loheia for the exportation of coffee. TheSultaun of Aden also procures a small quantity, and will probably increase his territories at the expence of the Imaum. His port is so far superior to any other in Arabia, that I cannot but believe it will soon become the mart for all that is exported, except to Suez. The rise of Mocha has been owing to accidental circumstances, which now no longer operate, and its trade will probably remove to Loheia and Aden. As the dynasty of the present Imaum may be thus at an end, I have been induced to bring down the history of his family from the time of Mr. Niebuhr, to whose accuracy on this and on every other occasion, I am bound to pay the tribute of approbation.

According to Mr. Niebuhr, in the year 1763, the eleventh Imaum, El Mahadi Abbas, reigned in Sana. His eldest son Abdallah died before him ; according therefore to the usual Mussulniaun custom, he was succeeded by his second son Ali, the present Imaum, who assumed the title of Elman- soor, on his accession in the year 1774. El Mahadi Abbas left, beside Ali, the following issue. 3d, Khassem. 4th, Mohammcd. 5th, Achmed. 6th,Yusuff. 7th, Ismael. 8th, Hassan, pth, Hossein. 10th, Abdulrachman. llth, Jachia. 12th, Ibrahim. 13th, Soolimaun. 14th, Saduc. 15th, Salauddien. 16th, Saleb. 17th, Yacoub. 18th, Sherifuddien. 19th, Shumsuddien. 20th, Abdulkerim. The present Imautn has only nine sous. 1st, Achmed, 2d, Hassan. 3d, Abdallah. 4th, Mohammed. 5th, Jachia. 6th, Ismael. 7th, Khassem. 8th, Abbas. 9th, Saiid. Achmed has three sons, Khassem, Ibrahim, and Abdallah ; while his brother Abdallah has already fifteen. It is supposed that at the death of thelmaum the succession will be disputed by Achmed and Abdallah; the former,though the eldest, is the son of an Abyssinian slave; he is rich, but avaricious, is the favourite of his father, and has great power as commandant of the military force at Sana. The latter is the son of an Arab wife, is in his manner open, in his character liberal, and consequently a great favorite of the soldiers.,.

The Imaum is, at least, seventy-eight years old, and fast approaching to dotage; he will not hear of any danger, and endeavours still to amuse himself in his sooty harem of four hundred Abyssinian slaves. The Vizier attaches himself to the party of Abdallah, though, before the Imaum, he treats them with equal respect. As the powers of the old man decay, their hostilities become more open, and the Hadje Abdallah informed me, that, during his residence at Sana, they actually drew their jambeas on each other, in their father's presence, but were separated by the Vizier. If, while disputing about the succession, they do not exert themselves to raise a force sufficient to resist the Wahabee, they will have no kingdom to succeed to. The whole disposable force of Yemen did not then exceed six hundred horse, and three thousandfoot; not a tenth part of the force that their enterprising enemy could bring against them.

Although Sir Home Popham failed in his attempt to reach Sana, Mr. Pringle, the present acting Resident, has twice visited that capital, without meeting with any insults or difficulties. He informed me that Sana is in latitude 15 20' N. and longitude 46 45' east of Greenwich, and described the town as handsomely built, and surrounded by gardens. The palace is a residence not unworthy of a prince, and a considerable degree of dignity and splendour is kept up. On his first visit he carried presents to the amount of thirty thousand rupees, in shawls, satins, muslins, and other rich articles for the harem. These were extremely acceptable to the Imaum, and Mr. Pringle's reception was consequently most gracious. On his second visit he unfortunately changed his plan, and took handsome sabres and pistols, which were by no means suited to the present taste of the Imaum. He was however very polite, and even assured Mr. Pringle, that he would issue orders that the French should receive no supplies in any of his ports. Had they actually appeared, I believe that he neither possessed the power, nor the inclination to refuse them.

The difference of climate between the Tehama and the hills of Yemen is so great, as, generally, to produce illness in those who change from one to the other. The air at Sana is cool, and, in the nights, even cold. Grain grows in abundance, and a profusion of fruit adds greatly to the luxuries of the table. A portion of these find their way to Mocha, where I have tasted apples, peaches, apricots, plums, and a variety of grapes. Of the latter, a small kind was particularly admired, which was called kismis, and had no stones.

It has been argued by Mr. Bruce and others, that polygamy is necessary in the East, in consequence of two females being born to one male. 1 inquired of the Hadje Abdallah if this were true, according to his experience; and he assured me that it was. I confess, however, that I received the information from the Mussulmauns with some doubt, as it is evidently used by them as an argument ia support of their law, which gives them the privilege of having more than one wife. Dr. Russell, who, from his long residence at Aleppo, had better opportunities of investigating the truth, not only expresses a strong doubt on the subject, but also gives, in a note, the report of a Maronite priest, who was employed in 1740, to number that nation in Aleppo ; by which it appears that there were one thousand five hundred and thirty-three females and one thousand five hundred males ; a disproportion that cannot serve as the ground for an argument in favour of polygamy. Mr. Niebuhr also gives several lists, made by the Christian missionaries, of the children annually baptised by them in India ; and here the males and females were nearly equal to each other, but rather in favour of the males ; and though in the list of those baptised in Persia there are only one hundred and nineteen to one hundred and fifty-one females, yet this difference is far from conclusive, even if it were not supposed to be owing to some accidental circumstance : a conjecture that may by no means appear improbable, when it is observed, how greatly this list differs from the others, taken in equally hot climates, and where polygamy is as common as in Arabia. Were the fact, as asserted by the Mussulmauns, to be proved, I should still doubt whether polygamy was not the cause, instead of the effect, of the birth of the supernumerary females.

It is now above forty years since a new sect started up in Arabia, which has rapidly increased, and is likely to cause a greater change in the political situation of that country, than any event since the time of Mohammed. Abdul Waheb, a private individual, born, according to Niebuhr, in El Aiane, a town of the district of Darale, in the province of Nedjed-el-Ared, has given his name to his followers, who are from him called Wahabee. This extraordinary man, for many years, studied the sciences in Arabia; and after travelling through Persia, and residing for some time at Basra, returned to his native country and proclaimed himself the reformer of the Mussulmaun religion. The province of Nedjed was at this time divided into a multitude of smaller tribes, each governed by its own Sheik. To these, Abdul Waheb pointed out the abuses which had crept into the Mussulmaun religion, particularly the worshipping of saints, and the use of spirituous liquors and other exhilarating articles. He reprobated the doctrine of the two sects of the Sunnis, with respect to the denying that the Koran was either created, or existing from all eternity, but admitting that it was inspired by God, as a guide for the conduct of mankind. However, as the greater -part of the Sheiks-were. Sunnis, he conciliated them by acknowledging the authority of the sayings of Mohammed. My good friend the Hadje Abdallah, who was avowedly a Wahabee, and was in Mecca at the time it was taken by Suud, gave me their profession of faith, which is as follows.

" There is only one God. He is God ; and Mohammed is his Prophet. Act according to the Koran, and the sayings of Mohammed. It is unnecessary for you to pray for the blessing of God on the prophet, oftner than once in you life. Youare not to invoke the Prophet to intercede with God in your behalf, for his intercession will be of no avail. At the day of judgment it will avaii you. Do not call on the Prophet; call on God alone."

These doctrines rapidly spread among the different tribes, whose power was nearly equal, and tended gradually to the recognition of a supremely controlling power in the person of the Reformer; which completely destroyed the former balance of power, and gave to Abdul Waheb a preponderating influence in the north-east part of Arabia. The Sheiks, who did not acknowledge either his spiritual or temporal power, at length united against him, and, under the command of the Sheik of Lachsa, who was alarmed for his own safety, attacked him in his native city. Abdul Waheb defended himself successfully on this occasion ; and on another, when his enemies marched against him with four thousand men. He from this time gradually extended his territories, and his faith. Sheik Mekrami of Nedjeran was one of his most powerful followers, and, according to the conjecture of Mr. Niebuhr, contributed greatly to his prosperity ; a circumstance that was confirmed by Hadje Abdallah, who met the Sheik twenty-seven years ago at Mecca, and had much conversation with him.

Abdul Waheb was too able a man to leave neglected any means of increasing the activity of his followers; obeying, therefore, the example of Mohammed, and fully aware of the influence which self-interest has over the human mind, he added to the inducements of religious zeal, the temptation of plunder, *by* declaring, that all the property belonging to those who were uncoverted, was unholy, and to be confiscated for the use of their conquerors.

Numbers, therefore, to save their property, professed themselves Wahabee before he marched against them, and immediately began to attack their neighbours, in order to oblige them to change their religion, and give up their property. By these means Abdul Waheb secured to himself the supreme power over the whole province of Nedjed, while, by his most powerful servant, Sheik Mek- rami, he carried his hostilities into Yemen. On his death he was peaceably succeeded in his spiritual and temporal power by his son Abduluziz.

I have not been able to learn the date of Abdu- luziz's accession, but he reigned till May 1803, when he was assassinated, while at prayers in a mosque at Darail, his capital, by an Arab, whose daughter he had forcibly carried away from her home many years before. The Arab had immediately sold all his property, and with a patient perseverance followed the footsteps of his oppressor, whom, at length, though his spiritual and temporal sovereign, he sacrificed to his private revenge.

During the reign of Abduluziz, the religion of his father was extended over the greater part of the peninsula of Arabia, either by the arms of his son Suud, or by his followers. Many Arab tribes of the Great Desert also recognized him as their religious head ; and even in temporal concerns, indirectly admitted his authority, by remitting him a proportion of their plunder, for charitable purposes, when they took possession of the celebrated burying place of Hossien at Arbela, and, according to their invariable practice, destroyed his magnificent tomb, so highly venerated by the Persians, and by the other followers of Ali.

The Sheriffe of Abou Arish had, as I have formerly mentioned, been appointed by the Imaum of Sana, Dola of Loheia, where he soon became in-

voi. 11. B B

dependent. The different Sheiks, who held many of the districts of Yemen, under a kind of feudal tenure, which admitted the right of the soil to be in the Imaum, but who hardly paid him any thing for it, were encouraged by the success of the Sheriffe of Abou Arish, and threw off even the appearance of obedience. The Imaum was too weak to conquer them; but they had a more powerful opponent in the Wahabee, who soon reduced the Sheriffe of Abou Arish to obedience, and to the necessity of adopting their religion, plundered him of his whole property, and then told him to go and indemnify himself in Yemen. He followed their advice, or rather orders ; and, recognizing Suud as his sovereign, carried devastation in his name, to the gates of Mocha. Beit-el-Fakih, and the greater proportion of the coffee country, are his, and Ho- deida alone prevents him from securing the Te- hama from Loheia to the straits of Bab-el-mandeb. Although this place remains to the Imaum, as a possession, it is useless ; since the Dola was obliged to burn the town, to prevent the houses from being occupied in the attack on the forts. In the latter his soldiers remained perfectly safe, as the Wahabee had no cannon; but he will probably soon be obliged to embark, and fly to Mocha in search of food, when Mocha itself must expect to be attacked.

Mecca and Medina have been so long recognized as the two principal cities of Arabia, that the Wahabee who aspired to the sovereignty of the whole' country, were particularly anxious to secure them. Galib, the present Sheriffe, is a monster of iniquity,, having scrupled no means to accumulate treasure,, and having poisoned two Pachas, and a young prince of the Maladives, who came in a vessel of his own to Jidda, on his way to Mecca. He wasof course unpopular, and his subjects by no means inclined to defend him. Even his brother-in-law, Mozeife, had so little confidence in him, that, on being sent on a mission to Daraie, he quitted his own party, and became a Wahabee. Abdu- luziz, conceiving this a good opportunity to attack the holy cities, early in January 1803, intrusted Mozeifi6 with the command of twelve thousand men, who fought several battles with his brother- in-law, and constantly defeated him. In February of the same year he laid siege to Tayif.

Galib, who had here his finest palaces and most flourishing gardens, hastened to its relief, and defended it for several days, till his nephew Abdullah secretly retired in the night to Mecca, when, conscious of the detestation in which he was held by his subjects, and dreading lest they should place Abdullah in his stead, he abandoned Tayif, having set his palaces on fire. Mozeife" immediately entered, and his followers commenced their usual devastation. Eight hundred males were put to the sword, but the harems were respected. Many houses were burned, and the whole were plundered ; but the treasure of the Sheriffe had been conveyed to Mecca with his wives and followers. All the holy tombs were destroyed, and among them that of Abdullah Ebn Abbas, the uncle of the Prophet, an edifice celebrated throughout Arabia for its pre-eminent beauty and sanctity. The grave itself, and the stone which covered it, were not disturbed. Mozeife, as a reward for his treachery, was appointed Governor. Abduluziz had no intention that Mecca, Medina, and their sea ports of Jidda and Yarnbo, should be held by any descendant of the Prophet as a viceroy under him ; he therefore sent his eldest son Suud to command the victorious army at Tayif, which marched so unexpectedly against Mecca, on the 26th of April 1803, that the Sheriffe, panic struck, determined to retire, with all his treasures, to Jidda. He effected this in the night, leaving his brother to make the best terms he could with the enemy. On the following day Mecca, for the first time since Mohammed entered it in 629, was obliged to submit to a hostile invader, who, however, strictly conformed to the terms of capitulation, and neither plundered nor injured the inhabitants. The religious prejudices of the Wahabee were greatly offended by above eighty splendid tombs, which covered the remains of the descendants of Mohammed, and formed the great ornament of Mecca. These were levelled with the ground, as was also the monument of the venerable and respected wife of the prophet, Kadija. The coffeehouses next felt the desolating zeal of the reformers. The hookahs were piled in a heap, and burned ; and the use of tobacco and coffee prohibited under severe penalties. The holy places were plundered of their valuable articles, but the Caaba remained uninjured. The Wahabee have asserted, that the veneration paid to the black stone was idolatrous; and disapproved of the ceremonies practised by the pilgrims at the stone of Abraham, which is placed near the well of Zemzem, and is supposed to have on it the mark of the Patriarch's foot, formed while he stood there to build the Caaba. Into this mark the water is poured from the well, for the pilgrims to drink. Suud seems to have justly estimated the benefits which Mecca enjoyed from the annual influx of pilgrims; he therefore acted with moderation, and confirmed the Cadi whom the Grand Seignior had appointed. He also wrote to him the following letter.

" Suud to Selim.

" I entered Mecca on the 4th day of Moharem, in the 1218th year of the Hejira. I kept peace towards the inhabitants. I destroyed all the tombs which they idolatrously worshipped. I abolished the levying of all customs above two and a half per cent. I confirmed the Cadi, whom you had appointed to govern in the place agreeably to the commands of Mohammed. I desire that, in the ensuing years, you will give orders to the Pachas of Shaum, Syria, Misr, and Egypt, not to come accompanied by the Mahamel, trumpets, and drums, into Mecca and Medina. For why ? religion is not profited by these things. Peace be between us, and may the blessing of God be unto you ! Dated on the 10th day of Moharem." This answers to our 3d of May.

On the llth of May Suud marched against Jidda ; but the delay at Mecca had given time to the Sheriffe to prepare for his reception, by bringing on shore all the cannon from the vessels in the harbour, and planting them on the walls. An attempt was made by the Wahabee to storm the town, but it failed ; Suud, however, contrived to cut off all supplies, even of water; in consequence of which numbers perished Jby thirst, in the nine days that the blockade continued ; and at length the Sheriffe was forced by the inhabitants to offer a sum of money to Suud, on condition of his abandoning the siege. The arrangements were actually made for the payment of a lac and thirty thousand dollars, when the intelligence arrived of the death of Abduluziz, which induced Suud to return instantly to Daraie, lest any rival should dispute the succession. Jidda was thus saved, and even Mecca fellagain under the controul of the Sheriffe; but Tayif, the most lovely spot in Arabia, a spot so unlike the surrounding country, that the Arabs believe it to have been a part of Syria, detached and dropped during the general deluge, still remained in the hands of Mozeife.

The richly ornamented covering for tte Caaba.

In 1804 Medina, with its treasure, which had accumulated for ages by the donations of the faithful, became a prey to the Wahabee : and the tomb of the Prophet shared the fate of those of his descendants. Jidda was again attacked, but without success, as the Sheriffe had received supplies from Egypt. Yambo fell, but was retaken on the sea side. The Pacha of Syria forced his way through the undisciplined troops of Suud, and the usual ceremonies were performed by the Faithful at the holy Caaba; probably for the last time; for the numerous hordes of the Wahabee now cover the Desert with their flying squadrons, and render a passage too dangerous to be attempted.

The Johassen Arabs, who acknowledge the religious supremacy of Suud, have occasionally entered the Red Sea, and, should they obey his call, and appear with their powerful naval force before Jidda, resistance would be unavailing, and the descendants of the Prophet would cease to reign in Arabia. The Imaum of Muscat has perished in battle, and his son is said to be under the control of a Wahabee guardian. Yemen has no natural means of resisting the vast power of her opponent, and must sink under the imbecility of her government. In the vast peninsula of Arabia, the little state of Aden alone offers any rational means of resistance to the power of the Wahabee, by the wisdom of her sovereign, and the bravery of his little army. Gratitude calls upon the British to prevent his ruin; for to them he has ever been an attachedand useful ally. During the expedition to the Red Sea, his port was open to them ; and, on General Murray's quitting Perim, the British troops were, with an unbounded confidence, admitted within his walls. On the appearance of the Jo- hassen fleet in his harbour, in 1804, while a large Surat vessel was lying there, he sent his soldiers on board to protect her from the pirates, and obliged them to put to sea, without receiving any supplies, though they offered him the half of the plunder they had already made, if he would permit them to remain. These repeated acts of friendship now call for a return, which it is perfectly in the British power to afford.

The Wahabee, conscious of their want of arms and ammunition, and fully convinced of the benefit they would receive from a trade being opened between India and their ports, have made repeated offers to the Bombay Government, of granting immunities and exclusive privileges to the British merchants, if they would establish a factory at Loheia; they would therefore willingly comply with any request in favour of the Sultaunof Aden as an ally of the British, and would, with little regret, give up an attack on a power, whom they have hitherto found capable of resisting them.

No answer has yet; been given to the applications of the Wahabee; and the Bombay Government behold, without concern, a revolution, which is again connecting the disunited Arabs under one supreme master. It is a circumstance well worthy of remark, that this has, for the first time since the death of AH, occurred at a moment, when the surrounding kingdoms of Asia and Africa are sunk into the same state of imbecility and distraction, to which they were reduced under the Romans, when the dissolute and lukewarm Christians were obliged to yield to the ardent and zealous followers of Mohammed.

Low as the power of the Turkish empire is now fallen, I do not expect that the Wahabee will completely prevail against it, unless, by a communication with Europeans, they obtain supplies of arms and ammunition, and, with them, learn a proportion of European discipline. I consider Arabia, however, as lost for ever to the Sultaun ; and, consequently, that he has ceased to be the head of the Mussulmaun religion. The order of Mohammed, that his followers should, once in their lives, visit Mecca, can no longer be performed. The sacred city has heard the dim of hostile arms, and is in possession of a Prince who denies to Mohammed that veneration which he has received for twelve hundred years. His descendants will soon cease to reign ; and although the Koran may be revered for a longer period throughout a portion of Asia, the mighty fabric of Islamism must be considered as having passed away, from the moment that Suud entered Mecca on the 27th of April, 1803.

8

SECTION 8

CHAPTER IX.

Proceedings at Mocha during my absence.\Massacre of the officers of the Alert Jby the Arab crew.\Sureeyand condemnation of the Assaye.\Disputes with the Do/a. | Captain Court's survey of the Straits of Bab-el-mandeb and the neighbouring islands.\Incorrectness of Sir Home Popham's chart.\Observations on the Factory.\Preparations for the visit to Abyssinia.\ Departure of Mr. Salt, Captain Rud- land, Mr. Carter and their attendants for Abyssinia.\Arrival of Captain Barton from Suez.\Conduct of the Americans.\Incursions of the Wahabee.\Alarm at Mocha.\Conduct of the Do/a.\Arrival of two vessels under Seid Mohammed Akil from the Isle of France.\Departure from Mocha.\Visit to Ait.\Arrival at Massowah.\Return of Mr. Salt with the Baharnegash,

ON my return to Mocha, it was with very great pain I discovered that an unfortunate attachment to spirituous liquors, brought on originally by the solitude of the Factory, had so greatly gained on Mr. Pringle, that, instead of conducting himself with the prudence and discretion, which had heretofore conciliated the natives, and given respecta bility to the British character, he had, during myabsence, thrown every thing into confusion, and was on the worst of terms with Devage and the Dola.

Soon after my departure, a letter was received by Mr. Pringle from the Nakib, or native chief, of Macullah, informing him, that he had detained in his harbour a vessel which had entered under Arab colours, but which he had discovered to be English ; that the Arab part of the crew had risen on the officers, had murdered them all, and had pira- tically changed the destination of the vessel. The Nakib concluded with professions of esteem for the English nation, and desired Mr. Pringle to send some person to Macullah, to receive and take charge of the property. Captain Benzoni, a respectable Italian, who had been in the service of Seid Mohammed Akil, but was discharged by him because, as Captain, he would not take a false oath that a ship, which the Seid had intentionally run on shore to cheat the underwriters at Bombay, was lost by stress of weather, was then at Mocha, and was immediately sent down to Macullah, with a letter to the Nakib.

Mr. Pringle, nevertheless, made a bargain with art American captain, to carry him there in his way home, and followed Benzoni, who had in the mean time prepared the ship for sea, which proved to be the Alert, from Bengal, loaded with rice and piece goods. The Nakib had immediately given Captain Benzoni possession of the ship, and had assured him that he would account for the rice, which he had landed and consumed. Mr. Pringle, however, on his arrival, was seized with a groundless panic, and ran away in the night, without concluding any arrangement with the Nakib. He next proceeded to Aden, with the Arab colours hoisted below the English, to the great mortification of the Sultaun, whom he abused and threatened. The Alert had very little water, her casks were therefore landed for a supply; but in the night Mr. Pringle again moved off, leaving them behind. On reaching Mocha, he remonstrated with the Dola for his former ill conduct, and threatened to fire on the town. Fortunately he did not carry his folly so far, and he was brought to his senses by discovering, that he had neither water nor provisions on board. He was obliged to hoist signals of distress, when the Dola permitted him to receive supplies, and at length to return to the Factory.

Immediately on my arrival, the Dola, and the Banian of the Sultauu of Aden, waited on me, to complain of the conduct of Mr. Pringle, and I felt it my duty to assure them, that nothing could be more contrary to the orders of the India Government, than the whole of his proceedings. He was indeed perfectly convinced of this himself, and, as his many amiable qualities had now recovered their former influence, a reconciliation was established without difficulty: poor Devage was deeply incensed ; nor could I do more than induce him to come to the Factory on business while I was there; Mr. Pringle having, in one of his fits, struck him on the cheek with the sole of his slipper, the deepest insult that can be offered to an Asiatic, among whom it is considered as a mark of disrespect to show even the sole of the foot.

The Assaye was surveyed by the officers and the carpenters of the American ships ; who reported, that the whole of her iron-works were totally decayed, her timbers deficient in number, and together with her bows and upper works, very bad, her bottom worm eaten, and rotten, and not a

bolt to be discovered in her; they therefore declared it was impossible for her to go again to sea. It is really astonishing how Mr. Sutherland, and the committee of survey, could have reported her fit for the service of the marine, since she could not have been in a much worse state than when she entered the Red Sea. I reported the circumstances to Lord Wellesley, Mr. Duncan, and Captain Money, the new superintendent of marine; and as Mr. Maxfield was now thrown out of his command, and his crew were to be returned to Bombay, I suggested to Mr. Pringle the eligibility of their being turned over, marines and all, to the Alert, and th;t the Assaye should be broken up. This was agreed to ; and on the 2d of April, Mr. Maxfield entered on his new command, and began to prepare for sea. On the 8th arrived the Company's cruizer Princess Augusta, Captain Bennett, having on board my friend Captain Sparks, as commissioner to Macullah, for the recovery of the Alert, dispatched by the Government of Bombay, who had learned the fate of this ship, by the means of a Banian at Muscat. The owners had turned her over to the underwriters, who had appointed Messrs. Forbes their agents at Bombay, by whose authority a Captain Loan was deputed to take the command. Mr. Maxfield was of course superseded, but, with Captain Court's permission, returned to Bombay with my dispatches for the Government there, and for his excellency the Governor General. He also took rough drafts of our discoveries, which Captain Court had paid me the highly flattering compliment of dedicating to me. Mr. Hurst being an acting Lieutenant, I thought it would be pleasanter for him to return, than to lo duty with us as a midshipman ; I therefore exchanged him for an officer of the Augusta of the

name of Denton, who was reported by Mr. Griddle to be a friend of his, and of whom Captain Court spoke favourably. He turned out a fine, manly lad, who had been educated at Eton.

Captain Sparks declined settling the accounts of the Alert, with which he was by no means satisfied, the expence of bringing her up, and preparing her for sea, amounting to five thousand dollars. As he was also not quite convinced, that Mr. Pringle was right in leaving Macullah in the way he did, without settling with the Nakib, he thought it his duty to return to that place. Mr. Pringle determined to accompany him in the Augusta, he having engaged Captain Bennett to return to Mocha, and convoy the trade to Bombay in August. The underwriters had sent about ten thousand rupees in presents for the Nakib; but as it was evident he had so large a sum in his hands, Captain Sparks disposed of the articles here. I purchased two telescopes, and some pieces of muslin. I again wrote fully to the Governor General respecting Arabia, and the Red Sea, and took the liberty of suggesting that Mr. Maxfield should be sent back in a small vessel, to survey the outsid? of the shoals from Jibbel Tier to Macowar, and the coast thence to Cosseir.

The arrival of so many English had driven the Americans from the Factory; we had to regret the absence of Captain Bancroft, but certainly it was not decorous that so large a party should live at the expence of the East India Company, as they had hitherto done, even during Mr. Pringle's absence at Macullah.

Though the Dola and I were on most friendly terms, it was not possible for him to leave off his old tricks of seducing our seamen. Lynch, a Mulatto, who was formerly Captain Vashion's cook, but

who, having ran away from him, was now a seaman of the Princess Augusta, and Gardner, a marine boy, were reported this morning as being in the Dola's house. I was on the Pier when I heard of it, and returned to the Factory by the Square, Gardner scrambled over a wall, and came running towards me, followed by several of the Dola's people. He conjured me to protect him, declaring that he had no intention to turn Mussulmaun; that the night before he had been drinking in the Jews' town, and that he knew not how he had been carried to the Dola's; that on awaking he had requested to be liberated, but without success, and that Lynch had endeavoured to persuade him to stay. The Dola's servants were unwilling to use force to carry him back, while I was present; I therefore got him safe into the Factory. The Dola was a little ashamed, and pretended he knew nothing of the business. The ships sailed this day, leaving me to act as Resident at Mocha.

Messrs. Forbes having again obtained a contract from the Bombay Government, to supply them with two thousand bales of Mocha coffee, had sent pne of their confidential servants, Mohammed Ali, to superintend the purchase. The Wahabee having in a great degree cut off the supply from Mocha, Mr. Pringle determined to comply with the request of the Dola of Hodeida to send there and purchase. On Mohammed All's attempting to embark, he was put in irons by the Emir Bahar. I instantly sent to the Dola to demand his release as a British subject, and to ask by what right he prevented any of our nation from going where they pleased. He immediately liberated the man, who he said had been arrested by mistake; but added, that he had positive orders from the Imaum, not to permit any one to go to Hodeida ;

that, as he was but a servant, and must act as he was ordered, he hoped I would not be angry with him. I believe he spoke truth, and consequently felt no resentment against him ; but as I considered the Imaum's orders as a violation of the neutral privileges of the British flag, I thought it my duty to send *off* a dow to Aden, where she would certainly overtake the Alert, communicating the whole business to the Governor General of India and Mr. Duncan. It would seem, from the conduct of the Imaum, that he considered Hodeida as lost to him; or determined, in spite of all difficulties, to keep up the old custom of not permitting any coffee to be exported through the Straits, except from Mocha.

The Americans by no means felt themselves bound by the orders of the Dola. There were no less than eleven vessels of this nation in the harbour ; for, as each captain kept his destination a profound secret, they were not aware of the intentions of each other. The arrival of so many vessels raised the price to fifty dollars per bale, and only about one hundred and fifty bales a week were procurable, chiefly from Oudien, in consequence of the conquests of the Wahabee in the neighbourhood of Beit-el-Fakih. The Americans have a private agreement, by which each ship purchases in rotation, according to the time of her arrival. A captain, whose turn would not arrive these ten months, sailed to the northward, evidently to Hodeida, or Loheia. The adventurers of the present season must have found themselves in a very different situation from their predecessors; for, independently of paying nearly double the price for their coffee, as they had only money enough to lay in half a cargo, the expences of freight would bedouble also. Many had suffered even more severely, having been obliged to quit without any coffee, and to seek for a cargo elsewhere.

I do not know whether it be of much consequence, as Yemen is changing masters, that the Americans are spoiling the road of Mocha by throwing over their ballast. The evil has already- become great, for there is now no clear spot, under four fathom, and at a great distance from the shore. In another season not a ship will be able to anchor in safely. Mr. Pringle spoke to the Dola about it; but he did not seem to consider it as of any consequence.

The southerly gales moderated on the 25th of April, and gave us an opportunity of getting fresh ballast on board the Panther, preparatory to her going to the Straits of Bab-el-mandeb, which I wished to examine during the present leisure time.

Captain Court returned from his cruize, having completed his survey, and discovered more errors in Sir Home Popham's chart, than even the leaving out of Jibbel Anish had given reason to expect. These will appear most plainly by a comparison between the two charts; but to those who may have no such opportunity, I will only observe, that the actual distance between the Island of Perim, and the nearest part of Africa, is ten miles and a half, instead of sixteen, as laid down by Sir Home Popham; that the distance between the two shores in latitude 13" is only thirty-five miles, instead of fifty-two; and that there exists a shoal in that latitude, which narrows the channel to fifteen miles, and which is entirely omitted by Sir Home Popham. This latter error is as unaccountable, as it is dangerous; for the shoal lies in the direct course between the Straits and Mocha, andwas actually discovered, during the expedition in the Red Sea, by the Antelope cruizer, upon which she was nearly lost.

I took advantage of Mr. Pringle's absence to regulate the Factory, and introduce a reformation among the Arab servants, who are the worst in the world ; stealing every thing which lies in their way. Not half the articles issued for daily use at the Factory were actually employed. The meat sent away from the table vanished in a moment, so that our European servants could rarely get any. Sugar, flour, fruit, were fair plunder; even wine and pork were not safe from these harpies. They came in a morning just before breakfast, and, so soon as they had secured the remains, they disappeared, and returned again when dinner was ready. They waited at table, indeed, but it was only till the meat was removed, and the cloth taken away, when they divided the spoils. This, however, I remedied, by having the dishes placed on a side table till we had quite finished. Much dissatisfaction was at first expressed; but I carried the business through triumphantly by the assistance of the Dola, who directed that any servant, on my complaint, should be put in prison. Indeed, on every occasion, where the orders of his master left him at liberty, I uniformly found him extremely obliging.

The British Factory has a pleasant view from the upper windows, but the ruins of a house in front keep off the breeze from the lower apartments. The Dola's stables are also a great evil, from the excuse which it gives to his followers, to be lurking about the door, and endeavouring to seduce the seamen who come on shore, to go and drink at the Jew's town, which so frequently leads to desertion. The danger of fire is great, from

VOL. II. C C

the vicinity of these buildings, which consist of wood and mats. If once they should be in flames, it would be impossible to save the Factory and its contents, which, at some seasons, are valuable. The building itself must also be replaced by the Company, as it is obliged at present to do all repairs, paying only five hundred dollars, instead of a thousand, when the landlord took these on. himself.

If the stables were removed, and the ground on which they stand, together with that of the ruined house, converted into a garden, the comfort and respectability of the Factory would be greatly increased, and the danger of seducing the seamen diminished. But Arabia seems too much neglected; her trade is considered as of little value, if not as an incumbrance , and her rapidly rising political consequence is overlooked. The guard of sepoy s which formerly protected the gates of the Factory, is removed, and the Resident is obliged to employ Arabs in his establishment, who are the licensed spies of the Dola. Though the consequence of Arabia, in a commercial and political view, may at length force itself on the British Government, it is improbable that Mocha will continue to be the residence of its Factor, since Aden and Loheia offer infinitely greater advantages. I hope, however, that wherever her Factory be established, it will be placed on a footing worthy of the British name.

I received a letter from Currum Chund, saying that he had forwarded my message to the Ras Welleta Selasse, who had sent the accompanying answer. This was in Arabic, expressing his wish that I would come up myself, or send some one to him; but it seemed doubtful whether he had not confounded me with Mr. Pringle the Resident, at Mocha, as the address would suit either, or rather neither, of us. As, however, I considered it anobr ject of the greatest importance, as well as interest, to obtain some positive information of the state of a country, which during a century had been visited only by Mr. Bruce, I determined to send Mr. Salt, with such presents as I could procure at Mocha. Captain Rudland and Mr. Carter having expressed a wish to accompany Mr. Salt, I consented most willingly; and every thing was hurry and preparation for their departure, as the season was so far advanced, and it was necessary they should be back by the end of October to take advantage of the monsoon, which is for so short a time favourable in the upper part of the Red Sea.

On consulting Captain Court and the rest of our party, it was decided that they should go up to Massowah in the Panther, to protect them from the impertinence of the Dola of Arkeko, and to give them more importance in the eyes of the natives ; and that Captain Court might afterwards examine the north of Dhalac. Andrew, a renegado boy, who had formerly attempted to escape to the Fox frigate, was, nevertheless, permitted by the Dola to attend Mr. Salt as his servant. He spoke good English, Hindostane', and tolerable Arabic. An Arab, by name Hamed Chamie, was hired to act as interpreter, a very respectable man, born at Mecca, and for some time in the service of Mr. Pringle. When he applied to the Dola for leave, he sent Devage to me to ask who would be answerable for the Arab, if the natives put him in prison. I assured him he should have the same protection from the Panther that Mr. Salt and the other gentlemen had. With this he was perfectly satisfied. A dow was sent off with letters for theHas and Curmm Chund, announcing my intentions.

The Augusta having returned with Mr. Priugle, I learned by a letter from Captain Sparks, that as the S. W. monsoon was set in, it was unsafe to carry the ship to Macullah, which was open to that point, though admirably protected from the opposite; that they proceeded thither in their boats from Broom bay, where they anchored. The Nakib was extremely civil. He restored fifty bales of broad cloth, and other articles, to the amount of half a lac, and debited himself six thousand dollars for rice. He declared, that he had received from the ship no other goods. This was probably false, as a large quantity of blue, scarlet, and green cloth, had found its way to Mocha, where it sold for three dollars the gudge. He made a demand of five thousand five hundred dollars for the expences of Ascari and men on board. Had Mr. Pringle staid and settled with him, it is probable a much greater proportion of the goods would have been recovered, as they were not then sold. Captain Sparks considered the Nakib's conduct as altogether meritorious for an Arab. He had given the first intelligence of the ship's being there; had professed the greatest regard for the English nation; and had tried to secure the murderers. He had willingly given the ship to Benzoni, when he arrived at Macullah alone, and unsupported : he had not stolen so much as he might have done, and possibly not even so much as we suspected; for those about him might have plundered unknown to him. Captain Sparks, therefore, made him a present of the five hundred dollars balance, and they parted excellent friends on the 27th, when the Alert set sail for Bombay, and the Augusta for Mocha. The length of her voyage was owing to light airs, and strong adverse currents. At one time Captain Bennett feared he should be obliged to bear away for Bombay, which he wished to avoid, as the Augusta is a grab, and ill adapted for the heavy sea that breaks on the Malabar coast in the S. W. monsoon. Yet the Company's Marine Board have had three built; the Queen, Princess Royal, and Princess Augusta, though so perfectly conscious of their defects, that they are regularly laid up at Massagong during the rainy monsoon.

The waste of wine had been so great in the Factory, and on board the Alert, during our absence, that there was every reason to fear we should soon be totally destitute of every liquor, except indifferent spirits. By reducing ourselves to a short allowance, we hoped to have some till August, when possibly our wants might be relieved from Bombay, whither we had written to state our situation on board the Panther, and to request, if possible, a supply of necessaries for the ship, such as biscuit and spirits; the latter were procurable here only from Mr. Pringle, ata monstrous price, and the former at a still greater. Our boat was also nearly worn out, and several naval stores were wanting. Mr. Pringle wrote to one of the tradesmen to send a large assortment of things for the Factory, almost sufficient to load a vessel. However, in the mean time, we tried what we could procure from the Americans. One captain admitted he had ten pipes of Madeira on board, but said it was meant for his owner's private use, and that therefore he could not venture to sell it but at a very high price, a price that would justify his violation of orders. At length he wrote to say, that on his return it would be worth at Boston six or eight dollars per gallon, but that he would let us have a cask at one thousand dollars. The impudence of this assertion in the first part of the letter, could only be equalled by the folly of sending, at the same time, a Boston newspaper, in which were the current prices of every article at that port. I there found that London Particular Madeira was between three and four dollars per gallon, after the duty was paid. It was mentioned as plentiful, and a dull sale. Now this wine certainly was not London Particular, for I knew that ten pipes of that quality were not sent to all America in the course of the year. But even if they had, the profit was most enormous ; nearly three hundred pounds for what cost forty three pounds. Convinced that it was a mean attempt to take advantage of our situation, to which we had been reduced by entertaining his countrymen, I positively refused to have any thing to do with it.

A few days afterwards a Portuguese ship arrived direct from Lisbon. I made application to them, and offered the enormous price of five hundred dollars for a pipe of port. The captain very liberally answered that he had no wine for sale, but that he would give us all he could possibly spare, taking an order on Bombay for a similar quantity. What a contrast to the American !!! I respect a merchant; I consider him as one of the great props of our nation : but when every idea of honour and liberality is absorbed in the pursuit of profit, he becomes one of the most despicable of animals ; and if his country should adopt his principles, it must inevitably sink into insignificance. Of this, Holland has been an awful example; and if America does not take care, her decline will follow with still greater rapidity.

On the 18th a brig arrived from Suez, bringingdispatches for India, from Major Misset, the British Consul General in Egypt. In his letter to Mr. Pringle, he mentioned that two French fleets had made their escape from the ports of France, and it was feared their destination might be India. He also forwarded dispatches that had arrived from Malta. However ill adapted for the sea the Augusta might be, it was thought necessary, as she was here, to send her off immediately: she sailed at four this morning. By her I wrote to my friends in England, and to Government. The Dola had received a letter from the Imaum, approving of his having stopped Mr. Forbes's servant; it now, therefore, became an act of the Government. I laid every thing before Lord Wellesley, and hoped that he would permit me to redress the evil.

By Captain Barton, who commanded the brig, I learned that the troubles in Egypt had induced Major Misset to remove to Rosetta, but that his agent was at Cairo. He assured me that the passing to that place from Suez was as safe as it ever was. The report of there being a British army at Alexandria was false, but had originated from Lord Nelson's appearing off that place. This was a great relief to my mind, and made me look forward with pleasure to my travels in Egypt.

On the 20th Mr. Salt, and the rest of the Abyssinian party, went on board, provided with presents for the King, and Has, and with such conve- niencies for their journey as the circumstances of our situation would allow.

The dow that we had sent to Massowah, and which was to have continued there, to attend Captain Court in his survey, returned with letters from the Nayib to Mr. Pringle and Devage", and also with letters from Currum Chundto me and Mr. Pringle. In the former, beside repetitions and extraneous matter, he observed, that he did not yet wish me to send my people ; that he had not given his consent to their going : and, without his permission, who could enter Habesh ? For " Avas not he the gates of it ?" That he must consult his brothers and soldiers, and would send the result by Currum Chund, who would be here next month. Currum Chund wrote and advised me to wait till his arrival, when my messengers might return with him ; that in the mean time, he would arrange every thing with the Nayib; but that if I sent them now, the Nayib would want five or six hundred dollars for permission.

The Panther had sailed, but the wind was contrary. I sent *off* a cutter early, but by neglect the boat was not ready till it was too late. The American boat tried to overtake them, but in vain. The loss of the dow would have been a serious inconvenience to Cap'tain Court, and it was advisable he should know my sentiments on this new occurrence ; I therefore sent Unus after him with letters who would probably overtake him before he reached Massowah, and would stay with him. I stated, that it was evidently a trick, of the Dola of Arke- ko, to get money from the messengers, under the idea that they would arrive there in a dow unprotected ; that I thought, when they saw the Panther, every thing would be well; but that, if not, I recommended their urging to the Nayib, that if he were the gates of Habesh, I was the gates of Massowah ;

and that if he shut the one against me, I could shut the other, by not letting a single dow enter the place. I left it to their discretion how they should act; but said I would give no present till my messengers returned. I felt perfectly easy, knowing that Captain Court would act inunison with Mr. Salt, in any transactions which might occur. We had this morning an alarm of the Wahabee, but it proved to be only some plundering Bedowee who had wounded a man at a village close to the town. The Dola immediately set off with his horse and infantry, but the robbers had fled.

July 5.|Was celebrated by the Americans as the anniversary of their Independence. On this occasion they obtained the Dola's permission to hoist their colours on their house. Mr. Prin- gle asked the Dola if an American factory were established here, and whether the Imaum had entered into any treaty with that nation. He said no ; that the Imaum knew nothing about it; that he had permitted it for one day only. That, as a nation, they knew not America; but that the merchants here had promised to bring, next year, the proper presents from their Government to the Imaum and Dola, and to establish an American Factory and Resident. That the Imaum wished to encourage all traders coming to his port. He asked Mr. Pringle if he wished it not to be done. He said that he could have no objection to it, or to the Americans trading here ; he only wished to know if they had a Factory, that he might communicate it to his Government. I was much amused by a few merchants making promises for their Government, which they must know would never be performed. Mr. Jefferson and his party are not so fond of trade, or Massachusetts, as to put the nation to the expence of one hundred thousand dollars to serve them.

The alarms respecting an attack of Mocha by the Sheriffe of Abou Arish gained ground. The Banian at Loheia had written to Devag6 to give him notice of it, and to advise him to be on hisguard. The Sheriffe was said to have at least fifteen thousand soldiers. We had then at Mocha about four hundred and fifty, as some arrived with an escort of coffee from Oudien on the 7th, and were detained. A few more came, in on the 10th, wretched looking animals, and rather injurious than serviceable, as provisions were extremely scarce. If the Wahabee had surrounded the town, in a week there would have been an absolute famine among the comrrion people. Fruit had been very scarce, and of grapes we had had no supply during the last fortnight. The weather had been extremely sultry ; calm in the day time ; the thermometer 90 to 95; at night occasionally a strong breeze from the north. One night we had a wind as hot as at Lucknow, which drove us all from the upper apartments to the rooms that could be shut up, It lasted about an hour. Hadje Abdallah told us it was the true Simoom, which blows all' day at Mecca during the summer months.

On the 15th in the evening the Wahabee carried off seventy camels, loaded with coffee and goods, between this place and Moosa. The garrison was immediately ordered out, but returned the next morning, bringing in with them only one lame camel. The party they went after being too powerful for them to attack, they contrived to go a wrong road. Two Ascari were put in prison for cowardice.

The Dola's new soldiers quarrelled with him, and marched off. There had been no provision of grain in the bazar for some days, and the people were in the utmost distress. The American Captain Elkins, who was in Mocha last year, arrived on the 10th. He found the markets strangely altered for the worse, and knew not what to do.

He brought some pumps for Mr. Pringle, whichthe Dola refused to let pass ; a black renegade having informed him, that they were instruments used by the English for drowning a country. He said such things were never seen there before, and he must write to the Imaum on the subject.

The weather for the last three weeks had been very pleasant, the nights being perfectly cool. The wind had been chiefly west, which comes from Habesh, where the tropical rains are in all their force, and had then to pass over the sea. If it change to the east for half an hour, the heat becomes very great. It is nearly as bad from the south, there not being a sufficiency of sea to cool it after passing the burning deserts of Africa. On the 24th we had a heavy squall in the night, when our friends the Portuguese lost,an anchor.

The Dola sent above half the garrison a few days before to Moosa, to bring in juwarry. They brought thirty camels' load, which vanished in a moment. He charged three dollars and a half escort money for each camel. This is one way of living on the distress of the country. The poor people have nothing but dates and fish, and not plenty of these.

The Portuguese ship Rosalia sailed on the 26th. Captain de Costa supplied us with five quarter- casks of Port, and took an order on Bombay for the same quantity. He also gave me some oil and some sweetmeats from Rio de Janeiro. I wrote by him to my friends in Europe, to the Governor General, and to Mr. Duncan, to whom I particularly recommended all the officers. We sent by her eight hundred bales of coffee for Mr. Forbes, and took dollars to the amount of fifty thousand on an advantageous exchange to them ; so that they would be no losers by their touching here.

The Americans buy their coffee without cleaning, and some of the worst quality; what we take is good. Six ships were there at that time, and Captain Elkins assured me six more were on their passage. He made last year two hundred per cent.

The Naquedaof adowfrom Massowah said that seventeen days ago the Panther was there ; that at first the Dola made objections to the gentlemen going into Habesh, but that every thing was settled. They had agreed to pay what was customary, and he had made himself responsible for their safety. The soldiers, he added, were all ready to escort them. From this account I hoped they were on their way. It accorded too well with what we knew to be fact, to be all an invention.

July 31.IThe Dola sent to prison every dealer in grain, till they should pay him two dollars each for the active exertions of himself and soldiers, in keeping off the Wahabee!!!

On the 28th it rained so heavily as to penetrate the upper apartments, and drive us below. The Dola's stables, which were thatched, sunk under it. The lightning was vivid, and the thunder loud; a dow was struck, and some damage done near the town. It had, for three days, being extremely close in the morning, till about eleven, when the sea breeze set in. After the rain the thermometer was at 80.

On the 30th, another American, Captain Lee, arrived. He sailed before Captain Elkins, and therefore brought no news, but was so kind as to share with us his Madeira. He thought there were fourteen more ships coming here!

The Emir Bahar, who had offended every one as well as myself, had been turned out of office. The soldiers were again gone to Moosa to bring in a cargo of provisions.

The Dola had notified to Captain Lee that the Imaum had appointed a brother of Seid Mahom- med Akil, agent to the Americans, and a Banian, to transact their business, having prohibited the others from selling to them under a penalty of five thousand dollars. This was partly done to annoy Mr. Pringle, but still more to benefit himself, by the large presents he exacts from the Seids. Captain Elkins had brought this on the Americans, by his requesting that some one, besides Devage, might be permitted to buy for them. He thought they should, by having an option of brokers, get it cheaper than from Mr. Pringle, who let them have it at thirty-five dollars, instead of which it was now up at fifty-two ; and they were more exposed to suffer from a monopoly than ever. The price was not likely to fall, and the trade was exposed to ruin. The Dola sent to tell me what had been done: I answered, that I was very happy to hear it, as I disliked the Imaum, for his conduct to the English, and that this act would punish him, by ruining his trade. He replied, that he hoped I was mistaken ; but if not, it was no fault of his, as he had positive orders from Sana on the subject. I desired Captain Benzoni to ask him, in confidence, respecting Mr. Pringle's pumps. He declared, he thought them very dangerous things ; that all the brass on the inside could be meant for no good. Captain Benzoni explained to him their real use; but he said he had written to Sana, and hoped, if the Imaum bought them, that Captain Benzoni would go and put them up.

Our Suakin friend, Emir Mohammed, arrived on the 5th with letters from Captain Court and Mr. Salt, which were on the whole sa-r tisfactory. He also brought a letter from theNayib. Captain Court had been extremely civil to him, and had saluted him on his coming on board ; with which he was highly pleased. They were in great distress at Massowab for provisions. The Emir dined with us on the 5th, and brought eight of his friends, who were very little at their ease. He said he had dined with us before, and was quite comfortable; so it seemed, for he devoured a prodigious quantity. He had brought slaves and gold. Since we saw him he had been at Senaar. He told me that country was in great confusion; that there had been four different sovereigns within three years : when deposed they are put to death, as Bruce describes, by one of their relations. He said, he could not be responsible for the safety of an European, who should go with him, as none have ever travelled that way, and the people are wild. I determined to pay him every attention, to conciliate the friendship of his powerful tribe.

The Panther was in sight on the 15th to the southward, but the wind being fresh from the north, and the current very strong in the same direction, she made but little way on that day, she was obliged to come to an anchor, just as she reached the sand heads. Captain Court sent on shore letters from Mr. Salt, dated from Dixan, which gave me the pleasing intelligence of his having reached in safety that frontier of Habesh.

Captain Court landed on the 16th. On the 17th another American ship arrived, commanded by Captain Rowe, whom I had seen before. He fortunately brought some flour for Mr. Pringle, which he turned over to the Panther. Knowing how very anxious Mr. Salt must be to hear of *us,* For an account of his voyage, vide Appendix.

and wishing to write to the Ras respecting his safe return, I spoke to Unus Barilla on the subject, who offered to convey a letter from a town by Amphila, where he had a wife, without its going through any part of the Nayib's territories. It was an important object to find another way to Habesh; I therefore agreed with him, and he was .. to set off that evening.

Seid Mahommed Akil arrived, with two very fine vessels, from the Isle of France on the 24th : one is the Pigeon, an English prize; the other a country ship, the Peggy, which he purchased on the Malabar coast. The Seid is a descendant of Hossein-ebn-Ali, by Fatima, thedaughter of Mohammed, and carries on trade. He hoists a green flag with a red border. I could not comprehend him. He had a quantity of arms and ammunition on board. His captains were French, and it was said, that he had brought assurances from the Isle, that a French resident would arrive in October. Last year he was a violent Wahabee, but this year he declared himself merely a- merchant, and of no party whatsoever. He has either sold, or given to the Dola twelve short six pounders, and some shot, for a new fort which he has erected to the north of the town, and to which he means to retire in case of a siege. I suspected the ship and all that it contained to be French property, and that the Arab flag was only a cover.

I was excessively hurt by the intelligence that an American boy, who had entered in the Panther from another ship, and of whom Captain Court had a very high opinion, had run to the Dola's house. He had by an accident broken his arm, in consequence of which he had remained on shore during the last trip, and been treated with the greatest kindness. His conduct therefore was unaccountable. Captain Court applied immediately to have permission to see him, which was granted, but in the Dola's presence. On first addressing the boy, the Dola interrupted Captain Court, by observing, that he had no business to say any thing, but to put the simple question, whether or no the boy were inclined to turn Mussulmaun. This Captain Court resented in high terms, and persevered in pointing out to him the madness of which he was guilty. The old Italian renegade attempted to answer his arguments; but was instantly silenced by Captain Court in the most peremptory terms. The lad, without hesitation, consented to return to us, on which they tried to hustle him out of the room ; but the Captain declared he should go with him, and immediately quitted the house.

August 28.|We had another dispute with the Dola. A Lascar had left the ship, but was met by the Serang, who, with an officer, Mr. Denton, was conveying him to the boat, when at the gate he claimed protection from the guard, which was immediately granted, and he was rescued from the officer. I immediately sent to the Dola, representing that this Indian subject of ours was already a Mussulmaun, and that consequently the usual plea of conversion could not justify his keeping him from us. He sent in reply, " that he would protect every body, who wished for his protection, and that I might send word of it to the Government of India." I answered, " that I would do so ;" for, that I considered his answer as insolent, and such as no servant of the Imaum ought to have dared to send to the Go.vernor of India. I could only attribute the alteration in the Dpla's language, to the confidence inspired by theinformation brought by the Seid from the Isle of France.

September 1.|Devag6's dow sailed for India : by her I wrote an account of the Dola's conduct. In a conversation with the Bas Kateb, he justified the measure of taking our men, and said, that if the Governor of India wrote to them about it, they should only answer, " it was their custom, and they would do it."

Unus's dow returned; he wrote by his son a joint letter to me, Captain Court, and Mr. Pringle, representing that he had sent off my dispatches, and that the man had promised to be back by the 5th of the next moon. He, however, added, that he had promised to pay him fifty dollars, and could not return till we sent it him. This was certainly an impudent attempt of our friend Unus, as I had before paid him for the whole. I therefore told his son I would not give a penny more, with which he appeared perfectly satisfied, and no more claims were urged.

We were again alarmed by the incursions of the Wahabee, who were certainly in great force. The road to Moosa was unsafe; and why this place was not attacked, I could not conceive.

We had so many delays in passing provisions at the gate for the use of the ship, that Captain Court applied to the Bas Kateb. He declared he knew nothing of it; assured us he would speak to the Dola and Emir Bahar, admitting it was positively contrary to the Imaum's engagement, by which all provisions and stores were to pass free to the Factory and British ships. He hoped it would not happen again. The Dola was angry about the boy's leaving him, and took this method of showing his resentment. : ..

Gardner, whom I have before mentioned, and,

VOL, II. D D

another white man, nearly, fifty years of age, ran away to the Dola's. Captain Court sent to the Dola, but he was invisible, and could receive no message. On the 6th the Hadje obtained an audience, and was told by the Dola, that he had found these men so determined to become Mus- sulmauns, that he made them so yesterday. This is with them illegal, as three days are allowed ; and it is necessary that a proper examination should take place, to prove their firm determination, and, that they should be instructed in the principles of the religion they wish to embrace. Here, however, the fear of Captain Court's inducing them to'return, outweighed the Dola's sense of duty, and he violated his own laws to secure two proselytes.

Captain Court sailed on the 10th to survey a part of the opposite coast. Captain Lee and another American also sailed for Bengal, since the price of coffee here rendered any hope of profit out of the question; the cessation of the English purchases having lowered the markets only to ninety-eight Mocha dollars. The Americans get between two and three hundred bales per week. The whole quantity sold at Mocha between August twelvemonth and last August, was twelve thousand bales. I wrote to Lord Wellesley by Captain Lee, stating all that had passed with the Dola.

On the 10th all the guns were fired to celebrate the raising of the siege of Sana. We never heard here that it had been attacked. It was not the Wahabee that were beaten, but some Bedowee tribes, who inhabit the hills, and are a brave and hardy race, that have had claims on the Imaum since the time they assisted in liberating the country from the Turkish yoke. Their loss, by theDola's account, amounted to twenty killed; the Imaum's loss was not mentioned. Most people believed it all a fiction to raise money; as the Dola generally, on those occasions, levies contributions for the expence the Imaum has been at in protecting his subjects.

The weather for some days had considerably changed. It was frequently calm, with easterly .winds ; we had in the morning a southerly light air, which gradually moved to the west by the middle of the day, to the north in the evening, and round by the

E. to S. in the course of the night. These light airs and calms on the 12th, saved the town of Mocha. As I was in bed that night, I was alarmed by a fire which consumed thirty or forty thatched houses, close to the American Factory. If the wind had blown from the south or west, the whole town would have been consumed; but as it was a perfect calm, our fears were over in a few hours. Some Samaulies exerted themselves in extinguishing the fire, in order to save their vessels, which were lying dry on the other side of the wall. The flames were stopped by the stone houses, as these people drove out the window frames, and kept pouring water on the walls. The Arabs did nothing but look on, with the Dola at their head.

On the iGth another American vessel sailed with half a cargo, having no more money. Burns, a seaman, who had run away from an American, and turned Mussulmaun, applied to my servant to get him off. I consented, and Captain Barton was so good as to send his boat, and take him at night on board the brig. Thus the Dola loses his converts as fast as he gets them ; for, of nearly one hundred within these five years, there are now only five remaining. Early in the morning we had a slight shock of an earthquake ; it was single, and seemed to proceed from the east to the west.

On the 18th Seid Akil sailed to the northward; for what purpose I could not conjecture. I heard he had been proposing to some of the Samaulies to assist him in getting possession of some place opposite to build a town; but this was probably only a pretext to conceal his real intentions. He must have had some secret plans, for it could never answer to keep a vessel of eight hundred tons, like the Peggy, in the Red Sea, a whole season, for the purposes of trade; particularly as she had nothing on board but ammunition and arms. The Waha- bee dows infest Camaran, and are continually cruizing off Jidda.

On the evening of the 19th, I was taxed by an Arab, who spoke English, with an intention of taking Mocha: it was done in a laughing way, and I replied in the same manner, that it was not worth having; and that I would not have it if they would give it to me. This, however, confirmed what I had before heard, that the people in general attributed to me intentions hostile to the place.

Another fire broke out about eleven in a stone house, and partly consumed it. The wind was fresh, and had the flames caught one house of thatch, the whole bazar must have been destroyed, as it was close to it, and built of the most combustible materials. Immediately after dinner we were nearly smothered by a sand storm from the east. It was not so terrible as the great north-wester at Lucknow, but no object could be distinguished at a distance of twenty yards. It blew very fresh; a few drops of rain fell towards the end; which sensibly cooled the air. Devag6 said it was the most violent he had experienced in eleven years, during which he had resided here.

Captain Court arrived this day. having finished his intended survey. He found Antelope shoal very different from what it was laid down. Assab is no cape, but a very lofty mountain, nearly forty miles inland. A very strong southerly current ran through the larger Straits of Bab-el-mandeb.

Captain Barton sailed for Jidda with a cargo. I wrote to my friends in England, and inclosed my letters to Major Missett, to whom I also sent copies of Lord Wellesley's dispatches to Mr. Jones at Bagdad, and of the Governor of Bombay's letter to Mr. Lock, who was appointed to succeed Major Missett, but died before his arrival. I requested his assistance to reach Cairo from Suez, and recommunicated the wants of the Panther. The wind was from the south, so that the monsoon might be considered as set in. The heat was greatly diminished.

September 25.|The Dola sent me a present of two baskets of grapes. This attention, after the late disputes, I attributed to a report in circulation, that the Capitan Pacha had arrived with a strong force in Egypt, and he possibly suspected that my return and stay here, had some connection with this event. There was another fire in the middle of this day. Captain Court with his boat's crew, and the Americans with theirs, saved the town by their exertions. A large number of thatched huts were consumed, and the tower by the wicket gate was once on fire, but was extinguished : a considerable quantity of gunpowder was said to be in the building. The Dola'was not there, and seemed to care little about an evil, by which he does not suffer, but on the contrary rather gains, for he hasa quantity of poles belonging to him, which he in consequence sells at an advanced price.

From the 24th to the 28th, the winds were again northerly, but on the 28th they returned to the south. The nights had been calm and sultry ; on the same day we had another fire, which only consumed three houses, and at night a man was sent to prison, said to have been caught in the attempt to set fire to the Samaulie town. The steward of the Panther, who had been degraded on account of the deficiency of rice, ran away to the Dola's, as did the black cook of the officers, and two American seamen.

Mr. Denton, in looking for some of the boat's crew in the Jews' town, met with Gardner and some others of the renegadoes, drinking. Gardner abused him very much, and threatened others of the officers. We immediately sent to the Dola, who, in the presence of the Hadje, told the Captain of the fort, commanding the renegadoes, that if the smallest complaint were again made, he would not only put the offender in prison, but flog him severely. The American captains were refused all access to the Dola respecting their deserters, and were absolutely thrust down the stairs by his attendants. I learned from Hodeida, that the American ship was still there, that she had been in danger from the piratical dows, and that the Dola sent troops on board to protect her.

I had notice from a renegado that one of the boys ashore who assisted in packing shells, meant to run away. We sent him on board with some boxes, where we designed that he should be kept. He had no idea that we were acquainted with his intentions. During my tedious confinement, I had amused myself in employing a great number of Arabs in collecting shells for me on the beach,I paid them generally a few komassis for their trouble, and a day rarely passed without their bringing me a new species. Mr. Macgie and I had packed them with infinite labour, and I now began to send them on board. ,

The custom-house officers wished to unpack all the boxes, to which I positively objected : they could hardly be persuaded that six large boxes were filled with articles they thought of no value. They at length took a few shells out of some of the boxes to show the Dola.

We had a slight shock of an earthquake on the 2d, in the morning; it lasted about a minute, with a tremulous motion.

Mr. Macgie heard to day from Captain Barton; he had been driven back to Hodeida when beyond Jibbel Tier, by strong north-westers. The American ship was still there, but had only procured fifty bales of three hundred and seventy pounds in the last two months, and for those she paid sixty- four German crowns. She had but three hundred and fifty bales, and lost her season. The place has suffered severely from the Wahabee, but sill belongs to the Imaum. Nothing but brackish water was to be had there.

In a conversation with Seid Akil's brother, he told me that the Dola was not very well pleased with an old Portuguese who had deserted to him|He said he was of no use, and cost four dollars a month. The Seid declared that it was contrary to their books to make Mussulmauns in this way. They could never be so in reality. I replied, that the Dola was very good to pay them four dollars a month till they had learned the language, when the good ones came back to the Europeans, and the others ran away to the Wahabee or Turks3 to fight against himThe conduct of the Arabs towards me was totally changed within this fortnight; not an Arab of any consequence met me without making his salaam.

October 10.|The nights for some time had been extremely sultry, and the wind light and variable. On the festival of Sheik Abdurrab, who, by his corpse, has sanctified the island on which the southern fort is built, the colours were hoisted on all the forts, and soon afterwards, to the astonishment of all the inhabitants of the Factory, the Americans also hoisted their colours. This compliment to a Mus- sulmaun saint was novel in a Christian power ; but it was carried still farther ; for on the Dola's departing to offer up his prayers at the Sheik's tomb, every ship saluted; some with two, some with three, and some with five guns : some twice, some three times. I was too much disgusted to speak to them myself on the occasion, but on their being laughed at by some of our officers, they replied, that they did not know what the colours were hoisted for; it was the Dola's doing; and was not he master of the roads ? I should not have cared for their degradation, had I not been afraid that the natives might confound these Americans with Europeans and Christians, in consequence of which we might have shared in the contempt they appeared so anxious to acquire.

On the 11 th, at night, Fowler, whom I have before mentioned as having ran away from Captain Keys, went on board the Panther, as my servant. He was anxious to escape from the wretched life of a renegado, and applied to me to take him. As he understood Arabic, he promised to be as useful as Abdallah was the last voyage. They were equally deserters from the Company's service.There were many circumstances in his case which rendered him an object of compassion, and his conduct in Arabia was good. He was to have gone up to Sana in a few days to be presented to the Imaum. More pains had been taken with his education than were ever before bestowed upon any one. The Dola had declared that he would not lose him for a thousand dollars; it was therefore, I must confess, a particular gratification to me, to find that he was punished for his inhospi- tality.

Unus Barilla returned on the llth, without the letters from Mr. Salt. This was owing to a mistake in writing to him to be here the 15th of the moon, instead of the 15th o' f the month. He brought an unpleasant report of the Ras's being engaged in repelling an attack of the Galla, and Mr. Salt's being still at Adowah. His account was so confused, that I did not give it much credit.

On the 15th, we agreed with Uuus to accompany us up the Red Sea for one hundred and fifty dollars per month. He begged us not to apply to the Cadi for a regular agreement, as the Dola made him pay one dollar for every ten he received from, us. We hired six Samaulies to act as Lascars on board the Panther, in preference to Arabs. The wind was to-day south the first time for many days. So late a northerly monsoon had not been, known in the memory of man; generally in the middle of September it changes decidedly to the south.

On the 21 st we had another fire close to the Factory, which alarmed us so much that the next day we were pulling down all our mat buildings on the roof. They were become the less necessary, as the southerly wind had continued since the 16th, and made a difference of seven degrees in thethermometer; in the morning it was at 84. The nights were very cold.

We prepared for our departure on the 1st of November. We had grown wise by our late trip, and Captain Court had at my request laid in white Surat cloth to barter for live stock, and some better articles to give to the Sheiks or other chiefs, who might oblige us. We had also taken in snuff, which was before much enquired after.

The officers of the Sheriffe's ship paid us a visit. TheNaqueda is a Seid, and offered us every assistance on our arrival at Jidda. They said, they would come on board the moment we arrived there. As they might have it in their power to serve us greatly, I gave the Seid a telescope. I was happy to learn by them that the Capitan Pacha was at Alexandria, where he would stay some time. He recalled the old Pacha of Cairo, and gave that office to the chief of the Arnauts, who cut off three Beys and two hundred and fifty Mamelukes. He told us the roads between Cairo and Suez were perfectly safe. I heard all the re- negadoes here meant to go with him.

We received positive information from the Banians, that Seid Mohammed Akil and his Frenchmen had paid a visit to the Sheriffe at Loheia, and presented him with four thousand dollars worth of presents, in the name of the French nation ; at the same time requesting permission to establish a Factory on the Island of Camaran. This island produces wood, water, and salt. Its situation is good for watching all vessels that go up or down the Red Sea, but would be of no use in a commercial view... The French seemed to intend attacking Egypt by the assistance of the Wahabee. Mr. Pringle proposed going up there when we sailed, and joining us at Massowah, to communicate theresult of his inquiries. At my request he also intended sending an express to India with the news. There can be no doubt that the guns left here by the Seid were a present from the French to the Imaum.

The Dola hearing that I wanted to buy a spear and shield of the cavalry, sent me his as a present; together with one of their battle-axes. They were all handsomely ornamented with silver. I sent to say, I would either pay him a formal visit the evening of my departure, if he would keep the gates open for me to go out afterwards, or I would pay him a visit without ceremony this evening. He preferred the latter; and we ail went accord- ly. The people at his doors said, he expected only me and Mr. Pringle ; but we all got up at last. He was, I believe, disappointed in not being able to talk on business. He enquired respecting the distance to England, how far I went by land, and how we travelled in Europe. The conversation then turned on Yemen. He informed me, that beyond Sana iron ore was found in sufficient abundance to supply all the upper country. It is smelted with wood, and is very soft, white, and tenacious. It is used for the rings of hookah snakes; and has the quality of not being corroded by smoke. There is also lead ore, but it is brittle, and of no use. He wished to present me with a piece of silver cloth manufactured at Sana, which I accepted.

He was chewing the buds of a plant which the Arabs call Kaad. It, is not unpleasant, rather bitter, and aromatic. He informed me that it is brought in weekly, from the hills, to the amount of two hundred dollars. The Imaum has a large duty on it. On parting, he expressed the usual anxiety for my welfare.

We had been delayed, that Mr. Pringle might accompany us to Ait, the place where Unus's tribe live, and where we expected Mr. Salt's letters. Mr. Pringle was to go thence to Loheia, and join us again at Massowah. Mr. Pringle being ready, I went on board on the 3d. It blew fresh, though we waited till dark, as it usually lulled in the evening. We were attended to the pier by an innumerable crowd of Jieggars. Captain Court and I gave a scramble of komassis, and to our friends a few half and quarter dollars. Seid Daud, the Sheriffe's captain, came to wish us a good voyage, but could not reach us for the crowd. At midnight the breeze freshened to a gale, but Unus and Mr. Pringle came astern in their dows.

November 4.|At four we weighed anchor in a stiff gale and heavy' sea. At eight we were up with Jibbel Anish, when the weather and sea both moderated. We sailed along very pleasantly till dark, when we anchored. Mr. Pringle came in at the same time, but went on shore, close to Ait.

November 5.|The night was very pleasant and moderate. Mr. Pringle and Unus came on board in the morning. No letters from Mr. Salt, nor any intelligence; we therefore determined to make the best of our way to Massowah. Mr. Pringle had a very rough passage; he came between the Abail Islands, and the main, in a passage not wide enough for any thing except dows. His Naqueda told him, that on the northern Abail was found a stone, which he describes as being like green glass. He promised me to visit it, and procure some, as the description suits the Opsian stone, which is probably found in many of the sandy islands of this part of the coast. Mr. Salt found some on Dhalac. At any rate I cannot suppose this the bay named by the ancients after that stone, for it is a fine one, with good anchorage, and by no means filled with sand, as the other is represented to be, neither will it agree with the distances in the PeriplQs. Ait is a wretched village of huts. The high hills behind it were once, we were told, part of Habesh. We weighed at one, and with a strong breeze rounded the northern Codalie rock, which forms the boundary of the bay on that side, as the southern does on the other. We then had a free wind and an excellent coast, along which we sailed all night in perfect se curity.

November 6.|At day light we were in sight of Saboo and Moora, which Unus, who kept well up with us, called Habou-beer; at twelve we were opposite Hovakil, with a pleasant breeze; we passed Antelope point at sun-set, and immediately bore up for Massowah, in a direction that would clear the shoals at the extremity of Valentia. At nine we were alarmed by getting into a quarter less three, when nearly four miles N. of it; we im- mediately stood to the eastward, and cleared the shoal, which seems to be detached. We anchored close to Massowah harbour;

November 7.|At day-light we tried to make the harbour, but the land wind did not permit us to enter till twelve. Unus had been on shore, and immediately came off to us with the unexpected, but highly pleasing intelligence, that Mr. Salt, and our other friends, were on the road near Arkeko, and would be with us this day. As he accompanied the intelligence with a demand of buxys, we suspected his veracity, and desired him to tell Currum Chuud we wanted him on board. A man of the Nayib's came off to deliver his master's compliments, from whom we learned that the Nayib did not wish Currum Chund to come to us. I sent Unus again to insist on it, and Fowler went withhim. The Nayib now said he might come, but Currum Chund himself refused, saying that he had made nothing by the English; that he was out of pocket by Mr. Salt, and by the horse and mule he had given Mr. Pringle; and, in short, that he did not choose to come. I immediately suspected that he was afraid of our resentment, now that Mr. Salt was so near, and would explain his real conduct, which I always suspected to be bad, in the Habesh business. The Nayib sent many professions of regard, but begged we would not land, as the Ascari were very angry with us. Soon afterward Mr. Salt arrived, attended by Captain Rudland, Mr. Carter, and the Baharnegash of Dixan. He had also with him a servant of the Ras. They all came on board, when we saluted Mr. Salt with eleven guns ; this the Baharnegash mistook for our firing on the town, and conjured us to stop. It was with some difficulty we explained to him, through the double interpretation of Andrew, andaMassowah boy, who spoke Tigre, what the cause really was. I received him as he deserved, for his attentions to our friends, with every mark of respect. He drank wine and ate sweetmeats. We sent Hamed Chamie on shore to provide every thing for him, and pay his expences while he staid. We ourselves examined with the greatest eagerness the drawings Mr. Salt had made in the country, and were never tired of asking him questions.

Till the morning of November 14, we were engaged in preparing dispatches for India, and in arranging for Mr. Carter's and our Arab servants return to Mocha. For this purpose we hired a dow to Hodeida, whence they were to proceed by land. I wrote to his Excellency the Marquis Wellesley, and Mr. Duncan, giving a short account of Mr, Salt's expedition. The RasWelleta Selass6' had sent a letter for his Excellency, which I abo forwarded.

The Sabbath of Habesh commences at sun-set. On the Saturday evening the Baharnegash was on board, and as soon as the sun went down, asked leave to say his prayers. He turned to the east, and in a kind of chant addressed himself to" the Deity, and a very long list of saints. His people occasionally joined him. He then prostrated himself three times, calling on God. He performed the whole in a very decorous manner.

The Nayib's conduct was such as greatly to displease me. He pleaded that he himself wished to do every thing that was kind and proper, but that his Ascari were very angry with us ; and he begged I would not then land; but that when the ship returned, every thing should be settled to our satisfaction. A fellow struck two of the boys who rowed the boat ashore with Hamed Chamie. The Nayib sent for them, and begged they would not tell me, in consequence of which, I did not hear of it till some days afterwards, when I was assured the man was in prison ; I could therefore take no notice of it. Our old friend the Dola of Dhalac paid us a visit on board. We made him several presents. He was ever steady to us; nor could the Nayib dissuade him from supplying the Panther with every thing she wanted during her last voyage. When on board during the gale of wind off Daguera, he owned to Captain Court, that he had received instructions not to do so. The Nayib thought he cculd drive away the Panther by depriving her of water and fresh provisions. This is the only act of the Nayib that proved any disinclination in himself towards us, for at Dhalac he is absolute master. Some excuse may be made for him, vexed and tormented as he always was by his brothers and the Ascari, whenever thevessel appeared. The Baharnegash used all his influence to induce me not to quarrel with -the Nayib. He went on his knees to me, and embraced my feet, nor would he rise till I had promised I would not fire on the town. I told him I felt it was a gross insult to refuse me permission to land ; that the conduct of the Ascari was so reprehensible to Mr. Salt, whom they had attempted to rob, that they ought at least to be punished, and the more so, as we had ever acted towards the whole tribe in the most friendly manner. He said it was very true ; that the Nayib himself was a very good man, but the people about him were great rascals, and ruled him in every thing. As I cared but little about the landing, compassion induced me not to drive things to an extremity, which might have ended in bloodshed; but I am convinced that no friendship can exist between them and us, till they are taught by dear bought experience, that it is humanity, and not fear, which prevents our resenting their insults.

Currum Chund's conduct has been such as to preclude the possibility of employing him; I therefore had recourse to a Mussulmaun merchant, Hadje Hassan Ben Mohammed Anja. This man was recommended to Mr. Salt by Pacha Abdallah, who is frequently mentioned by him in his tour to Antalou, as an active friend, and greatly in the Ras's confidence. From him I learned, that, independently of their anger, at Mr. Salt's having escaped so well from them, the Ascari were really alarmed by an idea that I was going on to Jidda to procure for myself the sovereignty of Masso- wah, from the expected Turkish Pacha, and that the English would garrison the island. He said that the Nayib had never received his investiture as Aga of the Ascari, which rendered these people more insolent, as he had no legal authority overthem. I pity the poor man; but he is still to blame individually in the transactions respecting Mr. Salt.

The Baharnegash visited us every day. We worked the guns for him, and made the Sepoys go through their exercise. He was much astonfshed, and delighted, and said that twelve such men would enable the Ras to beat the Galla. I represented to him that the arms were procurable from the English in abundance, if the trade could be opened. He would not eat with us, but drank spirits or wine, and was much pleased with sweetmeats. He was astonished at the number of pieces of china on the table at breakfast and dinner, and always counted them. He was in high spirits, and seemed greatly pleased with the presents we made him, which consisted of a fine piece of kincaub, one hundred dollars in money, a razor, some china, sweetmeats, coffee, snuff, and a number of other little articles. He told us that he had always supposed all the articles brought to Massowah were made in Arabia, but he now found they came first from us. The Ras had sent me his own knife, spear, and shield, and a very fine piece of Habesh cloth; in return I. presented him with my silver chourie, an article of great use in Habesh, a bottle of lavender water, of which I heard he was very fond, and a pair of razors.

Nathaniel Pierce, who had accompanied Mr. Salt, was induced by the Ras to stay in the country. Should any connexion take place between Habesh and India, his being there, and understanding the language, will be advantageous. Mr. Salt had left him every thing he could spare, and we sent him several other articles which he had mentioned in his letters. I also procured from Captain Court two of the ship's muskets, some pow-

VOL. II. E E

der, flints, and ball. He had a gun, so that he was the best armed man in Habesh. I wrote to Mr. Pringle to procure me six more, in consequence of the lias's promise to give him a district when he had six matchlocks. He is a clever fellow, and will, I have no doubt, do well. He had several female protectors, and they have as much power in Habesh as elsewhere. He draws a little, which pleased the priests, for whom he manufactured saints in abundance. I sent him some money, and secured him more, should he wish to leave the country. I intrusted every thing to Hadje Hassan to be sent to Pacha Abdallah, as the safest conveyance. The Baharnegash declared to me in the most solemn manner, that he would protect Pierce with his life. I also sent Pacha Abdallah a handsome present of kincaub, requesting his friendship for this poor fellow : from the same motive I gave another to Hadje Hassan himself, who, in an equally solemn manner, promised to be his friend. I have great hopes of this man's ultimately increasing our knowledge of the interior of Africa. He meant to return by Senaar ; he might then be induced to join the kafla to Tombuctoo, for which he is well qualified by his knowledge of Arabic, and by his having conformed to the reli- gio.n of Mohammed, and knowing their prayers perfectly.

The Ras had given Mr. Salt three mules, and he had purchased five more; so that I had now eight to dispose of. Formerly the Baharnegash had given Mr. Salt three; I now therefore gave him ;his choice of the same number. I sent two to Pierce; one I gave to Guebra Selasse, the Ras's man, another to Hamed Chamie, and the eighth I sent to the Dola of Mocha, to put him in good humour with my people.

On the landing-place opposite to Massowah we discovered a rude fluted column of black granite, with a capital, of which I have given an etching. It was unlike any other I had ever seen, and gave me hopes that, by it, we might discover the ruins of Aduli, from which it was probably brought. We were informed by some of the Shiho Bedowee, who bring milk every morning to the town, that there were quarries of a similar stone in the lower hills, lying due west from Massowah, but we could obtain no positive intelligence of any other columns. They spoke, indeed, of some ruins between us and the hills; but situated as we then were with the Nayib, it was impossible to make any researches at a distance from the vessel.

We were not able to procure a sufficiency of sheep, orwater, from the Nayib, which he excused by the want of rain: we were consequently obliged to go to Dohoole; however I sent the Nayib a frassel of coffee, merely as a proof that we parted friends.

The Baharnegash went yesterday. I sent letters by him to the Ras and Pacha Abdallah, and to Pierce.

I have given in the following chapters Mr. Salt's narrative of his expedition, which he delivered ta me on his return.

9

SECTION 9

CHAPTER X.

Mr. Salt's Narrative.|*Arrival at Massowahfrom Mocha.* |*Negotiations with the Nayib.*|*Difficulties experienced* in *procuring Mules, Camels,&$c.for our Journey.*|*Preparations for the Journey.*|*Passage from Massowah to Arkeko.*| *Transactions there.*

"JUNE28.|We arrived in the harbour of Massowah this day at noon, having been exactly a week in sailing up the coast from Mocha. During our passage we experienced a regular succession of land and sea breezes. As soon as we had dropped anchor, Captain Court sent his boat on shore for Churrum Chund, the Banian. He declined coming, and returned for answer, that the Nayib, without whose permission it was impossible for him to communicate with us, was at Arkeko; that he was much alarmed at our coming in the ' great ship;' especially as he had written to delay our expedition, in consequence of the country being in a state of confusion; but that he would acquaint the Nayib with our arrival, and would himself come on board as soon as had received permission.

' June 29.|Captain Court again sent his boat early in the morning for the Banian, who still excused himself on the plea of the Nayib's absence; it was therefore determined to send on shore Hamed Chamie, our Arab interpreter, who also spoke the language of Hindostan. He soon came back, bringing us an account that the Banian was greatly alarmed at our speedy return in the Panther, a ship offeree. Alt would have been well, he added, if we had come over quietly in a dow; but that now the Sirdar of the troops was again bringing in his claim of five hundred dollars for the anchorage of the vessel. He moreover assured Hamed Chamie that he had forwarded Lord Valentia's letter to Ras, Welleta Selasse'. This latter assertion, however, was not quite correct, as we knew, from private information, that it was still remaining at Arkeko in the hands of the Ascari. In the afternoon the Banian himself came on board; but was able to communicate to us little more than a confirmation of what we had heard before. All our present difficulties have arisen from the Sirdar of the Ascari, now in Massowah; we however declined having any communication with him, being determined to transact business only with the Nayib in person.

" June 30.|The Nayib came over in the morning from Arkeko to Massowah, and immediately sent Hamed Chamie to us, with his salaams, and an excuse for not having come sooner; fixing twelve o'clock for our public visit. Accordingly, I, and Captain Rudland went on shore with Captain Court, under a salute of eleven guns, with which the latter was kind enough to honour us for the purpose of giving importance to our mission. On landing, we were saluted with all the guns, both great and small, that they could muster on the island; and then proceeded to the divan, or hall of audience, attended by a havildar's guard of the Bombay marines. The ceremonies were precisely as heretofore, except that our sepoys were marched up and ranged along the lower end of the hall. The divan was crowded; the Nayib, the Sirdar, and the Dola of Arkeko being present. After the usual compliments, coffee was handed to all, not omitting even the sepoys. I and Captain Court then received caftans of blue cloth lined with satin, after which we departed, in the same order as we came, to the house of Abou Yusuff, Secretary to the Nayib, which had been prepared for us by Currum Chund.

" On going off to the ship the former compliment of eleven guns was repeated. After dinner we returned, and took up our abode on shore. The Nayib declared to Hamed Chamie that he had sent Lord Valentia's letter to the Ras.

" July 1.|The Nayib sent us a message in the morning desiring that the boat, which they observed conveying our baggage on shore, should land it at the wharf, in order that it might be examined at the Custom-house, instead of bringing it round immediately to our own house. Gap- tain Court remonstrated with them on the inconvenience of this plan, as the packages contained merely articles that were necessary to us on shore, and which would not be carried out of the house ; if, therefore, they meant us to stay on friendly' terms, he should persist in bringing the baggage by the most convenient way; but, that if they wished it, it should be opened at our own house for the inspection of any person whom the Nayib should think proper to depute for that purpose. This proposal gave satisfaction, and accordingly two men were sent down, but they appeared to be soon tired of their office, and went away again in the course of an hour.

" The Nayib's brother and the Vizier came to
us before breakfast, demanding, and that in no very delicate terms, the extravagant sum of one thousand dollars, half for the ship's anchorage, and half forpermittingusto pass through the country on our intended visit to Ras WelletaSelasse; and this I believe, exclusively of the expences of our three or four days journey through the country.

We stopped the conversation abruptly, by saying that we never discussed matters of business before a multitude of people, (for the room was full of strangers) and desired them to choose some more convenient opportunity, as we were then going to breakfast. They promised to do so, and departed. At eleven o'clock, instead of the return of the above chiefs, as had been agreed upon, the Banian came, accompanied by one of the Nayib's secretaries. They informed us that Hamed Chamie had already stated our willingness to pay what was proper; and in consequence, the Nayib had resolved to.reduce his demand to three hundred dollars, and to be paid down to the Ascari, and that the expences of our journey should be a subsequent consideration ; that he hoped every thing would be speedily adjusted to our mutual satisfaction; but if not, as we had come friends into the country, so he hoped we should depart. As they added that the Nayib wished to talk over the business personally, we declined returning an answer until we should see him; at the same time giving them fully to understand, that no such demand would be complied with, and that, as the indispensable condition of our paying any thing, was the being supplied with convenient means for passing through the Nayib's territory, we should make but one agreement which must comprehend a supply of mules, asses, a guard, and provisions for the journey. The evening was accordingly appointed for our privatevisit to the Nayib. After waiting till past seven o'clock, Currum Chund at last came, and endeavoured to put *off* our visit, stating, that nothing could be done without first settling with the Ascari. We paid little attention to him, and sent Hamed Chamie to the Nayib to enquire, whether he meant to see us according to his appointment, as we should enter into no farther negotiation until he should grant us a personal interview.

" From the situation of affairs, I perceived it was impossible to avoid paying exorbitantly for permission to pass through the country ; we therefore came to a determination not to exceed five hundred dollars; and we were induced to comply so far, merely from our extreme reluctance to return without having made every possible effort towards the accomplishment of our mission.

" Hamed Chamie returned with a message, that the Nayib was ready to see us. We found him in his cadjan-house, where Lord Valentia had had his first private audience. He was in a loose undress, sitting at the further end of the room, surrounded by all his principal people, in a similar dishabille : one small lamp hung from the centre of the room, shedding around so faint a light, that we 'were at a loss to recognize even the Nayib, till he was pointed out by one of the attendants.

" Having made our usual salaams, we were seated immediately opposite to him, and then (Hamed Chamie standing between us as interpreter, and Andrew, a servant, whom we had hired at Mocha, and who spoke Arabic, Hindostanee, and English, on my right hand) the following dialogue took place.

" Salt.lWe have now arrived in your territory for the third time; you have received us with the greatest honours; such, indeed, as we have alwaysexperienced from your friendship. For these we return you our thanks.

" Nayib.lIt has always been my wish to treat you well. You came here as friends; we have always continued as such; and I hope that we shall settle every thing amicably.

" Salt.lIt is for that purpose we have waited on you, and I will now explain the reason of our coming. Your friend, Lord Valentia, has received letters from Ras

Welleta Selasse", desiring that some persons should be sent to him, in order to open an intercourse of friendship with Abyssinia. We are, in consequence, proceeding to the Ras, having been selected by Lord Valentia for that purpose: we therefore request permission to pass through your country, and such assistance as may be necessary for the prosecution of our journey.

" Nayib.|I have no objection to your passing through my country, but you must satisfy my As- cari. Give them five hundred dollars, and I will supply you with every thing requisite, for which we will settle afterwards.

" Salt.|Why do you demand five hundred dollars for your Ascari ? You well know the vessel in which we have arrived is not a trader, but a ship of war, that never pays one single komeassm to the greatest Sultaun on earth. Even in this sea they go to Suez, to Jidda, and to Mocha, and nothing is ever demanded. It must be fully understood that not a komeassm will ever be paid on this account.

" Nayib.|I know the ship is no trader, and when you were here before this was understood ; nothing more shall be said on this head.

" Salt.|What, then, are these five hundred dollars for? We do not know your Ascari, and can have nothing to say to them : you are surely the Prince of this country, and it is with you only that we can treat. We are willing to give, for your assistance, even more than would be given in any other country, only let us know your demand.

The smallest money of Yemen.

" Nayib.|What assistance do you require ?

" Hamed Chamie then entered into an explanation of the number of mules, asses, camels, and attendants of which we should stand in need. Notice being now given that the hour of prayer was at hand, the Nayib and all his people went out, and prostrated themselves on a carpet in front of the house; after which the priest recited passages from the Koran. The moral effects, however, of this religious service were not very apparent: though the highest sum hitherto demanded had never exceeded eight hundred dollars, a message was now brought from the Nayib that he expected a thousand.

" I answered, that the idea of a thousand dollars was ridiculous, and that we would give no such sum, demanding where the Nayib was, and whether he did not intend to return? On this Hamed Chamie called out, not very delicately, I thought, " Nayib Edris, Nayib Edris !" on which the Nayib came in, and resumed his seat, when I thus addressed him.

" You have now made a demand of a thousand dollars; for what? for permitting us to march only three or four day's journey through your country. If you were in our country, you would be received with honour, without having any thing to pay for such permission; even in Arabia no such tribute is ever imposed.

" Nayib.|Three or four day's journey ! why itit is twelve. Moreover, I intend sending rriy people to insure your safety to the presence of the Ras.

" Salt.|This we do not want; when we arrive at Dixan we shall be met by the Ras's people; besides, what guard is necessary? We shall be safe even should we walk thither, as you well know that both Massowah and Arkeko will be answerable for our return. In one word, if you will provide us with every convenience to pass through your country, we will agree to give you five hundred dollars, which sum nothing shall induce us to exceed. If this offer be not accepted, there are other places through which we can communicate with the Ras, and all the fault of our not reaching him must rest with you. We expected that you would have acted as our friend, instead of which you place every obstacle in our way. We have been here three times; have we not always shown ourselves your friends? This conduct of yours, however, if persisted in, may bring upon you a very different treatment from what you have hitherto experienced from the English.

" This address seemed not a little to alarm our interpreter, for while translating it, he turned round and called upon Andrew to say whether each word, as he again repeated it aloud in Arabic, were not precisely what we had ordered him to deliver; to which Andrew made his repeated affirmations, " just so." The Nayib's countenance shewed that he felt the force of our remonstrance ; he was silent for a short time, then turning to his people, he spoke in the language of the country for upwards of five minutes: his manner was persuasive, his action apparently just, and upon the whole he seemed no inconsiderable orator. Afterwards, turning to us, he said, that uponconsideration of his friendship for Lord Valentia, and on consultation with his people, he would reduce his demand to seven hundred dollars, which being paid, every thing should be arranged to our satisfaction. We again assured him that we should not in the least vary from our original proposal. After some words between Currum Chund, Hamed Chamie, and the Nayib, he offered to accept of six hundred dollars, positively declaring that we should not pass through his country for less; that the camels, mules, asses, &c. were to be fetched from a distance; that his people were ravenous, and that he had a thousand mouths to fill. To this proposal Hamed Chamie and the Banian intreated us to accede, adding, that they themselves would rather pay the additional hundred dollars, than press the subject any farther This however, we declined, and again ordered them to repeat to the Nayib that we had but " one word;" that we had offered as much, nay more than we were authorised to do by Lord Valentia, and perceiving that the matter was not likely to be adjusted, we would, for the present, take our leave, hoping that, by the morrow, he would be convinced, not only of the fairness, but even of the liberality of our offer. To this the IVayib replied, " These are not the words Lord Valentia would use, but your own." This insinuation brought on a warm remonstrance on my part, which happily produced an apology from the Nayib, and a declaration that he would accept our terms. " God be praised," cried Hamed Chamie, raising his voice, that every one present might hear, " it is settled; five hundred dollars is the sum agreed upon." ,. –

- After our public business was arlnged, Captain Court mentioned, that, understanding rice was

exceedingly scarce in the Nayib's dominions, h would on the morrow send him as much as he could spare out of what he had provided for his own people. This offer was received with much thankfulness hy the Nayib and all his attendants, except the Banian, who would have prevented Hamed Chamie from mentioning it, doubtless from its not agreeing exactly with his immediate interest. The Nayib was displeased with the Banian's interference, and rebuked him sharply. We now arose, and departed, rejoiced at having brought this troublesome business to a conclusion.

" July 2.lA messenger from the Nayib came early in the morning for the money ; we returned for answer, that it was usual with us to pay one half on making a bargain, and the other half on its being fulfilled; that, however, we had no objection to send him three hundred dollars, and that the remainder should be paid on the day of our departure from Arkeko. This gave no great satis- fection ; the Nayib said that his soldiers would not leave Massowah till they saw the money: was I afraid of trusting him ? I asked the Banian, who brought the message, if he were willing to be security for the Nayib, which he refused. " What have 1 to do with it ?" said he, " I am your servant, and not the Nayib's."

" Previously to coming to a final determination on this matter, we sent to the Nayib to enquire how soon all things would be in readiness for our journey, and were told that it might be fifteen days, or more, as the mules were far up in the country. This assertion, so much at variance with our wish of losing as little time as possible, still further embroiled the discussion. At length, after spending the whole day in altercation, we submitted two propositions to the choice of the JNayib; either,that we would pay three hundred dollars immediately, and the remaining two hundred when every thing was ready; or, which was by far the most agreeable to us, that the whole five hundred dollars should be paid down, on condition of our receiving a written receipt for the money, and an agreement that all the preparations should be completed in ten days, at the end of which time, if there were any farther delay, we should consider him as having forfeited his word, and should employ such means as he well knew were in our power, to enforce the fulfilment of the contract.

" The Nayib at length acceded to this latter proposal, after an ineffectual attempt to evade giving a written agreement.

" July 3.lThe money was paid in the morning; and the written agreement made out by Hamed .Chamie in Arabic, was signed and sealed by the Nayib; in return, on his requisition, I gave him a counter-receipt.

. " July 4.lSome difficulty arose about the bags of rice which Captain Court offered to present to the Nayib. His people did not appear satisfied with the quantity, and therefore hesitated about accepting it; so insatiable are their desires, and so little delicacy have they in making them known. Captain Court repeated to them, that the rice now landed was all that he could at present spare, but that if, by the Nayib's expediting the party to Abyssinia, his stay here should be shortened, he would double the quantity. It will scarcely be believed that, notwithstanding this refusal to accept the generous offer of Captain Court, the people were at that time almost starving for want of grain. On account of a partial failure of the annual rains, not a drop of fresh water was left on the island, and that which came from Arkeko wasevery day becoming more and more brackish. The *boys* and girls gather the root of a kind of sea weed to eat; it is by no means unpleasant to the taste, and constitutes a great part of their food.

" About six o'clock this evening an unpleasant circumstance occurred to Captains Court and Rud- land. As they were walking through the town, an insolent fellow, lately arrived from Jidda, either from a religious frenzy, or some unknown cause, began to abuse them in a violent manner, as they passed the walled inclosure round his house; and taking up a large stone, was in the act of throwing it at them, when some of the inhabitants, who were near, laid hold of his arms, and prevented the assault, calling out at the same time, that the Nayib was at hand. This proved to be actually the case; for the circumstances having happened close to his residence, he himself, on hearing the noise, immediately came out, and with great kindness took our friends by the hand, and led them into his house. They sent directly for our interpreter, and one of the Nayib's sons came in great haste for me. On my arrival, Captain Court represented to the Nayib, in very strong terms, what had happened, and desired the offender might be brought forward.

" The Nayib said, that what had passed, had passed; he hoped it would be over-looked, as he could not answer for our safety when we went out, unless we were accompanied by some of his own people.

" After assuring him that a repetition of the offence should be punished as it merited, Captain Court informed the Nayib, that, from personal regard to him, he would pass over what had happened, trusting that his present forbearance would not encourage a repetition of the insult.

" While we were at the Nayib's, Unus Barilla, hearing that there was some distur-bance in which we were concerned, armed all his men, eleven in number, and drew them up in front of the Nayib's house, where he kept them on watch till the whole affair was settled: an instance of attachment to our interest, both in himself and his Samaulies, highly creditable to their fidelity.

" July 5.|Hamed Chamie waited on us at breakfast time, with the agreeable intel-ligence of the dispatch of a letter, which I had sent over to Arkeko to be forwarded to the Has, requesting him to send people to meet us on our arrival at Dixan. For the conveyance of this letter Currum Chund demanded no less a sum than thirty dollars ; but exorbitant as it was for the conveyance of a single letter, for so short a distance, I thought it best at the time to submit to the imposition, as it was a point of the greatest importance to acquaint the Ras with the success of our negotiation with the Nayib; particularly as, from several circumstances, we doubted whether Lord Valentia's letter to the Ras, announcing our intended visit, had been forwarded.

" July 6.|The weather since our arrival at Mas- sowah has been intensely hot; the thermometer varying for the most part from 96 to 99 during the day ; but we have been relieved by frequent breezes from the south. Nothing particular has occurred, and we have been reducing our baggage as much as possible preparatory to our journey. In other respects affairs are going on so well that we expect to set off by the thirteenth or fourteenth instant.

" July 7.|An attendant of the Nayib came to us in the afternoon, bringing with him a man just arrived from Dowarba. His mode of salutation

Vol. n. F F

differed from that made use of at Massowah. He first kissed the back of his hand, and then made a slight inclination of the head. We offered him coffee, which he refused : he called himself a Christian, and said that he was ' all one with us.' We were beginning to question him concerning the news in the upper country, when he was sent. for in a great hurry *by* the Nayib.

" Abou Yusuff came to us in the evening : he told me that he had written a second letter, by order of the Nayib, to hasten the mules; he had also sent two men, of the tribe of Shiho, to attend us. These people are very wild, and inhabit the mountains through which our road lies. He particularly mentioned the mountains of Gidam, Taranta, and Assooba, as frequented by them. He recommended us not to let the ship go away till our arrival at Dixan was announced; and to permit Hamed, the Nayib's son, to go over to Arkeko with us, as the people of this latter place are not to be depended upon; even the Nayib himself cannot trust them; but that if we had his son with us, they would not dare to molest the party. I told him that his thoughts were mine; that I would follow his advice, and that Captain Court had already determined to stay till our letters from Dixan should be received.

" July 8.|The Christian from Dowarba came to us again in the evening, accompanied by an attendant of the Nayib. He appeared to be a simple uneducated creature, from whom we could not expect to obtain any important information ; and it was not improbable that he had been selected on this very account, out of four who had arrived, as the Nayib's people were evidently shy of letting us know the object of their mission. From repeated questions, however, we learned, that theyhad brought from Welleta Sulimaun, Governor of Dowarba, an answer to a demand which the Nayib had made of some long forgotten tribute. The purport of the answer was, that the Governor was the Nayib's friend, and would prevent, so far as lay in his power, any of the neighbouring tribes from making plundering incursions into the territory of his ally, and that he would continue in all amity ; but not a word was said about the money. The Abyssinian Christian took coffee in the evening, on its being handed to him by ourselves, to the surprise, as it seemed, of the Mussulmauns. On his leaving us, I made him a present of a piece of Surat cloth, with which he was much pleased.

" July 9. We were under the necessity of troubling the Nayib at an early hour in the morning, in consequence of a melancholy occurrence, which took place yesterday evening; namely, the death of Woodward, one of the marine boys belonging to *the.* Panther. He neglected to take off his wet clothes, after having been in the water on the evening of the second instant, and was attacked the following morning with a locked jaw, and other violent symptoms, which baffled the effects of opium, and of every other medicine that it was in our power to administer. At Captain Court's desire his death was reported to the Nayib accompanied by a request, that a spot might be pointed out for his interment; which, with great civility, was immediately granted. Another boy was seized in a similar way, whom we were fortunate enough to recover by large doses of opium.

"July 10.|The Nayib left Massowah in themorning for Arkeko, where he meant to continue for some days. Before his departure he introduced an officer of the Ascari, with whom we might communicate, should occasion require; he also promised to dispatch a messenger on the arrival of the mules from Hamazin.

The Banian and Amed Yusuff informed us that the mission to the Nayib was from RasAylo, the Chief of Serawe, eight days journey beyond Dowarba. Ras Aylo, we understand, is a dependent upon Ras Welleta Selasse.

" July 11.|About 2 P.M. a dow belonging to Emir Mohammed arrived in the harbour of Mas- sowah, from Suakin, having on board three Arabian horses, intended, we understood, as a present for the Imaum of Sana, or the Dola of Mocha. Emir Mohammed himself was expected in the course of a day or two.

" July 12.|The Nayib came over in the morning from Arkeko, to settle the duties of thekafila and dows lately arrived. I sent to remind him of the near approach of the time which had been fixed for having the mules ready; stating, that from a reliance on his word, I had hitherto avoided troubling him on the subject, and hoped that all would be prepared by the morrow. He returned in answer, that he had already sent twice for the mules, that they were nearly at hand, and, by the blessing of God, all would be ready in three or four days. This manifest evasion and violation of his written engagement brought on much altercation, which was carried on during the whole day by messengers charged alternately with our complaints, and the Nayib's excuses. The particulars it is needless to detail; the result of the whole was, that the Nayib promised to give me a personal interview the next day.

" July 13.|At the appointed hour of our visit, twelve o'clock, we were informed that the Nayib was asleep; the interview was therefore postponed

Or caravan.

till the evening. At six o'clock we waited on the Nayib, and found him in the mosque, whence he proceeded with us to the Cadjan house, accompanied by two or three attendants. I opened the. conference by saying, that, as I was about to dispatch a letter to Lord Valentia, it would be necessary to state to his Lordship the reason of our still continuing at Massowah, after the day had elapsed on which by agreement, we were to have proceeded on our journey to Abyssinia. The Nayib replied, that it would be most agreeable to him to send us off the next morning, but that the mules and asses were not come down so soon as he had expected ; he trusted, however, that they would arrive in three or four days; after which there would be no further delay. I answered, that I well knew that the mules might, without difficulty, have been brought to Arkeko from the most distant part of his territory, by the time appointed ; I was both surprised and hurt at the delay ; that every day was now of importance to us ; and that the non-fulfilment of his deliberate and written engagement had placed me in a very disagreeable situation ; more especially as I had received private information that the mules were actually at this very time at Arkeko. To these remonstrances he answered as before, that he was as anxious for our departure as ourselves ; and that there was no foundation for the report which we had heard.

" I again urged the impossibility of delaying, day after day, without any thing being settled; that the vessel in which I came could not stay much longer, and that as I had determined to proceed, if all things were not ready in three days, I should set out on foot, with such assistance of asses and camels for our baggage, as tie might choose to supply; if, however, we were constrain ed to begin our journey thus unprovided with the stipulated conveniences, I should consider him as no longer acting the part of a friend. The Nayib said that if such were our determination, we certainly might have all his asses and camels, and one mule which he kept for his own riding; and that he would send us on the road where we should meet the other mules coming down. We then ended the conference, by repeating our fixed determination to act as we had informed him.

" July 14-|I went on board the Panther in the morning to make preparations for our departure. The day was extremely hot, the thermometer being at)6 a few minutes after sun-rise, in the shade of a house with stone walls. In the course of the day, three of the Christians, who came down with the kafila, paid their respects to us. They seemed much pleased at the idea of our visiting their country, and answered with, great willingness all our inquiries, in spite of Abou Yusuff, who was greatly displeased at their coming, and spoke to them with much harshness. They told us that all was well on the road, and that the Tacazza was passable at all times and seasons, on rafts kept for that purpose. Each of the men had a blue fillet of silk round his neck, a badge of Christianity mentioned by Bruce; they were stout, robust people, with short and almost woolly hair.

"July 15.|We were engaged all the morning in packing and securing our baggage. In the evening some Mussulmauns from Gondar paid us a visit, one of whom spoke Arabic, and appeared to be a man of much information. Among other particulars we learned from him, that the present Ras of Abyssinia is a son of Kefla Yasous, thatAxum is one day's journey from Adowa, and has many curious ruins, some of which are in good preservation. The lake Dembea, he tald us, is about the same distance from Gondar, as Arkeko is from Massowah. The head of the Nile gushes out generally from one spring, but when there is much rain it forces its way through many. It is only five days journey from Gondar, and is perfectly easy of access, as all the country belongs to the king.

" 'July 16.|We went on board the Panther in the morning, and brought on shore such fire arms, ammunition, &c. as Captain Court could spare: on leaving the ship we were highly gratified at being cheered by the ship's company, a pleasing testimony of its good wishes. In the mean time I sent Hamed Chamie to the Nayib, to inform him that the day fixed upon for our departure having arrived, we were all in readiness, that we wished to know if the mules were at Arkeko, otherwise the ship would proceed thither to-morrow, and that we should go on to Dixan, with the asses and camels only, as before staled : to this he an- awered that there would be no necessity for the ship's going, that he himself would conduct us in the course of the day, and begged that we would get all things ready for our departure : he added, that it would be necessary to prepare provisions for our guard ; beside which, if we gave them five dollars each, they would, he thought, be satisfied.

" To this I replied, he might rest assured, that I would never give his Ascari a single dollar more, nor would I provide them with provisions on tlie road..

" Captain Court at the same time told the Nayib, that he had but one word to say on theoccasion; if we were not at Arkeko by the day after he had once taken us in charge, he should go down thither with his ship. The Nayib now took up another ground; he said the road Avas extremely bad, that the Simooms were raging; and that a great many people were dying daily from these causes ; if we therefore persisted, he must detain Emir Hamed as a witness to Lord Valentia, if any accident occurred: that the mules would be ready in three or four days, and that if that were not the case, he would then collect his Ascari, and conduct us himself. We replied, that he knew our minds, and we had no more to say. In the evening we again demanded at what time he proposed to be ready, and after much difficulty extorted an answer from him, that he would go with us the next morning.

" July 17.|I sent a message this morning to know the hour he meant to accompany us to Arkeko: after waiting about three hours, Hamed Chamie, Emir Hamed, and

Currum Chund came to bring us the Nayib's answer, which was, that he was busy at the custom-house, and could not fix upon any hour; he also added, that if we chose to go without waiting for the mules, we must pay extra for all the asses and camels he might procure for us, as they belonged to other people at Arkeko, ProVoked at these repeated attempts at extortion, I informed them that, having been already acquainted with Captain Court's determination and my own, they might now do as they pleased ; they had experienced the good effects of the friendship of the English, and if they were wise, would not brave their enmity. They returned almost immediately with a message from the Nayib, that he would be ready to accompany us at day-break the next morning; in consequence of which Captain Court at my request deferred sailing. In the evening Captain Court went on board; the Banian's boat was loaded with our baggage, and the guard stationed over it for the night.

" July 18.lAt day-break the Nayib's boat passed us, under way for Arkeko, upon which we immediately put the few remaining packages into our own boat, and then nnding it so full that we were unable to accommodate ourselves, we sent Pearce and two seapoys on with it, and waited till Captain Court came on shore, we then returned with him to the ship, breakfasted, and set off immediately afterwards in Unus's dow, attended by a naig and seven sepoys under charge of Lieutenant, Crawford, whom Captain Court had been kind enough to send with us, for the protection of our baggage and persons, which, from all that we knew of the character of the inhabitants of Arkeko, appeared to be by no means a superfluous precaution.

" The sea breeze sprung up and carried us over very pleasantly to the landing-place at Arkeko; on our way we passed over a shoal not known before, Ras Gidam and Valentia being both in one, and Sheik Seid and Massowah open. There is plenty of water for ships of any size till within a quarter of a mile of the shore.

" It was eleven o'clock when we landed, and the intense heat of the sun reflected by the burning sand made our walk up to the house prepared for us, which was half a mile distant, the most oppressive that I ever experienced; we were all much exhausted by it on our arrival, but were soon refreshed by the attention of the Nayib, who was waiting to receive us. Our people were engaged till two o'clock, in getting up the baggage, which was effected without any loss or accident.

" As soon as the boat was ready to return, I sent Harned Chamie to the Nayib, wishing to know when we were to leave Arkeko, as I was desirous of conveying the intelligence to Captain Court; he replied, that nothing could be done on. the morrow, it being their Sabbath ; that it would take up the whole of the next day to arrange the baggage, and that on the following morning we should commence our journey. By remonstrating with him, however, on this unnecessary delay, I prevailed so far that the day after the Sabbath was fixed on for our departure. We procured for our day's supply a quantity of water and a sheep ; the water was well tasted, but of a whitish colour, and deposited much sediment. In the evening we received two sheep from the Nayib, and in return presented the servant who brought them with a dollar.

" Some of our party wishing to walk at sunset, I requested the Nayib would send one of his people to attend them. He said the women and children would be alarmed, and that the boys would be very troublesome; he therefore begged that we would not go beyond the walls of the enclosure As we were retiring to rest, the Nayib placed an

Ascari as a guard at the door of our house, and desired us on no account to go out during the night, as wild beasts were abroad, and evil minded persons, who would molest us. We slept within our enclosure in the open air, only using the precaution of having our fire arms near at hand. Pearce and one of the sepoys sleeping on the outside of the gate, but with their heads on the threshold; were awakened about eleveno'clock by the Nayib himself, who insisted on their coming in and bolting the door. As a proof that this was not an unnecessary precaution, it may be mentioned, that the Nayib's sentinel, who was stationed at the door, sent in his cap and shoes, lest they should be taken from him in the night. We heard the cries of hyaenas, and other wild beasts, prowling about, which, from the noise they made, must have been very numerous; nevertheless, we passed the night without molestation.

"July 19.|Early this morning the Nayib came, with some of his people to look at our baggage; and in the afternoon the packages were sorted by the camel drivers, and an account taken. There seemed to be much dispute among the parties as to the number of animals required. Much diffi culty was made about the tent, and I was at length obliged lo determine on leaving the fly behind. At mid-day the thermometer was 110.

" We Avere, as usual, pestered in the evening with a number of messages concerning provisions for the Ascari and camel drivers. I told them we had very little for ourselves, and that I should therefore not take upon myself the care of providing for them. As we were retiring to rest, the same disturbance again occurred about the door of our house being closed and bolted; but the night being intensely hot (and our party much increased by the arrival of Captain Court with his boat's crew, making altogether twenty-six in number, and crowded into a space of not more than forty feet square) we determined to protest against it, and at length prevailed on the Nayib to give up the point; but, as what had passed in our conference with him was not particularly pleasant, wethought it prudent to be on the alert during the remainder of the night.

" July 20.|The circumstances already mentioned caused us to pass a most unpleasant night; we could neither sleep nor rest, so closely were we pent up, and so oppressive was the state of the air.

" Early at day-break some of the camels arrived, and the Nayib came for the purpose of iinally settling every thing. On a repetition of a demand for provisions for the people who were to accompany us, we gave him the same answer as before; but added, that wishing to make it easy to the camel drivers, we would give each of them a small sum of money, to furnish them with provisions as far as Dixan.

" At eight o'clock all the camels were loaded, aad proceeded on their way, guarded by Pearce, and Mr. Carter, who volunteered upon the occasion. For myself, I thought it not prudent to brave the mid-day sun at the commencement of a journey, which would doubtless prove sufficiently fatiguing. There were also a few matters yet remaining to be arranged ; in consequence of which Captain Rudland and the rest of the party still continued with me at Arkeko.

" Captain Court, completely weary of the place and of the Nayib, returned very early in the morning to the ship, leaving however with us Lieutenant Crawford and the guard. We felt great regret at parting from this valuable friend, whose kind assistance in farthering every object of our mission had been such as to claim our warmest gratitude. With respect to his private stock, there was nothing which he would not have given us; and so far as lay in his power hefurnished us, in his public capacity, with those articles which it was impossible for us to procure at Mocha of elsewhere in the Red Sea. Indeed from all our friends on board the Panther we received every kind attention and assistance.

10

SECTION 10

CHAPTER XL

Mr. Salt's Narrative coNTiNUED.–Deparfwre *from Ar- keko to Dixan.|Numbers and description of our party.| Illerbehey.|Shillikee. | Weak. | Hazorla Encampments.| Meet with mules sent down from Dixan.|Hamhammo.| Sadoon.|Tubbo.|Illilah.|Foot of Taranta.|Passage over that Mountain.|Arrival at Dixan.|Proceedings at Dixan.*

" JULY 20.|Our party, on quitting Arkeko, consisted of the following persons. Myself; Captain Rudland ; Mr. Carter; Hamed Chamie, an interpreter from Mocha and born at Mecca ; Andrew, another interpreter, likewise from Mocha, who spoke English well; Pierce, an English servant, who spoke a little Arabic; two Arabian servants, Seid and Ageeb ; a boy from Massowah, who spoke the language of the country arid Arabic : and an old man who carried our pedometer : total in number ten. We were accompanied also by an old Mussulman Sheik, and his little boy, going up into the country on a trading expedition, both of whom continued with us the whole of our journey, and proved very attentive and useful. Our guard consisted of about twenty-five of the Nayib's Ascari; besides whom we had a guide belonging to the Shiho tribe, and about ten camel- drivers, natives of the country. .

" The baggage with its escort had already left Arkeko fas mentioned in the preceding Chapter), and the rest of the party were preparing to follow, when I found that no animals had been provided, except a mule for myself. This was not the time to enter into a long discussion with the Nayib on the subject, I therefore hired an ass for Captain Rudland, four camels for our servants, and four more to carry the tent poles, for which I agreed to pay eight dollars. At four P. M. one camel only arrived, and many excuses were made to detain us. After enquiring into the full extent of the Nayib's demands, the charge of twelve dollars was made out by the Dola and the Nayib's son, for which I gave a draft on Currum Chund. The Nayib now, without assigning any reason whatever, declared he would have twenty-two dollars ; provoked at this new and unexpected instance of knavery, I replied in Arabic, before his son and the Dola, that if he said so he told an untruth, for that I would not, on any account, pay a single dollar more. In the midst of the wrangling which this occasioned, the ship most fortunately moved towards Arkeko. Upon the Nayib's demanding the reason of this, I replied, " Captain Court is coming to see that I am safe, and though, if he finds that all is well, he will immediately go away, yet, he will return in ten days for intelligence which I have agreed to send him from Dixan." The Nayib's son replied in a haughty tone, " Let him come;" but liis coming was not equally pleasing to the Dola and the inhabitants of the place; for the former immediately went out

This, as we found on our return, was merely accidental, the ship having been driven from her anchor by a partial Simoom. It was one of the many lucky coincidences, that occurred in the course of our expedition.

in great alarm, taking the Navib's son with him, and made so forcible a representation of his fears, that in a few minutes, without more words, every thing was prepared, and we set off.

" After I had mounted the mule and had proceeded a few yards, Captain Kudland and his ass were completely hustled by the members of the divan, one of whom had actually employed a boy to steal his fowling piece; he only escaped by urging forward his beast, and pouring forth in Arabic all the abuse that he could muster on the occasion. Of Arkeko I have little to say; it is an assemblage of miserable huts, among which are two stone houses with walled yards, belonging to the Nayib : before that in which we resided was a verandah covered with mats.

" We passed out to the southward through gardens, which are cultivated with a degree of care unusual in this country. Immediately beyond lies a burying-ground, and to the right a village, where most of the Ascari reside. In passing along the plain, which is upwards of a mile in breadth, reckoning from the sea to the nearest rising ground, 1 had an opportunity of observing that the bottom of the bay forms a considerable bight. About a mile and a half from Arkeko are six wells, near twenty feet deep, and above fifteen in diameter. It is from these that the town receives its scanty supply of fresh water. By the evening the wells are so nearly drained, that the water, as it rises in the middle of each, is taken up with a flat vessel like a skimming-dish; it is then put into skins, and brought up a broken ascent by men, women, and children in a state of perfect nudity. The name of these wells is Illerbehey, Bruce's first stage. Having watered the mules and came is, we proceeded on our way, in the course of which, we *voi.* ii. G o

saw several red deer exceedingly tame, and some small wolves, that bore a near resemblance to the large paria dog of India. We passed another village, beyond which two large flocks of goats were feeding; and observed that all the villages, and gardens, were carefully fenced round with large branches of the thorny Acacia. By the time that we had quitted the plain, it became too dark to make any observations, except such as were forced upon us by the ruggedness of the road. We arrived at length at the rising ground, called by Bruce, Shillokeeb, but pronounced by the natives Shillikee, where we slept undisturbed in the midst of our camels and baggage. There is no water at this place.

" July 21.lAs soon as the moon arose, which was about half past two, we commenced our morning's march. The air was pleasantly cool, and tha road, which was good, winded among the gullies of the mountains, at times crossing the dry beds of the torrents. There was at this time little variety of vegetation, almost every thing being burnt up: the Acacia, which grows to the height of about forty feet, nearly covered the face of the country; round the trunks of this tree were twined the stems of various climbing plants, which were completely leafless.

" We were much gratified, after being wearied .with the sun-burnt foliage of the Acacia, with the sight of green trees at a distance, indicating the presence of fresh water. We accordingly soon found ourselves on the bank of a torrent called Weah, much discoloured by the dirt and rotten wood brought down by it from the hills whence it rises. By the side of this stream we hung up the walls of our tent on the branches of a tree, resembling the cedar in its general growth, exceptthat the boughs droop like those of the weeping willow. The quill of a porcupine was brought me by one of our attendants. Here also we first saw the dung of elephants, though the natives deny that these animals ever frequent this place. Hitherto we have journeyed in nearly a south course, varying a little to the west, and are, I conjecture, about eighteen miles from Arkeko.

" Our Ascari now conceiving that we had advanced so far into the country as to be entirely at their mercy, began to display their insatiable rapacity and insolence. The camel master and drivers also made common cause with them, so that, had they not been deterred by the superiority of our fire-arms, I am persuaded that even our lives would scarcely have been safe. They made demarids of tobacco, rice, coffee, and liquor, on the plea that the Nayib had given them nothing but a little ju- warry. These we resisted; but, at length promised to buy them some goats and juwarry, if we met with any, and to give them a small quantity of tobacco ; but to satisfy such villains was impossible. We quitted Weah at three P. M. and passing the torrent, which was shallow, and running in an easterly direction, proceeded over the plain to the south a little westerly. Captain Rudland made an excursion with his gun, and saw many deer of different kinds, hares, partridges, and guinea-fowl; he was attended by a famous Shan- galla hunter, armed with his spear and shield, the latter of which was of a circular form, two feet and a half in diameter, and made of the skin of the rhinoceros. He was a very handsome young fellow, straight-limbed, and appeared to be a truly brave man, for he was well behaved, and despised the wrangling of the Ascari.

" We saw a few people of theShiho tribe on thehill, and some wolves: after passing a second stream as muddy as the former, we encamped for the night. The name of this station is Markela; it was at that time occupied by a tribe of the Ha- zorta, which had come down with its flocks into the low country for water. The Sheik of the tribe called himself a Dancalle. Their encampment was nearly circular, and about a hundred yards in diameter, well fenced with thorns and brushwood: within was a circle of rude huts composed of sticks and mats, and placed at equal distances from each other; while the vacant space in the centre formed a secure resting place during the night for their goats and sheep, of which they had an ample stock.

" After we had settled our encampment, the Ascari came round me, headed by their chief, and in a very insolent tone repeated their former demands, declaring that unless these were complied with, they would instantly leave us, take the cattle, and return. I told them, that they might themselves depart as soon as they pleased; but that I would certainly shoot the first person whom I should see meddling with the camels. I now sounded the man. in charge of the camels, and found him more tractable than the Ascari, which. convinced me that the whole was an attempt to alarm us. In consequence of what had passed, I ordered all our fire arms to be loaded, and a two-hours watch was kept during the night, by myself, Captain Rudland, Mr, Carter, and Pearce.

" The villagers about this time brought in their goats and sheep, consisting in the whole of at least five hundred. I purchased three for two dollars, and distributed them among our guard and drivers; we ourselves supped heartily on rice and salt-fish, having eaten nothing but a little biscuit in thecourse of the day. The water has hitherto been very muddy, though not ill-tasted. Our computed distance from Arkeko is twenty-four miles.

" July 22.|Our attendants made no preparation for commencing our journey at the time appointed; we found, on inquiry, that the delay was occasioned by the non-arrival of the long promised mules of the Nayib, which were to have joined us at this place. Very intelligible hints were also thrown out by the Ascari, that none of them would move until their former demands were satisfied. From this disagreeable state of suspense we were happily relieved soon after, by the arrival of an Abyssinian Christian with ten mules in his charge, from Dixan. He was sent, by the express command of the Ras, to convey us and our baggage, with all possible speed, to his presence at Antalow, and the strictest orders had been issued to ensure our personal safety during the remainder of the journey. On receiving this welcome intelligence, I called the chief of the Ascari to me, and acquainting him with what had happened, gave him and his followers full liberty to quit us as soon as they pleased. This they none of them chose to do; but finding that all hopes of obtaining any thing by force were now at an end, they promised better behaviour for the future ; upon which we consented to their continuing with us.

" By this time it was ten o'clock, and the intense heat of the day induced us to defer our journey for a few hours; we therefore hired, for a little coffee, the hut belonging to the Sheik of the tribe near which we had encamped: it was just large enough to hold our two beds, which we covered with mats, and thus obtained a comfortableretreat from the rays of the sun. The old Sheik and his wife paid us many begging visits in the course of the day, with which we could readily have dispensed, as the lady was neither young nor handsome, and possessed a most invincible volubility of tongue. Before our departure she came in to examine all her valuables, and gave us a vociferous scolding for having drank some water without leave.

Two small beds taken from our sea cots, which Captain Rudland and myself had found very serviceable to us.

" This tribe seem to fare tolerably well; they have milk and butter, and a fruit called Gersa, which when boiled greatly resembles the common pea ; they also kill two goats for their daily consumption. The Nayib's two servants, with his mule, quitted us at this place, and at three P. M. the rest of the party set out, mounted on the mules from Dixan, which with our thirteen camels made a very respectable appearance. The road seemed perfectly secure, and well frequented, as we saw, almost every hour, small kafilas of twenty or thirty people passing with merchandize to Ar- kefco.

" After winding about among the acacias, for three miles or more, we turned into the dry bed of a torrent, where at first we suffered much from the heat. Our servants having neglected the most necessary precaution ot filling the skins with water, we were in the course of our march incommoded with thirst, the heat being intense. I was for a time relieved by the kindness of a poor fellow coming down from the hills, who gave me a portion of a small quantity that he carried in a cruise upon his back. As we proceeded, the valley became contracted to a rocky gully not more thau one hundred yards wide, bounded on each side, and overshadowed by steep and lofty hills.

" We passed a small burying place on our left;and soon after, the two ridges of mountains apparently closed, having at their foot a little rising ground called Hamhamou, a few yards distant from the bed of the torrent, where we halted for the night. We had just unloaded our camels, and were congratulating ourselves on having arrived at the end of a harrassing day's journey, during which we had taken no refreshment, except breakfast, when our guide told us that a storm was at hand. We accordingly collected our baggage in haste, covered it over with the walls of the tent, and were in the act of pitching the tent itself, when the rain came on with great violence, accompanied by loud thunder and vivid lightning. We all huddled together in the tent for shelter, but could not boast much of the protection which it afforded. To add to our trouble, it had no sooner grown dark, (the storm being now at its height), than an alarm was given by the Ascari, who were on the outside, that the natives were coming upon us. W"e instantly seized such fire-arms as were at hand, and rushed out to receive the enemy, into so drenching a rain as would presently have rendered our fire-arms entirely useless. Fortunately, however, it proved to be a false alarm, excited, I have no doubt, by our Ascari, who, if we had not shewn ourselves ready to repel aggression, would in all probability have taken the opportunity of at least plundering us.

" About an hour after this disturbance, we heard the torrent come rushing down, while the thunder still continued roaring in tremendous peals among the mountains. The air was now become so cold as to render both a cloth coat and camoline very acceptable, although the thermometer, when we

An Arab cloak

first arrived at this station, was as high as eighty- four degrees.

" The storm continued for four hours, during which some of our party, exhausted by fatigue, fell asleep, and the rest of us soon after, notwithstanding our uncomfortable situation, followed their example.

" July 23.lIt was curious to observe, in the morning, how completely our tent was filled, there being not only ourselves and servants, but the As- cari, camel-drivers, and three asses, that had crept in during the night for shelter.

" The hills that here seem to close, run nearly in a south direction; they are composed of large strata of burnt brown stone, with here and there layers of white spar; they are thinly covered with stunted Acacias and brushwood, and rise so steep as completely to shut out all distant hills. The rising ground on which we are encamped, is at present only a heap of bare gravel and loose stones, covering a rocky base, out of the crevices of which shoot forth a few green bushes. Bruce passed a night on the same spot; and it was his fortune, as well as ours, to encounter here a terrible storm, which, as usual, he describes with some exaggeration ; although he was here on the 17th ot November, a very different season.

" From this place there is a winding path of a mile or more,leading up the mountain on the eastern bank of the torrent, to some springs and natural cisterns in the rock, from which the tribes on the hills supply themselves with excellent water of a crystalline clearness. While we were at breakfast, a few miserable naked wretches, who live somewhere in the neighbourhood, came to us begging; We willingly made them partakers of our meal.

we recommenced our journey, Guebra.Michael, our Abyssinian guide, came to us, and recommended, as provisions were beginning to fall short, to dismiss the Nayib's Ascari. I was not sorry for the opportunity, and therefore ordered them immediately to depart, with which, as they now found all their consequence was gone, they reluctantly complied, on receiving two dollars each as a bribe.

" We quitted Hamhamou about ten A. M. the water having nearly subsided, and occupying only a small part of the bed of the torrent along which, as before, we took our way. As ve advanced, the gully gradually became narrower, and our guides urged us to make all possible expedition, fearing that more water might come down from the mountains. This actually took place about noon, though there had been no appearance of rain ; but fortunately it was not in such quantity as materially to impede our progress. Indeed our mules were so well trained, that it was no small obstacle which could disconcert them ; and it was continual matter, both for surprise and satisfaction, to see with what care thev passed over the rocks and loose stones that incumbered the road, as we repeatedly crossed and re-crossed the stream.

" We passed by a cave inhabited by a family of the natives; in it was a woman grinding corn, and some children playing about her. The general face of the country began to improve, the vegetation was fresher, and we observed a considerable variety of plants ; some of them seemed to belong to the liliaceous tribe, and made a very beautiful appearance. Captain Rudland killed a curious bird, of which I have a drawing.

" At half past four we arrived atSadoon, distant, from Hamhamou, according to our computation, About ten miles. This station is a small green plat,shaded by the same kind of trees as those which we saw at Weah ; it is within a few yards of the stream, and is entirely surrounded by woody mountains. As there seemed to be a probability of rain, we pitched our tent, and stowed within it all our baggage for the night. From the time that the Ascari had left us, the nightly watch, which had been kept before by ourselves, was entrusted to Pearce, Hamed Chamie, and the Abyssinian Christian, and muskets fired at stated intervals. The thermometer at day break was 77, and at noon 86.

" July 24.|Our expectations of rain were happily disappointed, for the night proved very fine, though cold. In the morning we observed that the stream had deposited the mud by which it was discoloured the evening before, and was now running quite clear : we saw in it a number of small fish resembling gudgeons.

" Between six and seven o'clock we recommenced our journey along the stony border of the stream, sometimes turning off into groves of trees, beneath the shade of which the ground was covered with green turf. Captain Rudland shot a small deer of the same kind as those we met with at Massowah, and a large bird of the grouse kind. After passing a small bury ing-ground, named Willo, we arrived at a thick grove, not unlike the mango topes of India : the trees of which it was composed also reminded us of the mango trees, from the form of their leaves and manner of bearing their fruit; this latter, however, was not a pulpy berry, but a hard nut inclosed within a thin husk. The natives all declared that it was poisonous ; but Mr. Carter eat three or four of the kernels without experiencing any inconvenience.

" Soon after, we arrivdd at Tubbo, a verypicturesque station, abounding in groves of various shady trees, and surrounded by abrupt clift's and precipices. Bruce has well described this place ; but though there were a great variety of birds around, their notes did not appear to me to be different from what we had often before heard. The mountains hereabouts are inhabited by the Ha- zorta, Welleihah, and above fifty other tribes, according to the concurrent reports of the people of Dixan and Arkeko; whence it may be inferred that almost each hill has its distinct tribe. The Hazorta are at present, and have been for many years, on friendly terms with the Nayib of Mas- Bowah; but a tribe to the eastward, called Hartoo, is at open war with him. A man of the former came down to us unarmed, accompanied by his little boy; they were both of them black, and very thinly clad, and were very grateful on being presented with a small piece of tobacco.

" We saw here two large trees of the sycamore fig, being about nineteen feet in girth at their bases; out of the sides of the larger boughs were growing great bunches of figs, which, however, were for the most part devoured by the black ants before they were ripe: a species of Asclepias also grows here in great abundance, as indeed it does all the way from Arkeko; of its wood the inhabitants make handles for their knives and swords. We remained at Tubbo, enjoying the grateful coolness of its shade, till half-past five, and then it was not without difficulty that I prevailed on our people to go another stage. Our road still continued along the bed of the torrent; but besides the trees already mentioned, the tamarind now began to make its appearance: we also saw several monkeys on the hills; they were chiefly of three species; one was the kind common at Mocha; another wasdistinguished by its large size, and white hair oft the head and beard; the third was much smaller than the others, and had a white beard, and white rings on the tail. We also saw the rock rabbit, which appeared to be like the Ashkoko of Bruce. In less than an hour we arrived at Illilah (Lila of Bruce), where we took up our quarters for the night under a tree, without taking the trouble to pitch the tent, there being no appearance of rain. We slept unmolested by wild beasts, and undisturbed by noise of any kind, but found the air very cold towards morning, especially during the strong gusts of wind which came down at intervals from the hills. Our computed distance from Sadoon was eight miles. The thermometer at 5 A. M. was *IT.*

" July 25.|We resumed our journey at an early hour, notwithstanding the appearance of the sky foretold heavy rain. The road, which had been very perceptibly ascending all the way from Ar- keko, now rose more rapidly ; much elephants dung lay scattered about, and the branches of most of the fig-trees were lopped off nearly to the top, to give an opportunity to the cattle]of browz- ing on the leaves and tender shoots, the grass being entirely burnt up: on the sides of the hills we perceived a few huts, and several of the inhabitants.

" After a march of nearly two hours we reached a place called Assubah, where there was a burying ground. We saw here a few men attending a large herd of cattle, of whom we purchased, for four dollars, a cow to serve as provision for our people during the ascent of Taranta. In about a quarter of an hour more we reached our station at the foot of that mountain. We had now proceeded with our camels as far as the unevenness of theground would permit, it was therefore necessary to seek for some other method of getting our baggage conveyed to Dixan. For this purpose we opened a negociation for the use of some bullocks, with some of the Hazorta tribe, who inhabit the mountains; but not being able to agree on terms, we procured only one of these animals, and finally concluded a bargain with some men and boys, for the conveyance of our packages on their shoulders. During this transaction a man of some consequence among them, called Sheik Ummar, had been making a demand of tobacco, coffee, &c. for allowing us to pass the mountain; this claim not being mentioned to me immediately by those to whom the chief had stated it, he thought himself neglected, rose up in a violent passion, and seizing his spear and shield, rushed down the hill with his attendants, muttering threats as he went. Being unwilling needlessly to hazard the serious consequences which this affair might produce, I sent after him, and in an amicable conference explained the mistake, and gratified him with the trifling presents required. In the evening the Hazorta chiefs all returned, accompanied by an old man of great authority among them. This venerable patriarch, who was said to have around him three hundred relations, placed himself on a rising ground, and having raised his garment on the end of a spear, and demanded silence, made a speech to the following effect.

" Be it known to all, that these people who are passing are great men, friends of the Nayib of Massowah, friends of the Sultaun of Habesh, friends of the Ras Welleta Selasse, and friends of the Baharnegash Yasous ; we have received and eaten of their meat, drank of their coffee, and partaken of their tobacco, and are therefore their friends;let no man dare to molest them." On this there was a general buzz of approbation, and ail was quiet and settled. We were however again disturbed by the Nayib's people in the evening, who made fresh demands upon us, backed with threats; to these, however, we paid no farther regard than arming ourselves as usual for the night, which we passed without molestation. The thermometer in the evening was 76.

" July 26.|The Hazorta chief being this morning in a very friendly humour, I availed myself of the circumstance to make some enquiries concerning the tribe to which he belonged. He told me that they married four wives ; that he himself had that number, and nine children, five girls, and four boys; that the population of the tribe amounted to about five thousand ; that they possessed maqy cattle, but seldom killed them, unless they were likely to die from disease or accidents, these animals forming the chiefmedium of barter for grain with the Abyssinians. On enquiring why they did not raise corn themselves, he replied, that they were ignorant of the art of doing so, otherwise they would willingly supply their own wants, without having recourse to others. He further informed me, that they never stripped the branches from the trees, except for the purpose of feeding their cattle, when the grass was burnt up or consumed. Hence it appears not improbable that these people might, by gentle means, be brought to a much higher state of civilization than that in which they are at present; with regard to their population, if their number be only half so many as the chief represented them, they must be considered as a very powerful tribe; and being a brave, though rude people, and in possession of a very strong country, throughwhich lies the only practicable passage into Abyssinia from this quarter, they might assume and maintain an importance much superior to what they actually possess.

" At half past eleven, after about five hours continued wrangling with our people, during which we were several times on the point of proceeding to blows, we at length prevailed on them to fetch the mules, and we began to ascend the mountain ; Sheik Umma, from whom I had obtained the preceding information, taking his leave with many expressions of friendship and humility. The first part of the road was smooth and easy ; but, as we advanced, it became steeper and more incommoded with loose stones and masses of rock, over which however our excellent mules carried us with great facility, and in perfect safety. Such of the Nayib's people as we had still retained with us to serve as guides, knowing that when we should have crossed the mountain, they could no longer with safety continue their insolence and rapacity, resolved to throw every obstruction in the way of our farther progress; accordingly they began by deserting us ; we fortunately however met with a young Sheik descending the mountain, who, fora small recompence, agreed to be our guide, upon which we continued our journey. In about a quarter of an hour afterwards we were overtaken by the Nayib's guide, who had already given us so much trouble : he now insisted on our halting, giving us to understand that there was neither water, provisions, nor resting-place to be found above, and therefore that we must take up our station where we were, and proceed over the mountain the next day. Having said this, he immediately seized Captain Rudland's mule veryroughly, and on my. passing him he came forwards to lay hold of mine ; this however 1 prevented by drawing my hanger, and threatening him to cut him down if he ottered the least molestation. On this he desisted, and seated himself on a stone by the road side in a violent rage. But we had not yet entirely got rid of him, for by the time that we had advanced half a mile farther, he again overtook us, having by some means or other got Captain Hudland's sword from the Sheik, who had been entrusted by that gentleman to carry it up the hill. He now began to abuse Mr. Carter, who had resisted the attempts made to stop the mule on which he rode, and was on the point of drawing the sword, when Mr. Carter took a pistol from his girdle and presented it at him; at the same moment Captain Rudland jumped from his mule and wrested the sword from him. Having thus failed in all his attempts to detain us another day, and being probably intimidated by the result of the last, he gave up the point in despair, and we experienced no farther trouble.

" The whole of this mountain was thickly set with kolquall, which grows nearly to the height of forty feet: towards the top the berry-bearing cedar of Bruce, (called by our guide Cereder) began to make its appearance, and became more abundant in proportion as we ascended; the summit of the mountain being covered with a thick copse of this tree. In the most rugged path of the road we dismounted, to ease our mules, and walked for about half a mile ; we then remounted, and gained the top without any further difficulty. As soon as we arrived we found, on looking at our watches, that it was only half past two; so that, notwithstanding ajl our delays, we had been occnpied only three hours in overcoming the exaggerated perils and toils of the passage of Taranta. We now directed our course into a beautiful little green valley shaded by cedars, and adorned by a pool of water; the sight of which was particularly grateful to us, as we had been repeatedly told that there was none on the top; near it was grazing a large herd of cattle. Wandering about the valley we discovered a great profusion of mushrooms, of which, notwithstanding they were considered by the natives as poisonous, we collected a large quantity: part we stewed for immediate use, and the remainder we bottled, and found them both wholesome and highly grateful, in the total want of vegetables which we afterwards experienced. Soon afterwards, Captain Rudland shot an owl of a very large species, and Mr. Carter and myself collected a number of flowers, several of which had bulbous roots; among the shrubs were the sweet briar, and several others highly aromatic. We were soon overtaken by the men and boys, who had charge of our baggage; one of our heaviest boxes, containing ammunition and dollars of considerable weight, was, to our surprize, brought up by a boy about thirteen years of age; and one of the walls of our large tent, together with the two poles, were conveyed by one man from the bottom to the top of the pass in about four hours. It is not easy to reconcile these facts, with Bruce's representation of the extraordinary difficulties- with which he had to contend during two days in going over the same distance, unless the re-establishment of peace between the Nayib, and the tribe of Hazorta, had been attended by a surprizing improvement of the road, which is not probable, as by Bruce's own account the trade, if we may judge by the number of slaves, was then fully

VOL. II. H H

equal tr what it is at present. Besides, we did not meet with a single hyaena or troglodytical cave; and luckily " had not our hands and knees cut by frequent falls, or our faces torn by thorny bushes ;" which last, indeed, appears scarcely possible in so open and frequented a path. The only part of our baggage that did not reach us till late at night, was the fly of the tent, and my bed, which were carried on the back of an ox; in consequence of which, the evening being very cold, we arranged our baggage in a half circle, made a good fire in the centre, and slept on the walls of the tent, having previously regaled ourselves with salt-fish, rice, and stewed mushrooms. The thermometer in the evening was 64.

" July 27.IA shower fell in the course of the night, and when we awoke, the sky was so lowering, that, though our guide declared it was only the common morning mist, we thought it prudent to pitch our tent, under which we obtained shelter from a smart shower of rain which fell soon after. The tops of Taranta, surrounding the little valley in which we slept, had hitherto been obscured by fleeting clouds; at seven they began to clear away, upon which we dispatched the baggage forward, and about eight o'clock set out ourselves. We had not however ascended the first rising ground before heavy rain came on, and continued, with very short intermission, during the whole of the day. Thence the descent became very rapid, and the road lay through gullies, down which the waters were beginning to run with great force; but none of these obstacles seemed to delay our mules; they descended almost like goats from rock to rock, and not one of the whole number made a single false step in the course of the day. Notwithstanding our clothcoats and camolines, we were all wet to the skin, and, on account of the difficulties of the road, were not able long to keep together; so that, while Captain Rudland and myself were proceeding on the direct road, Mr. Carter and Pearce were wandering wherever the mules chose to carry . them, and, as it afterwards appeared, they had actually arrived within half a mile of Dixan, when they turned, and made a circuit of about five miles.

" Captain Rudland and myself took shelter in a village about three miles from Dixan, under a hut divided into many compartments, and inhabited by several families. They paid us every attention that their miserable means would allow; and an old woman, who spoke a little Arabic, brought us some water which was much discoloured ; among the group we observed two handsome young women, who had fine teeth, and silver rings in their ears. House-sparrows were seen to fly from under the roofs of the huts ; and the cattle were lodged in the same apartment as the women and children. The mode of building here is by raising walls of the required height, adjoining, and at right angles, to a steep slope on the side of a hill, and then laying on a roof of sods, pitched so as to correspond with the general descent of the hill, which gives the appearance of caves to these habitations. We much regretted having nothing with us to give these poor people but an empty wine bottle; with this, however, they were well satisfied.

" Our companions soon after joined us, and about two in the afternoon, after the most unpleasant day we had yet experienced, we reached Dixan, completely wet, and without any of our baggage, which was all scattered upon the road in proportion to the strength or willingness of thosewbxcarried it. We were received by the Bahar- negash Yasous, and the head men of the town, who were waiting at the house prepared for us.

" Soon after our arrival,, the Baharnegash sent us some large flat barley cakes, some honey, and hydromel; and upon this, with a little of our Dhalac cheese, we were glad to make our dinner.

" July 28.IThe thermometer in the morning at day break on Taranta was 59; in the course of the day it varied from 61 to 66. We passed a most miserable night, the air being extremely, cold, (thermometer 59) and the few cloaths we had with us completely wet; for my own part, I sat till nearly morning with my feet in the embers of a small fire which occupied the centre of our cave. I call it so, because being constructed on the same plan as the habitation before described, it is evidently copied from natural or artificial excavations. It may be said, in favour of this mode of building, that there is hardly any other better suited to the hilly nature of the country, or which, with so little labour, will afford an equally secure protection to the inhabitants and their cattle from the inconveniences of the weather, and the wild beasts that are continually prowling about during the night. We all found ourselves unwell in the morning, in consequence of the fatigue of yesterday ; nor did the gloominess of the weather, for the rain still continued, contribute to raise our spirits. At about ten o'clock, Hamed Chamie, and the rest of our servants, arrived in as wretched a condition as ourselves ; they had however been, better accommodated during the night, at a village where they had procured a sheep, and were well treated by the inhabitants. Our boxes were brought in one by one, most of them drenched with water; but, fortunately, the cloth and presents designed for the Ras, and my smaller box of valuables, escaped undamaged. Towards evening the greater part of our baggage arrived, and an additional demand of five dollars was made by Guebra Michael: this Hamed Chamie resisted. The Baharnegash at first expressed his displeasure at this new charge; however, he afterwards came to me and stated, that his nephew had promised the money as a gratuity to the bearers, some of whom he had pressed into the service on the road. To this Guebra Michael gave his hand as a pledge ; on which I ordered the money to be paid to him. It rained the whole day; the thermometer varied from 61 to *63'*.

" July 29.|We were kept awalce during the greater part of the last night by the barking of dogs, which were alarmed at the near approach of hysenas and other wild beasts.

" I had a conversation this morning with the Baharnegash respecting our conveyance hence to Adowa. He said that his orders were to pay us every possible attention ; and added, that my letters had been forwarded to the Ras ; but as he was unacquainted with their contents, he should be glad of some information respecting the object of my coming. I replied, that the English was a very powerful nation, which had complete command of the sea; and that an English nobleman, then at Mocha, had sent me for the purpose of promoting an intercourse of friendship with Abyssinia; which, if properly encouraged, could not fail of proving most beneficial to the whole country. I was induced thus far to explain myself, not only from the generally friendly manner in which he had behaved towards us, but also to secure his good offices in furtherance of our views. He expressed his entire satisfaction with my communication, and proceeded to inform me, that it was necessary to write immediately to Basha Ab-dallah, Secretary to Nebred Araur, Governor of Adowa, stating what animals we should want for our own riding, and for carrying our baggage, which, on my requisition, would be immediately sent down; that he himself had only three mules, but that they were all at our service. I told him, whatever had been arranged by the Ras, would meet with my hearty concurrence, and begged that he would hasten the messenger ; and also urge to Basha Abdallah the necessity of sending the mules as speedily as possible, since I was obliged soon to return to Massowah. Accordingly I wrote a letter, which he promised to dispatch immediately, requesting to be furnished with twenty-five mules; to which I was led to expect an answer in six days. For the carriage of the letter I paid two dollars. I found the Baharnegash himself was under orders to attend me up to the Ras, which he professed he should do with pleasure. I was informed that, after we had ascended the mountain of Taranta, the natives, headed by that rascal the Nayib's guide, had assembled for the purpose of detaining our baggage, but our friend Guebra Michael, by his very strenuous exertions, succeeded in getting it up in safety. This, joined to the very insolent manner in which our guide had endeavoured to stop us on the ascent, as already mentioned, gave us good reason to suppose that some serious mischief was meditated, which our promptitude in crossing the mountain enabled us to avoid.

" The day being tolerably clear, we collected some plants, dried all our things, and made ourselves in other respects as comfortable as our situation would admit.

" July 30.lI was engaged all the morning in writing letters, copying my journal, and preparing a packet for Lord Valentia, containing an account of occurrences up to our arrival at Dixan, which was dispatched in the afternoon, and, as I afterwards learned, arrived safely. Towards evening Captain Rudland walked out with his gun, in hopes of meeting with game or hyaenas ; he however met with no success, having seen only two large spotted deer, which were exceedingly shy : during his absence I employed myself in taking a sketch of the mountains of Tigre1. The day was clear and fine, though with much thunder and lightning in the evening. The thermometer was 66. We were none of us well, which I attributed to change of food and climate.

" July 31.lA letter, of which the following is a translation, was received by the Baharnegash from the Ras's Secretary at Adowa, whom the natives style Bashaw Abdallah. After the usual compliments, ' Expecting that by this time the English are arrived at Dixan, I shall send my man Negada Moosa for them with horses and mules. I desire that you will pay them all the attention in your power, and will dispatch a messenger as soon as possible to acquaint Ras Welleta Selasse", with their safe arrival. The Ras commands that all care may be taken of them ; that you will provide them with houses, with meat, and with drink of the very best, as your head must answer for it. In short, take as much care of them as you would of Ras Welleta Selasse", and so soon a& they arrive, send me instant intelligence thereof.'

" In consequence of the receipt of this letter, I thought proper to make remonstrances about the high price that we were charged for provisions.

The Bahaniegash told me that he would very willingly give whatever he had of his own, but that the articles which we wanted, were such as they themselves did not consume ; and, owing to a late scarcity, which had been felt very severely so far as this place, they were extremely difficult to procure; it was not therefore in his power to afford us any relief in this particular; a representation, which, from the poverty of the place, I had afterwards reason to consider true.

" The day was tolerably fine: about eleven in the forenoon, however, there fell a smart shower, during which au alarm was given of an hysena being seen near our cave, by Mr. Carter and Pearce. Captain Rudland went out with his gun in pursuit of it, but was unsuccessful. I was myself too unwell to stir out, and was therefore engaged in drawing. More rain fell in the evening.

" August 1.lThis morning the messenger who was dispatched with my letter to the Ras from Massowah, arrived hither on his way back from Antalow. He reported, that on the receipt.of the letter the Ras issued immediate orders to a chief at Adowa to have in readiness the same number of animals as we had engaged from the Nayib ; and to send them to meet us at this place as soon as he received intelligence of our arrival. The Nayib's charge to me for the conveyance of this letter, was, as I before mentioned, thirty dollars, of which the bearer declared that he was paid only two, Frequent showers fell during the day. The thermometer in our cave was 70. . .... - -

August 2.ıI walked out in the morning with Captain Rudland; collected a few plants, and killed a bird called by the natives Warre, of which I look a sketch. Our people were engaged in repacking the baggage preparatory to our departure. The day was fine without rain. The thermometer in our cave was 75.

" The Baharnegash, attended by his brother and Guebra Michael, paid us a visit at a late hour in the evening, and after some conversation on common occurrences, began mentioning the names of several, supposed English, gentlemen, who had formerly passed this place ; these we imagined to have been Bruce and his attendants : they soon concluded their discourse by saying that our countrymen had made the inhabitants of the place a present of one hundred dollars, and therefore they hoped that I would do the same. Upon my evading this, and referring the Baharnegash to the lias, he went so far as to assert that he had a rightful claim to the money, and being an independent chief, would demand it in the Ras's presence. I replied, that to my certain knowledge no English gentlemen had ever given any such sum ; that one only had ever passed through this town before, and that he had given only forty dollars to the late Baharnegash, for which sum he had received in return a fine black horse : that we had already been at a very considerable expence, and as we were going up by desire of the Ras, and looked for no advantage ourselves from the journey, I should certainly not give him any thing at present, but should on my arrival at Antalow report the affair to the Ras, and guide myself entirely by his determination.

" After this had been explained, the brother began to raise his voice and interfere ; but I stopped him at once, by telling him that I would not suffer him to meddle with the affair ; on which he rose from his seat in a violent passion and left the house, followed, to our great satisfaction, by the Baharnegash and his nephew, who seemed happy

thus to get rid of a demand which they found themselves too weak to support.

" In a few minutes Hamed Chamie returned with a message from the Baharnegash, saying, that his people were very hungry, and that it was on this account only that he had asked for money; he hoped, notwithstanding, that we should con tinue good friends, and that he was ready to accompany us as soon as the mules arrived ; he also begged that what had passed might not be mentioned to the Ras.

" August 3.ıI took a walk, as usual, after breakfast, and collected a few specimens of plants. The day was fine, and without rain. In the course of our walk we saw a large bird much resembling the Abba Gumba of Bruce; but a shower coming on at the moment, prevented our sportsmen from pursuing it. When the rain was over, Captain Rudland went out again, and killed a large bird called by the natives Derhomai (or water fowl, from Derho, a bird, and mai, water), of which I made a drawing. This bird inhabits low marshy grounds, and feeds on worms. We had it cooked, and found the flesh tender and well flavoured.

" At a late hour in the evening the brother of the Baharnegash waited upon Hamed Chamie, repeating his demands for money in the name of the town's people, declaring that it was their right, and that they were determined to be paid. Hamed Chamie said, that an answer had already been given by me to the Baharnegash; and he very properly got up, called for him, and brought him to me, complaining of the behaviour of the people. The Baharnegash, after desiring Hamed Chamie to pay no attention to them, said, that as our food and lodging had been providedby himself, no other person could possibly have any demand upon us.

" August 5.|Nothing particular occurred this day. The weather was bright and mild, like a May day in England.

" August 6.|So much rain, accompanied by thunder and lightning, fell this day, that we were scarcely able to stir out of doors. I amused myself with drawing, and Captain Rudland in collecting information from the inhabitants.

" The Baharnegash was very urgent to have a picture for the church: accordingly I set Pearce to work, who painted one of the Virgin Mary and the infant Christ, in most flaming colours, which gave great satisfaction. The thermometer in our hut at noon was 64.

" August 7.|A letter was received from Basha Abdallah at Adowa, stating, that the mules were not to leave that place till to-morrow, and would therefore probably not arrive here before Sunday. This delay was attributed to the necessity of sending to the Ras at Antalow, for an order to have more mules purchased, as the people at Adowa refused to send their mules for our accommodation.

" A kafila came in from Massowah, by which the Baharnegash received a letter from Currum Chund; but no anwer arrived to either of our letters sent to Massowah. Reports were in circulation that Captain Court had been firing on Massowah, as the natives described an iron kettle which burst over the town.

" We heard that the dead bodies of three men had been found, washed down by the torrent on this side of Taranta.

" Our sportsmen, having seen a dead horse and an ass lying in the skirts of the town, were out for two hours in the evening in pursuit of the hyaenas, which they supposedwould be attracted by the carcases. They discovered a great number of these animals growling and fighting over their food, and making at times a hideous roaring; they must be possessed of gre'at strength, as a single one was observed dragging along the entire carcase of the horse; in size they varied considerably, but Captain Rudland and Pearce both agreed that one of them, which they wounded, was quite as large as a small ass. Some dogs of the village were gnawing the carcase, but they retired, snarling, to a small distance, on the approach of the hyaenas, who in their turn did not seem to have any inclination to attack the dogs. Intermixed with the bycenas, and feeding on the carcase very amicably at the same time with them, were smaller animals, supposed to be jackalls. The morning was cold and foggy, but the weather cleared up about breakfast time, and continued tolerably fine for the remainder of the day.

" Intelligence arrived that a kafila, on its way hither from Massowah, had suffered severely by the sudden rise of the torrent at Elleilah, one man, ten camels, and a great part of the baggage were washed away.

" August 8.|I walked out in the morning, and collected some plants. In the evening we all sallied forth on an alarm of an hysena. We saw. two, one of which Captain Rudland was lucky enough to shoot; the ball passed through the right shoulder and lodged in the neck, on which the animal immediately fell. Pearce ran up to it, and threw large stones upon its head, and Mr. Carter thrust his sword down its throat, which soon dispatched it.

" On hearing the shot, the people of the village all came out, many of them armed with spears;but we could not prevail on any of them to assist in carrying our game home, as all the Abyssinians hold the hyaena in utter abhorrence. Our servants, however, brought him in great triumph, and hung him up to one of the posts before our door, that I might take a drawing of him in the morning.

" August 9.|My first care in the morning was to examine the hyaena that we had shot the preceding night: it was a male, of the spotted species (canis crocuta), and is called by the natives Zubbee; its prevailing colour is a dirty light brown inclining to yellow, with black spots : the extremity of the tail is covered with long and coarse black hair, like that of a horse's tail; on the back is a ridge of long hair, of which that part between the loins and head inclines forwards, while the rest points towards the tail, shortening by degrees, so that it lies quite smooth on the rump. The length of this animal from the nose to the insertion of the tail was four feet three inches ; its height, from the top of the shoulder to the sole of the fore foot, was two feet four inches and a half; and from the crown of the rump to the sole of the hind foot was two feet one inch and a half. We afterwards saw several considerably larger, and of a darker colour.

" When the inhabitants came out to us last night, on hearing the report of Captain Rudland's gun, they were accompanied by several of their dogs, which, as soon as they perceived the hyaena stretched out and roaring on the ground, fell upon him, and seized him with great fury; but as I liave already mentioned, these two animals, in ordinary circumstances, though mutually inimical, seldom venture on a contest. We have more than onceobserved their passingandrepassing, each suarKing, but neither venturing to begin an attack; and, one evening, both were seen feeding on the same carcase. The hyaena, however, always retires from the presence of man; and the dogs, by barking, give notice to their master of its approach.

" While we were touching and skinning the hyaena, the inhabitants looked on with evident signs of horror and disgust; the Baharnegasb, however, begged the liver of the animal, which forms one of the ingredients of an ink in which charms are written, that are worn round the arms as amulets from all evil. The man who was sent for the liver seemed as much afraid of it as of a snake, and carried it away with great caution on the end of a long stick.

" After we had skinned the hyasna, we left him on the grass about one hundred yards from our hut, where he remained untouched by the dogs or vultures during the whole day ; but as soon as it became dusk, the carcase was dragged off and devoured by other hya?nas.

" Having finished these observations, we took a walk of about three or four miles, but met with little worthy of observation. We killed a lizard of a light blue colour, of which I made a drawing, and took a camelion alive. On our return we were overtaken with very heavy rain, hail, thunder, and lightning.

" I was engaged during the afternoon in making drawings of some plants that we had collected in Qur walk.

" News arrived that Captain Court had been under the necessity of landing fifteen men from the Panther at Massowah, and of threatening the Nayib, before he could get possession of the packet which we dispatched hence : to this no answer has as yet been received.

" August 10.|I wrote a letter this morning to the Ras, informing him of our delay at Dixan, and that, as we had received no intelligence with respect to the time when the mules from Adowa would probably arrive, we should within in three days proceed with such conveyances as we might be able to procure at this place.

" Five dollars were required by the Baharnegash for the carriage of this letter to Antalow ; with which demand, having no alternative, I was obliged to comply.

" We rode a short distance out of town, but the weather compelled us very soon to return ; on our way back we passed over the highest part of the irregular hill on which Dixan is built; and which Bruce has not very accurately described, when he compares it to a sugar loaf, as may be seen in one of my larger views.

" On our return, we found that a fresh demand had been made on Hamed Chamie for some pepper for the messenger about to depart with our letter to Antalow; but this, being too valuable an article to part with, we absolutely refused. The letter, in consequence, was returned by the Baharnegash with the five dollars to Hamed Chamie; I immediately sent for the Baharnegash, and represented to him my surprise at what had passed : assuring him that I should leave Dixan in three days, and, if the letter should not arrive at Antalow before me, the blame would fall upon him. I afterwards thought it expedient to inclose the letter to Bashaw Abdallah, as the communication from Adowa to Antalow appeared more open than from this place.' The Baharnegash attempted, but in vain, to prevent the letter being sent, by telling us he had information that the mules would be here to-morrow.

" In the evening there arrived a man from the village of Dagozie, two days journey hence, with intelligence that the mules from Adowa were near at hand. He brought also a lean cow from his uncle, who is Kantiba, or chief of the village above mentioned, as a present; in return for which I gave him two pieces of cloth. This, however, did not satisfy him; for, when we had retired to rest, he came to inform me, that, as he was about to set off for Hamazen, if I had any thing to give him, he begged to receive it immediately. After enquiring what were his demands, I learned that lie had the modesty to expect a gift of an equal value with the mule he rode upon, which he estimated at the trifling sum of forty dollars ; upon this I referred him to Hamed Chamie, as was invariably my custom on such occasions, and he soon got rid of him, by recommending him to take his cow back again, for which he thought he had already been most amply paid.

" August 11.|In the course of this morning two men arrived, bringing intelligence from Ne- gada Moosa, that the mules would be here on the morrow ; but we had so many similar accounts, that I told the Baharnegash I should pay no farther attention to verbal messengers, and, as these people might have come merely for the purpose of getting the usual recompence of a piece of cloth, I did not choose to comply with the custom any longer.

" Heavy rain attended by thunder came on at noon, and the remainder of the day was so dark and dismal, that in our hut we could not see to do any thing without a candle. Our whole party was unwell with violent colds. We killed a vulture, which upon examination, we pronounced " to be a bird of passage," since we could not discoverany of that powder which, Bruce says, the hill birds of this country are provided with, and which, it is to be observed, all the birds that we have hitherto killed have been without.

"August 12.|We passed the morning in anxious expectation of the arrival of the mules, and in preparing our fire.arms, &c. for the journey. About twelve o'clock intelligence was brought us of their approach, and soon after, the Baharnegash introduced Hadjee Hamed, and Negada Moosa; they brought each of them a letter from the Ras, in Arabic, mentioning the former as a man in his confidence, to whom we were to make known all our wishes, and the latter as appointed to take charge of our persons and baggage. They seemed to be men of more respectability than any we had hitherto met with since we left Mocha, and their retinue and attendants were numerous, and decently clad. They brought us information that the Ras and his family were well; that he was himself exceedingly anxious to see us, and had given orders to bring us up, without delay, by the nearest road, to his presence; that all things were prepared for us by his special orders in the villages through which we had to pass; and that if any man should dare to molest us, his head must answer for it. They likewise mentioned, that when we arrived within two days march of Antalow, an additional retinue would meet us. Hadjee Hamed, immediately on his coniing into our hut, recognized me, and I soon recollected that we had met at the village of Badoor, on one of the islands of Port Mornington, and that he then informed me he was on his way from the Sheriffe of Mecca to Ras Welleta Selasse'. After having taken coffee, they retired with Hamed Chamie, and I *Vol. u. I i*

gave an order for the purchase of five sheep for the better accommodation of the party.

" Dixan was now extremely full of strangers, for besides our attendants from the Ras, there wert kafilas hourly coming in both from Massowah and Adowa. The day was cloudy with a little thunder.

" August 13. I Hadjee Hamed and Negada Moosa sent Hamed Chamie early in the morning to deliver me the mules sent by the Ras ; I therefore went to the door of our hut, and all the mules, in number twenty-one, were brought before me; sixteen of them were of a large and coarse breed, for the conveyance of baggage, and five of a lighter, for our riding. This ceremony being over, the Baharnegash informed me, that he would provide me with three more, a sufficient number to accommodate all our people. I gave orders to have every thing prepared for setting out by daylight on the morrow, having consented to remain here this day at the request of our new attendants, who were anxious for a little rest, and with whom I felt desirous to commence our journey on as good terms as possible. They afterwards brought me flour and other necessaries, and informed us that every thing in future, would be provided for us, free of expence, by the Ras's commands.

" In the evening the Baharnegash visited us with his brother, who had been a very troublesome fellow; and as we knew that he could not come for any good purpose, we evaded all communication, on the plea of our interpreter being out of the way. The cause of their visit, as we afterwards learned, was this: the Baharnegash had promised us three mules, but being himself inpossession of only two, he expected to obtain the third from his brother. This man, however, positively refused to accommodate him, saying, that as we had made him no present we should have nothing belonging to him.

-The Baharnegash tised the most urgent entreaties; but all in vain. The only terms on which he would agree were, that his brother should give him an equal share of what he might receive from us. The Baharuegash told him that he was going on with us to Antalow, and that it might be very long before he should receive any thing; he was nevertheless willing, to give him half, so anxious was he to keep his word with us. His brother, however, demanding immediate payment, the Baharnegash was under the necessity of sending to a neighbouring village to purchase a mule, which was brought in the evening.

" The houses of Dixan are flat-roofed, and without windows, and, instead of chimneys, have two pots of earthenware rising out of the roof, but so narrow as to give vent only to a small portion of the smoke : the houses are built round a hill commanding an extensive prospect of the mountains of Tigre and country around, which consists almost entirely of rocky mountains, on many of which are to be observed villages constructed much in the same style as at Dixan.

" The only public building in this place is the chapel, which we visited. It is a place of a mean appearance, with a conical thatched roof, and mud walls. On entering the door of the inclo- sure (A) the boys who conducted us kissed the door posts : and we, in conformity to their customs, pulled off our shoes and hats, on entering the door of the building itself (B). The inner bailding was shut. The aisle that surrounded it(c c) was strewn with rushes; and on the walls were painted rude figures in glaring colours of St. George and St. Haimonout on horseback, with spears, and various other strange figures in as many strange postures. The priests bear large keys in their hands, like that which the painters place in the hand of St. Peter. The natives all appear fond of crosses. The Baharnegash was highly pleased with one given to him by Captain Rudland. Most of the Christians here have a cross marked upon their breast, or their right arm, or forehead, which with a blue silk string round their necks, they seem to think indispensable badges of their religion. They kiss every thing that has the least claim to sanctity or respect, a strong instance of which was. the Baharnegash's kissing the letter which I delivered to him for the Ras's Secretary, Bashaw Abdalla.

" The people whom I have hitherto seen, with few exceptions, are idle, ignorant, and dirty; they are of a very dark complexion, few having a claim to the appellation of copper-coloured given them by Bruce. It is usual for them to say prayers over every thing they eat, drink, receive, or give away, concluding the ceremony with blowing upon it, in the same way as a conjuror does on his balls.

" In these prayers they always turn the face to the east, as they turn the heads of the animals which they kill to the west. They refuse to taste of any thing killed by Mahomedans, whom they hold in great contempt.

" Boys marry at fourteen years of age, girls at ten, eleven, and twelve; both are circumcised on the eighth day after their birth; this operation is performed by women.

" The number of wives possessed by each manvaries from one to ten, according to their property, or as they are able to support them, as each woman must be furnished with a separate place of residence.

" Most of the laborious occupations, both abroad and at home, devolve upon the women; such as grinding the corn, bringing in wood and water, which is brought from a valley about a mile from the town, cultivating the ground, and picking herbs for the consumption of the day. They carry their children on their backs, and wear tanned hides round their waists; their necks and arms are ornamented with beads, and white shells; and the women of the higher class allow the nails on the left hand to grow to a great length, wearing cases of leather on their ringers several .inches long, to preserve them.

" Slaves are very dear at this place, if we are to be guided by the report of the inhabitants; but the price of these animals, like that of every other put up to the highest bidder, is greatly regulated by their outward appearance. If nature has been favourable, and given them fine features, with a tolerably fair skin, they sell for a great deal more than those of a darker colour.

" The proportion of land capable of cultivation, as far as we had an opportunity of observing, is scanty, consisting of a few spots on the sides of the hills, and the drier parts of the valleys.

" The present seems to be the season of spring in this country ; some of the inhabitants are now ploughing their fields with wooden ploughs. These are rudely shaped out of the root or branch of a tree, and sometimes the shares are formed of iron. After twice ploughing the land, the clods are broken with rude hooked instruments by the women, who at the same time pick out theweeds ; the grain is then strewn upon and they seem to make choice of the worst samples for seed. There are a great number of goats belonging to this place, but they are now mostly dry, in consequence of which milk is not to be obtained without great difficulty - the whole that we have been able to procure has not exceeded a pint per day. A small goat costs half a dollar. The sheep are most of them black, but some of them have white faces: the skins of all are valuable commodities, as they make excellent coverings ; and no man moves a hundred yards from his house without having one hung over his shoulders.

" We have as yet observed but few cows, and those miserably poor. There is plenty of barley andjuwarry, but we have not hitherto seen any wheat.

" White cloths are preferred at Dixan before any other colour. Tobacco, black pepper, looking-glasses, snuff, spirits, and large beads, are good articles for barter : green beads are at present in fashion, and therefore fetch a better price than any others.

" The musical instrument that we heard at Massowah, and which I imagine to be Bruce's lyre, is in use here ; it was played upon by one of the young priests. Their singing is, if possible, ruder than their music, and both together are intolerable.

" Bruce says that they allow no figures in re-. lief; the few that we have yet seen are two faces at the head of the couch on which I sleep.

" The duties arising from the merchandize that passes through Dixan are collected by the person, at whose house the travelling merchanthooses to put up. Travellers are housed and fed during their stay, for which the landlord is recom- penced either in goods or money. The rate at which they pay on these occasions is said to be so very exorbitant, that I could give no credit to the report.

The Baharnegash seems to preside over Dixan and six or seven adjoining villages ; these appear to have agreed among themselves to continue in peace with, and faithful to, each other. If at any time an offence be committed, the whole body assembles, and the affair is discussed ; but punishment is seldom inflicted, because the offender has an easy mode of evading it, by joining another hill tribe. It has been repeated to us by many of them, that they pay no tribute to the Has ; and they asserted more than once that they were entirely independent of the Tigre " government. This, however, from several circumstances that occurred, we did not believe to be strictly the case; they may not pay him any revenue, but it is evident that they stand in awe of his authority.

" The Baharnegash carries on the affairs of his government entirely by verbal messages. Judging from the little attention that the Geesh characters in Brace's book excited when we shewed them to him, I do not believe that he is himself capable either of writing or reading.

" There are no schools for the education of youth, in any language, that I could find out, at Dixan : we met with only a few persons who could read the church Bible, which I apprehend is the sole book in their possession; and those who have obtained even this degree of knowledge are considered as priests; at least in their own opinion. Of this order, upon trial, not one intwenty could write the characters which they read; indeed we found but one man in Dixan who attempted to write the native tongue : from this person we begged the different characters of the Geesh alphabet; but his obvious ignorance in this respect, gave us evident proof of his inability. Upon enquiry, we found that this person was not a resident at Dixan, but travelled about the country in the character of a physician as well as priest, and had for some time past been exercising his skill in the former profession.

" The present Baharnegash is a tall elderly man, with a mild countenance; the top of his head bald, and his hair bushy round his ears. His dress, like the rest of his people, consisted of a single garment wrapped round his body, and his only ensign of office was a peeled staff about six feet long, which was also borne by his relations, and those in authority under him. He performs the duties both of chief priest and governor, and recites prayers to his people both morning and evening, on which account he incurs some ridicule at court. The form of prayer commences with chanting three times over Jehu Arozoo (praise be to Jesus), in which he is joined by the whole assembly. This is followed by Binta Mariam Arozoo; then Haimanot Johan- nim, Georgis, Welleta Selasse &c. which are all in like manner three times chanted by the congregation. To this succeeds the invocation, with which it began, Jehu Arozoo; the chief then recites several prayers, to which the congregation answer, Amen. The service ends with the whole congregation prostrating themselves three times, with their faces to the ground, calling out on the name of God|Tabbait|Tabbait|Tabbait. After this prostration the Baharnegash generally continues praying by himself for a short time, and immediately after issues orders for the day, which chiefly relate to the care of the cattle, and similar employments.

APPENDIX.

11

SECTION 11

Si

."2 3 ill x-:.6. CHIMSAGEE. il d. *lit* .D3 1 AAD0 S g I JARRAIN 1 ceeded MHDU RAO K ! -*f3l* 3 s- *4* qQJ o *JS* y V *a* = '3 '*34 S* DA S I -*i* 1AIS,A;8 S SRAGONAUT RAO. 1*l*. 3AJEE R,3. HHADU RAO, P HH- Ph I H i E H If s O ll 1*C* w w .Sa a 1 I,1l P a a C 9 g 1-r If S illJ W -S2I as Si .3 Ml

Duties proposed to be levied by the Nayib of Masso- wah ; referred to in p. 230.

Four dollars for a bale of tobacco of fifteen mauncls. One-fourth of a dollar for one Bengal bag of 16Glb. of

rice. One dollar and twenty-two komassie for nine frassel of pepper. Three dollars for twelve Bombay maunds, (28 Ib.) of cotton.

One-fourth of a dollar for one frassel of kalai (block tin).

One fourth of a dollar for one frassel of gessel (tutenac).

Three dollars for twenty frassel of red copper.

Two dollars for four guz (twenty-eight inches) of red or

blue broad-cloth. Eight dollars for one corge (twenty pieces) of fine piece goods.

Five dollars for one oorge of blue cosses.
Two dollars, and a half for one corge of coarse cloth

Baftas.
One dollar and a quarter for one corge of chintz, coarse

or fine.
One dollar and a half for eight guz of kincaub or silk.
Two dollars for eight guz of velvet.
No duty on .iron or gunpowder.

from Captain Court's ftepOrt on his 'return from Massowah ; referred to in p. 398.

On the 20th of July, having left Mr. Salt, with a guard of sepoys under Mr. Crawford, at Arkeko, I reached the vessel about eleven o'clock ; and as the land wind almost ceased to blow before we left Arkeko in the cutter, I suffered much from the intense heat which prevails during the interval of calm between the land and sea breeze. I had hardly been on board one hour, when a hard squall of hot wind off the land suddenly arose, in which we parted our cable. Enveloped in a cloud of dust, and suspecting from the appearance of the sky that we were about to encounter very severe weather, I thought it unsafe to let go another anchor, and at once determined to avail myself of the opportunity then afforded me, by the wind blowing from the north-westward, to run the vessel out of the harbour, and endeavour to get sea-room, before the gale should become too violent; and, in the event of the weather clearing up, it was my intention, as well with a view to intimidate the Nayib from raising any more obstacles to Mr. Salt's immediate departure, as to facilitate Mr. Crawford's return to the vessel with the guard of sepoys, to have tried to effect a passage into Arkeko Bay, and bring the Panther to an anchor abreast that town. The squall continued with great violence till half past four P. M.; and it was not till half past seven o'clock that we had accomplished the purpose above- mentioned.

As soon as the vessel was anchored, I sent the cutter on shore well manned and armed, under charge of Mr. Denton, and was much pleased, about nine o'clock, toee her returning with Lieutenant Crawford and the sepoys, all safe. I had also the great additional gratification to learn from Lieutenant Crawford, that the appearance fthe Panther standing into Arkeko Bay had produced, in the minds of the Nayib and his faithless and rapacious As- cari, the exact sensation and effect that I had hoped, and expected it would ; and that it was not until she hove in sight, that they ceased to importune Mr. Salt for more money upon new pretences, to which every fresh instant gave birth.

On the 21st, I quitted Arkeko Bay to proceed to the Island of Dohul, where we had been informed that provisions and fresh water might be obtained. As we passed Massowah, I hove the vessel to, and sent an officer on shore in the cutter with a message to Currum Chund, respecting the anchor we had left in the harbour, and at the same time desired him to inform the Nayib that I should be back in six days, when I hoped to receive, without delay, Mr. Salt's dispatches for Lord Valentia from his hands, as I had not the least doubt of their arriving from Dixan by that time. Having received a satisfactory answer from Currum Chund, I proceeded on to Dohul, and anchored the Panther in safety off the N. W. side of it at sunset. Being informed by the islanders that the proper anchorage was on the east side of the island, and the account I had received at Massowah, " that plenty of horned cattle, sheep, and goats, with abundance of good water, might be procured at this place," being confirmed, we weighed anchor, and worked round the south side to the proper anchorage, where we came to in three fathom at the distance of one and a quarter from the island. A spit of sand which runs off the south end of Dohul breaks the sea, and shelter the roads in some measure, in that direction, and a similar one to the northward protects it from the violence of the N. W. winds ; but it would be dangerous riding here wlien the wind blows hard from any point on the eastern-board.

On our first coming among them, we found the inhabitants of this island, who in number did not exceed thirty grown persons, inoffensive, mild, and hospitable; and I was in hopes that my presents of rice, tobacco, and bluecloth, might have made them so much our friends, that they would have cheerfully supplied us with water, and such live stock as we wanted, at a reasonable price ; that is to say, at the rates we had been accustomed to procure them, at Massowah. I was led, however, very soon, to entertain a different opinion : for the islanders, in consequence of injunctions, no doubt brought from the Nayib by a boat which arrived here shortly after the Panther, entirely changed their conduct towards us; and from being very forward and willing to render us every service in their power, became quite the reverse, and seemed extremely desirous to get rid of us assoon as possible. In addition to this vexatious circumstance, I had the mortification to find that, in consequence of the long drought universally complained of in the Red Sea, the Dohul wells, which are, I believe, in number about twenty, several off which however were dry, could not supply us nearly so expeditiously as I wished and expected, with the large quantity of water we required to replenish our stock ; I therefore determined upon going to Dhalac, where I was certain that we could, in two or three days, procure as much as we wanted. ,

After purchasing a few young goats, which are here, as well as at Valentia Island, excellent, I left Dohul on the 26th of July P. M.; but owing to contrary winds and threatening weather did not reach Nockara Roads, until the next day about noon, at which time it blew a hard gale from the westward. At five P. M. the wind began to veer round to the southward, and the weather to wear altogether so threatening an aspect, that I was induced to strike the lower yards and topmasts. This and every other possible precaution being taken, and all our anchors down, saved us, under God's providence, from shipwreck. Since I have been at sea, I never have in any vessel rode out a harder gale of wind at anchor; nor was I ever in my life at anchor on a lee-shore with so awful a prospect of inevitable destruction, had an accident happened to one of our cables. The gale continued with

Vol. H. K K

unabated violence from four P. M. of the 21th, until ten A. M. of the 28th. During the whole of the night loud peals of thunder, vivid lightning, and a sea of fire, encreased the terrific horrors of our situation. Thanks be to God! we rode the storm out, which began to abate considerably about noon on the 28th ; and in the evening Unus brought us *off* sixteen casks of water.

At five P. M. on the 30th, having replenished our stock of this article, we weighed and made sail for Mas- sowah harbour, in which we anchored in safety a quarter before ten A. M. on the 29th, and were fortunate enough, with the assistance of a diver, procured us by Unus, to recover the bow anchor we had parted from, and left behind us on the 20th.

Having learned that a kaiila was arrived from Dixan, I applied to the Nayib to know whether letters had not come by it for Lord Valentia; but received an answer that none had arrived. On the 31st, having gained intelligence from Unus that dispatches from Mr. Salt were certainly in the possession of the Nayib, I wrote to him by Unus to demand them, and to say that I would not wait any longer, but should proceed to Mocha, with or without them, and would there receive Lord Valentia's instructions how to act, in consequence of such wanton and unmerited perversity, but that I would leave Unus for forty-eight hours, in hopes that the Nayib would perceive the injustice of his conduct, and the unpleasant circumstances to which it must lead ; and in consequence, be induced to send the letters by him.

By the assistance of a fair spirt of wind we got out of the harbour at eleven o'clock P. M.

On the 1st of August we found in the morning that we had been driven by the strong northerly currents in sight of Dohul. We beat against these currents and a strong S. E. wind for another twenty-four hours, and found ourselves in precisely the same situation on the following morning.

On the 2d, I had the pleasure of seeing Unus's dow leave the harbour of Massowah, and make directly for us. In a few hours he came on board, and delivered me letters from Mr. Salt, announcing his safe arrival at Dixan. For the six following days we beat against ad- verse winds and currents without being able to get round Hurroo point. At length we rounded it in the burst of a land gale from W. N. W. under a fore staysail, at midnight. We had afterwards a fair wind, and passed the Aroes at sun-set on the 10th.

.At three o'clock on the llth we were abreast of the town of Mocha in nineteen fathom. At five it became so black and threatening over the land, that although in six fathom, we could see neither shipping nor town. Having no land mark to guide us, we erroneously supposed ourselves to be to the north of the town ; but on the weather clearing, discovered that we were ten miles to the south of it. Trifling as was the distance, it was six days before we were able to beat up against the strong northwester, which generally kept us under our close reefed top sails. On the 16th we anchored in Mocha roads.

(Signed) CHARLES COURT.

END OF VOL II.

T. C. HANSARP, JTinttr, jglerborough Court, Fleet Street, London.
hrvt

LaVergne, TN USA
01 February 2010
171729LV00010B/16/P